The Journal Articles of
Hermann Sasse

Sasse and Friends

Description taken from correspondence between Drs. Matthew Harrison and Jobst Schöne. Dr. Schöne knew the men in the picture. No date.

. . . As to the photo you attached to your email, I know almost all of these men in the picture. They are (from left to right): the late Rev. Dr. Gerhard Gesch, pastor of Augustana Lutheran Church, Berlin, SELK; Rev. Ludwig, former pastor of SELK in Berlin, St. Pauls Church, but converted to the Roman church; the late Rev. Rudolf Hein, pastor of Trinity Lutheran Church Berlin-Steglitz (now Gottfried Martens' church); Dr. Hermann Sasse; the late Rev. Dr. Matthias Schulz, Pastor of Holy Cross Lutheran Church Berlin-Wilmersdorf of SELK (the Photo was taken right in front of his church building); the late Rev. Heinrich Willkomm, Pastor of Trinity Lutheran Church Berlin-Reinickendorf (church and congregation are not existing any more, the congregation merged with Augustana Lutheran Church); the late Rev. Heinrich Petersen, former President of the Evangelical Lutheran Free Church (when the photo was taken, he was already in retirement); the late Rev. Dr. Wilhelm Hopf, Director of SELK's Lutheran Church Mission; and finally the US army Chaplain of the US Army Berlin Brigade, an LCMS clergyman, whose name I have forgotten. At least 8 of the nine (if not all) are already in the church triumphant. —Jobst

The Journal Articles of
Hermann Sasse

Edited by
Matthew C. Harrison
Bror Erickson &
Joel A. Brondos

An imprint of 1517.the Legacy Project

The Journal Articles of Herman Sasse

© 2016 Matthew C. Harrison

Published by:
New Reformation Publications
PO Box 54032
Irvine, CA 92619-4032

Printed in the United States of America

ISBN: 978-1-945500-52-7 Hard Cover
ISBN: 978-1-945500-51-0 Soft Cover
ISBN: 978-1-945500-53-4 e-book

NRP Books is committed to packaging and promoting the finest content for fueling a new Lutheran Reformation. We promote the defense of the Christian faith, confessional Lutheran theology, vocation and civil courage.

TABLE OF CONTENTS

PREFACE FROM MATTHEW HARRISON
President of the LCMS

This publication of Sasse's RTR articles marks yet another milestone in the continued publication of the works of one of the great Lutheran theologians of the twentieth century. Much has been written elsewhere about Sasse's life and work.[1] Sasse taught at the University of Erlangen from 1933. When his Bavarian Church in 1948 joined the EKiD (a union of Lutheran, Reformed, and United Churches in Germany), he went into a state of confession, and left the territorial church for a small Lutheran Free Church. Soon after this, he received a call to teach in the United Evangelical Lutheran Church of Australia, which merged with the Evangelical Lutheran Church of Australia in 1966 to form the Lutheran Church of Australia. Sasse taught at its Luther Seminary until his death in 1976.

To be sure, Sasse was something of a Jeremiad. He rejected the approach of Karl Barth, his main nemesis in the early years under Hitler, which called for a union of Lutherans and Reformed to fight Hitler. After the war he was dismayed when even his own bishop, Hans Meiser, supported entry into the EKiD. From the 1930s he had reached out to the Missouri Synod, which he called "our last hope" for world confessional Lutheranism, but Missouri

---

[1]See *Letters to Lutheran Pastors*, vol. 1, 1948–1951. St. Louis, Concordia Publishing House, 2013, pp. xlix–lxxxv; Ronald Feuerhahn, "Hermann Sasse as an Ecumenical Churchman." University of Cambridge unpub. diss., 1991; and Lowell Green, *Lutherans Against Hitler: The Untold Story*, St. Louis, CPH, 2007.

was soon busy, as Sasse often quipped, "moving straight out of the ghetto into the ecumenical movement." He wrote voluminously and was eager to be published where possible. His *Letters to Lutheran Pastors* were published seriatim by his friend Friedrich Wilhelm Hopf in Germany in mimeographed form. He was published occasionally by the journal of Concordia Seminary, St. Louis, but there too he felt that the door was mostly closed to him, as he was a persistent critic of Concordia's ever-stronger move to the ecumenical left and the loss of the dogmatic substance of the Lutheran Confession. In his personal correspondence in the fifties and sixties, he often complained that Lutheran doors were closed and that all but the *Reformed Theological Review* were uninterested in his work.

The RTR essays in several cases mirrored the topics and sometimes the content of his *Letters to Lutheran Pastors*. Sasse had written all of these essays in English. We are fortunate to have them, in addition to the several articles published for *The Springfielder*, of Concordia Theological Seminary then in Springfield, now Ft. Wayne.

The churchs that will survive into the future are those that dare to confess their dogma, Sasse noted. The RTR essays are replete with this thought and conviction. They are winsomely ecumenical in the best sense. Sasse was an early key participant in the Faith and Order Movement (more engaged than any other continental theologian according to Feuerhahn), but increasingly the ecumenical movement succumbed to forces devoid of doctrinal substance. Several RTR essays deal with the dogma of Scripture, and "Inspiration and Inerrancy" especially demonstrates how far Sasse had moved from his position expressed ten years earlier in Letter 14 that only those matters in Scripture that dealt with faith and life are inerrant.

There remains much to mine in the deep riches of Sasse's work. The *RTR* and *Springfielder* articles and the many book reviews have been all but inaccessible for decades. All of them bear witness to Sasse's deep knowledge of Church history, the New Testament, Luther, the Reformation, the Eastern Church, and Rome. Though writing as a very convinced confessional Lutheran, Sasse nevertheless affirms the breadth and scope of the Una Sancta. He dispels myths such as the "ancient undivided church" and untangles the riddles of Roman Catholicism with deepest respect and truth.

In the late 1990s, when Joel Brondos and I served Zion Lutheran in Ft. Wayne, Joel had possession of a scanner. I had photocopied the *RTR* articles of Sasse on an old machine in the Loehe Library of Luther Seminary in Adelaide, Sasse's former institution. The copies were far from perfect, and Joel's scanner even less so! After years of pecking away, and now with the help of Bror Erickson and Wade Johnston, we now offer another hefty batch of classic Sasse.

Two weeks ago, my dear father in Christ and fellow Sassephiliac, Ron Feuerhahn, was laid to rest here in St. Louis. He knew this volume was coming and was delighted. Even as he now with Sasse no longer has to have that apostolic "concern for all the churches," may all who read these pages be strengthened in these last days.

In the blessed and strong name of Jesus!

Matthew C. Harrison
Holy Week 2015
St. Louis

THE REFORMED THEOLOGICAL REVIEW
Vol. XII, No. 2, June 1953

Some Remarks on the Ecumenical Movement

The editors of this review have asked so kindly and so persistently for a contribution on some problems of the Ecumenical Movement that the author could not decline their kind invitation, though he is afraid the readers will not like at all what he has to say. But the situation of Christendom is so serious and the crisis of the Ecumenical Movement so obvious that all true believers in the *Una Sancta* of whatever denomination, inside and outside the World Council of Churches, should exchange their thoughts and share their concern for what each one must understand as the true unity of the Church.

I.

The Ecumenical Movement is more than the organizations it has produced and in which it has found its most conspicuous expression, like the great world conferences on ecumenical problems and the World Council of Churches (W.C.C.). Later Church historians may describe it as one of the great religious movements, which from time to time, like an irresistible flood, sweep over all Christendom and by transcending all national and denominational frontiers prove that there is a unity of Christendom. Like Puritanism around 1650, Pietism around 1700, and the great awakening of the idea of the Church around 1830, so the Ecumenical Movement of the twentieth century has penetrated all denominations of the Christian world, though, of course, it finds different expressions in Anglicanism and Lutheranism, in American Methodism and Roman Catholicism. Indeed, even the Roman Church of today would not be what it is but for the influence this movement has exercised upon it.

In stating that, we do not think so much of the farsighted politics of the Vatican, which, convinced that the endeavors of the W.C.C. are bound to fail, prepares for the day when it can present the Roman solution of the ecumenical problem to disappointed Anglicans and Protestants; we rather think of the fact that all leading Roman Catholics, from the pope to the last parish priest in Europe, have quite a different attitude towards the Christians of other denominations simply because the whole of Christendom is in their thoughts as it was not in the thoughts of Pius X and his contemporaries. This aspect of the Ecumenical Movement is perhaps less perceptible in England and in countries in which religious life follows the English pattern. There the fifth of November does not seem to have passed entirely, while on the European continent—this has been called the only real achievement of Hitler—Catholic and Protestant theologians are able to discuss in a very friendly manner all controversial issues, including such an interesting question as whether or not the pope is the antichrist, which he, of course, is for us Lutherans, notwithstanding the antichrists in our own churches.

As one who has given practically some years of his life to the World Conference on Faith and Order and has also taken part in the discussions between Roman Catholic and Evangelical Lutheran theologians, I am not quite sure which of these two movements has brought more fruit. Hopeless as such discussions between Roman Catholics and Lutherans necessarily are if one looks upon a possible rapprochement of the churches, they are no more hopeless than the conferences on Faith and Order like Lund 1952. On the contrary: in their utter hopelessness which cannot be concealed behind utopian dreams, clever compromises, or the painstaking work of the architects of a future "Reunited Church," they reveal the real situation of Christendom, a sickness which human endeavors cannot heal. For the absolute helplessness of the churches, their inability to overcome the divisions, point to the only hope the Church has in this world: the second advent of Christ.

Is it by accident that also in the W.C.C. the eschatological hope of the New Testament has become one of the main topics under discussion? Professor Schlink's moving address on "The Pilgrim People of God" [*The Ecumenical Review*, Vol. V, No. 1. (Oct. 1952) pp. 27–36.] at Lund 1952 shows how that "*salutaris desperatio*" is growing:

> "Let us direct our eyes towards the much deeper division which the Returning Lord will effect in all churches, and towards the unity of the eternal splendour which he will bring with him" [*loc. cit.* p. 36.]. It is most significant that the Ecumenical Movement with this eschatological outlook in a certain way goes back to its beginnings. It was born out of the great missionary movement at the turn of the century with its slogan "Evangelisation of the world in this generation," which originally meant that the rapid proclamation of the gospel throughout the world should prepare the Second Advent of our Lord according to Matt. 24:14. At Edinburgh in 1910, Mark 9:1 was twice quoted on very solemn occasions, by Archbishop Davidson of Canterbury and by John Mott, who in his closing address referred to the great speech of Dr. Davidson, in the last words spoken at the great conference: "It may be that the words of the Archbishop shall prove to be a splendid prophecy, and that before many of us taste death we shall see the Kingdom of God come with power." [*World Missionary Conference 1910*, vol. IX, p. 351 cf. p. 150.]

The kingdom of God did not come as it was expected then and as some people wanted to establish it after World War I. The "*theologia gloriae*," if we may use Luther's terminology, of those days was refuted. Again Christendom is being taught the "*theologia crucis*." Thus it is not only a return to the old eschatology of 1910, but a new and deeper understanding of the Last Things which we observe in the present stage of the Ecumenical Movement. And does not the Church of Christ belong to the Last Things (Acts 2:17; 1 Peter 2:9f.)? Is not ecclesiology, rightly understood, a chapter of eschatology?

II.

Why is it impossible to organize the whole Ecumenical Movement of our time in the World Council of Churches? Why do not all those who are seriously asking for the "*Una Sancta*" join it? It is not, as some people seem to think, because some churches regard themselves as the "*Una Sancta*" and can, consequently, imagine a union only in the form of a submission to that one church. It has been stated expressly that also for such churches there is room within the council, for example for the Eastern Orthodox churches or even for Rome if she wanted to join. On the other hand, there are Lutheran churches that strictly refuse to join the W.C.C. although the Lutheran Church even at the time of the strictest orthodoxy has never identified itself with the "*Una Sancta*" but has recognized the Church of Christ even in the Church of Abyssinia or in the mission churches of the Jesuits in America, and, of course, also in the Reformed churches of France or Scotland. What, then, is the deepest reason for the refusal to join the W.C.C.? What is the reason for the dissatisfaction even many member churches feel?

The Ecumenical Review of July 1952 (p. 427) reports an answer the Archbishop of Canterbury, Dr. Fisher, gave to the objection that a certain church would not feel at home in the World Council: "Not at home—precisely. There is no member church of the council which feels at home there. The Orthodox churches often feel unhappy. The Anglican Communion has much heart-searching about what goes on. Of course we do not feel at home. That is just why the World Council is so important. If we all felt at home the unity we seek would have been already found and the World Council could give way to a united church."

This reply, wise as it may seem, is not sufficient. It does not answer the real problem looming behind that feeling of uneasiness: Why is it that the Eastern Orthodox Church no longer allows her theologians to take part in the discussions of the Commission on Faith and Order except to "inform the heterodox about the contents of her faith and teaching"? Why is it that just the churches that represent a great ecclesiastical heritage either do not belong to the W.C.C. or do belong to it with a bad conscience? Why on the other hand do churches without a great doctrinal or liturgical heritage and with a shallow theology feel very much at home in the council? Is the reason to be found, as some of the "younger churches" and their friends in the "older churches" seem to think, in the fact that the older churches have to carry the burden of a long history?

It is easy to sneer at serious ecumenical conversations as "the Church Ruminant, placidly chewing the cud of ancient controversy in the meadow of academic leisure" [quoted in *The Ecumenical Review*, Vol. V, No. 2 (Jan. 1953), p. 121]. But what if this "cud of ancient controversy" should contain the Gospel itself? When does a controversy become ancient and when does a younger church cease to be young? Some people seem to think of the Ecumenical Movement in terms of the European "Youth Movement" at the beginning of this century that regarded youth as a virtue in itself and old age as a vice or at least as a regrettable misfortune. One wonders how such disdain of historic Christianity could arise just with the Christians in those peoples of Asia who used to appreciate very old religious traditions. This was by no means only a reaction against the Western divisions, but it was, to a large extent, the result of an education by missionaries who brought to the mission fields that contempt of history and that dogmatic indifference in which they themselves had been trained. It should have been the task of the Ecumenical Movement to assist these younger churches in understanding the one great truth by which the Church of Christ has lived in so many nations throughout the ages. Instead the great tragedy is that as this movement has found its expression in so many ecumenical organizations and conferences, it has been instrumental—certainly against the will of its leaders—in silencing the quest for truth.

The whole extent of this tragedy becomes obvious to one who looks at the way of the World Conference on Faith and Order from Lausanne to Lund. "This is a conference about truth, not about reunion ... We seek God's truth about the whole of Christendom. We must necessarily begin by stating what we have learned in our part of it" [*Faith and Order, Proceedings of the World Conference Lausanne*, 1927, ed. H. N. Bate, p. 223]. Thus the unforgettable Dr. Palmer, then Bishop of Bombay, defined the task of the conference at the beginning of his paper on the highly controversial topic "The Church's Ministry." "This is a conference about reunion, not about truth" could have been said of Lund 1952. Otherwise the conference could not have failed to answer the question of what the basis not only of a future reunion but also of the common work of the churches should be. Lausanne in 1927 said quite clearly what the common ground was: "Notwithstanding the differences in doctrine among us we are united in a common Christian faith which is proclaimed in Holy Scriptures and is witnessed to and safeguarded in the Ecumenical Creed, commonly called the Nicene, and in the Apostles' Creed." [*op. cit.* p. 466.] This common ground has obviously been lost in the twenty-five years between Lausanne and Lund, as the "Report" of Lund declares under the heading "Consensus in Doctrine" (p. 19):

> All accept the Holy Scriptures as either the sole authority for doctrine or the primary and decisive part of those authorities to which they would appeal. Most accept the ecumenical creeds as an interpretation of the truth of the Bible or as marking a distinctive stage in the working-out of the orthodox faith. Some assign a special importance to the creedal documents of the early ecumenical councils. Some would say that to found unity on any creeds is to found it on something human, our understanding of the gospel or our theological work in formulating its meaning. Some judge in accordance with the Inner Light and the leadings of the Spirit and are therefore concerned to witness against the use of outward creeds when these are held to be necessary or sufficient. Many denominations possess confessional documents in which they express the Christian faith as they read it in the Bible. It would generally be admitted, however, that these last documents would not be regarded as irreformable and they do not in fact occupy the same position in the Rule of Faith of all churches which possess them. We acknowledge the importance of theological study. . . . In listening to one another in ecumenical discussion we move towards a deeper understanding of each other in faith and doctrine.

One must read this confession of doubt and uncertainty even about the Nicene Creed twice in order to understand the unspeakable tragedy of modern Christendom. These modern churches no longer know what the faith is which was once delivered to the saints. They no longer know whether the Bible is the sole authority or whether tradition and the inner light are also sources and standards of doctrine. They do not know whether what the Church for sixteen centuries has confessed with the words of the Nicene Creed is true. "The Church by its very nature is an evangelising fellowship with an inescapable missionary obligation," so we read on the same page. But how can the Church preach the Gospel if it does not know exactly what the Gospel is? How can it satisfy the hunger of modern mankind, Eastern and Western, for truth, if it cannot distinguish between truth and error?

On the previous page, the report discusses the problem of heresy and defines *heresy* as "an error of doctrine persistently proclaimed against an established norm of the Church." But the question of what this norm may be is left open. "It is agreed that there are *necessaria* (necessary articles) in the Christian faith and we would restrict the word *heresy* to this sphere, but we are not unanimous about their number and nature"; in other words, we know there are doctrines that must be taught and others that must not be taught, but unfortunately we are not able to distinguish them. Does anyone believe that a hundred years of continued discussion, study, and "listening to one another" would change this situation? Ecumenical discussions can be fruitful but only if carried on between those who have a common doctrinal basis, be it the Nicene Creed or the "*sola scriptura*" of the Reformation. Without such expression of common convictions and a common faith, the ecumenical discussions will lead not to a new Pentecost, but to a Babel-like confusion of tongues. That is the tragedy of the modern ecumenical organizations. What was meant to be a means of overcoming the divisions of Christendom has practically destroyed the unity that already existed.

The celebration of the Lord's Supper in the Cathedral of Lund—where general intercommunion was practiced against the Confession of the Lutheran Church and the rules of the Church of Sweden, but sanctioned by the Bishop of Lund and the Primate of Sweden—has forever destroyed the bond of unity that for several hundreds of years had united the Lutheran churches of the world not in what today is called a denominational "family" (we Lutherans are not united by family resemblances), but in the "*magnus consensus*" of a real faith. What Anglicans and Orthodox Christians who for conscience's sake could not join in such Communion think about it, we will not ask. At the end of the "Word to the Churches" (*Report*, p. 6) we read, "The Lord says once again: 'He that gathereth not with me scattereth.'" The Last Judgment only will reveal who has gathered and who has scattered in the ecumenical labors of our time and in the strife of the Christian people of all ages for unity in the truth. It should never be forgotten that in John 17 "that they all may be one" is preceded by "sanctify them in thy truth; thy word is truth."

III.

It has been said and will be said that the W.C.C. and the Commission on Faith and Order are no churches or super churches. However, it cannot be denied that they act and speak as if they were churches. "We believe" and "we confess," says the Report of Lund several times, as on p. 46: "We confess our faith in the One, Holy, Catholic and Apostolic Church" (why not in the whole Nicene Creed?). The W.C.C. has a confessional basis, even if only a very weak and doubtful one. Celebrations of Holy Communion are arranged by its assemblies. The council and its commissions promote evangelization: the proclamation of the Gospel, which is the main function of the Church of Christ. And they help to organize churches. It is, indeed, left to the individual churches whether or not they want to accept the suggestion put forward by the Faith and Order Commission.

The W.C.C. is indeed, as Dr. Leipor said on his visit in Australia, no marriage office for churches. But it is a sort of marriage guidance office. Here lies the deepest practical problem of the Ecumenical Movement today. Is it a mere union movement, as so many before? Or is it a movement whose meaning is quite independent of the attempts to bring about church unions? Undoubtedly, the W.C.C. today encourages unions irrespective of their doctrinal aspects, thus endorsing with its authority also such church unions that might lead to a deterioration, if not destruction, of the Christian faith.

We, the Christians in Australia, are especially interested in that problem. The churches of this country, small in number compared with their sister churches in other continents, are separated by vast oceans and by the large islands and countries of Asia from the rest of the Christian world. North of Australia the Church is represented by comparatively small "younger churches" only, which themselves are minorities in their pagan, Muhammadan, or Buddhist nations. Perhaps the Roman Church is right in considering Southeast Asia the part of the earth where the final battle of Christianity is to be fought. For in this area the Church has to fight not only primitive paganism, but also the great high religions of mankind, which so far hardly have been touched by the Christian missions, and, in addition to that, atheistic communism, the most effective substitute for all religion, which seems to divert its main attacks from the Christian world to Asia. Maybe our Catholic fellow Christians are right if they ascribe to Southeast Asia the same importance for the future of the world that Europe once had in the Middle Ages. Christian Australia is for them what Ireland was at the dawn of the Middle Ages, and they try to live up to the great missionary opportunity given by its geographical position to the Church in this country. What is non-Roman Christendom in Australia doing in order to solve one of the greatest missionary tasks of the history of the Church?

We see how, more or less with the blessing of the W.C.C., if not under its auspices, "united churches" are being organized out of Anglican and Reformed, Methodist, and other Protestant mission fields. They stretch from Pakistan and North India via South India and Ceylon to Indonesia, New Guinea, and perhaps Australia. They are meant to solve, in the interest of more effective evangelism, the problems of unity and ecumenicity in their respective areas. Can they really do it? Or will the tragedy of the union churches of Europe and America repeat itself in this part of the world? For the attempts to overcome the divisions have so far always ended in the creation of new denominations (e.g., the Disciples of Christ) and even of new divisions, as in Germany, where in 1817 two Protestant denominations existed, the Lutheran and the Reformed. After strenuous attempts to unite these two, fifty years later there were still existing Lutheran and Reformed churches, and in addition to them six or seven union churches with different types of doctrine that up to this day nobody has been able to unite. But even if such tragedy could be prevented, if actually one "reunited church" would replace the present Anglican and Reformed churches—Roman Catholics and most Lutherans would not be able to join it—in the mission fields of Asia, would such a church be spiritually strong enough to preach "*magno consensus*," the Gospel as the answer to the longing of the multitudes of the Asian peoples for the "way," the "truth," and the "life"?

IV.

With this question in mind, if we look at the "younger churches" that have come into existence or are being organized in Southeast Asia, we find faithful Christians with deep personal convictions, men and women who are real confessors of their faith and witnesses to Christ. Everyone who has had the good fortune to meet people from these churches knows that. It is, however, quite another question whether these churches as churches are able to confess the full truth of the Gospel and whether, if a weakness in this respect should exist, this must not inevitably lead to a decay also of the faith of the individuals. We do not want to discuss here any particular church since this could be misunderstood as a criticism of the members of that church. There are, however, some problems common to all of them, and there are plans of a "Reunited Church" that partly have been carried out in them and partly are under discussion in ecumenical circles in Australia and abroad. As the plans are of vital interest for all Christians in this part of the world, a word or two may be said about them.

First of all, a word is necessary on the problem of the faith of a "Reunited Church." General agreement is expressed that such a church must have a common faith and a common expression of that faith in a creed. This faith is defined as faith in Jesus Christ, which implies faith in the Triune God. As creeds witnessing to and safeguarding that faith, the Apostles' and Nicene Creeds are accepted or suggested. Later confessions like those of the Reformation churches may be used for theological and catechetical purposes, but they are not regarded as essential expressions of the faith of the Church.

This idea is untenable. As a matter of fact, the Nicene Creed loses its original meaning if it is under-sufficient for all times, a minimum confession containing that on which there must be agreement in the Church of Christ and leaving open all questions not expressly mentioned therein. Not merely a minimum requirement, but the fullness of faith is thought of in the Eastern liturgy when after the exhortation "Let us love one another that we in unanimity may confess the Father, the Son and the Holy Ghost, the consubstantial and indivisible Trinity" the creed is spoken, not as a beautiful liturgical text only, but also as a simple statement of facts. Therefore, it has its place not only in the solemn worship of the Church, but in the streets as well—in spite of all *"disciplina arcani"*—where its content is preached to the world. It has its place in the dungeon where it is said in prayer by a lonely confessor and at the stake and on the scaffold where a martyr stammers with his last breath some of its mighty words. Thus the creed must be understood as a confession of the one faith God the Holy Ghost gives to the whole Church as to every single believer. It was, indeed, formulated at a certain time, but it expresses the one great truth confessed earlier by the Church of the apostles and martyrs in primitive formulas and that had to be confessed later in more elaborate form in the doctrinal statements of Ephesus and Chalcedon against the heresies of Nestorianism and Monophysitism, which readily accepted but unfortunately misinterpreted the Nicene Creed.

In later centuries, again the creed had to be safeguarded against new misinterpretations. This is the meaning of all great confessions of the sixteenth century, which, though contradicting each other, each one in its way tried to express the real meaning of the Nicene Creed (e.g., what the words "for us men and for our salvation" actually mean) over against new errors and heresies. As the Eastern Church cannot but read the Nicene Creed in the light of the doctrinal decrees of the later ecumenical councils, as Rome cannot but understand it in the light of the councils of Trent and the Vatican, in a similar way the churches of the Reformation have in their Confessions, in the *Confessio Augustana*, in *The 39 Articles*, in the various Reformed confessions, that interpretation and application of the Apostles' and Nicene Creeds that they, on the basis of God's Word and in view of the errors and heresies of their time, could not but confess *"in conspectu Dei omnipotentis et coram tota ecclesia, quae nunc est et quae aliquando in posteritate erit"* (Formula of Concord, closing paragraph). They can discard these confessions, as some Reformed churches have done, or they can silently abandon their authority, as seems to have been done by the Anglicans with regard to *The 39 Articles*, regarding them as merely historical documents with a certain practical value even for today. It is, however, a great error to think if all these churches, Eastern and Western, Catholic and Protestant, would give up their interpretations of the ancient Creed, it would be restored to its old and even a higher dignity. Without such interpretation the creed would become a dead formula. How can I confess the truth contained in a creed in living faith unless I understand it? The mere text means nothing if it is not accompanied by an interpretation, even if it be a silent interpretation. And such interpretation cannot overlook what has occurred in the Church since 381.

They who want us to give up the confessions of the sixteenth century as real confessions (theologically there is no difference

between a creed and a confession) actually replace the confession of
the Reformation by a confession of their own, stating that the issues
of the sixteenth century—problems like the nature of man and of
God's grace, the authority of Scripture, the Sacraments and other
questions that have occupied the deepest thinkers of Christendom
for more than a thousand years—do not really matter. They try to
restore the unity of the Church by wiping out from the history of
the Church the sixteenth century and by going back to the "ancient
undivided church," which actually has never existed, as every historian knows, but is a dream of seventeenth century theologians who
were tired of controversies and of nineteenth century Romanticism,
which read its own ideals into the past. For Christians today it is
impossible to ignore, as not touching the real substance of the faith
expressed in the Nicene Creed, such questions like the "*sola fide*"
the "*sola scriptura*," the real presence, the nature of Baptism, and the
Ministry of the Church.

Whether we take sides with Luther or Calvin, with Cranmer
or Trent, or whether we try to find a better answer of our own, it is
impossible to avoid answering such questions. How can we hope to
win India for Christ if we refuse to answer the questions put to us
on the mission field: What is the Bible as compared with the Koran
and the Sacred Books of Ancient India? What is the highest authority in the Church? These people ask us today what Baptism and Holy
Communion are. We cannot say, "The Nicene Creed does not answer
these and similar questions; thus everybody is free to form his own
opinion, but the Church cannot tell you what you receive at the Lord's
Table and whether Baptism is really the washing of regeneration. These
are rites to be performed but not to be speculated on." A church with
no better answers to give would do better to withdraw from the mission
field. And a "younger church" which would not be able to answer these
questions; an indigenous church without a definite commentary to the
Nicene Creed would soon lose this creed too. We are fully aware of
the immense tragedy of modern Christendom that comes to the mission fields with various and even contradictory answers, which, by
the way, was the tragedy of the ancient churches also. But even contradictory answers are better than no answer at all. It is one of the
greatest errors of all mankind, ancient and modern, Christian and
non-Christian, to find truth only in that "in which we all agree."

A second word must be said on the constitutional aspect of the new "Reunited churches." If our friends in India tell us of their vision of a Reunited Church in which the episcopal, the presbyterial, and the congregational order of the Church are united and Christians of Catholic and Protestant persuasions may find their spiritual home, we must ask them whether it is really their vision and not an English theory on home reunion brought to them by their missionaries. If they would ask Roman Catholic Christians on the one hand and Christians from churches in which the heritage of the Reformation is still strong on the other hand what they think of these plans for a united earthly church of the future, they would soon realize that they are striving for a utopia. Instead of encouraging them to go on with what many think to be an interesting experiment, we should warn them of the impending disappointment that might become a catastrophe for the Christian faith in their countries. For nothing is more detrimental to the Christian life of individuals and churches than disappointed hopes and fruitless efforts.

The situation becomes clear if we try to understand the act that is to inaugurate the union. It has been performed in some churches, and it is provided for in the various plans of new unions. Its latest and most perfect form seems to be the "Ceylon-Formula" on which Father A. G. Hebert reports in "Impressions of the Post-Lund Consultation." [*Ecumenical Review*, Vol. V, No. 2; January 1953, p. 124] According to this formula, which was discussed at an unofficial meeting in connection with the World Conference at Lund, "an act of unification is to take place, which cannot be called Reordination or Supplemental Ordination or Mutual Commissioning, but which will be what we called 'a Rite without a name': no name is possible because the occasion is unique. No one is to be asked, no one is to be allowed to deny any ordination or grace which he believes that he has already received: in the Rite the Lord of the Church is prayed to make good, through the imposition of episcopal hands, whatever is defective in any of these ministries, and make them real and valid presbyterial ministries according to the historic order of the Church."

The learned Anglican theologian admits "that the Rite involves a certain ambiguity, in so far as different people will attach different meanings to it: thus for instance a Congregationalist on whom the hands are being laid may think that he is already a minister, but is now receiving a wider sphere of ministry, while an Anglican may think in his heart that this Congregationalist is now receiving ordination." Father Hebert thinks that this ambiguity can be tolerated since this rite is an anomalous act that should help the Church to return "to visible unity from the anomalous condition of schism and disunion." But would it really do that? Supposing the clergy not only in Ceylon, but also in other countries, would undergo such "a Rite without a name," what would be the difference? Would the Catholic churches of the world, Eastern and Western, recognize this as a substitute for an ordination as they understand it? Most certainly not. Even Anglo-Catholics would probably have their doubts. Can a person receive a grace or an order he does not want to receive? Even an infant is asked in Baptism whether he desires to be baptized. And what should the young Christians on the mission field think of it? What assurance would these new bishops, priests, and deacons have of the validity of their orders in view of the fact that four hundred million Roman Catholics do not and never can recognize the Anglican orders and that even the Orthodox churches of the East have not yet definitely recognized them? All these ministers would have to rely on the assurance given by the Church of England that the succession was not broken in the sixteenth century and that their orders are valid. As these mission churches are unable to examine historically and dogmatically the claims of the Church of England, their whole structure would rest on the "*auctoritas ecclesiae Anglicanae.*" And what would the Protestants think of the "Rite without a name"? There would be a variety of opinions. Some would easily accept it as a solution of their union problems. Others would ask what the future of a Church must be in which rites are performed which may be understood by different persons in quite a different way. This would be true not only of this particular "Rite without a name." For as soon as this ambiguous rite has been accepted, every ordination, every consecration of a bishop must become ambiguous. Confirmation would also be a rite of very ambiguous character, and so would Baptism be, for the Ceylon plan includes Baptist churches. Thus in the "Reunited Church," infant Baptism and adult Baptism would be a practiced side by side, both to be completed by episcopal confirmation. As nobody would know what the "Rite without a name" really is, so the Sacraments of our

Lord would become mere rites the understanding of which would be left to the individual. This kind of "private judgment" and religious individualism has nothing to do with the freedom of the Christian the Reformation has discovered. For this freedom is bound to and limited by the Word of God. To help the younger churches in Asia to find and understand the Word of God as the authority on which a church can really rely and out of which the *"Una Sancta"* is born, this is the task of all Christians in this country who still believe in the *"sola scriptura"*: Anglicans, Methodists, Presbyterians, Lutherans, and whatever their name may be.

THE REFORMED THEOLOGICAL REVIEW
Vol. XIII, No. 1, February 1954

Ecumenical Responsibility

Nothing is more painful for a theological author than the fact that what he has to say might or even must hurt another Christian heart. This was the reason why only reluctantly I complied with the kind request of the editors of this review to write on the Ecumenical Movement. I am deeply indebted to the readers that they took so patiently what must have sounded very strange to many of them. I am not less indebted to the Rev. John Garrett whom we all like and whose work we admire even when we must differ from him for the way in which he has voiced his criticism. It was, of course, his duty as Secretary of the Australian Council of the World Council of Churches to reply to my article. My answer to his letter is not to be of a controversial nature. Nor am I going to repeat what I have written. I want to make only a few points that inevitably will come up in the ecumenical discussions during the next generation and that must be answered also by the churches in Australia.

First of all, I want to assure the readers that I have studied the literature produced by the modern Ecumenical Movement, including the writings Mr. Garrett recommends to me. It is not from lack of information that I speak, but rather from a different understanding of the facts and the documents. I know that the World Council of Churches as such cannot celebrate the Lord's Supper. But the fact that it invites churches of various convictions to arrange celebrations in connection with its meetings is not denied even by my worthy opponent. He also knows the discussions concerning this question that have preceded and followed meetings like that of Amsterdam. Was Karl Barth really wrong when he expressed the idea that it might be better to have no Communion service at all instead of several communions, the participants of which were not quite sure whether all of these celebrations were really the Sacrament instituted by Christ?

If the World Council arranges in this way such celebrations it presupposes that they are one and the same Sacrament under various human forms. Supposing the Reformation was right in its judgment on the sacrifice of the Mass, how can a Lutheran or a Presbyterian encourage the celebration of such Mass? How can, on the other hand, an Orthodox or an Anglo-Catholic encourage a celebration he must regard as an adulteration of the true Sacrament? With all due respect for the deepest conviction of another Christian and all that is sacred to him, I am not allowed to encourage that which I cannot but regard as heresy. Here lies the deepest problem of the W.C.C. It does not and cannot see that within Christendom there are not only differences that may be overcome by discussions, but also heresies that never will give way to the truth voluntarily and that must be excluded from the Church.

There are, indeed, traces of the Church also in heretical communions. Nobody would deny that, and I as a Lutheran would not dare to find much more than such *vestigia ecclesiae* in my own church. But this fact that traces of the Church are to be found in almost all denominations does not entitle me to pass over what the New Testament clearly teaches of my duty to separate myself from heresy (1 Tim. 6:20f.; 2 Tim. 4:3ff.; Titus 3:10f.; 1 John 4:1ff; 2 John 7ff.; Rev. 2:9f.). I wonder what St. Paul, St. John, and the Fathers of the Church would say about the document "The Church, the Churches and the World Council of Churches," which carefully avoids speaking of that mortal danger that threatens the existence of every church, also my own church?

This leads to the question of "Evangelism." One can say, of course, that the council does not evangelize itself except where officers may be invited. If, however, one of the tasks of the council is "To support churches in their task of evangelism," the council must know what evangelism is, and this presupposes that it knows what the Gospel is. What, then, is the Gospel if it can be proclaimed irrespective of the fact that there is no agreement among the members of the World Council of Churches as to what the doctrinal basis of the council "Jesus Christ as God and Savior" actually means? The divinity of Christ is obviously not understood in the same way by modern Protestants who deny the Virgin birth and the bodily resurrection of Christ and by Eastern Orthodox Christians who strictly adhere to the Nicene Creed. The understanding of Christ as the "Savior" is not the same with Quakers and Lutherans, with Catholics and Baptists, with Methodists and Monophysites. Even such fundamental facts like the incarnation and the atonement are interpreted differently. What is the doctrine taught at the Institute at Bossey? According to what principles are articles on Evangelism and other highly theological subjects selected for or rejected from the "Ecumenical Review"? For nobody would say that the individual author has the sole responsibility for what is said and not said.

As to the organization of churches, church federations, and church unions, I have never said that the World Council itself is doing this work. What I have said and what I must repeat is that the World Council supports and encourages the establishment of such organizations. In the great struggle in Germany after the war between the unionistic "Evangelical Church in Germany" and a solution of the church problem along confessional lines, the World Council was not neutral. The various "National Councils" from the NCCCUSA to Indonesia in which an "essential oneness" of the churches is presupposed that does not exist and, at any rate, is not the oneness of the Church according to the New Testament, had at least the moral support of the World Council of Churches. The same is true of the "United Church of South India," as shown by the articles in the "Ecumenical Review" and the older publications of the World Conference on Faith and Order (e.g., the report for Edinburgh, 1937, "A Decade of Objective Progress in Church Unity 1927–36" by H. P. Douglass). The fantastic plan of a future Reunited Church of Australia, which has caused this whole discussion, is another example of the activities of the World Council of Churches in the field of church union. It has never been heard that Geneva has disapproved of this plan and the various similar plans for the churches of South East Asia.

This criticism in no way interferes with the plans of the churches of Anglo-Saxon background for a home reunion that would cover all these churches throughout the world. On the contrary, we can only wish that some of those divisions that more or less have become obsolete might be overcome. What we Lutherans object to is only the attempt to see the divisions of Christendom mainly from the point of view of these churches. We are aware of the danger of seeing the history of the Church from the point of view of the Lutheran Reformation only. What we are interested in is not our Lutheran Church as a separate body. But we are interested in the Word of God and in the Sacraments of Christ. We cannot think of a real union of churches apart from the true unity which the New Testament clearly teaches, Eph. 4:1ff. Maybe that the churches fail to reach agreement as to what the "one baptism" is. Such tragic failure could never justify an attitude that leaves the question open. A Catholic and a Baptist who, each in his way, take seriously their beliefs concerning this Sacrament are perhaps nearer to one another than two members of a modern union-church who have agreed to disagree.

One last word may be permitted with respect to the problem of responsibility. The great global organizations now coming into existence as ecclesiastical parallels to the global political organizations are in great danger of leaving the responsibility for what they do fail to do to their constituent bodies. It is very easy to say that the World Council of Churches is no super-church. At any rate it is more than a mere council or federation, and nobody knows whether or not the future of these organizations—I would say that also of an organization like the Lutheran World Federation—will be a striking parallel to those "super-states" like the U.S.A., the U.S.S.R., the Commonwealth of Australia, and similar political bodies that in the future may arise in Europe and Asia. At least one "super-church" has already been formed, the "Evangelical Church in Germany."

The Roman pope, an Anglican bishop, the General Assembly of the Church of Scotland, a Lutheran or a Methodist synod have their responsibilities. Who is responsible for the actions of the World Council or the Lutheran World Federation? The constituent churches will be the answer. But how can they speak? How often have they the opportunity of speaking? How can the member churches supervise that which their young people learn at Bossey and in groups and meetings especially arranged for them? Concerning the pope, can 1556 C.I.C. says, *"Prima sedes a nemine iudicatur."* This, however, does not exclude that he is a poor sinner who has to go to confession each Friday. Who confesses the sins of the great committees of the Ecumenical Movement? Obviously nobody. Their sins are attributed to the member churches. They themselves are as sinless as the great political organizations of modern mankind.

This is perhaps the most urgent question put to all Christians by the rise of the modern ecumenical organizations: what can be done to prevent a new invasion of the world into the Church by an imitation of secular forms of mass organizations and methods of government? And this implies the other question: what can be done in order to preserve the offices and institutions to whom the Lord has entrusted the responsibility for his Church on earth? The ministry of the Word and the Sacraments and the Christian congregation are the strong pillars of the Church. Wherever anonymous global organizations arise with the good intention to serve the ministry and the congregation—even the pope calls himself *"servus servorum Dei"*—everything has to be done in order to protect the rights and duties of the divinely appointed offices and institutions. Otherwise the Church must decay.

THE REFORMED THEOLOGICAL REVIEW
Vol. XIV, No. 1, February 1955

A History of the Ecumenical
Movement 1517–1948

German—Edited by Ruth Rouse and Stephen Charles Neill
(published on behalf of the Ecumenical Institute Chateau
de Bossey by S.P.C.K., London), 1954, pp. 822; 32/6.

If a team of fifteen authors, some of whom are scholars of world fame, undertakes to write a voluminous symposium on a highly important subject, one might well expect a really good book. The present book contains, indeed, excellent contributions. We mention here only the chapter on ecumenical bearings of the missionary movement by Prof. Latourette, the contributions by the Eastern theologians Dr. Florovsky and Dr. Zernov on the ecumenical relationships of the Orthodox churches prior to and after 1910, furthermore the excellent presentation of the history of the World Conference on Faith and Order by Canon Tissington Tatlow and the movement on "Life and Work" and the ecumenical endeavors connected with it by the Swedish scholars N. Karlstrom and N. Ehrenstrom. In these chapters that deal with the modern Ecumenical Movement since 1910, personal reminiscence and careful study of the rich sources still available have formed a solid basis. Unfortunately, one of the most complete collections of documents and especially letters seems to have been lost. Shortly before his death, A. Deissmann told me he was going to

bequeath his great ecumenical archive to the State Library at Berlin.
I tried to persuade him to leave these documents not to a library controlled by the Nazi government but rather to a church archive. The
vast correspondence of this great champion of ecumenical Christianity in Germany and Europe will, if it can still be found, help many
to realize what an important role has been played by individual
Christians, and not only by conferences, organizations, and church
leaders. Thus one misses with regret the name of Jules Rambaud and
his "French Unity"—at least I could not discover the name of this
great French Reformed Christian and pastor. Without the sacrifices
of such men and of many an unknown soldier in the rank and file of
the Ecumenical Movement of the twenties, the great rapprochement
of the churches would not have been possible. In this respect even
the best parts of the large book share the shortcomings of all Church
history. If the reader keeps that in mind, he will gladly make use of
the wealth of firsthand information contained in these chapters. It
may be that the silent passing over of men and events is partly due
to the strict limitation of the space available for the single chapters.
In many cases the reader is informed that a certain contribution had
to be shortened. Sometimes, however, one has the feeling that the
whole story is intentionally not told. Not all leaders of the Ecumenical Movement have seen right from the beginning the danger of the
totalitarian state. There have been men of high standing in England
who believed that the acceptance by Hitler's new "bishops" of the
apostolic succession would cure the apparent disease of German
Protestantism, just as in Germany some very ecumenically minded
high church people were not far from the new political millennium.
The current story of the "Confessional Church" in Germany and the
struggle for the freedom of the Church in other European countries
has to a large degree become a fabled convenu that needs urgently
a "de-mythification," especially since these events are closely linked
with the progress of the Ecumenical Movement. But these remarks
are not meant to minimize the merit of the chapters dealing with
the twentieth century. Almost half of the book is devoted to the
development since 1910 (chapters 8–16, pp. 353–724), from Edinburgh to Amsterdam. The critical reader will be grateful for the vast
amount of information on the various branches and aspects of this
great movement, the details of which are hardly known to many of

our contemporaries after the beginners of the great movement and most of the witnesses of the first conferences have departed from the *ecclesia militans*. We can only wish that future Church historians will re-examine the sources and not be satisfied with an account that naturally must be streamlined, and therefore incomplete.

The great weakness of the book lies in its understanding of what the Ecumenical Movement is. It is, indeed, not easy to define the great spiritual movements that from time to time sweep throughout Christendom irrespective of national or denominational borderlines. How many various answers can be and have been given to the question of what the Reformation is or what Pietism is? The present book sees here no problem at all. The foreword, written by Remold von Thadden-Trieglaff, a Christian layman of high reputation, in his capacity as Chairman of the Board of the Ecumenical Institute, takes it for granted that the Ecumenical Movement is the sum total of church union movements, comprising "(1) co-operation between Christians belonging to different confessions and churches, (2) co-operation between the several churches and confessions, (3) union or reunion of separated churches, (4) the full and final restoration of the unity of all Christendom." Thus understood, the Ecumenical Movement accompanies the whole history of the Church since the apostolic age, or rather it is one aspect of the history of the Church. It is for practical reasons only that "Division and the Search for Unity Prior to the Reformation" is dealt with by way of an introduction on twenty-four pages by Bishop Stephen Charles Neill with the help of an editorial group. Of special value are the remarks on the Middle Ages. The real history starts with the Age of the Reformation, Prof. J. T. McNeill writing on "The Ecumenical Idea and Efforts to Realize It, 1517–1618," Prof. Martin Schmidt on ecumenical activity on the continent of Europe during the seventeenth and eighteenth centuries, and Prof. N. Sykes on the Ecumenical Movements in Great Britain during the same period. This third chapter is one of the most illuminating of the whole work because it makes visible some of the roots of the modem Ecumenical Movement, which would not be what it is but for the fact that English-speaking Christendom has carried its own problems into all parts of the world. The same cannot be said of the preceding chapters on the Reformation period and on the seventeenth and eighteenth centuries on the continent, the reason being the simple fact that the strength of the churches of the Reformation lies in what the Ecumenical Movement, as it presents itself in this book, combats: a strict confessionalism. It is certainly not by accident that among the reformers, Bucer, the church politician and negotiator whom even his friends called a fox, as well as the real founder of what later became known as Pietism, appears to be the hero of Ecumenism. While Dr. McNeill tries to do justice to Luther, his presentation of the Marburg Colloquy and the Wittenberg Concord needs correction. In Marburg, Luther made an amazing concession Bucer was prepared to accept, and in Wittenberg, Bucer accepted Luther's doctrine. For a local presence of the body of Christ had never been taught by Luther (as it is even not taught by the Roman Church), and the words in Luther's instruction of 1534 "torn by the teeth" (p. 45) are apocryphal. If Luther at Wittenberg accepted the biblical word "*indigni*" for "*impii*," this cannot be interpreted as showing "that he had caught the spirit of Bucer" (p. 46). We mention this example to show that the ideas and ideals of later centuries should not be read into the history of the Reformation. It was Emil Brunner who at the fourth centenary of the Marburg Colloquy warned against measuring the reformers with the standards of modern Christianity, which is so far from the Reformation that it cannot discover the real differences between the reformers, and which no longer understands that the strength of the Reformation lay in the inexorable seriousness with which the reformers regarded their confessions. The problem of intercommunion did not exist at all. All churches of the sixteenth century, as the Church of all ages, were convinced that intercommunion is possible only where the *consensus doctrinae* exists. The point at issue between the Reformed and Lutheran churches of the sixteenth and seventeenth centuries has never been whether or not members of other churches could be admitted to the Lord's Supper. It was solely the question of where the borderline of the Church was to be found. When Strassburg accepted the Wittenberg Concord and the Augsburg Confession, the Church of Zurich no longer allowed their students to receive the Sacrament at Strassburg. The idea that there could be intercommunion with the Baptists would have been quite inconceivable even to Zwingli. The churches of the Reformation continued simply the usage of the Church since the beginning. There is not and cannot be a *communicatioin sacris cumhaereticis aut schismaticis*.

This principle of the Catholic Church of all ages was maintained until at the end of the seventeenth century the division of Christendom was taken for granted. One must never forget:

Luther was not a Lutheran, nor was Calvin a Calvinist. Either wanted to be; and was in his way, as he understood himself, a Catholic. There is an astonishing amount of common medieval heritage in the great confessions of the sixteenth century. This common doctrinal heritage in connection with the general conviction that the unity was only temporarily lost made the great debate possible that went on up to the later part of the seventeenth century between Romans, Lutherans, and Reformed and which cannot be understood as controversy only. It may be that the shortening of Prof. Schmidt's contribution is responsible for the fact that the truly ecumenical work of seventeenth century orthodoxy is not mentioned at all. Neither Johann Gerhard's great *Confessio Catholica*, nor the *Historia Syncretistica* by A. Calov, nor E. C. Cyprian's book on Church union with its valuable and otherwise not accessible documents are even mentioned. One of the most important aspects of the life of the Church in the sixteenth and seventeenth centuries has been neglected completely: the common liturgical heritage. Not only did he common canonical hours continue in some German monasteries or chapters that survived the Reformation adherents of the Augsburg Confession and of the Roman Church (the material has been collected and partly published by Prof. Nottarp at Koenigsberg, now Kaliningrad), but also in purely Lutheran churches. Much of the old Latin liturgy lived on to the turn of the seventeenth and eighteenth centuries. Just as for Johann Gerhard, Thomas Aquinas's *Adoro te devote* was an expression of the evangelical doctrine concerning the Lord's Supper, so the *Lauda Sion salvatorem* was sung in the Lutheran churches, with slight alterations, in Latin or German. It has been stated that the real disruption of Western Christendom, at least on the continent, took place at the end of the orthodox period, not at the time of the Reformation. This importance of orthodox theology has not been understood in this book. Instead the men of minor stature— Christian humanists like Acontius, Calixtus the discoverer of the *Consensus quinquesaecularis*, religious adventurers like Labadie and the leading characters of Pietism—all of whom are distinguished by a lack of understanding of the Church of the New Testament and by an individualism quite foreign to the Reformation, appear here as heroes of ecumenism. Even a religious genius like Zinzendorf has never been able to overcome the idea of the Church as a society of pious individuals. This understanding of the Church together with the idea that the essence of Christianity is "the religion in which we all agree" (be it the Apostles' Creed or the consensus *quinquesaecularis*, or the natural religion of enlightenment) was the heritage left to the nineteenth century.

This important century is dealt with in three chapters: "Christian Unity in Nineteenth-Century America" by Dr. Yoder; "Approaches of the Churches Toward Each Other" by H. R. T. Brandeth, Priest of the Oratory of the Good Shepherd in Paris; and "Voluntary Movements and the Changing Ecumenical Climate" by Dr. Ruth Rouse. The chapter on America is, despite its brevity, highly interesting, though the author does not seem to realize that the real contribution to the understanding of the *Una Sancta* was not made by the enthusiasts of the union movements, but rather by those who took seriously the European heritage of doctrine and liturgy. Father Brandreth makes a good start in observing (p. 263ff.) in a similar way as Dr. Florovsky (p. 195f.) the real origin of the Ecumenical Movement in the years since 1828 when the Great Awakening—which originally in the early nineteenth century had been a renewal of Pietism—turned into a new discovery of the Church. Moehler's famous book on *Unity in the Church*, which led the Roman Church back from a pietistic or ethical understanding of the Church to a new realization of the doctrine on the Body of Christ, Chomjakov's discovery of the Orthodox doctrine on the unity of the Church, the beginnings of the Tractarian Movement in England, and, we could add, the revival of Lutheranism and of the Reformed understanding of the Church on the continent: all this produced the real Ecumenical Movement, which is not interested in increasing the number of Christian denominations by establishing new and various union churches, but in the *Una Sancta, Catholica et Apostolica Ecclesia*. In this sense the foundation of the great world denominational fellowships is rightly regarded by Father Brandreth as one of the most outstanding features of the nineteenth century. But why does he not mention the *Allgemeine Evangelisch-Lutherische Konferenz* of 1868, which for the first time brought together the Lutherans of Germany, Scandinavia, and America and thus has become the mother of the later world organizations of Lutheranism? In a history of the Ecumenical Movement, it belongs together with the corresponding world organizations of the Anglicans, Reformed-Presbyterians, Methodists, Congregationalists and Baptists. Dr. Ruth Rouse, in a later chapter titled "Other Aspects of the Ecumenical Movement, 1910–48" (pp. 399–641) gives among most valuable information another review of these world denominational fellowships. Here the General Lutheran Conference is mentioned together with the Lutheran World Convention of 1923, but its importance has not been fully realized. Also about the unions in Germany the learned Father Brandreth is not very well informed. The Prussian Union, like the corresponding unions in Baden, the Palatinate, Nassau, and so on, are results of that dogmatical indifference that prevailed during the eighteenth century and the Erastian idea of Enlightenment that it is up to the state to determine the order of the Church. Otherwise these various union churches would not have adopted quite different doctrinal statements and catechisms. Thus far it has proved to be impossible to unite these union churches, and Spener's warning against the plans of a union between Lutherans and Reformed has been confirmed by history. Repeatedly he predicted that such union would not lead to one, but to three or four churches. It is much to be regretted that the history of the Church in Germany in the nineteenth century seems to be unknown. Otherwise it would be a serious warning to other churches. Sometimes it seems that all the mistakes made in Europe during the nineteenth century, including such futile enterprises as the Anglo-Prussian Bishopric of Jerusalem (p. 288)—the establishment of which was one of the blows that drove J. H. Newman to Rome—are being repeated in our time on a worldwide scale. One gets this impression from a later chapter of the book written by Bishop Neill on the plans of union and reunion, 1910–48 (pp. 445–95): "To What Does It All Lead?" This question is put by the learned bishop at the end of his review of the unions made in our time in Scotland, Canada, Germany, China, South India, Ceylon, and other countries. It is a question to be thought over, not to be answered. At any rate it will not lead to a "future reunited church" on earth. It is a grave misunderstanding of John 17 if the eschatological character of Christ's *ut orrmes unum sint* is not realized. It is a misunderstanding of the New Testament doctrine on the Church if the biblical warnings against heresies are no longer taken seriously. It is the greatest misunderstanding of the history of the Early Church if the fact is overlooked that Christendom has never been a visible unity. The people of God sojourn in this world, it appears here and there, in Corinth or in Rome, in larger or smaller communities, even where two or three are gathered in Christ's name, the greatest reality in the history of mankind, but hidden to our human eyes under the cross, under false Christians and soul-destroying heresies.

Here lies the greatest weakness of the World Council of Churches, the genesis of which is narrated by Dr. Visser't Hooft (pp. 697–724). This council is not able and never will be able to distinguish between truth and error, Church and heresy. It has to take into full membership every Christian community that accepts a formula that says nothing at all. If one of the great creeds of the Ancient Church would be the basis—such as the Nicene Creed, which was accepted by Lausanne in 1928—the WCC would break asunder. Certainly, the WCC can speak to the world and to the churches. Its pronouncements, however, are made in *futuram oblivionem* only. Who remembers the pronouncements of Amsterdam, of Oxford and Edinburgh in 1937, of Jerusalem, Tambaram, and Willingen? Who will remember in one or two years' time what Evanston had to say about the Christian hope? But what the Apostles' Creed and the Nicene Creed say about that hope will sound through the ages until the coming of Christ in glory because it is the content of God's Word. In spite of all publicity, secured by modern means of communication and by the highly developed art of influencing the masses, the simplest papal encyclical is of greater importance than all the papers of an Ecumenical Conference. What is the reason for that? Is it perhaps the fact that the real strength of the churches is not to be found in the "religion in which we all agree," but rather in those things in which we disagree? These are questions every thinking reader of this volume must ask. No greater damage could be done to the cause of Christianity in the world then if this book would get a sort of canonical dignity. It does not claim that. But uncritical readers, especially in the younger churches and in the Christian youth movements, might overlook the statement of the foreword that nobody is responsible for the work. "This history is in no sense an official publication of the World Council of Churches; the council is not responsible for anything contained in the volume except the quotations from its official publications," although the WCC has promoted and discussed at its meetings the book for years. This happy irresponsibility is shared even by the Board of the Ecumenical Institute, which "in sponsoring the writing of the history has not accepted responsibility for all or any statements contained in it" (p. XXI). If anywhere, then in this evading responsibility the deepest weakness of the modern Ecumenical Movement becomes evident, a real tragedy of the Protestant churches, for no Catholic, no Eastern Orthodox church, not even the few remnants of Eastern Christendom that are still members, will ever accept this attitude that reveals the profound disease of the churches, which with their confessions have abandoned the quest for truth. It will be the great task of those churches that still know the authority of Scripture and of the confession of the biblical truth to call their sisters back, in all humility, from a road that otherwise must lead to a catastrophe.

[Postscript] Some suggestions for a future new edition may be added. The problem of unity, schism, and heresy in the Ancient Church has lately been discussed in very valuable monographs, two of the most important being the books by the late Dr. W. Elert: *Abendmahl und Kirchen-gemeinschaft in der alien Kirche, hauptsaechlich des Ostens* (Berlin, 1954) and S. L. *Greenslade Schisms in the Early Church* (London, 1953). Nicolaus Cusanus and his great work *De concordantia catholica* (1433) must be mentioned. The Lutheran Church—Missouri Synod is not a daughter of the Lutheran Church in Prussia, but in Saxony; the Prussian Lutherans founded the Buffalo Synod and the Lutheran Church in Australia (p. 325). Whether the Missouri Synod "has proved a serious obstacle to union even amongst Lutherans" or not depends on what by true union is to be understood. A book like this should avoid censuring churches for not joining the W.C.C., especially if the contributor does not know exactly the Lutheran doctrine of the Church. The remark on Dollinger (p. 293) as the most powerful mind among the old Catholics should be formulated more cautiously. Dollinger was never a member of the old Catholic Church whose development especially after the abolition of celibacy he very much regretted. Finally, a question may be put to our Anglican friends. Nobody would like to minimize the importance of the Anglican Communion. But has not the time come when this great branch of Christendom owes it to the whole of Christendom, and especially to the younger churches, to make it quite clear what it means by apostolic succession, what it understands a "priest" to be in contradistinction to a minister of a Lutheran or Reformed or Methodist Church? These questions must be answered on the basis of the New Testament. Furthermore it must be made clear what the claims of the Anglican Church mean in view of the fact that the Roman Church can and will not recognize the Anglican Orders and that the same is true of the Orthodox churches. For a recognition based on "economy" is no recognition at all. It would be better to drop the distinction between the interpretation of canon law *kat' akribeian* and *kat' oikonomian.* The Western Church does not know such *oikonomia,* which in Latin would be *pia fraus.* The poor patriarchs and bishops of the East could perhaps not exist in view of the tyranny of their emperors and sultans without such doubtful means of saving face. We Christians of the West, of a free world, should not employ such methods.

THE REFORMED THEOLOGICAL REVIEW
Vol. XIV, No. 3, October 1955

Sacra Scriptura: Observations on Augustine's Doctrine of Inspiration

The quest for the authority of Holy Scripture has become one of the foremost problems for all Christendom, for Catholics and Protestants, for the churches in countries with an old Christian tradition as well as for the younger churches on the mission fields throughout the world. This fact indicates the presence of a deep crisis within Christianity itself. It is a universally accepted doctrine of all churches, with the exception of some modern Christian bodies that have more or less severed their bond with historic Christianity, that Holy Scripture is given by inspiration of God and is, therefore, the infallible Word of God in writing. This doctrine is either silently presupposed or expressly testified to in the great creeds and confessions of Christendom from the Nicene Creed (". . . who spoke by the prophets") to the confessions of the sixteenth century and to the *Constitutio de Fide Catholica* of the Vatican.

The deep difference that exists between Catholicism, Eastern and Western, on the one hand, and the churches of the Reformation on the other, concerning the *sola scriptura* and the authoritative teaching office of the Church, must not lead to the widespread misunderstanding that the churches of the Catholic tradition did not accept the dogmatic authority of the Scriptures for the Church. Rome expressly declares in the Constitution on the Catholic Faith that she accepts the books of the Bible as "sacred and canonical," not because they have been approved by the authority of the Church or because they contain the revelation without error, "but rather because these books, written by inspiration of the Holy Spirit; have God as their author and have as such been *given to the Church*."[1] During the last 250 years, it is true, the impact of modern historical research seemed often to endanger or even to destroy the old view, founded upon the biblical statements themselves, of the Bible as being in its entirety—from cover to cover, so to speak—the inspired and infallible Word of God.

In our days, however, the fight between "Fundamentalism" and "Modernism" is becoming more and more obsolete because the tacit *philosophical* presuppositions of either view have proved untenable. A "Bible Movement" is proceeding throughout Christendom, the deeper reason for which is the fact that all churches are confronted with the task of finding a new theological understanding of the written Word of God. The great encyclicals on the Bible by the modern popes, such as *De sacrorum Bibliorum studiis* of 1943 (Denziger 2293f.), or the new Latin translation of the Psalms reveal something of the amazing work being done in this direction by Rome. The fresh approach to a theological understanding of the Bible on the part of Anglican and Reformed scholars, Karl Barth's *Church Dogmatics*, and the rediscovery of Luther's Christological understanding of the Bible—all this shows that the churches are beginning to realize their precarious situation, as it became manifest at Evanston and as it is keenly felt on the mission fields. How can the churches meet the challenge presented by the revival of the great religions of Asia and by the powerful political substitutes for religion in our age unless they know what they are saying when they claim the Bible is God's Word?

They should help to elucidate the problem of Holy Scripture by furnishing some observations on the doctrine of that Church father who through his authority has determined the thoughts of all Western Christendom on the inspiration and inerrancy of Holy Writ.

---

[1]Denziger 1787: "*sed proptera, quod Spiritu Sancto inspirante conscripti Deum habent auctorem, atque ut tales ipsi Ecclesiae traditi sunt.*"

These pages were first published in German in a symposium for Dr. Franz Dornseiff, Professor of Classics at the University of Greifswald (*Festschrift Franz Dornseiff zum 65. Geburtstag* 1953, pp. 262–73). They are printed here by kind permission of the publisher (VEB Bibliographisches Institut Leipzig) in a translation for which the author is deeply indebted to Mr. R. F. Hosking, B.A., Tutor at Ridley College, Melbourne. The following pages are not meant to be more than the title intimates.

I.

The view of Scripture inspired by the Spirit of God as the source and record of revelation is not, as we know, simply a creation of Christianity. Jesus and the apostles took it from Judaism together with the Old Testament as an obvious truth not requiring any proof. This is shown by the way in which the Old Testament is quoted as an authority. An express doctrine of the *Theopneustia* of the Scriptures, with reference to the prophetic message of the Old Testament, is found in 2 Timothy 3:16 and, on the border of the canon, 2 Peter 1, 19ff. On the way in which this inspiration is to be understood, the New Testament makes no direct statement. So it came about that when the early Christian theology of the apologists felt it necessary to make statements on the inspiration of the Holy Scriptures, it was, to begin with, content to take over Jewish theories as they had developed in the Aramaic and Greek synagogues, partly through the influx of Oriental-Hellenistic concepts.[2]

Not all Judaism's notions of the origin of Holy Scripture were taken over. For example, the rabbinic theory of the pre-existence of the Torah, which has parallels in the various conceptions of a book or books in heaven, never took on Christian form, whilst it reappeared in the Islamic doctrine of the Koran. But it is different with the Jewish ideas of the inspiration of the books of the Old Testament

---

[2]Material for the rabbinic doctrine of inspiration has been collected with remarkable completeness by Paul Billerbeck in H. Strack and P. Billerbeck, *Kommentar zum NT aus Talmud und Midrash*, vol. IV, pp. 415–51. Excursus 16: "*Der Kanon des AT und seine Inspiration*." The value of this great work for the history of religion is still to be extracted.

following the Pentateuch. As an example of Jewish teaching on inspiration, the description of Ezra's copying of the lost Holy Scriptures in the Ezra Apocalypse (2, Vulg. 4, Esdras 14) may be quoted. God, as an answer to the prayer, "Send the Holy Spirit into me"[3] (v. 22) lights "a lamp of understanding"[4] (v. 25) in Ezra's heart for the period of copying, forty days. The process of inspiration is itself described thus: "my heart uttered understanding, and wisdom grew in my breast, for my spirit retained its memory: and my mouth was opened, and shut no more"[5] (v. 40f. R.V.). Endowed with this divine understanding, wisdom, and strength of memory, in forty days Ezra dictates to his scribes the twenty-four books of the Old Testament, and in addition seventy more apocalyptical writings that were to be kept secret.

Philo understands inspiration as a fate of ecstatic enthusiasm that can only fall to the lot of the sage:

> The prophecy of Holy Scripture bears witness to every sage. Yet a prophet preaches nothing of his own, but thoughts that come outside of himself and with which someone else inspires him. It is not given to a fool to become an interpreter of God, so that in point of fact no person morally bad does come into a state of ecstasy, for that befits the sage alone, for he alone is a sounding instrument of God, invisibly played and struck by him.[6]

Thus does H. Leisegang translate the well-known passage *Quis rerum divinarum heres* (259 Mangey 510) and rightly adds to it, "With these words Philo demonstrates his complete misunderstanding of

---

[3] *Inmitte in me spiritum sanctum.* (Vulg.)

[4] *Lucerna intellectus.*

[5] *Cor meum cruciabatur intellectu, et in pectus meum increscebat sapientis. Nam spiritus meus conservabatur memoria, et apertum est os meum et non est clausum amplius.*

[6] *Der Heilige Geist,* (vol. I, I. p. 146); *Jedem Weisen bezeugt die Heilige Schrift Prophetie. Ein Prophet aber verkuendet nichts Eigenes, sondern ihm fremde Gedanken, die ein anderer ihm eingibt. Einem Toren ist es nicht verstattet, ein Dolmetscher Gottes zu werden, so dass tatsaechlich kein sittlich Schlechter in Enthusiasmus geraet, allein dem Weisen ziemt sich das, da ja auch er allein ein klingendes Instrument Gottes ist, unsichtbar gespielt und angeschlagen von ihm.*

Old Testament prophecy," which indeed knows of no nexus between the Holy Spirit and the prophetic message with a particular degree of education. For the first time we find here, within Alexandrian Judaism, the disastrous apposition of revelation and philosophy, of prophecy and ecstatic enthusiasm that soon was taken over uncritically by the Christian apologists.

It is not to be wondered that in a movement such as the Montanist, in which heathen ecstasy found its way into the Church, there should become possible such an understanding of inspiration as is conceived in the utterance of the Paraclete in Montanus: "Behold, man is like a lyre and I come rushing down like a plectrum" (Epiph. *Panarion haer.* 48:4). But one is surprised that over such misunderstanding of prophecy the healthy reaction exhibited in the title of Miltiades's work, "That a prophet ought not to speak while in a state of ecstasy" (cf. Eusebius, h.e. V, 16f.) did not triumph. The contemporary apologists did not accept this approach. Rather they took over with startling assurance from paganism and the Jewish literature the old picture of the lyre and the plectrum and applied it to the biblical authors. Thus Athenagoras (*Legatio pro Christianus* 9) suggests that Moses, Isaiah, Jeremiah, and the other prophets, "being removed from their own mind (in the state of ecstasy), would have uttered under the influence of the Holy Spirit that with which they had been inspired, the Spirit using them like a flautist playing a flute."[7] In Chapter 7 the apologist proves by this the necessity of recognizing such revelations, for it would be "absurd to withdraw from faithful surrender to the divine Spirit that touches the prophet's mouth like a musical instrument and turn to human opinions." Even pseudo-Justin, in *Cohortatio ad Graecos* 8 (Migne SG 6,256) makes use of the same illustration in order to render inspiration intelligible: the divine Pneuma descends from heaven and uses the holy person as an instrument (*organon*) like the plectrum that causes a zither or lyre to sound.

Such illustrations are directed, if need be, to the "prophets" and "Sibyls" of ancient paganism—one thinks of the classic description

---

[7] Cf. The Commentary of J. Geffecken, *Zwei Griechische Apologeten* (1907) pp. 177 and 179f. Here he traces back the picture of the prophet's mouth as the *organon* of God to the above quoted passage in Philo, *quis rer. div. h.* Mangey, I:510.

of the Sibyl of Cumae in the sixth book of the Aeneid. The result is that the biblical prophets are placed on a par with the heathen prophetesses. Judaism led the way with its sibylline literature. The Church followed on from here since Christian authors adapted the Jewish sibylline oracles. The logical conclusion of this mantic conception of inspiration is reached by pseudo-Justin (*Cohoratio ad Graecos* 37) and Theophilus (*ad Autolycum* 11, 9) when they see revelation in the prophets and revelation in the Sibyls to be in "fine harmony with each other" (Theophilus *ad. loc.*).

What was not noticed by those time-honored theologians of the second century was that this interpretation of inspiration was directed neither to Old Testament prophecy, which was not restricted to states of ecstasy, nor to what the New Testament, with great sobriety, says or implies of its origin (cf. Luke 1:1; John 21:24; the Pauline Epistles). Their blindness to the originality and reality of the biblical Word largely explains itself by their being apologists who had to explain in discussion with alien religions a doctrine of the Scripture and its inspiration, as the Jewish apologists before them had already done in a similar situation. But what proves the downfall of every apologist is that it is not simply that the questions of the opponent are being accepted unthinkingly, but that in the framing of the questions part of the answer is effectively taken over from him. So it becomes clear that the early Christian doctrine of the inspiration of Scripture as developed first of all by the apologists is for the main part nothing else than a heathen theory taken over via the synagogue, and which was only superficially given Christian appearance. It was a disaster that later theology, especially in Alexandria, took over this doctrine and developed it instead of contenting itself with the plain teaching of Justin (e.g., *Dial. cum Tryph.* 58, 4) and Irenaeus (e.g, *adv. haer.* 11, 28, 2), according to which Scripture is inspired by the Logos or the Holy Spirit and is therefore true, only these fathers did not attempt to explain the "how" of inspiration.

II.

Only against the background of the old apologetics can Augustine's doctrine of inspiration be understood. It is no accident that the most important thing that he, the last great apologist of the Early Church, said about the Holy Scripture and its inspiration is extant in two works of apologetics: in that huge work *De Civitate Dei,* and in *De consensu evangelistarum,* which, though compared with the former is slight and paltry, yet even today is an effective attempt at a harmony of the Gospels. From these works emerge the phantoms of the great heathen critics of the Christian religion and its claim to revelation—men such as Celsus, Porphyry, and Julian.

The work on the evangelists is especially directed toward the criticism of Porphyry. How far Augustine is able to go into the province of his opponent is shown by the fact that he, too, like his predecessors, groups the prophets of the Bible and the Sibyls together.[8] Hence he tries to demonstrate the existence of the true God to the pagan by comparing the predictions of the prophets and the Sibyls: "If they give the name of god to that being under whose inspiration the Sibyl sung of the fates of the Romans, how is not he (to be called) God, who, in accordance with the announcement aforetime given, has shown us how the Romans and all nations are coming to believe in himself through the Gospel of Christ as the one God, and to demolish all the images of their fathers?

Finally, if they designate those as gods who have never dared through their prophets to say anything against this God, how is not he (to be designated) God, who not only commanded by the mouth of his prophets the destruction of their images, but who also predicted that among all the Gentiles they would be destroyed by those who should be enjoined to abandon their idols and to worship him alone, and who, on receiving these injunctions, should be his servants. Or let them aver, if they are able, that some Sibyl of theirs, or any one whatever among their own prophets, announced long ago that it would come to pass that the God of the Hebrews, the God of

---

[8]"Augustine should be regarded as the author of *Teste David cum Sibylla,*" says Heinrich Scholz in *Glaube und Unglaube in der Weltgeschichte: Ein Kommentar zu Augustins De Civitate Dei.* (1911) p. 95, note 3. Yet he himself refers to the Sibyl of Cumae in the Shepherd of Hermas (vis I, I, 3); neither should the older apologetics be overlooked. For all that, Augustine, together with Virgil's 4th *Eclogue,* did actually prove a basis for the medieval respect for the Sibyls.

Israel, would be worshiped by all nations"[9] (*Nicene and Post-Nicene Fathers*, vol. VI, p. 88).

While here prophets and Sibyls are still contrasted, the Erythraean or Cumaean Sibyl, on account of the clearness of her prediction, is regarded as belonging to the *Civitatis Dei*. For this Sibyl, who had foretold Jesus Christ as Savior, in her whole poem not only has nothing "that can relate to the worship of the false or feigned gods, but rather speaks against them and their worshipers in such a way that we might even think she ought to be reckoned among those who belong to the city of God"[10] (*Ibid*, vol. II, p. 373).

Of course even if Augustine in other respects deeply distinguishes between the prophetic revelation in Scripture and the chancy or absurd predictions of heathen seers and Sibyls, the single exception of the Cumaean Sibyl shows that there can be true prophecy even outside the Bible. The same process of inspiration that occurred in the realms of biblical prophecy can occur and has occurred even outside the biblical revelation. That is the inference from the apologists' concept of inspiration. There can be a state of ecstasy brought about by God both within and without the biblical sphere. Prediction is still prediction whether it is proclaimed by prophet or Sibyl. It is the foretelling of future events whose occurrence or non-occurrence can be ascertained from the events of history. What must remain obscure with this way of thinking is that prophecy in the meaning of the Bible is something more than the foretelling of future events, and

---

[9]*De consensu evang.* (I, 19f. CSEL 43, 26, Iff): *Si deum dicunt, quo impleta Sibylla fata cecinit Romanorum, quomodo non est Deus, qui et Romanos et omnes nationes in se unum Deum per Christi evangelium creditruas et omnia patrum suorum simulacra eversuras, sicut praenuntiavit, exhibuit? Postremo, si illos deos dicunt, qui numquam ausi sunt per vates suos contra istum Deum aliquid dicere, quomodo non est Deus, qui per vates suos istorum simulacra non solum everti iussit, verum etiam in omnibus gentibus eversuiri praedixit ab eis, qui illis desertis se unum Deum colere iuberentur et iussi famularentur? Aut legant, si possunt, vel aliquam Sibyllarum vel quemlibet aliorum vatum suorum praedixisse hoc futurum, ut Deus Hebraeorum, Deus Israel ab omnibus gentibus coleretur.*

[10]*De civ. Dei* XVIII, 23. *quod ad deorum falsorum sive factorum cultum pertineat, quin immo [?] etiam contra eos et contra cultores eorum loquitur, ut in eorum numero deputanda videatur, qui pertinent ad civitatem Dei.*

that it is the content of the word alone and not the form of its origin that makes this word prophecy the pure Word of God.

There are two ideas that Augustine took over from the late Hellenistic and apologetic doctrine of inspiration and which he applied to the biblical Word: the view that the author of a book of the Bible was, as an inspired person, only the *instrument* of the Godhead (whether speaking or dictating), and the understanding of inspiration as a *suggestio* of thoughts, words, and phrases. So the evangelists' activity as writer of the tidings of Christ is to be understood as the writing down of what Christ, the head, dictates to the evangelists, as his limbs, or more exactly his hands: "When those disciples have written matters which he declared and spake to them, it ought not by any means to be said that he had written nothing himself; since the truth is, that his *members* have accomplished only what they became acquainted with by the repeated statements of the *head* (literally: through the dictation of the *head*). For all that he was minded to give for our perusal on the subject of his own doings and sayings, he commanded by those disciples, whom he thus used as if they were *his own hands*"[11] (*Ibid.* vol. VI, p. 101). If the idea of the writer as an instrument—as in the illustration of the lyre and flute in the older apologists, or in the picture found in Gregory the Great[12] of the writer being the *calamus* (pen) of the Holy Spirit—is emphasized so strongly it would seem there could no longer be any talk of the biblical author's personal contribution. However, this personal contribution does not seem fully to have been effaced where the activity of the divine Spirit is understood not as *dictare* but as *suggerere*. In

---

[11]*De consensu evang.* 1, 35, 54; CSEL 43, 60, 17ff: *Cum illi scripserunt, quae ille ostendit et dixit, nequaquam dicendum est quod ipse non scripserit, quandoquidem membra eius id operati sunt, quod dictante capite cognoverunt Quidquid enim ille de suis factis et dictis nos legere voluit, hoc scribendum illis tamquam suis manibus imperavit.*

[12]*Moralia Praef.* c. I, n. 2 (Migne SL 75, 571): *Si magni cuiusdam viri susceptis epistulis legeremus verba sed quo calamo fuissent scripta quaereremus, ridiculum profecto esset epistularum auctorem scire sesumque cognoscere, sed quali calamo earum verba impressa fuerint indagare. Cum ergo rem cognoscimus, eiusque rei Spiritum Sanctum auctorem tenemus, quia scriptorem quaerimus, quid aliud agimus nisi legentes litteras de calamo percontamur.*

this way Augustine explains the differences in the Gospel accounts with regard to the sequence of events, "that each of the evangelists believed it to have been his duty to relate what he had to relate in that order in which it had pleased God to *suggest to his recollection* the matters in which he was engaged in recording. At least this might hold good in the case of those incidents with regard to which the question of order, whether it were this or that, detracted nothing from evangelical authority and truth"[13] (Ibid. vol. VI, p. 127). A memory aided by the Holy Spirit, judgment concerning what is to be related, free in its consciousness even if actually directed from above, this and no more remains of human authorship. As slight as this seems to be at first sight, how great is it in comparison with the theory that in inspiration the human mind is a mere mechanical tool like a musical instrument or a typewriter?

Augustine's teaching on inspiration is not uniform. It is governed by the tension between *dictare*, which makes man a mere tool, and *suggerere*, which does not exclude human cooperation. In this tension is revealed a contradiction between what the Bible actually is and what it ought to be according to both the heathen and Jewish concept of the inspiration of Scripture. Augustine saw that in Holy Scripture there is such a thing as the human individuality of the biblical authors. He could not get away from the fact that the evangelists give different accounts and that they show differences in ability to remember. His mistake was the same as that of the earlier apologists. Instead of starting from what the Bible is and what it says itself about its origin and building upon this a Christian doctrine of *Theopneustia* (cf. 2 Tim. 3:16; 2 Peter 1, 19ff.), he went on from what the ancients understood by inspiration and inspired writings and laboriously endeavored to show that the Bible conforms to these conceptions.

At the same time, it must have appeared a great advantage for the Christian apologists to be in a position to strike back at heathen opponents with their own weapons, since they *proved* to them that

---

[13]*De consensu evan,* 11, 21, 51; CSEL 43, 153, Iff: *quod unusquisque evange-listarium eo se ordine credidit debuisse narrare, quo voluisset Deus ea ipsa, quae narrabat, eius recordationi suggerere in eis dumtaxat rebus, quarum ordo, sive ille sive ille sit, nihil minuit auctoritati veritaque evangelicae.*

the Holy Scriptures of the Christians possess all the marks of a perfect book of supernatural origin. But just as soon as this proof lost its credibility, this weapon instantly recoiled on the Church itself. It is one of the greatest tragedies of Church history that Christianity, through the authority of the Fathers of the Church, had to drag along through the centuries a theory that is simply the painfully Christianized form of a pagan doctrine of inspired writings.

III.

From the earliest times, the understanding of the inspiration of Holy Scripture has been connected with the understanding of its inerrancy. Clement of Rome had already called the Holy Scriptures "true [sc. given] by the Holy Spirit" (1 Clem. 45, 2), and the chorus of Western and Eastern fathers writing on this question witnesses to the belief of early Christendom that the Holy Scripture, as a revelation of the truth of God, was free of error. Hellenistic-Judaism's doctrine of inspiration as depicted most impressively in the legend of the origin of the Septuagint owes its origin to the desire to possess a guarantee of the accuracy and truth of a given text. In the Old Testament, a saying was established as God's Word by its content, in Hellenistic Judaism, by the manner of its origin. The prophet proclaims God's Word and demands belief in it: *Haec dixit Dominus!* The Jewish and Christian apologist wanted to prove that a certain message was not of human but divine origin and therefore must be believed by every thinking person.

Nothing is more characteristic of Augustine's apologetic comprehension of inspiration than the lack of discrimination with which he accepts from Jewish apologetics, in its late form, the legend of the Septuagint. According to this, the seventy-two translators independently of each other had translated the whole of the Old Testament in such a way that "an agreement in their words so wonderful, stupendous and plainly divine"[14] (Ibid. vol. II, p. 386) furnished the proof that one spirit, the Spirit of God, had been effective in all. About

---

[14]*De civ. Dei* XVIII, 42: *mirabilem et stupendum planeque divinum in eorum verbis . . . consensum.*

this legend, it says the opposite to what the older form in the letter of Aristeas recounts, that is to say, that the translators had worked together in one building and "through mutual collation had agreed on one wording" (Aristeas ed. P. Wendland, 301f.) Augustine let nothing make him waver, not even Jerome, with whom he had conducted a long correspondence concerning the Septuagint, and who states, "I do not know who was the first writer who by his falsehood built those seventy cells at Alexandria in which they, separated from each other, wrote the same words,"[15] particularly since Aristeas and Josephus have them collating their text as writers working in one hall and not writing as prophets. Yet Augustine insisted on his seventy-two prophets and sharply criticized Jerome because he translated the Old Testament out of the Hebrew instead of the equally inspired Septuagint.

Yet if inspiration is to be understood in such a way that man is only the tool of the Holy Spirit and that the Spirit alone determined content and form, then even in the smallest detail the principle that the Bible is free of inaccuracies, mistakes, and contradictions must be valid. In his eighty-second letter (to Jerome, no. 116 in Jerome's letters), which represents a vast treatise on the doctrine of Holy Scripture, Augustine expounds his fundamental position on this question: "I have learned to yield this respect and honor only to the canonical books of Scripture: of these alone do I most firmly believe that the authors were completely free from error." If in these writings he is perplexed by anything that appears to him to contradict the truth, he does not hesitate to suppose "that either the manuscript is faulty, or the translator has not caught the meaning of what was said, or I myself have failed to understand it"[16] (Ibid. vol. I, p. 350,

---

[15]*Apol. adv. libros Rufini* 2, 25: *Nescio quis primus auctor LXX cellulas Alexandriae mendacio suo exstruxerit, quibus divisi eadem scriptitarint.* (Cf. *praef in vers. Gen.* and other places quoted in E. Schuerer, *Gesch. des Juedischen Volkes im Zeitalter Jesu Christi* III, 1898, p. 471).

[16]*Ep.* 82, 1, 3; CSEL 44, 354, 5ff: *Solis eis scripturarum libris qui iam canonici appellantur, didici hunc timorem honoremque deferre, ut nullum eorum auctorem scribendo aliquid errasse firmissime credam . . . vel mendosum esse codicem vel interpretem non adsecutum esse, quod dictum est, vel me minime intellexisse.* Cf. *Contra Faustum* XI, 5 (CSEL 25, I, p. 320: *Non licet dicere:*

Augustine's Letters, no. LXXXII, I, 3). This passage represents many others in which Augustine acknowledges the inerrancy of Scripture as a foregone conclusion.

IV.

It is extremely instructive to observe the painful efforts by which Augustine tries to reconcile the belief in the basic infallibility of the Bible with the actual state of the biblical text. We choose the two most difficult problems that he has to solve in this regard: the relation of the Septuagint and Hebrew text of the Old Testament, and the differences between the Gospels.

That the Septuagint is the inspired Word of God just as much as the Hebrew Bible, Augustine was certain throughout all his life, even though later he abandoned his negative judgment on the Vulgate's being translated from the Hebrew, declaring it useful, and using it himself (e.g., *De doctrina christiana* IV, 15, where he quotes Amos 7:14f. from the Vulgate and gives his reason for choosing that text). The deeper reason for his holding firm to the authority of the Septuagint lies not so much in the legend, the veracity of which he never doubted, but in the esteem the LXX text enjoyed among the apostles in the New Testament.

So Augustine is confronted with the superhuman task of harmonizing the Greek and the Hebrew Old Testament that was open to him in the Vulgate. How he accomplishes this masterpiece of apologetics may be demonstrated by one example. According to the Hebrew text of Jonah 3:4, the prophet announced the destruction of Nineveh within forty days, whilst the LXX reads three days. That the prophet obviously could not have said both at once Augustine points out in *De Civ. Dei* XVIII, 44 and explains that he himself inclined to the forty days of the Hebrew text. The much later seventy translators with their divergent statement could have said something different that was yet to the point even if under another figure, and amounted

---

auctor huius libri non tenuit veritatem, sed: aut codex mendosus est, aut interpres erravit, aut tu non intelligis etc.); *De Genesi ad litteram* I, 21, 41; *Ep.* 28 (*ad Hieronymum*) III, 3, CSEL 34, 1, 107.

to the same thing, exhorting the readers not to despise either authority but to raise themselves above its historic content to the meaning of
it signified by the historic event, and which it attempts to record. The
events that took place in Nineveh hint at what the Gentile Church,
symbolized by Nineveh, experienced. Jonah was held to be a type of
the Savior, who lay for "three days" in the tomb and communed with
the apostles for "forty days." "Because that which could be most suit-
ably signified by both numbers, of which one is used by Jonah the
prophet, the other by the prophecy of the seventy translators, the one
and the self-same Spirit has spoken"[17] (Ibid. vol. II, p. 387). In this
instance Augustine was able to solve the problem of harmonization
only by falling back on a meaning to be found deeper than the letter
of the text. For him the truth of the Scripture was hidden behind an
apparent contradiction. Thus, when in his youth he devoted himself
to the Scriptures, he was at that time unable to understand them:
"And behold, I perceive a thing not comprehended by the proud,
not disclosed to children, but lowly as you approach, sublime as you
advance, and veiled in mysteries"[18] (Ibid. vol. I, p. 62). It is this very
discovery, which he made in Milan when Ambrose opened up the
Scriptures to him *remoto mystico velamine*, by which he learned to
understand the saying "the letter killeth but the Spirit quickeneth!"

Any explanation other than the mystic allegorical one was indeed
impossible if both the Hebrew text and the Septuagint were to be held
as inspired and infallible. But the question of how it was then possible to maintain the absolute trustworthiness of the history related in
the Bible has not been answered by Augustine. In the explanation of
Jonah 3:4, he himself follows the Hebrew text as the correct reading
of what the prophet said. But then is not the reading of the Greek
text erroneous whatever there may be of deeper meaning behind
the mistake? The historical problem, the historian's question, "how
it really happened," was even more pressing in the Gospels, which are

---

[17]*De civ. Dei* XVIII, 44: *Propter quod utroque numero significari convenien-
tissime potuit, quorum unum per Jonam prophetam, alterum per septuaginta
interpetum prophetiam, tamen unus atque idem Spiritus dixit.*

[18]*Conf.* III, 5; CSEL 33, 50, 59: *Et ecce video rem non compertam superbis
neque nudatam pueris, sed incessu humilem, successu excelsam et velatam
mysteriis.*

certainly not amenable to an allegorical typographical interpretation such as is always possible with the Old Testament.

So it is that the great apologetic attempt at a harmony of the Gospels in *De consensu evangelistarum* is among the most unsatisfactory of what the great father of the Church wrote. His sparkling intellect here develops into cold acumen, seeking artificial pretexts to bring the theory that there should be no contradictions within the Gospels into harmony with the reality of the differences in the transmission of the Gospels. Unable to solve the problem with a clear doctrine of the nature of the Gospel and its historic form, he has to try to harmonize each particular case where a contradiction or mistake appears to exist. So he discovers that the cleansing of the temple, which according to the Synoptics takes place at the end of Jesus' ministry, and according to John, at the beginning, took place several times (*De consensu evan.* II, 67; CSEL 43, 231, 9ff.).

The explanation of Mark's statement about the crucifixion of Jesus at the third hour (Mark 15:25), whereas according to John 19:14 Pilate delivered the Lord for crucifixion at the sixth hour, is that the Jews had asked for the crucifixion at the third hour. "Mark judged most truly that the Lord's murderer was rather the tongue of the Jews than the hand of the soldiers"[19] (Ibid. vol. VI, p. 199). That is, of course, no explanation of the difference.

One example that has been particularly difficult for apologists of all times is Matthew 27:9, where a quotation coming from Zechariah is attributed to Jeremiah. Origen, if we are to trust Rufinus's translation—otherwise the statement would have to stand to the credit of Rufinus alone—indicates that this is an error of the Scriptures (*errorem scripturae*, Migne SG 13, 1709) in his commentary on Matthew *ad loc.* Jerome expresses himself very carefully in the letter to Pammachius that is so important for his attitude to the Bible: "May they then accuse the apostle of a fault because he neither agrees with the Hebrew text nor with the seventy translators; and, what is more than this, because he errs in the name, insofar as he put Jeremiah instead of Zechariah? But far be it to speak thus of a man who

---

[19]*De consensu* III, 13, 42; CSEL *ad loc.* 327, 2 f: *Marcus ostendit verissime iudicans magis fuisse Domini necatricem linguam Judaeorum quam militum manus.*

accompanied Christ and whose business it was not to chase after words and syllables, but to explain sentences containing doctrine."[20]

This means by the strict standard of history the apostle has made a mistake. But one must not charge him with falsehood on this account, because it is not his function to catch words and syllables, but to put forward the doctrine. Augustine in his intricate discussion comes to the conclusion that it may so have happened that the name Jeremiah instead of Zechariah occurred to the evangelist, as often happens (*ut animo Matthaeievangeliumconscribentis pro Zacharia Hieremiasoccurreret, ut fieri solet*). Later he would certainly have corrected these mistakes had he not reflected that the falsity of his memory, aided by the Holy Spirit, would not have occurred unless God willed that the text should so read (*nisi cogitaret recordationi suae, quae Sancto Spiritu regebatur, non frustra occurisse aliud pro alio nomen prophetae*).

Augustine saw the deeper reason for God's willing it in the fact that at bottom all prophets compose a unity because it is one Spirit who speaks through all and effects a *mirabilis consensio*. This is the doctrine to be extracted from the confusion (*De Consensu evang.* III, 7, 30; CSEL 53, 305f.). Accordingly, what appears to us as a mistake in the presentation of Holy Scripture is effected by the divine will with a quite definite purpose. "How, then, is the matter to be explained, but by supposing that this has been done in accordance with the *more secret counsel of that providence of God* by which the minds of the evangelists were governed"[21] (Ibid. VI, p. 191).

V.

These examples may suffice. In conclusion we attempt to answer the question of what we may learn from Augustine's attempt to prove

---

[20]*Ep.* 57, Migne SL 22, 568ff: *Accusent apostolum falsitatis, quod nec cum Hebraico nec cum Septuaginta congruat translatoribus: et quod his maius est, erret in nomine, pro Zacharia quippe, Jeremiam posuit. Sed absit hoc de pedissequo Christi dicere: cui curae fuit non verba et syllabas aucupari sed sententias dogmatum ponere.*

[21]CSEL *ad loc.* 305, 9ff: *Quid ergo intellegendum est, nisi hoc actum esse secretiore consilio providentiae Dei, qua mentes evangelistarum sunt gubernatae.*

the inerrancy of Holy Scripture apologetically. This essay shows that it is impossible to apply to the Bible that Hellenistic, pagan-Jewish understanding of inspiration that makes the human mind an impersonal instrument. As a matter of fact, the great Church father has not at all been able to prove that absence of mistakes or contradictions he had maintained. Either he must be satisfied with clumsy and unconvincing attempts at harmonizing narratives that defy harmonization, as in the case of the cleansing of the temple or the time of the crucifixion, or he must have recourse to "the reality veiled in mysteries" (*res velata mysteriis*) in Holy Scripture or to a "more secret counsel of the providence of God," which has guided the biblical writers and allowed them to give the divine revelation in a disguise that to our human reason must appear as error or contradiction.

The question arises why he makes this step as *ultima ratio* only. Is it possible to understand the doctrine of the Word of God as given by the Holy Spirit otherwise than by the belief in the "reality veiled in mysteries"? Is it not necessary right from the beginning to make the step Augustine makes at the end when he, driven into a corner by the facts of the biblical text, does not know a way out? Does it not belong to "the more secret counsel of the providence of God" that the Gospel is given us not in the form of one book without contradiction, but rather in four Gospels that often are at variance and defy harmonization? Indeed, just as in the Old Testament almost every important narrative is given in several accounts?

None of the Church Fathers, not even Augustine, the greatest among them, was able to grasp the idea that the Word of God is always hidden, "veiled in mysteries," and not merely, only where our reason fails to grasp it. The heritage of ancient philosophy and indeed the religious bud from which the Fathers came were too strong. Only eleven centuries after Augustine, when the Christian West had passed through all possible forms of a synthesis of ancient philosophy and Christian faith, a member of a monastic order called after St. Augustine was able to express the truth of the "veiled reality" in words that contain a new doctrine of the Word of God: "God's wisdom is hidden under the appearance of foolishness, and his truth under the appearance of a lie. . . . The word of God, as often as it comes to us, comes in a form contrary to our mind which thinks very highly of its own ability to see truth."[22]

We may ask whether at least traces of this insight are found with the Fathers of the fourth century. With Augustine one may find it, without being troubled by the problems of apologetics, where in his personal experience he finds what he calls "the reality veiled in mysteries" (e.g., in the passage quoted earlier from *Conf.* III, 5). Among the theologians of that age there is, as far as we can see, only one man who had at least hinted at the possibility of solving the problem of Holy Scripture with its divine and human side in still another way without applying the pagan theory of a divine and, therefore, obviously most perfect book to the Holy Scriptures of the Church. This man was Chrysostom, the great doctor of the Eastern Church. He has done that in his teaching of the *synkatabasis*, the *condescensio* of God. "Behold the condescension of the divine Scripture, see what words it uses on account of our weakness," he says, commenting on Genesis 2:21 (in Gen. Hom. XV—Migne SG 53, col. 121). In a similar way, he says commenting on Genesis 3:8 (Migne *loc. cit.* col. 135) of Holy Scripture that it shows such great humility (*tapeinotes, humilitas*) of speech. In Homily 15 on John (Migne SG 59, col. 97f.), he explains the passage Hosea 12:11[23] in this way: "This means I have condescended and I did not appear as that which I was." *Neque id, quod eram, apparui.* In such sentences a new doctrine of Holy Scripture begins to become manifest that, to use Luther's terms, is no longer a *theologia gloriae*, but a *theologia crucis*: a doctrine in which the gracious condescension of God in Holy Scripture becomes a parallel to the incarnation of the eternal Word, because he who is the Word is content and Lord of the Bible.

---

[22]*Roemerbriefvorlesung zu Roem.* 12, 1ff. WA 56, 446, 31ff. *Dei sapientia abscondita est sub specie stultitie et veritas sub forma mendacii . . . verbum Dei, quoties venit, venit in spetie contraria menti nostrae, que sibi vera sapere videtur.*

[23]LXX: *en chersin propheton homoiothen*; Vulg., v. 10; *in manibus prophetarum adsimilatus sum*; A.V. v. 10: I . . . used similitudes by the ministry of the prophets.

THE REFORMED THEOLOGICAL REVIEW
Vol. XVI, No. 3, October 1957

Concerning the Origin of the Improperia

One of the most moving and truly evangelical pieces of the liturgy of Good Friday are the Improperia, the reproaches of the Crucified against his people. Since they present some important theological problems and seem to have deeply influenced the *theologia crucis*, which is so significant for Western Christendom, an attempt to trace their history back to the Church of the second century might be of more than mere historical interest.

The "Improperia" are closely connected with the adoration of the cross and with the "Trishagion" and can be understood only in this context. In the present Roman rite, which goes back to the Middle Ages—a somewhat simpler form is presented by the Sarum Missal—the priest shows the veiled crucifix and, while unveiling it more and more, sings three times, "Behold the wood of the cross (*Ecce lignum crucis*) on which the Savior of the world hung," whereupon the choir each time replies, "Come let us adore" (*venite adoremus*). During the adoration the Improperia are sung. They consist of two parts, the first being regarded as the more important one that seems to have been used exclusively in the Middle Ages, as the Sarum Missal and other sources suggest. It comprises three reproaches, based on Old Testament pages in which God complains of the ingratitude of his people. "My people, what have I done unto thee and wherein have I offended thee? Answer me. Because I brought thee out of the land of Egypt, thou hast prepared a cross for thy Savior." (*Populae meus, quid feci tibi? aut in quo contristavi te? Respondemihi. Quia eduxi te de terra Aegypti, parasti crucem salvatori tuo.*) This is, apart from the last words, literally taken from Micah 6:3f. (comp. Jer. 7:22). The second reproach has its roots in Jeremiah 2:6f. (comp. 7:22) and reads, "Because I led thee (*quia eduxi te*) through the desert forty years, and fed thee with manna, and brought thee into a land exceedingly good, thou hast prepared a cross for thy Savior." The third reproach stems from Isaiah 5:2,4 (comp. Jer. 2:21): "What could I have done more unto thee that I have not done? I planted thee, indeed, my most beautiful vineyard, and thou has become exceeding bitter unto me. For in my thirst thou gavest me vinegar to drink, and with a lance thou piercedst the side of thy Savior." (*Quid ultra debui facere tibi et non feci. Ego quidem plantavi te vineam mean speciosissimam, et tu facta es mihi nimis amara. Aceto namque sitim meam potasti, et lancea perforasti latus salvatoris tui.*) Each of these reproaches is answered by two choirs alternately singing in Greek and Latin the "Trishagion":

Agios o Theos	→	*Sanctus Deus*
Agios ischyros	→	*Sanctus fortis*
Agios athanatos	→	*Sanctus immortalis*
Eleeison imas![1]	→	*Miserere nobis.*

"O Holy God, O Holy Strong One, O Holy Immortal One, have mercy upon us."

The second part consists of nine further reproaches in which the Crucified reminds his people of the benefits he has bestowed on them from the liberation from Egypt to their entrance into the Promised Land, and of the acts of ingratitude committed by Israel in the Passion, each of these reproaches being followed by the "*Populae meus*" with which the Improperia begin. In a most impressive way, each act of divine mercy is contrasted with a corresponding act of human ingratitude. In each case a certain word or thought provides the parallel between what has happened in the deliverance of Israel

---

[1]We give the text here in the Latin transcription of the Missale Romanum. The Gallican and Mazarabic have older forms of the "aius" that try to render the pronunciation of the later Greek, which is almost the same as today. The reader is asked to follow up our quotations in a Latin missal.

and in the Passion of Christ. Leaving out the constant refrain "my people . . . ," these reproaches read as follows:

> For thy sake I scourged Egypt with its first born; And thou hast scourged me and delivered me up.

> I brought thee out of Egypt having drowned Pharaoh in the Red Sea; And thou hast delivered me to the chief priests.

> I opened the sea before thee;
> And thou with a lance hast opened my side.

> I went before thee with a pillar of cloud;
> And thou hast led me to the judgment hall of Pilate.

> I fed thee with manna in the desert;
> And thou hast beaten me with blows and scourges.

> I gave thee the water of salvation from the rock to drink; And thou hast given me gall and vinegar.

> For thee I struck the kings of the Canaanites; And thou hast struck my head with a reed.

> I gave thee a royal scepter;
> And thou hast given to my head a crown of thorns.

> I have exalted thee with great power;
> And thou has hanged me on the gibbet of the cross.

The Improperia are followed by an antiphon that resumes the idea of the adoration of the cross. Then Venantius Fortunatus's great hymn on the cross "*Pangue lingua gloriosi lauream certaminis*" with the "*Crux fidelis*" as refrain is sung.

II.

The Improperia in connection with the adoration of the cross and the Trishagion in Greek and Latin are first to be found in the

Mozarabic liturgy. The *"Missale Mixtum secundum Regulam Beati Isidori"* (Migne PL 85, 430f.) has the text of the three reproaches with negligible variations, while the *"Breviarium Gothicum"* (Migne PL 86. 610f.) contains after the first reproach—*"Popule meus, quid feci tibit in quo contristavi te? Responde mihi. Quia eduxi te de terra Aegypti, parasti crucem mihi"*—seven other Bible passages, most of them taken from Micah 6 so that practically the whole context Micah 6: is quoted, each passage being set into the framework *"Popule meus," "Quia eduxi."* This seems to be a secondary form, as some of these verses, such as 6, 7, and 8, are not reproaches. The reason for this form with its admonitions may be the fact that in the Mozarabic liturgy this service of Good Friday (*Parasceve*) was connected with the reconciliation of the penitents as definitely prescribed by the Fourth Synod of Toledo (A.D. 633).[2] Since the Mozarabic rite has been derived from the Gallican liturgy, the question arises whether the reproaches have their origin there. There is, however, no trace of them to be found in Gallican sources before the ninth century, though the Trishagion and adoration of the cross belong to the Gallican rite. The fact that the *"Pangue lingua"* belongs to the liturgy of *"Parasceve"* in the *Breviarium Gothicum* shows Gallican influence. For this hymn, composed at Poitiers by Venantius Fortunatus not later than A.D. 600, belongs to the most precious gifts the Church of the Visigoths in Southern France and Spain received from her Frankish sister church after Rekkared had accepted the Catholic faith in A.D. 583.

Before we can go on with further investigations of possible earlier traces of the Improperia, we have briefly to speak of their inseparable companions, the Trishagion and the adoration of the cross. The Trishagion belongs to the liturgy of the Greek Church. Its origin is unknown, but the beautiful legend with which John of Damask (*De fide orthodoxa* III, cap. 10) concludes his explanation of this hymn suggests that it may have been introduced into the liturgy of Constantinople at the time of the Third Ecumenical Synod. It must be

---

[2]See L. Duchesne, *Christian Worship*, trans. by M. L. McClure, 5th ed., London, 1949, p. 442f. Duchesne's assumption that the reconciliation took place in Milan on Good Friday has been challenged. It could have belonged to the ceremonies of Maundy Thursday.

much older, for it occurs also in the Nestorian liturgy before the lessons as in the other Eastern liturgies. From the East it came into the Gallican liturgy, where it appears in Greek and Latin, its place being before the lessons as in the East. Whatever its history in the West may be,[3] it proves the close connection between the Eastern and the Latin churches of Gaul and Spain. There is no trace of a connection between the Trishagion and a passage in the liturgy of Good Friday in the present Eastern Church, which corresponds to the Improperia of the West, a chant by the priest after Isaiah 53 has been read. There the Crucified reproaches Israel: "In what have I grieved you? Or wherewith have I caused you anger? Who has before me liberated you from distress? And now, how do you requite me? Evil for good. For the pillar of fire you prepared me the grave, for the manna you have brought me gall, for the water you have given me vinegar. Now I call the Gentiles, and they will glorify me with the Father and the Holy Ghost."[4] We shall come back to this text, the origin of which I have not been able to trace. It is a complaint against the Jews, while the combination of the Latin reproaches with the Trishagion identifies the people of God with the Church. It is the Church, and especially the penitents, who ask for reconciliation, listen to the reproaches of the Savior, and answer with the invocation of the holy, mighty, and immortal God: *"Eleison umas," "miserere nobis."* While what we could call the Improperia in the Eastern Church remain an accusation of the Jews, the Improperia of the West are an expression of penitence. This is warranted by the Trishagion. Good Friday in the Eastern Church is a day of deepest sorrow and compassion. In the Western Church it becomes through the Improperia a day of repentance.

Also the connection with the adoration of the cross is of highest theological significance. We sons of the Reformation are inclined to look at such "adoration" as a subchristian, if not superstitious and even pagan, form of devotion. However, two things should not be

---

[3]See Gregory Dix, *The Shape of the Liturgy*, p. 463ff., and the literature quoted there.

[4]I have translated this from the German text in F. Heiler *Urkircheund Ostkirche* (1937), p. 348, after a reliable and competent Orthodox priest kindly examined the text.

forgotten. First, that even within the Catholic churches the problem of such worship has been felt, and Catholic scholars have called our attention to the fact that *"crucem adorare"* and *"crucem salutare"* are used in rubrics interchangeably. *Adoratio* is in the Latin of later antiquity what in Greek is called *"proskyneda,"* the deep reverence due even to emperors and kings, as also the English "worship" can be used in a similar sense. Luther in his writing on the adoration of the Sacrament of the Blessed Body of Christ (1523) complains that there is no real translation of *"adorare"* in the secular sense. If even Jesus in John 10:35 can accept the Old Testament usage of "God" for "ruler," we must admit that it was not so easy, for the Bible might have pagan implications. Even if we can never approve of the veneration of human beings or icons, we should at least as historians admit that such forms of devotion are not simply "idolatry," though they easily can become that. Second, we should never forget that the veneration of what was regarded as the holy cross, allegedly rediscovered by Helena, or particles thereof, was the beginning of a development that led to the great theology of the cross of Western Christendom. It is astonishing how little the Early Church, the Church of the martyrs, made use in its art of the cross as a symbol. For Constantine the sign of the cross was not much more than a magic symbol, the swastika of a ruthless and superstitious ruler. It became popular with the pagan masses that then entered the Church. The discovery of what became since the fourth century the most sacred relic for Church and Empire stirred up the imagination of the people who slowly were transformed from pagans into Christians. The veneration of the holy cross in the elaborate ceremonies of Holy Week in Jerusalem, as indicated first by Cyril about 350 and so vividly described by the Spanish pilgrim Aetheria in her famous Peregrinatio was one of the ways in which the pagan souls were Christianized. Who will say how much paganism and how much Christian faith lived in the souls of those who on Good Friday kissed the cross in deep emotion, the deacons watching that no one tried to bite off a splinter of the relic. The accompanying hymns and lessons, the stations along the traditional way of Christ to Calvary, all this made the Passion a reality. Still today the words "Behold the wood of the cross on which hung the Savior of the world" point back to the time when the relic itself was shown. The same process went on when the Germanic peoples were Christianized. The splinter of the holy cross that Radegunda, the pious queen of the Franks obtained in 569 at Poitiers from Emperor Justin II became not only the object of veneration by the people, but inspired also Venantius Fortunatus to compose his great hymns "*Vexilla Regis prodeunt*" and "*Pangue lingua,*" just as later the famous Cross of Ruthwell in Scotland inspired Cynewulf's "Vision on the Holy Rood." The popularity of the relics of the cross and their veneration with all Germanic peoples, particularly the Anglo-Saxons, is evidently connected with the old Teutonic cult of sacred trees, the last triumph of which is the spread of the Christmas tree throughout the world today. How the old pagan cult was "baptized"—who would not think of the wise instructions Gregory I gave to Augustine when he sent him to Kent?—is illustrated by this verse:

> *Crux fidelis, inter omnes Arbor una nobilis:*
> *Nulla silva talem profert Fronde flore, germine*
> *Dulce lignum, dulces clavos, Dulce pondus sustinet.*[5]

Or one may think of how in the "*Pangue lingua*" the story of Adam's fall and the story of the incarnation and Passion of the Second Adam are told in the manner and even in the terms of Irenaeus and how this Christian message, together with the legend of the cross having been made from the tree of Paradise, is blended with the remnant of that cult when the cross is poetically addressed:

> *Flecte ramos, arbor alta Tensa laxa viscera,*
> *Et rigor lentescat ille, Quem dedit nativitas.*
> *Et superni membra Regis Tende miti stipite.*[6]

The adoration of the cross has here become adoration of the Crucified, just as the pagan adoration of the light at winter solstice

---

[5]Faithful cross, O tree all beauteous, Tree all peerless and divine / Not a grove on earth can show us / Such a leaf and flower as thine, Sweet the nails and sweet the wood / Laden with so sweet a load.

[6]Lofty tree, bend down thy branches / To embrace thy sacred load / O relax the native tension / Of that all too rigid wood. Gently, gently bear the members / Of the dying King and God.

has become in our Christmas the adoration of him who is the light of the world. This is the way in which the cross of Christ has become the center and theme of Western Christianity. It is a long way that led from the old relics to the Romanesque *Crucifixus*, the King who stands rather at, than hangs on the cross, to the man of sorrow in the Gothic cathedrals and to Grünewald's and Dürer's pictures of the Passion, from Fortunatus and Beda to St. Anselm and St. Bernhard and to the *theologia crucis* of Luther, Zinzendorf and the Wesleys, from the first hymns addressed to the cross to Bach's passion music. The connection of the Improperia with the adoration of the cross has helped to overcome the primitive, pagan background of that adoration, as vice versa the Improperia gained their full meaning when they were sung in the spirit of "*Salve caput cruentatum*."

III.

Where is the origin of the Improperia to be found? If we try to go back to the earlier centuries, we cannot find them at the time when the adoration of the cross and the Trishagion are traceable. A happy discovery of one of the lost writings of Melito of Sardes, however, makes it possible to prove that at least the beginnings of the Improperia are as old as the second century. In 1936, Professor Campbell Bonner of the University of Michigan at Ann Arbor announced in a symposium for Franz Cumont that Melito's Homily on the Passion ("*Peri tou Pascha*"), which was known only from some small quotations, had been in a papyrus codex, some leaves of which were in the possession of Chester Beatty in England, while others belonged to the University of Michigan. Bonner's ingenious reconstruction produced one of the most important documents of the Church of Asia at the end of the second century. In 1940, Dr. Bonner published the work in a masterly edition ("The Homily on the Passion by Melito Bishop of Sardis with some fragments of the apocryphal Ezechiel" edited by Campbell Bonner, London: Christophers, Philadelphia: University of Pennsylvania Press) that contains an elaborate introduction, the text with notes, and a translation. It seems that this masterpiece of modern scholarship has not yet found the attention it deserves, and we would like to call the attention of all those interested in the history of the Ancient Church, its theology, and its liturgy to this book.

Bonner, though mentioning in a footnote (p. 148) Micah 6:1–2 as a parallel to a passage in paragraph 87, has not seen the connection with the Improperia. But from the text as a whole, it appears that the complaints of the Crucified against his ungrateful people belong to the liturgy of the Christian "*Pascha*" of the second century, at least in the Church of Asia. This "*pascha*"[7] was the celebration of the deliverance of the new people of God through the death and resurrection of the Savior, the fulfilment of what had occurred in the Exodus of Israel from Egypt. The Exodus is the type of the redemption, as already Paul suggests in 1 Corinthians 10:1ff. The Christian "*pascha*" is the commemoration of the death and resurrection of Christ. It is, so to speak, Good Friday and Easter celebrated on the same day, the Christianized Passover of the Jews. The word "passa" is rendered by the LXX as "*pascha,*" which suggests the "*paschein,*" the suffering of the "*Kyrios,*" as "*Jahve*" is translated. In this sense "*pascha estin kyrioo*" (Ex. 12:11; comp. Lev. 23:5; Num. 28:16) is understood. Already Paul in our epistle for Easter, 1 Corinthians 5:6–8, has this understanding. It was the common understanding of all Christians in the second century, the quartadeciman controversy centering solely around the question whether the *pascha* must or must not be celebrated on the day of the Jewish Passover. If the Church of Asia retained the Jewish date, she did so on the basis of its Johannine tradition according to which Jesus died at the very hour when the Passover lambs were killed, and not on the fifteenth of Nisan. This tradition, which is irreconcilable with the narrative of the synoptists, was so strongly defended, even at the risk of a schism, because it confirmed the mysterious parallel between the deliverance from Egypt and the final redemption of the new people of God. But also they who held that the Christian *pascha* must be celebrated on a Lord's Day as the day of resurrection did at this time not distinguish between what later was called Good Friday and Easter. Both events were celebrated as one festival, the *pascha*, as the liturgical name for Easter is still today. A fasting of a day or some days was

---

[7]See Gregory Dix, op. cit. p. 338ff. and the most important article on the Pascha of the Ancient Church by the late Benedictine Odo Casel, *Jahrbuch fur Liturgiewissenschaft*, vol. xiv, (1938), pp. 1–78. It has remained unknown to Dix.

terminated during the night of *pascha* with the Eucharist. Then the "*pentecoste*" began, which was the name not only for the fortieth day, but rather of the whole period of seven weeks following "*pascha*." These are well-known facts, corroborated by all early fathers (*Epistula apostolorum*, Irenaeus, Hippolytos, Clemens Al., etc.[8]), but we must recall them in order to understand Melito's homily, which was preached after the narrative of the Exodus (Ex. 12) has been read, and which still belongs to the lessons of Good Friday. The homily begins with the words, "The Scripture of the Hebrew Exodus has been read, and the words of the mystery have been proclaimed, how the sheep (*probaton*) is sacrificed and how the people is saved." The events of the Exodus are told and explained as "mystery," as "type" of the redemption brought about through the sacrifice of the true Lamb of God. "For indeed the salvation and truth of the Lord were foreshadowed in the people, and the ordinances of the Gospel were proclaimed beforehand by the Law. So the people became the pattern of the Church, and the Law the writing of a parable, and the Gospel the setting-forth and fulfilment of the Law."[9]

A most important theological feature of Melito's understanding of the Exodus as well as of the entire Old Testament history is the way how he sees Christ already present in this history: "He is the *pascha* of our redemption, he it is who in many men suffered many things. This is he who in Abel was slain, in Isaac was bound, who in Jacob dwelt in a strange land, who in Joseph was sold, who in Moses was cast out, in the lamb was sacrificed, in David was hunted, in the prophets was dishonored. This is he who was made flesh in a virgin, whose bones were not broken upon the tree, who in burial was not resolved into earth, who arose from the dead and raised man from the grave below to the heights of the heavens." This remind of

---

[8](*Epistula apostolorum* 15; Irenaeus adv. haer. IV:10, 1; Hippolytos, Ref. VIII, 18, and many other references, especially his Homily for Easter, which has been discovered by Ch. Martin among the writings falsely ascribed to Chrysostom, Migne PG 59, 735–46; Tertullian, e.g., *De idol.* 14; Origenes, e.g., *Contra Celsum*, VIII, 22).

[9]With kind permission I follow the translation of Bonner except in cases where theology seems to demand some clearer expression. The quotations are given according to Bonner's paragraphs.

Paul's "that rock was Christ" (1 Cor. 10:4). The type is not an empty symbol. It does not only signify the reality to which it points. It contains it already as a *"mysterion"* to be later revealed in the fulfilment.

We cannot discuss here the theology of Melito any further. Suffice it to state that his Christology, to say the least, lacks clarity. He regards Christ as God incarnate (*"theos endysamenos ton anthropon"*) (par. 100 Bonner). This can be understood as modalism. He speaks of him as "buried as man he arose from the dead as God" (par. 8), which sounds like Nestorian formulas. He distinguishes between Christ and the Father when he makes Christ say: "Come hither all ye families of men . . . for I am your remission. I am the pascha of salvation, the Lamb that was sacrificed for you . . . I am the resurrection, I am your king, I lead you up to the heights of heavens, I will show you the Father (who is) from the ages" (103). This again seems to be a dangerous subordinationism. It is not surprising that later theologians found all sorts of heresies with Melito. But Melito was not a heretic. He was a profound religious thinker, as some of the fragments show, but his theology was still undeveloped. By his contemporaries he was regarded as a prophet, and a prophet he was. His style is that of ancient Christian prophecy out of which the language of the liturgy has grown. His homily is perhaps after the Gospel of John and Revelation, the greatest example of such prophetic language.[10] He was "theologos" in the same sense in which St. John was called "The Divine," "ho theologos," which means primarily "the liturgist." The *"eucharistia,"* the solemn prayer of the Eucharistic liturgy, used to be spoken by the prophets (1 Cor. 14:16), until the prophetic office more or less subsided and its functions were taken over by the bishops (Didache 10:7; 14:1). It is characteristic of Melito's charism language that it is impossible to distinguish between the preacher and the liturgist.

In this document we find for the first time the solemn reproaches of the Crucified against His people, which seem to have belonged to the liturgy of the early Christian "pascha" of the second century long before what the Greek theologians have called *"pascha staurosimon"*

---

[10]In this respect, Bonner's excellent discussion of Melito's style (p. 20ff.) needs supplementation.

(Good Friday) and *"pascha anastasimon"* (Easter) were separated from each other. We have quoted a passage from the Eastern liturgy of Good Friday that corresponds to the Latin *improperia*, proving that both have the same source. The reader is asked to compare this quotation and the *improperia* of the Roman missal, including the second part with the following passages from Melito:

> "Ye have returned unto me evil for good" (72). "Why, O Israel, hast thou done this strange wrong? Thou hast dishonored him who honored thee, thou hast held in contempt him who glorified thee, thou has denied him who acknowledged thee, thou hast renounced him who gave thee life. Thou hast done an impious deed, O Israel" (73f.).

> "Come, he says, Israel, thou hast slain the Lord" (74). "Thou didst put . . . *thorns upon his head.* Thou didst bind the beautiful hands with which he (shaped) thee from the earth; and his beautiful mouth, the mouth that fed thee with life,[11] thou hast fed with *gall"* (79). "Thou wast of good cheer, while he was hungry; thou wast eating bread and drinking wine, while he drank *vinegar and gall* . . ." (80).

> "*He it was who guided thee on the way to Egypt and preserved thee and sustained thee there.* This was he who gave thee light by a *pillar of fire,* and shelter by a *cloud,* he who *divided the Red Sea and led thee across and destroyed* thine enemy. This is he who gave *manna from heaven,* who gave thee *water to drink from a rock,* who made laws for thee in Horeb, who gave thee an inheritance in the *land* . . . who *raised up thy kings"* (64i).

> "*Come hither, Israel, and plead thy cause against me concerning thine ingratitude* . . . How didst thou esteem the ten *plagues?* How didst thou value the *pillar by night and the cloud by day, and the crossing of the Red Sea?* How didst though value the *gift of manna from heaven, the gift of water from the rock* . . . and *the land of thine inheritance?"* (87f.)

We have italicized the most convincing parallels, but one must read the entire text to see the close relationship existing between the

---

[11]This resounds still in St. Bernard's *"Salve caput cruentatum."*

Improperia and this homily. The reproaches of *Jahveh*, the *Kyrios* of the Old Testament, become the reproaches of the Crucified, the *Kyrios* of the New Testament. The idea underlying the second part of the Latin Improperia, the parallel between the Exodus and the Passion, is striking. As to the Eastern liturgy of Good Friday, there is still another passage to be mentioned. After the Gospel has been read, which closes with Jesus bearing the cross, a crucifix is carried in a sort of "entrance" through the church and is shown from the Royal Door to the people, the priest chanting, "Today he hangs on the tree who hung the earth above the waters. . . ." In the homily we read, "He who hung the earth in its place is hanged, he who fixed the heavens is fixed upon the cross, he who made all things fast is made fast upon the tree" (96). A very important parallel between Melito and the Eastern liturgy is the fact that the reproaches are directed against the Jews. There is an anti-Jewish attitude in the Eastern churches that probably goes back to terrible experiences the Church of Asia Minor had met since the days of Paul and John and that resounds even in the Gospel of St. John (comp. also Rev. 2:9 and 3:9; Acts 21:27). It belongs to the greatness of the Latin Improperia that they, by the insertion of the Trishagion with its "*eleison imas,*" "*miserere nobis*" have referred the reproaches to the Church as the people of God, thus making them one of the most powerful expressions of the penitence by which the true Church of Christ lives.

THE REFORMED THEOLOGICAL REVIEW
Vol. XVII, No. 3, October 1958

Hexaemeron: *Theology and Science with the Church Fathers*

In his book *The Oriental Religions in the Roman Empire*, Franz Cumont quotes Renan's famous statement that, if the growth of Christianity in the Roman Empire during the third century had been brought to a standstill by some fatal disease, Mithraism would have become the religion of Europe. Discussing the consequences of such a development, Cumont points out that in this case European culture would never have been able to get rid of a wrong physics. "Astrology would have been indelible, and still today heaven would move around the earth, as that physics would require." Unbelievable as it may seem to many of our contemporaries, it is a fact that in the last analysis Christianity has saved the freedom of science to search for truth. We who have seen how easily philosophers and scientists can be enslaved by a totalitarian state understand better than former generations that all true human freedom and all serious search for truth is deeply connected with the freedom and the truth of which the New Testament speaks.

I.

This may sound strange in view of the conflict between theology and science that has been going on for so many centuries. "Is the knot of history to be untied in that way that Christianity goes with barbarism and science with unbelief?" So Schleiermacher has formulated the problem confronting the modern world since the Renaissance. In point of fact, this problem existed already in one of the most critical periods in the history of the Church when around A.D. 1200 Averroism began to penetrate into Christendom with its contention that wherever the authority of Aristotle clashed with the authority of religion, one must follow the "*philosophus.*" At that time Thomas Aquinas was able to so solve the problem by building up his system that tries to render to philosophy the things that are philosophy's and to theology those that are theology's. Whatever one may think of this attempt to solve the problem, it has to be admitted that it was one of the greatest ever made, and one can well understand the deep impression it has made not only on the contemporaries of Doctor Angelicus, but also on future generations, so much that even today Roman canon law (CIC can. 1366,2) demands that all philosophical and theological instruction must maintain the principles of Aquinas. The Thomistic solution was possible because the Church had brought to the new nations of Europe not only the theological, but also the philosophical heritage of the ancient culture in the midst of which it had grown up, one of the superstitious sects from the Orient, as men like Tacitus and Celsus regarded it, not to be taken seriously by anybody except the police. But soon Christianity asserted itself also in the field of philosophy and science. No one can read Origen's great apology *Against Celsus* without feeling the superiority of the Christian thinker. "Jesus was silent" when he was falsely accused, so Origen begins, but he was no longer silent when he was asked whether he was the Son of God. Then he replied with his great confession "*Ego eimi*," (Heb. 3:1) "I am" (Mark 14:62). So the Church, this is Origen's point, cannot be silent when asked for its confession. An answer must be given in the interest of the unbelievers as well as in the interest of "him that is weak in the faith" (Rom. 14:1). Thus the encounter between Christianity and "modern science," whatever science may be just modern, takes place at all times. The encounter will assume various forms from peaceful co-existence to a cold war that may become hot and will be very hot when the Great Inquisitors on either side prepare the stakes for their *auto-da-fes* to crush the heretics of the other side.

II.

One of the burning issues of these encounters and the conflicts arising from them has always been the meaning of the *Hexaemeron*, the work of the six days, the story of creation in the first chapter of the Bible. Already Philo had to reconcile his philosophical ideas of the origin of the world, which were mainly based on Plato's *Timaios*, with the narrative of Genesis. He did so by explaining the text allegorically, as also the Christian thinkers of Alexandria later did. It is not accidental that the conflict began in Alexandria, the center of natural science and the center of allegorical interpretation of texts with pagans, Jews, and Christians. It is significant that all thinkers and fathers who are connected with Neoplatonist Alexandria make use of the allegorical method, while the great theologians of the school of Antioch, following the Aristotelian tradition of this city, prefer the literal interpretation. As it is neither possible nor of interest to our readers to describe or enumerate the countless attempts to interpret Genesis 1, we confine ourselves to a few documents and to two problems, the problems of time and space in the *Hexaemeron*.

The problem of time is posed by the "six days." But in order to understand the attempts to understand the "days," we begin with the question that arose in the second century: how old is the world? John Lightfoot, one of the greatest scholars of the learned seventeenth century has found out that Adam was created on October 23, 4004 B.C. at nine o'clock a.m. Behind this date there is a venerable tradition of Christian chronography.

Our Christian era (*ab incarnatione Domini*) goes back to Dionysius Exiguus in the sixth century. He assumed that Jesus was born in 754 of the Roman era (Varro's era *ab urbe condita*). Though adopted by the Church, it was not very much used. Only since 1431 the papal documents are regularly dated *ab incarnatione Domini.* The splendid idea that the years before the incarnation could be called years B.C. was conceived only in the late seventeenth century. Up to that time other eras had to be used. While the Jews used the Seleucidian era for many centuries, it seems to have been Julius Africanus who after A.D. 200 created for the first time an era "after the creation of the world." Still medieval chronographers accept his theory that Jesus was born 5,500 years after the creation. Several other attempts have been made. Thus in Egypt a very similar chronology was made that spread as far as Ethiopia, while the most important era was that of Byzantium, which assumes that the creation began (to use our chronology) on September 1, 5509 B.C. It was the official era of the East until Russia introduced the Christian era in 1700. But still around 1800 there are complaints that people in Germany are slow in accepting the way of the historians of dating the years B.C. This explains not only Lightfoot's attempt, but also the fact that the German reformers found it desirable to investigate the question. Luther and Melanchthon arrived at dates that would correspond to our 3690 B.C. and 3963 B.C. respectively. They have been influenced by the Jewish era, which seems to go back to the fourth century but was accepted only in the Middle Ages. The Jewish date is October 7, 3761 B.C.

What does all this mean? It means that the *supputatio annorum mundi* (Luther 1541 and 1545, *W.A.* vol. 53) belongs to the sphere of private speculation. The Church has never made a dogma of the age of the world. The Byzantine era appears officially for the first time in the dating of the decrees of the *Quinisextum*, that synod of 692 that is for the Eastern Church a highly important supplement to the fifth and the sixth ecumenical synods. But the Eastern Church would never regard such assumption as dogma, just as John of Damask in describing the *Hexaemeron* and giving details of the earth would not regard it as an orthodox doctrine that there are thirty-four provinces or countries in Europe and forty-eight in Asia (*De fide orthodoxa* II, 10). None of the Church Fathers would ever have admitted errors in the narrative of creation or in the Holy Scriptures as a whole. But they were far away from that biblicism or "fundamentalism" that makes a doctrine or a dogma of every statement of the Bible and tries to understand nature and history from the Bible only. This is a grave abuse of the *sola scriptura* of the Reformation. The great freedom of the Ancient Church in interpreting the Scriptures is especially obvious in the attempts to explain the six "days" of creation. Already Gelaus had seen that Genesis 1 speaks of six days, while 2:4 mentions one day. He had blamed Moses for this contradiction. Origen, who gives an allegorical explanation (i.e., the light of the first day means the angels), teaches a simultaneous creation, the days meaning only the diversity of the things created (*Contra Celsum* VI, 50f.; 601f.). The simultaneousness of creation has been taught even by Athanasius (*Or. contra Arianos* II, 60; Migne PG 26; 276) and is also the doctrine of Augustine. Three times he has started explaining the *Hexaemeron* literally. "But each time he ended with an allegorical exegesis" (*Cath. Encyclopedia*, vol. VII, p. 315). He repeated the question of Celsus whether there could be days before there was the sun. He asked himself whether it took the whole day to create the things assigned to a special day. How the great father has wrestled with the problem may be seen from the twelfth book of his *Confessions* where he in the sight of God—for the *Confessions* are written in the form of a prayer, and they are a prayer, a prayer of praise—discusses all the difficulties and develops his own thought without condemning those who come to different conclusions: "So when one says, 'Moses meant as I do; and another, 'Nay, but as I do,' I suppose that I speak more reverently, 'Why not rather as both, if both be true?' And if there be a third, or a fourth, yea if any other seeth any other truth in those words, why may not he be believed to have seen all these, through whom the one God has tempered the Holy Scriptures to the senses of many who should see therein things true but divers (*Deus unus sacras litteras vera et diversa visuris multorum sensibus temperavit*)? . . . I will not therefore, O my God, be so rash as not to believe, that Thou vouch safedst as much to that great man (i.e., to Moses). He without doubt, when he wrote these words, perceived and thought on what truth so ever we have been able to find, yea and whatsoever we have not been able, nor yet are, but which may be found in them" (*Conf.* XII [31], 42, translation by Pusey). In other words, Augustine realizes the impossibility of giving a full and sufficient exposition of the *Hexaemeron*. Submitting fully to the inerrant Word of God, he sees that the things of which it speaks are hidden in mysteries. Such a mystery that no man can solve is the mystery that human reason cannot understand the "time" in creation.

III.

From the problem of *time* we turn to the problem of *space* in the *Hexaemeron*. Again we look at John of Damask, the Aquinas of the Eastern Church, and we look into the *Hexaemera* by Basilius the Great and Ambrose. Both are series of sermons on Genesis 1, preached like the homilies on Genesis by John Chrysostom (Migne

PG 53) to congregations consisting of people of various degrees of education. An interesting observation may be inserted. Genesis 1:1–2:2 is the first of the "prophecies" in the Liturgy of Holy Saturday, which has now become again the Vigil of Easter. In the Roman breviary this lesson appears on Septuagesima Sunday. The custom goes back to the Ancient Church, where in the East sermons on the *Hexaemeron* were preached at the beginning of Lent, while the West had these sermons preached at the beginning of Holy Week. This becomes quite clear from Basilius, who makes repeated references to the fasting of his congregation, which attended the sermons twice a day. It is confirmed by Chrysostom, whose first homily explains the situation of the preacher as well as of his hearers who joyfully begin the Quadragesima as the beginning of a new life. For Ambrose, on the other hand, "In the beginning" refers mystically to the Pascha as the beginning of the New Year (Ex. 12:2). Ambrose repeats many thoughts from Basilius. It is interesting to compare the two preachers. Throughout the *Hexaemeron* of Basilius, one notices the Greek sense of the beauty of the world. His description of the sea is rightly regarded as one of the finest expression of that sense in Greek literature. The greatness of Ambrose lies in the solemn dignity of his speech.[1] Both praise the wisdom of the Creator. Both make use of the Psalms, of Job, of the Prophets, and of the New Testament, thus taking the doctrine of creation from the entire Bible, not only from Genesis 1. Both emphasize over against the Jewish interpretation of the Bible, the connection between the First and the Second Articles of the Creed: Genesis 1:26 cannot be understood as if the Father held a monologue or addressed the angels. Here "the light of theology shines through the window" and puts the Jew and the denier of the *Homoousios* to shame, as Basilius points out (*Hex.* IX, 6, comp. Ambrose *Hex.* VII). For here the Father speaks to the Son, who is "of one substance with the Father," "by whom all things were

---

[1] *Hex.* V, 24f. (88ff.) is one of the most touching calls to repentance. Speaking of the birds, the preacher mentions the cock crowing at Peter's denial and asks for the forgiveness of his Lord: "Give me the tears of Peter, I do not want the pleasures of the sinner." Then follows the admonition that shows this sermon is connected with the reconciliation of the sinners that took place in Milan perhaps on Maundy Thursday rather than on Good Friday.

made." Both take issue with the pagan theories of an eternal world and with the myths of ancient cosmologies. Their criticism, however, is, as far as I can see, nowhere directed against science as such. They take over what then was regarded as the result of scientific research, (e.g., in the fields of botany and zoology,) mainly from Pliny. They also accept the theories concerning the structure of the universe. For Basilius the earth is a globe. He accepts this view from the science of his age. He does not blame the scientists for their theories but for their blindness that prevents them from believing in God the Creator. He would like to know with them what stars are being seen by the inhabitants of the Southern Hemisphere (I, 4). He leaves it to his hearers to accept or to reject the theories about what we would call the law of gravity (I, 9). This is not a matter of faith. All these fathers know that the words "greater" and "lesser" of the lights created on the fourth day refer only to what appears to our eyes. They know of the immense distances between earth, moon, and sun. They know that stars are bigger than the moon. They do not fight ancient astronomy, but only the deification of the heavenly bodies and astrology, which is bound up with it. Not science, but idolatry is rejected, adoration of the creature instead of worship of the one true God, the Creator.

How free from any prejudice the fathers were appears clear in a passage by John of Damask in *De fide orthodoxa*: "Some declare the earth to be a globe, others to have the shape of a cone. In any case it is lesser and much smaller than the heaven, a point, as it were, hanging in the midst of it. But also it will perish and be transformed. Blessed is he who inherits the earth of the meek (Mt. 5:5). For the earth that will receive the saints is imperishable" (II, 11). Who will say that these fathers were bound to an antiquated view of the world, to the imagination of a flat earth with heaven above and hell below? These men were in exactly the same situation as modern Christians who find themselves realizing the size of the universe and trying to interpret the creation in such a way that they do not deny the facts established by scientific research, which, however, are to be distinguished from the theories put forward to explain these facts. Also these men lived in a world of science. Erotosthenes had computed the circumference of the earth with an astonishing approximation. Would they have accepted the Copernican view of the universe, which made the earth move around the sun? There would not have been any reason to reject it as the Church later did with detrimental consequences. Heliocentric systems are known also to ancient scientists. At least Aristarchos of Samos, who made his observations in Alexandria in 288–77 B.C., had established such a system, probably on the basis of earlier theories he improved by means of astronomical observations and exact mathematical calculations. It was not the Church that prevented this system from being accepted. There was not yet a Church to do that, and the Ancient Church would never have done it. It was merely the overwhelming authority of Aristotle who at that time and throughout the Middle Ages made the acceptance of a heliocentric view of the world impossible. It was suggested by Nicolaus of Oresme who died in 1382. So powerful was the authority of Aristotle still at the time of the Reformation that Luther also rejected the theory of Copernicus, and soon after the Reformation, Aristotle became again the philosopher of all Western Christendom in the age of orthodoxy. This could happen although Luther already had overcome the medieval idea of space in his "*Dextera Dei ubique est*," in other words, "God's right hand is everywhere," a conviction he shares with John of Damask, who understood the right hand of God as God's glory and majesty. Both Luther and Damascenus know that God is "beyond all mathematics," as Luther puts it (we would today use the word "physics").

IV.

We cannot enter here how today the problem presented by the *Hexaemeron* of the Bible must be solved. Whatever modern theology has to say, why should we not study the fathers and learn from them? The churches that today want to preserve the heritage of the Reformation must find a new approach to the Bible, and this means also a new solution of the problem of "reason and revelation." We cannot accept the solution of Thomas. Already Aquinas's great friend Bonaventura had his misgivings about the wonderful harmony Thomas found between reason and revelation. In Santa Maria sopra Minerva, the main church of the Dominicans in Rome—what a significant name—there is to be seen the famous painting by Filippino Lippi (1489) showing the triumph of Doctor Angelicus over Averroes. Seated on his cathedra surrounded by scholars, he puts his foot on the vanquished Averroes and the books of the Averroists. Pointing with his right hand to the defeated foe, he holds in his left hand another book with the words *"Sapientam sapientum perdam,"* "I will destroy the wisdom of the wise" (1 Cor. 1:19). Thomas was able to overcome Averroes at the high cost of receiving Aristotle, as far as he seemed not to contradict the Bible. However, this meant that the creation became more or less a truth of reason. Luther was right when in one of the Heidelberg Theses of 1518, the first thesis on philosophy, he says, *"Qui sine periculo volet in Aristotele philosophari, necesse est ut ante bene stultificetur in Christo."* "If one wishes to be a philosopher in Aristotle without danger, one must first become a good fool in Christ." That is what Basilius called the "light of theology" that must shine through the window. Belief in God the Creator must always be belief in the Triune God. Otherwise, God becomes a *demiourgos*, a mere action, or a *prima causa*, the first cause, according to Aristotle. Then the *Hexaemeron* loses all meaning. It becomes a mere cosmogony. Its true meaning can only be understood by him who is of one substance with the Father: *"per quem omnia facta sunt,"* "by whom all things were made."

THE REFORMED THEOLOGICAL REVIEW
Vol. XVIII, No. 2, June 1959

The Rise of the Dogma of Holy Scripture in the Middle Ages

I.

Unbelievable as it may seem to modern Christians, Catholic or Protestant, it is a fact that the Church existed for fifteen hundred years without a dogmatic definition of the nature and authority of Holy Scripture. This does not mean, of course, that it had no strong and generally accepted convictions on that subject. On the contrary, during all these centuries no one doubted that the Bible in its entirety was God's Word, that God was the principal author of the Scriptures, as their human authors had written under the inspiration of God the Holy Spirit, and that, therefore, these books were free from errors and contradictions, even where this did not seem to be the case. The Middle Ages had inherited this view from the fathers who had established it in numerous exegetical and apologetical writings. These again had not wanted to establish a new doctrine. They meant to render faithfully the doctrine of Jesus and his apostles to whom, like to all people of the Old Covenant, the Old Testament Scriptures had been the undoubted Word of God. How self-evident this understanding was appears from the fact that comparatively few writings of the fathers deal expressly with the doctrine of Scripture, as for example, Augustine's *De consensu*

76   THE JOURNAL ARTICLES OF HERMANN SASSE

evangelistarum, which has played such a great role up to our own time. Most of the innumerable patristic references to the divine character of the Bible occur in the vast mass of exegetical writings. Theology proper has always been exposition of the Scriptures even before a professor of the Bible at Wittenberg became the reformer of the Church. In the New Testament we find three great offices that are valid in all churches and not only in a local church, and which are conferred not by men, but by God directly. They are the offices of the Word: the apostles as the witnesses to the Word Incarnate, the prophets who are entrusted with the proclamation of the oral Word that God "puts in their mouth," and the teachers ("*didaskaloi*," Vulg. "*doctores*") whose task it is to explain the written Word. Thus Paul, before he took up his great mission work as apostle, had acted as teacher in Antioch (Acts 13:1). When in the Middle Ages with the rise of the universities the ecclesiastical doctorate was renewed, its content remained the same. The exposition of Holy Scripture was entrusted to Bonaventura and Thomas when on the same day they received their degrees in Paris in 1256. Theology is for Bonaventura *scientia Sacrae Scripturae*. If Paris were his, said Aquinas, he would give it for Chrysostom's homilies on Matthew. His theological work proper was to him his lectures on the Gospel and on Romans. Dogmatics was still at the time of Luther a subject for beginners, as also Thomas wrote his *Summa theologica*, as he points out in the prologue, as a book for beginners (*incipientes*), "milk for babes in Christ." It was not necessary to tell these babes what Holy Scripture is. They were supposed to know that, and only incidental remarks in the *Summa* reveal what they were supposed to know. Thus Thomas calls God the author of the Scriptures (part 1, q. 1, art. 10). The relationship between the principal author and the human authors is dealt with in the doctrine of inspiration in the *Quaestiones* on prophecy (II/II, q. 171–77). Several times he states that Holy Scripture cannot contain even a historical error (I, 32, 4; 102, 1). Such truths were regarded as self-evident. If occasionally they are expressed or hinted at in a doctrinal statement, like the Creed of Leo IX (A.D. 1053), which is still read at the consecration of a bishop, no new doctrine is introduced.

II.

As is to be expected, the dogma of the Scriptures has been least developed in the East. John of Damascus, the Aquinas of the Eastern Church, has in his presentation of the Orthodox faith no chapter on the Scriptures, but simply states in the chapter on Faith (IV, 10) after quoting Romans 10:17: "We hear the Holy Scriptures and believe the doctrine of the Holy Spirit." Since for the Orthodox Church dogma can only be a doctrine defined by one of the ecumenical synods, an elaborate definition comparable to the decisions of Trent and the Vatican Council is impossible. What this difference between East and West created by the last two Roman Councils means or does not mean we cannot discuss here. We have to state that during the Middle Ages no real difference was found by either side. This is all the more important as East and West had different Bibles as far as the Old Testament is concerned. The difference between the Septuagint and the Vulgate that had played such a great role in the discussions between Augustine and Jerome is essentially the continuation of the difference between the Bible of Jesus and the Aramaic-speaking synagogue and church on the one hand, and the Bible of Stephen, Paul, and the Greek-speaking church on the other. While the Koran ceases to be Holy Scripture if translated into another language, while also other holy books in the Orient are bound up with a certain language and even a certain alphabet, the Bible can be translated, and has even been translated already by the Jews, without ceasing to be the Word of God. This is, of course, not true of any translation. There are translations in which the Word of God is destroyed.[1] But the way in which the New Testament confirms the Septuagint or another translation

---

[1] As an interesting example, we quote from the Ethiopian text of Acts 27:33–37: "And they called upon the Lord, beseeching Paul, all of them, that they might eat food, and he said to them, 'On the tenth and the fourth day since ye ate, on the day that ye ask me for food, anoint and make ready your souls, for that which is lacking in them will be a loss to yourselves.' And having thus said, he took the bread of the Lord and giving thanks, he blessed and [broke] before them, and took and ate, and they all rejoiced, and two hundred and seventy-seven souls were anointed and were satisfied" (from S. A. B. Mercer, *The Ethiopic Liturgy*, 1915, p. 331).

shows that even varieties that to our reason seem to be contradictory can exist side by side in the Word of God.[2] Thus one and the same Word of God can exist in various forms, as also the biblical narratives show and the two churches in the Middle Ages were quite right when the question of the Bible was not made one of the issues between them.

In order to understand the dogmatic problem of the Scriptures in the Middle Ages, we look at the first dogmatician who deals expressly with the problem of Scripture. While Peter Lombard's famous *Sentences*, the official textbook for dogmatics still at Luther's time, does not deal with the Bible, one generation earlier Hugh of St. Victor (d. 1141) in his profound *De sacramentis*, a dogmatics under the title "on the mysteries of the faith," starts with the Scriptures. He begins the prologue with the statement that theology is "*divinarum Scripturarum lectio*," the reading of the divine Scriptures. He then speaks on the nature of the Scriptures and enumerates the "books of the holy word" ("*de numerolibrorum sacri eloquii*"). Following the traditional Hebrew canon, he enumerates the twenty-two books of the Old Testament, then what we call the Old Testament Apocrypha (Hugh does not use this name; "apocrypha" are for him Old and New Testament "pseudepigrapha," heretical forgeries) as "books that are read but are not written in the authoritative canon" ("*in canone autoritatis*"). "The New Testament contains the Gospels, the apostles, the fathers. There are four Gospels of Matthew, Mark, Luke, John. Similarly four apostolic volumes (namely) the Acts of the Apostles, the Epistles of Paul, the Canonical[3] Epistles, Revelation, which, conjoined with the twenty-two books of the Old Testament, make thirty, thus completing the body of the divine book. The Scriptures of the fathers are not computed in the body of the text, because they do not add other things, but rather extend in explaining and clarifying that which is contained in the Scriptures mentioned" (Migne PL 176, 186). Apart from the interesting division of the New Testament into eight books,

---

[2] E.g., 1 Cor. 15:55—the Greek text reads, "Death is swallowed up in victory." The Hebrew text reads, "*lannezach*" (forever). Theodotion transcribed "*nezach*" by "*nikos*." Such variation is not supposed toz alter the true meaning.

[3] In the Middle Ages, our "Catholic" epistles are often called "canonical."

remarkable is the negative judgment on the Old Testament Apocrypha that are contained in the Vulgate (Hugh was well acquainted with the Hebrew canon and knew the Hebrew names of the books), and the positive evaluation of the church fathers who in his opinion belong to the "New Testament." In the introduction to his exegetical writings (*De scripturis et scriptoribus Sacris*, MPL 175, 9–28), Hugh enumerates again the twenty-two books of the Old Testament, some "books like Wisdom, Sirach, Judith, Tobit" and the books of the Maccabees, "which are being read, but not written in the canon," and the eight books of the New Testament. While the Gospels form the first class of the New Testament writings and the apostolic writings the second class, corresponding to the Law and the Prophets in the Old Testament, there is a third class that would correspond to the "Scriptures," the hagiographa of the Hebrew canon. Hugh describes this third class thus: "In the third order the first class take the decretals[4] which we call 'canonical,' i.e., establishing rules (*regulares*). Then follow the innumerable writings of the holy fathers, as Jerome, Augustine, Gregory, Isidor, Origin, Bede, and other doctors. However, these writings of the fathers are not computed in the text of the divine Scriptures, just as in the Old Testament there are certain books that are not contained in the canon and yet are read. . . . In these orders the convenient structure of either Testament appears. For as the Law is followed by the Prophets, and the Prophets by the Hagiographa, so the Gospel is followed by the apostles, and the apostles in due order by the doctors." We have given these details to show how a great theologian of the early twelfth century has wrestled with the problem of the canon. It is noteworthy that the Eastern Church was not alone in being unsure about the content of the biblical canon—the synod of 692 had confirmed several and varying lists of the books of the Bible—but that even in the Latin Church the same problem existed in spite of the official lists that existed since Damasus (A.D. 382; Denzinger 32) and Innocence I, who had confirmed the canon of Carthage A.D. 397 (Denz. 92). Actually the definite canon of the Western Church was proclaimed only at Trent, though the list of Trent appears

---

[4]Church Orders, like the "Apostolic Constitution," were also in the East sometimes included in the New Testament.

already in the Decree for the Jacobites of 1441 (Denz. 706). In the last analysis, the biblical canon cannot be defined, except by an arbitrary act. This is born out by an interesting debate at the Vatican Council on the constitution "On the Catholic Faith." The question was raised what the words "sacred" and "canonical" mean if the new definition (Denz. 1787), following the decree of Trent (Denz. 783), called the books of the Vulgate "sacred and canonical." One of the most learned theologians of the council, Bishop Gasser, replied: A sacred book is a book written by the inspiration of the Holy Spirit, a canonical book is a book which is recognized by the Church as sacred and therefore received into the canon. This led to the question whether all canonical books are sacred and all sacred books canonical. The first part of the question must be answered by the Roman Church in the affirmative. What about the second part? While Gasser expressed the belief that all sacred books have been received into the canon, others thought that this could not be said with certainty. The Jesuit, T. Granderath, the historian of the Vatican Council, remarks (Vol. II, p. 466) cautiously, Gasser's assumption may be correct, but it would be very difficult to prove it. In fact, it cannot be proved that a sacred book cannot have been lost. It is a question that helps to clarify the issues in the discussion of the doctrine on Holy Scripture if we ask: What would it mean to the Church if in this age of unexpected discoveries some of the lost epistles of Paul would turn up, or texts that would historically prove the authenticity of some of the growing number of the agrapha of our Lord in a similar way as Luke and Paul warrant the authenticity of the logion quoted in Acts 20:35? One is tempted to wish for such discovery simply to cause the churches to rethink their doctrine of Scripture and the biblical canon.

III.

Behind the question of the canon, there looms another great problem, the real issue between the Catholic and the Protestant churches: the relationship between Holy Scripture and the Church. The issue is obscured if we ask for the relationship of Scripture and tradition, which for the Western Church has become the great problem since Trent has put Scripture and tradition on the same level as sources of doctrine. This was the real revolution of the sixteenth century and

not the "*sola scriptura*" of the Reformation as far as this means that
Holy Scripture alone can be the source of articles of faith. A glimpse
at the doctrinal definitions of the Middle Ages quoted by Denzinger
as teaching the ecclesiastical tradition as the second source of revelation (see Index syst. I f) shows that they do not contain this doctrine,
but that it has been read into them. They speak of the preservation
of the doctrine of the fathers and councils. Only once in a papal
document seems to occur the word *tradition* (viz., in an admonition
addressed by Gregory IX to the theologians of Paris in 1228 to retain
the classical terminology, since they have to teach theology according to the "approved traditions" of the holy fathers.) Otherwise the
word *traditio* occurs only as translation of the Greek *paradosis*, such
as in the decrees of the Seventh Ecumenical Council (787). It is
worthwhile to look at them because they reveal that during the Middle Ages East and West had a different approach to the idea of the
"tradition." The synod gives the decision on the images "following
the divinely inspired teaching of our holy fathers and the tradition
of the Catholic Church, for it is the Holy Spirit who dwells in it"
(Denz. 302 with the Greek and the Latin text). The Greek "*theadoros
didaskalia*," the doctrine in which God speaks, is rendered "*divinitus
inspiratum magisterium.*" The next paragraph (Denz 303) speaks of
the preservation of the doctrine of our holy fathers, in other
words, the tradition of the Holy Catholic Church, which from one end
of the earth to the other has received the Gospel. Thus we follow Paul
who has spoken in Christ (2 Cor. 2:17) and the divine circle of the apostles and the holy fathers, keeping the traditions (*paradoseis, traditiones*, 2 Thess. 2:14) "which we have received." In another document of
the same synod, we read, "If any one rejects the ecclesiastical tradition,
written or unwritten, be he anathema" (Denz. 308).

Here we find again a significant difference between the Eastern
and the Western Church, at least as regards the terminology. While
the Latin Church in the Middle Ages does not use very much the term
tradition, at least not in the technical sense, *paradosis* has remained
a keyword in the Eastern Church. While in the West, and not only
with Hugh of St. Victor, there is a tendency to include the writings
of the fathers in the "Holy Scriptures" —time and again one can find
quotations from ecclesiastical authorities introduced with "Scripture
says"—in the Eastern Church Scripture becomes "tradition." Already

the canon of Nicea II quoted (Denz. 308) contains the distinction between *paradosis engraphos*, which means Holy Scripture, and *paradosis agraphos*, which means tradition not contained in Holy Writ. Roman theologians must understand this in their way after the decree of Trent has declared that the Gospel is contained in "written books and unwritten traditions" (Denz. 783). In the time between Trent it did not make much difference whether tradition was understood as belonging to the Scriptures, or Scripture as being written tradition. Even modern Roman theology could approve of the statement of the Confession of Dositheos (1672): "As the author of the Scriptures and of the Church is one and the same Holy Spirit, it does not matter whether one has as teacher the Church or the Scriptures." The danger of the Eastern view is that the difference between Scripture and tradition, both canonical and non-canonical books disappears completely. The fact that nobody is able to define the border of the canon with absolute certainty does not mean that there is no such border. This is the mistake of Eastern theologians who would say with Chomjakow: "As Holy Scriptures are regarded the Old and New Testament writings as accepted by the Church, Scripture, however, has no border. For any Scripture that the Church recognizes as hers is Holy Scripture. Of such nature are mainly the confessions of the ecumenical creeds."

In contrast with the East, the Western Church of the Middle Ages has not only avoided the term *tradition* in a surprising way, but she has also refrained from dogma on tradition. In vain one seeks for a theory of tradition with Aquinas or anyone else among the great schoolmen. The idea that tradition could be a second source of revelation is absolutely foreign to them. The doctrine Hugh finds in the fathers is nothing else than an elaboration of the doctrine of the earlier parts of the "New Testament." In this sense only can the sentence of Leo's Creed be understood. "I accept the four councils and venerate them like the four Gospels. . . ." (Denz. 349). Also, though Thomas assumes that human reason can know certain "preambles to the faith" such as the existence of God, he makes it quite clear that Holy Scripture alone can be the source of any article of faith. Referring to Augustine's saying that he could attribute inerrancy only to the canonical books and to no other writers (Ep. 82; MPL 33, 277), he says, "Our faith rests upon the revelation that was given to the apostles and prophets. It cannot be based on a revelation which might perhaps have been given to another teacher" (*Summa theol.* I, q. 1, art. 8 ad 2). If in this sense the "*sola scriptura*" is the common doctrine of the Latin Church of the Middle Ages, how, then, could the dogma of Trent arise that made tradition a second source of revelation, to be received and venerated "with equal pious affection and reverence"?

IV.

This new dogma is the result not only of the Reformation. Its roots are to be found in the first of three centuries about the highest authority in the Church. While outwardly the medieval papacy reached its climax after 1200, it became obvious that its authority was declining. Since that time the question has been asked whether the pope is the antichrist. The heretical movement threatened the existence of the Church in several parts of Europe. The recovery of the Church in the fifteenth century was transitory, as the age of Boniface VIII, of the great schism, of Wiclif and Hus, and of the Conciliarist Movement proved. That this development was not only the result of political, social, and cultural movements, not only a revolution against a divine order, is proved by the fact that it is accompanied by a deep spiritual movement hidden under the turbulent surface of the late Middle Ages. The disintegration of the papal authority is accompanied by a rise of the authority of Holy Scripture, as the downfall of the political power of the pope is accompanied by the rise of the new national powers. And yet that spiritual process means more than the transition from one authority to another one, more than the transition from papalism to conciliarism. If the Waldensians criticised the papal church for not living up to the Law of God as contained in the Scriptures, if Wiclif criticized the Roman antichrist for having invented and introduced human traditions contrary to the Word of God, this could be understood and was understood by the Church of that time as a clever attempt to combat the foe with his own weapon. Actually it was infinitely more, as the facts show that the Waldensians in France and the Lollards in England knew by heart entire books of the Bible or even the whole New Testament in the vernacular. There was a hunger and thirst for the Word of God, that holy famine of Amos 8 sweeping through Europe.

Against this background one must read the statements of the schoolmen since Duns Scotus and Occam and their disciples about Holy Scripture as the only source of doctrine. What Hugh and Thomas had taught in this respect was developed into a theology of *"sola scriptura,"* which, however, did not mean an anticipation of the Reformation. As the Waldensians, the Wiclifites and Hussites remained with the medieval understanding of the Gospel as the Law of God, so the theologians of the *via moderna* remained loyal adherents of the Papal Church and its dogma. But there was a reaction on the part of Roman theologians against what they regarded as a wrong use of Holy Scripture. For them the Bible is a dark book. It can be understood correctly and interpreted authoritatively only by the teaching office of the Church. This is what the schoolmen stated against the Waldensians. They did not appeal to a tradition as another source of doctrine, but to the authority of the Church. In the trials against Wiclif, Hus, and Luther, the idea of "tradition" plays no role whatever. What is maintained against them is solely the authority of the Church in interpreting the Bible. It seems that in these discussions some apologists of the Roman position have gone so far as to deny the absolute inerrancy of Holy Scripture. When Luther at Augsburg 1518 appealed to the *sola scriptura*, Cajetan, the legate of the pope to the Diet, one of the most learned Thomists of that time, called Luther's attention to the famous "error" in Matthew 27:9, where a quotation from Zechariah is ascribed to Jeremiah, which shows, by the way, how many questions concerning Holy Scripture at that time still were open questions.

V.

Many of our contemporaries may look at the situation on the eve of the Reformation with the question: Would it not have been better for Christendom if all those questions that at that time were open still—including the *sola scriptura* and *sola fide*—had never been answered by dogmatic decisions, especially since these decisions in the various churches that arose out of the Reformation were different and even contradictory? But the wheel of history cannot be turned back. Christendom cannot go back behind the Reformation, including the reformation of the Roman Church made by the Council of Trent and finished by the Vaticanum with its *"irreformabilis."* And even if we could forget the answers given in the sixteenth century, the questions would remain and demand answers: What is Holy Scripture? What do we mean when we call it God's Word? What do we mean when we speak of its inerrancy? What is the relationship between the Bible and the Church? Whatever the answers the churches of this century will have to give, we cannot hope to give a real answer without having studied and understood the dogmatic decisions the various confessions of the age of the Reformation have given to a problem that has occupied the hearts and minds of Christendom for so many centuries and that will remain a problem for mankind to the end of the world. For if the Bible is, as we believe, God's Word, then its right understanding is a matter of life and death.

THE REFORMED THEOLOGICAL REVIEW
Vol. XIX, No. 2, July 1960

Inspiration and Inerrancy:
Some Preliminary Thoughts

I.

Future Church historians will show how the three great movements that have shaped the inner life of Christendom in the twentieth century are interrelated: the Ecumenical, the Liturgical, and what has been called the Bible Movement. What we observe today is the fact that the ecumenical as well as the liturgical endeavors of our age have led to a new search for the nature and authority of Holy Scripture as the Word of God. To ask for the reality of the Church means to ask for the objective reality of the Word of God by which it lives. Thus all Christendom seems to be returning to the great issues of the first decade of this century when Rome's fight against the Modernist Movement reached its climax in 1907, and when in 1909 with the appearance of "The Fundamentals" in America the great controversy between "Fundamentalism" and "Modernism" began in Western Protestantism. What would the modernists whom Pius X excommunicated have to say about the sweeping revolution in which Rome since Pius XII accepts almost the entire results of the historical investigation of the Bible?[1] And what would the Protestant modernists of

---

[1] The greatness of this revolution may be seen from some volumes of the series *Faith and Fact Books: Catholic Faith in the Scientific Age* (translated from

the same period who interpreted the Bible as a collection of historical documents of the greatest of all religions think of their successors
who have begun to realize that the historical approach to the Bible is
neither sufficient nor the only one?

The theology of Karl Barth in Europe, "Neo-orthodoxy" in
America, and the new "Biblical Theology" in England are remarkable
attempts to rediscover the divine side of the Bible, which remains
inaccessible to any merely historical research. Thus all churches of
Christendom are confronted with the same great problems. If we
mention some of them here, our aim is not to present a solution,
but to clarify questions that can find an answer only through the
thorough and patient work of decades and in the co-operation of
historians, exegetes, and dogmaticians of the various churches.

II.

The Bible is the written Word of God. For seventeen hundred years
this has been the conviction of all Christians. It is still today the
dogma, the public doctrine, of all Catholic churches and of those
Protestant churches that claim allegiance to their old confessions.
Whatever difficulties this dogma may present to men of our time,
as long as we claim historic continuity with the Church of all ages,
our task cannot be to abolish this dogma based on the doctrine of
Jesus and the apostles. We have rather to interpret it not in the light
of modern theories and hypotheses but facts established by scientific and historical research. It would be destroyed by any theory
meant to limit the statement that the Bible is the Word of God. It is
not enough to say that the Bible contains this Word and that some
parts of the Scriptures are given by inspiration and others, perhaps
a very little portion, not. This has been suggested not only by Protestant theologians but it is even, in principle, the solution suggested
by such a great Catholic thinker as John Henry Newman in one of

---

French; London: Burns and Oates): *Biblical Criticism* by Jean Steinmann; *The
Religion of Israel* by Albert Gelin; *The Origin of Man* by Nicolas Corte (pseud-
onym), 1959. The new approach to the Bible was made possible through the
encyclicals *Divino afflante Spiritu* (1943) and *Humani Generis* (1950).

his last publications, an article on inspiration in "The Nineteenth Century" (1883). Deeply concerned with the situation of modern man between the claims of science and those of the Church, and in view of the fact that the decrees of the Tridentine and the Vatican Council "lay down so emphatically the inspiration of Scripture in respect to faith and morals," but "do not say a word directly as to its inspiration in matters of fact," the Cardinal assumed that there are in Holy Scripture "*obiter dicta*," certain incidental statements, such as in geographical or historical matters, which do not "bear directly upon the revealed truth" and do not come "under the guarantee of inspiration." This would contradict the dogma that the Bible as such, and not only parts of it, is the Word of God. Nor is it possible to make the Bible only indirectly the Word of God. That happens if one says the Bible can become to us the Word of God. Certainly the Scriptures must become to us the Word of God, meaning we ought to accept it, by the grace of God, as his Word he speaks to us. But it remains God's Word even if we do not accept it. The Scripture the eunuch of Ethiopia read was the objective Word of God even before he was led by the grace of God to its understanding. And even if he had not found the help of Philip, he would have brought the Word of God in writing to his homeland.

Another attempt to understand Scripture is to regard it as the "record" of God's revelation in the history of salvation. No one denies that it is such a record, and a most faithful one at that. But it is impossible to separate the record from what is recorded. Just as the Word of God preached today as the faithful exposition of the Scripture is the Word of God ("*Verbum Dei praedicatum est verbum Dei*," as Luther puts it), so the Word of God that came to Jeremiah remains the Word of God when it is written in a book (Jer. 36:1ff., 28ff.). "For the word of God is living and powerful" (Heb. 4:12; cf. Jer. 1:9f. 17:7, 23:29): this applies to the Word of God in its various forms. If we call Scripture the Word of God, we do not deny that there are also other forms of the Word. The Bible itself tells us that before there was a human ear to hear or a human eye to read, there was the "Word of God" (Rev. 19:13), the Logos through whom all things are made (John 1:3; cf. 1 Cor. 8:6), who was from eternity with God and was God and was made flesh in Jesus. As this Eternal Word is living and powerful, so the oral word of the prophets and apostles, the written

Word of Scripture, and the faithful preaching of this Word of Scripture through the Church are something living and powerful. They share the life and power of him who is the Word. Holy Scripture is never a dead letter.

III.

How can a book or a series of books written by men be the Word of God? The first theologians confronted with this question were the scribes of the synagogue who collected and interpreted the Old Testament. It has often been overlooked that they in answering this question distinguished between the Torah on the one hand and the Prophets and the Scriptures on the other. While the latter were regarded as given by the inspiration of the Holy Spirit, the divine character of the Torah as the primary and principal Word of God was explained in a different way. The Torah had been created by God thousands of years before the creation of the world.[2] It existed unlike other pre-existing creatures (e.g., paradise, hell) not only in the mind of God, but in reality, a real book in heaven written with black fire on white fire. The content of this book was brought down to earth and given to Israel. God himself has proclaimed the Ten Commandments to the people. With his own finger he has written them on the tables. The rest of the Torah he has given to Moses directly, without the mediation of the Spirit. Either he has taught Moses the words of the Pentateuch as a teacher teaches his disciple, or he has dictated it, or written it, too, for Moses on the two tables. Angels are sometimes mentioned in this connection by the rabbis, but not in the sense of mediators as in Acts 7:53, Galatians 3:19, Hebrews 2:2, and sometimes in apocryphal books. The rabbis have never forgotten that there was not a prophet like Moses whom Jahveh knew face to face (Deut. 34:10). It was the Hellenistic synagogue that understood Moses as a prophet who spoke by inspiration of the Spirit. If Rabbinic theology thus distinguishes between the Torah and the rest of the Old Testament, this does not mean that the eight "prophets" (Joshua, Judges, Samuel, Kings, Isaiah, Jeremiah, Ezekiel, the Twelve— without the later distinction between "prior" and "later" prophets) and

---

[2]For the references, see Strack-Billerbeck, Vol. IV, p. 435ff.

the "Scriptures" are not God's Word. In them God speaks through the mediation of the Holy Spirit. The term "spoken from the mouth of God" is applied not only to the words of the Torah (e.g., Sifre Deut. 1:6), but also to the Prophets (Is. 61:6 Pesiq 126 a Billerbeck op. cit. 439-44. Comp. also Matt. 4:4 and Deut. 18:18).

The distinction between two ways that a book can be the Word of God belongs to Rabbinic and not to Christian theology. It is an attempt to explain the divine character of the Torah by applying to it an Oriental idea of a heavenly book we can trace in several religions up to the Islamic doctrine of the Koran. The idea is not biblical. It is, however, related to the biblical doctrine of the pre-existent Word. In Ecclesiasticus 24:31, the Torah is more or less identified with the Chokmah, the pre-existent Word of God. Since the hypostatised Wisdom (Prov. 8 comp. Ecclus 24) was understood by the Church as identical with the Logos on account of the obvious parallel between Proverbs 8:22ff. and John 1:1ff., we may find behind the strange Jewish speculation on the pre- existent Torah an anticipation of the New Testament doctrine of the pre-existent, eternal Word.

IV.

For Jesus, the apostles, and the Primitive Church, the differentiation between Torah and the rest of the Old Testament had lost its meaning. All Holy Scriptures of the canon, Law, Prophets, and Scriptures (Luke 24:44), constitute now "the Scripture" (*he graphe*). Though the singular can mean an individual passage or a single book, "Scripture" and "Scriptures" can be interchangeably used for the entire Bible of the Old Testament (comp. Matt. 22:29 with John 5:3; 10:35). Whatever differences concerning the understanding of the Scripture may exist between Jesus and the scribes, between the apostles and their Jewish adversaries, between Church and synagogue, on either side, the Scripture is accepted as the Word of God. There is a strange agreement as to the inspiration of the Scriptures. The way that Jesus quotes Psalm 110 as words David spoke "in the Spirit" (Matt. 22:43), or that Peter (Acts 1:16) quotes a "Scripture . . . which the Holy Spirit spoke beforehand by the mouth of David" corresponds exactly to the way that the rabbis quote the Old Testament. The two passages of the New Testament that teach expressly inspiration, 2 Timothy 3:16 and

2 Peter 1:21, could have been written in the synagogue. Here the question arises: What is inspiration? What does the Church mean when it teaches that *the Bible is the Word of God because it has been written by inspiration of the Holy Spirit*?

In order to find an answer we must first ask, What is this inspiration not? We must be aware of the fact that words like "inspire" and "inspiration" are used in modern English in a very general and indefinite sense. But even when used in a specific and pregnant sense, they do not do justice to the facts the Bible and the Church have in mind when they speak of the "*theopneustos*" [lit. God-breathed] Scripture. Inspiration in this sense is the work of the Holy Spirit and consequently something that defies any psychological understanding. Psychology knows such phenomena as the "inspiration" a poet or an artist experiences when suddenly insights, words, or artistic visions are given to him. Nietzsche's description of the "inspiration" in which his *Zarathustra* was given to him is perhaps the most illuminating testimony of such experience. No one would be tempted to regard this "revelation," as Nietzsche, comparing his experience with those of former ages, calls it, as wrought by the Spirit of God. The same is true of the "inspiration" claimed by prophets, Sibyls, and religious writers in many religions of the ancient world. The prophets whom Jeremiah and Ezekiel called false prophets claimed to be true prophets, to have been called by God, and to be entrusted with his Word. Psychology cannot discover the difference between true and false prophecy, between that which is truly Word of God and that which is not, between true prophetic experiences and what Jeremiah called dreams. Therefore, it cannot know what inspiration in the sense of the Bible is, let alone explain it.

The psychological misunderstanding of inspiration is very old. It begins in the Hellenistic synagogue. To Philon, Moses is a prophet, filled with the Spirit of God, full of wisdom and virtue. One must read Philon's *Life of Moses* in order to understand the greatness of the Old Testament as a book of real history. Philon reads his own ideals into the stones of the Pentateuch. It was the "blameless deed" of a virtuous philosopher when Moses killed the Egyptian (*De Vita Mosis* I, 44). This great man becomes what the Greek calls a "*theios aner*" [lit. a man of God] when he is in ecstasy and the divine Spirit speaks through him, the last of these ecstasies taking place immediately before his death when he prophesies his own death and burial (II, 291). In another context[3] we have shown how this psychological misunderstanding of the biblical inspiration by Hellenistic Judaism has deeply influenced the Early Church and how even still Augustine tries to apply this idea of prophetic inspiration and of a divine book produced by such inspiration to the Bible. It is one of the great tragedies of the history of the Church that the early fathers, and even still Augustine, instead of taking the doctrine *de Sacra*

Scriptura from the Scriptures themselves approached the problem with a preconceived idea of a divine book that must bear all the marks of a book claiming divine origin, a most perfect book without what our human mind would call "error," without contradictions, a book whose divine origin can and must be recognized by any unprejudiced reader. For everybody can see the perfection of the Bible, for example, if he observes how all prophecies of the Old Testament have been fulfilled in the New. "How is not he to be regarded as God whose prophets have not only given the congruous answer on subjects regarding which they were consulted at the special time, but who also, in the case of subjects respecting which they were not consulted, and which related to the universal race of man and all nations, have announced prophetically so long a time before the event those very things of which we now read, and which indeed we now behold?" (*De consensu evang.* I, 19 quoted from Nicene and Post-Nicene Fathers VI, p. 88). This view of prophetic inspiration that puts the biblical prophets into one category with the pagan prophets is untenable. The inspiration of Isaiah is something quite different from the inspiration of the Sibyl of Cumae whom Augustine regarded as a true prophetess. If this is so, then the psychological explanation of inspiration Augustine gives and has left to future centuries up to our time must be abandoned. All these venerable pictures in which the relationship between the divine and the human author is described and which go back to Augustine and Gregory the Great—head and hands, author and secretaries, the *amanuenses* even as pens (*calami*), the process of inspiration as "*suggerere*"

---

[3]"Sacra Scriptura: Observations on Augustine's Doctrine of Inspiration," *Reformed Theological Review*, Vol. XIV, No. 3, Oct. 1955, pp. 65–80. See the reprint of this article in this volume.

or "*dictare*," and so on—must be seen as what they are: attempts to understand psychologically what no psychology ever can grasp.

For if inspiration is a work of the Holy Spirit, it is like all works of the Spirit, beyond the sphere of what our reason can understand. A real conversion can be accompanied by deep emotions. These emotions may be studied by a psychologist, but not the conversion itself. The same emotion may be present in an imaginary conversion. The work of the Holy Spirit in a human soul may be accompanied with such phenomena as we find in the Primitive Church: prophecy, glossolaly, miraculous healing, and the like. But the same phenomena may accompany experiences definitely not caused by the Holy Spirit. Who will explain how faith, hope, and charity are created in a human soul? Who will explain the effects of the Word of God and of the Sacraments of Christ in the depth of our souls? It is very dangerous, to say the least, to speak of the "experience of the Holy Spirit" or of the guidance of the Spirit, as we so easily do. How often has the Spirit who was experienced or whose guidance was acknowledged not the Holy Spirit but another spirit? If we confess, "I believe in the Holy Spirit," we admit that the Holy Spirit is an article of faith and not an object of observation.

V.

If we apply this truth to the problem of the inspiration of Holy Scripture as one of the great works of the Holy Spirit, we may define inspiration as that action of God the Holy Spirit by which he causes chosen men to write his Word in the form of human writings. It would not be sufficient to define this action as assistance, as sometimes has been done. Many books have been written with the assistance of the Holy Spirit. We would claim that for Augustine's *Confessions* and other works of Christian writers, or for the great deeds of the Church or for many confessions of faith. Such books and documents, however, remain human writings. The Roman Church, which regards the final definitions of doctrine by the pope as infallible exposition of the doctrine entrusted to the Church, would nevertheless not ascribe "inspiration" to the one whom she regards as vicar of Christ and to his decisions. The Vatican Council speaks of "divine assistance." Inspiration is ascribed to the Scriptures only, though the work of the

Holy Spirit in the interpretation of the "tradition" may practically come very close to his work in the inspiration of Scripture.

The divine inspiration of the Scriptures must be distinguished from the way in each case the will of the Holy Spirit was carried out. In some cases we hear that the writer received the direct command: Write! (e.g., Ex. 17:14; Jer. 30:2, 36:2; Rev. 1:11). There may have been cases of real dictation, comparable to the phenomenon of "automatic writing," which has been described by psychologists of religion. Just as biblical prophecy is not bound to any definite psychological experiences (visions, auditions, etc.), so there is no definite form of inspiration. Leviticus has been written and composed in quite a different way from the way in which the *Miserere* came into existence. John 17 has not been written in the same frame of mind as the Epistle of James. A variety of ways of inspiration must be assumed in view of the variety of writings, styles, and literary genres found in the Bible. And yet the inspiration itself was in all cases the same. God the Holy Spirit caused his Word to be written in the form of human writings. In a "variety of operations," the Holy Spirit created the Bible in which the song of Lamech and the Lord's Prayer, Song of Songs and the Epistle to the Romans, the Gospel of St. John and the story of the conquest of Canaan belong together and nothing is superfluous, not even the cloak that Paul left with Carpus at Troas.

The Bible is *one* in virtue of the inspiration. Without the belief that God the Holy Spirit has created it, we could regard it only as a collection of writings of greater or lesser religious or historical value produced and gathered in the vicissitudes of history. For even the view that the unity of the Bible rests upon the decision of the Church that defined the canon is untenable. According to the belief of the Church of all ages, even the Roman Church, the Church has not produced but received the Scriptures. She has canonized the books, and only such books that she firmly believed to have been written by the inspiration of the Holy Spirit.

VI.

If Holy Scripture can be understood properly only as the work of the Holy Spirit, then *the doctrine of inspiration is an essential part of the doctrine of the Holy Spirit.* This is borne out by the Nicene

Creed, where both are connected in the words, "I believe in the
Holy Spirit . . . who spoke through the prophets." What this means
is shown by the "according to the Scriptures" of the preceding sentence. This again must be read in the light of 1 Corinthians 15:3f.[4] If
our observation is correct, how could anyone expect from the synagogue a real understanding of the inspiration of the Scriptures? How
could anyone understand the Holy Spirit before Christ's promise of
the Paraclete was fulfilled at Pentecost? If we, moreover, remember
that only after three hundred years, at the synods of Alexandria 362
and Constantinople 381, the divinity of the Holy Spirit was recognized, we can hardly blame the fathers of the first centuries that they
were not able to overcome the view of the pneuma as a divine power
or divine influence enabling and causing men to speak divine words
and to write divine Scriptures. The full meaning of the fact that the
name *Parakletos* is given in the New Testament to Christ as well as
to the *Pneuma Hagion*, and that in John 15:26 and 16:7ff. the Spirit is
referred to as a person was realized only by the fathers of the fourth
century. Very rarely, however, they mention the Scriptures among
the work of the Holy Spirit.[5] We must not forget that the doctrine
of the Holy Spirit has never been finished in the Ancient Church.
Otherwise the great dissensus between East and West about the
Filioque could not have happened. It is significant that the history
of the liturgy also shows a strange neglect of the Holy Spirit. "Who
with the Father and Son together is worshiped and glorified," says
the Nicene Creed, confirming the rule that every dogma appears first
in the liturgy. The Holy Ghost is indeed mentioned in the conclusion of the prayers of the Church. But the logical conclusion from
the Trinitarian dogma that prayers can also be directed to the Third

---

[4]This basic creed of the Church would be understood better if the biblical
Pauline background were taken more in account. It has grown out of the binitarian formula of 1 Cor. 8:6, which is the Pauline, Christian version of the basic
confession of the O.T., the "Shema" of Dt. 6:4. Still the creed of 325 is binitarian
like the Great Gloria of the Western liturgy. Pauline is the "one God . . . and one
Lord Jesus Christ through whom all things are," as also the "one baptism" (Eph.
4:5) and the connection of the Spirit with the Lord (2 Cor. 3:17).

[5]Gregory of Nyssa and Didymos seem to be the only theologians who do
that, but they do not elaborate on this thought.

Person of the Trinity has never been drawn in the liturgy. The orations are directed to the Father and Son, even at Pentecost and in the Roman Mass of the Holy Ghost. This shows the antiquity of the Christian liturgy, which still today celebrates Pentecost as a feast of Christ as in the first centuries. The liturgy knows only the invocation of the Holy Spirit in the "*Veni sancte Spiritus . . . ,*" out of which the medieval hymns and those of the Reformation churches directed to the Holy Spirit have grown. If we must state that the doctrine of the Holy Spirit is unfinished in the Church, can we then be surprised that the same is true of the inspiration of Scripture? All churches of Christendom feel today this great gap in their doctrines.

VII.

If Holy Scripture is the work of God, the Holy Spirit, its main task is that ascribed to the Paraclete by Christ: "he will teach you all things and will bring to your remembrance all that I have said to you" (John 14:26); "he will bear witness to me" (15:26); "he will guide you into all truth . . . he will glorify me, for he will take what is mine and declare it to you" (16:13f.). Christ is the real content of Holy Scripture. This was not only Luther's understanding of the Bible. It appears already in the Middle Ages, as with Wiclif. Scripture, he points out, can be understood only by him who believes "that Christ is true God and true man because he is the Messiah promised to the fathers." Scripture must be understood from those parts that clearly testify to this truth. Then "the entire Scripture and each part of it "teach" that Christ, God and man, is the Redeemer of all mankind, the a\ Author of the whole salvation, and he who gives the last reward."[6] The Jews could not, and the synagogue today cannot, understand the Old Testament, because they have rejected Jesus as the Messiah. No one can understand the Scriptures of the Old Testament unless he knows Christ and understands what it means that "To him all the

---

[6]"*Conclusio autem finalis totius scripturae et cuiuslibet partis suae est, quod Christus, deus et homo, est humani generis . . . redemptor, totius salutis autor et ultimus praemiator,*" De Veritate Sacrae Scripturae III cap. 31 (ed. Buddensieg vol. III, p. 242, 18ff.).

prophets bear witness that everyone who believes in him receives forgiveness of sins though his name" (Acts 10:43). As in the great vision of Revelation 5, "the Lamb that was slain" alone is "worthy to take the book and open the seals thereof" (5:9), namely the heavenly book in which the events of the future are written, so the Old Testament is a book sealed with seven seals till the Risen Lord opens it to men, until the Risen Lord "opens their understanding that they might understand the Scriptures" by showing them how "all things must be fulfilled which were written in the Law of Moses, and in the prophets, and in the Scriptures concerning me" (Luke 24:44f.). As a stained window is meaningless until it is seen against the light, so the Old Testament becomes clear to him only who sees the light of Christ shining through it.

This connection between the inspiration by the Holy Spirit and Christ as the content of the Scriptures corresponds to the New Testament doctrine of the Holy Spirit. Apart from the passages on the Paraclete (John 14–16), Paul's utterances have to be taken in account. It is the Holy Spirit who enables us to confess Jesus as the Lord (1 Cor. 12:3, comp. Matt. 10:19f.), as also the Holy Spirit enables us to call God our Father (Rom. 8:15), see the words in the "*Veni Creator Spiritus*" that express this truth: "*Per te sciamus da Patrem, noscamus atque Filium.*" Christ and the Holy Spirit belong for Paul so closely together that in 2 Corinthians 3:17 he almost seems to identify them: "The Lord is the Spirit." This is, however, as the immediately following words "The Spirit of the Lord" show, no real identification, but rather the expression of an inseparable connection as the later Church has it expressed in the "*Filioque.*" It could be formulated, "Where Christ is, there is the Holy Spirit. Where the Holy Spirit is, there is Christ."

As in the Gospel Jesus and the Holy Spirit belong together since the incarnation, so in the entire Bible Christ and the Holy Spirit belong together from the first chapter of Genesis, where we read that the Spirit of God moved upon the face of the waters when God created all things through his eternal Word (Gen. 1 read in the light of John 1:1ff.; 1 Cor. 8:6; Heb. 1:2), to the last chapter of Revelation, where the Spirit and the Church say, "Come, Lord Jesus" (22:17-20). This understanding of Holy Scripture does not mean that we can find in any passage a Christological meaning, or that we even should look for it. Only those passages of the Old Testament that are clearly interpreted in this way in the New Testament can be regarded as clear testimonies to Christ. But they are sufficient to convince us that Christ is the content proper of the entire Bible even there where we cannot perceive him with the limitations of our human mind.

VIII.

This understanding of the inspired Bible as the Scriptures in which God the Holy Spirit testifies to God the Son frees us from many a false understanding of inspiration. Men of the sixteenth and seventeenth century who thought of books and their authors in terms of humanism were embarrassed by what seems to be the very bad Greek of some of the New Testament writings. A perfect book must be written in a perfect, flawless language.

The apologists of all times since Origen's "Against Celsus" have had to defend the Bible against those who found in it moral deficiencies, inaccuracies, contradictions, and errors. The Church fathers as well as the medieval and modern theologians were confronted with the fact that the story of creation cannot be understood in terms of natural science.

The conviction is growing that the time has come when the Church has to give up definitely the well-meant attempts to reconcile the first chapter of the Bible with "modern" science. Since theology moves very slowly, "modern" science proves in each case to be the science of yesterday. The Church defended the geocentric view of the world when it long since had become obsolete. It accepted the heliocentric view when the center had already moved to the center of our galaxy and from there to other galaxies. How detrimental to the Christian faith this has been is now generally recognized. The rapid development of modern physics has led to serious warnings on the part of Roman theologians as well as such an outstanding leader of conservative Reformed theology as Professor Berkouwer against the repetition of the great mistakes made in the case of Galileo and on other occasions. It may be a heroic act of faith to accept the story of creation as a substitute for a scientific view of the origin of the universe, but to demand that from a Christian means to excommunicate all scientists who in firm belief in their God and Savior do the work of their calling that is based on the dominion over all the earth given to man by his Creator. How many souls have been lost through the failure of the Church to do justice to the facts established by solid research, by experiment and observation.

We have shown on another occasion what we could learn in this respect from the fathers of the Church.[7] This does not imply any denial of a dogma of the Church. Neither the creation of the world "out of nothing" is abandoned, nor the special creation of man and the fall of the first man as an historic event. What must be admitted by the Church is that the Bible in speaking of such things uses a language different from ours. It speaks to men of very ancient times in a way that was even by the church fathers felt to be very old and simple. How could men of such times have understood a story of creation told in the terminology of Aristotle or Augustine, let alone of twentieth century science, which probably will be obsolete in another century? This is what Chrysostom has called the "*synkatabasis*" ("*condescensio*") of God. "Behold the condescension of the divine Scripture, see what words it uses on account of our weakness," he says, commenting on Genesis 2:21 (Migne SG 53, col. 121, cf. col. 34f., 135; vol. 59, col. 97f.). In a similar way, Jerome and other fathers have solved the problem.

If we say that, we do not think that the way of thinking and speaking in those very early times was inferior to ours. It was different, but we would by no means dare to say that our scientific view of the world gives us a deeper insight into the nature of the world. They were very far from our rational thinking. They saw realities we no longer see, just as primitive people today still observe things we no longer perceive. What they said about such realities must not be regarded as myth, though it sometimes may remind us of the language of mythology, the reason being that pagan mythology is a deteriorated and paganized echo of such wisdom.

In addition to the "law of condescension" in the Bible, we must take in account what we could call the "law of parallels" in Holy Scripture. As we find in the Hebrew language the *parallelismus membrorum* in poetic and prophetic texts, so we find the strange fact that

---

[7]"Hexaemeron: Theology and Science with the Church Fathers," *The Reformed Theological Review*, Vol. XVII, No. 3, October 1958.

almost every important event is told several times and always with variations. There are two stories of creation. There are all the other parallels in the Pentateuch, due to the different sources. We have two great histories of Israel, one written from the prophetic, the other from the priestly point of view. In the New Testament even, four lines run parallel in the Gospels. What does it mean that we have parables and other sayings of Jesus in the Gospels, even the Lord's Prayer and the eucharistic words in various forms? Two baptismal formulas also appear in the New Testament. This must have a meaning. How easy would it have been for the Church to agree on one Gospel or to create an official harmony of the Gospels.

Why have all attempts at such a harmony failed? The Church of Syria, which used the Diatessaron, became heretical and its return to orthodoxy coincided with the return to the Four Gospels. The Gospel harmonies created in the sixteenth and seventeenth centuries or those to be found in some Catholic Bibles have proved to be failures. The picture of Jesus they give is always unrealistic and lifeless, as when, for example, a twofold cleaning of the temple is assumed or even several healings of the same person. No one has been able to harmonize the apparent "contradiction" regarding the chronology of the Passion and the events of Easter. But are these real contradictions? If we compare paintings of the crucifixion by four great painters, who would find "contradictions" and "errors" in them? Have not Grunewald and Durer seen more than a photograph could show? The strange idea of the sacred history underlying the apologetic attempts to harmonize all differences goes back to an age that no longer was able to understand the biblical idea of history. Neither the Jewish rabbis nor the fathers of the Church nor their pagan adversaries like Celsus and Porphyrius have been able to think in terms of history. This is to a large degree due to the fact that Greek philosophy had no understanding of history.

What we have to learn again is to measure biblical history by its own standards. Instead of asking whether a certain narrative corresponds to our standards, we should ask, why did the biblical writer tell events and record words just the way he did it? Luke, for example was a critical historian who evaluated his sources (1:1ff.). Why has he given or inserted in Acts three reports on the conversion of Paul that are not in full agreement? He must have been aware of this.

Instead of finding fault with his method and accusing him of errors, we should rather ask: What was his intention when he wrote these passages? Why did he not regard as intolerable contradictions what later centuries have called that? The great concern of the Church in factual historical truth is deeply rooted in the Bible. How carefully are the events in the history of salvation dated (e.g., Is. 6:1, Amos 1:1, Luke 3:1, 1 Cor. 15:1ff.) lest anyone might deny the facts.

The words "under Pontius Pilate" belong to the Nicene Creed just as "according to the Scriptures." What, then, is factual historical truth for the holy writers? This is one of the great problems biblical theology has to investigate and to answer. It cannot be answered by the statement that "truth" in the Bible has a deeper and more comprehensive meaning than *"veritas"* with Aquinas (*Summath.* I qu. 16 *"De Veritate"*). However, biblical truth cannot be without what we understand by propositional truth, because otherwise the revelation of the Bible would become myth.

All creeds of the Church from the first creedal statements of the New Testament present facts (see 1 Cor. 15:1ff.). Without this factual, dogmatic character Christianity would be a mystery religion. How and why the holy writers transmit to us one truth in several parallel records and what the variety means, this is one of the foremost problems of biblical hermeneutics. It is a most comprehensive question, for the fact also that the New Testament knows and uses two "Old Testaments," the Hebrew and the Greek, comes under the "law of parallels."

IX.

Whatever the answer to these questions may be, one thing Christian theology can never admit, namely, the presence of "errors" in the sense of false statements in Holy Scripture. The holy writers may have used, as they actually have, sources, traditions, methods of a prescientific historiography, and literary forms of the ancient Orient we do no longer possess. Their language may be figurative, their narratives sometimes bordering on legend and poetry or even using such forms of expression. Yet all this has been written by the inspiration of the Holy Spirit. In a way that is and always will remain inscrutable to human reason these truly human writers wrote God's

Word. The inspiration of Holy Scripture has often been understood as an analogue to the incarnation. It seems that this view is becoming more and more the common possession of Christendom, especially since it has been introduced into Roman Catholic theology and approved by the encyclical of 1943.

To the dilemma formulated by Paul Claudel, "either the Bible is a human work . . . or else Scripture is a divine work," Steinmann (*op. cit.* p. 14) has rightly replied, "One might as well say: Either Jesus Christ is man or he is God." We cannot go into this theological problem here. The time may come when the Christological decision of Chalcedon will become the pattern of a solution of the doctrine of Holy Scripture and its inspiration. Between the Monophysitism of Fundamentalists who fail to understand the human nature of the Bible and the Nestorianism of modern Protestant and Anglican theology that sees the two natures but fails to find the unity of Scripture as a book at the same time fully human and fully divine, we have to go the narrow path between these two errors. But we must never forget that the Chalcedonense has been authoritatively explained in the doctrine of the "*enhypostasia.*" The human nature has its hypostases in the divine. So Holy Scripture is first of all and essentially God's Word. The human word in the Bible has no independent meaning. What would the Books of Samuel and even the Epistle to the Romans mean outside the Bible? God has given us these writings as his Word.

"What is Holy Scripture without its content, Christ?" "*Tolle Christum e scripturis, quid amplius invenies?*" as Luther wrote against Erasmus: "Take Christ out of the Scriptures, what remains?" As we humbly bow before the mystery of the incarnation of the Eternal Word, so we accept in great humility the mystery of Holy Scripture as the written Word of God in which the Father through the Holy Ghost testifies to Christ: "This is my beloved Son in whom I am well pleased: hear ye him."

THE REFORMED THEOLOGICAL REVIEW
Vol. XX, No. 2, June 1961

The Second Vatican Council (I)

1.

Shortly before World War II, rumours were abroad about a new ecumenical council to be summoned by the pope in connection with the fourth centenary of the Council of Trent, which was opened on December 13, 1545. If such plans existed for 1945, they were frustrated by the war. It is, however, most likely that the last period (January 18, 1562 to December 4, 1563) of that great council that has created modern Roman Catholicism will coincide with the Second Vatican Council. Shortly after his succession, Pope John XXIII announced to the College of Cardinals assembled in the Basilica of St. Paul on the Feast of the Conversion of Paul, January 25 1959, his intention to convene an ecumenical council. The announcement, made in deep emotion, as the allocution itself stated, was received with joy and unanimous approval. At Pentecost, May 17, an "Antepreparatory Commission for the Ecumenical Council" was appointed with Cardinal Tardini as moderator.

In his first encyclical, "*Ad Petri Cathedram*," of Peter and Paul, June 28, the pope referred right in the beginning to the announcement. In the section dealing with the "Unity of the Church," he gives the following information[1]:

---

[1] The documents are quoted from the official English translation as contained in "Catholic Documentation," Sydney Sept 1959 and Dec. 1960. Those

Bishops from every part of the world will come to discuss matters important to religion. The council's chief business will be concerned with the growth of the Catholic faith and the renewal along right lines of the habits of Christian people and the adapting of Christian discipline to the needs and conditions of the present time. That event will surely be a wonderful manifestation of truth, unity and charity; a manifestation indeed, which it is Our hope that those who behold it, but are separated from the Apostolic See, will receive as a gentle invitation to seek and find that unity for which Jesus Christ prayed so ardently to his heavenly Father.

The strong plea for reunion with Rome made in the following paragraphs shows that the reunion of Christendom will be, though not a topic of the agenda, yet one of the great thoughts pervading the whole work of the council.

With these actions began the first, the "antepreparatory" phase. All bishops in communion with Rome were asked to make suggestions and to express wishes. More than two thousand replies were received, carefully digested and supplemented by the suggestions and opinions of the various sections of the Curia and of the universities. In the surprisingly short time of one year, the work of the "Antepreparatory Commission" was finished. On Pentecost 1960, the next stage began with the Motuproprio "*Superno Dei nutu*" and a discourse (in Italian) by the pope after Vespers on Pentecost Sunday in St. Peter's. Here he declared the "introductory" or "antepreparatory" phase finished and opened the second, the "preparatory" phase, which is to go on until the third phase begins, "the celebration of the distinguished and general assembly: the council in its most resplendent solemnity," to be followed by the fourth stage, "the promulgation of the acts of the council." This classification shows what importance is attached to the two phases of preparation.

Actually the council is already at work. The Motuproprio announces that the official name of the council shall be "The Second Vatican Council" ("*Concilium Vaticanum Secundum*"). Technically it could have been summoned as a continuation of the Vatican

---

not contained therein are translated directly from "*Acta Apostolicae Sedis*" 1959 and 1960.

Council of 1869/70, which has never been solemnly closed but only adjourned. The document repeats from *Ad Petri Cathedram* the definition of the purpose of the council as quoted above. It establishes ten "Preparatory Commissions" whose number later may be increased, each to be presided over by a cardinal. They have to deal with (1) Theology (Scripture, tradition, faith, morals), (2) Bishops and government of the dioceses, (3) Discipline of clergy and laity, (4) Religious orders, (5) Discipline of the Sacraments, (6) Liturgy, (7) Studies and seminaries, (8) The Eastern churches, (9) Missions, (10) Lay apostolate; Catholic action, religious and moral. Their work is coordinated in a "Central Commission."

There is no commission so far to deal expressly with matters of reunion. But a special office is created together with the commissions:

> "In order to show more our love and goodwill toward those who claim the title of Christians (*"qui Christiano nomine decorantur"*), but are separated (*"sejuncti"*) from this Apostolic See, and to enable them to follow better the labours of the council and make it easier for them to find the way to attain that unity for which Jesus Christ prayed so ardently to his heavenly Father, a special body (*"coetus"*) is established which will have as its moderator one of the Cardinals of the Holy Roman Church to be named by Us. It will be constituted in the same way as the commissions mentioned above."

Cardinal Bea, a German Jesuit, has meanwhile been appointed to that office.

An amazing amount of work has been done since Pentecost 1960. Already in July of that year, a volume was published containing all official documents up to that time. It is to be followed by three more volumes in which the whole work of the Antepreparatory Commission will be made available. Vol. II will contain the correspondence from the bishops all over the world. The indexes will give cross-references of the 8,987 suggestions submitted. A second series of volumes will contain the documents and acts of the Central Preparatory Commission and the special commissions and secretariats.

The whole work is so well advanced that the pope has asked the faithful to pray that the council can be held in 1962. No definite date has as yet been announced, no "bull of convocation" issued. In the case of the First Vatican Council, which began on December 8 (the Feast of the Immaculate Conception) 1869, the *"bulla convocationis"* appeared on June 29, followed by the invitation of the schismatic Oriental churches on September 8 and the letter addressed to "all Protestants and other non-Catholics" five days later. The only indications of the possible date are special prayers requested from the faithful and approved by the pope. While the prayer in July is still for those who will take part in the council, the intentions for the months from August are directly for the council. If the Vatican Council began on the day that commemorated the dogma of the Immaculate Conception, this time August 15, the Feast of the Assumption of Mary, might be regarded as the proper day in remembrance of the dogma proclaimed by Pius XII.

2.

The preparatory work has been tackled with an admirable promptness and efficiency. While this was possible thanks to the modern means of communication of which no one would have dreamt when the First Vatican Council was prepared in the years 1864–9, it is obviously also due to the desire to accelerate the work, the completion of which depends to a large degree upon the political situation of the world. The "intention" for the prayers in September 1962 is "that the work of the ecumenical council may proceed unhindered and be brought to the desired conclusion." It is not necessary to go far back to the history of Trent and even to the ancient synods to realize what the political situation can mean for a council. Even the Vatican Council of 1869/70 could do its work only as long as Rome and the Papal State was protected by a French occupation force. The constitution *"Pastor Apterous"* with the dogma of the pope's direct episcopal power over the entire Church and his infallibility in defining a dogma was accepted and proclaimed as it were in the last possible moment on July 18, 1870. The next day war broke out between Prussia and France. The bishops of the countries involved had to go home. The French troops had to be withdrawn. In September the Italian army occupied Rome. In October the council was adjourned *sine die*. What could happen to the Second Vatican

Council if a major political conflict should break out with the council still in session? In this connection it may be observed that the pope seems to have in mind a very brief council, as the prayers mentioned would indicate.

It was this difficult situation, in which any council in the modern world might find itself, that prompted a champion of the papal infallibility like Manning, then Archbishop of Westminister, to force the decision of July 18, 1870. To the minority who declared the dogma to be inopportune, he replied that the question was not whether it was opportune or inopportune to proclaim that doctrine, but whether or not it was true. If it must be regarded as true, then it had to be declared just in view of what could happen in the future when wars and revolutions as Manning anticipated would make it impossible to hold another council. The new dogma would make it possible for the Church not only to survive, as it had survived more than three centuries since Trent without an ecumenical council, but also to carry on its business in proclaiming the divine revelation to the world by defining new dogmas, if necessary.

The weight of this argument becomes evident if one thinks of the situation of the Eastern Church that locates more or less the infallibility of the Church in the ecumenical council and, thus, is unable to proclaim a doctrinal decision of binding force because she cannot summon such council. It is easy to criticize the Roman doctrine of the Ecumenical Council as codified in the Codex Iris on the basis of the Vatican decrees. Canon 220 says, "1. There can be no ecumenical councils which were not summoned by the Roman Pontiff. 2. It belongs to the Roman Pontiff to preside over the ecumenical council either in person or through others, to determine the matters to be dealt with and the order in which they have to be treated, to transfer, suspend, dissolve the council and to confirm its decrees." Canon 229 adds that in case the pope should die during the ecumenical council, this would be automatically interrupted until the new pope —who, of course, can be elected only by the cardinals—orders it to be resumed and continued.

We must ask what, then, an ecumenical council actually is and whether it is not superfluous, especially since canon 227 states that its decrees cannot be of any obligation, unless they have been confirmed by the Roman Pontiff and promulgated at his command, and since canon 228,2 states that there cannot be an appeal from a sentence of the pope to the council. What does, in view of all these limitations, can. 228,1 mean: "The Ecumenical Council possesses the highest power over the Church Universal"?

Not only we are asking this question. It is the great problem for the Roman Church itself since 1870 when the dogma of the papacy was finished: Can the unique authority of the pope be reconciled with the "*suprema potestas in Universam Ecclesiam,*" which Rome, following the tradition of the Church of all ages, attributes to a council? This question will have to be answered by the forthcoming council. Its answer will determine the future relationship between Roman and Eastern Catholicism. It will open or forever close the door to a reunion of East and West. In this respect the Second Vatican Council will be one of the most momentous events in the history of the Church. The decision of the First Vatican Council is, as any doctrinal decision made by the pope, irreformable, as the fateful constitution "*Pastor Apterous*" states. Will it be possible to interpret it in such a way as to restore to the episcopate and to the ecumenical council such an amount of authority as would satisfy the Eastern churches? This is the first and paramount problem of reunion. For the Eastern churches are the only ones which Rome, outside of its own orbit, counts as parts of the Church Universal. Whatever possibilities of reunion may exist with those Christians who are separated, according to the view of Rome, not only from the Apostolic See, but also from the Church, such as Anglicans, Lutherans, Presbyterians, and so on, the reunion of the Church means the reunion between Rome and the Orthodox churches of the East, which must precede the reunion with us "separated brothers," as we are called in "*Ad Petri Cathedram.*"

3.

As Rome will have to answer the question of what an ecumenical council is that is completely dominated by the pope, so the East will have to say what it understands by an ecumenical council and why it should not be governed by the pope. What makes a council ecumenical? The word "ecumenical" itself does not say that. "*He oikoumene (chora* or *ge)*" means for the Greeks the earth as far as it is inhabited by the Greeks in contradistinction to the countries inhabited by the barbarians.[2] In Luke 2:1;

Acts 17:6; 19:27; and 24:5, it means the Roman Empire, in other passages the entire world. It is similar as in the case of the words "catholic" or "universal," which by no means always must be understood in the strict sense. A synod of Carthage, if it is held for all North Africa, like that of 418, can be called "universal" or "general." The word "catholic" soon became identical with "orthodox," perhaps already in the second century.

To Augustine the communion to which he belongs is in contradistinction from the Donatists, the "*communio catholica.*" Constantine II writes a letter "to the people of the Catholic Church in Alexandria" (Theodoret, *Hist. eccl.* II,2). In the liturgy of St. Mark, the Patriarch of Alexandria who still today bears the title "pope," which originally belonged to every bishop, is mentioned in the following prayer: "The most holy and blessed pope N. who according to Thy foreknowledge rules also Thy Holy, Catholic, and Apostolic Church, and our Most Reverend Bishop N. Thou mayest preserve for many years and in peaceful times so that they may discharge the holy office of Thy High Priesthood which Thou hast entrusted to them . . ." (Brightman, Liturgies I, p. 129). "The holy, catholic, and apostolic Church" which the Pope of Alexandria governs is the church of his patriarchate, which covers all Egypt and the countries south of Egypt.

Hence it is impossible to give an exact definition of what an ecumenical council is from the meaning of "ecumenical." There have been many synods in the Ancient Church. Some have been summoned as ecumenical (e.g., Sardica) but have never been recognized as such. There is at least one regional synod that has been regarded as ecumenical. This is our Second Ecumenical Council, Constantinople 381. Theodosius who called it invited only bishops from the East. No Western bishop, not even Damasus of Rome, received an invitation. No representative of any Western church was present. Another synod held at Constantinople 382 has called it "ecumenical," but this was not accepted until Chalcedon 451 approved the

---

[2]See the essay by G. Racoveanu quoted later.

creed of "the 150 fathers" of Constantinople, our so-called "Nicene" Creed, which only since the decision of Chalcedon replaced the old Creed of Nicea 325. And it is the authority of that creed that caused Rome in the sixth century to join the East in calling the synod of 381 "ecumenical."

What, then, is for the Eastern Orthodox Church the essence of an ecumenical council? This question has been thoroughly debated by modern Eastern theologians and philosophers since Chomjakow's *The Unity of the Church* (around 1840). Chomjakow, Florenski, Arseniew, Bulgakow, and others have tried to show that there is no individual institution of the Church, not even the ecumenical council, that can speak with infallibility. This infallibility belongs to the entire Church. According to Bulgakow the decisions of the councils have only a relative authority. Absolute authority they receive only when they are received by the Church Universal. This is rejected by others who maintain that the council speaks the truth as it is given by the Holy Spirit.

We can here only state the fact that even in the Eastern Orthodox Church for which the Seven Ecumenical Synods are of binding authority there is no full agreement as to what an ecumenical synod is. There can be no dogma about that because no ecumenical synod has ever defined its own nature. The Rumanian theologian George Racoveanu has made an interesting contribution to the discussion of the problems of the forthcoming council in *Lumiere et Vie* (Nr. 45, 1959, pp. 124 45): "L'Oecumenicite. Point de vue de l'Orthodoxie roumaine." He reaches the following conclusions: "The ecumenicity of a council is not determined by the number of bishops participating. — The ecumenicity of a council is not determined by the participation of bishops from all churches. — The ecumenicity of a council is not determined by the participation of all churches or by the proportion of such representation. — The ecumenicity of a council is not determined by the fact that it has been formally convened by the emperor, or by the imperial confirmation of its decrees" (*loc. cit.* 141). These negative sentences, the last of which refers, of course, to the ancient councils, are followed by the positive statement, "*The ecumenicity of a council is determined by the fact that the episcopate of the Church of Christ recognizes its decrees as infallible. Ecumenicity means infallibility.*" The author goes on, criticizing the view of Russian theologians who assume that the ecumenicity depends on the reception by the whole Christian people and seem to neglect the unique office of the bishops as successors of the apostles: "The seal of the ecumenicity of a council is the orthodoxy of its teaching. All merely formal criteria . . . are of no avail if this indispensable condition is not fulfilled: The recognition of its infallibility by the episcopate of the Church."

In other words, *an ecumenical council is a council the Church recognizes as ecumenical.* This is the only possible definition. In the West it must be recognized by the one bishop who has as successor of Peter in Rome the *plenitudo potestatis* and the *magisterium* over the whole Church. In the East it is the *numerous episcoporum.*

4.

We who are "separated" from the Church, as Rome understands it, whose "churches" are no real churches, should watch the great discussion between Rome and the East with deepest interest. The breach between Western and Eastern Catholicism was and is one of the greatest tragedies in the history of the Church. In the last analysis, it was not doctrine which split the Catholic Church. Nontheological factors, the cultural and political differences and contrast between the Greek East and the Latin West, facts are older than the Church, are the real cause of what later became a great theological issue. Today the one great theological question dividing both churches is the ecclesiology. Will the Second Vatican Council be able to finish the doctrine *De ecclesia Christi*, which could not be finished in 1870? And will the dogma at which it may arrive or which it will prepare be acceptable to the East? Will again nontheological, political factors separate those who recognize each other as parts of one Church?

When we watch this discussion and the work the council will have to do in regard to the reunion between East and West; we cannot be mere onlookers. For what happens in one sector of Christendom affects all the others. For there is a solidarity of sin and guilt, of divine judgment and human suffering, that still binds together those who confess Christ as Lord and Savior, even if other bonds have been broken. We shall later discuss what the council will mean to us poor "non-Catholics" who cannot be invited because we have no bishops recognized by Rome, and what the existence of such separated brothers means to the conscience of our Roman Catholic fellow-Christians, as a reminder of their sins and as a cause of profound sorrow. What we must do in preparing ourselves for the great discussion with Rome that will come in connection with the council is to thoroughly examine our own thoughts on the Church and its unity. We must clarify the meaning of words such as "catholic" and "ecumenical," which we use often so carelessly. The word "ecumenical," for instance, has received among us a new meaning during the last generation that it never had before. Today one would in Protestant circles not call worldwide organizations of one denomination "ecumenical" as the Methodists did when they founded in 1881 their "Ecumenical Methodist Conference." This word is now used for interdenominational, interchurch movements and organizations. For modern Anglicans or Protestants an ecumenical council would be a council in which many, if not all, churches were represented, not only Rome and the Eastern churches, but also Anglicans, Methodists, Baptists, Quakers, Lutherans, Presbyterian and Reformed, Disciples, and the various union churches of all parts of the world. From this point of view, an Assembly of the World Council of Churches would be much more ecumenical than any council of the Vatican could be. If this understanding of ecumenicity is correct, then the Vatican Council could not claim any more ecumenicity than a World Assembly of one of the great non-Roman denominations. But this would then apply also to the great ecumenical councils like Nicea. In Nicea there was present, at the request of the emperor, the Novatian Bishop of Constantinople, but the Novatian Church was not represented. Why not? Why had it never occurred to the Ancient Church that the great divisions of Christendom, which were not less scandalous than the present ones, could be overcome by negotiations at a synod? Because the lawful synod can always be only a synod of the Orthodox Church. Heretics and schismatics have no place in a synod of the Church, and if they appear they are solemnly excommunicated. *Ecumenicity is orthodoxy.* This rule is correct and applies to all ages and to all Christians. The convictions may differ as to who is orthodox, who a schismatic or a separated brother, as they differed in Africa when the Donatists regarded the Catholics as heretics while Augustine and Optatus of Mileve tried to prove that

the Donatists were not heretics, but only schismatics and even separated "brothers." Modern Protestants may laugh at distinctions and
accuse the Ancient Church of lack of love and brotherliness. They
should ask whether this reproach would not also be directed against
the apostles John and Paul. They should ask what it means that
even the World Council of Churches—at least it has given up, probably to the interest of the Eastern churches, the proud name of an
"Ecumenical Council"—has retained a last remnant of that principle
in its basis that excludes Unitarian churches and similar communities. Thus the preparation of the new council compels us to rethink
our own ecclesiology in the light of the Word of God.

THE REFORMED THEOLOGICAL REVIEW
Vol. XX, No. 3, October 1961

The Second Vatican Council (II)

5.

The main task of the forthcoming council will be to finish, in a world that is totally different from the world in which the First Vatican Council met, what had to be left unfinished in 1870. A scheme for the "Constitution on the Church of Christ," which contained in fifteen chapters a full doctrine of the Church, was distributed and comments were solicited. But the scheme was never debated. Only its eleventh chapter, "On the Primacy of the Roman Pontiff," was taken up. Augmented by a statement on the infallibility, it became the basis of what on July 18 was proclaimed as the "First Constitution on the Church of Christ" (*Pastor Apterous*). All other ecclesiological problems were left to a future "second constitution," which is to be expected from the Second Vatican Council.

One of the most serious criticisms with which *Pastor Apterous* met already at the council was the objection made by outstanding bishops of the minority that one cannot define properly the office of the pope without defining also the office of the bishop. If the Scripture passage is quoted in which the office of the keys is entrusted to Peter, one must also take into account the passages in which the same function is given to all apostles. It seems that today there is general agreement among Roman Catholics that the decision of 1870 needs to be supplemented in this direction. At that time the attention was so exclusively focused on the doctrine of the papal infallibility as taught in chapter 4 of *Pastor Apterous* that the implications of what chapter 3 teaches on the nature of the primacy were not fully realized.

If the power (*potestas*) the pope exercises over the entire Church and all its pastors and faithful is a direct, an immediate (*immediata*) and truly episcopal (*vere episcopalis*) power, how is this office of the bishop universal related to the office of the local bishop? Are not the bishops, as it was said already in 1870, actually vicars general of the universal bishop in their dioceses, especially since according to can. 329 CIC, which is based on the decree of the Vatican Council, only the pope can nominate a bishop? *Pastor Apterous* claims that "this immediate power of the Supreme Pontiff" does not obviate "that ordinary and immediate power of jurisdiction of the bishops by which they, made bishops by the Holy Spirit (cf. Acts 20:28), as successors of the apostles feed and rule as true pastors the individual flocks entrusted to them." The power of the bishops is rather "asserted, strengthened and vindicated by the supreme and universal pastor" (Denzinger 1828). How this claim is to be understood, how it is possible that within the Church two "immediate" episcopal powers co-exist that do not interfere with each other but rather belong together, this question will have to be answered by the council in a doctrinal statement on the nature of the episcopal office.

From the ongoing discussions, it may be concluded that the emphasis will be not on the office of the diocesan bishop only and his power to rule his flock, but on the episcopate as a body that subordinate to and in communion with "the first of the bishop" rules the entire Church. In a thought-provoking essay, "Le premier des eveques" in *Nouvelle Revue Theologique* (Paris), June, 1960, Father G. Dejaifve, S.J., has tried to suggest such a solution on the basis of thoughts expressed by some outstanding fathers of the First Vatican Council:

> Christ has put Peter over the whole Church in the midst of an apostolic college to which he has confided a saving mission to be carried out in unity. He alone remains the last source, the fullness (*pleroma*) of all apostolic power. If the souverain pontiff inherits this plenitude, as the Council of the Vatican has called to mind, this can be meant

only in the sense of an administrator, a *minister generalissimus*, as the Bishop of Granada put it at the Council of Trent, and with the intention that he should communicate what Christ gives him to his brethren who are his associates and corresponsible for the carrying out of his mission proper. (loc. cit. p. 579)

The author adds a quotation from Laynez at Trent who, while believing that Christ has given directly (immediate) to the apostle their jurisdiction, claimed, "To him (i.e., Peter) Christ gave all jurisdiction in order that he might confer it to others." Will this or a similar suggestion be acceptable to the Eastern churches? The Eastern patriarchs and bishop can never admit that the episcopal power is in any way communicated by the pope. They can never accept as a lawful and valid decision the anathema expressed in the canon added to the third chapter (Denz. 1831) against those who deny "the full and supreme power of jurisdiction over the Church universal, not only in matters pertaining to faith and morals, but also in those which pertain to the discipline and the government of the whole Church on earth," and even against those who deny, "that this his power is an ordinary and immediate power over all churches and each single church and over all and single pastors and faithful" (Denz. 1831).

How can any Eastern church accept that without denying what it has taught and confessed throughout all centuries about the episcopal office? Rome, on the other hand, has never refused to recognize not only the orders of the schismatic churches of the East, but also the power of jurisdiction the schismatic bishops exercise, at least in connection with the administration of the Sacraments. What is the relation between such episcopal office, conferred on behalf of the whole Church outside the Roman orbit, to the episcopal office in the Roman Communion? Can there be a connection of such bishops with the pope of which they are not conscious and that has never been expressed in words or deeds? The law that the pope must name a bishop (can. 329) and that no episcopal consecration can be given without the papal mandate (can. 953) applies only to the Latin Church, for which alone the *Codex Iris Canonici* is binding law, and to the Eastern churches in communion with Rome as far as the existing canons demand that. These circumstances make it possible and imperative for Roman theologians to try to find an interpretation of the primacy that would do full justice to the dignity of the bishops as successors of the apostles and their immediate power of jurisdiction without violating the "irreformable" decree of the Vatican Council? With Christian sympathy we must follow these discussions. Will they lead to the reunion of the two great branches of pre-Reformation Catholic Christendom whose tragic separation was not caused by doctrinal reasons but by "nontheological factors," which are, in the last analysis, a version of a cultural and political contrast, Greece and Rome, East and West, and go back into pre-Christian times and underlie our whole civilization?

6.

A new doctrine on the office of the bishops will be a chapter of "The Second Constitution on the Church of Christ," for which the Roman Church has waited since 1870. Such a constitution would have to take up the whole content of the scheme, questions like the nature of the Church, its unity, visibility, necessity, and its relation to other societies. At first sight it might seem strange that the Roman Church with its elaborate doctrinal system has so far no dogma on the question of what the Church is. It is not surprising that the Eastern Orthodox Church possesses no ecclesiological dogma except the article of the Nicene Creed, "I believe (the Greek text adds: 'in') one, holy, catholic and apostolic Church," because none of the ecumenical councils has said more. The fathers have dealt with the Church in their exposition of the symbol (i.e., Cyril of Jerusalem cat 18, 22ff.) and occasionally when rejecting heresies. But in vain one would look for an article on the Church in the dogmatics of the Eastern (John of Damask) and the Western Church. It was the Reformation only that caused theological definitions of the Church. The reformers who found themselves excommunicated by Rome had to show that they were not excommunicated from the true Church. Hence we find since the seventh article of the Augsburg Confession of 1530 in all Reformed confessions, including the Anglican nineteenth article, doctrinal statements on the nature of the Church. Trent did not take up that matter, but the *Catechismus Romanus* of 1566 gave in Part I an elaborate explanation of the ninth article of the Apostles' Creed, "I believe the holy Catholic Church, the communion of saints." This important document, however, is not regarded as dogma. What all statements on the Church in the sixteenth century have in common is that they start with the idea of the Church as "congregation," "assembly" of the faithful. This corresponds to the original meaning of the word "ecclesia." It is the method of the Greek fathers who always started from the meaning of "ecclesia" in the Greek Bible of the Old and New Testament (see Cyril *loc. cit.*). It is even followed by the *Catechismus Romanus*, which begins with the etymology of the Greek word: *ecclesia* means *evocatio*. In contradistinction from "*synagoga*," it is used to denote the "Christian community" (*rem publicam Christianam*), the "congregations of the faithful" (*fidelium congregationes*), the "Christian people" (*Christianus populus*). "In one word, the Church (*ecclesia*), as St. Augustine says, is the faithful people (*populus fidelis*) dispersed over the whole earth" (qu. 2, 2). As do the Lutheran and the Reformed confessions, so the *Catechismus Romanus* mentions the designation of the Church as "Body of Christ," but along with other terms (bride, house, family, flock) and not as the description proper from which the definition has to start. This older usage is confirmed by the liturgy. In the *De tempore* orations of the Roman Missal, *populus* is used for the Church more than fifty times, *corpus* explicitly only once. In the Canon Missae, the Church as the whole family of God (*cuncta familia tua*), as God's holy people (*plebs tua sancta*), offers, together with the clergy (*nos servi tui*), the sacrifice. The modern idea that the Church as the Body of Christ offers the body and blood of Christ in the sacrifice of the Mass is foreign to the liturgy and to the dogma (Trent Sess. 22; Denz. 938ff.) of the Roman Church. This is a conclusion from the idea that "Body of Christ" is the essential designation of the Church. It seems to be a product of the modern Liturgical Movement.

It will be a great event in the history of Christian doctrine when the Second Vatican Council takes up the dogma of the Church. Eastern Orthodox theology is satisfied with the present state of things. The Eastern churches confess the article of the Nicene Creed and leave it to the theologians to explain it. They even find it appropriate to refrain from dogmatizing on it. "The Church defies definition because it is a living reality." But no Christian theology and no church can abstain from answering the question of how the great passages of the New Testament on the Church are to be understood.

As the Church in the sixteenth century had to say what it meant by the words of the creed, "Who for us men and for our salvation came down from heaven," so the Church in the modern world has to say what it means when confessing "One, Holy, Catholic and Apostolic Church."

Ecclesiology is one of the great theological problems for all Christendom. How will Rome approach this problem? The scheme prepared for the First Vatican Council started with the definition of the Church as the mystical Body of Christ (chapter 1) and developed the ecclesiology from this concept of the Church. This met with strong criticism, as the written opinions of almost three hundred bishops show.[1]

It seems that only since the middle of the nineteenth century the emphasis has been shifted from the Church as the people of God to the Church as the Body of Christ. This is obviously a result of the great rediscovery of the Church and the corresponding revival of ecclesiology that took place since the end of the Napoleonic wars in all Christian nations and in all denominations of Christendom, not only in Roman Catholicism (France, Germany, Spain), but also in the Church of Russia (since Chomjakow), in the Tractarian Movement in England, and in all Lutheran and Reformed churches of Europe. It is the great counter-movement against the dissolution of the idea of the Church in the pietistic and rationalistic movements of the eighteenth century. The connection with the development of secular sociology from the eighteenth century understanding of all human society as based on a "social contract" of individuals to the new understanding of the social life as a life of social organisms in the philosophy of Romanticism is obvious. In European Catholicism, J. A. Möhler is the great turning-point who under the influence of German Idealism (Schleiermacher, Hegel)—which must make his theories suspect to the theologian—had developed the new idea of the Church as the embodiment of the Spirit of Christ, and later in his Symbolics (1832), which has influenced all churches of Europe, as "Jesus Christ living

---

[1] *Mansi Collectio Conciliorum* Vol. 51, 731–930. Since *Mansi* is not available to the author, he takes this from M. D. Koster, *Ekklesiologie im Werden*, Paderborn, 1940, p. 20. The documents of the council itself, including the *Ischema De Ecclesia Christi*, are available in Fredberg's collection of 1872.

on in the history of mankind." This idea is to be found already earlier, for example, with Bossuet who could say, "What is the Church?
. . . The Church is Jesus Christ, but expanded and communicated."
But only since Möhler's "Symbolics" has this view been generally
accepted. It has become the common possession of Catholics and
Protestants. Not only the Anglicans claim that the Church is Christ
living on in the history of mankind. Even an outstanding leader of
American Liberal Protestantism spoke in his essay on "the Nature
of the Church" at Lausanne 1927 of "the Church as the extension of
her Lord's Incarnation"—whatever he may have understood by
"incarnation"—and Dietrich Bonhoeffer calls the "collective person"
of the Church "Christ existing as a congregation" (*Sanctorum Communio*, p. IIIff.). The Church, he says, is "Christ himself present." So he
understands the term "Body of Christ" for the Church. The Church
"is not only a means to an end, but it is at the same time an end in
itself; it is Christ himself present; hence 'to be in Christ' and 'to be
in the Church' is one and the same thing."

In this context it must be understood that modern Roman ecclesiology no longer starts from the concept of the Church as the people
of God, the assembly of Christians, as the *Catechismus Romanus* in
harmony with the entire Western theological tradition did,[2] but from
the idea of the mystical Body of Christ. One notices a certain embarrassment in the great Catholic works on dogmatics. Where is the
place of ecclesiology in the dogmatic system? Scheeben, who now is
generally regarded as the greatest dogmatician in German Catholicism at the time of the Vatican Council, a man of flawless orthodoxy,
was never quite sure where the doctrine of the Church belongs. He
dealt with the Church partly in connection with the Christology—
where it belongs if the Church is the continuation of the incarnation,
as also Aquinas deals with the Church as the mystical Body of Christ
and head of the Church in the Christology (*Summa theol.* III *quaes-
tio* 8)—and partly, in "The Mysteries of Christianity", in connection
with the Eucharist.

---

[2] J. H. Newman has given in paragraph 4 of Tract 90 an impressive enumeration of testimonies.

The real place of the doctrine of the Church is, as the creeds show, in the "Third Article," between the doctrine of the Holy Spirit on the one hand and the Sacraments and the Last Things on the other. Since all these articles have an eschatological meaning—the Holy Spirit is poured out "in the last day" (Acts 2:17), and in the sacraments our future salvation is anticipated—here the Church finds its proper place. For the Church also belongs, according to the New Testament, to the Last Things as the true people of God redeemed from this aeon. If this is not realized, if the ecclesiology is not treated in its essential context with eschatology, the doctrine of the Church becomes homeless in the whole of the Christian doctrine and loses its biblical content. This danger becomes obvious in modern Catholic dogmatics, which put the ecclesiology into the prolegomena, the "fundamental theology," as, for example, Lercher does in his *Institutiones*, the first chapters of which deal with "the true religion," "the Church of Christ," and "Scripture and Tradition." This then leads to such an impossible question as 'Holy Writ or Holy Church?' (G. T. Tavard), which none of the apostles would have understood.

Warning voices have been raised against the attempts to understand the nature of the Church from the concept of the Body of Christ. The profound doctrine of Paul on the Church as "one body in Christ" (Rom. 12:5), "the body of Christ" (1 Cor. 12), and the body whose head Christ is (Eph.; Col.) will in all its implications be understood only when we shall see Christ in his glory. It is the last, not the best word of all ecclesiology. Where it is made the first, the inevitable consequence is a *theologia gloriae* in which we sinful men—by trying to make visible that which will become visible only on the Last Day when Christ's glory will become manifest—are unknowingly wiping out the borderline between Christ and the Christian, and this means in the last analysis, the borderline between God and man, the Creator and the creature.

It makes no difference whether this is done in Rome or in Geneva, in the Augustinian identification of the Church on earth with the kingdom of God, or in the chiliastic endeavors of certain forms of modern Ecumenism to make this world the kingdom of God or at least to make visible in a fellowship of the various churches the *Una Sancta*, which is the Body of Christ, or whether a small body of Christians claims to be and to act as the Body of Christ.

Serious warnings against the identification of the Church with Christ—it cannot be justified from passages like 1 Corinthians 12:12 or Acts 9:5—have been made by Roman Catholic theologians. They have raised objections against *defining*, not only describing, the Church as the Body of Christ.[3] The situation has, however, completely changed since the encyclical "*Mystici Corporis Christi*" of 1943. Though an encyclical is not a decision *ex cathedra* and, consequently, its doctrinal statements must not be regarded as dogma, this important document indicates in what direction the coming dogma *de ecclesia* is being developed. It gives an elaborate doctrine of the Church, but it does not say one word on the Church as the people of God, the original meaning of the word *ecclesia*, which so strongly emphasized in the New Testament, also by Paul, and is the meaning in which Jesus himself has used the word in the fundamental passage Matthew 16:18. This is a deliberate omission, a well-considered abandonment of the old ecclesiological tradition the *Catechismus Romanus* still shared with the confessions of the Reformation. Since the theologians of Pius XII must have had in mind the scheme of 1870 and the criticism it met with, "*Mystici Corporis*" may be regarded. The pattern of that will be put before the Second Vatican Council. We cannot discuss here the highly important encyclical that presents a full doctrine of the Church under various aspects of the idea of the Body of Christ: the Church a Body, the Church the Body of Christ, the Church the Mystical Body. This part I is followed by a second part, "The Union of the Faithful in and with Christ," and by practical conclusions. This document should be studied by all those who want to understand the decisions to be made by the council on the dogma of the Church. But it should also be studied as a challenge to us. That the Church as Body of Christ is a visible social organism is taught today by many Protestants. Is this really the understanding of Paul to whom one single local church can be the Body of Christ, as in the entire New Testament two or three assembled in the name of Jesus can be the Church of Christ, just as well as all local churches and the whole "brotherhood" is

---

[3]Details are given by Koster *op. cit.*, see especially his protest against the identification, p. 104.

the Church of Christ. Does not the term "Body of *Christ*" indicate that the Church can never be understood as a social organism? Is it allowable to conclude from the word "Body" that the Church of Christ *must* be visible? Could it not be that the mystical Body of Christ is hidden in, with, and under the earthly society we see, just as the sacramental body of Christ is hidden in, with, and under the species of bread? If we address these and similar questions to our "separated brethren" in the Roman Church, we must direct them also to ourselves. There is so much talk, well meant, but at the same time confused talk, about the Church as the Body of Christ that we must first clarify our own thoughts before we can enter a discussion with others. Catholic theologians have been aware, as we have seen, of the danger of identifying Christ and the Church, Christ and ourselves. Even Pius XII was aware of this danger when he rejected the idea that "the divine Redeemer and the members of the Church are united to form one physical person" and when he reminds of the "statement of the Apostle of the Nations, who, though he combines Christ and his mystical Body in a marvelous union, yet contrasts the one with the other, as Bridegroom with Bride." We must ask whether this error is confined to some extravagant representatives of the Liturgical Movement whom the pope had in mind, or whether it underlies the whole idea that the Church is Christ living on in the world, which the encyclical employs so strongly. But this question we must also first ask ourselves: do we really believe that the church body to which we belong is the continuation of the incarnation? Can we really with Möhler apply the Christological doctrine of the two natures of Christ to the Church? Is it really so, as "*Mystici Corporis*" maintains, that, when the Church prays the Lord's Prayer, she prays not for herself but in the name of "some of her members" who are "sick and wounded in their sins": "Forgive us our trespasses" (English Translation par. 65). Of course, if the Church is Christ, then it is sinless and does not need to repent. Since the visible Church is Christ, then it is not only infallible, but also holy in the sense of "sinless" and need not repent. In the New Testament, the Lord calls also his Church to repentance, as Revelation 2 and 3 shows where the *seven* churches represent the *whole* church. Or have we no longer an ear to hear what the Spirit says to the churches?

7.

Who are the members of the Church as the mystical Body of Christ? According to the scheme of 1870, all baptized Christians who are in unity and communion with the Church, though they may be sinners. The idea that the true Church is invisible or hidden (*latens*, i.e., what the Lutheran doctrine calls *ecclesia abscondita*) is rejected. Christian bodies not in communion with the Church cannot be called parts or members of the Church, which is Christ's Body. To belong to this Church is necessary to salvation, though they who suffer from invincible ignorance concerning Christ and his Church should not be eternally condemned on account of this ignorance because this does not make them guilty in the sight of God, who wills all men to be saved and denies not his grace to him who does what he can do with his powers (*facienti quod in se est*). "But no one can attain eternal life who is culpably separated (*culpabiliter sejunctus*) from the unity of the Faith or the communion of the Church." Pius XII in "*Mystici Corporis*" had to maintain this over against theologians of the Liturgical Movement who tried to establish a closer relationship of non-Catholic Christians with the Body of Christ on the basis of Baptism. "Only those are to he accounted really members of the Church who have been regenerated in the waters of Baptism and profess the true faith, and have not cut themselves off from the structure of the Body by their own unhappy act or been severed therefrom, for very grave crimes, by the legitimate authority" (21). "Schism, heresy, or apostasy are such (*scil.* sins) of their very nature that they sever a man from the Body of the Church, but not every sin, even the most grievous, is of such a kind . . ." (22). What, then, is the relationship of Christians in schism or heresy with the Church? In their Baptism, if it was valid, they have become members of the Body of Christ. They have received the indelible character of those who belong to Christ, as children of their heavenly Father. But as long as they are not in communion with the true Catholic Roman Church, "the full use of their rights as children is impeded since they are separated visibly from her" (Cardinal Bea, quoted from "Catholic Documentation," Sydney, March 1961). They are, as Pius XII puts it in "*Mystici Corporis*" (101), "those whom an unhappy breach of faith and unity has severed from us, who, however unworthily, represent on earth the person of Jesus Christ." This breach is either made by themselves—then it is a most grievous sin—or it is an unhappy inheritance. Of these the encyclical (102) says that "they may be related to the mystical Body of the Redeemer by some unconscious yearning and desire." But they are in no sense members of it. They are separated, though they may be called "separated brethren" (*fratres sejuncti*).

This term is not yet to be found in "*Mystici Corporis*," though it is used at that time already in apologetic and devotional literature. It has been introduced into the official terminology of the Curia, as far as we can see, in the documents of the council since "*Ad Petri Cathedram*." Here John XXIII appeals to the non-Catholics: "We address you, then, as brothers, even though you are separated from Us. For, as St. Augustine said: 'Whether they like it or not, they are our brothers. They will only cease to be our brothers when they cease to say: Our Father.'" He adds another quotation from Augustine with an exhortation to love God as Father and the Church as Mother. Both passages from the "*Enarrationes in psalmos*" (Pss. 32 and 82), written about A.D. 400, remind of very similar words written some twenty years earlier by Optatus of Mileve in the fourth of his books "On the Schism of the Donatists" (IV, 2f; Migne PL 11, 1049ff.). It is most touching to read how the great fathers have wrestled with the problem of the relationship between the "*catholica communio*" (Augustine), which recognized the Sacraments of the Donatists as valid, and the Donatists who regarded themselves as the true Church and denied the validity of the Sacraments of what to them was the sect of the *traditores*. Optatus insisted on calling the Donatist bishop Parmenianus his brother, while this man refused to recognize the Catholic bishop of Mileve as a member of the Church. One must remember the history of the great African schism, the hostility and hatred of Donatist fanatics who went even so far as to desecrate the Catholic Sacrament on the one side, and the patience and charity of the great Catholic fathers on the other, in order to realize what the great call to never-failing charity toward separated brethren means, which the present pope, following the example of his predecessor, has issued time and again.

The theological problem of "separated brethren" becomes clear if one realizes that this term is now used not only for schismatics— that means for Christians who according to the Roman doctrine have a valid priesthood and valid Sacraments, as, for example, the "separated" churches of Eastern Orthodoxy—but also for heretics, as Anglicans, Lutherans, and various groups of Reformed Christians are for Rome. How is that possible? Could the pope call Luther, Calvin, Cranmer, and all the rest who came under the anathema of the Roman Church in the sixteenth century his separated brethren? Obviously not. For, according to the Roman view, these heretics or heresiarchs willfully and culpably destroyed the unity of the Church by refusing to obey the Vicar of Christ. Others have only inherited the heresy. They are the separated brethren who are called back to the Church whose members they were at the moment of their Baptism.

But what about those who have not only inherited a certain doctrine, but have made it their own on the basis of a thorough study of Holy Scripture? If they, though knowing and historically understanding the claims of Rome, take their stand with the Reformation on the authority of the Word of God, the Gospel of Christ and his apostles, is it possible to dissociate them from the reformers whose decision against the papacy they are repeating. Against whom is the acclamation directed with which the last session of the Council of Trent on December 4, 1563, came to an end when the Cardinal of Lorraine spoke the solemn "anathema to all heretics," and the members of the council responded unanimously, "anathema, anathema"? It is directed against us who confess today the *sola fide* and the *sola scriptura*, which were condemned by that council. So the differentiation between heretics and conscious heretics and unfortunate Christians who have inherited a heresy collapses. This is probably true also of the distinction between "heresy" and "schism." Donatism is by the Augsburg Confession rightly condemned as a heresy, and one has only to ask whether or not the schism between Rome and the East, which originally was not caused by doctrinal differences, has developed in the course of a thousand years into a split where on either side grave doctrinal issues are at stake. If the Filioque is not regarded as such, it should not be overlooked that the Eastern Orthodox Church has not accepted, and cannot accept, the dogmas of Trent—for example, the condemnation of Pelagianism—and the Vatican and the Mariological dogmas of 1854 and 1950. He who denies these doctrines, as, for example, the Vatican dogma on the papacy, is for Rome a heretic, not only a schismatic.

8.

The Second Council of the Vatican, whether it can meet according to schedule or must be postponed, will be a historic event of the first magnitude. Christianity is facing its greatest crisis since the fall of the Roman Empire and the victory of the crescent over the cross in the Orient. It is losing more and more of its historic strongholds and is becoming the religion of a shrinking minority in a rapidly growing population on the earth. It may well be that the churches in most parts of the world will exist, as the churches in the Mohammedan world have existed for many centuries, in poverty and distress, in a state of oppression and persecution. We Christians of the West have always looked upon the history of the Church as advancement and victory. The cross has become to the West since the day of Constantine the sign of victory: *In hoc signo vinces.* Our history was accompanied by the battle-hymns of a victorious army from the *Vexilla regis prodeunt* of the sixth century to the hymns of the missionary movements of the last century. Now we all have to learn what the second line of that old Latin hymn implies, *"Fulget crucis mysterium."* Even our optimistic American friends begin to realize the mystery of the cross, the real cross that the Church of the Crucified must bear in this world in following Christ. Luther was right when he always emphasized the holy cross as a mark of the true Church.

If one compares the atmosphere of the First Vatican Council with the atmosphere in which the Second Vaticanum is prepared, the difference is striking. The "spectre" of Communism was "haunting Europe" already when Pius IX condemned it in the "Syllabus" of 1864 along with other "pests," such as secret societies and Bible societies (Denz. 1718). A few months after the adjournment of the council, one of the leaders of the minority, Archbishop Darboy of Paris, became a victim of the first small Communist revolution in Europe. He died as a martyr, blessing his murderers. Today's situation becomes clear if one thinks of the destiny of the strongholds of Roman Catholicism in Eastern Europe, the churches of the Lithuanians, Poles, Czechs, Slovaks, Hungarians, Croats, of the weakness of French and Italian Catholicism, of the unsoluble problems of Latin America where one third of all Roman Catholics are supposed to live, of the tragedy in China, and of the problems faced by Rome in all Asia and Africa. One must keep this external situation in mind in order to understand the spiritual background of the plans made for the new council. "We are reminded of Our many Brethren in the episcopate and of Our dear priests and faithful people, who have been driven into exile or are detained in prisons and concentration camps for resisting to desert their episcopal and priestly duties, or to defect from the Catholic faith," says John XXIII in "*Ad Petri Cathedram*" (90) and he adds, while pleading for that lawful freedom to which everyone—God's Church included—has a right": "We have no desire to offend anyone. On the contrary, We freely pardon all and pray God for their pardon" (91).

It is at a time when confessors arise and martyrs die in all parts of Christendom irrespective of their denominational affiliation that Rome pleads for unity. She can understand unity only in terms of her understanding of the Church and the truth entrusted to the Church, as we, on the other hand, can think of Church unity only as unity in what we cannot but regard as the truth of God's Word, which must not be abandoned. Our age has become aware, more than former centuries, of the tragedy of a divided Christendom. The forthcoming council will help us to realise the depth of this tragedy. It is to be expected that it will definitely destroy the dream of a "reunion" of all Christendom in a visible Church. Also the American Protestants will have to learn that a united church built on compromise and "comprehensiveness" would not be the Church of Christ. For such a "church" would lose with the distinctive doctrines any doctrine. It would not be able to distinguish between truth and error, Church and heresy. Even bound to fail is the idea underlying the present World Council of Churches that it *must* be possible to reach visible unity by bringing the churches together for common work and worship and for a serious search of the truth.

We men of this age of conferences have a superstitious belief in discussion, as if we must come to a common understanding of the divine truth if only we continue long enough to discuss our respective doctrines humbly, frankly without prejudice, and with the earnest prayer that the Spirit must lead us into the truth. This can be so in many cases. But it can also be otherwise, and just in those points of doctrine where the deepest mysteries of God's revelation are at stake. As long as we live on this earth and in the limitations of our sinful human existence, it will happen again and again that something stands against conscience in the most vital doctrinal decisions. Why this is so, we do not know. We must have a conscientious decision, and we can and must not act against conscience. This is one of the doctrines about which Thomas Aquinas and Luther, the Roman Church and the churches of the Reformation, agree.

Much can be done in the way of Christian unity: union of those who are one in the faith, practical co-operation wherever it is possible without violation of consciences, and in any case more common work, more repentance for our sins, more mutual charity, more prayer for one another, more solidarity over against a hostile world. As *separated* brethren we enter the historic period of the Second Vatican Council and the ensuing theological and ecclesiastical discussions. But even where our separation remains, we shall be separated *brethren*.

THE REFORMED THEOLOGICAL REVIEW
Vol. XXII, No. 1, February 1963

"The Sources of Revelation"

A new chapter in the history of Christian doctrine was opened when the Second Vatican Council at its Nineteenth "General Congregation" on November 14, 1962, began the discussion of the *schema* "The Sources of Revelation." The preceding fifteen meetings had discussed the *schema* "On the Sacred Liturgy."[1] Now the first of the great dogmatic issues was taken up by the council. Cardinal Ottaviani,

---

[1] The discussion was interrupted on November 13. Votes taken on the seventeenth and during the last meetings in December resulted in the almost unanimous acceptance of the preface and the first chapter of the constitution. This means that the basic ideas and the principles of the reform of the liturgy have been approved. These parts of the constitution may be published by the pope after the Commission has considered the last suggestions for improvements. No constitution, dogmatic or otherwise, has been finished so far. A project on Church unity with special reference to the Eastern churches and the all-important constitution on the Church have been briefly touched upon during the last meetings of the First Period of the council, which was closed on December 8 without a solemn "*Sessio*" since no decree was ready for proclamation. By a special decree of the pope, the name of St. Joseph was for the first time included in the "*Communicantes*" of the *Canon Missae* on that day. The quotations in this article are taken, where no reference is given, from the official press reports and correspondences, since the documents will not be available for a long time. Space did not permit to discuss here the debate

chairman of the "Commission on Faith and Morals" and who presided over the meeting, introduced the document. The Committee's
secretary, Salvatore Garafalo, Rector of the University of the Propa-
ganda, gave the explanation. A lively discussion ensued that went on
at the subsequent congregations and led to what was called a crisis
of the council. The *schema*, which has not been published yet, met
with the opposition of the majority of the bishops. While none of the
critics seems to have doubted the dogmatic correctness of the document, which had been approved by the Central Committee, made up
largely by Cardinals, serious objections were raised not only against
its form ("too lengthy," "savoring too much of the classroom"), but
also against its content. The document "did not take enough account
of the growth of the dogma and was therefore not mature enough
from a theological point of view."

The main objection raised by many of the speakers was that
it did not serve "the purpose of the council in respect to separated
brothers." "The dialogue with separated brothers, Orthodox as well
as Protestant, which has been placed on a new basis in recent years,"
demanded, so it was pointed out, "to respect the position of others
and to seek a manner of expression that does not divide, but unites."
"This manner of expression would be the authentic ecumenical style,
which the Secretariat for promoting Christian Unity also has clearly
demonstrated as being its chosen usage." The reference to this Secretariat, which meanwhile has been elevated to the rank of one of
the Commissions (which means that it now can, through the Central Commission, put motions to the council), points to the growing
authority Cardinal Bea is exercising on the members of the council.
This learned German Jesuit, for many years the leader of the Pontifical Biblical Institute and as such the venerated teacher of many of
the bishops, is at the same time the champion of the "ecumenical"
trend of the council and the leading mind of modern Catholic biblical theology.

While the defenders of the scheme made the point that it had
been prepared by learned bishops and priests and presented the

on the inspiration of Scripture in the Roman Catholic Church today, especially
the book by Rahner quoted below. This must be left to a later article.

Catholic truth, which "does not give offense to the separated brothers who also are in search of it," the opponents claimed that the document "gave little encouragement to scientific research in theology and scriptural studies." Thus the ecumenical approach to the problem of the sources of revelation is closely linked up with the new biblical theology asserting itself within the Roman Church. It seems to the outside observer that the new biblical research was the real issue at the bottom of the exciting debate that continued at the subsequent meetings. While the objectors demanded that the draft be sent back to the Commission to be rewritten in its entirety, the supporters regarded it as a sound and sufficient basis for a dogmatic *constitutio* to be finalized through continued discussion by the council in assembly.

In view of the deep differences of opinion that appeared in the debate, the presidents decided a vote should be taken on the question of whether or not the discussion of the scheme should be terminated. The vote was taken on November 20. Of the 2,211 fathers present, just around 1,400, more than 60 percent, voted for the discontinuation of the discussion. This meant that the rejection of the scheme barely fell short of the two thirds majority necessary in this case. Strength and weakness of the "more progressives" became manifest at this critical moment. They were in the majority, but the "more traditionalist" minority was strong enough to prevent any sweeping changes. The deadlock was broken when on the following day, before the discussion was resumed, the Secretary General of the Council, Archbishop Felice, intervened on the instruction of the Secretary of State. The pope, who does not take part in General Congregations, had ruled that the scheme should be referred to a new Special

Commission under the joint presidency of Cardinals Ottaviani and Bea. Thus the discussion of the subject was terminated. It will be resumed at the next period of the council, which has been fixed for the time from September 8 to December 8, 1963. In the meantime the Special Commission in which both the Theological Commission on Faith and Morals and the Secretariat for Christian Unity are represented will have to redraft the scheme. They have been instructed to make it shorter and to lay special emphasis on the doctrine already treated at the Council of Trent and the First Vatican Council.

II.

It is most remarkable that the great discussion of the "Sources of Revelation" at the council is going on with constant reference to the "Catholic-Protestant dialogue" and in view of a possible reunion with those who thus far have emphatically confessed the *sola scriptura* of the Reformation—at least when criticising Rome. Strong objection has been raised at the council against the very title of the scheme that prejudices the outcome. Are there really two sources of revelation, or is there only one?

Father George Tavard, whose *Holy Writ or Holy Church: The Crisis of the Protestant Reformation* (1959) is one of the most important books written in preparation for the council, has been a consultant of Cardinal Bea's Secretariat on Christian Unity and has now been named by the pope one of the experts to advise the members of the council. He has defined for the Catholics of the United States the two existing views in the following way: "1. That Scripture and tradition appear as two sources of revelation. 2. That tradition and Scripture are not two sources standing side by side, but that tradition is the explanation of Scripture by the Church." He adds the statement that "the council's stand on the matter can affect the movement for Christianity." The first of these views has been almost universally accepted as the doctrine of the Roman Church since Trent. Not only the Protestant critics of the Tridentine decree on the Scriptures, but also its defenders since Canisius and Bellarmine have understood it in this way. It is the normal view of Catholic dogmaticians.[2]

Tavard is the spokesman of a new school of thought represented mainly by German (Geiselmann, Karl Rahner, Hans Küng) and French (de Broglie, Bouyer) Catholic theologians. This school holds that the "two sources theory" is not the doctrine of Trent, but rather an interpretation of Trent that has grown up among Catholic theologians in the post-Reformation controversies with Protestantism. Neither Tavard nor Rahner nor, as far as I can see, any representative of this view would reject the old view of the two sources, which is also

---

[2]Even M. Schmaus declares it to be a dogma that tradition is a separate source (*Kath. Dogmatik*, Vol. I, p. 46).

held by the scheme proposed to the council, as un-Catholic and unacceptable. But they are very outspoken in rejecting it as dangerous.

In an article that has been widely published also in Australia by the Catholic press (e.g., *The Australian Sunday Visitor*, Brisbane, December 30, 1962), Tavard sees two dangers. First, he thinks that the apologetical and polemical distinction between Scripture and tradition might influence the piety and devotion of Catholics, giving them a less biblical aspect. The council might run into trouble if it urged a biblical, liturgical piety on one hand and separated Scripture and tradition on the other. Second, the separation of Scripture and tradition would interfere with what he regards as a promising development in the World Council of Churches, where the concept of tradition is being rediscovered: "If we adopted a theology seeing tradition as something completely separate from Scripture, we should run the danger of moving too far away from a position which the Protestants are approaching." This refers, as it was made clear in the debates, to the discussions on "Tradition and Traditions" going on in the World Council's "Commission on Faith and Order" and to the new evaluation of tradition by O. Cullmann, especially in *Die Tradition als exegetisches, historisches und theologisches Problem* (1954).

Hence Tavard and the new school of "Biblical Theology" favor the alternative view: Scripture and tradition are not two sources, but substantially one source, tradition being essentially nothing else but the interpretation of Holy Scripture by the teaching office of the Church. This is, as Tavard tries to show in his book, the older view held by the Church fathers and still recognized by the schoolmen until the Late Middle Ages raised new problems that led to the various doctrines of the sixteenth century.

This is the issue that will be thoroughly investigated and discussed by the "Special Committee" during the coming months. Either side will consult its best theologians. By the end of 1963, the council is supposed to have made the great decision. The way is open for either view, for both are possible within the framework of Catholic dogmatics, as also the Eastern churches have always accepted the "two sources."

At first sight it might be hard for the observer from outside to understand the passion with which either side is defending its position if everyone is prepared to submit to whatever the council may decide. What both sides fear are the consequences of the decision.

What Cardinal Ottaviani seems to fear is that the new "biblical" theology will prove to be a new form of that Modernism the Church had to condemn at the beginning of this century because it led in fact to the destruction of the Catholic dogma. If the distinction is made by these modern theologians between dogma and its expression, how can the traditional Thomistic theology be maintained, as well as the philosophy with which the Catholic dogma is so closely bound up?

Cardinal Bea and the theologians behind him, on the other hand, are aware of the great danger that the Roman Catholic Church will be unable to communicate the dogma, the Christian message, to the rapidly changing world in the outgoing twentieth century if it preaches anything but the eternal Word of God or wraps this Word in a philosophy modern man cannot possibly understand and in a view of the world that is untenable because it contradicts the established facts of the universe. The fact that this school of thought has found the approval of the majority of the council and the moral support of the pope, who has shown remarkable fairness and justice to everyone, was the great surprise of the first period of the council. Whether it will prevail depends on its ability to convince the whole Church of its unimpeachable orthodoxy.

III.

Any discussion of the problem of the sources of revelation must start from the dogma defined in the decree of the Fourth Session of the Council of Trent on April 8, 1546:

> The Holy Ecumenical and General Synod of Trent . . . having this aim always before its eyes, that errors be removed and the purity of the Gospel be preserved in the Church, which was before promised by the prophets in Holy Scriptures and which our Lord Jesus Christ first proclaimed with his own mouth and then commanded to be preached by his apostles to every creature as the source of all saving truth and moral discipline, and perceiving that this truth and this discipline were contained in written books and in unwritten traditions which were received by the apostles from the lips of Christ or, by the same apostles, at the dictation of the Holy Spirit, and were handed on and have come to us; following the example of the orthodox fathers,

this Synod receives and venerates, with equal pious affection and reverence (*pari pietatis affectu acreverentia*) all the books both of the Old and the New Testaments, since one God is the author of both, together with the said traditions as well those pertaining to faith as those pertaining to morals, as having been given either from the lips of Christ or by the dictation of the Holy Spirit and preserved by unbroken succession in the Catholic Church.

The fact that the word "source" (*fons*) occurs here in the singular must not be adduced, as it has been done, in support of the "one source theory." It is a modern line of thought that Tavard reads into the text when he interprets it in this way:

> The dynamic element which constitutes the source (*fons*) of all saving truth and all Christian behaviour is the Gospel of Christ, the Word spoken by Christ and communicated to the Church through the apostles. It is a living Word. It carries the Holy Spirit. This dynamic element uses two sets of vessels: Holy Scripture and traditions. In as far as they carry the same Gospel of Christ, in as far as they channel the original impetus whereby the Spirit moved the apostles, both Scripture and traditions are entitled to the same adhesion of faith. For faith reaches Christ and the Spirit whatever the medium used to contact us. (*Op. cit.* p. 208)

But does the text say that? It speaks of the Gospel as the source of dogmatic and ethical truths. It does not speak of one source of the Gospel. The question to be answered is this: where do we find the Gospel? The answer of the decree is this: in written books and unwritten traditions. These again are divided into traditions the apostles have received from the lips of Jesus, and others they have received at the dictation of the Holy Spirit.

It should always be kept in mind that the entire revelation was finished with the apostles. Nothing has been added to that revelation except an interpretation of its contents by the teaching office of the Church. All churches, Catholic and Evangelical, agree on that. The assumption of an ongoing revelation contradicts the New Testament doctrine of the eschatological character of the revelation of Christ (Heb. 1:2, Acts 2:17) and the finality of Christ. The idea that there is a third source of revelation (reason or experience) which was held by ancient and modern sects has been rejected by all churches which claim "apostolicity" in the sense of the Nicene Creed.

The decree speaks neither of one nor of two sources of revelation. The careful enumeration of the Scriptures of the Old and New Testaments and the two kinds of traditions justifies the traditional understanding of two sources of revelation. It is the natural sense of the decree, not a theory read into it. Theology may ask how Scriptures and traditions are related and may come to the conclusion that they are essentially one.

But this is a later interpretation of the text. The decree does not answer how much of the divine revelation is contained in Scripture and how much in the traditions. (Trent uses the word still in the plural; it does not know strictly speaking, the *modern* concept of "tradition"). It does not say that there are truths contained not in Scripture, but in the traditions only. Nor does it deny that.

Much has been made of the fact that the decree does not contain the *partim-partim* of the original draft, which spoke of the truths contained "partly" in the written books and "partly" in the unwritten traditions. The council rejected that because some of the fathers held the opinion that "Scripture is complete as to its content and contains all truth necessary for salvation" (H. Jedin, *History of the Council of Trent*, Vol. II, p. 75). Even Tavard (p. 20) cannot say more than that the decree "respects" the view that tradition is the authoritative interpretation of the Scriptures. It does not exclude, but rather favors, the view held by the majority of the Catholic theologians since Trent. The First Vatican Council, which has expressly confirmed the decrees of Trent (Denz. 1787), has enlarged on the doctrine of Holy Scripture but added nothing concerning tradition. It says in defining the objects of faith (Denz. 1792): "With divine and Catholic faith all those truths must be believed which are contained in the Word of God written or given by tradition (*in verbo Dei scripto vel tradito*) and which have been proposed by the Church either through a solemn judgment or through the ordinary and universal teaching office as divinely revealed articles of faith." Scripture and tradition are here summed up and distinguished as two forms of the Word of God. Hence the Catholic dogmaticians are perfectly justified with the problem under the title "*Revelationis fontes*" (see the *Index systematicus* of Denzinger).

Are there revealed truths not contained in Holy Scripture but only in tradition? The majority of the Catholic theologians since Trent assumed that, and this is still the prevailing view. The theologians speak of tradition as far as it is compared with Scripture in a threefold sense. *Traditio constitutiva*, in other words, tradition constituting doctrine, is that tradition "the object of which is not in Scripture." Tradition can be *inhaesiva*, if its content is inherent, explicitly contained, in Scripture. It can be *declarativa* as far as it explains some doctrine implicitly contained in Scripture (*Sacrae Theologiae Summa*, Madrid, 1958, Vol. I, p. 765). Even a modern German dogmatician like M. Schmaus could not deny the existence of some dogmatic truth based not on Scripture but on tradition. He protests against the erroneous view as if Scripture were written tradition only, which would make tradition the proper and only source of revelation, and states,

> In reality the divine revelation which is testified to by the preaching of the apostles flows since the apostles in two river-beds through the ages, in Scripture and in the oral gradition. However, one can say that tradition has a certain precedence in so far as it guarantees the authority of Scripture by testifying to the canon and its inspiration. For the rest, the advantages of gradition should not be exaggerated at the expense of the written Word of God. The content of tradition extends, as far as one can state that today, only a little beyond that of the Scriptures. This 'more' of tradition concerns, apart from the canon and inspiration, especially Infant Baptism. (*Katholische Dogmatik*, Vol. I, 2nd edition, 1940, p. 52)

Also Karl Rahner, who is one of the protagonists of the "one source theory," leaves in the Introduction to the series *Quaestiones Disputatae* (No. 1 *Über die Schriftinspiration*, p. 7) the question open "whether there is . . . in addition to Scripture interpreted by the Church's teaching office . . . still a tradition that has handed on concrete contents of the revelation that are in no way contained in Holy Writ and yet are revelation proper and obligatory object of faith." "Be that as it may," he continues, "practically Scripture is always the primary starting point of new theological work on problems on which we have not received yet an answer from the teaching office of the Church."

The book itself is an impressive defense of the "one source theory" and the superiority of Scripture over tradition. Rahner accepts even the term "sufficiency" of Scripture, of course in the sense that Scripture must be interpreted by the Church. Hans Küng, who gives in his book on Justification (*Rechtfertigung. Die Lehre Karl Barths und eine Katholische Besinnung*, 1957, pp. 116ff.) a picture of the discussion of the problem in present European Catholicism, regards the Word of God as the source of Catholic doctrine and theology and says: "The Word of God in its strictest sense is the Holy Scripture only." He emphasizes "the unconditional precedence of Holy Scripture, which is directly and in a very concrete way in every sentence the Word of God, while the documents of tradition do only contain the Word of God" (p. 121). To understand the full meaning of such a statement one must compare it with the thesis I. Salaverri defends in the Spanish *Summa* quoted (pp. 764ff.): "The primary source of revelation is the divine tradition of the apostles which excels Holy Scripture in antiquity, plenitude, and sufficiency."

IV.

Thus two theories on the meaning of the Tridentine dogma of Scripture and tradition are competing in the great discussion between the first and the second period of the Second Vatican Council. While we accompany the debate with Christian sympathy and with the sincere desire to learn from it whatever we can, we owe it to our "separated brethren" just in view of the ecumenical implications of their endeavors to find a solution of the problem of the authority of Holy Scripture, to say a word about how the two theories look in the light of the Reformation and its *sola scriptura*. The questions we put to them we must put in all frankness also to ourselves and our churches. For the *sola scriptura* is, as our Catholic brethren clearly see, no longer an undisputed, self-understood possession of Protestantism today.

What actually is the difference between the theories of "one source" or "two sources" if both are regarded as possible interpretations of the decree of Trent as affirmed by the First Vatican Council? We try to answer this question by looking at the latest of the dogmas proclaimed by Rome, the doctrine of the Assumption of the Blessed Virgin Mary (in the constitution *Munificentissimus Deus* of November 1, 1950; Denz. 2331ff.). In this dogmatic constitution, the first issued since the First Vatican Council, Pius XII announced, declared, and defined it to be "a divinely revealed dogma that the Immaculate Mother of God, always Virgin Mary, after her earthly course of life was completed, has been assumed with body and soul to heavenly glory." Where is this revelation to be found? The constitution cannot give and does not try to give a direct proof from Scripture, nor does it give a real proof from tradition. According to the dogma of Trent, the "truth of the bodily assumption" of Mary here proclaimed must be contained either in Holy Scripture or in the unwritten traditions the apostles have received and handed on to the future generations of the Church, or in both. The tradition, however, cannot be traced back to the first four centuries. The pope had to confine himself to the statement that that truth "has been approved by the cult of the Church since the oldest times."

That the apostles, or the last of the apostles, have known of Mary's assumption and have handed on this tradition cannot be shown. It is an assumption of the teaching office of the Church that supplies what is missing in the tradition. The source of this knowledge is, consequently, the Church. "The Church Universal in which the Spirit of truth is alive who guides the Church infallibly so that she may more perfectly understand the truths given in the revelation" has, as the constitution says, "in many ways in the course of the centuries made manifest her faith, and all the bishops of the world have now almost unanimously asked that this truth might be defined" (Den. 2332). And as the gap in the tradition is as it were filled by the faith of the Church, so the Church also provides what is missing of a scriptural proof of the new dogma.

The truth of the bodily assumption of Mary finds *support* in the Scriptures: *Sacris Litteris innititur*. No direct proof can be given but an indirect proof:

> Since our Redeemer is the son of Mary, he who is the most perfect observer of the divine Law could certainly not fail to honor beside the eternal Father also his most blessed mother. And since he *was able* to adorn her with such a great honor that he preserved her from the corruption of the grave, it must be believed that he *has done* it in reality. But especially it must be kept in mind that since the second century

the Virgin Mary is shown by the holy fathers as the new Eve closely connected with, even if subordinated to, the new Adam in the fight against the hellish fiend which, as it was signified in the protevangel (Gen. 3:15), was to culminate in the fullest victory over sin and over death, which in the writings of the Apostle of the Gentiles are always interconnected (Rom. 5 and 6; 1 Cor. 15:21–26, 54–57). Therefore, as the glorious anastasis of Christ was an essential part and the last sign of this victory, so the fight which was common to the Blessed Virgin with her Son had to be concluded with the glorification of her body. For thus saith the same Apostle: "When . . . this mortal will put on immortality, then shall come to pass the saying that is written: Death is swallowed up in victory" (1 Cor. 15:54).

What kind of proof is this? It is an argumentation of the theologians that Mary who had conceived Christ, given birth to him, and nursed him, and thus was so closely connected with him, could not be separated from him bodily after her earthly life. Since he was able to do the great miracle, and since his complete love and obedience made it his duty to do it, it must be concluded that he did it. This conclusion is in harmony with what St. Paul teaches about the victory over death. These are "argumentations and considerations of the holy Fathers and the theologians," as *Munificentissimus Deus* states. But it is claimed that these human thoughts "are supported by the Holy Scriptures as, so to speak, their ultimate fundament" (*Sacris Litteris, tamquam ultimo fundamento, nituntur*). In other words, the source of the dogma is not Holy Writ, but pious human reasoning, conclusions that are in harmony with the rest of revealed truths ("*ceteris revelatis veritatibur summe consona*").

Nobody would deny that there are dogmas not explicitly found in Holy Scripture but deduced from it by way of conclusion, such as the dogma of the Trinity. What matters is whether the content of the dogma is taken from Holy Scripture. This is most certainly true of the dogma of the Trinity; it is not true of the dogma of the Assumption.

We have chosen this example to clarify the issue. What do Catholic theologians like Tavard, K. Rahner, and H. Kung mean if they maintain that Holy Scripture is the one and only source of revelation and tradition is the authoritative exposition of the Scriptures by the Church? They mean obviously something quite different from the *sola scriptura* of the Reformation. If they make the point, and Tavard makes it most impressively, that the adherents of the scriptural principle of the Reformation are in disagreement as to the individual doctrines of the Scripture and that this proves that Scripture without an authoritative teaching office is not sufficient, we have to ask whether there are rules to which the teaching office is bound and whether these rules allow to teach as binding dogma doctrines not clearly taught in Scripture.

If it is possible for the teaching office to teach doctrines not taken from, but only regarded as being in harmony with, Holy Writ, then there is another source of binding doctrine, however it may be called, tradition or the implicit faith of the Church. It would be wrong to call the infallible teaching office, be it the Ecumenical Synod or the papal office, the source of revelation. For the revelation is given in the apostolic "*depositum*" ("*paratheke*" 1 Tim. 6:20; *cf.* "The faith which was once delivered to the saints" Jude 3). But by making the faith held since immemorial time by the Church ("*das Glaubensbewusstsein der Kirche*") the source of doctrine, as is being done in the decision of 1950, and by assuming that this faith is developing and that its content is understood by the Church only in a process of development, even the theologians who today favor the "one source theory" admit in fact a second one: the Church.

"Holy Writ or Holy Church?" This title of Tavard's book is an excellent formulation of the problem, as it was at issue between the Reformation and Rome. Our reformers have never denied the authority of the Church as far as it is obedient to the Word of God. They have not established the kind of "private judgment" that later in an age of individualism was ascribed to them. What they have taught was the clarity and perspicuity of Holy Scripture, which makes it possible for everyone who believes in Christ to understand the great truths of salvation in the Bible. They have, indeed, been aware that Holy Scripture can be also misunderstood and falsely interpreted. They have known that this can happen and has happened not only with individuals, but also with whole churches and synods and that it can happen even with the majority of Christians.

The remedy against this was to them not an infallible *magisterium* — where was this *magisterium* when in Jerusalem Jeremiah and the prophets whom he called false prophets contradicted each other and the poor people did not know who was right and who was wrong? And where was it when Paul and the "apostles" of Judaism fought for the souls of the Christians in Galatia? The infallible *magister* who makes us understand the Scriptures is Christ who is Lord, center and content of the whole Bible, and who opens it (Luke 24:24; John 5:39; Acts 10:43; 2 Cor. 3:15ff.) revealing himself as the Savior from sin and death. This is how Luther understood the authority of Holy Writ. And Calvin added the emphasis on the Holy Spirit, who as the author of the Holy Scriptures gives us the assurance of the truth of the Bible through the *testimonium Spiritus Sancti internum.*

The reformers have, moreover, never denied that there are traditions in the Church, not only man-made traditions, but traditions based on God's Word in the Bible or compatible with it and therefore to be maintained. What they have rejected was any equation of Scripture and tradition, of Scripture and the Church. Also Rome teaches that the Bible is not made by the Church but given to the Church (*Vaticanum* I; Denz. 1787) by the inspiration of the Holy Spirit. Would it not be the greatest service to the cause of Christian unity if we on all sides began to realise what this consensus means in an age when we all are asked by the non-Christian world what the divine revelation is which we all want to proclaim?

It is certainly not accidental that the nature and authority of Holy Scripture has become again the central problem of all Christian theology. We cannot hope to find a solution to it unless we try seriously to understand what the great churches of Christendom teach about it and why they do so. As we who come from the churches of the Reformation have to study the doctrine of Trent and the Vatican Councils on the sources of revelation with great seriousness, is it too much if we ask the theologians in Rome to try to understand the *sola scriptura* of the Reformation by reexamining this doctrine and the deepest motives behind it? If Hans Küng was able to write from a definitely Catholic standpoint a fair and profound book on Karl Barth's doctrine of justification, it should not be impossible that some day we shall get from a Catholic scholar an equally able book on Luther's doctrine of the Word of God.

HERMANN SASSE

THE REFORMED THEOLOGICAL REVIEW
Vol. XXII, No. 2, June 1963

Rome and the Inspiration of Scripture

I.

The starting point for all discussions of the problem of the inspiration of Holy Scripture in modern Roman Catholic theology is the statement of the dogmatic constitution *De fide catholica* of the First Vatican Council that the Church accepts the books of the Bible enumerated by the Council of Trent "as sacred and canonical not because, having been composed by human industry, they later have been approved by its authority, and not only because they contain revelation without error, but because, having been *written by the inspiration of the Holy Spirit, they have God for their author* and as such have been delivered to the Church" (Denz. 1787). This is the dogma of the Catholic Church, contained already in the decrees of the councils of Trent and Florence (Decree for the Jacobites. Denz. 706). It comprises two propositions: (1) God—The Triune God as in all divine works *ad extra* —is the author of Holy Scripture. (2) This authorship is appropriated in a special way to the Holy Spirit. From these two propositions a third is derived, which, though never especially formulated in a dogmatic constitution, is taken for granted. (3) Holy Scripture is free from error.

This dogma is supplemented and limited by the Tridentine doctrine of traditions as a source of revelation to be accepted in addition to the Scriptures with equal pious affection and reverence,[1] and by the Rule, established by Trent and reaffirmed by the Vatican Council, concerning the interpretation of Scripture, *to wit.* that "in matters of faith and morals which pertain to the teaching of Christian doctrine, the sense of Holy Scripture which must be considered as the true sense, is that which has been held and is being held by our holy mother, the Church, to which it belongs to judge of the true sense and inspiration of the Holy Scriptures" (Denz. 1788).

With this dogma Rome had to meet the challenge of the modern world against which the First Vatican Council was directed, that revolutionary world of Atheism, Pantheism, Indifferentism, Latitudinarianism, Rationalism, and other enemies of the Church that the Syllabus of 1865 had exposed. Behind them, Pius IX and the majority of the bishops of 1870 saw as the real source of all errors and cause of all revolutions in the modern world the great heresy of the Reformation, which, as Rome has always seen it, with its *sola scriptura* has destroyed the authority of the Church with the result that Protestantism has eventually lost with the authority of the Church also the authority of the inerrant Bible. It is certainly not accidental that the same council that tried to safeguard the authority of the infallible Scripture has also established the authority of the pope and his infallible teaching office. For Rome these two authorities belong inseparably together.

II.

Soon after the decision of 1870, it became evident that not only those enemies of the Church were challenging Rome's doctrine of Holy Scripture. Within the Roman Church itself with its wonderful structure of authorities that are supposed to support each other, the question arose of what that doctrine really meant and how it would be upheld in the nineteenth century. The men who raised that question were theologians who could not possibly be accused of making concessions to the unbelieving world or of leanings to Protestantism. The greatest among them was Cardinal Newman, who with an

---

[1]See "The Sources of Revelation," This Review, 1963, no. 1. [note above].

article "On the Inspiration of Scripture" in the "Nineteenth Century"
(1884, pp. 185–99) started a discussion on what he called "a burning
question of the hour."[2] Starting from the council's emphasis on the
inspiration of Scripture in respect to "faith and morals," he found
it "remarkable that they do not say a word directly as to its inspiration in matters of fact." He refused to conclude "that the record of
facts in Scripture does not come under the guarantee of its inspiration." However, he regarded it as possible that certain *obiter dicta*—
incidental statements of a factual character but of minor importance
and in no way connected with matters of faith and morals—would
not be covered by the inspiration. This included passages such as
2 Timothy 4:13 and Judith 1:5. It has been said that Newman was not
very well acquainted with the terminology of the theological schools.
This may be so. In any case he has in the touching seriousness of this
essay called the attention of the Church to the fact that problems
were turning up that demanded an answer, problems not posed by
objectionable theories but by irrefutable facts of nature and history
unknown to former centuries but known to our age.

This was at the time of Leo XIII (1878–1903) who, in contrast
with his predecessor, tried to reconcile, as far as possible, the Roman
Church with the modern world. Only reluctantly he took up the fight
against those who went too far in their attempt to adapt Catholicism
to the needs of the modern world (Hecker's *Americanismus*, Schell as
apologist and dogmatician, Rosmini as philosopher). Among these
forerunners of what later was called Modernism were also exegetes,
especially in France, who as loyal Catholics tried to apply historical scholarship to the interpretation of the Bible. One of them was
the young Loisy, who taught since 1884 at the Institut Catholique,
Paris. His *L'enseignement biblique* of 1892 was still defended by the
conservative d'Hulst who shared Newman's view on inspiration. But
it was this book that caused Leo XIII to issue in 1893 the encyclical
"On The Study of Holy Scripture," *Providentissimus Deus*, the first
of the three great Bible encyclicals that have determined the biblical
studies in the Roman Church during the last generations. The pope

---

[2]See W. Ward, *Cardinal Newman*, vol. II, pp. 502ff. W. Gives excerpts from
the article and from the ensuing correspondence.

defends the Bible against those who attack its authority. "There has arisen, to the great detriment of religion, an inept method, dignified by the name of 'higher criticism' (*criticae sublimioris*) that pretends to judge of the origin, integrity, and authority of each book from internal indications alone."

In historical question[s] the witness of history is of primary importance. Internal evidence can only support that witness. Otherwise "this vaunted 'higher criticism' will resolve itself into the reflection of the bias and the prejudice of the critics." The second point made in this apologetical part is the relationship between Scripture and Natural Sciences. Here the encyclical refers to Augustine and to Aquinas:

> There can never be any real discrepancy between the theologian and the physicist, as long as each confines himself within his own limits, and both are careful, as St. Augustine warns us, not to make rash assertions, or to assert what is not known as known. If dissension should arise between them, here is the rule also laid down by St. Augustine for the theologian: "Whatever they can really demonstrate to be true of physical nature we must show to be capable of reconciliation with our Scriptures; and whatever they assert in their treatises, which is contrary to these Scriptures of ours, that is to the Catholic faith, we must either prove it as well as we can to be entirely false, or at all events we must, without the smallest hesitation, believe it to be so" (*De Gen. ad litt.* 1, 21, 41; M.P.L. 34, 262).

Following Augustine, the encyclical maintains that the sacred writers "did not seek to penetrate the secrets of nature, but rather described and dealt with things in more or less figurative language, or in terms which were commonly used at the time ... Ordinary speech primarily and properly describes what comes under the senses; and somewhat in the same way the sacred writers—as the Angelic Doctor reminds us—'went by what sensibly appeared' (*S. th.* 1 q. 80 ad 1, ad 3)—or put down what God, speaking to men, signified, in the way men could understand and were accustomed to it" (Denz. 1947). The rule of St. Thomas is quoted: "When philosophers are agreed upon a point, and it is not contrary to our faith, it is safer in my opinion, neither to lay down such a point as dogma of faith, nor to reject it as against faith, lest we thus give to the wise of this world an occasion of despising our faith" (*Opusc.* 10, *praef.*; Denz. 1948).

Concerning the problem presented by natural science, the encyclical was thus able to pave the way for a reconciliation between theology and science. For this problem had already occupied the fathers in East and West as well as the schoolmen.[3] It was different with the problems presented by modern historical research. The problem of history in our sense was unknown to the Ancient and Medieval Church, as also to the reformers, though we find in the sixteenth century the beginning of historical criticism applied to the documents of Church history. Hence *Providentissimus Deus* was not able to answer what Newman had called the burning question of the hour. The Thomist Leo would never even understand the question how the inerrancy of the Scriptures can and must be maintained in view of the existing discrepancies between the biblical narratives and established facts of history. "It is absolutely wrong and forbidden either to narrow inspiration to certain parts only of Holy Scripture or to admit that the sacred writer has erred."

Also the limitation of inspiration to the matters of faith and morals is not allowed (Denz. 1950):

> For all the books which the Church receives as sacred and canonical are written wholly and entirely, with all their parts, at the dictation of the Holy Spirit; and so far is it from being possible that any error can coexist with inspiration, that inspiration not only is essentially incompatible with error, but excludes and rejects it as absolutely and necessarily as it is impossible that God himself, the supreme Truth, can utter that which is not true. This is the ancient and unchanging faith of the Church. . . .

Here follows the reference to the decrees of Florence, Trent, and the Vatican (Denz. 1951f.).

During the remaining years of his reign, Leo XIII had to recognize that these strong assertions were not sufficient to keep theology

---

[3]See our article "Hexaemeron: Theology and Science with the Church Fathers," This Review, October 1958 [see above].

in the traditional path. In his Apostolic Letter *Vigilantiae* of 1902, he states, "We remark that the causes which prompted us to publish the previous letter are still persistent and more serious. It is therefore necessary to insist more emphatically on what has already been enjoined." In order to help the bishops to watch with the greatest vigilance over the biblical studies, he established by this document a Biblical Commission in Rome, consisting of some Cardinals and other churchmen and scholars. This commission, furnished with all available help, should serve as a sort of clearing house in exegetical matters. Its task is "to regulate in a legitimate and suitable manner the principal questions which are pending between Catholic doctors in order to arrive at a conclusion. To settle them, the assembly will lend sometimes the light of its judgment, sometimes the weight of its authority."

Their investigations will also furnish "to the Holy See an opportune occasion to declare what ought to be inviolably maintained by Catholics, what ought to be reserved for more profound research, and what ought to be left to the free judgment of each." This institution has proved of great benefit to the Roman Church in so far as it guided the discussion of certain controversial issues and prevented it from becoming a *bellum omnium contra omnes*. The price to be paid for it was high. It prevented a free discussion, without which there is no progress in whatever branch of human knowledge, and it often silenced the real experts. The decisions made by the Pontifical Biblical Commission in the time of Pius X (e.g., on tacit quotations contained in Holy Scripture; the Mosaic authorship of the Pentateuch; author and historical truth of the Fourth Gospel; the character of the book of Isaias and its author; the historical character of the first three chapters of Genesis; author, time of composition, and character of the Psalms; problems of the Synoptic Gospels, the Pastoral Epistles; author of Hebrews; the Second Coming of Christ in the New Testament) were very conservative. On the other hand, they had not the character of infallible decisions of the Church and could be rescinded in the light of deeper research.

This, then, has happened with most of the decisions, in a most conspicuous way in the case of the decision of the decree of the Sacrum Officium of 1897 (before there was a Biblical Commision) concerning the authenticity of the *Comma Johanneum* (1 John 5:7), which was practically rescinded by the Holy Office in 1927.

III.

Before biblical theology of the Roman Church could face in a new way the problems of history, it had to go through the ordeal of the pontificate of Pius X (1903–14). Perhaps only he who has still a memory of the ecclesiastical situation in the years preceding the First World War can understand the profound sadness that pervaded Roman Catholicism at that time. These were the years of the Modernist controversy, which caused not only numerous personal tragedies, but threatened also to develop into a tragedy of the Church itself.

For the censures expressed mainly in the Decree *Lamentabili* of 1907 with its syllabus of sixty-five errors of the Modernists (Mirbt, *Quellen* 652; Denz. 2001) and the *Motu proprio* of the same year *Pascendi* (Mirbt 653; Denz. 2071ff.) with its description of the docutrines of the Modernists, furthermore the *Motu proprio Sacrorumantistitum* of 1910 with the anti-Modernist oath to be taken and repeated again and again by all priests and teachers of theology did not only condemn propositions more or less contradictory to the dogma of the Church, but they seemed to condemn at the same time any application of the methods of historical research to the Bible and the history of the Primitive Church.

Pius had all the virtues of a pious parish priest and treated the Church as his parish. But he had little understanding of the intellectual problems that confronted the Church in the twentieth century. He did not understand Newman's last question, but seemed to execute the testament of Manning: "one must overcome history with the dogma." His fight against those who had given up the Catholic dogma, such as Loisy, was justified, and he made some very good points against the modern attempts to understand Jesus by means of historical research only. He rightly criticised those who under the pretext of objective historical research produce a picture of Jesus that is the product of their subjective wishes. The weakness of Pius X in this whole matter becomes evident in the fact that according to objective Catholic historians[4] he is at least partly responsible for the

---

[4] J. Schmildin, *Paptsgeschichte der neuern Zeit*, Vol. III (1936), pp. 162ff; see also: Jean Levie, *The Bible, Word of God in Words of Men*, 1961, pp. 72ff.

rise of that strange conspiracy of the "Integralists" whose leader was Benigni in Rome.

The whole story of "La Sapiniere," as this secret society called itself, was revealed when in 1915 a whole correspondence was found by the German occupation forces at Ghent, Belgium, and turned over to the church authorities. A systematic campaign of slander had been going on for years against men like Cardinal Mercier and Bishop Faulhaber, against whole faculties, against Dominicans and even the Jesuits in Rome. Already in 1914, Benedict XV had right after his accession warned against such a campaign, which obviously was going on in high places, denouncingmen of impeachable orthodoxy as secret Modernists. It was a tense atmosphere of suspicion and distrust created by these controversies in which both the "Modernists" and their adversaries were convinced they were fighting for the very existence of the Church.

The positive contribution Pius X made to the future work in biblical theology was the creation of the Pontifical Biblical Institute in 1909. Its task was to be a center of higher scriptural studies to promote biblical learning and subsidiary sciences as effectively as possible and in accordance with the spirit of the Catholic Church. Entrusted to the Jesuits, this institute has become the great instrument for the renewal of the study of the Bible and of an inner reform of the Catholic Church. Its quiet work replaced the turbulent controversies that were bound to subside with the outbreak of the war in 1914.

Another center of biblical studies had been founded at Jerusalem by the Dominican theologian A. M. H. Lagrange (1885–1938) who is today regarded as the greatest of the biblical scholars of modern Catholicism. He defended in a famous book the application of the historical method to the Old Testament. A member of the Biblical Commission in 1902, he was soon suspected of Modernism. Though he regarded stories like those of the flood and the tower of Babel legends, he maintained the historicity of all passages on which a dogma was based, for instance the story of the fall. From the study of the Old Testament, he turned to the New Testament and wrote famous conservative commentaries on the Gospels. "The Bible of Jerusalem," which we have to mention later, is the greatest monument of his school.

IV.

After the end of the Great War, in 1920, Benedict XV issued the second of the great biblical encyclicals, "On the Fifteenth Centenary of the Death of St. Jerome," *Spiritus Paraclitus*. Starting from Jerome's doctrine of the inspiration and inerrancy of Scripture, the pope compares this doctrine with modern views. "We warmly commend . . . those who with the assistance of critical methods, seek to discover new ways of explaining the difficulties in Holy Scripture. But we remind them that they will only come to miserable grief if they neglect our predecessor's (i.e., Leo XIII in *Providentissimus Deus*) injunctions and overstep the limits set by the fathers" (Denz. 2186).

"Certain recent writers" distinguish between "the primary or religious and the secondary or profane element in the Bible" and restrict absolute truth and immunity from error to that primary element. Leo's assertion is emphatically repeated: "It would be wholly impious to limit inspiration to certain portions of Scripture or to concede that the sacred authors themselves have erred." "Jerome maintains that belief in the biblical narrative is as necessary to salvation as is belief in the doctrines of the faith." He would sharply reject "people who set aside what is the mind and judgment of the Church and take too ready a refuge in such notions as 'implicit quotations' or 'pseudo-historical narratives,' or in 'literary genres' (*genera litteratum*, Denz. 2188) in the Bible such as cannot be reconciled with the entire and perfect truth of God's Word, or who suggest such origins of the Bible as must inevitably weaken—if not destroy—its authority."

Benedict refers especially to "the treatment of the Fourth Gospel" and quotes John 19:35. A whole chapter is given to the sayings of Jesus on the Scriptures: "Whether teaching or disputing he quotes from all parts of Scripture; he quotes it as an argument that must be accepted. He refers without discrimination to the stories of Jonas and the Ninivites, of the Queen of Sheba and Solomon, of Elias and Elisaeus, of David and Nathan, of Lot and the Sodomites, and even of Lot's wife. . . . How solemn his witness to the truth of the sacred books: 'One jot, or one tittle shall not pass of the law till all be fulfilled' (Matt. 5:18); and again: 'The Scripture cannot be broken' (John 10:35)."

These are touching words. They could have been written and have virtually been written during those years at Princeton when the Fundamentalist-Modernist controversy raged through the Protestant churches of America with the same passion we found in the church of Pius X. And yet, there is a difference between the Fundamentalism of Benedict XV and the Fundamentalism of American Protestants, just as the Modernism in the Roman Church cannot be compared with the Modernism of America, which was only the Liberalism of European theology uncritically taken over by men who had no theology of their own.

Behind *Spiritus Paraclitus* as behind *Providentissimus Deus*, there stands the scholarship of centuries, Patristic and Thomistic scholarship indeed, but it was scholarship, and the Church had built up the institutions in which a new generation should be trained for the solution of problems to which in the first half of this century no church, Catholic or Protestant, had a solution.

V.

Fifty years after *Providentissimus Deus*, on the feast of St. Jerome, September 30, 1943, Pius XII issued the third of the great Bible encyclicals, *Divino afflante Spiritu*. The expert who had written it for him was the Rector of the Pontifical Biblical Institute, Augustine Bea, S.J., now Cardinal and one of the leading men of the Second Vatican Council. It was the fruit of the patient work done by the scholars of this Institute through forty years, and especially since the death of Benedict XV, during the pontificate of Pius XI (1922–37) and the first years of Pius XII.

The document begins with a historical part reviewing the endeavors of the popes since Leo XIII to further the biblical studies and reminding of the rule established by Pius XI in the *Motu proprio* "*Bibliorum scientiam*" "that no one should be appointed professor of Sacred Scripture in any Seminary, unless, having completed a special course of biblical studies, he had in due form obtained the academic degrees before the Biblical Commission Institute" or Biblical Institute and "that these degrees should have the same rights and the same effects as degrees duly conferred in Sacred Theology or Canon Law," furthermore that no one should receive "a benefice having attached the canonical obligation of expounding Sacred Scripture to the people, unless among other things, he had obtained the licentiate or doctorate in biblical science."

As regards the doctrine of Scripture, the encyclical reaffirms the traditional doctrines of the inspiration and the inerrancy of the Bible, but it makes now an attempt to overcome the deadlock concerning the claim for absolute inerrancy in matters where the established historical facts seem to contradict the Bible. *Spiritus Paracletus* had still rejected the assumption of "implicitquotations," "pseudo historical narratives," and "literary gen[r]es," to solve the problem. Now this door is opened:

> "For the ancient people of the East, in order to express their ideas, did not always employ those forms or kinds of speech (*formae et modi dicendi*) which we use today.

> What those exactly were the commentator cannot determine as it were in advance, but only after careful examination of the ancient literature of the East" (Denz. 2294).

> "No one, who has a correct idea of biblical inspiration, will be surprised to find, even in the Sacred Writers, as in other ancient authors, certain fixed ways of expounding and narrating, certain definite idioms, especially of a kind peculiar to the Semitic tongues, so-called approximations, and certain hyperbolical modes of expression, nay, at times even paradoxical, which even help to impress the ideas more deeply on the mind. For of the modes of expression through which, among ancient peoples, and especially those of the East, human language used to express its thoughts, none is excluded from the Sacred Books, provided the way of speaking adopted in no wise contradicts the holiness and truth of God, as with his customary wisdom the Angelic Doctor already observed in these words: 'In Scripture divine things are presented to us in the manner which is in common use amongst men' (*Comm. ad Heb.* cap I, lectio 4). For as the substantial Word of God became like to men in all things, 'except sin,' so the words of God, expressed in human language, are made like to human speech in every respect, except error.

> "In this consists that 'condescension' of the God of providence which St. John Chrysostom extolled with the highest praise and repeatedly declared to be found in the sacred books."

This recognition of various "literary genres" and of ancient modes of historiography does indeed remove many difficulties, but not all of them. Hence the encyclical admonishes the exegetes to grapple with the difficult problems, hitherto unsolved, and to try to find a solution "which will be in full accord with the doctrine of the Church, in particular with the traditional teaching regarding the inerrancy of Sacred Scripture; and which will at the same time satisfy the indubitable conclusion of profane sciences."

This encyclical has made it possible to Roman theology to accept the results of modern biblical criticism to an astonishing degree. Within a few years a real revolution has taken place in the understanding of the Bible. Not only the sources of the Pentateuch have been recognised and the literary criticism of the Psalms and the prophetical books (Isaiah, Ezekiel, Jonah, Daniel), but even a really historical interpretation of the first eleven chapters of Genesis has been attempted (Bruce Vawter, *A Path through Genesis*, 1955, following hints given in a decision of the Biblical Commission of 1948). What modern Catholic understanding of the Bible is becomes evident from "*La Sainte Bible, traduite en francais sous la direction de l'Ecole Biblique de Jerusalem*," with its illuminating comments and introductions. Even the literary criticism of the New Testament has been widely accepted (see Jean Steinmann, *Biblical Criticism*, Faith and Fact Books No. 63, 1959). Within a few years, the Roman Church has accepted and assimilated the results of generations of Protestant biblical scholarship.

VI.

Pius XII knew what a revolutionary venture his step was. He concludes his remarks on the unfinished tasks of the theologians with the admonition:

> "Let all the other sons of the Church bear in mind that the efforts of these resolute laborers in the vineyard of the Lord should be judged not only with equity and justice, but also with the greatest charity; all moreover should abhor that intemperate zeal which imagines that whatever is new should for that very reason be opposed or suspected."

How necessary this admonition was appears from the critical remarks by Cardinal Ruffini on the new doctrine: "How can one suppose that the Church has during nineteen centuries presented the divine book without knowing the literary genres in which it was composed, if this is the test to exact interpretation? Such an assertion becomes absurd when one takes in account that a large number of these superior-minded critics not only call for new applications of the theory of literary genres in regard to the inspired books, but to remit to the future a definite explanation. . . ." What Ruffini in his unhistorical way of thinking overlooks is the fact that there is indeed in the Church of Christ a progress in the understanding of the Scripture, though it belongs to the nature of the Bible as God's Word that its essential content, its message, remains the same in all times and can be understood by all men without fallible or infallible teaching authorities.

We have quoted Cardinal Ruffini because his words shed light on the inner situation of the Roman Catholic Church as it has been revealed at the first period of the Second Vatican Council. The two conflicting theological schools whose presence became manifest to the world, represented by their leaders, Cardinals Ottaviani and Bea, are not simply the continuation of the parties that at the beginning of the century clashed in the Modernist controversy. Though it is obvious that the deepest motives underlying the Modernist Movement have been revived, on a higher level, in the new biblical theology of the Pontifical Biblical Institute, this theology is not a new form of Modernism. Between this new theology and the conservative Modernists lies the development of half a century that saw the rise of two other movements that have changed the Christian world. One is the Liturgical Movement, which began under Pius X.

It is remarkable that the same pope who had to fight Modernism has become the father of the modern Liturgical Movement, directly through his liturgical reforms, indirectly by causing the best minds of Catholic theology to shift their interests from fields in which historical research had become dangerous to the less dangerous research in liturgiology. In this way modern Catholic theology has been able to train a whole generation of theologians in the application of historical research to one of the essential aspects of the life of the Church.

At the same time the study of the liturgy was bound to pave the way for a new understanding of the Bible. For the Scriptures are not primarily books meant to impart theoretical knowledge, but liturgical books meant to be read or chanted "*en ekklesia*" to make men wise unto salvation. Even the Law was read in the solemn assembly of God's people (2 Kings 23; Neh 8f.), and the liturgical formulas in the conclusion of the Pauline Epistles (e.g., 1 Cor. 16:19ff.) show that even this kind of literature was read in the solemn assembly of Christ's Church.

How closely the new biblical theology is linked with the Liturgical Movement becomes obvious in the new Latin translation of the Psalms for the use of the priests and in the remarkable fact that the new translation of the Psalms in the Bible of Jerusalem is sung on the streets of France in Gelinaud's wonderful setting. Freed from the fetters of a mere schoolbook, the Bible has become again the book of the Church.

The second movement is the Ecumenical Movement, which must not be identified with the forms it has developed in modern Protestantism, where it has degenerated into an unprecedented process of church amalgamations in which the substance of the Christian faith is rapidly vanishing. Essentially it is a process going on in the innermost soul of Christendom, a new discovery of the *Una Sancta* in the common experiences, defeats, and victories of all Christendom. This movement has now reached the Roman Church and is changing its attitude toward the rest of Christendom. It has the same strange effects as in the Protestant churches: the enthusiasm of young theologians (Hans Küng, *Thatthe World May Believe*, 1963), the attempts of the older ones to find formulas of compromise (e.g., the new doctrine of the relationship between Scripture and tradition), and the businesslike efficiency of church politicians who figure out how long it would take to reunite the churches by way of individual conversions and how soon this goal could be attained by way of corporate reunion.

No one can take this seriously. But what we have to take very seriously is the encounter between Rome and our churches that is taking place in our time. Rome is discovering us as "separated brethren." There is a strange lack of clarity and certainty in the way the great Roman Church is approaching her small sisters. At the opening of the council, the observers from the non-Roman churches were treated as honored guests, as representatives of the separated brethren in the world. But in the solemn act of confession of faith, each of the nearly three thousand bishops repeated not only the Nicene Creed, which still binds together the greater part of all Christians on earth, but also the serious pledge of the *Professio Fidei Tridentina*, "I, condemn, reject and anathematise" the doctrines of the Reformation. In this certainly unavoidable contradiction lies the question Rome addresses to us: We have essentially the same Bible; what then separates us?

Are we still able to answer this question with the clarity with which Luther made it clear to Erasmus, who claimed that the Bible needs the authoritative interpretation by the Church, that the inspiration, inerrancy, and sufficiency of the Scriptures can be understood only from their content, which is Christ, the Savior of sinners: *Tolle Christum e Scripturis, quid amplius in illis invenies?* Take Christ out of the Scriptures, what else will you find in them? If the inspiration is the work of the Holy Spirit, it can never be separated from the proper work of the Spirit to "bring to remembrance," to "witness of," and to "glorify" Christ (John 14:26; 15:26; 16:14). Then the Bible is the Book of the Triune God in which from the first (Gen. 1:3 comp. John 1:3; 1 Cor. 8:6; Heb. 1:2) to the last page (Rev. 22:20f.) the Father testifies through the Holy Spirit of Christ: "This is my beloved Son, in whom I am well pleased; hear ye him."

THE REFORMED THEOLOGICAL REVIEW
Vol. XXIII, No. 1, February 1964

The Ecumenical Movement in the
Roman Catholic Church

Paper read at The Tyndale Fellowship, Melbourne, November 21, 1963.

L.

The Ecumenical Movement, as one of the great spiritual movements of the twentieth century, must not be identified with any of the organizations it has produced and in which it has found an expression. It began outside Europe in America, where as a consequence of the great migrations from the Old World churches and denominations, those who in Europe and the Near East were separated by national and linguistic borders, now found themselves living as neighbors in the same city, in the same street, and even in the same house. The second starting point lies on the mission fields of the entire world, where all denominations of Christendom met and each of them claimed to represent the one true Church of Christ. The third root of the movement lies in Europe, the Europe of the years 1914–1918, war-torn and haunted by the Bolshevist Revolution.

Ten years after the World Missionary Conference of Edinburgh and, after that, the Anglican Convention of Cincinnati, which started the Faith and Order Movement, the seed of the ecumenical idea was germinating in the blood-soaked soil of the Old World. The appeal "To all Christian people" issued by the Lambeth Conference of 1920 was preceded by one of the most touching documents of modern

Church history, the encyclical that the Patriarchate of Constantinople addressed in January, 1920: "Unto all the churches of Christ wheresoever they be" (G. K. A. Bell, "Documents on Christian Unity 1920–24," Oxford 1924, pp. 44ff.). Under the motto "See that ye love one another with a pure heart fervently" (1 Peter 1:22), the Locum Tenens of the Patriarchal Throne with his metropolitans expressed the opinion "that a closer cooperation with each other and a mutual understanding between the several Christian churches is not prevented by the doctrinal differences existing between them."

"The other brothers in the East" and "the venerable Christians of the churches in the West" are admonished to follow the example set by the political powers in the establishment of the League of Nations and to establish among the churches a closer relationship, which, in an explanation of the appeal, was later defined as a "*koinonia ton ekklesion*," a league of churches. Very concrete, practical suggestions for such co-operation are made, among them the convening of "pan-Christian conferences." It is regrettable that this document has not found the attention it deserves. It provides the key to the understanding of the participation of the Eastern Orthodox churches in the ecumenical conferences and councils. It was by no means only caused by the need for help after the catastrophe of the Russian Revolution and the destruction of the Church in Asia Minor by the new Turkey. In these catastrophes the Eastern churches had discovered the fact that all Christian churches are bound together by a common destiny: "A frank and vivid intercourse between the churches will be all the more beneficial to the whole body of the Church as many dangers threaten no longer any particular church, but all of them generally, because these dangers attack the very foundation of the Christian faith and the very composition of Christian life and society" (p. 47).

It is this solidarity of a common destiny experienced in the greatest persecution the history of the Church knows that has stirred up the Ecumenical Movement in the Eastern churches. Before the judge who pronounces the death sentence and in front of the execution squad, the boundaries between the confessions become unimportant. What becomes all-important is the love of Christ and the love that binds together also those who are separated by denominational borders, as Orthodox, Baptists, and Lutherans were in Russia.

Something of the appeal to Christian love that later pervaded the speeches of Pope John XXIII already sounds in this great document of Eastern ecumenicity.

That it did not find a great echo has several reasons. The Church of England was too much pre-occupied with its own Lambeth Appeal and with the attempts made in the following years to have the Anglican orders recognized by the Orthodox churches. So it was mainly the Lambeth Quadrilateral, which had been redrafted in the Appeal of 1920, that determined the ecumenical discussions of the twenties, especially the discussions of Faith and Order. The Ecumenical Movement became thus a movement among Anglicans and Protestants in which some Eastern churches participated, but it was not that pan-Christian movement the Ecumenical Patriarchate had envisaged.

Rome was not prepared to participate in any co-operation and intercourse, let alone in any theological dialogue with other churches. As it declined the invitation to the World Conference on Faith and Order, so it confined itself to a brief acknowledgment of the Encyclical Letter and the Report on Lambeth in 1920.

The Encyclical of the Patriarchate seems to have found no echo at all in Rome. The Curia was in the years following World War I interested in establishing diplomatic relations with the Balkan states, especially with Greece, rather than in improving relations with the Ecumenical Patriarchate, which, being not interested in diplomatic relations between Rome and the governments of the Orthodox nations, was accused of political maneuvering (J. Schmidlin, *Papstgeschichte der neueren Zeit*, Vol. III, p. 310). It may be assumed that Archbishop Roncalli—who under Pius XI in 1925 was sent as Apostolic Visitor to Sofia and in 1934 transferred to Instanbul—came to see that the difficult problem of the relation between Rome and the Eastern churches cannot be solved by political and diplomatic means and that his experiences have helped to prepare the ecumenical attitude toward the East that he took as Pope John XXIII.

II.

There was a long way to go until Rome reached the insight that had found an expression in the encyclical of the Ecumenical Patriarchate of 1920. In the encyclical *Ubi arcano Dei*, which Pius XI issued after his accession in 1922, the pope speaks of "the many who, either not knowing Christ or not fully holding his teaching or the unity established by him, are still outside the fold, though destined for it by divine providence." His ecumenical program is contained in the words "The Vicar of the Divine Shepherd cannot but repeat and make his own words which, with their simple brevity, are redolent of love and tender pity: 'Them also (the other sheep) must I bring,' and must rejoice, too, in the happy prophecy of Christ himself: 'And they shall hear my voice, and there shall be one fold and one shepherd'" (Bell p. 30f.).

As a "good augury for this religious unity," Pius XI regards the fact "that the representatives and rulers of almost all the States of the world . . . have turned to this Apostolic See either to resume old friendly relations or to inaugurate such relations of concord." Not one word is said about the non-Roman churches and their longing for ecumenicity. Also the encyclical *Ecclesiam Dei*, issued in 1923 for the commemoration of the 340th anniversary of St. Josaphat the Martyr, Archbishop of Polock (of the Oriental Rite), though referring to the touching prayers for unity in the Latin and Oriental liturgies, knows only one way of reaching the desired unity, the submission of the Eastern Church to the Vicar of Christ: "Let us therefore invoke our most gracious Mother . . . that she may lead our separated brethren back to the health-giving pastures, where Peter, never failing in his successors, the Vicar of the Eternal Shepherd, feeds and rules over all, both the lambs and the sheep of the Christian flock" (Bell, p. 43).

One must read this document, the first, as it seems, in which the term "separated brethren" officially is used, at least for the Eastern Orthodox Christians, to understand the development that has gone on in Rome in our time. The answer to the great World Conferences of Stockholm and Lausanne was given in *Mortalium animos* of Epiphany 1928, which spoke of the ecumenical conferences in a most unfair way and forbade all Catholics participation in conversations with non-Catholics such as had been going on at Malines with Anglicans, and with Protestants in other places. "There is but one way in which the unity of Christians may be fostered, and that is by furthering the return to the one true Church of Christ of those who are separated from it; for from that one true Church they have in the past fallen away."

III.

No one can deny that the attitude of Pius XI is doctrinally correct, seen from the standpoint of the Roman Church. And it must be admitted that the practical conclusion, the prohibition for Catholics to take part in such movements and to engage in any ecclesiastical activities with non-Catholics was logical. How, then, is it to be explained that the Roman Church has been able to change its attitude towards Christians of other denominations and toward the ecumenical organisations in such a striking way? This change cannot be explained as church politics. Church politics, plays, of course, always a role in a church, which is by nature a political body. But church politics is being made also in Lambeth and Uppsala, in Geneva and New York, even if not with the efficiency of Rome and certainly with less success.

The only explanation is the fact that the great Ecumenical Movement of our age has meanwhile taken hold also of the largest of the Christian churches. *Mortalium animos* has stopped or prevented the active participation of Roman Catholics in ecumenical organisations, but it could not stop the Ecumenical Movement in the souls, the growth of a deep concern for the Christians outside the Roman fold, the longing for true unity between those who confess the same Lord. This spiritual movement went on during the remaining years of the pontificate of Pius XI, who died shortly before the outbreak of the Second World War, and continued during the eventful years of Pius XII. It found its expression in the theological literature, especially in Germany and France, in personal contacts that were beyond the legislation of the Church.

Pius XI could forbid formal organizations in which Catholic priests and evangelical pastors met. But he could not prevent Catholics and Protestants from meeting in the concentration camps. The *Codex Iuris Canonici*, which in canon 1258 forbids any participation in the worship of non-Catholics has a strange way of becoming unimportant and losing its authority in the night before one's execution. The common experiences of the churches in the totalitarian states of Europe and in the horrors of the

Second World War have created the atmosphere in which men who were separated through the boundaries of their churches became brethren again. What the Eastern churches had experienced after

1917 was to become the experience of the Western churches too, the solidarity of a common destiny. If still in the twenties, Roman Catholic writers—and perhaps the Curia itself—could think that the fall of the Russian Church or the disintegration of Protestant churches would lead the members of these churches to Rome, such thoughts were not corroborated by the history of the following decades. On the contrary, we had to learn that the sin and guilt of one church is visited upon all churches, that the shame and glory of one are the shame and glory of all.

The decay of the Church of Sweden or the Church of England does not mean that the people in these countries will turn Catholic. Some will, but the masses will fall into indifference and perhaps atheism. The decay of the Roman Church in Latin American countries does not mean that the people there will turn Protestant. Some will, but the masses will perhaps sink into a new paganism. In these experiences lies the deepest secret of true ecumenicity, which defies definition and explanation as the Church of Christ itself defies definition and explanation.

IV.

These discoveries are closely connected with the development of Christian theology during the last few decades. It is certainly not accidental that the Ecumenical Movement is closely connected with the Liturgical Movement, which since the First World War has changed the spiritual life of the Roman Catholic Christians in many countries and has, at the same time, deeply influenced the Protestant churches. This movement meant for Catholics and Protestants the overcoming of the religious individualism and subjectivism of the eighteenth and nineteenth centuries and the rediscovery of the objective facts on which the Christian life rests: the Word of God, the Sacraments, the Church. It is closely connected with the overcoming of a mere subjective theology in the rediscovery of the theology of the Bible, the fathers, and the reformers. Hence theology became in all churches again what it had been in the sixteenth and seventeenth centuries: a dialogue between the churches of Christendom.

The "new theology" in the Roman Church is hardly thinkable without the influence of Karl Barth as, on the other hand, Lutheran,

Reformed and Anglican theology of today shows everywhere the influence of Catholic thought. The most important and most promising encounter is taking place in the field of biblical theology, especially since the Encyclical *Divino afflante Spiritu* Pius XII issued in 1943 opened for Catholic scholars the wide field of a truly historical investigation of the Bible. Protestantism, on the other hand, is slowly beginning to learn again from Roman Catholic Theology—what an irony of history—that the Bible is in its entirety the Word of God; the Book of the Church, however, is not made by the Church, but written under the inspiration of the Holy Ghost and, as such, given to the Church. It is certainly not accidental that the leader of the Bible Movement, the learned biblical scholar Cardinal Bea—who for many years was the head of the Pontifical Biblical Institute and who wrote for Pius XII the encyclical of 1943—is at the same time the leader of the Ecumenical Movement in the Roman Catholic Church and the head of the Secretariat for promoting Christian Unity.

V.

Seldom in the history of the Roman Church has a movement met with so much enthusiasm and with such initial success. This is, of course, due to the fact that Pope John XXIII identified himself with it and that the majority of the council has greeted it enthusiastically. Neither the acceptance by the pope nor the approval of the council would have been possible if this movement did not really represent the mind of the Church, which has entered a new epoch of its history. The election of Paul VI confirms this. Whatever the final outcome of the council may be, whatever the majority of the bishops may attain against a considerable conservative minority, Rome has entered its ecumenical era, and the reunion of all Christians will henceforth be one of its great aims, perhaps the supreme aim to which all other aims in fields of doctrine, liturgy, missions, pastoral care, and canon law will be subordinated. This is a turning point of Church history, perhaps the greatest since the Reformation.

There is little likelihood that Rome will achieve its aim in this century, and probably the "reunion" of all Christians is a utopia that never will be reached on earth. But even so, it is an event of first magnitude that Rome takes up the task of reunion. It will pursue this task with all its resources, spiritual and material. A new vision will be before all Catholic Christians, and a new purpose will inspire all activities of the Church. It is an event also in the history of the Ecumenical Movement. It is a challenge to the World Council of Churches. Henceforth our ecumenical conferences and councils will no longer be able to indulge in the easy-going theological dilletantism that is satisfied with producing papers, writing formulas of compromise, and drafting schemes for the younger churches, which are supposed to solve the problems the older churches have not been able to solve. Already now it is obvious that the presence of Roman Catholic observers in each of our meetings compels us to ask ourselves some searching questions.

What is the actual result of the conferences of half a century? They have certainly meant a lot to Christendom. But what have we reached in the way of "reuniting" churches? Is the Church of South India really such an achievement as we are inclined to believe, even if not all Anglican churches can recognize its orders? What has Faith and Order attained in so many decades of earnest, scholarly discussion? It remains to be seen what Rome will achieve. In any case they will select the best scholars in every field under discussion to prepare the solutions. And they will work with great patience and not expect that a conference of two weeks' duration will solve problems to which in the course of centuries no solution has been found. Patience is one of the things that distinguish a church from a sect. A sect must have everything at once. It cannot wait, because it has no future. The Church can wait, for it has a future.

VI.

What are the means by which the Roman Church hopes to achieve the aim of a reunion of all Christians? The first is the renewal of the Roman Church itself, the *aggiornamento*, the bringing up to date as John XXIII called it. It is a complete reform of the church in its spiritual life, its liturgy, its constitution and church law, and in the presentation of its doctrine. Sweeping changes in the liturgy are envisaged, such as a wider use of the vernacular in the Mass and in the administration of the Sacraments. To achieve this a change in the constitution is necessary—a decentralization of the church that gives more powers to the episcopate in various parts of the world and to the episcopate as a whole. A complete reorganization of the Curia, which includes an internationalization of this still predominantly Italian body, has been announced by Paul VI.

The *aggiornamento* concerns also the intellectual life of the Church. One may think of the pathetic figure of Teilhard de Chardin, that great scientist and humble Christian and priest, of the courage with which he undertook the great task of reconciling the theory of evolution with the Catholic faith, the Christian resignation with which he bore the frustration of his life's work, the patience of the Church, which abstained from any condemnation, and the love his Jesuit brothers showed him; also one thinks of the success of his magnum opus when it appeared posthumously—what a tremendous longing for a reconciliation of science and faith becomes manifest in this case. The Church wants to avoid the repetition of the mistakes made in the past by the rejection of the truth discovered by scientific research. She wants to get rid of that narrow-minded apologetics that defends in constant retreat one untenable position after another. She wants to regain that leadership in the life of the spirit it had possessed in past centuries. This is a tremendous task that perhaps would require a mastermind of no lesser stature than Thomas Aquinas.

One may doubt whether the present Catholic theology is able to solve even the problem that must be solved if that *aggiornamento* is to succeed, namely, to express the truth of the Christian faith without the Thomistic-Aristotelian philosophy to which it is bound not only by tradition, but also by the canon law (can. 1366). Do the theologians who today demand this separation of the truth of the Gospel from its expression in the traditional doctrinal form realize the greatness of this task, which is not less than a Reformation of the Church, and which involves the danger to which so many modern Protestant churches have succumbed, namely, to lose with the alleged old form its eternal content?

VII.

The second means by which modern Catholicism hopes to reach its aim is a new attitude towards Christians of other denominations as "separated brethren" or "brethren," and even "brethren in Christ." It is not our intention here to examine the theological relevance of these terms that have become official terms since the bull *Humanae salutis* by which John XXIII convoked the council. Cardinal Bea has given the theological basis of this terminology in several publications (collected in "The Unity of Christians," ed. by B. Leeming, London, 1963) that try to determine the border of the Church beyond what Pius XII had said in *Mystici Corporis*, where the Roman Church was still equated with the mystical Body of Christ.

In the address with which John XXIII opened the council on October 11, 1962, he spoke of the duty of the Church to defend the truth entrusted to her against errors: "The Church has always opposed these errors. Frequentlyshe has condemned them with the greatest severity. Nowadays, however, the spouse of Christ prefers to make use of the medicine of mercy rather than that of severity. She considers that she meets the needs of the present day by demonstrating the validity of her teachings rather than by condemnations" (Catholic Documentations, Dec. 1962, p. 9). It is quite astonishing how suddenly in the entire Roman Church the polemics against non-Catholics has been stopped and replaced by an irenical ecumenism that even perturbed good Catholics, especially in countries where the Christian churches were at loggerheads, as in England. When Archbishop Heenan of Liverpool— who meanwhle has been transferred to the See of Westminster—in a public address had voiced the opinion "that being a Christian was more important than being Catholic or Protestant," he met with severe criticism on the part of clergy and laity, as he himself reported at the Heythrop Conference on Christian Unity of 1962 (see the Report *Christian Unity*, ed. by J. C. Heenan, London, 1962, Sheed and Ward.)

It is a fact that the number of conversions to Rome has considerably decreased in England and that the English Catholics look with suspicion or anxiety at the new policy. But Archbishop Heenan, while admitting that the situation in England was quite different from that on the continent, made it quite clear that the new course, which was already inaugurated by the Instruction on the Ecumenical Movement given by the Holy Office in 1949, must and will be followed also in England, even at the cost of a temporary setback for the Catholic cause. Since Newman's "Second Spring" has not been followed by a summer and an autumn, and since individual conversions cannot bring about reunion, no other way is possible.

The Report on the Heythrop Conference, which met in the presence of Cardinal Bea, is one of the most illuminating documents of the Ecumenical Movement in the Roman Church. This movement started on the continent, in German and Austrian, Dutch and French Catholicism. There it was indigenous and consequently understood by the people. It had to be transplanted to the English-speaking countries like Britain, America, and Australia, and to the Spanish- and Portuguese-speaking churches. This is being done by way of an ecumenical education of the clergy and the laity in conferences, publications, and especially through the council, where the bishops of the entire world meet and the relation between the "more conservative" and "more progressive" gives a pretty fair picture of the progress the movement has made in the various parts of the Church. It is quite obvious that the ecumenical education under the leadership of the Secretariat for Promoting Christian Unity is really changing the climate of interchurch relations.

One point deserves special attention. In his contribution at Heythrop, Father B. Leeming, S.J., says, "I would like to endorse the desire of many Catholics, if not of absolutely all, for more opportunities of praying with our separated brethren. . . . I do not think that common prayers will solve the problems of disunity; but I think a more open attitude would greatly help to dissolve some of the non-doctrinal factors in our divisions" (*Loc. cit.* p. 160f.). Up to 1949, prayer with non-Catholics was regarded as *communicatio in sacris*, which was forbidden by canon law. The encyclical on the Ecumenical Movement allowed the common praying of the Lord's Prayer or a prayer approved by the Church. M. Bevenot, S.J., who at Heythrop spoke on *Communicatio in Sacris*, quotesthe late canonist Canon Mahoney who, after the instruction of 1949, wrote, "It must follow that those among us have held that a united prayer with heretics . . . *is always of its nature wrong*, have been defending a too rigorous interpretation of the law in Canon 1258, an outlook due to our conditions in this country (i.e., England), to the traditions received from our forefathers, and to the necessity, as we conceived it, of discouraging the faithful from any religious contact whatever with non-Catholics" (*Loc. cit.* p. 114). The question is very old, whether the prohibition of the *communication in sacris cum haereticis* is in itself sinful and against God's command or whether it is forbidden by the Church to avoid certain dangers. As a matter of fact, common prayer with heretics and schismatics was forbidden in the Ancient Church since the Apostolic Constitutions (can. 10–11). It may be assumed that Rome, in dealing with the problem in the Ecumenical Movement, will come to conclusions similar to those of the Eastern Orthodox churches.

VIII.

The third means is the ecumenical dialogue.

> "Dialogue with separated brethren is necessary and must be encountered with them on the theological level. It ought to be well-prepared and undertaken by only competent theologians, always with the explicit or tacit approval of the Hierarchy. We ought not even to seem to impose our doctrine upon separated brethren. A real dialogue is sought, not a monologue; but, at the same time, the Catholic should be able to show that our doctrine is really founded in Scripture and ancient tradition."

In these well-balanced words, Cardinal Bea has given at Heythrop the Roman program of the ecumenical dialogue (loc. cit. p. 187). The emphasis on the necessity of having the dialogue undertaken by competent theologians must be welcomed, for one of the weaknesses of our ecumenical discussions is the lack of competent theologians. Here lies one of the reasons for the failure of Faith and Order. Each of the large conferences suffered from the fact that many of the delegates sent by the churches were not competent at all. A very serious setback for the Protestant churches is that many of their theologians are no longer able to read a simple Latin text. How is a discussion even on the problems of the Reformation possible without this ability? The decline of knowledge of the ancient languages is not limited to Protestants. The serious problem it presents caused John XXIII to issue his Apostolic Letter *Veterum Sapiens*, with its touching appeal to save with the classical languages the very foundations of our civilization. But it is not only knowledge that makes a person competent for real dialogue: knowledge of language, of history, of the Scriptures, of theology. He must be also aware of the prerequisites of any true dialogue. A dialogue must start from certain presuppositions that are *extra controversiam*.

One of the reasons why the discussion of the great problems of the Sacraments in Faith and Order has remained fruitless is the fact that since Lausanne any discussion between the churches ended with a statement by the Quakers, later also by the Salvation Army, in which they praised and accepted the statements reached, with the proviso that outward sacraments are not necessary. One could say this is just the reason why we include the Quakers in the dialogue. They will eventually see that they are wrong. But suppose the individual Quaker delegate accepted our view; this would mean that he ceased to be a Quaker and would have to be replaced by another Quaker. So the dialogue with the Quakers would go on until the last Quaker had changed his view, which is obviously impossible.

Another case in point is the Basis of the World Council of Churches. It is evident there must be some basis expressed that is accepted by all and can, therefore, be the starting point of the theological dialogue, as well as of the common work. The old basis ("the W.C.C. is a fellowship of churches that accepts Jesus Christ as God and Savior ...") was regarded as unclear and not sufficient. Lutherans demanded a reference to the Scriptures as its basis. Eastern Orthodox demanded a clear statement of the trinitarian faith. Liberals in Europe and America rejected any binding dogmatic statement. So New Delhi found the diplomatic solution: "The World Council of Churches is a fellowship of churches that confess the Lord Jesus Christ as God and Savior according to the Scriptures, and therefore seek to fulfil together their common calling to the glory of one God, Father, Son, and Holy Spirit."

This masterpiece of church politics mentions the Scriptures without saying anything about their nature and authority. It mentions the Trinity, but in a doxological formula that even the most liberal American bishop can accept. It uses the term "confess the Lord Jesus Christ as God and Savior" but allows at the same time all deniers of the divinity of Christ and of the Trinity to declare that they do not regard the Basis as having any dogmatic significance (see the debate on the Basis in "The New Delhi Report" pp. 151–59).

Will our Catholic brethren understand why orthodox Lutheran and Reformed churches are not able to join a council based on such ambiguous formulas and that grants equal rights to faith and unfaith? Or have we reached that degree of ecumenicity that the weekly of the American Jesuits, *America*, revealed when it criticized some

Lutherans who did not participate in a that which would have brought them into the World Council of Churches: "While having the delicacy to withhold judgment on the complex issue involved in this dispute (is doctrinal purity threatened by the merger?), no Catholic should consider that an issue of this kind, involving his brothers in Christ, is none of his concern. Much less should he take pleasure in the thought that Protestant Christianity is in the last stages of dividing itself to death." The editorial then tells these conscientious Lutherans that "the tide towards Protestant fragmentation was reversed half a century ago, and Protestantism has been steadily gathering strong momentum in the other direction." It tells them that their attitude "springs from thinly veiled tribalism, which has nothing at all to do with Christianity. . . . Christ our Lord solemnly prayed . . . that all his followers might be one, and no one who calls himself a Christian can be happy to see his Master's deepest desire frustrated anywhere" (quoted from *The Lutheran Standard*, Minneapolis, August 13, 1963).

We mention this case of a well-meant but pointless fraternal admonition because it shows what more than anything else jeopardizes the true dialogue between the churches: the lack of knowledge of the faith of separated brethren, the untheological thinking in terms of modern church politicians who regard any merger under whatever conditions as a step towards the fulfilment of the High-Priestly Prayer of Christ. Church politics is the death of any true Ecumenical Movement.

9.

This leads us to the fourth of the means by which Roman Catholicism hopes to bring about the reunion of all Christians. This is the confession of faith. He who has taken part in ecumenical conferences remembers those moments when, after endless discussions and fruitless endeavors to find a comprehensive formula to cover views that seemed to be, and actually were, irreconcilable, a man arose who on behalf of his Church declared what was the faith on which they were not prepared to compromise. . . . Shocking as this was to the majority, it was actually the greatest relief. One was reminded of Luther's word *Non in doctrina, sed in disputatione veritas amittitur,* "The truth is lost not in teaching, but in disputations."

Occasionally, at least in the beginning of the movement, such a dogmatic statement could be heard from Lutherans or from Anglicans with firm convictions. But soon it was left to the Eastern Orthbdox to be the confessors. Whatever concessions the Eastern Orthodox churches have made in their membership in the World Council of Churches, they have never compromised on doctrine. They have never given up their belief that the Eastern Orthodox Church is the true Church of Christ. A firm confession remains never without fruit. The voice of the Orthodox Church, which after New Delhi has become even stronger, especially in Faith and Order, has always been a challenge to the Anglican and Protestant churches. Even we who cannot share so many beliefs of the Eastern churches and find in them errors and heresies must admit that they in the hard shell of their dogmatism have preserved doctrines essential for the Christian faith, such as the great truths of the Nicene Creed. Why we have not been able to preserve them must be a serious question for us Protestants.

There was a time when the conflict with the totalitarian state created a new understanding of the confession of the Church. Even confessors and martyrs arose in the Protestant churches in various parts of Europe. But why has this revival of a personal confession not renewed the churches as a whole? Why belongs the "confessing Church" today in past history? And why has a new undogmatic Christianity again prevailed in the Protestant churches of the world? Why are the confessions the Ecumenical Movement has produced in South India and similar younger churches so noncommittal and, therefore, lifeless? They reflect the doubts of the theologians of older churches rather than the fresh faith of new converts.

If we have not realised yet this situation of the Protestant churches in our encounter with the churches of the East, then it will become clear to us when Rome asks the churches that claim the confessions of the Reformation, "What is your faith? What do you believe?" We must be quite clear about the fact that the new ecumenical era of the Roman Church will mean to Rome, as we have seen, a new appraisal, perhaps even a new formulation of her dogma, but never an abandonment of what she believes to be the deposit of faith entrusted to her once for all. What Rome can do is abstain from defining new dogmas. Rome may and certainly will interpret and clarify existing dogmas, as is being tried concerning the relationship between Scripture and tradition. This can and will be done also concerning the existing Mariological dogmas. They will be interpreted in a Christological sense. The dogma of the First Vatican Council on the papacy will be supplemented by a dogma on the episcopal office and its functions in the Church Universal. Even the infallibility of the pope will be interpreted in a way that gives to the episcopate its share in the infallible teaching office. Though Rome can never rescind a dogma once proclaimed, such additions and interpretations will, this is the hope of the Roman Church, make the reunion possible of which Pope Paul VI in his first address on June 22nd, 1963, spoke in the touching words: "We open our arms to all those people who glory in the name of Christ. We call them by the sweet name of brothers. May they know that they will find in us constant understanding and goodwill, that they will find in the Church of Rome the paternal house that exalts and values with new splendour the treasures of their history, of their cultural patrimony, of their spiritual heritage" (*Documentations*, September 1963, p. 6).

10.

An analysis of this program shows that it contains all thoughts characteristic of the modern Ecumenical Movement, the idea of the brotherhood of all those who believe in Christ, the idea of a visible Church of Christ in which all Christians should find their home when they return to the lost unity. This unity is not uniformity. In the "future reunited church," there will be room for the treasures of the history of the separated brethren, their cultural and spiritual heritage. The Church of the future will be richer than the Church before separation was. If the separation was sin and guilt, then it may be said of this guilt: *O felix culpa . . . o vere necessarium peccatum.* O happy guilt, O truly necessary sin! This ideal will appeal to many who see the fulfilment of Christ's *Ut omnes unum sint* in a great visible Catholic Church on earth.

Where lies the difference between this ecumenical ideal and that of the Ecumenical Movement as it presents itself in the World Council of Churches? One could say this: The Roman Church knows separated brothers. She does not know separated sisters. The pope can recognise us as Christian brothers in virtue of our Baptism, but he can never recognise our churches as branches of the Church, with the exception of the Eastern Orthodox. This is true, but the same is also the attitude of the Eastern churches in the Ecumenical Movement. And are we, whatever our confession may be, sure that all Christian groups that claim the name "Church" are really Church of Christ? Do we not all differentiate between Church and heresy? Does not even the World Council of Churches make this difference by excluding the Unitarians?

We do not know what Rome's entry into the Ecumenical Movement of our age and what the ecumenical program of the Roman Catholic Church may mean to future generations. No one can predict decisions to be made by the Christians of the next century. But we know what this turning point of the history of the Church means to us. The Roman ecumenical program grows out of a deep doctrinal conviction; it is the expression of deep faith. The question for us is not whether this program is great, attractive, and practicable. The question is solely this: Is the doctrine on which it is based true? If the dogma of the Church, the ministry, and the papacy is true, then we must accept it with all its consequences. If we cannot accept it as true, then we owe to our Catholic brethren an answer, given in deep concern for the Church of Christ and the souls of men—the answer of a deep faith in him who has called himself the Truth and whose prayer, "That they all may be one," is preceded and inseparably connected with the prayer "Sanctify them through thy truth; thy word is truth." The Word of God, which judges us all, is also the judge of the Ecumenical Movement in the Roman Catholic Church.

THE REFORMED THEOLOGICAL REVIEW
Vol. XXIII, No. 2, June 1964

Concerning the Nature of Inspiration

When the present writer began his theological studies in the years preceding the First World War in Germany, the inspiration of Holy Scripture did not play any role in theological discussions. It was regarded as a doctrine of the past that had definitely been abandoned by the Protestant churches, even by those of conservative character. The Modernist controversy raging through the Catholic churches of Europe seemed to demonstrate the untenableness of this outmoded doctrine. When first news of the rise of the Fundamentalist movement in America reached the continent, no one took the revival of the classical doctrine of inspiration seriously. But great theological problems are never dead issues. They have a strange way of coming back and demanding a new answer. Nothing perhaps shows more clearly the greatness of the theological and ecclesiastical changes during the last fifty years than the fact that today all churches, Protestant and Catholic, are facing the problem of the inspiration of Holy Scripture again and that theologians of all denominations are working together to find a new solution to the old problem in which the legitimate claims of truly historical and truly dogmatic research are met.

We add to former contributions in this Review[1] a brief discussion of the doctrine of the nature of inspiration as we find it in modern Roman Catholic theology.

I.

The Roman dogma of the inspiration of Scripture, as it has been defined in the Constitution on the Catholic Faith of the First Vatican Council, asserts that the Scriptures, "having been written under the inspiration of the Holy Spirit, have God for their author" (Denz. 1787). The corresponding canon anathematizes those who deny that the entire books of the canon as defined at Trent are divinely (divinitus) inspired in all their parts (Denz. 1809). Nothing is said about the nature of inspiration. It was Leo XIII who in *Providentissimus Deus* of 1893 explained the dogma of 1870. "All the books which the Church receives as sacred and canonical are written wholly and entirely at the dictation of the Holy Spirit" (Denz. 1951). This "*Spiritu Sancto dictante*," however, must not necessarily be understood in the sense of a mechanical dictation that would make the holy writers mere secretaries (*amamuenses*) or even pens (*calami*) of the Holy Ghost. The same word is used by Trent (Denz. 783) just for the "unwritten traditions" the apostles have received "either from Christ's own mouth or at the dictation of the Holy Ghost (*a Spiritu Sancto dictatas*)." The word *dictare* has a wider meaning and is often used for *inspirare*. However, a few lines later on, the encyclical says of the Holy Spirit using men as his instruments, "By supernatural power he so moved and impelled them to write. He so assisted

---

[1]"Sacra Scriptura: Observations on Augustine's Doctrine of Inspiration" (Oct 1955); "Hexaemeron Theology and Science with the Church Fathers" (Oct. 1958); "The Rise of the Dogma of Holy Scripture In the Middle Ages" (June 1969); "Inspiration and Inerrancy" (July 1960); "The Source of Revelation" (Feb 1963); "Rome and the Inspiration of Scripture" (June 1963). We quote Denzinger according to edition 31 (Rahner). The new enlarged edition gives also the old numbers of the paragraphs. Quotations not found in Denzinger we give from the *Enchiridion biblique*, 4th ed, Naples-Rome 1961. English translations of the documents are now easily accessible in "Rome and the Study of Scriptures," St. Meinrad, Indiana.

them when they were writing, that the things which he commanded and those only, they first rightly understood, then willed faithfully to write down, and finally expressed in apt words and with infallible truth. Otherwise it could not be said that he was the author of the entire Scripture." In these words Leo affirms that the Vatican dogma of God as author of the Holy Scripture implies the classical theory of inspiration we find with Jerome, Augustine, and Gregory the Great.[2] Leo quotes expressly Augustine ("Since they wrote the things which he showed and uttered to them, it cannot be pretended that he was not the writer, for the members executed what their head dictated" [*De consensu evang.* I, 33, M.P.L. 34,1076]) and Gregory the Great ("Most superfluous it is to inquire who wrote these things—we loyally believe the Holy Spirit to be the author [*auctor*] of the Book [scil. Job]; he wrote it who dictated it for writing, he wrote it who inspired its execution"; *Praef. im Job* M.P.L. 75,517).

II.

For every Catholic theologian the question arises what authority this affirmation of the patristic theory possesses. That God is the author of Holy Scripture because it has been written under the inspiration of the Holy Ghost is a dogma, defined by the highest teaching office of the Church as a divinely revealed truth. It must be accepted by every Catholic *fide divina*, that is, by the faith that is a supernatural gift of grace. This faith man owes to God who reveals that truth. But is the exposition of the dogma of 1870 in the encyclical of 1893 de Jidey? In other words, does the theory of the nature of inspiration the pope found with Augustine and Gregory the Great belong to the content of divine revelation? This is obviously not the case. A dogmatic definition meant to supplement the dogma of 1870 would require a different and

---

[2]For lexicographical details see Syneve-Benott, *Prophecy and Inspiration, a Commentary on the Summa Theologica* II-II, Questions 171–78 (1961), p. 88. In connection with this important commentary, another great work on Aquinas's doctrine of the grace of prophecy (which includes always the inspiration of Scripture) deserves to be mentioned, the commentary on the same question by Urs von Balthasar in *Deutsche Thomas-Ausgabe* Vol. 23. It gives a wealth of information on the history of the doctrine.

much more solemn form of proclamation than a simple encyclical—a letter addressed to the bishops of the whole world—can be. Only a solemnly proclaimed dogma is "irreformable." It is not unthinkable that this affirmation of a patristic theory will at a later date be modified or even rescinded.

But until this happens, every member of the Church, and this includes all theologians, must accept the statement, certainly not "by divine faith," but by Catholic faith, "a pious inner assent" (*assensu interno religioso tenenda*) as M. Nicolau (Sacrae Theolo-auK Summa, Madrid 1958, Vol. I, p. 1039) puts it. It is a Catholic doctrine imposed by the pope and therefore to be accepted as a certain theological proposition in that obedience the Catholic owes to the pope. Thus indeed all Roman Catholic theologians accept the Patristic theory, which was renewed by Leo XIII more or less joyfully. Sometimes it is stated with an audible sigh of relief that "an encyclical is not infallible" (comp. M. Schmaus, Kath. Dogmatik I, 1940, p. 38). Karl Rahner may be quoted as the most representative dogmatician of present-day Roman Catholicism that tries to combine absolute loyalty to the dogmatic heritage with the serious endeavor to free the Church from the fetters of a false traditionalism. He says,[3] "We assume the acceptance of the traditional concept of inspiration, which is partly defined, partly laid down by the official teaching of the Church, and is partly the concept formed by the common opinion of scholastic theology. It is not our purpose to criticize this concept of inspiration, nor to propose to change it. If we had any intentions in this regard, it would be only to show by raising some questions that this concept of inspiration, implicitly acceptable as it seems to us, has a certain formal abstractness. Easily overlooked as it is, this abstract concept is sometimes regarded as an adequate, material, and factual description of the process of inspiration, though on closer examination we might prefer it to be more meaningful in the way we hope to propose." It would be unfair to judge the great dogmatician who has done so much to clarify the doctrines of the person of Christ, of grace, and the Church

---

[3]"Inspiration in the Bible" (*Quaestiones Disputae*, Nr. 1), 1961, p. 9. The title of the German original is *Ueber die Schriftinspiration*. See the review by K. Runia in this Review. Vol. XXII, No. 1, Feb. 1963, p. 25ff.

from this sentence that betrays the embarrassment in which every Catholic theologian finds himself when he tries to investigate the nature of inspiration and finds himself bound to the Patristic theory sanctioned by *Providentissimus Deus*. He wants to propose a better understanding of the dogma of 1870. But he cannot do that by questioning the correctness of Augustine's and Gregory's theory.

To understand the authority of Leo's decision, one must remember the seriousness with which the pope spoke at the eve of the Modernist controversy. "We shall not be silent," he said to those who expressed their concern for the Church as guardian of the divine revelation. What he said about the nature of revelation was the doctrine of the fathers—especially that of the great doctors of the Western Church, of Jerome, Augustine, and Gregory, who were not only the great authorities for the Middle Ages, but in many respects even for the churches of the Reformation—and for the old Protestant orthodoxy was just the doctrine of Holy Scripture. If even in the old Protestant churches the traditional doctrine of Augustine and the formulas of Gregory were regarded as in full harmony with the Bible and were used to safeguard the authority of the Word of God against the modern world, which rejected it, who will blame the modern popes for their loyal adherence to that great theological tradition? Leo's encyclical was, moreover, solemnly reaffirmed by Benedict XV and even by Pius XII, who published "*Divino afflante Spiritu*" in 1943 to commemorate the fiftieth anniversary of "*Providentissimus Deus*." It was his wish, so he declares in the introduction, to do this "by ratifying and inculcating all that was wisely laid down by our Predecessor and ordained by his successors for the consolidating and perfecting of the work, and also by adding such instructions as the present time seems to demand."[4] The new encyclical, however, while thoroughly discussing the problem of inerrancy and opening new avenues for a future reconciliation between "the teaching of the Church's tradition regarding the inerrancy of Sacred Scripture" with "the inevitable conclusions of profane sciences,"[5] did not repeat what had been said by Leo about the nature of inspiration. The only passage that touches the problem speaks of the "inspired

---

[4]*Ench. Bibl.* 538.

[5]*Ench. Bibl.* 564.

writer" who "impelled by divine motion (*divina actione aetus*) so uses his faculties and powers that from the book composed by him all may easily infer 'the special character of each one and, as it were, his personal traits."[6] This concession of the human side of the inspired writings is taken almost literally from "*Spiritus Paraclitus*" (1920).[7] But the strong words used by Benedict XV in this context concerning the concept of inspiration ("suggestion and even dictation") are left out, and the description of the process of inspiration Benedict gives in the same paragraph on the basis of Jerome ("God illuminates the mind, moves the will, assists in writing") are no longer found in the encyclical of 1943. But they are not modified, and so remains the Patristic theory official doctrine of the Roman Church even today.

III.

To understand the classical theory of inspiration, one must be clear about its source. Roman theology knows that it is not a biblical doctrine but a venerable theory established to explain the doctrine of the Bible. The Bible teaches that Holy Scripture is the Word of God written under the inspiration of the Holy Ghost. This is the doctrine of Jesus and his apostles that the Church confesses in the Nicene Creed. Holy Scripture contains no doctrine regarding the nature of inspiration beyond what is stated in 2 Timothy 3:16 and 2 Peter 1:19ff. The first passage says that Scripture is "*theopneustos,*" which the Vulgate correctly renders with "*divinitus inspirata,*" inspired by God. In 2 Peter 1:19ff, the apostle admonishes his readers in view of false teachers and false prophets who come with their myths, their arbitrary interpretations of the Scriptures, and their destructive heresies to adhere to the testimony of the apostolic eyewitnesses and to pay attention to the written prophetic Word. This cannot be understood arbitrarily, by man-made interpretations. It can be understood only by him who submits to its divine authority. "No prophecy came ever by the impulse of man, but men moved by the Holy Ghost spoke of God." Because God *moved* the prophets, the prophetic Word is divine. It is noteworthy that this is

---

[6]*Ench. Bibl.* 556.

[7]*Ench. Bibl.* 448.

true not only of the Word when it was spoken, but also of the written Word. The modern idea that the true Word of God is the revelation in "mighty acts" of God or in the original proclamation of the prophets, and that the written Word is "only" a record of God's revelation of himself is absolutely foreign to the Bible. It is a product of modern theology and appears wherever the biblical doctrine of the Word is endangered or has even been abandoned. The juxtaposition of the spoken and the written Word as equally divine is to be found also in the Nicene Creed where "according to the Scripture" and "who spake by the prophets" supplement each other. No one can understand the biblical and ecclesiastical doctrine of inspiration who does not know that the spoken and the written Word of God are essentially identical. The loss of this truth in modern Protestantism under the influence of the enthusiastic and idealistic contraposition of "spirit" and "letter" has destroyed the understanding of the Bible's doctrine of inspiration.[8]

---

[8]The first ecclesiastical document that contains the idea of the Scriptures as "record" seems to be the "Statement of Doctrine" by the American Congregationalists of 1883: "V. We believe that the Scriptures of the Old and New Testaments are the records of God's revelation of himself in the work of redemption . . ." (E.F.K. Muller, *Die Beknenntnisschriften der Reformierten Kirche*, 1903, p. 928). In this case the Scriptures as records may be highly valued, but the true Word is to be found in that of which they are a record, the Word spoken in the past to and by the prophets or, as we hear today, "The mighty acts of God" in history. But mighty acts of God are such events only for the believer who accepts their interpreation through the prophetic and apostolic Word. Whether this Word is spoken or written makes no difference, at least not for the Bible (see the treatment of the Old Testament in the New Testament) and in the Church. The differentiation between the "*viva vox*" and the "dead letter" goes back via the young Schleiemacher ("Every Holy Scripture is a mausoleum of religion," *Discourses on Religion*) to the "enthusiasts" of the seventeenth and sixteenth centuries. The misuse of 2 Cor. 3:6, where "gramma" means the Law, as in Rom. 2:27, 29, should cease. For the New Testament writers, the Scriptures of the Old Testament, "*ta hiera grammata*," are filled with the Spirit. It is one of the deepest insights of Luther that the Holy Spirit always uses outward means to communicate himself to man: the Sacraments and "Scripture or the oral Word." Whether the Word of God comes as spoken or written words makes no difference to the Church up to the reformers. This is also the reason why the fathers and schoolmen deal always with the inspiration of Scripture in their doctrine of the charisma of prophecy. Connected with these problems is the question of

IV.

If the Bible does not reveal to us anything about the nature of inspiration beyond the fact that God the Holy Spirit moved holy men to
write and that what they spoke and wrote is God's Word, what, then,
is the source of the classical theory of inspiration? This theory is a
venerable tradition of the Church that goes back to the great fathers
of the fourth century, especially the four great doctors of the Western Church and Chrysostom. In a previous article,[9] we have tried
to show how even these greatest of the fathers have not been able to
overcome entirely the concept of inspiration that was common
to the religius world of the Hellenistic-Roman civilization. The
Greek-speaking Jews in Alexandria had taken it over from paganism
and had passed it on to the Christian apologists of the second century.
This "mantic" theory that made man a mere mechanical instrument,
moved by the divine spirit, like a flute or a lyre, had to be modified or
abandoned when the Montanist movement shook the Church to its
very foundations. We should like to know the arguments of the lost
writing of Miltiades when he wrote against the alleged saying of the
Paraclete, "Behold, man is like a Iyre, and I come rushing down like
a plectrum," in which he developed the thesis that no true prophet
speaks in a state of ecstasy. We know how Origen met the claims of all
mantic prophets. Against Celsus's praise of Pythia's and other pagan
oracles, he described[10] the inspiration of the biblical prophets as an
illumination of the mind by the Spirit of God. In contrast to Philo's
mantic theory, the prophet is regarded as fully conscious of his office.

---

whether we should not be much more careful in our use of the word "revelation." The idea that God reveals *himself* belongs to the theology of Calvin and
stems probably from his humanistic heritage. It occurs in the Reformed confessions influenced by him (*Gallicana II* "Dieu se manifest"; Westminster II: "to
reveal himself"). However, this should not prevent us from re-examining the
concept of revelation in view of the fact that the New Testament never says that
God reveals *himself* ("*theos*" in 1 Tim. 3:116 is a false reading of the *Textus recep-
tus* for "*hos*). The Son reveals the Father to whomever he wills (Matt. 11:27), to
those whom the Father has given him (John 17:6). A new investigation of the
problem is necessary. Oepke's article in THWB (Kittel) needs revision.

[9]This Review, 1955, pp. 65ff.

[10]E.g., *Contra Celsum* I 48: VII, 3.7.

Willingly he lends himself to the service of God. In the state of illumination, he sees and hears what he has to proclaim and to write. He delivers his message after careful deliberation. The prophet and the holy writer are to Origen, as it were, a kind of higher gnostics— the word understood in the way of orthodox, churchly gnosticism of the school of Alexandria. It is easy to see why this view of inspiration could not satisfy the Church. It finds the inspiration in the inspired writers rather than in inspired books. It does not do justice to the "*pasa graphe theopneustos.*" And it does exclude a verbal inspiration, which is obviously implied in the decision of Leo XIII.[11] The fathers of the fourth century found Origen's theory unsatisfactory. They ascribed, it is true, to the holy writers an activity of their own. They realised that inspiration does not extinguish the personality of the writer. Man was not a dead but a living instrument. But if these writers may be called authors, this can be done only in a very limited way. Everything that makes an author in the literary sense is ascribed to the Holy Spirit. He moved or impelled the writers to write the book he wanted to be written. He gave them the "illumination" of the mind that an author must possess. He assisted them by providing them not only with the content, but even with the words to be used and preventing them from erroneous statements. In other words, the real author (*auctor principalis*) of the Scriptures, even

---

[11]The question whether inspiration must be understood as verbal inspiration or whether God has left the formulation of what he wanted to be written to each particular author is regarded as an open question by Roman Catholic theologians, because no definite answer has been given by the teaching authority of the Church. Both views are to be found. While Scheeben (*Dogmatik* I, p. 116), Schmaus (*Kath. Dogmatik*, Vol. I, 1940), and Nicolau (*Summa I*, p. 1071) speak for the *inspiratio verbalis*, Lercher-Schlagenhaufen (*Institutiones I*, p. 354) reject it. There can be no doubt that Jerome, Augustine, and Gregory the Great taught verbal inspiration. This is evident from Augustine's explanation of Matt. 27:9, where he expressly states that the Holy Ghost had given to the apostle the name Jeremiah. Still Luther accepts his explanation that the evangelist might have later noticed the "slight error" but did not dare to alter the text, assuming that by this mixing up of Jeremiah and Zechariah the Holy Spirit spoke the words quoted because all of them spoke by one and the same Spirit. If this is the view of the fathers, verbal inspiration must have been in the minds of Leo XIII and Benedict XV.

in the sense of literary authorship, is the Holy Spirit. Inspiration of Holy Scripture means here that God the Holy Spirit exercises all functions—apart from mere writing—necessary to compose a book.

Here a great theological problem arises. Are we entitled to ascribe to God such human functions? Is not this whole theory an answer to the question of how I should act if I were God and wanted men to write for me Holy Scriptures. But I am not God, and God is not the author of earthly books, at least not in the sense of literary authorship. The Patristic theory is an attempt to understand the inspiration of the Scriptures psychologically in analogy to the psychology of human authorship. In this sense the encyclicals of 1893 and 1920 ascribe to the Holy Spirit "the three psychological steps involved in the composition of a book" (Benoit, op. cit. p. 90). But if the Inspiration of the holy writers is a work of the Holy Spirit, and one of the greatest at that, must we not apply also to the doctrine of inspiration the theological rule that the Holy Spirit and his works are never an object of observation, but always an object of faith. *Credo in Spiritum Sanctum, Dominum et vivicantem*: if we consider what this great confession means as the continuation of "I believe in one God the Father Almighty . . . and in one Lord Jesus Christ," then we shall be a little more careful in our theological terminology. We shall be more reluctant to call every religious emotion an experience of the Holy Spirit and to speak of the "guidance of the Spirit" without realizing what this means. The casual use of the words "the Spirit," "to inspire," and "inspiration" in the English language—which has no parallel in the other European tongues and seems to be rooted in the religious history of England in the seventeenth century—must not be allowed to obscure the profound meaning of these words. If we cannot understand the way how the Holy Ghost works in a human soul in what we call conversion and regeneration and how he is acting in our souls when we hear the Word and receive the Sacrament, how much less shall we be able to understand and describe the process that went on in the soul of the author who wrote the Fourth Gospel or in the soul of the writer of the Psalm Miserere. Even if we try to comprehend this process by comparing it with an analogous process in the soul of a great poet whose inner life is revealed to us by his confessions in a reliable autobiography, we come necessarily to a point where the analogy vanishes and the mystery inaccessible to human reason begins.

Christendom has reached the point where one of the greatest endeavors of its theology has come to an end, the attempt to explain the inspiration of Holy Scripture by means of philosophical thought and psychological investigation. This is the result of nearly eighteeen hundred years of theological research. All available means were employed: the psychology of Hellenistic Mysticism that the Church found in Alexandria, the anthropology of Neoplatonism from Origen and Augustine to the great mystics of the Middle Ages, the Aristotelian understanding of the soul, its powers, and its functions. Even Jews and Arabs had to make their contributions. The theory that grew out of these roots has survived the Reformation. The formulas of Jerome, Augustine, and Gregory the Great have lived on even in the Protestant churches. The churches of the *sola scriptura* fought for a great tradition that could not be proved from Scripture but was supposed to safeguard the authority of the Bible. As so often has happened in the history of the Church, the *ecclesia militans* fought and did not admit defeat even where this defeat was manifest to the world. The time has come when we have to recognise that the weapons with which we fought were partly borrowed from the enemies of God and his Word and, therefore, ineffective. The doctrine of the inspiration of Holy Scripture is what Luther says of the doctrine of original sin: No human reason can understand it; it must be believed on the basis of God's Word. It is the Bible itself that tells me that the Scriptures are written under the inspiration of the Holy Spirit and therefore the Word of God. This and nothing else is taught concerning the inspiration in the written Word of God. This, therefore, is the dogma of the Church, to be accepted by faith, just as we accept the dogma of the incarnation or any of the great doctrines confessed in the creed. We shall never know in this world how the virgin birth of Christ or his bodily resurrection was possible. So we shall never understand in this life the inscrutable miracle expressed in the words "according to the Scriptures" and "who spake by the prophets."

V.

What have we to say about the proposition that God is the author of Holy Scripture? This belongs to the dogma of the First Vatican Council and presents the greatest problem to Roman Catholic theology.

The formula was used by the Protestant theologians of the classical "orthodoxy" who, in the Ariatotelian-Thomistic way, distinguished between God as the *auctor principalis* and the bibllical writers as secondary or instrumental authors. But it is not an official doctrine of our churches. The embarrassment it creates to modern Catholic thinkers can be studied in K. Rahner's book. We have quoted his remarks on the patristic theory on the inspiration of Scripture as it was reaffirmed by the modern popes. It is the example of a loyal acceptance of a doctrine that presents problems that in the future must be solved. His main interest is concentrated on the dogma of 1870, which cannot be rescinded as perhaps that theory can. Rahner must show how God can be called "author" of Holy Scripture in the full sense of authorship, while, on the other hand, God's authorship must imply that the biblical writers are literary authors of their writings in the full sense of the word. The great merit of his penetrating analysis of authorship is the proof that the old classical theory of the two authors, the divine and the human, is untenable. It limits, in spite of all endeavors to maintain the share of the human writer, his authorship to such a degree that he is not the literary author in the full sense of the word. In this we agree with Rahner. One cannot say that God wrote the letter to Philemon, which is obviously understood as a private letter.[12] We must recognise that the Scriptures are real human writings written by human authors. The doctrine of inspiration says nothing about their human origin. What it says is that their authors were moved by the Holy Spirit—which does not imply that they always were aware of it and which must not be con-

---

[12]Strangely enough, Rahner puts always Rom. 16:1-23 side by side with Philemon as a private letter which has later been incorporated in Romans. Why does he accept this wholly unfounded thesis? Does he not realise the liturgical character of the "greetings" which make no sense in a private letter? Does he not see the parallel with 1 Cor. 16:19ff.? As a matter of fact, this chapter is a precious monument of the pre-Neronian Church in Rome with their house churches. That Aquila and Priscilla have returned to Rome can have ecclesiastical reasons. Is perhaps the reason for the ready acceptance of the thesis of some Protestant scholars to be found in the fact that it does away with Rom. 16 as one of the strongest arguments against the legend of Peter's early arrival in Rome? Also other Catholic scholars are inclined to accept this theory, e.g., O. Karrer, *Peter and the Church*, p. 115.

founded with the divine concurrence (*concursus divinus*) that makes all actions of the creatures dependent upon the creator—and that what they wrote was, in virtue of the inspiration by the Holy Spirit, God's Word.

We agree also with Rahner in assuming that he has not only caused the writing of the Scriptures, as he is the cause of all things and of all actions. There is a very special will, a *voluntas specialissima*, behind the origin of these books and the Bible as a whole.

But we disagree if Rahner finds the last intention of God when he caused these books to be written in his will to create the Church. For Rahner, the Bible and the Church belong together already in the fact that only the Church, through its infallible teaching office, can say which books can be received into the canon because they are inspired.

The synagogue could not determine the Old Testament canon, but the Church could do it and did it at Trent when she accepted, for example, 2 Maccabees as sacred and canonical. We would say that just this case shows that the judgment of the Church is not infallible. The Church can never say with infallibility what belongs in the canon and what not. There has always been an element of incertitude as far as the borders of the canon are concerned. One may only think of Mark 16, of the *Comma Johanneum*, of the corruptions of the text in Old Testament passages. Why did God allow that? It was his will that we should not have a Bible as we perhaps would like to have it, free of any doubtful passage, of any corruption of the text. Congar has raised the objection against Rahner's co-ordination of the Bible and the Church that the danger exists that we forget the Bible is given to the Church and not made by it.

What would we suggest if the question arises of how the doctrine of inspiration should be built up again after the old psychological categories have proved untenable? We must return to the theological categories of the New Testament. The doctrine of Holy Scripture belongs in the doctrine of the Holy Spirit and his works. The Holy Spirit, "the other Paraclete," belongs together with Christ, the Paraclete. "*Ubi Christus, ibi Spiritus Sanctus; ubi Spiritu Sanctus, ibi Christus.*" This is one of the fundamental rules of the theology of the New Testament: Where Christ is, there is the Holy Ghost; where the Holy Ghost is, there is Christ. How can one speak of Holy

Scripture without mentioning its content? Rahner is right when he criticises the "abstract" character of the classical theory of inspiration. Why is it so abstract? "You have all the time been talking about the manger and forgotten who lies in the manger," Luther might say to us. How is it possible that Thomas Aquinas can deal with the problem of prophecy in his astonishing scholarship—referring to authorities including Avicenniaand Maimonides, from whom he takes over the classification of the prophetic experiences—without mentioningthe New Testament passages on the Paraclete? Can anyone understand the prophets of the Old Testament, the prophetic and apostolic Word of the Scriptures, without realising what, or rather who, the content of the inspired word of the prophets and apostles is? *Universa Scriptura de solo Christo est ubique.* "The entire Scripture deals every-where with Christ alone" (Luther).

H. SASSE.

THE REFORMED THEOLOGICAL REVIEW
Vol. XXIV, No. 1, February 1965

Peter and Paul: Observations on the Origin of the Roman Primacy

L.

"The doctrine which distinguishes Roman Catholicism from all other Christian communities is the primacy of the bishop of Rome." So begins a highly important article ("The Roman Primacy in the Second Century and the Problem of the Development of Dogma") by Professor James F. McCue (Lehigh University, Bethlehem, Pa.) which has just appeared in "Theological Studies," the theological quarterly of the Theological Faculties of the Society of Jesus in the U.S.A. This statement explains the fact that the problem of the Roman primacy is moving more and more into the center of the ecumenical dialogue.[1]

---

[1]Strangely enough, it is necessary to remind the younger generation of the Ecumenical Movement that "dialogue" is not the same as "duologue," but rather means a conversation between any number of persons. This everybody knows who has read a Platonic dialogue or the "*Octavius*" by Minucius Felix. *The Christian Century* of April 29, 1964, reports on a dialogue held by Orthodox, Protestant, and Roman Catholic seminarians in Boston area under the title "A Seminar in Ecumenical Trialogue," thus reviving the impossible word used by Wiclif, who did not know Greek. Neither the leader, Professor Ehrenstroem, nor any of the participants seems to be responsible for that title. The

It is the great issue between Rome and Eastern Orthodoxy, since the claims of the rising medieval papacy destroyed the unity between East and West. It is also the issue between Rome and the churches of the Reformation, Lutheran, Reformed, and Anglican. What separates them from Rome is the anathema with which the papacy has excluded from the Church such doctrines as the *sola fide* and *sola scriptura*. Rome would do well to enter into a true dialogue not only with that modern Protestantism that has lost or never possessed the confessions of the Reformation, but also with those churches which still believe, teach, and confess along with the ancient creeds the doctrines condemned by the Council of Trent. Just as the Eastern Church has marvelously survived, in spite of all divisions and confusions in their own midst, the persecutions that seemed to extinguish it, so the faith of the Reformation is still a very living reality in spite of all disintegration and even apostasy that has occurred in Protestantism. It would be a grave mistake if Rome, while taking seriously what Eastern Orthodoxy has to say about the primacy, refused to listen to what the heirs of the Reformation have to say about the claims of the papacy.

II.

In the dialogue about the primacy, the great Petrine texts of the New Testament (Matt. 16:17ff.; Luke 22:32; John 21:15ff.) will be the center of all discussions and investigations. In contrast to the Mariological dogmas of 1854 and 1950, which are predominantly based on tradition, the dogma of the papacy, as defined by the First Vatican Council in the constitution *"Pastor Aeternus,"* rests on what to the Roman Catholic is a firm scriptural proof, the proof from tradition being only subsidiary. Tradition plays a role here mainly in the sense

---

misunderstanding is obviously caused by a confusion of "dialogue" and "dialectics." Here lies the great danger of the mistake. The dialogue between the churches is not a dialectical process in the sense of Hegelian philosophy (Ferd. Chr. Baur's understanding of Church history) in which the encounter of thesis and antithesis necessarily results in a synthesis. The ecumenical dialogue must not necessarily lead to the "One Church" of which Catholics and Protestants, either part in its own way, are dreaming today.

in which the "new theology" wanted it to be understood during the first session of the present council, namely as the interpretation of Scripture by the teaching office of the Church. Scripture, we are told, is the source, the only source of doctrine. But Scripture needs the authoritative exposition that comes to us in the tradition of the Church. Otherwise we end in a chaos of various interpretations as Protestantism does. But just the dogma of the primacy is the classical example for the insufficiency of tradition. As Protestants differ in the understanding of the Bible, so the Catholics differ in the understanding of the tradition of the Church. The Eastern Church, which represents an older form of Catholicism, would agree that the New Testament teaches a primacy of Peter and that this primacy lives on in the bishops of Rome, as the second chapter of *"Pastor Aeternus"* teaches without being able to give anything like a Scripture proof. But the East cannot find in Luke 22 ("I have prayed for thee that thy faith fail not" the doctrine of the infallibility of the bishop of Rome). Nor can it find in John 21 ("feed my sheep, feed my lambs") a primacy of jurisdictions. The dialogue between East and West will concentrate on the question of which of the two traditions is right and whether it is possible to harmonise them.

It would be quite wrong if, on the other hand, we as adherents of the Reformation looked at this discussion as uninvolved spectators. Any serious doctrinal dialogue between two churches is essentially a dialogue between all churches. We are involved. We must make clear to ourselves and to others what *sola scriptura* means. It is not an invention of the Reformation. Our Catholic brethren should ask themselves why it sounded so vigorously through the centuries of the later Middle Ages, and not only as a slogan of heretics, but as the watchword of pious Christians and blameless Catholics.

It was not only the result of the breakdown of the existing ecclesiastical authorities, the papacy, and the ecumenical council. In connection with the despair of Christendom of the authority of pope and council, there arose that hunger for the Word of God that is the work of God the Holy Spirit (comp. Amos 8:11). It was a mighty movement that found its crowning climax in the Reformation, which in many respects is the harvest of the Middle Ages, an event that took place within the Roman Catholic Church. Only slowly modern Catholicism begins to understand its positive meaning, which could not be understood by the councils of Trent and the First Vaticanum. The rediscovery of the Bible in present-day Catholicism goes hand in hand with a new evaluation of the events of the sixteenth century that we call with a word that by no means exhausts its meaning: "Reformation." This new movement in the Roman Church puts some heart-searching questions to us, and we do well to try to answer them for ourselves before the great dialogue about the authority in the Church begins. The *sola scriptura* of the Reformation was based on a great love for the Scriptures. Luther was married to the Bible, says a Catholic Church historian. It was based on the overpowering experience of the Scriptures as the living Word of God. The reformers and the Church of the Reformation knew what it means: "The word of God is living and active, sharper than any two-edged sword, piercing to the division of soul and spirit, of joints and marrow, and discerning the thoughts and intentions of the heart; and before him no creature is hidden, but all are open and laid bare . . ." (Heb. 4:12f.) This is the reason why they could translate, preach, and expound the Scriptures while many of us are dissecting what has long since ceased to be to us the living Word of God, God's actual revelation to us, but has become a "record" of a revelation that has come to others in the past. Luther always maintained that God can take away his Word from whole nations and churches and give it to others. Could not the time come in which the Scriptures are held in higher respect as the Word of God in the Papal Church than with us? In what sense, then, shall we be able to appeal to the *sola scriptura* against Rome? These questions we should seriously ponder before we call back Rome to the authority of Scripture.

III.

We turn to the historic problem of the primacy of Peter and the primacy of the Roman bishops. That Peter had a primacy among the apostles cannot be doubted. The question is only what the nature of this primacy was. He heads the catalogues of the apostles as the first: *protos Simon ho legomenos Petros* (vulg.: *primus Simon . . .*). That Jesus himself has given him the name Cephas no serious historian can doubt. The surname is already, in the Aramaic and in the Greek form, testified by the early epistles of Paul to the Galatians and Corinthians long before the first Gospel was written. This proves the authenticity of the unanimous tradition of the four Gospels that Jesus himself has given this name to Simon. There is no reason to doubt that Matthew 16 has preserved a reliable account of the occasion. We hear of several groups of followers of Jesus. The "Seventy" are mentioned and "the women." The most important group is the college of the Twelve, whose number was meant to correspond to the number of the tribes of Israel, thus indicating the connection between the old and the new people of God. The Twelve are the representatives and leaders of the people of the Messiah ("my church" Matt. 16:17). Within this group we find a narrower circle of the three whom we see on certain occasions (the raising of the daughter of Jairus, the Transfiguration and Gethsemane) as the closest companions of our Lord: Peter and the "sons of thunder," John and James. Is it accidental that a group of three appears later in Jerusalem as the "pillars," Peter, John, and James, the brother of the Lord. But Peter is always the first. In what consists his "primacy?" It cannot be a "primary of jurisdiction." A hierarchical misunderstanding of the organization Jesus gave to his disciples was constantly threatening the real meaning of it. Jesus himself had to reject the ambitions that very soon became manifest among the disciples (Mark 10:35ff.) According to Luke 22:24ff., immediately after the Last Supper "a dispute arose among them which of them was to be regarded as the greatest," which means that even in this solemn hour the quest of the primacy comes up again. The answer Jesus gave should have been sufficient to settle the matter for all times: "The kings of the Gentiles exercise lordship over them . . . but not so with you." There is no primacy of jurisdiction among his disciples.

What, then, is Peter's primacy? He is the spokesman of the Twelve in his confession of Caesarea Philippi—"Who say ye that I am?"—and later in the confessions before the Jewish authorities (Acts 4:8ff. and 5:29ff.). He takes the initiative in the appointment of an apostle in Judas's place to bring the college of the Twelve again to its full strength.[2] But it is this college that ruled the Church as long as

---

[2]One must always remember that the concept of an "apostle" in the New Testament is wider than the concept of the "Twelve." The Twelve are apostles, even "the twelve apostles" (Matt. 10:2). But there are apostles outside this college, such

it existed in Jerusalem. Peter was their "first" and their spokesman. He acted in their name. In Acts 8:14 we read, "Now when the apostles at Jerusalem heard that Samaria had received the word of God, they sent to them Peter and John . . ." And when "the apostles and brethren" in Jerusalem heard that in Caesarea "the Gentiles had also accepted the word of God" (11:1) and the strict Judaists were dissatisfied with the Baptism of uncircumcised people by Peter, he went up to Jerusalem and defended his action successfully by reporting what had happened. He appears as the man who is responsible to the Church. Nowhere he appears as having a jurisdiction over the Church. The jurisdiction, if one may use this word for the responsible leadership, is vested in the college of the Twelve as the representatives of the Church as the people of God. The Twelve again are always acting in conjunction with the "*plethos*," the assembled "brethren." For the Church of Jerusalem is not to be understood as a local congregation only, but as the mother church of all Christians in the world, as the Jewish diaspora has its center in the holy city. This is how the Church in Jerusalem understood itself. It may be that they, or at least some of them, understood the collection Paul had agreed to take up in the mission field for the poor saints in Jerusalem as the Christian version of the didrachma the Jews in the diaspora had to send to John. But this position of Jerusalem came to an end when the persecution of the year A.D. 44, the execution of James, the brother of John, and the imprisonment of Paul, which caused his departure from the holy city, terminated the first period of the Apostolic Age of the Church. By and by the college of the apostles disappeared. Henceforth, they no longer supervised the growing Church from

---

as Paul, Barnabas, perhaps Andronicas and Junias and others who have seen the risen Lord and have been sent by him. For only he can call an apostle, as he does also in the case of Matthias in answer to the prayer of the Church (Acts 1:24ff.). This wider concept appears also in 1 Cor. 15:7. Also James is an apostle, though in his case his relationship to Jesus plays a particular role. Underlying his special authority is the oriental view that the spirit can be bound to the blood. We have in Jerusalem, after the college of the Twelve disappeared, since A.D. 44 the beginnings of what has been called a Christian "caliphate"; for James was succeeded by other relatives of Jesus. A parallel case is the succession in the later Nestorian Church, where the Katholikos used to be succeeded by a nephew.

Jerusalem by sending their delegates to the mission fields, as they did in the case of Samaria by sending Peter and John or in the case of Antioch where they sent Barnabas (comp. Acts 11:22 with 8:14). It seems that henceforth their activity is centered in mission work, even if they occasionally returned to Jerusalem.

This was at least the case with Peter. Paul describes in Galaltians 2:7 his own and Peter's position as it was definitely recognized by the Church of Jerusalem in the words: "I had been entrusted with the Gospel to the uncircumcised, just as Peter had been entrusted with the Gospel to the circumcised. For he who worked through Peter for the mission to the circumcised worked through me also for the Gentiles." As Paul was the great Apostle of the Gentiles, so we find Peter as the great Apostle to the Jewish diaspora (see 1 Peter 1:1). This is what O. Cullmann has rightly seen (*Petrus*, Second German Edition pp. 72 and 237). However, he is not right in assuming that he accepted this new office in dependence from James, the brother of the Lord, and that James was his successor in the primacy. Otto Karrer (*Peterandthe Church. An Examinationof Cullmann's Thesis*, 1963, pp. 22ff.; 32ff.) has seen that this assumption of a translation of the primacy from Peter to James is the weakest point in Cullmann's theory. However, this does not mean that the primacy was trans-ferred to another person, namely to the bishop of Rome. Cullmann's exegesis of John 21—according to which the commission given to Peter means his reinstitution into the office he had forfeited by his denial of the Lord—is correct. He is also right in assuming that the close connection between the commission and the prediction of the martyrdom of Peter indicates that the commission is "chrono-logically limited" (p. 72). But to assume that James became in his stead the leader of the Church and so his successor in the primacy is untenable. The primacy is bound up with the college of the apostles. Peter is the first in this college. With the dissolution of the college, the position of the first lapses. What remains is the name "Peter," which is now, at least in the Greek language, a name, as the word "Christ" has become a name. For all times Peter will remain the man who as spokesman of the Twelve was the first who confessed Jesus as the Christ and received the title of kephe in that memorable dia-logue: "Thou art the Christ. . . . Thou art *kepha*." To him as the first was given the office of the keys of heaven, which in John 20 is given to all apostles and in Matthew 18 to the whole Church, even in the appearance of the smallest local congregation (vv. 15–20). On him the Church is built, but it is also built on the rest of the apostles (Eph. 2:20). His primacy was never more than a primacy between equals. He was the "first" of the college of the Twelve. He ceased to be that when the college ceased to exist.

But what about the position of James? He was the leader of the Church of Jerusalem, its first bishop according to the list of the succession of Jerusalem (Eusebius, H.eccl. IV, 5), perhaps the proto-type of the monarchical episcopate that spread via Antioch and Asia through the Church. It seems that in this second period of the Apos-tolic Age, a new conception of the local church became prevailing. The individual local church is no longer a daughter or a branch of the Church in Jerusalem, but rather a replica of Jerusalem. This would explain the fact that each church has seven deacons and can have no more, even if, as it was the case in Rome, seven cannot cope with the tasks a large church presents.[3] In any case James is not more than the leader of Jerusalem. The so-called "apostles convention" (Acts 15) is not an assembly of all apostles, though some are present; still less is it the first synod of the Church. It is a meeting of the Church of Jerusalem, naturally presided over by James. The issue is whether and under what conditions the Church of Jerusalem can recognise the Baptism of Gentiles. The controversy breaks out in Antioch when Judaists from Jerusalem appear and make a loud protest. Antioch decides to send a delegation headed by Paul and Barnabas to put the question before the Church of Jerusalem. The Church assembles, the "*plethos*," the apostles (which does not necessarily mean the Twelve, but apostles who were temporarily or permanently residing in Jerusalem and are there, under James, a ruling body—for an apos-tle can, like a prophet, exercise his office everywhere) and the presby-ters. The right to speak is obviously limited to the apostles, including the visiting apostles from Antioch, while the right to vote belongs also to "the presbyters with the whole church," which may mean that

---

[3]The idea seems to live on in "*Santa Crocein Gerusalemme*," one of the seven basilicas of Rome. The original name was "*Sancta Hierusalem*." According to the tradition, some soil from Mount Calvary had been used in laying the foun-dations. Helena presented the church with relics of the holy cross.

the *plethos* has the right of acclamation, after the presbyters as the representatives of the local church have given their vote. Peter makes the first speech, favouring the recognition. Barnabas and Paul (note this sequence as Acts 14:12) make their report. James as the chairman suggests the decision that is generally accepted. It is communicated to the Christians in Antioch, Syria, and Cilicia in a letter that is solemnly transmitted by two delegates of Jerusalem who accompany the legates from Antioch back to their church. Jerusalem declares itself to be in church fellowship with the Christians from the Gentiles and restores the peace that had been disturbed by Judaists from Jerusalem. This is the meaning of Acts 15. There is not the slightest trace of a "primacy," neither a primacy of James nor a primacy of Peter. Peter has only the privilege of being the first speaker.

From the New Testament we turn to the post-apostolic age and the early fathers. With great acumen Roman Catholic scholars have tried to find traces of the primacy of Peter in the documents of the second century from I. Clement to Irenaeus and Caius. All these attempts will have to be given up. Professor McCue in the article quoted shows that neither I. Clement nor Ignatius *ad Romanos* nor Irenaeus know anything like a primacy of Peter and that the apologetical attempts to interpret the pertinent passages in that sense as is still being done by O. Karrer are artificial and unconvincing. This view, presented in that outstanding journal of the American Jesuits, seems to be more and more accepted by the Catholic scholars also in Europe. On the whole, the picture of the development as given by the late Erich Caspar in his books on the subject, especially in the first volume of his unfinished *Geschichte des Papsttums* (1930) and also by H. Lietzmann *History of the Ancient Church, vols. I and II*; "Petrus und Paulus in Rome" (2nd Edition, 1927) seems to become the common possession of Catholic and Protestant scholarship. Matthew 16 is for the first time quoted by Tertullian (*de pud.* 21) in his Montanist polemics against Callistus's declaration that he was prepared to admit to a "second penance" Christians who had been excommunicated for the sin of adultery or fornication.[4] The text Matthew

---

[4]It has been assumed that the "bishop of bishops" against whom Tertullian writes was a bishop of Africa. But who but the bishop of Rome could in the West be addressed as "apostolic"?

16:17ff., says Tertullian, cannot be applied to the whole Church related to Peter, but only to Peter himself. Whether Callistus had appealed to Matthew 16 or whether Tertullian makes this objection to himself cannot be decided. Matthew 16 plays again a role with another African father. Cyprian quotes the passage in *De unitate ecclesiae* without referring it to Rome. Among the Bible passages he quotes for the doctrine that there is only one Church. there appears Matthew 16:18f. Cyprian explains it as meaning this: "On one he builds the Church. And although he gives after his resurrection the same power to all apostles (here follows John 20:2ff.), yet in order to emphasize clearly this unity he has ordained by his authority that the origin should begin with one. Certainly also the other apostles were what Peter was, sharing with him the same honor and power, but the beginning is with one to show that the Church of Christ is one" (*cap.* 4).[5] From a letter by Firmilian of Caesarea in Cappadocia, which is contained in Cyprian's correspondence (*ep.* 75c. 17), we know that Stephen of Rome in the controversy about the validity of baptism by heretics has used Matthew 16 as a weapon against Cyprian and the Church of Africa. He seems to have been the first Roman bishop who based the authority of the Roman See on Matthew 16, while Callistus had probably only thought of the power to forgive sins as taught in Matthew 16:19.[6]

Unfortunately we have not the text of Stephen's letter to Firmilian in which he made that claim. It seems that Stephen had claimed to be the successor of Peter on whom the Church is built. We

---

[5]This is undoubtedly the original text. It is not likely that the version presented by some manuscripts has been made by Cyprian himself. Its Roman origin is proved by the Roman custom to mention Paul together with Peter: "certainly the others were what also Peter was, but to Peter the primacy (*primatus*) is given so that the oneness of the Church and the oneness of the primacy might be shown. He who does not keep this oneness and that with Paul (*hanc et Pauli unitatem*) does he really think he is keeping the faith?" (*Cyprian* ed. Hartel, C.S.E.L., vol. 1, p. 212)

[6]It should always be kept in mind that among the Church fathers there has never been agreement concerning the exegesis of Matt. 16, especially the meaning of the words "on this rock." In the West Jerome seems to have been almost the only one who consistently referred the word "rock" to Peter.

find here an understanding of the primacy that is since that time slowly developing in Rome in the fourth century. It finds an expression in a statement, found in the *Decretum Gelasisnum* of the sixth century, but probably formulated at the Roman Synod under Darnasus in A.D. 372: "The Roman Church has received the primacy through the Word of the Lord, 'Thou art Peter and on this rock I shall build my church. . . .' *To this is added the communion with the blessed Apostle Paul*, the chosen vessel who with Peter on the same day under Caesar Nero in the city attained the crown of martyrdom" (quoted from Caspar, *Geschichte des Papsttums*, Vol. I, p. 247f.).

5.

This is a new conception of the nature of the primacy that was unknown to the Roman Church in the first centuries. It finds its expression in the list of the Roman bishops that appears under Liberius in 354. Here is Peter the first of the Roman bishops. This is an innovation, partly due to the influence of the lists of the great Oriental churches.[7] The first bishop in the official list of Antioch is also Peter, James is the first bishop of Jerusalem, and Mark of Alexandria. This was not so in the West. After the blessed apostles Peter and Paul had founded the Church in Rome, so Irenaeus writes (*adv. haer.* III, 3, 2), they handed over to Linus the office of bishop (*episkope*). Then follows the list of the bishops up to Eleutherus, the twelfth from the apostles. Here the first bishop is Linus.

The view that the office of an apostle is different from and higher than that of a bishop has led to the restoration of the old order. In the present official list of the popes, Peter is outside the

---

[7]Unfortunately, the East has not exercised an altogether wholesome influence on the papacy. Instead of moderating Rome's claims, Eastern theologians have showered the See of St. Peter with their rhetorical superlatives. Peter is for them the "*coryphaios*," even the "*exarchos*" of the apostles. Even Michael Caerularius could still say before the Roman anathema arrived in 1054, "On Peter the great Church of Christ is built." This was not meant in the sense of a primacy of jurisdiction. See Meyendorff in the valuable symposium, *La Primautede Pierredans l'Eglisc Orthodoxe*, by Afanasleff, Koulomzine, Meyendorff, and Schemann (Neuchatel, 1960).

bishops proper (the numbers have disappeared). The primacy of Rome is in the first centuries a primacy not of its bishop, but of the Roman Church. She has authority—this is the view of Irenaeus and Tertullian—because she is the apostolic Church proper, the only church in the West that can claim direct apostolic origin. This is the reason why according to a famous word of Irenaeus with this church every other church must agree in doctrine. This church is founded (in a spiritual sense) not by one apostle, but by two, Peter who was the first of the Twelve, and Paul whom Christ has chosen to become the great apostle lo the Gentiles. And both have been crowned with the martyrdom in the midst of their church. Their blood, shed for Christ has sanctified the pagan city. Their graves are holy places of the city. Where the Tiber enters Rome, there is on the Vatican Hill the grave of St. Peter. Where it leaves Rome there is, off the road to Ostia, the grave of St Paul. They are always mentioned together by I. Clement in the short report on their martyrdom in connection with the Neronian persecution. Ignatius writing on his way to Rome, where he is to die as martyr in the circus, to the church, "which presides in the regions of the Romans," shows that he knows it well. He knows, for example, that this church has not yet a monarchical bishop, like Antioch and the churches of the East, but a college of bishops. He asks that Rome may do nothing to save him from the terrible death he is going to suffer. "Not like Peter and Paul do I command you." So we could go over the writings of the second century that mention Rome. Always is Rome the city of Peter and Paul, the two great martyr apostles. In the controversy with Asia on the Christian *pascha*, the defenders of the Quartodeciman practice appeal to the great tradition of their church. Polykrates writes to Bishop Victor of Rome, "Also in Asia great stars have found their resting place and will be raised at the advent of the Lord." He enumerates some of the great Christian men and women who will be raised when the Lord comes to visit his saints, Philip the apostle—he should be "one of the Seven"—with his daughters, John, the apostles, Polycarp, and others (Eusebius, h.e. V, 24). To a similar appeal made in the Montanist controversy, the Roman writer Gaius replies, "I can show you the '*tropaia*' of the apostles. You may go to the Vatican or to the road to Ostia. You will find the *tropaia* of the apostles who have founded this church" (op. cit. II, 25). The *tropaia* can in this context be only the graves, not the places of execution, of Peter and Paul.[8]

We have seen how in Roman texts of later times where the primacy of Peter is referred to, also Paul is mentioned as if it were not possible to speak of one without mentioning the other. Still today it is a rule of the Roman Missal that on each feast of Peter, Paul must be commemorated with a special collect, and vice versa. Even Leo the Great, who otherwise has definitely established the dogma of the primacy of Peter on the three great Petrine texts, magnifies both as "the princes of the apostles" in his sermons. They belong together, the twin founders of the Christian Rome as Romulus and Remus in the saga of the founding of the old Rome.

The lasting expression of this conjunction of the two great apostles and Roman martyrs is found in the feast of the Holy Apostles Peter and Paul on June 29. According to the mass of that day—in the present Roman rite as in the older rites outside Rome—this is the day on which the two apostles suffered their martyrdom. But this tradition is not tenable. What we know is that since the June 29, A.D. 258, during the Valerian persecution, this feast was kept in the catacomb of St. Sebastian. We do not know what the original meaning of that day is. Leitzmann's hypothesis that on this day the holy relics were transferred from the original graves to the catacomb—where they remained until they were returned to the churches Constantine had built on the original sites—is despite all difficulties it entails so far the best explanation. The "graffiti" in the catacomb prove that both apostles were invoked there, in some cases even as "Paul and Peter." The day is still the feast of both, though in the post-Constantine time it could no longer be celebrated on one place only. Hence the celebration of the two in St. Peter was and still is followed by the commemoration of St. Paul on June 30 in St. Paul. This order is to be found in any Roman Missal. It was one of the great feasts of the Roman Church that spread through

---

[8]We cannot discuss here the questions of the authenticity of the sites of the graves. It cannot be proved, but it is very likely that they are authentic. Christians who later would have searched for them would have found them certainly in a Christian cemetery, side by side, and not remote pagan graveyards. There is good evidence for Peter having been toward the end of his life in Rome (see 1 Peter 5:13).

Christendom East and West. In the present Roman Mass of the 29th, both are mentioned, but the lessons refer to Peter, the epistle being taken from Acts 12, while the Gospel is Matthew 16:13–19. On the 30th the Epistle is Galatians 1:11–20, the Gospel Matthew 10:16–22. These pericopes were already used in the Middle Ages. They correspond to the division of the old feast into two festive days, one mainly dedicated to St. Peter, the other to St. Paul. Outside Rome and the Roman Church province, however, in the old Latin churches of Africa, Spain, Milan, and Gaul, we find still the one-day feast of the two apostles on June 29, preceded, of course, by a vigil. The lessons are different from the Roman Mass, which very early seems to have read Matthew 16. The Epistle is in Africa taken from 2 Timothy 4. In Milan it is 2 Corinthians 11:19ff. In Spain, Luxeuil, and Bobbio, lessons from various chapters of Romans are read. The Gospel in the Mozarabic liturgy is John 15:7–16, in Luxeuil Matthew 5:1ff.; in Milan Luke 5 is read, in Africa John 21. In each of the non-Roman liturgies, the Epistle is taken from Paul, while the Gospel refers either to all apostles or to Peter, but no liturgy outside Rome seems to have read Matthew 16. Thus the history of the liturgy confirms the fact that the authority of the Roman Church was based not on Peter, but on Peter and Paul. A primacy of the Roman bishops based on Matthew 16 was unknown to the Church of the first three centuries. Even Rome itself derived its authority from the two great apostles whom already the New Testament puts side by side and whose conjunction the great feast of the 29th of June confirms in the collect: "O God, who has made this day sacred by the martyrdom of thy apostles Peter and Paul, grant that thy Church may in all things follow the teaching of those from whom she received the first beginnings of the faith. Through our Lord Jesus Christ . . ."

HERMANN SASSE

THE REFORMED THEOLOGICAL REVIEW
Vol. XXV, No. 1, January–April 1966

After the Council

To Pius XII, the saying is ascribed that he was the last pope who was able to maintain the Roman Church as it had been in the first half of the twentieth century. After his death a great change was bound to come. Some of the inner problems of the church became manifest when Pius published in 1943 his encyclical "*Divino afflante Spiritu?*" which opened the door to a truly historical research of the Bible. Conservatives like Archbishop (later Cardinal) Ruffini expressed their deep disappointment at what seemed to them a new Modernism that was encroaching the Church via the Pontifical Biblical Institute under its rector, the later Cardinal Bea. "Liberals," on the other hand, came to the fore with views Pius had to reject in "*Humani Generis*" of 1950, theories on the Eucharist, for example, that led to the denial of transubstantiation. If one keeps in mind that this happened when Rome was deeply involved in the political events of the era of Mussolini and Hitler, the Second World War and its aftermath, the loss of the Catholic churches in Eastern Europe to Communist powers, and the rise of the Communist Party in Italy, the critical situation of Rome becomes evident. What was the remedy for the evils that threatened the Church from within and without? Perhaps a council? The idea of a council was in the air since many years in view of the fourth centenary of Trent in 1945. It had to be given up on account of the political events. Besides, it seems that Pius XII, after the war was over, did not believe that a council could do what the pope and the wise men of the Curia were not able to do. The cardinals were speechless when John XXIII surprised them with the announcement that he was to summon an ecumenical council. Great as Pius XII had been as theologian, canonist, and diplomat, a practical man was required to start the renewal of the Church. And this was John, the caretaker pope. As the successor of the great Pius, he did always just the opposite to what the great theoretician had done or might have done. Pius had seen all the difficulties. John had the courage to ignore them. The natural cleverness of his peasant ancestors blended in him in a wonderful way with the shrewdness and skill of a trained and experienced diplomat and with the sincere piety of a devout Catholic Christian and that wonderful love that has endeared him more than any other pope in modern times to the people of Italy, to Catholics and Protestants throughout the world, and even to many people beyond the Iron Curtain. He was a caretaker. None of the documents of the council bears his name. But his spirit pervades them all. He was called away before he could realize all the difficulties the council would have to encounter. But his successor who in many respects is more akin to the intellectual Pius VII is determined to carry out with his great conscientiousness what John's council has decided.

John's practical idea in view of the difficulties encountered by the Curia in ruling the vast Roman Church[1] was this: should I decide the way the Church has to go in future? The pope is not infallible, except

---

[1]The growth of the Roman Catholic Church between the First and the Second Vatican Council is illustrated by the following figures, which give a more reliable picture than the statistics based mainly on populations of entire countries. In 1870 of 1,050 prelates entitled to participate in the council, 774 were in Rome, the rest being prevented by sickness, old age, or other circumstances, such as the Catholic bishop in Russia who did not get a visa from the Russian government. The highest number present at any vote taken was 667 who accepted unanimously the constitution *De Fide Catholica* on Sunday after Easter, April 24, 1870. The session of July 18 was attended by 535 fathers, the bishops of the minority having left Rome with the permission of the pope. The Second Vaticanum was attended by 2,100 prelates. It seems that in no voting less than 2,000 took part. When at the first session the decisive vote was taken on the question of whether the discussion on "The Sources of Revelation" should be continued or not, 822 fathers voted for the continuation, and that

in those rare cases when he proclaims a new dogma to be believed by the entire Church, which happens perhaps once in a century. Even his encyclicals cannot claim infallibility, let alone the cardinals who have prepared them, to say nothing of the political blunders made by the popes and their curias. So let the Church herself decide which way she wants to go. The Lord will not let her down. Rome cannot do everything. The council must do it with and under the pope. Such a council has the promise of the guidance by the Holy Spirit. Hence the Second Vatican Council was from the outset an inner affair of the Roman Church. Whatever it would have to say about other Christians, other religions, and mankind as a whole, its primary aim would always remain the renewal and the *aggiornamento* of the Roman Catholic Church. The entire life of the Church and its members from its highest dignitaries to the last layman would come under the scope of the council. And indeed the documents accepted and published deal with all spheres of the life and activities of the Catholic Church: the nature of the Church and of its offices of the bishops, priests, and deacons and their functions, the various aspects of the life and activities of the "religious," the rights and duties of the laity. They deal with all activities of the Church, including missions, teaching in schools of every level, and the use of modern means of communications. The bishops who have now returned to their flocks from what in many respects has been a great retreat in which they have been stimulated and instructed for their ministry in its various aspects are now faced with the great task to communicate the results of the council to their priests and their parishes. An era of education will follow the conclusion of the council, and the fruits of this education of clergy and laity will be the real result of the council, a real renewal of the entire Church as it is being hoped for by the pope and the members of the council.

II.

This is not the place to review even briefly the decisions of the council. We mention only two of those that are of utmost importance

---

means, for the scheme, and 1,368 against. The final document "On Revelation" was adopted three years later with more than 2,000 voting for it.

for the future of Roman Catholicism. The first is the great liturgical reform allowing the use of the vernacular in the liturgy. If one
remembers that the victory of the Reformation in large parts of
Europe must be ascribed to the fact that the people who had been
silent onlookers at a solemn rite they did not understand now suddenly became active worshipers, one may well ask what the effects
of this change may in the future be. Writings in which the question
was cautiously discussed by leading men of the Liturgical Movement
of whether the time had come when the great European languages
ought to be elevated to the rank of a liturgical language could not
be published thirty years ago. Now the great change has come, and
everywhere the Catholic parishes are instructed about the true meaning of the liturgy and begin to understand what it means that "we, thy
holy people" are offering with the priest the sacrifice. It should not be
forgotten what a tremendous sacrifice the Western Church is making by giving up the Latin liturgy. For the time is coming when the
Latin Mass will continue to live as the old Spanish liturgy is still continued in a chapel of the cathedral of Toledo. Now one understands
the Apostolic Letter "*Veterum Sapientia*" in which John XXIII made
a touching appeal to save the knowledge of the ancient languages
as a basis of Western civilization. Will the Roman Church have the
destiny of so many Protestant churches that seem to have lost
the ability to think theologically when they lost the knowledge of
Latin, which after all was still the language in which the reformers
wrote and thought? For a language is not only a means of communication, but also a tool of thought.

The second great decision is the acceptance of the collegiality of
the bishops. To counteract the one-sided emphasis on the papacy in
the "*Constitutio Prima de Ecclesia Christi*" of the First Vaticanum, the
new doctrine elevates the office of the bishop. Apart from being the
shepherd of his diocese, each bishop is a member of the "college of
bishops." All bishops together form this college, which with the pope
and under the pope rules the Church universal. As the pope is the successor of Peter, so the bishops are the successors of the apostles among
whom and over whom Peter held the primacy. The notes that have
been added to the Constitution on the Church show already that
there is a lack of clarity in the new doctrine. A "collegium" in the strict
sense of the law appoints its own chairman. But even if one calls the

Twelve a college, what is the relation between the Twelve and the apostles outside this college like Paul? The new theory meets with the same historical difficulties that the theory of a Petrine primacy of jurisdiction in the Primitive Church encounters. Since the dogma of 1870 concerning the primacy and infallibility of the pope is "*irreformabilis*" and had to be reaffirmed time and again by the Second Vatican Council, the "collegiality" is an attempt to mitigate it by bridging over the gulf the decision of 1870 had created.

This understanding of the relationship between pope and bishops finds its expression in the form of the decrees. The decrees of Trent begin with these words: "This Holy Catholic and Universal Council of Trent, in the Holy Spirit lawfully assembled under the presidency of the three (papal) legates . . . decrees, etc." The decrees of the First Vaticanum begin, "We Pius, servant of the servants of God, with the approval of the holy council (*sacro approbante Concilio*) . . ." While in Trent the synod speaks, at the First Vatican Council the pope speaks. The decrees of the second Vaticanum begin, "Paul, bishop, servant of the servants of God together with the fathers of the Sacred Council." And he signs "I, Paul, bishop of the Catholic Church," and this signature is followed by that of all bishops. It is no longer the proud "We" of 1870, which distinguishes the pope from the bishops, but the "I" of the first of the long range of the bishops, as the present pope prefers the singular "I" to the *pluralis majestatis* when he speaks to his brethren, the bishops. This is the new style of the papacy. Paul VI has given away the precious tiara his people of Milan gave him for his enthronement, sold for the poor, as the newspapers wrote. It is probably now somewhere in America and no longer in Rome. Instead of the threefold crown, the servant of the servants of God, the bishop of Rome, wears now the mitre of a bishop. This belongs to the style of Pope John who emphasized his office as bishop of Rome and wanted to be buried in his cathedral, the Basilica of the Lateran, dedicated to the Savior and the two Johns, the Baptist and the Apostle. But as the first of the bishops he is never alone. Where he acts and speaks, even as the Vicar of Christ, he does so "together with" (*una cum, cf.* the use of this term in the first prayer of the *Canon Missae*) his brethren in the episcopal office.

If the primary task of the council was to inaugurate a renewal of the Roman Catholic Church, and an "aggiornamento," a bringing up to date of the Church, which for a century and longer had lived in a ghetto and ought to come to the fore again to take its place in modern civilization, then this task is inseparably linked to the ecumenical task of the Church as Rome must understand it. Several great ecumenical programs have been put forward in modern Christendom. Anglicanism has its Lambeth Quadrilateral, which regards the acceptance of the Scripture of the Old and New Testament, the Apostles' and Nicene Creed, the Sacraments of Baptism and the Lord's Supper, and the "Historic Episcopate" as necessary and sufficient to restore the lost unity of the Church. This program is regarded as insufficient by the Catholic churches as well as by the churches of the Reformation because it ignores completely the issues of the Reformation. Even the Eastern Orthodox churches do not regard it as sufficient. American Protestantism has put forward the program of unity in service, in practical application of the Christian ethics to the life of the world, that then would lead to mutual recognition and to a unity in what is really essential in the Christian faith. Since this program neglects entirely the doctrinal aspects of the Christian faith, the "Faith and Order" movement tried to bring about a thorough discussion of the agreements and disagreements of the Christian churches in the hope that this would lead to the discovery of deeper unity. These thoughts were blended in the program of the World Council of Churches with the pietistic idea of an existing unity that binds together the children of God in the various denominations and will become manifest when they unite in worship, in common works of Christian love and in serious study of the Bible. It was obvious that Rome could not take part in any of these movements due to the belief of the Roman Christian that his church is the *Una Sancta Catholica*. To restore the lost unity of all Christians could mean to him nothing else but the return of those who have left their father's house to the one flock under the one shepherd. What hurt the rest of Christendom in our ecumenical era was not this conviction based on the Roman understanding of Holy Writ, but how it was presented to the other churches. No Catholic today would defend the lack of Christian love and humility with which the invitations to attend the ecumenical conferences were received by Rome. The great change of the ecumenical climate occurred in Rome only after the Second World War. It was brought about by the Catholic Christians and their bishops in the countries that had suffered under Hitler's totalitarian state and had been the battlefields of the war: Germany and Austria, Holland, Belgium, and France. How deeply the new attitude toward other Christians has determined the council is obvious. It was held in the presence of representatives of many churches of various denominations who were treated not only with extreme courtesy but, as separated brethren or even "brethren in Christ," in a spirit of real brotherliness. The last session of the Council of Trent on the fourth of December 1563 was concluded after the fashion of the ancient councils with acclamations praising the popes under whom the council had met, the emperors, the cardinals, the bishops, and the council itself. The last of these acclamations was "*Anathema cunctis haereticis. – Anathema, Anathema.*" These were the last words of Trent, and even the constitutions of 1870 ended with anathemas. No anathema was heard this time. Instead Pope Paul held a special service with the separated brethren, who according to the canon law are schismatics or heretics, in the Basilica of St. Paul. This is the "Testament of John," who in the address with which he opened the council mentioned the errors that in former times the Church had to condemn with the greatest severity. "Nowadays, however, the spouse of Christ prefers to make use of the medicine of mercy rather than that of severity."

What under these circumstances can the ecumenical program of Rome be? Unity of the Church requires the acceptance of the entire Catholic faith, as it is professed by Rome, and the entire order of the Church, an essential part of which is the primary of jurisdiction of the pope. Rome could never accept the minimalism of the Lambeth Quadrilateral nor the doctrinal relativism of the World Council of Churches. No one should expect anything else. This is not lack of ecumenicity. On the contrary, it is a service Rome renders to all churches of Christendom if it reminds them of the fact that there is a Christian faith, once delivered to the saints, from which nothing can be abandoned. It is a different question whether this faith is purely taught and preserved without violation in Rome. Insofar as the Roman Church with its ecumenical program belongs now to the great Ecumenical Movement of our age, which is not identical with any particular organization it has produced. We should also cease to understand Roman ecumenicity as a clever device to bring all Christians into the Roman fold. First of all, if modern Roman Christians think of a "future reunited church," they do not think in terms of uniformity. The Church of the future, as they see it, will have room for a variety of liturgies, customs, languages and national peculiarities. It will never be a sort of monolithic block. It will give to the various nations and cultures the possibility of developing their church life. They all will have the same dogma. But, as already Pope John said in the address quoted, "The substance of the ancient doctrine of the deposit of faith is one thing. The way in which it is presented is another." Why should the Church not on the mission fields, along with other features of the cultures of Asia and Africa, also use new patterns of thought to express truths of the Christian faith? As a matter of fact, the problem of adaptation with which all Protestants are confronted in their mission work was already a problem for Rome centuries ago in the controversies about the Chinese rites. The problem of "unity in variety," which has plated such a great role in our ecumenical discussion, was taken up by Cardinal Leger (Montreal) in one of his speeches at the council when he said, "We all know that many Catholics and non-Catholics think the Catholic Church favours too monolithic a unity. And perhaps we could admit actually, that the Church, especially in recent centuries, has cultivated an exaggerated uniformity in doctrine, in worship, and in her general discipline. For frequently we have somewhat neglected certain legitimate demands of freedom and diversity within the bonds of unity."[2]

This ecumenical program, however, cannot be carried out by the Roman Church as it is today. It presupposes the great renewal of the entire Church, which is expected to be the fruit of the council. A real reformation of the Church is required. "For although the Catholic Church has been endowed with all divinely revealed truth and with all means of grace, yet its members fail to live by them with all the fervor that they should. As a result the radiance of the Church's face shines less brightly in the eyes of our separated brethren and of the world at large, and the growth of God's kingdom is retarded. Every Catholic must therefore aim at Christian perfection and, each according to his station, play his part that the Church, which bears

---

[2]Council Speeches of Vatican II, ed. by Congar, Küng, and O'Hanlon, 1964, p. 147.

in her own body the humility and dying of Jesus may daily be more purified and renewed . . ." (*Decree on Ecumenism* 1,4). "There can be no ecumenism worthy of the name without interior conversion." "St. John has testified, 'if we say we have not sinned, we make him a liar; and the word is not in us' (1 John 1:10). This holds good for sins against unity. Thus, in humbled prayer we beg pardon of God and of our separated brethren, just as we forgive them that trespass against us" (*ibidem* II,7).

The churches of Christendom would do well to realize the greatness of the changes that are going on in the Roman Catholic Church. It would not do to say that, after all, the Roman dogma remains the same. The dogma is not everything in a church, not even in Rome. Much depends on what use is made of it. Even if the reform that is obviously going on cannot be called a reformation at this stage, where is the Protestant Church that has the inner strength to undergo a reform of this magnitude? While our claim to be "*ecclesia semper reformanda*" remains often a mere theory, the "*irreformabilis*" the First Vaticanum wrote over the dogmatic decisions of the papacy has not prevented Rome from a real reform. And we should consider what Rome's entry into the Ecumenical Movement means to us all. The program presented by Rome is the only one that could bring together all Christendom. For the Lambeth Quadrilateral, which goes back into the time before the First Vaticanum, would always leave out the largest of the Christian churches, while the endeavors of the ecumenical council would lead, as the experience shows, only to local unions and never to a union of all Christendom. If John 17:21 should really mean, as Rome and the World Council in a remarkable unanimity think, that Jesus wanted all Christians to be united in one Visible Church, then the question should be seriously considered whether or not Rome's program is the only feasible one, the reunion of all Christians in one decentralized Catholic Church that would give reasonable freedom to each of its sections but would be united in the doctrine of the Roman Church under a pope who would really be servant of the servants of God. The appearance of the Roman program must and will have one tangible result already now. The discussions going on between the theologians of the various denominations under the auspices of the World Council of Churches will be supplemented by the serious dialogue with Rome.

This will have the beneficial result that the non-committal theological conversations between professors of theology, each of whom can speak only for himself and perhaps for his school of thought, will have to be raised to a responsible dialogue from church to church.

IV.

To give a brief example of what will have to be discussed in the forthcoming dialogue, we mention the constitution on "Divine Revelation" ("*Dei verbum*") of November 18, 1965. We have mentioned the scheme "*De fontibus revelationis*" that was put before the council at its first session and rejected by a majority of fathers. Written in the traditional style of theological documents of the Curia, it presented the traditional doctrine of Scripture and tradition as the two sources of revelation without taking into account a discussion that years since had been going on between Catholic theologians on the meaning of the pertinent document of the Council of Trent. The truth and the discipline of the Gospel, so Trent declares (*Sessio IV*, Denz. 783) "are contained in written books and in unwritten traditions." "This synod receives and venerates with the same sense of loyalty and reverence all the books of the Old and of the New Testament, since one God is the author of both, together with the said traditions, as well as those pertaining to faith as those pertaining to morals, as having been given either from the lips of Christ or by the dictation of the Holy Spirit and preserved by unbroken succession in the Catholic Church." This has always been understood as teaching that there are two sources from which the Church takes its doctrine, Scripture and tradition, until in our time modern Catholic theology has tried to give another interpretation. Starting from the fact that the final form of the decree left out the words *partim-partim* ("contained partly in written books and partly in unwritten traditions"), the theory was proposed that Trent knows only one source of revelation, namely Holy Scripture, and that tradition is only the interpretation of the Scriptures by the Church. It is astonishing that scholars like Geiselmann and Jedin, historians of high reputation, could accept this view, which then readily was adopted by the dogmaticians (e.g., Congar, Küng, and with reservation also by Karl Rahner). There was indeed a great diversity of opinions among the fathers of Trent, a definite hesitancy to put Scripture and tradition on the same level, especially since the word "traditiones"—Trent uses always the plural, and the modern combination "Scripture and tradition" was not yet in use—covered also outward ecclesiastical rites. But a text like this must be interpreted not from what some men said in the discussion, but from what it clearly says. The omission of the partim-partim is sufficiently explained from the fact that in many cases a doctrine is contained in either source.

Why then this attempt to read into the text of Trent another meaning? The first reason is to be found in the new appreciation of Holy Scripture in the modern Catholic Church. It has a deep symbolical meaning that the old oriental custom of enthroning the Book of the Gospels at the beginning of each meeting of the council was introduced. The Catholic Church of today is a Bible Church as it has not been for many centuries. If one compares the constitution on the Church with its elaborate chapters on the biblical doctrine of the Church with the *Constitutio Prima de ecclesia Christi* of 1870, where the Bible was only used to furnish the *dicta probantia*—it has a deep meaning that the new constitution is not called *Constitutio Secunda*—it becomes clear that the great changes within the Roman Church are to a large degree due to revival of the biblical studies on the level of theological scholarship as well as on the level of the pastoral care in the parish. It is certainly not accidental that the leader of the "progressives"—to use this catchword—at the council was Cardinal Bea, who for many years had been the head of the Pontifical Biblical Institute, one of the great Bible scholars of our time, a man whose spirituality has been shaped by a lifelong study of the Scriptures. This has given him an authority probably no other man in the council could exercise.

Again it is not accidental that this man became the great ecumenical leader of his church. There is a saying among Catholic Christians in Germany from where Bea hails: "It was Scripture that once had divided our fathers. It is Scripture that will reunite us." One of the reasons why the "one-source theory" in the interpretation of Trent has become so popular among ecumenically minded Catholics was the possibility that it might help toward an understanding with Protestants. A new understanding of the tradition of the Church was awakening among Anglicans. Was not, after all, the New

Testament written tradition of the Church? This idea is incidentally not acceable to Rome. For the First Vatican Council makes it quite clear that the Bible is not made by the Church but written under the inspiration of the Holy Spirit and given to the Church. Protestant New Testament scholarship had meanwhile discovered the biblical concept of *paradosis* and had found in the New Testament several "traditions." All this seemed to narrow the gulf the *sola scriptura* of the Reformation had created. Hence the "one-source theory" on the Catholic side and the discussions of "tradition and traditions" on the Protestant side, especially in Faith and Order circles, seemed to indicate that the old problem was not insoluble.

Now Rome has spoken. Pope John broke the impending deadlock of the council in 1962 by having the scheme "On the Sources of Revelation" withdrawn. He appointed a new special committee to deal with the problem under the joint chairmanship of Cardinals Ottaviani (the main author of the first draft) and Bea. The result was after thorough debates on November 18, 1965, the council adopted the "Dogmatic Constitution on Divine Revelation." Its first words by which it will be known, "*Dei Verbum*," indicate already the solution. The Word of God comes to us always as Scripture and tradition. Based on the doctrine of the fourth session of Trent and on the "*Constitutio de Fide Catholica*" of the First Vaticanum, it presents what henceforth will be taught as the Catholic doctrine of revelation. The doctrine of 1870 on the general revelation of God is expressly reaffirmed: "God, the beginning and end of all things, can be known with certainty (*certo cognosci posse*) from created reality by the light of human reason (Rom. 1:20)." It has to be kept in mind that the constitution of 1870 in canon I (Denz. 1806) even speaks of "the one and true God, our creator and Lord." The new constitution speaks in detail of the special revelation of God in words and deeds to our first parents before the fall, to Abraham, Moses, and the prophets. In a later chapter on the Old Testament, we read more on the history of the Old Covenant as the preparation for the full revelation in the New Testament. But on the whole the Old Testament is treated very briefly. One has the impression that the authors of this document have not been aware of the fact that, as Luther puts it, the Old Testament is the Bible proper, the Scripture that is followed by the glad tidings of its fulfillment. No doctrine on the inspiration is sufficient that does not keep in mind that everything the New Testament and the fathers say about the inspiration and authority of the Bible refers to the Old Testament. This is true even of the Nicene Creed: "*Qui locutus est per prophetas,*" "*secundum scripturas*" (cf. 1 Cor. 15:3f.).

The divine revelation reaches its climax and its final perfection in Christ. He has commissioned the apostles to preach the Gospel to all men. "This commission was faithfully fulfilled by the apostles who, by their oral preaching . . . handed on what they had received from the lips of Christ . . . The commission was fulfilled too, by those apostles and apostolic men who under the inspiration of the Holy Spirit committed the message of salvation to writing." "In order to keep the Gospel forever whole and alive within the Church, the apostles left bishops as their successors, 'handing over' (Trent, Vatican I) to them . . . 'the authority to teach in their own place' (Irenaeus III,1). This sacred tradition, therefore, and Sacred Scriptures of both the Old and the New Testaments are like a mirror in which the Pilgrim Church on earth looks at God from whom she has received everything, until she is brought finally to see him as he is, face to face (1 John 3:2)" (7). Thus the sacred tradition and the Holy Scriptures belong inseparably together and constitute the Word of God. "Both of them, flowing from the same divine wellspring, in a certain way merge into a unity and tend toward the same end. For Sacred Scripture is the Word of God inasmuch as it is consigned to writing under the inspiration of the divine Spirit, while sacred tradition takes the Word of God entrusted by Christ the Lord and the Holy Spirit to the apostles, and hands it on to their successors in its full purity, so that, led by the light of the Holy Spirit of truth, they may in proclaiming it preserve this Word of God faithfully and make it more widely known. Consequently it is not from Sacred Scripture alone that the Church draws her certainty about everything which has been revealed. Therefore both sacred tradition and Sacred Scripture are to be accepted and venerated with the same sense of loyalty and reverence".

This, then, is the authentic interpretation of the doctrine of Trent and the final rejection of any attempt to limit the tradition to the function of interpreting the Scripture as the one source of the doctrine of the Church. On the other hand, the constitution, which bears the traces of long and difficult negotiations, avoids an unambiguous statement that the doctrine of the Church is not derived from Scripture alone. The *sola scriptura* was mentioned in connection with the certitude of the Church concerning the content of divine revelation. The answer to our question is contained in the following complicated statement: "Through the same tradition the Church's full canon of the sacred books is known, and the sacred writings themselves are more profoundly understood and unceasingly made active in her; and thus God, Who spoke of old, uninterruptedly converses with the bride of his beloved Son; and the Holy Spirit, through Whom the living voice of the Gospel resounds in the Church and through her in the world, leads unto all truth those who believe and makes the Word of Christ dwell abundantly in them (Col. 3:16)." Here we find first the great example mentioned in all schoolbooks of a doctrine the Church knows from tradition, the biblical canon. Then follows a somewhat enigmatic statement on what tradition means to the Church. It leads to a deeper understanding of the sacred writings. They are being activated—in several passages the fact is emphasised also that the written Word is living and powerful. And thus God, who spoke of old, converses uninterruptedly with the Church. How does he speak? In some other passages the idea of a conversation between God and us Christians is beautifully expressed. "In the sacred books the Father who is in heaven meets his children and speaks with them" (21). In an exhortation the faithful are reminded of the necessity to read the Bible prayerfully: "Prayer should accompany the reading of Sacred Scripture, so that God and man may talk together; for we speak to him when we pray; we hear him when we read the divine sayings" (25, quotation from Ambrose). Here everything is clear: God speaks to us in the Scriptures. But what about the uninterrupted conversation that is going on between God and the bride of his beloved Son? The context compels us to understand it as God speaking to his Church not only in the written Word, the living and powerful Word of the Scriptures, but speaking also in the living Word of the sacred tradition. In this mystic conversation it may happen—has it not happened?— that the Church hears a voice telling her wonderful things about Mary, all that is told of her in Holy Writ, but adding things that we do not find in Scripture: her immaculate conception, her assumption into heaven, her role as "Advocate, *Auxiliatrix, Adjutrix, Mediatrix*"

(*Constitution on the Church* 62), as Queen of Heaven and Mother of the Church. Was this really the "living voice of the Gospel"? Was this really the Holy Spirit who leads the Church into all truth? Or is it the Spirit of man, that natural man who cannot bear the idea that man can do nothing for his salvation?

We have briefly spoken on one of the theological issues of the great council, which will be one of the great topics of the dialogue to which the churches of the Reformation are called. Also we know of a "tradition" of the Church, the oral "paradosis" that precedes the writing of the sacred books, the living proclamation of their content in the preaching of the Word, the doctrine of the Scripture, which is summarized in the creeds and Confessions of the Church. We know of the sacred "paradosis" the Father has delivered to the Son and the Son delivers to the faithful (Matt. 11:27). At all times the written Word is accompanied by tradition, even in the entire history of the Old Testament. But there is true and false tradition. It was a false tradition concerning the Messiah that caused the Sanhedrin as the highest, responsible keeper of Israel's sacred tradition to sentence Jesus to death. It was the true tradition that lived on in Zechariah and Elizabeth, in Mary and Joseph, in Simeon and Anna, the sacred tradition that resounds in the Magnificat and the *Nunc dimittis*. The mark of the false tradition is that it tries to become Lord of Holy Scripture, while the true tradition remains always its humble servant. As our fathers in the Reformation put it: the tradition or confession of the Church is *norma normata* under the *norma normans* of the written Word.

We rejoice with our Roman Catholic brethren that, by the grace of God, it was possible for them to finish their council in an age of political unrest and human insecurity, when mankind always lived on the brink of another great war. And we promise to search with them the Scriptures in the dialogue of the coming years, mindful of the word of the Lord that he addresses to us all: "This is the man to whom I will look, he that is humble and contrite in spirit and trembles at my word" (Is. 66:2).

THE REFORMED THEOLOGICAL REVIEW
Vol. XXVI, No. 2, May–August 1967

Some Thoughts on Christian Hope

The voice of Christian hope sounds again, still feebly, but more and more distinctly, through a world of fear and hopelessness. More than enough has been written in our time by poets, philosopher,s and theologians on the situation of modern man who is experiencing the disappointment of all his hope, the frustration of his labours, the despair of the future, and lives in a state of anxiety, deprived of the comfort that men of former generations found in their religion or in the "consolations of philosophy." Has there been any other century in the history of the world in which mankind—not only individual nations—has moved between such extremes as the glowing optimism with which the Western nations entered the twentieth century and the deep pessimism of the Fifties and Sixties, which in turn found an expression in the existentialism that became the leading philosophy of our time? Mankind moved between an almost indestructible belief in the progress of man and his civilization and the deep disappointment of those who had to go through the catastrophies of the wars and revolutions that started in 1914. No century before had achieved such triumphs in science and technology, but we seem incapable of making any other use of them than to destroy our own lives. Never before have such serious attempts been made to prevent wars and to establish lasting peace and justice in the world, but the result has been that the wars became worse and worse and that even the primitive rules and principles of international law have been forgotten. These contradictions drive mankind, individuals, and nations, into an abyss of despair.

In such a time, the Church of Christ has to preach the eternal Gospel of hope. But are we able to proclaim this glorious message, the source of peace and joy in human hearts, the great antidote against the suicidal sin of despair? Or have we already also in the churches been affected by the poison of this sin to such a degree that we no longer understand the biblical message of hope? Our churches have yielded for a long time to the temptation of identifying the secular hopes of our modern civilization with the hope of the New Testament. The consequence was that the breakdowns of such worldly hopes that has led modern man into a state of despair has now a very dangerous effect on us. The "Death of God" theology is only the extreme form of a theology that, under the influence of modern existentialist philosophy, has lost the biblical message of hope and robs the preaching of the Church of the joy that belongs to the "glad tidings" of the Gospel. The whole New Testament is pervaded by great joy, from the joy proclaimed in the Gospel of Christmas to the joy of which Jesus spoke in his last discourses before the Passion (John 15:11; 16:20–24; 17:13), the joy of Easter, and the joy that for all apostles is one of the fruit of the Spirit (e.g., Gal. 5:22; 1 Peter 1:8; 1 John 1:4). The joylessness of so much of our preaching could have its deepest root in the hopelessness of so much of our theology.

But what is the hope that belongs to the nature of the truly Christian life? Christian hope is not simply the hope of a Christian. For every Christian within the depth of his heart is a believer, earnestly desires to live in the Spirit, and shares with all other men the hope that belongs to the nature of man. Also the apostles can use the words "elpizein" and "elpis" in an ordinary sense, as Paul dioes when he "hopes" to see the Church in Rome on his way to Spain (Rom. 15:24) or to spend a few days at Corinth (1 Cor. 16:7) or when he hopes "in the Lord" to soon send Timothy to Philippi (Phil. 2:19; comp. also 1 Tim. 3:14; Philem. 22; 2 John 12; 3 John 14). All saints of God, all believers, share the hope that according to the wisdom of all nations belongs to the very nature of man, because man lives by hope (e.g., Ecclesiastes 9:4) and cannot live without hope. The hope of the sick for the restoration to health, the hope of the prisoner for freedom, the hope for social justice in a nation and for peace between the nations of the world—all these human hopes are common to Christians and non-Christians, and no Christian should dissociate himself from the hopes of his fellow men, as long as these hopes are justified. It would be a grave violation of the great commandment to love our neighbour if we failed to understand these human hopes and if we refused our active participation in the lawful attempts to realize them under the pretext that there are higher things to hope for.

Human hopes, however, whether held by Christians or non-Christians, have one definite limitation. They may be fulfilled or not fulfilled, and even if they seem to have been fulfilled, their fulfilment is never final. Even the sick persons whom Jesus healed fell sick again and died. These healings were signs of the approaching kingdom of God. It cannot be far away if it happens "that the blind receive their sight and the lame walk, lepers are cleansed and the deaf hear, and the dead are raised up and the poor have the good news preached to them" (Matt. 11:4ff., comp. Luke 4:18ff). These "signs" announce the coming kingdom as the first dim light of dawn announces the coming of the new day. But the day is not yet there. If this is true even of the great works of Christ in the New Testament in which he showed his sympathy with sincere human hopes and helped to fulfill them, how much more is it true of human hopes in our ordinary lives. To live is not only to hope, as the proverbs of so many peoples say. To live means also to bury hopes, as a great German novelist says whose dictum is quoted by J. Moltmann in his remarkable book on the *Theology of Hope*.[1] One has only to think of the sadness and feeling of frustration with which the generation of those who built up the League of Nations and other organisations for world peace have seen their works crumble, of the *"Triatesse écumenique"* in which a good deal if not most of the Ecumenical Movement of our time ends, in order to understand what the "buried hopes" have meant to our century. It belongs to the richness of the Bible that it contains a book entirely built around the topic of this experience: "Vanity of vanities. All is vanity. What does man gain by all the toil at which he toils under the sun?" (Qoh. 1:2f.).

---

[1] Juergen Moltmann. *Theologie der Hoffnung*, Muenchen 1965, p. 17.

Between the human hope that is bound to fail and to end in despair and the Christian hope of the New Testament stands the hope of the old people of God. The Old Testament is a great book of hope. One may first think of the problem of human hope in the Psalms and in the Book of Job. The latter is the most exhaustive description of the wrestling of man in a hopeless situation with God "Behold he will slay me, I have no hope" (Job 13:15), until he resigns himself to the inscrutable will of God, not the God of pious sentiments and human theology, but the real, living God who comes to us as an overwhelming reality when we no longer know him from hearsay only, but when we hear him speaking to us: "I had heard of thee by the hearing of the ear, but now my eye sees thee. Therefore I . . . repent in dust and ashes" (42:5). The Psalms, the prayer book of Jesus and of the Church of all ages, have exercised an unequaled influence on the spiritual life of mankind because by praying them man has learned to overcome the hopelessness of his existence by faith in the living God: "Thou, O Lord, art my hope" (Ps. 71:5). In contrast to human hopes, which are bound to fail, this hope, God himself, cannot fail. In the Psalms the distinction between the individual and the people as a whole vanishes, though both are and remain realities. *Jahve*, Israel's God, is the never failing hope of his people. So the history of Israel becomes the history of hope. This hope is based on the sacred history in which God through his Word has called Abraham and established the covenant with the patriarchs. This sacred history went on when God, revealing his omnipotence and saving mercy, led Israel out of Egypt and renewed the covenant with the fathers in the covenant with his people on Mount Sinai. Henceforth Old Testament hope rests on two pillars, on the promise of God and on the history that accompanies and illuminates the promise. What God has done in the past in his power and mercy, this he can and will repeat in another form in the future. Hope, thus, becomes hope for redemption. Since there is no redemption without redeemer, it becomes hope in the Redeemer, God, who acts or may act through the Messiah. Hope becomes thus Messianic hope. It would be hard to understand that the author of the article "The Old Testament View of Hope" in Kittel's *Theological Dictionary of the New Testament* (English translation by Geoffrey W. Bromiley, Vol. III, p. 521ff.) does not mention the Messianic hope at all (except by implication when he uses [p. 523] the words "eschatological help" and "eschatological future") were not his name Rudolf Bultmann. A similar blindness for biblical realities we find in what he writes on the New Testament hope. The tragedy of a great scholar becomes manifest here.[2]

If hope is the great motor that moves the history of Israel, a history without parallel in the entire history of the world, hope gets a new significance in the New Testament. We begin with a linguistic observation. Who is the God who is invoked in the Psalms as our "hope"? What is the name of him in whom we hope? He can be called "*el*" or "*elohim*" or "*Jahve*." It seems today to be taken for granted that *Jahve* is identical with the New Testament "Father." This is often the case, but it is not the whole truth. Even if Moltmann identifies *Jahve* with the Father and can render the statement that God has raised Christ from the dead with "*Jahve* resurrects the Messiah," something is wrong. The New Testament, which followingthe Greek Bible renders *Jahve* with *Kyrios*, can also identify *Jahve* with the Son. We should not forget that for the Greek-speaking Christians, Psalm 23 referred to Christ. "The Lord is my shepherd" means to them the same as "I am the good shepherd." Who is *Jahve* whose glory Isaiah saw in the temple? According to the Gospel of St. John what Isaiah saw was Christ's glory: "Isaiah said this because he saw his glory and spoke of him" (12:41). Our exegetes should pay a little more attention to the history of the holy name of God and ask what it meant that the old *Jahve* was no longer pronounced but replaced by "LORD" in the reading of the Hebrew text as well as in the Greek-speaking synagogue and its Bible. *Jahve* is "God in his revelation," and this revelation is Christ. It is regrettable that even the English version of the Bible of Jerusalem compels now also the Catholic readers of Holy Scripture to use the word "Yahweh." Otto Procksch begins his profound *Theologie des Alten Testaments* (1950) with the statement: "All theology is Christology." But we modern theologians demythologize everything, also the blessed Trinity. Or in what sense do modern biblical scholars still find in Scripture the Triune God of the Christian faith? Do they not find at least "*vestigia trinitatis*" in the Old Testament?

---

[2]Compare with this the different treatment of hope in the O.T. by H. Bardtke in *Die Religion in Geschichte und Gegenwart* (3 Aufl. Bd. III, 1959), p. 415ff.

To remember this is important if we want to understand that "hope" in the New Testament becomes hope in Christ. When the Early Church read their Psalm 129 (our 130th) it was Christ or Christ also to whom they referred the word: "I wait for the Lord, my soul waits, and in his word I hope . . . O Israel hope in the Lord. For with the Lord there is steadfast love, and with him is plenteous redemption. And he will redeem Israel from all his iniquities." So Christian hope means always hope in God and hope in Christ simultaneously without distinction. In 1 Tim. 1:1, Paul calls himself an apostle "by the command of God our Savior and of Christ Jesus our hope." In Rom. 15:13, the apostle expresses the wish, "May the God of hope fill you with all joy and peace in believing so that by the power of the Holy Spirit you may abound in hope."

What is the nature of this Christian hope? It is given by God, by Christ, by the Holy Spirit. God, and especially Christ, is its content proper. No man can give it to himself. No man can give it to others. It belongs to the great *charismata* that God the Holy Spirit gives to those who believe in Christ. It belongs together with faith and love and constitutes with them the triad Paul mentions repeatedly, not only in 1 Corinthians 13, but also 1 Thessalonians 1:3 and Ephesians 4:1–6. While other *charismata* may be lacking, these three are present in every true believer. Faith cannot be without hope, hope not without faith. And also love belongs inseparably together with them.[3] The formula is, so to speak, the shortest description of the Christian life.

---

[3]Since Augustine, the theologians have tried to determine the relationship between faith, hope, and charity. They all agree that "in the order of perfection" (Aquinas) charity is the first. They all agree in the recognition of the close relationship between faith and hope. They disagree concerning the precedence "in the order of generation." In this order for Augustine, faith has the precedence: One cannot love what one does not believe to exist. One cannot hope for what one does not love (*De Doctrina Christ.* Migne PL, 34, 35). Thomas discusses the whole problem of what for him are the three "*virtues theologicae*" in the *Summa theol.* II-I, qu. 62. Hope in the full Christian sense, "*spes caritate formata*," is to him the longing for full communion with God, specifically the longing for the "*visio beatifica*." The finest expression of this hope is the last stanza of his "*Adoro te devote*." It is a perfectly legitimate desire contained in

The characteristic mark of hope is that it always looks into the future. Also faith and even love (1 Cor. 13:7) do that. Hope is in a certain way faith and love applied to the future (2 Tim. 4:8). The close connection between "faith" and "hope" becomes everywhere clear in the New Testament, so much that occasionally the words seem to be interchangeable. So we read 1 Peter 3:15, the admonition to "be prepared to make a defense to anyone who calls you to account for the hope that is in you" (comp. 1:21). Another example is the great chapter Hebrew 11, which begins with the definition of faith that has become so important to all churches: "Faith is the assurance (*hyposta-sis*, Lat. *substantia*) of things hoped for (*elpizemenon*), the conviction ('*elenchos*') of things not seen." This is followed by the enumeration of the great examples of faith from the beginning of the world, which, as faith only knows, was created by the Word of God "so that what is seen was made out of things which do not appear" (comp. the terms *phainomena, blepomena* with the juxtaposition of 'visible' and 'invis-ible,' 'transient' and 'eternal' in 2 Cor. 4:18). The long range of the examples of faith stretches from Abel, Henoch, and Noah to Abra-ham, Moses, and to the innumerable cloud of witnesses of all ages. The examples of "faith" are in each case also examples of hope. Faith and hope are always directed to things unseen, as also Paul empha-sizes that hope means the firm expectation of something that is not yet seen (Rom. 4:18; 8:24). In Paul as well as in the Epistle to the Hebrews, it becomes evident that the last aim of all Christian hope is the eschatological future promised in the Word of God, in the Gospel of Christ (Col. 1:5 and 23). As far as we hope for this future, God is our hope, and Christ is our hope.[4]

---

the Christian hope, as 1 John 3:2 and 1 Cor. 2:9 show, though the biblical con-cept of hope contains still more.

[4]Space does not permit a discussion of what the relationship is between the hope of the individual Christian and the hope of the Church as a whole. Both are essentially identical. Both are comprised in the article of the creed: "I believe in (*expecto*) the resurrection of the dead, and the life of the world to come.""I believe . . . the resurrection of the body (*carnis resurrectionem*), and the life everlasting." As the Church looks joyfully toward the Last Day despite the horrors of the last times that precede it, so the Christian looks toward to the day that will deliver him from this body of sin and death

Both hope and faith have to do with the past and the future, though faith in a special way with the first, and hope most certainly primarily with the latter. This explains why they belong together. The future of yesterday is the past of tomorrow. This is the reason why faith and hope belong to the very nature of the biblical and Christian religion. In contrast with all other religions that we know (excepting Islam, which has its origin in Jewish-Christian sects), the Bible and Christianity claim that not nature (as the pantheistic religions of all times think), and not the human soul (as the mystic religions of all ages assume), but rather history is the realm of divine revelation. Both faith and hope are bound to history to the assertion that certain historic events have occurred in our world. Abraham migrated from Harran to the land in which his descendants were to live, on the

---

(Rom. 7:24; 8:23; 2 Cor. 5:8; Phil 3:20) although he knows of the horrors of death, the last enemy (1 Cor. 15:26, 55ff.). As in the Old so in the New Testament the salvation of the individual is inseparably linked with the salvation of the whole people of God. This was to a large degree, though not altogether, forgotten when the Greek concepts of body and soul in their Platonic and Aristotelian forms (these are not quite identical) penetrated into the Church. The return of theology to the biblical understanding of man, however, cannot mean that we have to go behind the New Testament. The Old Testament, especially in its earlier parts, was very reticent about what happens after death, one of the reasons being the fact that Israel was surrounded by the great cults of the dead in ancient paganism. Jesus and the apostles certainly did not teach the "Immortality of the soul," which we find with Plato and with the Rationalists and Idealists of the eighteenth and nineteenth century. But they teach that the human person even after death stands before God. What Psalm 31:5 means is revealed when Jesus prays, "Father into thy hands I commit my spirit" (Luke 23:47, comp. the words of the proto-martyr in Acts 7:59: "Lord Jesus, receive my spirit."). "Spirit" (*pneuma – ruach*, Matt. 10:28 has "soul," *psyche*) must be understood in the sense of the New Testament terminology. The "spirit of man," in contrast with the Holy Spirit who is God himself, is not the "soul" man has in common with other creatures but that innermost being core of the the soul that he has as created in the image of God, see 1 Cor. 2:10ff., where the terminology is fully developed. The believing Christian commits his spirit in the hands of his heavenly Father knowing that (not how) he will be "with Christ" after death. No theological speculation should rob any Christian soul of this great hope (see also Luke 23:43; 2 Cor. 5:8f.; Phil. 1:20.).

basis of a divine call. The covenant between God and Abraham is an historic fact. The same is true of the Exodus under the leadership of Moses, the covenant between God and Israel, and all the other essential facts of the history of salvation. They are the presupposition of the history of the New Testament, which began with the incarnation of the Son of God who is the Christ, the Messiah whose appearance was promised in the Old Testament. The biographical facts of the life of Jesus from the incarnation to the resurrection and ascension, which the Church confesses in its creeds as articles of faith, are historic events. They must be believed as such, whatever can and must be said about the literary form of the sacred historiography of the Bible. It is a most significant fact that this history is given in the form of various traditions. Every great event in the history of salvation in the Old and the New Testament is related twice (comp. the relation of the history of the patriarchs in the various books of the Old Testament and in the Greek Bible, which Stephen uses in his great discourse Acts 7). Also in the New Testament this "law of parallels" is valid. Three times we read in Acts the story of the conversion of Paul, and each time with small variations of which the author was, of course, aware. At the climax of the sacred history, we have the four strands of the Gospel. Whatever this may mean for the interpretation of the biblical writings, the sacred history of Israel, of Jesus and the Church of the New Testament remains one indivisible unit. Its dogmatic content must be believed. This means that Christian faith as well as Christian hope can never exist without the recognition of historical facts. If the migration of Abraham is a mere saga, if the exodus has not taken place, then the whole faith of the Old Testament collapses. If the saving events of the New Testament are legends, then the entire Christian faith breaks down, as St. Paul has rightly seen: "If Christ has not been raised, then our preaching is in vain. We are even found as false witnesses who testify against God that he raised Christ whom he did not raise. . . . If Christ has not been raised, your faith is futile and you are still in your sins." It must be understood that no one in the ancient world, neither Christians nor non-Christians have ever been able to understand this message of the resurrection of Christ as not including the empty grave.

If this is so, then we understand the difficulties the *kerygma* of the Church presented to the world. When Paul preached to the people of Athens, they listened until he said that "God commands all men everywhere to repent, because he has fixed a day in which he will judge the world in righteousness by a man whom he has appointed, and of this he has given assurance to all men by raising him from the dead" (Acts 17:30f.). This is exactly the point where the modern man voices his loud protest. Those people were prepared to listen to him when he seemed to be "a preacher of foreign divinities— for he had preached Jesus and the anastasis" (v. 18). They would have raised no objection against a new couple of those divinities in whose myth and ritual the eternal truth of rebirth was symbolically proclaimed in the story of the death and resurrection of a God, such as Artis and Kybele, Osiris and Isis. But to speak of repentance and judgment is offending the dignity of every Athenian in the world. And on top of that to speak of a man as judge and of the resurrection of a real man from the dead must seem to Greeks to be such hair-raising nonsense that their patience was exhausted. "When they heard of the resurrection of the dead," they said what amounts to a courteous or less courteous "Never again." The sacred history of salvation is unacceptable not only because it contains miracles that seem to our reason to be unbelievable, but because it is history. A historic event can finally never be proved with the certainty with which we can prove a fact of nature. And secondly it cannot help us. What helps us is not what has happened or may have happened once upon a time, but what happens today. This is what all "Athenians" feel, also the modern Athenians like Lessing and Fichte, and the man of Athena who lives in every one of us.

Wherever the historic character of the Christian revelation is rejected or the historicity of the great saving events of the sacred history is denied, there the Christian faith collapses. The inevitable consequence is that the Christian hope also fades away. One of the most promising young theologians in Germany in the nineteenth century was Heinrich Thiersch. After he finished a brilliant course in classics at Munich, he studied theology at Erlangen. After graduation in 1837 he went, for some time, to Tubingen for studies, especially with Ferdinand Christian Baur, the famous leader of historical-critical theology in Germany. He got the shock of his life when shortly after his arrival he heard the celebrated scholar preaching in the university church service an Advent sermon on the topic "Jesus will never come again." This made him a strong believer in the Second Advent of our Lord and a development started that later made him, who had meanwhile become a professor at Marburg, an adherent of Edward Irving and a leader of Irvingism on the continent. History of modern theology shows that wherever the historic facts of the history of salvation as confessed in the creed are no longer acknowledged, the great hope falls that is also confessed in the creed. If Christ is not risen from the dead, if he did not ascend into heaven, then he will not come in glory to judge the living and the dead and we can cease to confess, "I expect the resurrection of the dead and the life of the world to come."

As faith can decay and as this decay will lead to the destruction of hope, so the breakdown of Christian hope can and must lead to the failure of faith. The great danger for the loss of faith lies in the fact that we can never have an absolute certainty of the facts of past history. We must rely on the witnesses who report these facts from their own personal experience. This explains the strong emphasis the New Testament always places on the testimony of eyewitnesses. It belongs to the nature of the apostolate that the apostle is a witness to the Word Incarnate, at least a witness to the resurrection of Christ (Acts 1:22, comp. 1:8; 2:32; 3:15; 5:32; 10:39–41; 1 Cor. 15:5–8; 15:15ff.; 1 Peter 5:1; 1 John 1:1–3). This is the reason why this office in contradistinction from the office of the prophet belongs to one single generation of history. The Church of Jesus Christ confesses itself in the creed to be an apostolic Church, built upon the revelation that was finished with the death of the last of the apostles. Is this witness reliable? Why did the risen Lord not appear to "impartial," "objective" witnesses? Why have the Jews not recognized the fulfilment of the Messianic promises in Jesus? Why did they never believe in his resurrection, though they have never denied that the grave had been found empty, which they explained in their way (the body was either stolen, or, as a Jewish tradition still maintained in the Middle Ages, the "gardener"—John 20:15—removed it). We can never fully prove that the mightiest movement in the history of mankind—for this is Christianity—is not a result of a conspiracy, a theft, or the mistake of a gardener, just as we cannot definitely prove that the greatest system of religious thought that ever has arisen on this earth was not the product of an anonymous group of men whose minds worked

according to the alleged laws of "*Formgeschichte.*" There will always
be historians who find it easier to explain the history of mankind by
assuming that behind each of the great world religions and systems
of human thought there has been a mastermind. They will find it
easier to apply this also to the Christian Church and its faith and to
assume that this mastermind was none other but Jesus Christ. Such
assumption is, of course, not the basis of our faith. We have nothing
to rely on but the witness. And this we accept as God's Word.

If the uncertainty of past history threatens faith, so hope is
threatened by the uncertainty of the future. "Where is the promise of
his coming? For ever since the fathers fell asleep, all things have continued as they were from the beginning of creation" (2 Peter 3:4) was
the anxious question to be heard toward the end of the Apostolic Age.
How could the Church survive the delay of the parousia, the "advent"
of Christ in glory? Humanly speaking, it was perhaps the greatest disappointment ever experienced in human history. One must think of
the truly remarkable phenomenon, the Church praying unceasingly
the "maranatha," "come Lord Jesus" throughout the centuries in order
to know what Christian hope and Christian faith are. This is truly
the hope and faith of Abraham, of whom St. Paul says, "In hope he
believed against hope" (Rom. 4:18). This looking "not to things that
are seen, but to the things that are unseen" (2. Cor. 4:18) belongs to
the nature of the Christian hope. "Hope that is seen is not hope. For
who hopes for what he sees? But if we hope for what we do not see,
we wait for it with patience" (Rom. 8:24f.). We cannot discuss here the
important concept of patience (*hypomone*) that belongs to the New
Testament concept of hope. The greatest example of it is the patience
with which the Church waits for Christ's advent in glory, undisturbed
by what, in the eyes of men, must be the greatest disappointment. The
Church could survive that. For she has the promise of Christ: "Surely
I am coming" (Rev. 22:20).

It is perhaps not accidental that the "Maranatha" of 1 Cor. 16
and the "Come Lord Jesus" appear in a liturgical context. The admonition to greet one another with the holy kiss, the Pax, the "anathema"
against the schismatics (in Rom. 16 we find the same combination,
in this case the warning against heretics) and the *charis*-formula
("The grace of our Lord Jesus Christ be with you"), with which still
today in the Eastern Mass the celebration of the Eucharist begins,

are the framework in which the great petition "Our Lord, come" appears with St. Paul. Also at the end of Revelation, the Invocation of the Lord is followed by the *charis*-formula: "The grace of our Lord . . ." (in 2 Cor. 13:13, we already find the trinitarian form used in the Eastern liturgies). All this shows that one and the same prayer asks for the coming of the Lord in his advent in glory and for his coming in the Sacrament. Each celebration of the Lord's Supper is both memorial of the past, of his first advent when he died as the Lamb of God for the forgiveness of our sins, and anticipation of the future, of his advent in glory. So the Sunday, the day of his resurrection, becomes the "Lord's Day," which in the Old Testament means the day of the advent of the Messiah (Amos 5:18). He who will come in glory on the Last Day comes already now, on every Sunday, in every celebration of the Sacrament to his Church. This is the reason why the Sanctus belongs to the liturgy of the Eucharist. The Church on earth, which is still sojourning in the world of sin and death, and the Church in heaven unite in singing the "*epinikion*," the hymn of victory, the Sanctus sung in the presence of God (Is. 6; Rev. 4). So it is not only the Word of Christ in which he promises his coming, but also the Sacrament that sustains the Church on its journey through the desert of this present world into the promised land of the future. These are not theological speculations but biblical thoughts, as 1 Corinthians 10:1ff.; Hebrews 11:13; and the discourse of Christ on the bread from heaven in John 6:32–58 show.

Christian hope is always hope for the coming Redeemer. It is a serious question for all churches today whether we have not neglected this truth and lost something without which the Church of Christ cannot be, without which also for the individual Christian a true spiritual life is impossible. The appearance of more and more books and essays on the problem of Christian hope show that Christendom becomes aware of the great danger that something may be lost that is essential to the Christian faith. The book by Moltmann we have mentioned is one example. What is impressive is the energy with which he emphasizes the necessity to understand Christ and to speak of him as the coming Christ. "Christological statements do not only say who he was and is. They imply also statements on what he will be and what is to be expected from him. They all say, 'He is our hope' (Col. 1:27)" (p. 3). Whether Moltmann has been able to carry out this program is a different question.[5] But he has started a theological movement that will go on.

"Come Lord Jesus": in these words the entire content of the Christian hope is expressed. This is the hope for the great day when "every eye will see him, every one who pierced him" (Rev. 1:7), when all men will recognize him, also they who have seen him here, heard him speaking, and rejected him when he walked on this earth as the humble servant of God obedient to the Father unto death. This "revelation" of Christ in his glory (1 Cor. 1:7; Gal. 1:12; 1 Peter 4: 13) will inaugurate the end of the world, the resurrection of all dead, the Last Judgment, and the final redemption (Rev. 21:3f.). Joyfully the Church is looking forward to that day. But it is not only the hope of the Church of the New Covenant that will find its fulfilment, and not only the hope of the fathers in the Old Testament. The Church has always taught that this hope is as old as the Gospel and that means as old as the world. It has always been the doctrine of the Christian Church that also in the immemorial time before Abraham there has been true faith in the world. Among those believers of old was Adam. One of the great icons of the Eastern Church shows Christ's *descensus ad inferos*, Christ entering as victor the realm of the dead. There he meets Adam, who through the endless ages has been waiting for the Second Adam, his Redeemer. A deep biblical truth is contained in this scene. The hope for the Redeemer is as old as fallen mankind. It is certainly permissible to find in the many myths who speak of a Redeemer traces of a truth that was known to mankind. Paul calls those who

---

[5]His strength is the thorough systematic discussion of the problem, also with modern philosophers (especially Ernst Bloch, *Das Prinzip Hoffnung*, Vol. I, 1959). One definite limitation lies in his understanding of the Sacraments (see p. 301). The congregation that celebrates the Lord's Supper is not only "Waiting and expecting congregation, seeking communion with the coming Lord." In the Sacrament (this applies also to Baptism) the future is really anticipated. The Presence of Christ is not to be understood as a sort of Hellenistic cult mysticism that has replaced the original merely eschatological sacrament. What is the Church if Christ is not really with us? More exegetical studies and a deeper understanding of the New Testament as Word of God are required before we can expect to reach a new understanding of the New Testament concept of hope.

do not know Christ men "who have no hope" (1 Thess. 4:13). This applies most certainly also to pagans who had been initiated into certain mystery religions and wrote on their graves "reborn in eternity" ("*renatus in aeternum*"). There is no hope apart from Christ. But even behind the demonic perversions of paganism, there may be a last reminiscence of a redeemer who saves from death, as the Buddha of the Northern Buddhists, who is regarded as a sort of savior, shows still traces of that Christ who was once preached in Central Asia and was forgotten when the Church was destroyed. Mission work means to call those "who have no hope" to him who is also their only hope, and in some cases this call may mean to call them back to him whom their ancestors may have known.

Thus hope in the New Testament has a worldwide horizon. The most astonishing fact, however, is that St. Paul finds hope even in the entire creation, which "waits with eager longing for the revealing of the children of God; for creation was subjected to futility . . . by the will of him who subjected it in *hope*" (Rom. 8:19ff.). The salvation Christ brings will also include the redemption of the creation from the curse of death. This means, since we know no life in nature without death, that a new world will replace this universe, a new heaven and a new earth (Rev. 21).

Thus Christian hope opens to us the vast horizons of the redemption brought about by the death and resurrection of Christ, which will be consummated "soon," as he says in Revelation 22:20. But this great work of redemption comprises the life of every one who believes in Christ and shares the hope of all believers. We should never forget the significance of each individual in the sight of God. The Te Deum, the mighty praise of God in which angels and archangels, cherubim and seraphim, and all heavenly powers with the Church in heaven and the Church on earth praise, confess, and magnify the Triune God closes with the voice of hope of the individual Christian soul: *In te Domine, speravi, non confundar in aeternum,* "In thee I have hoped, O Lord, let me never be put to shame."

H. SASSE

THE REFORMED THEOLOGICAL REVIEW
Vol. XXVII, No. 1, January–April 1968

Apostles, Prophets, and Teachers: Some Thoughts on the Origin of the Ministry of the Church

Paper read at an open meeting of The Tyndale Fellowship of Australia at Ormond College, University of Melbourne, July 11, 1960.

The Primitive Church knows three offices that never can be transmitted by men, but are given solely and immediately by God: the offices of the apostle, the prophet, and the teacher (*didaskalos*, doctor). This is the innermost nature of these great offices that have been discussed so often since the discovery of the "Didache" and its publication by Harnack in 1884. It is misleading to characterize them as "pneumatic" or "charismatic" in contradistinction from other offices. For in the Early Church, every office presupposes a "charisma," as, for example, the gifts of "helps" and "governments" (1 Cor. 12:28) belong to the offices of the "deacons" and "rulers" ("*proistanenoi*" or "*episkopoi*," Rom. 12:7ff., comp. Phil. 1.1) in the local church "*Pneumatikoi*," filled with the Spirit, are all office bearers, and even all members of the Church (Gal. 6:1), for the Church as the "Israel after the Spirit" is the people of God in which the prophecy of the Spirit that is to be poured out upon all flesh has been fulfilled (Joel 3:1ff., Acts 2:16ff.).

The fact that all offices of the local church are transferred by men does not abolish their charismatic, pneumatic character. It is the general conviction of the Early Church that the same Spirit that "bloweth where it listeth" is given by the laying on of hands through men. The local church decides who should have the *"protokathedria"* (comp. Matt. 23:6) and be received into the state of the elders. The individual church can elect and ordain bishops and deacons (Did. 15:1), or it confirms their election where this is the privilege of the presbytery as the representation of the Church (e.g., Rome, 1 Clem. 44:3). Also an individual office bearer, be it an apostle (Paul, 2 Tim. 1:6) or a representative of an apostle (1 Tim. 5:22), can appoint and ordain a minister (the congregation through its presbyters concurring, 1 Tim. 4:14).

However, in the cases of an apostle, a prophet, or a teacher, it is God who calls immediately. These offices are not transmitted by way of an ordination. It was not an ordination when the Church of Antioch "set apart" Barnabas and Saul with prayer and laying on of hands for the work whereunto the Holy Spirit had called them (Acts 13:1ff.). Both had been for a considerable time at Antioch, Barnabas obviously as a prophet, Paul as a teacher, when they were sent out to the mission field on the basis of a prophetic utterance (comp. 1 Tim. 4:14). Paul would never have regarded this as the beginning of his apostolic office. It was a commissioning for a special task of men whose ministry went back immediately to the call of God. The fundamental difference between such divinely given office and another one into which men may call must be upheld, even if it is up to the Church or to a local church to examine whether a man claiming to be an apostle is a real apostle of Christ, whether the prophet is a true or a false prophet (1 John 4:1f) or the teacher a teacher of truth or a heretic, a man who has received the divine charisma or one who has made himself a teacher (Hermes, Sim. IX 22, 2, comp. James 3:1). It may be that the recognition of the divine call into one of the three great offices looks very much like the action in which a person is called by the assembled congregation into one of its offices. But the difference remains and must be recognized as essential.

Still in another respect the unique character of those three offices becomes evident. All other offices in the Church are offices of a local church. The offices of the *presbyteros, proistamenos, hegoumenos, episkopos*, and *diakonos* are limited to one place. Polycarp was bishop of Smyrna. When he came to Rome, he was honored as such. He was even allowed to celebrate the Eucharist. But he could do that only by permission and on behalf of the local bishop. The apostle, by contrast, can exercize the functions of his office everywhere, irrespective of local office-bearers, as, for example, Paul and Peter did in Rome. This universality belongs to the nature of the apostolic office (Matt. 28:19; Mark 16:15; Acts 1:8). But also the prophet and the teacher belong to the entire Church. Even if they are no longer migrating, itinerant prophets and teachers occur still for some generations, or if they exercise their office in one place and are there even leaders of the local church, yet their authority as prophets and teachers transcends the limits of this individual church, as the authority of Hermas and the claims of the Montanist prophets show.

II.

Though the "triad" is clearly distinct from all other offices in the Church, it is not always easy to draw the borderline between these three. Already the concept of the "apostle" defies an unambiguous definition, as is shown by the remarkable fact that even among the apostles themselves there was no full agreement as to who could claim that title. Paul certainly did not measure up to the standards of Acts 1:21f., where it is regarded as necessary for an apostle to have been an eyewitness of the earthly days of Jesus. Yet even James recognized him, in contrast with strict Judaists. James the brother of the Lord (Acts 15:13, 22; 21:18; Gal 1:19) is himself an exceptional case. What does the word "apostle" mean in the cases of Barnabas (Acts 14:4, 14; 1 Cor. 9:6) and Andronicus and Junias (Rom. 16:7)? Who are "all the apostles" (1 Cor. 15:7)? It is obvious that apart from the ordinary use of "*apostolos*" (*shaliach*) as "messenger" in the widest sense (e.g., 2 Cor. 8:23; Phil. 2:25) this word has a theological meaning. Though any messenger may be called *apostolos*, and especially any missionary, as the Didache seems to do, (Eph. 4:11 introduces the term "evangelists" for such missionaries), the biblical concept of an apostle implies that he is a messenger of the Gospel sent directly by Christ and a "witness of the resurrection" (Acts 1:22; 1 Cor. 15:7). This explains why this office belongs to one generation of the

Church. And only a very limited number of persons within this generation were "chosen by God as witnesses, who ate and drank with him after he rose from the dead," and were commanded to preach to the people and to testify that he is the one ordained by God to be judge of the living and the dead," as Peter puts it in Acts 10:41f. Thus the apostles are preachers of the Word in a particular sense. They proclaim that "which we have seen with our eyes, which we have looked upon and touched with our hands, concerning the word of life. . . ." (1 John 1:1) *The task of the apostle is to testify to the Word Incarnate of which he has been an eyewitness.*

If the apostolic office has to be understood in this way, it is clear why this office is the first in the triad. The sequence "apostles, prophets, teachers" is not only a logical one, as Rengstorf thinks. (Kittel WB z. NT vol. II, p. 161, 13ff.). The "first," "second," "third" (1 Cor. 12:28) indicates rather a "hierarchical" order, just as in the *Te Deum* the "*gloriosus apostolorum chorus*" precedes the "*prophetarum laudabilis numerus*" and the "*martyrum candidatus exercitus*" (see already Cyprian, *De mortalitate* 26: "*Illic apostolorum gloriosus chorus, illic prophetarum exultantium numerus, illic martyrum innumerabilis populus ob victoriam coronatus*"). This is confirmed also by Eph 2:20, where the Church is said to be built upon the foundation of the apostles and prophets. The message of the apostles is more than any prophetic message can be, as to bear witness to the incarnation is more than to proclaim the coming of the Messiah. Both, however, belong together. There would not have been the apostles of the New Testament without the prophets of the Old. And the New Testament prophets had to stand side by side with the apostles. Even if the content of the prophetic message after the Incarnation has become different, the nature of prophecy has remained the same. As in Israel, so in the Church the prophet is a man, or a woman, for there are female prophets in the Church (the daughters of Philip, Acts 21:8; Maximilla and Priscilla etc.), though they are not allowed to speak in the church service (1 Cor. 14:34), as we have prophetesses in the Old Testament (Miriam, Deborah, Hulda) through whom God speaks his Word to certain men at a certain hour. This is not only true of a man like Agabos, who reminds very much of the prophets of Israel, but of all prophets of the Church, of Judas and Silas in Jerusalem (Acts 15:32), of Barnabas, Simon Niger, and Lucius in Antioch, of the anonymous prophets who went down from Jerusalem to Antioch with Agabos (Acts 11:27), of the prophets whom we find in the Pauline churches and in the Church of the Didache, and it is true also of all prophets whom the Church has later recognized like Ammia and Quadratus (Eusebius, h.e. V, 17, 3). To all applies the simple definition of the prophet that we find Exodus 4:15 and 7:1. God puts his Word in a human mouth.

As always in the history of prophecy, there was the danger that a prophet might falsify the word given to him, that he might listen to the voice of his own heart rather than to the voice of God, that he might proclaim dreams instead of the revelation of God (Jer. 23:25ff.) and thus become a false prophet. Hence it was the duty of the Church from the beginning to distinguish between true and false prophecy. For fear of committing the sin against the Holy Spirit (Did. 11.7), the Christians were often hesitant to pass a definite judgment. It took a long time until the Montanist prophecy was rejected. Even Tertullian never did recognize the heresy of the prophets from Phrygia. It is significant that on this occasion the words of Jesus on the Paraclete, especially John 16:13f. became of importance. While Montanus (as later Mani and Mohammed) referred the promise of the Paraclete to himself, the Church saw that no genuine prophecy could go beyond the revelation of Christ. For the task of the Paraclete, the Holy Spirit, is to explain the revelation in Christ: "He shall glorify me: for he shall receive of mine, and shall shew it unto you" (v. 14). It is worth noticing that in this connection the enthusiasm of ancient Christian prophecy was rejected.

If Miltiades wrote in his book, "A prophet must not speak in ecstasy," he made the same point as Paul in his statement that "the spirits of the prophets are subject to the prophets" (1 Cor. 14:32). It has often been observed that prophecy for Paul is not essentially a speaking in a state of enthusiasm. The prophets who arise in the Church of Corinth are what we would call preachers and liturgists. The same is true also of the prophets who, together with the "teachers," act in the services of the Church according to Acts 13:1ff. and Didache 10:7; 15:1ff. To them is entrusted what Luther calls "the preaching office or oral word." Since the Holy Ghost teaches and helps to pray (Rom. 8:26f.), it is also the task of the prophets to say "in the spirit" (comp. the *"Dominus vobiscum"*—*"Et cum spiritu tuo"* before the liturgical prayer), the solemn prayer of the Church, especially the Eucharist, which the "unlearned" own with "Amen" (1 Cor. 14:16). While others are bound to the liturgical formula, the prophets are allowed "to give thanks as much as they will" (Did. 10). It seems that in the solemn language of the ancient liturgies the inspired prayers of the early Christian prophets resound.

III.

If it is not easy to draw a clear borderline between "apostles" and "prophets"—both can be united in some cases, as the book of Revelation, which is ascribed to an apostle, shows—it is still more difficult to distinguish between the offices of the prophet and the teacher. We hear that Paul was a "*didaskalos*" in Antioch before he went as a "missionary" to Cyprus and Asia Minor. In both cases he made use of his office as apostle, for it was by no means essential for an apostle to be a migrating missionary (see the Twelve and James in Jerusalem). That a teacher gave up his position in order to go to a mission field (see Matt. 23:15 for the synagogue) seems to have occurred more often, as in the case of Pantaenus, the first leader of the school of Alexandria, who went to "India." It might seem that the teacher was more inclined to a stationary life than a prophet or apostle, though his authority extends over the whole Church, even if he remains in one place. As Aquinas was "doctor" for the whole Church, whether he taught in Paris or in Naples, or Rome or Viterbo—the medieval usage of "doctor" for the magister who had the right to teach everywhere was in a way a restoration of the ancient office of the *didaskalos* ("doctor," *Vulg*)—so the authority of Origen was the same, whether he taught in Alexandria or in Caesarea. As the task of the medieval doctor of the church was the exposition of Scripture, so also the "doctor" in the Early Church was mainly an expositor of the Scriptures. While the apostle is the witness to the Word Incarnate, the prophet a man entrusted with the task to proclaim orally the word that God gives him, the *didaskalos* is the interpreter of the written Word. The Pauline Epistles, but also the Epistle to the Hebrews, which is the work of an unknown Christian teacher, show how this duty was discharged. It becomes at the same time evident that the Christian *didaskalos* is the succesaor of the Jewish teachers, the scribes. Paul's theological method, as well as the history of Jewish and Christian theology in Alexandria, prove this.

The dangers connected with this office had been seen by Jesus when he characterized the vanity of the scribes who "sit on Moses' seat," in other words, the cathedra of the synagogue from where the teacher, seated like Jesus when he taught (Luke 4:21; 5:3; Matt. 5:1; etc.) and like the Christian bishop later, interpreted the Scriptures. Proud of their liturgical vestments (Matt. 23:5), they demanded the *proto-kathedria* in the synagogue and the *protoklisia* at meals. They wanted to be addressed by their titles. "But be not ye called Rabbi; for one is your *didaskalos*, even Christ; and all ye are brethren. And call no man your father upon earth; for one is your Father, which is in heaven. Neither be ye called *kathegetai* (teacher—has the evangelist intentionally avoided the word *didaskalos*?), for one is your *kathegetes* even Christ." So strong was the oriental usage of "father" for the teacher that soon the Church was full of fathers (papa as title of the bishop, abbes, abuna, etc.) in spite of Christ's warning, and the vanity of the Christian rabbis (*didaskaloi, doctores*) was not less than that of their predecessors in the synagogue.

The first schools in Christendom of which we hear are the great gnostic schools in Alexandria. Within a generation or two, the *didaskaloi* had turned the Church upside down, so much so that in the middle of the second century, orthodox Christendom seems to have been a minority. When in Alexandria by the end of that century the Church began to recover, Clement was actually still a gnostic, and even the great Origen, a faithful Christian confessor, the greatest scholar and teacher of the Greek Church, was of so doubtful orthodoxy that nearly three hundred years after his death the Church had to excommunicate him.

IV.

The office of the apostle ceased with the death of the last "witnesses of the resurrection." Their work lived on in the apostolic writings, which now became Holy Scripture. The offices of the prophets and the teachers degenerated, but the functions of the "triad" continued. It was the great turning point in the history of the Christian ministry when the functions of the apostles, prophets, and teachers were taken over by the ministers of the local church. Ephesians 4:12 (apostles, prophets, evangelists, pastors, teachers) already seems to indicate this development. The Pastorals no longer speak directly of such offices. *Didache 15* shows how that process went on: "Elect for yourselves bishops and deacons worthy of the Lord . . . for they also minister to you the ministry of the prophets and teachers. Therefore despise them not; for these are they that are honored (*testimemenoi*) of you with the prophets and teachers."

If we want to understand this process, we must realize that the Church of the New Testament does not know the difference between what we call "Church" and "congregation," Church Universal and local church. It was in the beginning of the second century only that Ignatius made this distinction by introducing the term "Catholic Church" for the Church Universal in contradistinction from the "*plethos*" (see the usage in Acts) as the local church. *Ekklesia* (LXX for *qahal*) is the assembled people of God. There is only one people, the Israel after the Spirit, Christ's "*qahal*" (". . . *mou ten ekklesian*" Matt. 16:18). It is the same people in every place where it is assembled (comp. Matt. 16:1b with 18:15–20), as later for Paul each local church is the Body of Christ, not a body or a part of the Body.

This *Ekklesia* exists first in Jerusalem, and even when the faith has spread through Palestine and Syria to Damascus and Antioch, it remains the Church with Jerusalem at its center, where the apostles rule together with the presbyters as the representation of the "*plethos*." Here in Jerusalem the great question is decided that has risen in Antioch concerning the Gentiles who accept the Christian faith. It seems that for a long time the Church of Jerusalem as the "First Church of Christ" or the "Mother Church" has regarded itself as the Church, of which all other congregations are daughters to Jerusalem as the Jewish diaspora were to Jerusalem. Maybe the collection Paul took up for the poor saints in Jerusalem was regarded as a Christian version of the Jewish "*didrachma*," a sort of Peter's penny.

When the apostles left Jerusalem, and James, the brother of the Lord, became the first monarchial bishop, the beginning of a Christian "caliphate" that lasted to the end of this Jewish Church— the center of gravity shifted to the Church of the Gentiles. There was no longer a geographical center. The Church, the people of God, existed in each individual church, each local church being so to speak a colony of the people of God, whose home is the heavenly city, the New Jerusalem. "Our commonwealth is in heaven from where we await as savior the Lord Jesus Christ who will transform our lowly body . . ." (Phil. 3:20f., comp. Heb. 13:14; Rev. 21:2). As strangers and as sojourners, the people of God live in this world. "The Church of God which sojourns in Rome" writes an epistle "to the Church of God that sojourns in Corinth" (1 Clem. 1:1 "*paroikusa*"; it is strange to observe the development of the meaning of "*paroika*" from "exile" to "parish").

Each of these smaller or larger groups has to organize itself. Though Christ has not left a law in this respect (an "*ordo quo Dominus ecclesiam anam gubernari voluit*"), there are some patterns that are followed in freedom. There is the pattern of Jerusalem. The fact that the number of the deacons remains seven even where this number is insufficient shows a tendency to regard each local church as a replica of Jerusalem. From the holy city seems to stem also the institution of the elders. The *presbyteroi* are the "honored" men who have the *protokathedria* in the service, who as a body (*presbyterion* 1 Tim. 4:4) represent the "*plethos*," and out of whom the governing officers are elected, the *episkopoi* who with the *diakonoi* are responsible for the administration of the Church, especially for the arrangement of the Sunday service (in Rome the *diakonoi* are also taken from the presbyters). All this follows the pattern of the synagogue, but under the influence of Jerusalem.

It may have been also the influence of Jerusalem that caused the institution of the monarchial episcopate. As with all institutions of the Church, this also developed first in the East. At the time of Ignatius, we find it in Antioch and Asia, but not yet in Rome, where, as Ignatius knows, there is not one bishop but still the college of *episkopoi*. Only about A.D. 140 is the constitution of the East introduced here also. The college of the *episkopoi* has shrunk to one person. This bishop is in the Ancient Church not the ruler of a "diocese" but the chief pastor of a city, including its nearest environment. The colleagues of the bishop are now the presbyters (for a very long time the bishops have regarded their presbyters as colleagues, not as inferiors). The seven deacons are still the assistants of the bishop, who is in many cases elected from their numbers (Athanasius). The constitution was finalized when the local clergy, and among them primarily the bishop, took over the functions once exercised by the apostles, prophets, and teachers. In this sense a man like Polycarp is called (*Mart. Poll* 16, 2) "*didaskalos apostolikos kai prophetikos, episkopos tea en Smyrne katholikes ekklesia*" (the first example for the usage "*katholikos*" for "orthodox").

V.

A last word may be in place as to the way in which the functions of the old triad were conferred on the local ministry. There was no law about it, but in several customs, as in the beginning of all institutions in the Church, there is a variety that only later develops into uniformity. We know of cases when an apostle ordained his substitute or successor as Paul ordained Timothy and Titus. These, then, ordained other men (1 Tim. 5:22; Titus 1:5). In other cases, as indicated in Didache 15, the assembled Church seems to have acted without an apostle or prophet. In any case either the "plethos" or the "presbyterian" as the *ecclesia representativa* took part in the laying on of hands (1 Tim. 4:14; 2 Tim. 1:6). "Prophecy" seems also to have played a great role in ordinations (1 Tim. 4:14; Acts 13:1ff.). The laying on of hands was widely used and did not always mean the beginning of the ministry as such, as Paul's "ordination"' by the Church of Antioch shows. This laying on of hands is a pre-Christian custom practiced in the synagogue following the example of the ordination of Joshua by Moses. Jesus practiced laying on of hands in other cases, but not when he called or ordained his apostles. The Jewish rabbis, who used to ordain their disciples in this way, gave up that gesture after the Church had begun to ordain by laying on of hands. In John 20:22, we hear that Jesus instead of laying his hands on the apostles breathed on them. This gesture has been preserved at the ordination of deacons in the Ethiopian Church, as in many cases churches at the fringe of Christendom have preserved rites and institutions that have disappeared in the great churches due to the trend towards uniformity.

This has to be kept in mind in the discussions of the problem of the "apostolic succession." It is a dogmatic over-simplification of history if Clemens Romanus describes the origin of the Church's ministry in this way: God sent Christ; Christ sent the apostles. "Having received his instructions and being fully assured through the

Resurrection of our Lord Jesus Christ, they went forth with confidence in the Word of God: and with full assurance of the Holy Spirit, preaching the gospel . . . And so, as they preached in the country and in the towns, they appointed their first fruits . . . to be bishops and deacons of them that should believe. And this was no novelty, for of old it had been written concerning bishops and deacons; for the Scripture says in one place, 'I will set up their bishops in righteousness and their deacons in faith.' Our apostles knew also, through our Lord Jesus Christ, that there would be strife over the dignity of the bishop's office. For this reason therefore, having received complete foreknowledge, they appointed the aforesaid, and after a time made provision that on their death other approved men should succeed to their ministry . . ." (1 Clem. 43f.).

This is a dogmatic interpretation of history, not a report of what actually has happened. The artificial character of this reconstruction of what was supposed to have occurred is confirmed by the quotation from Scripture. For this quotation of Isaiah 60:17 is not literal. In order to make the passage prove what it ought to prove, the text is altered so as to speak of bishops and deacons. This is the first of the "forgeries" for which the Church of Rome has become famous: an authentic text is changed into what it ought to be. It is significant that this has happened in the first document we have from the Roman Church, long before there was a papacy, and even before there was one bishop in Rome. In the same way the famous list of the succession of the Roman bishops must be understood, which Irenaeus (*Ad haer.* III, 3, 2) has preserved. It is an artificial construction of a list of twelve names from Linus as the first to Eleutherus as the twelfth. All the names are genuine. It may even be assumed that all of them were bishops. But the first eight can have been only members of a college of bishops, as even Roman scholars admit today. But then the "succession" is artificial.

It must also be kept in mind that the succession here is not a succession of consecrations, as we today understand the *successio apostolica*, but rather a succession of incumbents of an episcopal see irrespective of how these incumbents were ordained and by whom. Though the Roman fiat, and also those of other churches, are much more valuable because they contain excellent historical traditions, they may be compared to the artificial list of successions with which the Mishna Treatise "*Pirqe Abot*" begins: Moses has ordained Joshua, Joshua the prophets, the prophets ordained the men of the "Great Synagogue"—a mere fictitious group of men—and from them the ordination has been given to the rabbis.

The truth behind the list of successions as they were made since Hegesippus and behind the various ideas of an apostolic succession, be it a succession of men who followed each other on a certain episcopal see, or of consecrations, is the continuation in the office of the bishop of the great offices of the apostles, prophets, and teachers. It is the continuation of the Word of God in its various forms, in the oral proclamation, in the interpretation of the Scriptures, in the witness to him who is the Word Incarnate.

THE REFORMED THEOLOGICAL REVIEW
Vol. XXVII, No. 2, May–August 1968

Erasmus, Luther, and Modern Christendom

The encounter between Erasmus and Luther in their controversy on free will has always been regarded as a major event in the history of the Reformation and, beyond that, in the history of human thought. It seems, however, that only now—after the Second Vatican Council and in the great crisis all Christendom is facing at the end of the second millennium of Christian history—the full implications of that encounter become manifest.

I.

If in 1517, the question was asked, Who will be the reformer of the Church? Who is the man able to help the Church bring about that reform for which all Christian hearts in Europe are longing, only one name could be mentioned: the great Erasmus of Rotterdam. Had he not all the qualifications for such a work? He was a man of the Church and has remained to be that, whatever else he was otherwise. Born as a son of a priest, he had some of those secret faculties one observes in the history of Protestantism with certain theological leaders who as sons of the manse have been able to exercise an influence on the Church, for better or in some cases definitely for worse, which seems to have been denied to others who had to confess that they were not "a prophet's son." One may think of men like Schleiermacher, Ritschl,

Harnack, Barth, and Tillich. Erasmus's love for the Church was unrequited. His unhappy youth, the wrongs done to the boy after the early
death of his parents, his experiences in the Augustinian monastery
where he had made his vows in 1488 without a real vocation to the
monastic life, the disappointments of the young priest who had taken
Holy Orders in 1492, the grave disappointment with the theology of
late scholasticism he studied at a poor college at Paris: all this could
not quench his secret love for the Church. This unrequited love speaks
even from the bitter Voltaire, like criticism of clergy and monks in
his "Praise of Folly" (*Moriae Encomnion*) of 1509. Since this book,
taken by its author later always slightingly, became the greatest literary success, its satire on the clergy—as on other dignities—became
most widely known. The Church has never forgiven that, though later
he published much more pungent writings, such as "*Julius exclusus*"
after the death of Julius II (1513), in which he shows the pope appearing in all his earthly glory at the gate of the heavenly paradise only
to find himself excluded. It was such sarcastic criticism that made
Erasmus suspect of being a heretic, though at the bottom of his heart
he always remained a man of deep catholic convictions, just as his
great friend Thomas Morus who in his "Utopia" anticipates the most
dangerous ideas of the later Enlightenment, but who died as a martyr
for the papal supremacy.

The depth of Erasmus's love for the Church became manifest
when the second great power entered his life: the new learning of
humanism. What the Church and the service in the Church could
not give him, this new movement offered him: the satisfaction of the
deepest longing of his mind, both intellectually and spiritually, and
a great life-work becoming this mastermind of Europe. This is not
the place to describe the rising of Erasmus as one of the stars of the
first magnitude on the sky of the new intellectual life of Europe. His
repeated stays in England led him into the highest strata of European society. In Italy he broadened his horizon and became the great
master of the classical languages and the connoisseur of the Greek
and Latin literatures. Latin was henceforth the language in which
he thought and wrote, the great European who was equally at home
in all countries of Western Europe. One must see this man reading proofs and writing in the great printers' shops from Venice to
Basel. Secular rulers as well as princes of the Church were seeking

his friendship and treated him as their equal. Though he had been freed by the pope of his monastic vows as early as 1517 and later ceased to wear the garb of a priest, he remained in his heart a son of the Church. As later for Kant the quest for God and the knowledge of God was the quiet motor behind his entire philosophy, so for Erasmus this learning was meant to serve the Church. His amazing knowledge of the great writers of pagan antiquity did not make him a pagan, as happened in the case of many humanists in Italy. He sided, as his great friends Colet and Morus in England, with the Christian Platonism of Pletho and Ficino at Florence. The ideal of later English and German classicism, the reconciliation of ancient culture and Christian religion, was the great program he left as his bequest to the coming centuries.

II.

Thus Erasmus developed a great program for the reformation of the Church. The new learning of humanism was supposed to be able to offer what the old sterile scholastic theology could obviously not provide: the means of carrying out the reformation of the Church. His program was the battle cry of the humanists: "*Ad fontes*" "back to the sources." The Church is corrupt. It is not only moral decay that is responsible for the state of the Church, which Erasmus knew better than anybody else, much better in any case than that pious and naive monk at Wittenberg who could not believe that such scandals as the indulgence trade had not the full approval of the pope. The real corruption is the corruption of true Christian piety. Erasmus is fully prepared to accept the dogma of the Church, all the Sacraments, and the ecclesiastical institutions. What he complains about is the deformation of the religious life into mere external practices and the failure of the clergy to lead their flocks back to true Christianity at that time. The "*Devotio moderna*" in the Lowlands, cultivated mainly by the Brethren of the Common Life at Deventer who had helped to educate him, as also Luther was at least for one year their pupil at Magdeburg, is the exception. The immortal "*Imitatio Christi*" is the lasting monument to this late medieval piety. But for the vast majority of the Christians Christianity had become a system of external rites. This was also the experience of Calvin who grew up in the shade of the Cathedral of Noyon. "You venerate saints; you are glad to touch their relics. But you condemn what good they have left, namely the example of a pure life. No worship of Mary is more gracious than if you imitate Mary's humility. No devotion to the saints is more acceptable and more proper than if you strive to express their virtue. You wish to deserve well of Peter and Paul? Imitate the faith of one, and the charity of the other—and you will do hereby more than if you dash forth and back to Rome ten times," says a famous passage in the "*Enchiridion Militis Christiani,*" written in 1501 (quoted here from "Desiderius Erasmus, Selected Writings, Edited and translated by C. Olin, 1965, p. 8"). In the same book, he points out that it is much better to understand one single verse of a psalm well and by this to deepen one's spiritual life than to chant the whole Psalter without attention.

This corruption of Christianity can be overcome only by the return to the sources of true Christianity in Holy Scripture and in the fathers of the first centuries. So he provides the Church with these means of a reformation. The first is his "*Instrumentum Graece,*" the Greek text of the New Testament with a new Latin translation of his own and annotations partly of a critical nature, for example, without the *Comma Johanneum* he later restored to please his conservative critics. The work is not a model of an edition. It was published in a hurry to put it on the market before the much more valuable text of Vol. VI of the "*Polyglotta Complutensis*" by Ximenes, a masterpiece of Spanish humanist scholarship (finished in 1514) had been published (it appeared with the whole work in 1520). The first printed editions of the fathers, beginning with his beloved Jerome, followed. Already here we notice that for Erasmus as for the medieval schoolmen the Scriptures and the fathers belong together. In contradistinction to Luther, for whom the Bible proper was always the Old Testament, he shares with modern Catholicism the one-sided emphasis on the New Testament. This every Christian should be able to read in the vernacular. Even the farmer behind his plough and the weaver at his shuttle should sing from it.

III.

What do we find if we go back to the sources? We find the true and uncorrupted Christian religion, the "philosophy of Christ" as

Erasmus likes to call it. He develops this idea for the first time for the laymen in his *"Enchiridion Militis Christiani,"* written at the request of a lady to help her husband to take interest in religion and published in 1503. This "philosophy" is, of course, not a philosophical system like that of Aristotle. It is practical religious and ethical wisdom. It includes the understanding of one's self, the understanding of Christ as the *Sanctus sanctorum* and teacher of all holiness. It comprises faith in God, trust in Christ, and belief in divine forgiveness. Besides Christ, Paul is the great teacher of Christianity. One favourite word was to Erasmus always Galatians 5:1: "For freedom Christ has set us free; stand fast therefore and do not submit to a yoke of slavery." In these and other words, he comes very close to the Reformation of Luther. The border was so fluent that adherents and foes of the Reformation began to see him as an ally of Luther. "Luther has only hatched the egg Erasmus has laid," said Erasmus's critics.

Nowhere Erasmus's program on reformation of the Church becomes clearer than in his "Paraclesis," the preface to his edition of the New Testament of 1516. Why is it that at a time when people devote themselves to their studies, "this philosophy of Christ alone is derided"—one is reminded of Schleiermacher's complaint in the first of his speeches—"by some, even Christians, is neglected by many, and is discussed by few, but in a cold manner . . . Platonists; Pythagoreans, Academics, Stoics, Peripatetics, Epicureans not only have a deep understanding of the doctrines of their respective sects, but they commit them to memory, and they fight fiercely in their behalf, willing even to die rather than abandon the defense of their author. Then why do not we evince far greater spirit for Christ, our Author and Prince? Who does not judge it shameful for one professing Aristotle's philosophy not to know that man's opinions about the causes of lightning, about prime matter, about the infinite? And neither does this knowledge render a man happy, nor does the lack of it render him unhappy. And do not we, initiated in so many ways, drawn by so many Sacraments to Christ, think it shameful and base to know nothing of his doctrines, which offer the most certain happiness to all? . . . Certainly he alone was a teacher who came from heaven. He alone could teach certain doctrine, since it is eternal wisdom, he alone, the sole author of human salvation, taught what pertains to salvation. . . . Why do not all of us ponder within ourselves that this must be a new and wonderful kind of philosophy since, in order to transmit it to mortals, he who was God became man; he who was immortal became mortal." And this philosophy should be made accessible and known to all men, also the peasant and the weaver.

> "Why do we restrict a profession common to all to a few? For it is not fitting, since Baptism is common in an equal degree to all Christians, wherein there is the first profession of Christian philosophy, and since the other Sacraments and at length the reward of immortality belong equally to all, that doctrine alone should be reserved for those very few whom today the crowd call theologians or monks, the very persons whom, although they comprise one of the smallest parts of the Christian populace, yet I might wish to be in greater measure what they are styled."

This seems to be, incidentally, the passage where Erasmus comes closest to the doctrine of the Reformation in the universal priesthood of all believers and where he differs more widely from the views expressed on *"De libero arbitrio"* about the role of the theologian in the Church: "If anyone under the inspiration of the spirit of Christ preaches this kind of doctrine, inculcates it, exhorts, incites and encourages men to it, he indeed is truly a theologian, even if he should be a common labourer or weaver" (Olin p. 97f.). This "philosophy," which is located more truly in the disposition of the mind than in syllogisms, life more than debate," "easily penetrates into the minds of all, an *action in special accord with human nature.*" "What else is the philosophy of Christ, which he himself calls a rebirth, than *the restoration of human nature originally well formed*?" (p. 100).

IV.

But why did Erasmus not become the reformer of the Church? Many reasons can be given and have been given why after years of wavering he made the decision against Luther and for Rome. The reluctance of the man of letters to sacrifice the quiet and peace of his study and the printing shop to the role of a fighter in the publicity of a tumult-ridden world has played a great role. "I prefer the present sad state of things in the Church to the new tumults" is one of his sayings. On the other hand, one should not forget that also Luther was not a fighter by nature either. He also resented being drawn out of his quiet cell in the monastery and from his studies into the scenes of public controversies and political fights. He was no revolutionary. By nature shy, he easily gave in during personal discussions, as Melanchthon critically observed. Also of Luther it might sometimes have been said what Paul's adversary said of the apostle: "His letters are weighty and strong, but his bodily presence is weak and his speech of no account" (2 Cor. 10:10). Repeatedly has Luther later expressed his regret that, at the advice of his well-wishers, at the Diet of Worms he spoke like a humble and modest monk instead of acting the Elijah. Luther was never the hero of a Luther film. What then was it that led him out of the monastery and the lecture hall into the wide publicity of the Reformation with all its implications? Why did Luther become the reformer and not Erasmus?

The answer to this question became evident in the great controversy Erasmus opened in 1524 with his "*De libero arbitrio Diatribe*," to which Luther gave his answer in what to the end of his life he regarded as his best book besides the Catechism: "On the Bondage of the Will," "*De servo arbitrio*." Although Erasmus tried to continuethe debate, it ended without further result. But the two books in which the two great men exchanged their views on the deepest question of the Christian faith, stand out, despite their literary weaknesses, as the monuments of one of these great debates in which the deepest questions of mankind is at issue.

V.

Erasmus chose a good topic when he decided to heed at last the numerous exhortations of outstanding adversaries of Luther to prove his orthodoxy by writing against Luther. The "*assertio*" 36 among the 41 articles, condemned by the Bull "*Exsurge Domine*" and defended by Luther so forcefully in his "*Assertio omnium articulorum*" of 1521 and its German version of 1522, had been: "Free will after the fall is a mere name; and he who acts according to his own power ('*facit quod in se est*') commits a mortal sin" (from his Heidelberg thesis 13). It is against this denial of the free will that Erasmus writes. He points out that he has read Luther's defense of his thesis without prejudice but that Luther has not convinced him. He confesses that he has approached the question with an open mind since it has occupied the philosophers and theologians at all times. What he does not like is Luther's way of making firm assertions even in matters on which the greatest scholars are not agreed, on mysteries that even the Bible does not teach with unambiguous clarity. There are passages in which the bondage of the will seems to be undoubtedly taught. There are others that seem to teach the freedom of the human will. He discusses Old Testament proofs supporting the free will, such as Ecclesiasticus 15:14–18; Genesis 4:6f; Deuteronomy 30:15–19; and admonitions in the prophetic books. From the New Testament he takes passages like Matt. 23:37 and 25:14–30, the calls and exhortations extended by our Lord and his apostles. A subsequent chapter (the book is not divided by the author himself) deals with "some scriptural testimony that seems completely to contradict the freedom of the will" (Winter p. 45), namely Paul's discussion of the election of Israel (Rom. 9–11) with the Old Testament references to the hardening of Pharaoh's heart, the destiny of Jacob and Esau, and the clay in the potter's hand. In his interpretation Erasmus follows mainly Origen. Luther, he says, "would be victorious were it permissible to interpret Scripture according to his momentary whim, while we would not be permitted to follow the interpretation of the church fathers nor produce our own" (60). Erasmus concludes his criticism of Luther's views with a refutation of the arguments in Luther's *Assertio*, heavily borrowing from the critique Bishop Fisher of Rochester had written and with a postscript on some more apparent arguments against the free will. There is hardly one pertinent passage of the Scriptures that is not at least briefly mentioned. He gives his own view in this statement: "We oppose those who conclude like this: 'Man is unable to accomplish anything unless God's grace helps him. Therefore there are no good works of man.' We propose the rather more acceptable conclusion: Man is able to accomplish all things, if God's grace aids him. Therefore it is possible that all works of man be good." He adds the summary statement on the Scriptures: "As many passages as there are in Holy Scripture mentioning God's help, as many are there establishing the freedom of the will. These passages are innumerable" (Winter 78). The final verdict of the great humanist is this: "It has been made plain that the opinion, as I have been elucidating it, when accepted, does not eliminate the pious and Christian things Luther argues for concerning the highest love of God; the rejection of exclusive faith in merits, works, and our strength, the complete trust in God according to his promises. Hence I want the reader to consider whether he thinks it is fair to condemn the opinion offered by the church fathers, approved of for so many centuries by so many people, and to accept some paradoxes which are at present disturbing the Christian world. If the latter are true, I freely admit to my mental sloth and inability to grasp. I know for certain that I am not resisting the truth, that I love from the bottom of my heart true evangelical liberty, and that I detest everything adverse to the Gospels."

VI.

The history of human thought knows of cases where two great men, occupied with the same problems, are simply unable to understand each other. They are unable, to grasp—to use Erasmus's word—one another's ideas. They talk to each other, but as it were on different wavelengths. No mutual understanding seems to be possible. A case in point in our time is the correspondence between Harnack and his former student Barth after the appearance of the latter's "Commentary on Romans." There is a certain truth in Barth's saying that they are not the worst theologians who simply do not have the ability to rethink the thoughts of others. But this does not explain the depth of the contrast between Erasmus and Luther. For Luther knew what Erasmus meant to say. He saw deeper than anybody else what was at stake. He saw behind Erasmus's concept of an undogmatic Christianity the coming neo-paganism of the modern world.

This is the reason why in his great reply in "*De servo arbitrio*," before entering the discussion of the individual Bible passages, he attacks his adversary's basic understanding of Christianity. Erasmus had confessed his dislike of not only Luther's firm "assertions" but of any religious dogma whatever: "You would," says Luther, "take up the skeptic's position if the inviolable authority of Holy Scripture and the Church's decisions permitted you to do so, so little do you like assertions. What a Proteus the man is to talk about 'inviolable authority' and 'the Church's decisions' as if you had a vast respect for the Scriptures and the Church, when in the same breath you tell us you wish you had the liberty to be a skeptic" (WA 18,603, quoted from Packer-Johnston, p. 68). Over against Erasmus's undogmatic Christianity Luther emphasizes in the most powerful way that Christianity is essentially a dogmatic religion and that he who destroys the Christian dogma or tried to play it down, as Erasmus does in his "philosophy of Christ," destroys the Christian faith: "*Tolle assertiones, et Christianismumtulisti*," "Take away the assertions, and you take away Christianity." "Why, the Holy Spirit is given to Christians from heaven in order that he may glorify Christ and in them confess him even unto death—and is this not assertion, to die for what you confess and assert?" (WA 18, 603; Packer 67). "The Holy Spirit is not skeptic."

Erasmus, who was always preoccupied with the practical, ethical aspects of his philosophy of Christ had no sense whatever for the dogma of the Church. This he left to the theologians—for whom he, on the basis of his experiences, had never much respect—and to the leaders of the Church to whose teaching authority he submitted though he was fully aware of all their weaknesses. Luther's conviction that a Christian must be prepared to die for the assertions, for the dogma of the true Churc,h almost seemed to be absurd to him. How can one die for what is not essential?

VII.

Erasmus based his rejection of the "assertions" on the fact that the Bible contains mysteries our human mind cannot grasp. He recognized the presence of a mystery also in the doctrines of the Bible on God's grace and the human will, but we should not speculate. For the Christian it is enough to do what he can to obey God's commandments, to repent where he has failed, to use the means of grace offered by the Church, to believe in the grace of "God who by nature is kindness itself" (Packer, 75). But we should not try to understand the divine mysteries that are beyond our understanding. Luther's answer to this is that you must distinguish between the mysteries of God he has not yet revealed to us and what he has revealed in his Word. Here the deep difference between Luther's and Erasmus's understanding of the Bible becomes evident. It is in this discussion with the great humanist that Luther has developed his profoundest thought on Holy Scripture and its authority and perspicuity. The entire argument of Erasmus's writing is based on the assumption that Holy Scripture must be interpreted in the light of the Church fathers and the teaching authority of the Church. Only thus he had been able to reconcile the various Bible passages. Without this necessary commentary, the Bible would be to Erasmus a dark book, full of irreconcilable statements. What Luther in "*De servo arbitrio*" calls the "*claritas Scripturae*" does not exist for Erasmus, because he, the great man of letters, can understand the "clarity" or "perspicuity" of a literary work only as "logical systematic harmony between its various parts and passages" (as H. Iwand puts it in his German edition of "*De servo arbitrio*" Munchen 1940, p. 317f.). This concept of perspicuity, which, unfortunately, has later become that of the old Protestant orthodoxy, is not identical with the "*claritas*" of Holy Scripture Luther teaches over against Erasmus. Luther knew always as an exegete how many problems the Bible poses to the interpreter, how many questions we cannot answer. Luther has never taken lightly the tasks the exegete has to face. During his whole life, he constantly tried to improve his own understanding of the Bible. But for him there was one thing in which the Bible is absolutely clear to the believing Christian who accepts it as God's own Word. Holy Scripture teaches with great clarity Christ. Christ is its proper content. "*Tolle Christum e scripturis, quid amplius in eis invenies*? (WA 18, 606). "Take Christ from the Scriptures and what more will you find in them?" (Packer 71).

But what does this mean? That Christ is the content proper of Holy Writ was known to every medieval theologian. The question is this: Which Christ? Is it Christ, the new Moses, the supreme lawgiver of the Middle Ages? Is it the Christ of Ritschl and Harnack who differed from all other men by his knowledge that God is a loving Father? Is it the demythologized Christ of Bultmann and his radical or less radical disciples? If we want to understand Luther's view, we have to remember first what he had to say against Erasmus concerning the "assertions," the dogmas of the Church. There is not such a thing as an "undogmatic Christianity," no faith in Christ without a definite Christology. There are assertions concerning

Christ in which the Christian rejoices and for which he is prepared to die. What these assertions are is clearly stated in the sentence that precedes the "Take Christ from the Scriptures . . .": "What solemn truth can the Scriptures still be concealing, now that the seals are broken, the stone rolled away from the door of the tomb, and that greatest of all mysteries brought to light that Christ, God's Son, became man, that God is Three in One, that Christ suffered for us, and will reign forever" (Packer 71). In other words, the great Trinitarian and Christological dogmas of the Church, the Blessed Trinity, the incarnation of the Eternal Son, his atoning death "for us," his bodily resurrectionm and his reign in glory—this saving Gospel is the content proper of Holy Scripture.

Why could Erasmus not understand that? What is the deepest reason for his rejection of Luther's Reformation? He believes in the Scriptures as the Word of God. He believes in God, in Christ. He believes in the grace of God, but he cannot accept the "*sola.*" Scripture, yes, but not *sola scriptura.* The authority of the fathers and the Church must be added. He believes in grace, but he cannot accept the "*sola gratia.*" Man has to do his share. In the last analysis, his doctrine of grace is contained in that medieval word Luther rejected in his famous thesis: "*Homini facienti, quod in se est, Deus non denegat gratiam.*" "To man who does what he can God does not refuse his grace." He believes in God, but he has not entirely lost his belief in man. He is fighting for the dignity of man who is not totally lost, who has retained free will and can co-operate with the divine grace. He has never been able to understand the depth of human sin.

For the depth of human sin, the misery of fallen man who cannot be anything but a sinner and cannot be saved except by the salvation brought by Christ is not a truth of human reason. Philosophers may teach the bondage of the will in the sense of determinism as the Stoics did. But they will never be able, as philosophers, to understand Luther's doctrine *de servo arbitrio* because they cannot understand what original sin is, that deep corruption of human nature that no reason can know, as Luther said, but which must be believed on the strength of God's Word. The Christian doctrine of sin is inseparably linked with the doctrine of Holy Scripture as the Word of God. For it is this book that we do not judge, but that judges us.

IX.

The great controversy between Erasmus and Luther has never come to an end. It goes on even today. We who belong to one or the other of the great churches that grew out of the Reformation may be inclined to side with Luther and Calvin—over against Erasmus. Not Erasmus, but Luther became the reformer in the sixteenth century. But who will be the definite victor in the great controversy remains to be seen. In the years after World War I, it seemed that a revival of the theology of the reformers would shape the future of Protestantism. Today Erasmus seems to be winning the day. His was the religion of Goethe, whose doctrine of salvation was a new version of the old "*Homini facienti, quod in se est . . .*" when we read at the end of Faust, Part II: "*Wer immer strebend sich bemüht, den können wir erlösen*" ("Whoever strives with ceaseless endeavor, him we can save"). Is not Erasmus with his moderation, his tolerance, and his dislike of any dogma the father of modern Anglicanism and Protestantism? And is not Erasmus also the father of modern Catholicism? It was his doctrine of sin and grace that prevailed at Trent. And who can read the documents of the Second Vatican Council without being reminded of Erasmus's great attempt to reconcile the Church and the rising modern world in a tolerant and broad-minded Catholicism? Modern ecumenicity with its compromise on Scripture and tradition and its belief in the ability of all men of good will to accept the Gospel, or what has been left of it, shows Erasmus as the man in whom Catholicism and Protestantism may meet today. But there are and will be Christians and churches who will maintain the doctrines of the Reformation, knowing that without this heritage modern Christendom would sink into a new paganism. For humanism, even Christian humanism, rests on the belief in man. It is the oldest heresy in the world, as old as the word of the tempter: "*Eritis sicut deus*," "You will be like God."

THE REFORMED THEOLOGICAL REVIEW
Vol. XXXVIII, No. 1, January–April 1969

Salvation Outside the Church?

In piam memoriam Augustin Cardinal Bea

In the early hours of November 16, 1968, Augustin Bea, Cardinal Deacon of S. Saba, died in Rome at the age of 86. Until the last days of his life, he had been working. Manuscript after manuscript, finished with the help of his indefatigable secretary, Father Stefano Schmidt, S.J., left the quiet apartment in the Collegio Brasiliano on the Via Aurelia. A short illness terminated his life as he had desired. He did not want to be a burden to anybody, but rather "vanish" when he could no longer work. His life went out like a candle. The pope visited him and they took leave in a touching way. The ceremonies observed at the death of a member of the Sacred College were kept to a minimum and held in great simplicity. Then the body was transferred through the rainy November of Italy across Switzerland, where the summits of the Alps shone in the glory of a late autumn day to Bea's hometown in Southern Germany, where the funeral took place in the old parish church. Church and state, ecumenical and other organizations were represented through their highest dignitaries. The secular as well as the church papers were full of eulogies, while in Australia the impending cricket season overshadowed even in some ecclesiastical papers the death of one of the greatest churchmen of our time.

The last publication the late cardinal made accessible to the present writer was the script of a talk he planned to give over Radio Vatican at the end of September to commemorate the twenty-fifth anniversary of the great Bible encyclical "*Divino afflante Spiritu*" in which Pius XII concluded an era of hot controversies and quiet work concerning the doctrine of Holy Scripture that Leo XIII had opened in 1893 with "*Providentissimus Deus*" (see our article "Rome and the Inspiration of Scripture," this Review, June 1963). Three great scholars stand out among the many theologians involved in this great endeavor to find a new understanding of the Bible. John Henry Newman saw in the last years of his life that it was necessary to interpret the doctrine of the inspiration of Scripture as it had been defined by Vatican I. Even if his attempt to answer "a burning question of the hour" may be regarded as unsatisfactory, he has not deserved the harsh treatment he received from his critics in Ireland. The whole material has now been published by J. D. Holmes and R. Murray, S.J., in a highly important book: "On the Inspiration of Scripture; John Henry Newman" (London, Dublin, Melbourne: G. Chapman, 1967.) Newman, the great humble Oxford don, was in contrast to his simple-minded brethren in Ireland always aware of the fact that Jesus Christ had died also for the academics and that the wise men of the modern world, historians and scientists, must be allowed to bring what gifts they may have to the child in the manger just as the magi of old. The second is the great biblical scholar Pere Lagrange, O.P., who did his quiet work at the Biblical Institute of Jerusalem while the modernistic controversy was raging through Europe. The Third was Augustin Bea, since 1924 Professor, later Rector of the Pontifical Biblical Institute. Under Pius XI and Pius XII, whose confessor he was, he succeeded in building up the Bible Institute as the center of all biblical studies in the entire Roman Church. The encyclical of 1943, which reflects his thought in every sentence, was the crowning success of his life work. In it Rome has definitely accepted and put into the service of the Word of God the literary and historical scholarship of the modern world without giving up the dogma of the Bible as the Word of God in writing.

Bea was fully aware of the multitude and complexity of the problems still unsolved. As the encyclical and the corresponding constitution "Dei Verbum" of the Second Vatican Council look still into the future, so also his last paper is more than a remembrance of the past. It envisages even the task of the future lexicography of the New Testament.

While his merits in the field of biblical scholarship will always remain undisputed as the real achievement of his life, it is doubtful whether the same can be said of the second work that has made him famous throughout the Christian and even the non-Christian world of today: his activity in the field of the Ecumenical Movement, and especially as the head of the Secretariat for Christian Unity. It fell to him to become the leader of the "progressives" at the council. A lot of misunderstandings have arisen out of this. The greatest perhaps is to regard him as a "liberal." Even Protestants should know he was a Catholic of blameless orthodoxy, a man with a deep devotion for Mary. He had been a member of the Commission for the dogmatisation of the Assumption of 1950. He was deeply sorry about the breakdown of ecclesiastical discipline and even of disintegration of the substance of faith in wider circles of the Roman Church. He regarded this as a transitory disease. His attitude toward Christians of other denominations must be understood from two great facts. The first is his knowledge of the true situation of the Roman Church. His experience in the long years of his teaching office in the Bible Institute—where he had become the teacher not only of the future professors of Scripture, but also of many future bishops, perhaps the majority of them—had given him an exceptional insight into the real life of the Church and its clergy. His close association with Pius XII during the most critical years of the Catholic Church in Europe and the world had revealed to him the true situation of the Church. He had come to see how utterly unfounded was that triumphalism that prevailed in

Rome still at the time of the rise of fascism, which coincided with the beginning of the Ecumenical Movement. He realized what the Ecumenical Patriarchate had already seen and proclaimed in 1920, that all churches of Christendom were facing the same problems and emergencies, bound together by a common destiny. The second fact one must bear in mind in order to understand him was his burning love for all men, Catholic and non-Catholic Christians and non-Christians. It made him the undisputed leader of the Ecumenical Movement in the Roman Church, which was slowly rising during the last decade of the pontificate of Pius XI and which became the official policy of the curia when the new pope, John XXIII, opened a new era of the Roman Church and summoned the Second Vatican Council to renew the Church.

One cannot understand Cardinal Bea's attempt to solve the ecumenical problem as he saw it unless one realizes the ecclesiological situation of the Roman Church as had been determined by another great encyclical of the year 1943, "Mystici Corporis." This document was the first attempt on the part of the papacy to finalize the doctrine of the nature of the Church, which had remained the great open question of Vatican I. The development of ecclesiology had meanwhile become one of the foremost theological problems in all Christendom, and the Roman theologians were waiting for guidance from Rome. Their hope that the basic understanding of the Church would be the Church as the people of God was disappointed. Pius XII started with the definition of the Church as the Body of Christ and regarded as members of the Church only those who have been baptized and profess the Catholic faith and are not separated from its unity by schism, heresy, or ex-communication. We have given an account of this document in this review (Vol. XX, Oct. 1961, p. 73ff. "The Second Vatican Council"). The true Church of Christ is, according to this view, identical with the Roman Catholic Church. Other Christians "may be related to the mystical Body of the Redeemer by some unconscious yearning and desire. . . . Let them enter Catholic unity . . . and be joined with us in the one organism of the Body of Jesus Christ . . . with open arms. We await them, not as strangers, but as those who are coming to their own father's house" (Myst. Corp. English Translation 102).

In the article noted, which was written during the preparations of the council, we mentioned what seems to be the great contribution of Cardinal Bea to the ecclesiology of the Second Vaticanum, the introduction of the term "separated brethren" ("*fratres sejuncti*") for baptized Christians who are separated from the Church in the sense of "*Mystici Corpori,*" by a schism or heresy they have inherited and not chosen by their own free will. We have discussed the origin of this term in the Donatist controversies of the fifth century and briefly examined its validity (*loc. cit.* 74ff.). Now after ten years have elapsed since Pope John accepted it and made it one of the basic concepts of the council, the time has come to re-examine it. It is fraught with great difficulties and contradictions. Optatus and Augustine could call the Donatists "*fratres sejuncti*" because they fully recognized their sacraments. Since the Donatists did not reciprocate this attitude, they declined to the Catholics as the communion of the "*traditores*" the name of brethren. The term may be applicable to schismatics, but it cannot be applied to heretics, to people who, even if in sincerity of their hearts, reject the orthodox Christian faith. This becomes evident if we look into the Constitution on the Church of Vatican II. It declares concerning membership in the Church: "They are fully incorporated into the society of the Church who, possessing the Spirit of Christ, accept her entire system and all the means of salvation given to her, and through union with her visible structure are joined to Christ, who rules her through the Supreme Pontiff and the bishops. This joining is effected by the bonds of professed faith of the sacraments, of ecclesiastical government, and of communion. . . ." This is what Pius XII taught in "*Mystici Corporis*." What about Christians outside the Roman fold? "The Church recognizes that in many ways she is linked (*conjuncta*) with those who, being baptized, are honored with the name of Christian, though they do not profess the faith in its entirety or do not preserve unity of communion with the successor of Peter." This would for instance refer to the Eastern Orthodox churches. "For there are many who honor sacred Scripture, taking it as norm of belief and action, and show a real religious zeal. They lovingly believe in God the Father Almighty and in Christ, Son of God and Savior. They are consecrated by Baptism through which they are united with Christ (*Christo conjunguntur*)" This would refer to Anglicans and Protestants in general, as far as their Baptism is recognized as valid. It is worth noticing that to them is not ascribed faith in the Triune God, which does not belong to the basis of the World Council of Churches. It is indeed true that many Protestants do no longer believe in the Holy Spirit as divine person. The text continues, "They also recognize and receive other sacraments within their own churches or ecclesial communities (*communitatesecclesiasticae*). Many of them rejoice in the episcopate, celebrate the Holy Eucharist, and cultivate devotion toward the Virgin Mother of God. They also share with us in prayer and other spiritual benefits. . . . Likewise, we can say that in some real way they are joined with us in the Holy Spirit, for to them he also gives his gifts and graces. . . . In all of Christ's disciples the Spirit arouses the desire to be peacefully united, in the manner determined by Christ, as one flock under one shepherd, and he prompts them to pursue this goal. Mother Church never ceases to pray, hope, and work that they may gain this blessing. She exhorts her sons to purify and renew themselves so that the sign of Christ may shine more brightly over the face of the Church."

The entire ecumenical program of the Roman Church is contained in these statements. Rome shares with the majority of the ecumenical leaders of non-Roman Christendom the conviction that the great "*Ut omnes unum sint*" of John 17 must and will be fulfilled in a visible united Church on earth. This will be achieved not simply by a return of the separated to the home church. For the Roman Church is not what it ought to be. The sign of Christ does not shine brightly enough over the face of the Church. A deep renewal of the entire Church is required if the separated brethren are to come to see the truth. This renewal must be accompanied by a dialogue with the rest of Christendom in which the Catholic truth will become credible and be accepted by all. A renewed Catholic Church will eventually be the spiritual home of all Christendom, a church which will be quite different in many respects from the present Roman Church and yet retain its undefiled heritage as it will embrace everything which is true and worthy of being preserved of the heritage of other churches and ecclesial communities.

This was the great ecumenical vision of Cardinal Bea, which was fully accepted by Pope John and confirmed by the Second Vatican Council. So the great Bible scholar became the great ecumenical theologian of Roman Catholicism. He was the true companion of Pope John. They supplemented each other theologically and spiritually. One of the secrets of Bea's success at the council was the deep humility that went hand in hand with his theological acumen and his ability to solve problems that seemed to be insoluble. Only the Church history of the future will bring out the full greatness of this man who has perhaps had a deeper influence on the Roman Church under four popes than anybody else.

What will be the future of this ecumenical work? The great danger of an ecumenical council lies in the undisputed assumption that its decisions have been made under the guidance of the Holy Spirit. This was the consolation of the dissenting minority at the First Vatican Council. The Holy Spirit had spoken. What the council wills is the will of God. So eventually all bishops accepted the decrees. The danger today is that again everyone acquiesces in the belief that the decisions of the council are the expression of the will of God for his Church and hence above criticism. No one seems to ask whether the College of the Apostles in which Peter and his successors in Rome hold the primacy can and must be regarded as the legitimate interpretation of *"Pastor Aeternus"* of 1870 and whether this theory is historically and theologically tenable.[1] What if this is not the case, as the Eastern Orthodox Church would maintain? There can be no doubt that a union between Rome and the East on the basis of Vatican II will not be possible. A Third Vatican Council would at least be required even for the clarification of the decisions made. Still more dangerous is the assumption voiced by many Catholic laymen that Vatican II has made the renewal or reformation of the Church that was overdue and that now nothing is required but to carry out the demands of the council concerning the spiritual life of clergy and laity and concerning the dialogue with the separated brethren. The merit of the post-Conciliar writings of the late cardinal lies not only in the clarification of the documents and their history, but perhaps mainly in the strong emphasis on the talks now to be faced by the Church. Stronger than any one else he has emphasized what the "Constitution on the Church" says of the Church, which "is at the same time holy and always in need of being purified and incessantly pursues the path of penance and renewal" (c.8).

But what does "penance" mean in this context? Is it the penance the Church does vicariously for "sinners in her bosom," much as Pius XII in *"Mystici Corporis"* explained the fact that the Church in the Lord's Prayer prays the Fifth Petition in the name of some of her members who are sick or wounded? Or is it the deep *"metanoia"* of the whole people of God in the sense of the New Testament? This is

---

[1] It excludes St. Paul, who could not fill the office of the lost twelfth apostle (Acts 1:20ff) and was, so to speak, treated as an unsalaried, extraordinary, part-time apostle (1 Cor. 9:1ff) until the dissolution of the college in A.D. 44 (Acts 12:2 and 17).

the question we have to put to our separated brethren in Rome. The great humble cardinal of the Roman Church was not angry when he was reminded of the word of Anselm of Canterbury: "*Nondum considerasti, quanti ponderis sit peccatum*" (*Cur Deus Homo* I, 21). How is this question of sin related to the fact of the disunity within Christendom and, consequently, with the restoration of unity lost? What else beside dialogue may be required if Christians should live in the unity of the faith?

In order to find an answer to these serious questions, we continue with the reading of the "Constitution on the Church." We have seen how non-Catholic Christians are even now "linked with" the Church. The subsequent chapter 16 goes on: "Finally, those who have not yet received the gospel are related in various ways to the people of God (*ad Populum Dei diversis rationibus ordinantur*). In the first place there is the people to whom the covenants and the promises were given and from whom Christ was born according to the flesh. . . . On account of their fathers, these people remain most dear to God, for God does not repent of the gifts he makes nor of the calls he issues (cf. Rom. 11:28–29). But the plan of salvation also includes those who acknowledge the Creator. In the first place among them there are the Muslims, who, professing to hold the faith of Abraham, along with us adore the one and merciful God, who on the last day will judge mankind. Nor is God himself far distant from those who in shadows and images seek the unknown God, for it is he who gives to all men life and breath and every other gift (cf. Acts 17:25–28), and who as Savior wills that all men be saved (cf. 1. Tim. 2:4)." We do not intend here to enter a discussion of the question of the Jews, which has played a great role at the council where the strong anti-Jewish tendencies of the Eastern churches clashed with those of Cardinal Bea who was opposed to everything that could encourage Antisemitism. The real issue between Judaism and Christianity was not even touched. It becomes clear in a confession that the great, pious Jewish scholar and Bible translator Franz Rosenzweig has made in a letter in 1935: "we do not go along with the world-conquering fiction of Christian dogma, because . . . it is a fiction . . ." and declares: "that we crucified Christ and, believe me, *would do it again at any time*, we alone in all the wide world (and *fiat nomen Dei Unius, pereat homo*, for "to whom will you liken me and make me equal?") (quoted from Kornelis H. Miskotte, *When the Gods Are Silent*. Translated by John W. Doberstein, London 1967, p. 315f.). We have to accept this statement. Between the Christian and the Jew stands a different understanding of the First Commandment. The only exception we would have to make refers to the proud "we alone." Also today there would be a Pontius Pilate, and how many Christians would recognize Christ if he came we do not venture to say. It has a deep significance that in the Western Liturgy of Good Friday the "Improperia," the reproaches of God against his people, are answered by the "misere nobis" of the Church.

One of the strangest passages in "*Lumen gentium*" is what it says about the Muhammedans. Have we really in common with them the belief in God, the Creator? "I believe in one God the Father Almighty, maker of heaven and earth . . . and in one Lord Jesus Christ . . . by whom all things were made." This is the Christian belief in the Creator. And what does it mean that the one and merciful God will judge on the last day the world? The Nicene Creed confesses of Jesus Christ, "He shall come again with glory to judge the living and the dead," and the new creed of Paul VI, published on the June 30, 1968, says, on the basis of the *Symbolum Quicunque*: "He ascended to heaven, and he will come again, this time in glory, to judge the living and the dead: each according to his merits—those who have responded to the love and piety of God going to eternal life, those who have refused them to the end going to the fire that is not extinguished—And his Kingdom will have no end" (Latin in Oss. Romano July 1–2, here quoted from "The 'Credo' of the People of God," Melbourne 1968). The works of God "*ad extra*" are always the works of the Triune God. The articles of the creed are not to be separated. The religion of Mohammed is not a less perfect, but a false religion; his God is not our God. The "Declaration on the Relationship of the Church to Non-Christian Religions," says of the Muslims: "Though they do not recognize Jesus as God, they revere him as a prophet. They also honor Mary, his virgin mother; at times they call on her, too, with devotion." Does this bring them closer to the Church? It is not reverence, but blasphemy to rob Jesus of his divinity and to regard him as a prophet, subordinate to Muhammed. And what has the virgin birth, of which Muhammed had heard from Christian sects to do with the "*Qui conceptus est de Spiritu Sancto, natus ex Maria Virgine"* of the Christian creed? If there ever was a false prophet in the world, it was that man who took away from the Church the vast majority of Christians in the Orient. The Church of former centuries has trembled at the mystery of iniquity, the Antichristus Orientalis. This has led to deplorable political conflicts no one wants to repeat. But has the Church not perhaps more to say than what the "Declaration on the Relationship of the Church to Non-Christians" says: "This most sacred Synod urges all to forget the past and to strive sincerely for mutual understanding. On behalf of all mankind, let them make common cause of safeguarding and fostering social justice, moral values, peace, and freedom." Is that the message of the Church of Jesus Christ to the world of Islam?

St. Francis of Assisi and Ignatius of Loyola were of a different opinion. So was Francis Xavier when he took upon himself the tremendous labours of preaching the Gospel to the nations of Eastern Asia. For he was of the naive conviction that without faith in Christ and without the Sacrament of Baptism no one can be saved. He believed that on the basis of the Fifth Session of Trent, where the Church teaches of original sin that it cannot be taken away by any other remedy except the merit of our Lord Jesus Christ and that this merit is applied by the Sacrament of Baptism, in the form of the Church rightly conferred (*per baptismi sacramentum, in forma ecdesiae rite collatum*, Denz. 790 = 1513). If the text leaves still any doubt whether there might be another way of conferring the merit of Christ than Baptism, such doubt is removed by the Sixth Session on Justification, where cap. 4 (Denz. 796 = 1524) clearly teaches that the justification of the sinner cannot, after the proclamation of the Gospel (that means after the coming of Christ) happen without the washing of regeneration or the desire of it (*sine lavacro regenerationis aut eius voto fieri non potest*), whereby John 3:5 is given as Scripture proof.

This is what Francis Xavier would have replied to Hans Küng, who tells us that the old great missionary could have saved himself the unspeakable trouble of walking through the hot sand of India believing that all those pagans would go to hell unless he had baptized them. The problem of the eternal destiny of the pagans who did not know anything of Christ and his Gospel has been a problem for the Church at all times. Origen's universalism was rejected, though it has remained a power in the Christian East. The West accepted Augustine's stern view of the unbaptized pagans as a *massa perditionis* in spite of the undeniable virtues of the great men of the ancient pre-Christian world which to Augustine were specious vices. Exceptions were made by the apologists who believed in the enlightening activity of the Logos in the pagan world. They knew of Christians ante Christum, as the Sibyls who prophesied the Messiah. Even Augustine had his pagan saint Plato, whose philosophy he regarded as having been influenced by Old Testament prophets. The great exception for Dante was Virgil, whose Fourth Ecloga with the Sibyllic prophecy of a savior has played a great role since Constantine made it a subject of an Easter Sermon. At the request of Mary and another heavenly lady freed from hell, Virgil is Dante's guide through the beyond. The Fourth Canto of the "Inferno" describes the first circle of hell in which the fathers of the Old Testament since Adam lived until Christ in his descent liberated them. But there are still the great men and women of the pagan world. They live there without pain, but without hope for redemption. This was the view of the Medieval Church. It could not believe that unbaptized persons could go to heaven. Hell was an indispensable part of God's creation, as Dante writes on the gate of hell:

> Fecemi la divina potestate,
> La somma sapienza e il primo amore.

"To rear me was the task of Power Divine, Supremest Wisdom and Primeval Love." Also hell, the place of eternal pain and hopelessness to those who are eternally lost, belongs to the good creation of the Triune God, the Father (divine omnipotence), the Son (highest wisdom, the logos), and the Holy Spirit (first love). This the Middle Ages had still the courage to believe. It was humanism that transferred the virtuous unbaptized pagans into heaven. In his last writing, a letter addressed to the King of France, Zwingli, the Christian humanist, wrote of heaven, "There, O King, you will see . . . the two Adams, the redeemed and the Redeemer, Abel, Henoch, Noah . . . Isaiah and the Virgin God-bearer whom he prophesied . . . Peter, Paul, Hercules, Theseus, Socrates . . . Numa." Luther was horrified. "Say, whoever wants to be Christian, what do we need baptism, the sacrament, Christ, the gospel and the prophets, the Holy Scripture if such godless pagans, even the horrible Numa who established idolatry in Rome by the inspiration of the devil . . . should be blessed and holy in heaven together with the patriarchs and apostles . . ." (WA54, 1431).

Incidentally, Luther also had his private saint among the ancient pagans. This was, strangely enough, Cicero, whose "Officia" he preferred to the ethics of Aristotle and whose proof for the existence of God impressed him more than Aristotle's classical proofs. The answer he gives to the question of whether pagans can be saved is the only possible one: "I hope," he says of Cicero, "our Lord God may be gracious to him and other people like him. However it is not up to us to make any definitions of such nature. We must rather stick to the revealed Word: He who believes and is baptized will be saved. But that God could not give dispensations and differentiate among men of other nations, this we cannot know now and say with any certainty. There will be a new heaven and a new earth, much larger and broader than it is now. God can give to anybody according to his good pleasure."[2] This is what a great theologian had to say about this problem. Hans Kung rejects the old idea that we must be satisfied with what the Bible tells us in this matter and leave the question to God. He wants to know more and claims that the Church must give an answer in view of the vast extensions of mankind in space and time of which former generations had no idea. But statistics cannot be a source of theology.

But we look again into the constitution and read the continuation of n.16: "Those also can attain to everlasting salvation who through no fault of their own do not know the gospel of Christ or his Church, yet sincerely seek God and, moved by grace, strive by their deeds to do his will as it is known to them through the dictates of conscience. Nor does divine providence deny the help necessary for salvation to those who, without blame on their part, have not yet arrived at an explicit knowledge of God, but who strive to live a good life, thanks to his grace. Whatever goodness or truth is found among them is looked upon by the Church as a preparation for the gospel.

---

[2] W. A. *Tischreden* IV No. 3926, Vol. II, No. 2412.

She regards such qualities as given by him who enlightens all men so that they may finally have life" (16).

Karl Rahner ("The Christian of the Future," *Quaestiones Disputatae* No. 18, p. 94) says of this and the preceding statement, "Anyone who knows the history of theology and of the Church's doctrinal pronouncements will be filled with amazement at the fact that it was accepted by the council without the slightest remark." Indeed, what becomes of the biblical doctrine that without faith no man can be saved (Mark 16:16; Heb. 11:6), what of Cyprian's *salus extra ecclesiam non est* (ep. 73,21) that rings through the entire history of the Western Church, what of Augustine's doctrine of original sin and its consequences, and what of the doctrine of sin and grace with Thomas Aquinas and at the Council of Trent? Every decent atheist who strives to live a good life—of course with the help of the ubiquitous divine grace—can be saved. The First Vatican Council has spoken its anathema against any atheism: "If anyone says that the One and true God, our creator and Lord, cannot be with certitude recognized by the natural light of human reason through the things that have been created, be he anathema" (Denz. 1806 = 3026). "If anyone denies the one and true God, the creator and Lord of all things visible and invisible, be he anathema" (Denz. 1801 = 3021). What has happened in the Roman Church that these doctrines can be so easily forgotten, though the Constitution on Divine Revelation, *Dei Verbum*, expressly repeats in 6 the doctrine of the natural knowledge of God (with the enthusiastic approval of a professor of Union Theological Seminary, New York, in the "Response" in the American Edition of the Council Texts by W. M. Abbot). Should perhaps the deepest reason for the present crisis of the Roman Church become manifest in the remarkable fact that none of more than two thousand bishops who accepted this text spoke one word in defense of the old doctrine but that all took it for granted that also unbelievers can go to heaven, provided they live a decent life? How can men be atheists "without blame on their part" if every man by the light of his natural reason can with certainty know God our Creator and Lord. Has the Catholic Church abolished the First Commandment? If unbelief is no longer sin, why should a Catholic layman or priest continue to believe what the Church proposes to him as an article of faith?

"Nondumconsiderasti, quanti ponderis sit peccatum." This is what the reformers had to tell the Church of the outgoing Middle Ages. This is what the churches of the Reformation in the weakness of their divisions told unanimously to the church of the Council of Trent. This is the witness we in this ecumenical age owe to our Roman brethren. The doctrine of sin and grace should be the first and foremost topic in the ongoing dialogue between the churches. This dialogue would reveal that we all are suffering from the same disease. What has become of the deep understanding of human sin, of the complete depravity and lostness of natural man in the churches of the Reformation? We men of the outgoing twentieth century have, this is true, lost that optimistic understanding of man and human progress that prevailed in years before World War I. But our pessimism and despair are just as self-centered as that optimism was. We indulge in the feelings of self-pity and of a tragic situation of which we are not guilty. This distinguishes the desperation of modern man from the *desperatio sui* of which the reformers knew. Even Trent states that the sin of Adam is in each individual as his own sin (*Adae peccatum . . . omnibus inest unicuique proprium*, Denz. 790 = 1513). But the doctrine of the fall as an event in the dawn of all history is no longer popular. It seems to contradict what today is regarded as the scientific view of nature and man. It is true that the fall is beyond our experience and, consequently, of our imagination. "No reason," says Luther of the original sin, "can understand it; it must be believed because of the revelation of the Scriptures." No human memory goes back into the mysterious "beginning" before the fall. No prehistory, no paleontology can ever discover the place and time in which God created man and man revolted against his Creator. We know man only after the fall. He who knows man only as a product of a natural evolution, even of a divinely guided evolution, cannot understand the sin of man. Here lies the weakness of the anthropology in the great scientific—or should we rather say, gnostic—system of Teilhard de Chardin.

Whatever Christ may mean to Teilhard, he is no longer the Savior who dies for the sins of the world. With the fall of the First Adam lapses the redemption through the Second Adam whose *"typos"* the First man is (cf. Rom. 5:14; 1 Cor. 15:22, 45–59). The Gospel ceases to be the forgiveness of sins, freely given to him who believes in Christ.

And the preaching of the Gospel to the world, which is the task of the Church, is no longer the call to repentance and belief, no longer the call of the apostles in the New Testament: "Repent and be baptized every one of you in the name of Jesus Christ for the remission of sins" (Acts 2:38); "Believe on the Lord Jesus Christ, and thou shalt be saved, and thy house" (16:31); "We pray you in Christ's stead, be ye reconciled to God, for he has made him to be sin for us who knew no sin, that we might be made the righteousness of God in him" (2 Cor. 5:20f.). Such a call might be issued to the last group of men mentioned in our text: "But rather often men, deceived by the Evil One, have become caught up in futile reasoning and have exchanged the truth of God for a lie, serving the creature rather than the creator . . . Or some are who, living and dying in the world without God, are subject to utter hopelessness. Consequently, to promote the glory of God and procure the salvation of all such men, and mindful of the command of the Lord, 'Preach the Gospel to every creature' the Church painstakingly fosters her missionary work." So these are the people who are called to repentance and faith in order to save them from hell. All the rest of mankind, the non-Catholic Christians, the Jews, the Muslims, Buddhists, Hindus, and decent atheists are called to dialogue rather than to repentance.

This was not the mission of the Church in the New Testament. There is one passage in which St. Paul comes close to what today is called a dialogue, his great missionary sermon in Athens, which is expressly quoted by the constitution. Attentively the hearers listen to the message of the Unknown God until the call to repentance comes (Act 17: 30ff.). When repentance, judgment, and the resurrection of Christ are mentioned, their patience is exhausted. The call to repentance is the end of the dialogue, today as at all times.

No one can read the documents of Vatican II without being touched by the attempt of the Roman Church to renew itself. This impression is strengthened if one reads Cardinal Bea's books on the council, which are an indispensable commentary on the documents (especially "Unity in Freedom, Reflections on the Human Family," 1964; "The Way to Unity after the Council," 1966; "Church and Mankind," 1967). It is certainly a "conventional theology" that speaks according to Karl Barth from them. But it is a theology dominated by that great love for all men, which was the charisma of this man who was a sort of "Holy Father" in Rome for non-Catholics. But the great question is what will become of the "renewal" the council has inaugurated. Will it end in a true reformation of Rome, a real rediscovery of the Gospel? Or will it end in a revolution in which the substance of the Christian faith is lost? The signs of such a revolutionary decay of the substance of the Christian faith can be seen in all churches of Christendom. In a thoughtful and thought-provoking book we have already mentioned, Karl Rahner has made some statements that must cause the greatest concern everywhere, especially because Rahner is perhaps the greatest of Catholic thinkers today. He describes the situation of the Christian of the future who lives in a Church that has become a small minority in a growing non-Christian mankind. "Everywhere will be diaspora, and the diaspora will be everywhere." "Nowhere will there be any more 'Catholic nations.'" "Everywhere the non-Christian and the anti-Christian will have full and equal rights . . . and may perhaps coalesce in powers and principalities as forerunners and manifestations of Anti-Christ." "The Church will be the little flock of brothers of the same faith, the same hope and the same love." What would be the consolation of the Christians in such a situation? We would perhaps think of the fact that the Church had to live in such situation for centuries and that we should learn from the Church of the apostles, from the Church of the New Testament, how to live and what to do. Instead the *Constitutio Dogmatica de Ecclesia Christi* of Vatican II is to be our consolation and the source of faith and courage. For this constitution understands the Church as the "sacrament of the world's salvation," the sign and efficacious means of the salvation of the world, as it is God's plan. "For Christendom in earlier times the Church was the plank of salvation in the shipwreck of the world, the small barque in which men alone are saved, the small band of those who are saved by the miracle of grace from the *massa damnata*, and the *Extra ecclesiam nulla salus* was understood in a very exclusive and pessimistic sense. But here in the conciliar text, the Church is not the society of those who alone are saved, but the sign of the salvation of those who, as far as its historical and social structure are concerned, do not belong to it." This makes it possible to look at pagans and atheists as such who have a real relationship with the Church, even in their present state. "God's salvific will includes them," as the constitution puts it. This has a great influence on the missionary practice. It will be much more tolerant toward pagan rites and beliefs. The theologians with whom we have been dealing here are mainly members of the Society of Jesus. We remember the broadmindedness of the Jesuit missions in East Asia, the controversies they had in the seventeenth century with the much stricter Dominicans, as well as the missionary politics in Japan and in the countries occupied by the Japanese in our time. This broadmindedness has grown out of the Pelagianizing tendencies of the Jesuits. One must remember that the Jesuits have determined the First and the Second Vatican Council. It is a great question for Rome whether this dominating influence will remain in modern Catholic theology.

The Bible passage on which all these theologians base their understanding of God's will to save all men is, of course, 1 Timothy 2:4, which states that God our Savior desires all men to be saved and to come to the knowledge of the truth. "The passage quoted," says Rahner, "is not easy to harmonize with the absolute necessity of faith, of revelation, and the necessity of the Church for salvation which cannot be denied either" (p. 95). So he envisages a theology of the future which would recognize the "possibility and existence of anonymous Christians," this is to say of people who are pagans and yet unconsciously already Christians. It is a theology that rests entirely on logical conclusions. If God wants all men to be saved, he must give them the necessary grace even without the ordinary means of grace, the Word of the Gospel, and the Sacrament of Baptism, an unconscious faith that can co-exist with the outward profession of atheism. Since the eternal destiny of every human being is decided before death, such divine grace must be offered to all men in this life. Rahner must leave it to the theology of the future to interpret in this way the *extra ecclesiam salus non est*. This is an impossible task, the end of all Christian doctrine.

What is our answer to the great problem of how God's will that all men should be saved can be reconciled with the fact that many souls, perhaps even the majority, will be lost? We call to mind the words we quoted from Luther. We are bound to the clear words of the Scriptures and to the teaching of our Lord and his apostles about the necessity of repentance, faith, and Baptism for the salvation of man. The seeming contradiction between the clear statements of Scripture about this and 1 Timothy 2:4 cannot be solved, so Luther points out at the end of "*De servo arbitrio*" (WA 18,785), in the *lumen naturate*, the light of reason. It can even not be solved in the *lumen gratiae*, the light of grace of the Gospel. It will be solved in the *lumen gloriae*, the light of God's glory in heaven. Up to the time when we shall see this light, we have to be satisfied with the word that limits all human theology: "My thoughts are not your thoughts, neither are your ways my ways, says the Lord. For as the heavens are higher than the earth, so are my ways higher than your ways and my thoughts than your thoughts" (Is. 55:8f.).

THE REFORMED THEOLOGICAL REVIEW
Vol. XXIX, No. 2, May–August 1970

Thoughts on the Centenary
of the First Vatican Council

Compare the previous articles in this review on the Council and its decisions: "The Second Vatican Council" I (June, 1961), II (Oct., 1961); "After the Council," Jan.–April, 1966; "Salvation outside the Church?" (Jan.–Apr., 1969); "The Ecumenical Movement in the Roman Catholic Church" (Feh., 1964).

The 18th of July will be a day of remembrance for the Roman Catholic Church. It should be a day of examination of conscience and of mutual intercession for all Christians. For if the century that has passed since the last solemn session of Vatican I has taught us one thing, it is that there is a solidarity or a common destiny that binds together a divided Christendom. Every great event in the history of one church is the concern of all. Church history should have taught us this long since. Today we are learning this better from year to year. Victory and defeat, glory and shame of one church are shared by all. Therefore, each individual church should be the keeper of her sisters. To know this is the beginning of true ecumenicity.

On the eve of that fateful day, the railway station in Rome was crowded even more than on the preceding days. The bishops of the minority were departing. In a letter addressed to the Holy Father, they declared: "In the General Congregation held on the 13th inst. we gave our votes on the schema of the First Dogmatic Constitution concerning the Church of Christ. Your Holiness is aware that 88 fathers, urged by conscience and moved by love of Holy Church, gave their votes in the words 'non placet'; 62 others in the words 'placet iuxta modum'; finally, about 76 were absent and gave no vote. Others had returned to their dioceses. . . . Thus our votes are known to Your Holiness and manifest to the whole world, and it is notorious how many bishops endorse our view; in this matter we have discharged the office and duty which lies upon us. Nothing has happened since to change our opinion, rather there have been many and very serious events which do not allow us to depart from our position." This refers to a further deterioration of the document on the 16th, mainly to an insertion that declares that the ex cathedra definitions of the pope are irreformable of themselves and not in virtue of the consent of the Church (*ex sese, non autem ex consensu ecclesiae irreformabiles*). The letter continues, "Confirming our votes, we have decided to be absent from the Public Session on the 18th. For the filial piety and reverence that very recently brought our representatives to the feet of Your Holiness do not allow us in a cause so closely concerning Your Holiness to say 'non placet' openly and in the face of the Father" (quotations from Cuthbert Butler, the Vatican Council, 1967–70, Fontana Library, p. 408f.).

Bishop Ullathorne, whose letters and diaries Dom Butler was able to use as an important source, gives a touching picture of that rainy and thundery Roman summer night when the last bishops of this minority left Rome with troubled consciences, among them some of the greatest characters of the Church, men who knew what it means to suffer for the Church. Germans and Frenchmen were among them whose countries would be at war two days later. The thunderstorm continued during the following day and reached its climax when the final vote was taken, 533 voting "*placet,*" two "*non placet.*" The lightning flashed into the aula, the thunder rolled over the roof, glass was broken. Candles had to be lighted for the reading of the *Constitutio*, which began with the words "*Nos Pius . . . sacro approbante Concilio.*" The weather caused several comments. While some regarded it as sign of the divine displeasure, others compared it with the thunder on Mount Sinai.

One of the reasons why the definition seemed to be necessary to Manning and others was the political situation. When the French troops under whose protection the council could meet undisturbed had to be withdrawn, Rome was taken by Garibaldi's army, the Papal State was dissolved, and Rome became the capital of the new Kingdom of Italy. Would it ever be possible to convene another council? If this should be impossible, the pope, now in possession of the full espiscopal power over the whole Church and able to act as the infallible teacher of all Christians, could rule the Church without an ecumenical council.

The First Vatican Council was in the mind of Pope John when he planned and opened the Second Vaticanum in 1962. As this remarkable Pontiff in every respect put the helm of Peter's barque over, so he summoned a council that would be quite different from that of 1869–70. Pius IX, originally a man of liberal persuasions, had become fully aware of the revolutionary tendencies in modern Europe. He tried to help Church and mankind by establishing the authority of the Vicar of Christ as the firm rock on which the tempestuous waves of the revolutionary movements of the modern world would break. On many occasions, especially forcefully in the encyclical "*Quanta cur a*" with the syllabus of errors in 1864, he spoke the anathema against the errors of the modern world, such as pantheism, "naturalism," "fideism" (the view that God cannot be recognised by human reason), socialism, communism, secret societies, and many others, even Bible societies. It was a declaration of war on the modern civilization by the Catholic Church of the restoration. A Catholic correspondent in an article commemorating the opening of the First Vatican Council on December 8, 1869 (quoted here from "The Advocate," Melbourne, Dec. 18, 1969), states, "Perhaps it was the apparent ineffectiveness of so many anathemas hurled at so many quarters that prompted Pope John to set a different tone for Vatican II." The writer refers to the address with which Pope John opened this council on the October 11, 1962. Speaking of the errors the Church has to combat, the pope said: "The Church has always opposed these errors. Frequently she has condemned them with the greatest severity. Nowadays, however, the spouse of Christ prefers to make use of the medicine of mercy rather than that of severity. She considers that she meets the needs of the present day by demonstrating the validity of her teaching rather than by condemnations" (quoted from Walter M. Abbott, The Documents of Vatican II, p. 716).

Thus the great change in the Roman Church began. What would the fathers of 1870 have had to say about this? A few days after the opening, it became obvious that the minority of 1870 had become the majority of 1962. Since it was not an absolute majority, a crisis developed over the proposed schema of the church. The wise pope succeeded in solving this crisis by way of a compromise. But the tension remained and reflects itself in all documents of the council. It underlies the great crisis in which the church found itself after the council. The great question for Rome is whether it will be possible to let this tension become the source of a healthy development that would lead to a real renewal or whether it would lead to revolution and disintegration. The present Roman Church is not simply the Church of Vatican II. It is also still the Church of Vatican I. Both wings of the church must learn to bear with one another, knowing that what they have in common is much more than that which divides them. If anything was great in the history of Vatican I, it was the way that the minority fathers took their defeat. The bishops who had left Rome with a troubled conscience were at the same time "the most devoted and obedient sons of the Holy Father," as they called themselves in the letter quoted.

Eventually all submitted, some sooner, some later, in the spirit of that Catholic faith the council had unanimously defined in the "Constitution on the Catholic Faith" on the Sunday after Easter, 1870. An illustration of this faith is the action of one of the two dissenting bishops at the last session. When the "Constitution on the Papacy" had been read and confirmed by Pius IX, he approached the papal throne, genuflected, and confessed: "Now I believe, Holy Father" (*modo credo, Sancte Pater*). Indeed if the ecumenical council has spoken, a Catholic knows what his duty is. The patience and humility of the minority fathers had borne rich fruit when ninety-two years later the incumbents of their very sees found themselves to be the majority of the Second Vatican. The question of the future of the Roman Church is whether the bishops and priests of our revolutionary age can afford that measure of humility and patience. Only then Rome and all Christendom may with confidence look at a Third Vatican Council in which the unresolved problems of today may find a real solution.

Great as the changes are which Vatican II has brought about, the real issue remains unsolved. It is the problem of the renewal of the church, a real reformation. It is astonishing how Rome was able to carry out the most striking reforms of the liturgy and the constitution of the church. The decentralization and what could be called the democratization of the government of the church and the restoration of the episcopal office are examples. But this is no reformation of the church, and we should not speak of the Catholic reformation brought about by Vatican II. Also our Catholic brethren should know that this type of reformation has been going on also in the past. Not even the spiritual renewal of the life of priests, religious and laity is something new. For centuries this has been the program of councils, bishops, and faithful monks in the late Middle Ages. "*Instaurare omnia in Christo*" was the motto of the papacy in the beginning of this century. The more the endeavors to achieve such a reformation will be carried out, the more our Catholic brethren will discover that it is in the long run impossible to exclude the doctrine of the Church from the Reformation they desire. Touching words have come from the mouth of Pope Paul VI complaining of the decline of the spiritual life in the Church, from the highest to the lowest ranks. What disappointments had this deeply conscientious pope to experience even in his own Curia. Whatever may be said about celibacy of the clergy, there is no and cannot be any reason for a bishop to become a layman and to marry. Have we forgotten that a servant of Christ must be prepared to sacrifice everything, all earthly happiness, all earthly possessions, and even his life for the Lord and his Church? We can have only the deepest respect for the cross this pope has to bear. I heard him at a public audience after the council develop his program: the decisions of the council will be carried out to the last letter. But no other reforms will come. Meanwhile, it has become evident that the decisions of Vatican II involve so many questions that they cannot be carried out without further decisions.

These decisions will concern the doctrine of the Church. This is true also of such decisions in the field of discipline and ethics that have caused so much discussion in the whole world. What is the *ratio legis* in the case of the compulsory celibacy of the priest? Why can a married man distribute the Sacrament but not consecrate? It is a medieval interpretation of the laws concerning ritual uncleanness caused by any sexual intercourse (Lev. 15:3–19; 22:3). As soon as the Mass has to be celebrated frequently or daily, celibacy is a logical consequence. All other reasons for the celibacy are of secondary nature. Or take the controversial question of birth control. The decisions made repeatedly by former popes rest in the last analysis on the understanding of the "natural law" that goes back to Stoic philosophy. Very serious and convincing arguments can and must be put forward against the modern methods of birth control with their detrimental consequences. But Roman theology must try to get rid of the arguments of ancient philosophy that play such a role in medieval scholasticism and canon law.

But the greatest original problem Vatican II has inherited from the council of 1870 remains the doctrine on the papacy. One cannot say simply that the schema on the Church contains many problems. Unfortunately the council had not the time to deal with all of them. Even if they had years, the doctrine of the Church would not have been finalized, and for the majority and the whole Ultramontane world, and even for Pius IX himself, the papal infallibility was the great issue. If the council of 1962–65 had had the freedom to rewrite "*Pastor Aeternus*," the chapter on the infallible teaching office of the pope would have been drafted along the lines of the minority of 1870. The insertion made at the last moment that states that the definitions of the pope are *ex sese, non autem ex consensu ecclesiae irreformabiles* is perhaps the most fateful dogma of Rome. For this terrible word "irreformable" makes any reformation that would also be a renewal of doctrine impossible. This sentence has made the Roman Church irreformable. The dogma of 1870 was preceded by the dogma of the immaculate conception, the great test case of whether the church would accept a dogma from the pope.

It was followed by the dogma of the assumption of Mary, proclaimed by Pius XII in 1950. In both cases the pope had made sure by inquiries that the bishops believed them to be true. But numerous priests have left the church as a consequence of the dogma of 1950. For in fact the pope had become a source of doctrines that are not contained in Holy Scripture and not in the tradition of the Church of the first centuries. The breakdown of the authority of the pope in wider circles of the Roman Church is the necessary reaction to the exaggerations of the First Vaticanum. Paul VI has to reap the storm sown by his predecessors.

How can the Roman Church overcome this predicament? It is not sufficient to interpret the doctrines of 1870 so as to make them say what they do not say. The attempts of Vatican II to give Vatican I a new meaning by reinterpreting and augmenting it are certainly remarkable. The best minds of Catholic theology have done what they could, but the result is that the old council stands, as ever before. The greatest achievement is the new evaluation of the episcopal office and with it the status of episcopal synods and an ecumenical council. This was possible by assuming that the bishops as the successors of the apostles have an office in the whole Church. As the Twelve formed a "college," which together with Peter the First and under him ruled the Church, so the pope stands always in the college of the bishops. This made it possible to give the episcopate a new status. But there remain problems. If the chapter of "*Pastor Aeternus*" on the nature of the papal office remains, then the pope can exercise his "*plenitudo potestatis*," his full episcopal power, without the bishops. He must not consult them. It is expected that he does everything after consultation of the bishops. But this was the practice already of Pius IX and Pius XII when they proclaimed their Mariological dogmas. The difference is only that the new organization of episcopal synods will actually give to the bishops more power and that a new organization of the Church will create better means to coordinate the pope and the bishops. But as long as "*Pastor Aeternus*" stands, the pope can act without the bishops. Has any pope the moral right to renounce a power given to him according to the dogma of the Church by Christ himself? Certainly he can refrain from making use of it if this is in the best interest of the Church. But what Christ has ordained must stand.

But has Christ ordained it? When the dialogue between Rome and the Eastern churches goes on, the question of the primacy will be the dominating question. No orthodox church can ever accept the Roman concept of the primacy. The East will recognize the primacy of honor, and they will do that with great seriousness as they always have done it. But the primacy of jurisdiction as defined in Chapter 3 of "*Pastor Aeternus*" they cannot accept, because they find it neither in the scriptural passages adduced by Rome, nor in the tradition of the Early Church. And they are right. It behooves us evangelical Christians not to look at this dissent between Rome and the

East with the self-complacency of certain Protestants who boast of the *sola scriptura*, which they long since have lost. We can only with deep sadness take cognizance of the fact that not only Holy Scripture is being interpreted differently, but also the tradition of the Church that is supposed to be the key for the understanding of Scripture. Pope Paul himself has recently stated: "I know that I, the pope, am the greatest obstacle in the way of Christian reunion." He said this to the members of the Secretariat for Christian Unity, and added, "I do not want to defend our claims. You should do it and convince the other churches that this is the true Christian doctrine."

In this dialogue on the primacy, the question will become the burning issue whether every dogma ever proclaimed by the Church is "irreformable." Every serious Church historian also in the Roman Church knows that the tradition about Peter's position in the Early Church is untenable. One has only to ask how the Church of the New Testament would look if Peter had been more than the first, the spokesman within the Twelve, had he and the Church known of his office. Nowhere in the first centuries the does the bishop of Rome claim to be the successor of Peter. There is one case in the third century; otherwise he is regarded as the successor of Peter and Paul. The authority of the Roman Church rests on the fact that the two great apostles, the apostle of the circumcision and the apostle of the Gentiles have together "established" (Iren III, 3.3) the Roman Church. They handed on the "*episkope*" to Linus, who is regarded by the old list of bishops as the first bishop of Rome. This is confirmed by the liturgy (the feast of Peter and Paul, the commemoration of Paul on the feast of Peter, of Peter on the feasts of Paul; still Leo the Great preaches on June 29 on the "Princes" of the apostles) and by the archaeological finds (St. Sabina, the iconography of both, the history of their basilicas). It is generally admitted today that the claims of the Roman primacy rest solely on the interpretation of the Petrine texts (Matt. 16; Luke 22; John 22). If this interpretation should be faulty, "*Pastor Aeternus*" would lapse.

When Doellinger after the First Vatican declared he could not accept the new dogma because it contained statements on history that could be proved to be false, Manning of Westminster replied, "One must overcome history with dogma." Harnack called this a frivolous statement. He was right. One must, however, not forget that every Church historian is in the danger of subordinating history to a dogma. Harnack's picture of Jesus is certainly a case in point. The same may be said of many a famous interpreter of the New Testament in our time. The difference lies only in the fact that it is not the dogma of Rome or of any other church that dominates this false presentation of the sacred history, but the private dogmas and prejudices of the modern scholar. Theology can never invent facts, but it has to interpret the facts of the sacred history given to us in Holy Scripture.

So the Roman Church faces today the tremendous task of examining its picture of the sacred history. This then would lead to the question of whether there will be in the future a possibility of revising certain dogmas. Rome has to face this question with the same seriousness and courage with which it has grappled with so difficult problems as the Church in the modem world. In the great debates on the infallibility in 1870, the bishops who lived in countries with a strong Protestantism or on the border of Orthodox churches (Strossmayer, the Patriarch of Antioch) claimed that the proclamation of the new dogma was inopportune because it would lead to a further estrangement of the Christian churches and prevent any possible reunion. Manning's answer was this: The question is not whether the dogma is opportune or not, but whether it is true. Truth is always opportune. Deeply convinced of the truth of the dogma on the papacy, he made it clear that, if it was proclaimed, the Roman Church must stand by it until the end of the world. The only way I can see for Roman theology is that it develops a hierarchy of its dogmas, corresponding to the various grades of censuring errors (heresy, "*haeresim sapiens*," offence for pious ears, etc.) and of classifying positive theological statements (e.g., "*fidei proxima*," etc.). The immaculate conception of Mary cannot claim the same degree of dignity as the virgin birth of Christ; Mary's assumption cannot stand on the same level as the ascension of Christ. In practice this differentiation is already made. I do not know whether the Catholic dogmaticians have the freedom to discuss this possibility. It seems to be the only way that the terrible "*irreformabilis*" of "*Pastor Aeternus*" can be overcome and the way can be paved for a real reformation of the Roman Church, which is not only an improvement of the constitution of the church but a spiritual renewal that makes the Roman

Church more acceptable to other Christians. It would pave the way also to a real dialogue between the churches that still have a dogma and do not want the terrific disintegration of Christian doctrine to go on. We see this process going on in all churches of Christendom. But the loss of the dogma is the loss of Christ. For the dogma of the Church is not an invention of clever theologians and churchmen. Christ himself has established it when he asked his disciples, "Whom say ye that I am?" when he asked his adversaries, "What do you think of Christ? Whose son is he?" and when he made himself the good confession before Pontius Pilate (1 Tim. 6:14).

The greatest service Roman Catholicism has rendered to the Protestant churches in the modern world was to remind them of the fact that Christ's Church is by nature a dogmatic Church and that there can be no Christian Church without a firm and definite doctrine. Modern Protestantism since the seventeenth century has been dreaming of "undogmatic Christianity" with the result that it has lost with a sound Christology, the living Christ, and with the trinitarian dogma, the living God of the Bible. Our great concern is that Rome today, following the path of an enthusiastic Ecumenical Movement, will go the same way. We know the dangers of dead orthodoxy. But we know also what happens to churches that, in order to avoid these dangers, lose that living orthodoxy without which the Church must decay and fall. Even at the risk that in this life we shall not be able to reach full agreement on all points of doctrine, we shall not cease to strive for unity in doctrine, searching for the one truth of the Gospel that binds us together, even where we are still on the way, sinners also in our theology, but justified by faith: separated and yet brethren.

THE REFORMED THEOLOGICAL REVIEW
Vol. XXXI, No. 3, September–December 1972

On the Theology of the Cross

1.

"*Unum praedica, sapientiam crucis!*" That is the answer (in a sermon-fragment of 1515; WA 1,52) Luther gives to the vital question of the ministry of all ages: "What shall I preach?" The wisdom of the cross, the word of the cross, a great stumbling block to the world, is the proper content of Christian preaching and is the Gospel itself. So thinks Luther and the Lutheran Church with him. The Christian world regards that as a great onesidedness. The cross is just one part, among others, of the Christian message. The Second Article is not the whole creed, and even in the Second Article the cross stands in the midst of other facts of salvation. What a narrowing of the Christian truth Luther is guilty of—so we are told by some Lutherans today—by limiting real Christian theology to the theology of the cross. Is not there also a theology of incarnation and a theology of resurrection? Must not the theology of the Second Article be supplemented by a theology of the Third Article, a theology of the Holy Ghost and his activity in the Church? Luther had, indeed, very much to say about these things also, for example, in his doctrine on incarnation and in his theology of the Sacraments. Besides, he had a more profound understanding of the article of creation than most theologians who preceded him.

Thus the question arises about the meaning of that alleged narrowing, that much criticised onesidedness of Luther's *theologia crucis*. The theology of the cross obviously does not mean that for the theologian the whole Church Year shrinks to Good Friday. It rather means that one cannot understand Christmas, Easter, or Pentecost without Good Friday. Luther was, alongside of Irenaeus and Athanasius, one of the great theologians of the incarnation. He was that because he saw the cross behind the manger. He understood the victory of Easter as well as any theologian of the Eastern Church. But he understood it because he understood it as the victory of the Crucified. The same can be said of his understanding of the activity of the Holy Ghost. It is always the cross that illuminates all chapters of theology because the deepest nature of revelation is hidden in the cross. This being so, Luther's *theologia crucis* wants to be more than one of the many theological theories that have appeared in the course of the history of the Church. It claims to be in contrast to another theology that now prevails in Christendom and that Luther calls *theologia gloriae*, the correct, the scriptural theology with which the Church of Christ stands and falls. Only of the preaching of this theology, Luther thinks, can it be said that it is the preaching of the Gospel. What then is this *theologia crucis*?

2.

The Church had to go a long way until in Luther's *theologia crucis* she gained the full understanding of the cross of Christ. It has often been observed how small a role the cross plays in the theology of the Ancient Church. To be sure, the Church of the first centuries as well as the Church throughout the ages has lived by the death of Christ and has known that. Every Lord's Day, every celebration of the Eucharist made the death of the Lord a present reality. There has never been another Eucharist. Hardly another passage of the Old Testament is quoted by the fathers as often as Isaiah 53. The sign of the cross was already in the second century an established Christian custom. Christian art of the time, however, represents our redemption by showing the types of the Old Testament, not the scenes of the Passion of Christ. Not till the fourth century, and then only hesitantly, does Christian sculpture begin to represent the narrative of the Passion as one of the many Gospel stories. And theology is not able to say very much of the death of Christ either. As soon as the great question is put, "*Cur Deus homo?*" it is understood as a question for the reason of the incarnation rather than of the death of Christ. The doctrine of the cross—not yet understood as a doctrine in its own right—is contained in the doctrine of incarnation. It is also contained in the mystery of the resurrection, since what we call Good Friday and Easter were celebrated by the oldest church simultaneously in the festival of "*pascha.*" The actual event of our salvation is the incarnation: "On account of his infinite love he became what we are, in order that we might become what he is" (Irenaeus, *ad. haer.* V *pref.*). And the beginning of our redemption, of our rising from the dead, is his resurrection.

Thus for the Ancient Church, as even today for the Eastern Church, the cross is hidden in the miracle of Christmas and in the miracle of Easter. The darkness of Good Friday vanishes in the splendour of these festivals. The cross is outshone by the divine glory of Christ Incarnate and the Risen Lord. Even for a long time after the Church begins to represent Christ Crucified in its art, the glory outshines the cross. When at the end of the ancient world and in the early Middle Ages Christ Crucified takes the place *of Christos Pantokrator* in the triumphal arch of the Church above the altar, he is still shown as King and triumphant. The Christ of the Ancient Church and the Christ of the Romanesque churches of the Middle Ages does not suffer. He remains triumphant even on the cross. And the cross, too, appears always as the sign of victory rather than of suffering and death: "*In hoc signo vinces,*" "*Vexilla regis prodeunt, fulget crucis mysterium.*"

Why is that so? How is that limitation of Ancient Christianity and its theology to be explained? Certainly it must not be forgotten that the divine revelation given in Holy Scriptures is so rich that whole centuries are necessary to understand its content fully. It cannot be expected that the Church of the first ecumenical councils should already have solved the problems of the medieval Western World. But even the selection of problems to deal with was determined by the horizon of the fathers' life and thought. The Greek would have considered it bad taste to represent the scene of the crucifixion. Would you hang a painting showing a criminal on the gallows in your dining room? As to the meaning of redemption, the Greek fathers could not get away from the idealistic concepton of man. Even the great Athanasius never considered, *"quanti ponderis sit peccatum."* They all are Pelagians. For them, as for Dostoevsky and the whole of Russian orthodoxy, the sinner is basically a poor sick person who is to be helped by patient love and heavenly medicine, not, as for the Romans, a criminal, an offender of the law who needed discipline and justification. But how can I understand the cross?

> I caused Thy grief and trembling;
> My sins, in sum resembling
> The sand-grains by the sea,
> Thy soul with sorrow cumbered,
> And raised those woes unnumbered Which press in dark array on Thee.

The lack of full understanding of the greatness of sin is the reason why the Ancient Church and the Church of the East never reached a *theologia crucis.*

The *theologia crucis* belongs to the Western Church, and it starts, as does every real theology, from the liturgy. These liturgical beginnings, it is true, point back to the Orient, and in fact to the Syrian Church rather than the Greek. Did the relationship of the Syrians to the language and thus also to the thought of the Old Testament lead to a better understanding of the Old Testament Gospel of the Lamb of God? The Agnus Dei was included in the Roman Mass by a pope of Syriac origin around 700 A.D.; so too the mentioning of the Lamb of God in the Gloria originates in the Orient. Besides the original Syrian territory, Jerusalem is the place where the death of our Lord, naturally, was commemorated in a special way. Here the Church of the Holy Scripture, built by Constantine, with the alleged relics of the holy cross, became the destination of pilgrimages from all parts of Christendom and the starting point of the veneration of the

Cross, which presently spread throughout the whole Church and found its first center in the West in the Church of the "Holy Cross in Jerusalem" at Rome.

This veneration of the cross, still today a part of the Roman Liturgy of Good Friday, is so to speak the oldest form of the *theologia crucis.* For it was by the roundabout way of the veneration of the cross and of the relics of the cross that the devotion for the Crucified became an important feature of medieval Western piety. The two great hymns of the cross that belong to the liturgy of Good Friday, even today, the *"Pange lingua, gloriosi"* and the *"Vexilla regis prodeunt,"* are hymns addressed not to the Crucified but to the cross. Venantius Fortunatus wrote them about A.D. 600, inspired by the enthusiasm for the relics of the cross Emperor Justin II had sent at that time to the Frankish Queen Radegunde. The *"Pange lingua"* praises the *"Crucis trophaeum,"* the cross as the sign of victory, and addresses it, the holy cross, as the holy tree of paradise that had become the instrument of salvation. The application of that old Christian idea reminds one of the cult of holy trees that was common to the Germanic peoples:

> *Sola digna tu fuisti Ferre mundi victiman*
> *Atque portum praeparare Area mundo nanfrago Quam sacer cruor perunxit Fusus Agni corpore.*

> Tree which solely wast found worthy Earth's great victim to sustain,
> Harbour from the raging tempest, Ark that saved the world again,
> Tree with sacred blood anointed Of the Lamb, for sinners slain.

In the same way the powerful hymn of battle and victory, *"Vexilla regis prodeunt,"* addresses the holy tree (*arbor*):

> *O crux, ave, spes unica Hoc pae&swnis tempore Piis adauge gratiam Reisque dele crimina.*

> Hail, cross, thou only hope of man, Hail on this holy passion-day!
> To saints increase the grace they have; From sinners purge their guilt away.

It was a long, circuitous way that finally led, after five hundred years, from this adoration of the holy tree to the *"Salve caput crucentatum,"* the salutation of the High Middle Ages to the Crucified.

On closer examination, this oldest *theologia crucis* appears to be a typical example of what Luther called *theologia gloriae.* The cross is

a direct revelation of the glory of God on earth. Triumphantly it precedes the victorious armies of the Christian emperors and the valiant
hosts of the Church Militant. As in the first centuries, the demons
fled from the sign of the cross, so now the enemies of the Church
flee in confusion where the banner of the cross or the relics of the
cross appear. Who can resist the power of this sign? The cross is the
sign by which unfailing victory is gained. In it God's power becomes
visible in the world.

3.

A deep change in the innermost life of Christendom took place when
in the churches and monasteries of Europe the suffering of the cross
was for the first time understood. This change becomes visible in the
crucifixes of the Middle Ages. The Crucified now no longer stands as
victor on the tree of the cross, as in the Romanesque period, but he
hangs on the cross, suffering, later even writhing in pains, and dying.
This change is complete when in the later Middle Ages the great crucifixes over the chancel in the Gothic cathedrals no longer show the
Crucified as the divine victor but realistically as the man of sorrows.
The depth of the suffering of Christ is felt. The *Christies humilis*, the
God-man in the state of deepest humility, becomes the brother of
man. And the *imitatio Christi*, even in the sense of a mystic feeling
of all pains of the Crucified becomes an ideal of medieval Christian
piety. Certainly it was only a small minority of the Church people who
experienced that. But all were at least touched by that idea. The liturgy
and the whole atmosphere of the churches already took care of that.

Now it is significant that this discovery of the suffering and
death of Christ as a terrifying reality went together with a more serious understanding of sin and the remission of sin than had existed
in the Ancient Church. A great deal may be said against the medieval
doctrines of sin and justification. It is true nobody had reached at
that time the depth of the biblical understanding of sin. The whole
system of penance was faulty and even a denial of the Gospel. In
spite of all that, the observation of Claus Harms[1] remains true, that

---

[1] In his *95 Theses for the Reformation Jubilee* of 1817.

those people at least took sin more seriously than modern Protestants, including the theologians. People knew that they were sinners and needed absolution. "How shall I find a gracious God?" For a thousand years, this question moved the theology of the Latin Church before it became the question of the Reformation. For many centuries it brought the most pious men of the Middle Ages into the monasteries before it became the vital question of the last great medieval monk.

In those thousand years, Christendom had learned that the two belong together: the sin of the world and Christ's suffering, my sin and Christ's death on the cross, although it was not yet possible to find an answer to the question of how they belong together. In pondering over this problem the Medieval Church develops its *theologia crucis*.

The greatest result of this theology is the small and simple, and yet daring and profound book by Anselm of Canterbury, "*Cur Deus homo?*" Much might be said in criticism of this work, and indeed must be: the attempt to prove that the miracle of miracles is reasonable, to speculate why God had to act as he did and what forgiveness cost him, and other things besides. It remains true, however, that here the great theological concept of the *satisfactio vicaria* was thought through for the first time. Medieval theology already criticized and corrected Anselm, and often more convincingly than modern theologians have done. But the Church never took notice of the protest that has been voiced again and again against the doctrine of satisfaction. It is a remarkable fact that the doctrine according to which the death of Christ is the satisfaction for the sins of the world is the only doctrine of the Middle Ages that eventually found general assent. The medieval doctrines on sin and grace have remained in dispute. The dogma of transubstantiation has been limited to the Roman Church. All doctrines developed in the sixteenth century are limited to certain sections of Christendom. But the doctrine of the *satisfactio vicaria* has been independently dogmatized in their respective confessions by the Lutheran, the Reformed, the Anglican, and the Roman churches. For never before was this doctrine declared a dogma of the Church; the Nicene Creed does not say anything about how the "*propter nos homines et propter nostram salutem*" ("for us men and for our salvation") is to be understood. It was the Augsburg Confession that first taught that Christ "*sua morte pro nostris peccatis satis fecit*" (CA IV). The Reformed confessions teach correspondingly, and likewise the Council of Trent (*sessio* VI, 7). The Thirty-nine Articles, as far as I see, do not have the word *satisfactio.* They teach that Christ died "*ut Patrem nobis reconciliaret, essetque hostia non tantum pro culpa originis, verum etiam pro omnibus actualibus hominum peccatis.*" But in the "Homily on Salvation" this is explained: "to make a sacrifice and satisfaction, or, as it may be called, amends to his Father for our sins." This, then, is the actual contribution of the Middle Ages to the theology of the cross.

4.

If the question is raised wherein Luther's contribution to the *theologia crucis* lies, one is at first inclined to find it in the strength of faith with which Luther appropriated the full comfort of Christ's atoning work. Luther indeed experienced and showed others what it means to believe in Christ crucified and that a soul in deepest distress and despair can find peace and real life in that faith. We must, however, not forget that there was faith in Christ's saving merit and the comfort derived from that faith also in the Middle Ages. Luther himself was deeply convinced that it was this faith by which the saints of all times, the Church of all ages, had lived. When Thomas Aquinas was taken ill on his way to the Council of Lyons (1274) and knew that he was going to die, he received his last Eucharist with the words: "I receive thee, ransom-price of my soul. Out of love toward thee I have studied, passed watchful nights, and exerted myself. Thee have I preached and taught. . . ." Thus the greatest thinker of the Middle Ages leaves his uncompleted work—he was not quite fifty years old. Forgotten is all the wealth of philosophical and theological learning. The great system of thought that comprises earth and heaven, world and super-world, has shrunk to the one thing needful. Now he, like St. Paul in 1 Corinthians 2:2, knows nothing save Jesus Christ and him crucified, whose body and blood he receives for the last time on earth, the ransom-price of his soul. This Christ is the content of all theology. Forgotten is the *theologia gloriae* of the semipagan proofs of the existence of God at the beginning of the *Summa Theologica.* Forgotten the belief in the abilities of the natural man, forgotten the "triumph of theology" that Thomas had won in the overcoming of Averroism and that had become a subject of Christian art.

This Christian, this truly evangelical side of the Middle Ages, must always be kept in mind if the Reformation is to be understood rightly. The evangelical core of the Mass, the "*Tu solus sanctus*" of the Gloria; the "*non aestimator meriti, sed veniae largitor*" of the *Canon Missae*; the *Kyrie* and the *Agnus Dei*; the words of the institution of the Lord's Supper and the baptismal formula; the "*Rex tremedae majestatis, qui salvandos salvos gratis*" ("King of majesty tremendous, who dost free salvation send us") of the Mass for the dead; the constant pointing to the thief on the cross: all these things have, according to Luther, preserved the Church in the Middle Ages and are preserving it at present in Roman Catholicism. The *sola gratia*, we should never forget, is a possibility also within the Roman Church, though only one possibility among others, and only when understood in such a way that it can never become the *sola fide*. For whatever the Roman Church may be otherwise, she wants to be and also is a church of the cross, a church of the Crucified, whose sacrificial death plays a greater part in its life and thought than in many Protestant churches. God alone knows whether perhaps in our time more Catholics meet death with faith in the saving merit of Christ than do Protestants.

Luther, however, was obviously more than a Roman Catholic Christian who, like many of his fellow-believers and perhaps in a specially strong way, believed in the Crucified as his only salvation. His *theologia crucis* is different from that of pious Christians of the Middle Ages. Where lies the difference? The difference becomes visible where Luther draws the demarcation line between the *theologia crucis* and the *theologia gloriae*, while Luther in the spiritual experiences of his strife for a gracious God learned to understand what the cross of Christ means for us men. He realized, as nobody before him had done, the deepest nature of the revelation of the cross. In the cross of Christ, he saw something that, as far as we know, no one had discerned since the days of the apostles. He saw not only the depth of divine wrath, not only the immensity of the divine love, but he saw with a complete understanding of both God's love and his wrath the deep mystery of the way God comes to man. He saw the secret of God's dealing with man, the mystery of the revelation itself.

5.

What is the secret of the divine revelation? Man wants to see God, but he cannot do so. Even the great saints of God cannot see him. "Show me thy glory" ("*Ostende mihi gloriam tuam*"), Moses asks the Lord, (Ex. 33:18). The answer is this: "Thou canst not see my face: for there shall no man see me and live." But one thing God grants his servant. God's glory shall pass by, and the Lord will allow him to see his "back parts," to gaze after him: "*Videbis posteriora mea: faciem autem meam videre non poteris*" (v. 22). It is well-known how often Luther made use of this passage to clarify the nature of the perception of God. We human beings cannot see the countenance, the glory of God, however strongly we may desire it and strive for it.

The attempt to perceive God as he is, whether by observation of the world, by mystical experience, or by philosophical speculation, is the *theologia gloriae*. It is the theology of the natural man, the theology of the heathen, of the philosophers, and, most unfortunately, also of the professors of theology. These, being Christians, ought to know better. But "we theologians," so Luther remarks, commenting on Psalm 66:17, "use the blessed name of God, by which we are baptized and at which heaven and earth tremble, in disputations, and even in prayer, very irreverently. We employ the arts of keen and loquacious disputing which we have learned from Aristotle on the divine truths, so that we talk about the Blessed Trinity as the shoemaker about his leather" (WA 3, 382,7ff.). That means God became an object, a thing about which one talks. But he who talks about a thing has to stand above the thing, has to "be in command" of it, and so all theology, as Luther rightly saw, is constantly in danger of losing the right relationship toward God. In Thesis 29 of the Heidelberg Disputation, Luther says, "He who without danger wants to be a philosopher in Aristotle ought to have become first a good fool in Christ" ("*Qui sine periculo volet in Aristotele philosophari, necesse est, ut ante bene stultificetur in Christo*") (WA 1,355). Otherwise he will become a *theologus gloriae*, and that would mean he is no theologian at all. For the two theologies Luther distinguishes, the theology of glory and the theology of the cross, are not two grades of one and the same theology that would supplement each other, as the natural and the revealed perception of God in those systems of Catholic and

Protestant theology determined by Aristotle. They stand rather in a relationship of irreconcilable contrast, as false and true theology.

"He does not deserve to be called a theologian who understands, and views God's invisible nature ("*visibilia Dei*" Rom. 1:20) by his works, but he who views and perceives that which God makes visible to sight when he allows us to gaze after him by the suffering and the cross of Christ" ("*qui visibilia et posteriora Dei per passiones at crucem conspecta intelligit*"). These are the famous Theses 19 and 20 of that Disputation of 1518. Luther does not deny that it is possible to perceive by the works of creation the "*invisibilia*" of God, namely (as he himself defines in his commentary to Thesis 19), God's power, his wisdom, his righteousness, his goodness, and so on. What he denies is that this perception of God is of any use. It makes "neither worthy nor wise." It does not change our relationship to God. Men have misused the perception of God by his works, as the explanation of Thesis 20 says, "They have become fools. The perception of God by his works has not hindered anybody from falling away from God and from becoming an idol-worshipper." Thus, "it pleased God by the foolishness of preaching to save them that believe" (1 Cor. 1:21). This preaching is the word of the cross (1 Cor. 1:18). While the *theologia gloriae* understands and views (*intellecta conspicit*), the *invisibilia* of God by the works of creation (*per ea quae facta sunt*), the *theologia crucis* views and understands (*conspecta intelligit*) the *visibilia et posteriora* of God by the suffering and by the cross (*per passiones et crucem*). The theologian of glory looks upon the world, the works of creation. By his reason he perceives behind them the invisible nature of God, his omnipotence, wisdom, and goodness. But God remains for him invisible. The theologian of the cross looks upon the Crucified. Here there is nothing great, beautiful, and sublime, as in the splendid works of creation. There is nothing but "humility," "shame," "weakness,"-"suffering," and "painful death." But this frightening and depressing aspect shows the *visibilia et posteriora Dei*, that which God lets us see of himself. Here God becomes visible who in the works of creation remains invisible. That is, he becomes visible as far as he can at all become visible to mortal men, as he became visible to Moses when he was allowed to gaze after him, to see the *posteriora Dei*. The *visibilia* are the *posteriora* of God.

Thus the singular meaning of the cross is established. We do not see God in creation, but we see him on the cross as far as human eyes are able to see him. Therefore, the cross is the revelation, and the theology of the cross is the only theology that deserves the name. In the explanation of Thesis 20, Luther continues, "When, according to John 14, Philip just like a theologian of glory said: Show us the Father! Christ at once called back those thoughts which wanted to see God elsewhere and focused them on himself by saying: Philip, he that sees me sees the Father. Therefore, in Christ Crucified is true theology and knowledge of God" ("*Ergo in Christo crucifixo est vera theologia et cognitio Dei*," WA 1,862). This is repeated in the following thesis by the sentence "*Deum non inveniri, nisi in passionibus et cruce.*" This then is a firm principle of the theology of Luther and the Lutheran Church. Theology is theology of the cross, nothing else. A theology that wants to be something else is pseudo-theology.

6.

The cross is the revelation. For it is the only place where God makes himself visible. What do we mean by that? What does Luther mean when he says that we can find God nowhere else than in Christ Crucified? How is it that God is present in a special way in the cross?

To understand that, we have to ask what revelation is. Revelation occurs when something hidden comes out from its hiddenness into the open. Revelation of God is God's coming forth from his hiddenness. For God is hidden as all objects of faith are hidden. Faith after all, according to the definition of Hebrew 11:1, which Luther quotes so often, has to do with things unseen. And God remains hidden for us as long as we live on earth. He dwells in the light that no man can approach, as his Word teaches us (1 Tim. 6:16). He also said "that he would dwell in the thick darkness" (1 Kings 8:12). He is a "hidden God" (Is. 45:15) whose face cannot be seen by any man (Ex. 33:20; John 1:18; 1 John 4:12) until we shall see him in the *lumen gloriae*, "as he is" (1 John 3:2), "face to face" (1 Cor. 13:12; Rev. 22:4). But although God remains hidden to our eyes, he still reveals himself by his Word. So the revelation in the Word is the way of divine revelation in this world.

"At sundry times and in diverse manners" God spoke to the fathers by the prophets, until "in these last days," in other words now, at the end of the world, he spake to us through the Son, who is more than a prophet, being "the brightness of God's glory and the express image of his nature." He is the eternal Word who was in the beginning. This Word is the content of all written and preached words of God. About him we are told, "And the word was made flesh . . . and we beheld his glory. . . ." Thus the revelation in the Word becomes incarnation. Therefore, Jesus Christ as the Logos Incarnate is the revelation of God on earth. Only in him, the Eternal Word, does God come forth out of his hiddenness. He is the content of all that is divine Word; his incarnation is the making-visible of the Word. The man Jesus is the *Verbum visible*. He who sees him sees the Father, as far as it is possible to see him in this aeon.

From here we understand Luther's doctrine of the cross. If God wants to reveal himself, to make himself visible to man, he cannot show himself as he is. He cannot show his glory unveiled. For no man would bear the sight of the *Deus nudus*. So he chooses the veil of human nature. Incarnation, therefore, is at the same time revelation of God and hiding of his glory. The *Deus absconditus*? The invisible Eternal God, becomes for us *Deus revelatus* in Jesus Christ. But the revelation, this unveiling—which is what *revelatio* originally meant—is at the same time veiling, hiding. This explains Luther's twofold use of the expression *Deus absconditus*. Luther can speak of the hidden God in the sense of God as he has not yet revealed himself and of God who has revealed himself by hiding himself in the humanity of Jesus Christ. The incarnation, therefore, is at the same time both revelation of God and veiling, hiding of God, in the human nature.

Nowhere does this disguise, this hiddenness of the divine nature, become so evident as in the Passion. Gethsemane and the cry from the cross "My God, my God, why hast thou forsaken me!" are the end of all attempts to misinterpret the Gospel as the message of the triumphant epiphany of a savior-god after the manner of ancient mystery religions or the epic of a religious hero. How often has such a *theologia gloriae* tried to take control of the Gospel. The miracles of Jesus have again and again been misunderstood in this way. Certainly Jesus manifested his glory thereby, as the story of the

Wedding at Cana testifies. But the text declares explicity, "And his disciples believed in him." Not the people of Cana, not the five thousand
whom he fed, not the sick whom he healed, not even those whom he
raised from the dead believed in him. For also these deeds were at
the same time revelation and disguise of his divine majesty. Only in
faith did his disciples see his glory. Even his resurrection was not a
demonstration for the world. The empty sepulchre as such convinced
no one who did not believe in him. Like the healings (Luke 11:18), it
too could be and has been explained differently (Matt. 27:64).

Faith always deals with hidden realities. Also the faith of the
apostles and the apostolic Church in Jesus Christ, the LORD, was
faith in his secret glory, in God hidden in the flesh, in the true divinity within the true humanity. This secrecy finds its deepest expression
in the cross: *Cruce tectum*"hidden under the cross"; that is Luther's
formula for this character of the divine revelation. Hidden under the
cross is Christ's divine majesty before his resurrection and exalta-
tion. Hidden under the cross is his royal office, his *regnum* ("That is
always the kingdom which he quickens by his Spirit, whether it be
revealed or be covered by the cross," ". . . *sive sit revelatum, sive sit tectum cruce*," Apology VII and VIII, 18); likewise the Church: "*Abscondita est ecclesia, latent sancti*," "Hidden is the Church, concealed are
the saints" (WA 18,652,23). That cannot be otherwise. For "*opus est,
ut omnia, quae creduntur abscondantur*," "Necessarily all objects of
faith are hidden" (WA 18,653). Hidden is the Word of God in the
letters and words of the Bible, in the human word of the preacher.
Hidden are the true body and blood of Christ in the earthly elements
of the bread and the wine at the Lord's Supper. Faith and the cross
belong together. The cross demands faith *against the evidence*.

If the cross is the place where God reveals himself, then it is
further the place where God's revelation *contradicts human reason*
most severely. Judged by everything called wisdom by the world, the
word of the cross, as already St. Paul has seen, is the most foolish
doctrine a philosopher can meet. That the death of one man is to be
the salvation of all, that this death on Calvary is to be the atoning
sacrifice for all sins of the world, that the suffering of an innocent
should assuage the wrath of God: these are claims contradicting all
ethical and religious feelings of natural man. Already beyond discussion for the world is the presupposition for these claims, namely,

the doctrine of man's universal sinfulness, because it means the end of all philosophical ethics. For all philosophical ethics rests upon the principle formulated by Kant: "*Du kannst, denn du sollst*," "Thou canst, for thou shalt." Now Holy Scripture claims that just this foolish preaching of the cross is the wisdom of God, which brings to nought the wisdom of the wise of this world. Between the wisdom of God and the wisdom of the world, there is a total and irreconcilable contrast. What for human reason is wisdom is foolishness for God, and God's wisdom is foolishness for the world.

Luther understood the whole depth of this contrast as no theologian before and after him. From here it becomes clear what the fight against the *theologia gloriae* means for him. It is the fight for the Gospel, for the *sola gratia*, for the right understanding of God and man. "*Theologus gloriae dicit malum bonum et bonum malum; theologus crucis dicit id, quod res est*," "The theologian of glory calls evil good and good evil; the theologian of the cross calls things what they are" (Thesis 21). What man regards as good, that may be sin in the sight of God, for example, the striving for virtue of the Aristotelian or Kantian moralists. What human wisdom thinks to be good fortune and gain for man, such as health, wealth, and success, precisely that may be regarded by God as hurtful for man and, therefore, denied to him. In the judgment of God, sickness, failure, and poverty may be much more precious, and this judgment of God is right, even if it contradicts all human reason. Our human judgment will see in an incurable sickness that after years of suffering leads to a painful death something definitely negative. But seen from God, such misfortune may paradoxically be something quite positive.

Thus Luther in "*De servo arbitrio*" ventures to say, "When God brings to life, he does so by killing (*occidendo vivificat*); when he justifies, then he does so by accusing us; when he brings us into heaven, he does so by leading us to hell" (WA 18,633). *Occidendo vivificat*—that is the adequate expression for the unreasonable way God acts. It is beneath the cross of Christ that we learn to believe that. There we see nothing but the suffering, the weakness, the torment of being forsaken by God, the shame, the defeat, the triumph of evil, and the victory of death. For the believer, however, all this is the *visibilia Dei*, that which God lets us see, his strange work behind which he hides his proper work of forgiving, saving, and life-giving. Deeply hidden in the events of Good Friday seen by human eyes is the great event of the reconciliation between God and mankind, is the victory of the Redeemer of the world that can only be believed in the face of all appearances and against reason with its doubting question: how is that possible?

7.

These are some, but by no means all, of the fundamental ideas of Luther's *theologia crucis*. If this theology, as it claims, is not the theology of a great Christian thinker but the faithful reproduction of a great New Testament doctrine, then it must be of importance not for one section of Christendom only, but for the whole Church. And I think this theology of the cross has a message for all Christians in this time of ours. May I say a few words about that in conclusion.

First, Luther's theology of the cross can help us to get rid of that *theologia gloriae* by which many of us have lived and which is not theology at all, but rather, as all *theologia gloriae* in the history of the Church, the revived natural religion of fallen mankind. Let us take one example: On the June 23, 1910, John Mott delivered the closing address of the World Missionary Conference of Edinburgh, that great meeting marking the beginning of the Ecumenical Movement of our age. His words were a powerful appeal to missionary action, inspired by the hope that the final aim of all Christian missions would be reached soon. He began with the words, "The end of the conference is the beginning of the conquest. The end of the planning is the beginning of the doing." He concluded by saying, "God grant that we, all of us, may in these next moments solemnly resolve henceforth so to plan and so to act, so to live and so to sacrifice, that our spirit of reality may become contagious among those to whom we go: and it may be that the words of the Archbishop—he refers to some saying of Archbishop Davidson of Canterbury at the opening session—shall prove to be a splendid prophecy, and that before many of us taste death we shall see the Kingdom of God come with power." Four years later, World War I broke out. Seven years after that conference, Bolshevism started the greatest persecution that ever has threatened the existence of the Church. Forty years later, China was conquered by Bolshevism, and the Christian missionaries were forced to leave the greatest mission field of the world.

Lead on, O King Eternal, The day of march has come.
Henceforth in fields of conquest Thy tents shall be our home.

That has been the battle song of the American missionaries in the time of Edinburgh. Today we all should understand better why Jesus never promised to his apostles glorious victories but the cross, the comfort of the *theologia crucis: occidendo vivificat.* The kingdom of God is in this world always *tectum cruce*, hidden under the cross. If we look through all those great statements and proclamations of the Christian churches and the ecumenical conferences regarding war and peace, church and state, disarmaments and rearmaments, League of Nations and United Nations, we shall understand why Christian theology today needs a rebirth of the *theologia crucis.* How many secular illusions have entered our thinking about the Church and the world! Among all the illusions that have taken the place of religion in the souls of modern man, there is also the *theologia gloriae* of the last decades. It is not only Nationalism and Pacifism, Liberalism and Socialism, Fascism and Communism, Militarism and Anti-militarism that today are deprived of the glory they used to have in the eyes of their adherents. It is also the Christianity that in all denominations prevailed in the past centuries, Christianity dreaming of a Christian nation or a Christian world, a Christian faith secularized by the *theologia gloriae.* Now the time has come for the theology of the cross. When the Church of today asks, "What shall I preach?" the only answer can be *Unum praedica, sapientiam crucis!*

To preach the Gospel as the wisdom of the cross—this second remark is necessary—presupposes that we understand that the *theologia crucis* can never be a philosophy. The *theologia gloriae* is always a philosophy, a Christian philosophy, of course, reconciling reason and revelation. But I cannot face the Crucified as a philosopher faces the object of his research, passing his judgment on this object. Before I can pass a judgment on Christ, stating who he is, he will have judged me. This is the reason why the *theologia crucis* has that practical aspect that makes it a vital affair for the theologian. A theologian of the cross cannot be without faith in the Crucified. And how can I believe in the cross of Christ if I am not prepared to take up the cross and follow him? It is not by accident that Jesus, whenever he speaks to his disciples about his cross, mentions also the cross they are to take up (cf. Matt. 16:21–24). According to Luther, it is one of the marks by which the true Church of Christ on earth is recognised that she has to go through persecution and suffering. The *theologia crucis* includes the yes of faith to the cross that Christ wants us to take up.

This aspect of the theology of the cross is expressed by Luther in an explanation of Romans 12:1ff.:

Sicut itaque Dei sapientie abscondita est sub specie stultitiae et veritas sub forma mendacii (ita enim verbum Dei, quoties venit, venit in specie contraria menti nostrae . . .) ita et voluntas Dei, cum sit vere et naturaliter "bona, beneplacens, perfecta," sed ita abscondita sub specie mali, displicentis et desperati, ut nostrae voluntati et bonae, ut dicitur, intentioni nonnisi pessima, desperatissima et nullo mode Dei, sed diaboli voluntas videatur.

In other words:

As the wisdom of God appears under the guise of foolishness, the truth of God under the form of a lie—for that is the way the Word of God comes, whenever it comes, in a form contrary to our reason— . . . so the will of God, which is truly and naturally a "good and well-pleasing and perfect" will, appears to us under the guise of evil so that it seems to us to be in no way the will of God, but the will of the devil.

Thus the gracious, living will of God is hidden, but only as long as man refuses to give up his own ideas of what is good, well-pleasing, and perfect. If he abandons his own will, then he will learn what Peter experienced, who according to John 21 let the Lord guide him where he himself did not want to go. "*Simul ergo vult et non vult. Sic Christus in agone suo voluntatem suam, ut sic dixerim, ferventissima voluntate perfecit,*" "He wills and at the same time he wills not, as the Lord himself in Gethsemane made perfect his not-willing by the most ardent will." "*Ita enim in omnibus sanctis agit Deus, ut faciat eos summa voluntate facere, quae summa nolunt!*" "So God is acting in all his saints that he makes them will what they do not will." And Luther continues, "*Et contrariatatem mirantur philosophi, et non intelligunt homines. Ideo dixi, quod nisi experientia et practica illud*

cognoverit, numquam cognoscet," "At this contradiction the philosophers are astonished, and people do not understand it. This is why I
said that it had to be understood by experience and practice" (lecture
on Romans, WA56, 4461).

This experience is the experience of faith. Of that faith that does
not see. Of that faith that like the faith of Abraham is faith in a promise that, humanly speaking, cannot be fulfilled. It is belief in what is
hidden to human eyes. It is faith that sees the light in the darkness,
as Luther describes it in a profound word he wrote in his commentary to Genesis 17 (WA42, 655) about the faith of Abraham: *"Clausis
igitur oculis abdidit se in tenebras fidei, in quibus mvenit aeternam
lucem,"* "With closed eyes he hid himself in the darkness of faith, and
there he found eternal light."

THE REFORMED THEOLOGICAL REVIEW
Vol. XXXV, No. 1, January–April 1976

Ten Years After the Council (I): Some thoughts for ecumenical discussion

Ten years have passed since at the closing session of the Second Vatican Council Archbishop Felice, the General Secretary of the council, read the papal breve which brought to its end the largest council ever held in the history of the Church. For whatever councils may be held in the future, they will hardly reach the size of this vast assembly of 2,500 bishops in communion with Rome. It is worthwhile to remember in our fast living time this event that has inaugurated a new era not only in the history of Roman Catholicism, but probably of all Christendom. No Christian church, whatever its name may be, can live in the future as if this event had not taken place. Whether we know it or not, whether we like it or not, the Second Vatican Council has been a turning point in the history of every church. So it may be well to remember this anniversary.

I.

This council brought to its end the epoch in the history of the Roman Church that began with the Reformation and found its first climax in the Council of Trent and its second in the First Council of the Vatican, 1870. This epoch was determined by the fact that the Church had to fight against two enemies that seemed to threaten its very life. The first was the Protestant Reformation, which destroyed the unity, or what seemed to be the unity, of Western Christendom after the Middle Ages had already caused the loss of unity with the Christian East. The second enemy that arose at the same time, but gained more and more prominence in the following centuries, was the modern European civilization that drifted slowly away from its Christian foundations. The great gains the Roman Church made during these centuries on the mission fields throughout the world, whose extension had been unknown to the Middle Ages, could not make up for the losses it was suffering in the Old World. Its claim to be the Catholic Church, the *una sancta ecclesia* Christ had established for all mankind, had lost its credibility. Even the small branches of the Eastern churches that had submitted to the papacy while retaining their national, constitutional, liturgical and, as they were convinced, also their dogmatical heritage could not be more than a reminder of the old catholicity lost by Rome. Even the great churchman Maximos, the Patriarch of the Melkite Church with the impressive title of Antioch, Alexandria, and Jerusalem, who belonged to the truly great members of the Second Vatican Council, was not much more than a remembrance of what the ancient patriarchs had been at their best. He was listened to as no other of the council fathers. But his presence did not alter the overall situation.

For the first time, the Roman Church had realized the full meaning of its status. It had become obvious in the political development under Pius XII, who in his way was perhaps the greatest representative of the Roman Church, this last Romanus ex Romanis. His policy as Cardinal Secretary of State under his predecessor, as that of his own pontificate, had ended in a breakdown of the papal policy in Europe. Both Pius XI and XII had been the strongest opponents to communism. They were convinced that fascism in Italy and National Socialism in Germany would destroy its political philosophy and would conquer the communist danger that threatened the Christian character of Europe. The Lateran Treaties with Mussolini and the concordate with Nazi-Germany indicated the hopes of the Vatican. But these hopes were bound to fail. When the Second World War ended, the strong wall of Catholic nations in Eastern Europe, from Lithuania and Poland to the Croats in Yugoslavia, found themselves behind the Iron Curtain. Today it has become obvious that the Catholic countries of Southern Europe, Portugal, Spain, and Italy can no longer be regarded as Catholic states, a concept that had to be given up definitely by the council. How far these nations can still be regarded as Catholic remains to be seen. In any case the concept of a Christian Europe belongs to past history.

II.

It took the ingenuousness of Pope John to terminate an era of centuries and to start a new epoch of the Roman Church. Unburdened by the traditions and inhibitions of his predecessor, who had been certainly one of the greatest popes in his own right, he started a completely new course. The leading men of the curia were shocked by the absolute certainty with which he made decisions no one else would have dared to make. His wisdom was not the *sapientia* you gain through profound philosophical reflections. It was the practical wisdom of a man who had shared the life of the simple soldiers in the barracks, where you learn to know men, and on the battlefields, where you see the crude realities of this world. Such was the man who was able to shock the solemn assembly of cardinals on January 25 at St. Paul's with his answer to the problems of Church and world: "A council." It seems that he was not aware that the question had been discussed in the highest Roman circles for some years. They had asked whether or not the Vatican Council of 1869–70 could be reconvened that had to be adjourned *sine die* but was never formally closed. But then an eminent canonist discovered that council had died of a natural death when the last of its fathers departed this world. John's council would be different from all previous ones. It would not be a repetition and continuation of Vatican I. The concluding breve called it the richest in view of the wealth of "questions that had been discussed." It was the most opportune because, bearing in mind the necessities of the present day, above all it sought to meet the pastoral needs and, nourishing the flame of charity, it has made a great effort to reach not only the Christian still separated from communion with the Holy See, but also the whole human family.

It is probably for the first time that a council of the Roman Church addressed itself not only to the churches in communion with the Holy See, but also to the rest of Christendom and even to the whole of mankind. As at the beginning, the fathers of the Second Vatican Council issued, with the endorsement of the Supreme Pontiff a message to humanity ("To all men and nations"), so at the closing ceremonies Pope Paul in his closing messages addressed not only the council fathers, but he spoke also "to rulers," "to men of thought and science," "to artists," "to women," "to the poor to the sick and the suffering," "to workers," and "to youth," offering to all mankind the service the Church can render to the world on a turning point of history. The Church wanted to take the definite step out of the ghetto into which it had drifted, to a large degree through its own faults. In his opening address, Pope John obviously had in mind the development since the era of the French Revolution, when the gulf between Rome and the modern world had grown deeper and deeper, until since the First Vatican Council any hope for a reconciliation seemed to have vanished. It was a tremendous task Pope John had begun to tackle when he proclaimed his program of an *aggiornamento* of the Church to enable her to gain again the confidence of the modern world and to render the service Christ's Church owed to a proud but ailing world. An updating of the church law and of its theology would not be sufficient. What was required was a spiritual revival, a renewal of the deepest spiritual potentials of Catholic Christianity. There were certainly gifts and treasures that had to be kept inviolate because the entire life of the Church was depending on them. But otherwise no sacrifice should be shunned, nothing should be regarded as inviolable that would not be required by the dogma of the Church.

So Pope John called the council mainly as a pastoral council, not as a synod to define new doctrines. In his opening address, he made some basic statements that always should be kept in mind by those who want to understand the nature of this unique council. "The greatest concern of the ecumenical council is this: that the sacred deposit of Christian doctrine should be guarded and taught more efficaciously." Hence, "it is necessary first of all that the Church should never depart from the sacred patrimony of truth received from the fathers. But at the same time she must ever look to the present, to the new conditions and new forms of life introduced into the modern world which have opened new avenues to the Catholic

Apostolate." To express this heritage "a council was not necessary. But from the renewed, serene, and tranquil adherence to all the teaching of the Church in its entirety and preciseness, as it still shines forth in the acts of the Council of Trent and First Vatican Council, the Christian, Catholic, and apostolic spirit of the whole world expects a step forward toward a doctrinal penetration and a formation of consciousness in faithful and perfect conformity to the authentic doctrine, which, however should be studied and expounded through the methods of research and through the literary forms of modern thought. The substance of the ancient doctrine of the deposit of faith is one thing, and the way in which it is presented is another."

No objection could be raised against this program. On the contrary, it had to be welcomed and was welcomed not only in the Catholic Church, but even in the non-Roman churches. Somehow the future of all Christendom is bound up with the destiny of the largest of the Christian churches. Most astonishing was the echo that the program of the council as proclaimed by the pope found even outside the Christian world. Our age was full of great leaders who were worshiped by the people whom they infallibly led into unheard of glory that soon ended in catastrophes. It is perhaps not accidental that just a man won the admiration and love of men of all nations and creeds who was a very simple man and remained so in the glorious pomp surrounding the supreme pontiff. His predecessor could speak to kings and dictators, to the leaders in politics and in the field of science. John, too, could speak to them, but also to the man in the street, to the tradesmen and the little shopkeepers, to soldiers and prisoners. But it was not only the undefinable human qualities that attracted his contemporaries, but the spiritual authority of a loving pastor for which even modern man is unknowingly longing.

III.

What Pope John perhaps did not fully realize is the fact that even a mere pastoral council cannot avoid entering the field of the dogma of the Church, least of all in the Roman Church where not only the constitution, but also every ethical decision is rooted in an unalterable dogma. What was possible and what John's council would do in a remarkable way is the avoidance of anathemas previous councils and popes had hurled so liberally against anything that was supposed to smell of heresy, from socialism to Bible societies. However not even the humblest and friendliest of popes and a truly spiritually minded council can avoid far-reaching dogmatic decisions. So at least two of the documents issued are by nature dogmatic: the "Dogmatic Constitution on the Church" (*Lumen gentium*) and the "Dogmatic Constitution on the Divine Revelation" (*Dei verbum*). Both contain very important doctrinal decisions that every Catholic is obliged to accept, though it is never stated which articles are to be accepted *fide catholica* and which may be open for further theological investigation, and though never an explicit condemnation is added. Thus the question remains of how far the decisions are binding except in such cases where a former decree of the magisterium is solemnly reaffirmed. Hence the Mariological dogmas of 1854 and 1950, which were solemnly proclaimed, are unalterable dogma. The chapter on Mary with which the constitution on the Church is concluded mentions among the titles of the Mother of God also the title "Mediatrix," which had been in controversy between the theologians. Also the controversial title "Mother of the Church" is contained in "*Lumen gentium*" (53 cf. 61 and 62) and was expressly confirmed by Pope Paul in the concluding Breve of Dec. 8, 1965 ("Mary . . . whom we have declared Mother of the Church"). The question of whether or not the acceptance of these terms is *de fide* remains open. To deny them would be, if not blank heresy, at least a grave violation of the obedience every Catholic owes to the Church.

It is not a lack of that clarity, which otherwise at all times has been characteristic of a doctrinal statement by the Roman magisterium, that causes even theologians of the Roman Church to disagree on the proper interpretation of certain texts, but a deeper intention lies behind all actions of the council. Rome wants to get rid of the strictly juridical language of former times. In this respect it has learned from the Christian East. The Feast of Mary's Conception and of her *Assumptio* (*koimesis*) are celebrated also in the Eastern churches. There is hardly anything in the official Mariology of Rome that is not to be found in Eastern Christendom, including the title "Mediatrix." But this remains in the sphere of the liturgy and of personal piety as it is nourished by the liturgical life of the Church. To proclaim the doctrines of 1854 and 1950 a solemn dogma would be unthinkable in the East, one reason being that these pious opinions have no basis on Holy Scripture. One has only to compare the articles on Mary in *Lumen gentium* with the text of *"Ineffabilis Deus"* and *"Munificentissimus Deus"* to see the great difference of the terminology. Rome wants to express the divine mysteries no longer in the technical language of dogmatics and canon law, but rather in the language of the liturgy and of pastoral care. This is a tremendous change. The embarrassment of many Catholic priests that in some cases led them to leave the priesthood is partly due to their failure to understand the full implications of this change. Many may have thought that this is not only a change of language and terminology, but that a profound change in the nature of the dogma may be hidden in the ways of expressing it. One might ask whether Pope John himself was aware of the problems contained in his statement that the deposit of faith must be distinguished from the way in which it is presented. As an example of how the interpretation of a dogma can contradict its content, we quote the famous"Extraecclesia nulla salus," which Pius XII called *"illud infallibile effatum"* (Letter to the Archbishop of Boston of August 8, 1949; Denz.-Sch. 3866ff.). Over against a Catholic priest who as a *"defensor fidei,"* as he called himself, maintained the literal interpretation of this word, the pope demanded that it must be interpreted in the sense of the Church that understands it to mean not any unbeliever, but those who knew of Christ and the Sacrament of Baptism and refused to receive it. (The only Bible passage quoted in this context is Heb. 11:6, while Mark 16:16 and John 3:5 are not mentioned). This has become the doctrine also of the Vatican Council, and the basis of the present attitude of Rome to non-Christian religions and unbelievers.

We might be inclined to criticize this method of dealing with Scripture passages. By way of a theology of conclusions, they are supposed to say something contrary to their original and natural meaning. If God wills the salvation of all men (1 Tim. 2:4), he must give to every man the opportunity to "respond to the love and pPiety of God"—as the Credo of the People of God, published by Pope Paul in 1968, puts it—in this earthly life, because the eternal destiny of a soul is decided at death. How the grace is offered to people outside the Church we do not know. The acceptance of this grace must then be the substitute for faith and Baptism. By way of such conclusion, the Baptism with water is replaced by what could be called "*baptismus in voto*," baptism by desire (see Trent VI, 4: Denz. 797, 1525). But Protestant critics should not be too confident. We have our own way of removing the washing of regeneration by declaring the word "water" in John 3:5, together with the rest of all references to the Sacraments in the Fourth Gospel" as a later addition to what the first author wrote. This is what we call "scientific research" (see Bultmann's commentary). We have no reason to claim any superiority to the theology of the Roman Church.

<h1 style="text-align:center">IV.</h1>

From the vast material of the Second Vatican Council, we select two topics of greatest importance for the dialogue with our Catholic brethren. We look first into the Dogmatic Constitution on the Church, which claims to be and certainly is in many respects a clarification of the *Constitutio Prima de Ecclesia Christi* of 1870. The nature of the Church was in the nineteenth century one of the great problems for the theology of all Christian churches. It was not only lack of time that in 1870 prevented a full and exhaustive statement on the doctrine of the Church. No church was at that time able to produce a convincing ecclesiology in spite of the amazing work done also by the fathers of the First Vaticanum. In some respects their thoughts have not yet been fully exhausted, neither in the Encylical of Pius XII "*Mystici Corporis*" (1943), nor in the present "*Lumen gentium*." Ecclesiology remains the great problem of theology in all churches. The constitution starts with a chapter on the mystery of the Church. The Church is understood as "a kind of sacrament, or sign of intimate union with God and of the unity of all mankind. She is also an instrument for the achievement of such union and unity. For this reason, following in the path laid out by our predecessors, this council wishes to set forth more precisely to the faithful and to the entire world the nature and the encompassing mission of the Church" (1). One has always to keep in mind this practical purpose of the constitution to understand its nature—a strange mixture of theology and practical personal aims—to understand it fully in its distinction from the *Constitutio Prima* and from the learned encyclical "*Mystici Corporis*."

While Pius XII built his ecclesiology on the concept of the Church as the Body of Christ, the council, obviously taking in account the rich literature provoked by Mystici Corporis, built its doctrine mainly on the understanding of the Church as the people of God. Nothing can be said against this way of procedure, especially since it has a firm biblical basis in the entire Scripture while the concept of the Body of Christ is limited to the theology of St. Paul. But if one follows this pattern, the entire Bible has to be taken into account with its varied use of the term. What was the meaning of the people of God at the time of the Exodus and the revelation on Mt. Sinai? What was the understanding of the people of God with the prophets, for example with Amos and Hosea? "Are you not like the Ethiopians to me, O people of Israel . . . Did I not bring up Israel from the land of Egypt, and the Philistines from Caphtor and the Syrians from Kir," complains the Lord (Amos 9:7). "Hear this word that the Lord has spoken against you. . . . You only I have known of all the families of the earth; therefore I will punish you for all iniquities" (3:1f.). "*Lo ammi*" is the name of one of Hosea's sons, "Not my people," for you are not my people and I am not your God" (Hos. 1:9). The faithless Israel ceases to be God's people, and only God's overwhelming mercy can restore it to become God's people again. In what sense is Israel God's own people, in what sense one of the nations of the earth? The New Testament distinction between Israel after the flesh and Israel after the Spirit is not applicable to the Israel of the Old Testament.

What, then, has to be said about Israel at the time of Jesus and the apostles? Did the Jewish people cease to be God's people when it rejected the Messiah? The apostles did not cease to belong to the people of the old covenant. One must go on and ask, "Has the Jewish people ever ceased to be God's people, and if so, when?" Chapters 14ff. contain highly important statements concerning the question of who belongs to the Church, as the people of God. "They are fully incorporated into the society of the Church who, possessing the Spirit of Christ, accept her entire system and all the means of salvation given to her, and through union with her visible structure are joined to Christ, who rules her through the Supreme Pontiff and the bishops. . . ." Also the catechumens who seriously want to be baptized are recognized as full members. The much-discussed chapter 15 enumerates those who in various ways are linked (*conjuncti*) with the Church, Catholics outside the Roman fold, and various groups of Protestants. Chapter 16 speaks of those who have not yet accepted the Gospel but are related to the Church (*ad Populum Dei ordinantur*). They are primarily the Jews, but also the Muslim and true Godseekers in other religions. The Jews are mentioned as "that people to whom the covenants and promises were given and from whom Christ was born according to the flesh (Rom. 9:4f.). On account of these fathers, this people remains most dear to God, for God does not repent of the gifts he makes nor of the calls he issues (Rom. 11:28.)." Here a question arises that will come up as soon as a dialogue begins between Rome and the Jewish scholars in Jerusalem and Israel, and with pious Jews throughout the world, a dialogue bound to fail utterly. For the Jews would claim that they are still the people of God as in olden times. If you Christians claim to be the true people of God to whom covenants and prophetic promises are given, which even you believe to be valid still today, we would fully understand that you try to convert us by the way of mission, but we cannot recognize and shall never recognize your claim that this Jesus was the Messiah of Israel. We cannot accept that "myth" because it would be the gravest violation of the First Commandment, nor do we recognize your "Scripture proofs" that rest on a false interpretation of the Holy Scripture we have in common with you. We would not again sentence him to death, as even today it has been suggested by at least one of our great scholars.[1] We see in him a really great man and teacher, whose doctrines we accept as far as they agree with the Torah. But more we cannot do. As we regard the Church as one of the greatest and most successful sects that have grown out of Judaism, we must claim that you recognize us as a people, as the Western nations have done until the laws of the modern states gave us citizenship in the Christian nations and degraded us from a nation that lived under its own law to one of the monotheistic religions of the world. Quite apart from the existence of the state of Israel that has made the Israelis one of the modern nations, the question must be answered: When have we ceased to be the people of God?

---

[1] Franz Rosenzweig, quoted by K. Miskotte, *Wenn die Goetter schweigen*, p.317.

This is one of the theological problems raised by "*Lumen gentium*," a very serious question because it seems to indicate that the council, here as in other constitutions and decrees has never been fully aware of the importance of the Old Testament, which after all was the Bible of Jesus and the apostles and the whole Church of the New Testament. Wherever the New Testament writers refer to Holy Scripture, they speak of what we call the Old Testament. The whole question comes up again in the "Declaration on the Relationship of the Church to Non-Christian Religions" of October 1965, one of the last documents of the council that bears the marks of controversies that had gone on since the beginning of the council. Pope John in conjunction with Cardinal Bea wanted the council to say a strong word against anti-semitism. The declaration deals elaborately with the attitude toward the Jews while it is very brief concerning other religions. In point of fact, it is a declaration against anti-semitism. The statement on the Old Testament people of God in "*Lumen gentium*" is repeated but not altered. "As Holy Scripture testifies, Jerusalem did not recognize the time of its visitation (Luke 19:44), nor did the Jews in large number accept the gospel; indeed, not a few opposed the spreading of it (Rom. 11:28), . . . In company with the prophets and the same apostle, the Church awaits that day, known to God alone, on which all peoples will address the Lord in a single voice and 'serve him with one accord' (Zeph. 3:9; cf. Is. 66:23; Ps. 65:4; Rom. 11:11–32)." In view of this common spiritual heritage, the synod recommends "that mutual understanding and respect which is the fruit of all biblical and theological studies, and of brotherly dialogues." Indeed, if Judaism is one of the non-Christian religions but has so much in common with Christianity, dialogue seems to be the key to the solution also of this knotty problem. One wonders why neither Jesus nor the apostles have recommended that.

But has not a dialogue started in the New Testament? The Gospels are full of reports of the constant dialogue that went on between Jesus and the scribes. Was it perhaps not brotherly enough? Should not the Lord have employed a more lenient terminology than we find in Matthew 23? And what about the dialogue between the Jewish authorities and the synagogues in the apostolic age? Might Paul not have been a little more brotherly when he debated with his former colleagues in Corinth and other cities? Why used this dialogue to end in riots that caused the police to interfere. Things became still worse when the Jews spread the rumors of ritual murder (and cannibalism). What had a Roman policeman to say if he was shown a passage like John 6:53? What if he heard of the "agape" held behind closed doors by these "brothers" and "sisters." How could the policeman understand the "holy kiss" with which these celebrations used to be opened? It was most certainly undefensible if the Christians later for many centuries reciprocated with equal slanders against the Jews. But the problem remains as to why just religious differences and controversies had to be fought with more than ordinary cruelty. The worst wars of human history were at all times the religious wars, from the conquest of Palestine by ancient Israel through the crusades of the Middle Ages to the holy wars of the Muslim in our time.

V.

The short declaration on the relationship to non-Christian religions contains a statement on anti-semitism that had been requested from the Church for a long time. It bears still the marks of long and bitter controversies. The matter had been brought before the council right from the beginning, but only in one of the last meetings in October 1965 was it in its final form adopted. Far too long the Church has delayed an authoritative statement against the theological arguments that bolstered the hatred against the Jews and the persecutions they suffered. Especially the mass murder committed by Hitler's crude and criminal anti-semitism necessitated a clear and unambiguous clarification of the relationship between Christians and Jews. The creation of the new state of Israel, with its political implications in the Middle East as well as in the world, confronted the churches with new questions. That the problem had become especially urgent in Germany is partly due to the political circumstances. German territories, especially the Lowlands, had become a sort of sanctuary for the Jews who had been expelled from Western Europe during the Middle Ages. Where they were tolerated they were regarded as members of a foreign people until since the eighteenth century their emancipation began, which made them slowly citizens of the "Mosaic faith." This tragic destiny led to the Zionistic Movement and to the establishment of the modern state of Israel. Even this development was for a long time and still is controversial among the Jews who had been assimilated into other nations and retained nothing but "the Jewish religion."

The sad history of the Jewish people throughout the centuries is one of the greatest tragedies of mankind and remains one of the darkest spots in the history of the Church, which was not able and probably not willing to find a Christian solution other than the conversion of the Jews to the Church. This was also the only solution of the problem in the eyes of Luther, whose inexcusable invectives against the Jews were his human reaction to the refusal of the Jews to become Christians, whereby it must not be forgotten that Luther believed the end of the world to be near. But the whole question cannot be solved in the terms of modern enlightenment as a question of the relation between various religions. Here lies the mistake of the document of the Vatican Council. It is a synthesis of Christian faith and modern enlightenment. "The Church repudiates (*reprobat*) all persecutions against any man. Moreover, mindful of her common patrimony with the Jews, and motivated by the gospel's spiritual love she deplores the hatred, persecutions, and displays of anti-semitism directed against the Jews at any time and from any source." A stronger word of repentance might have been expected. It follows the positive statement that "the Church has always held and continues to hold, Christ in his boundless love freely underwent his passion and death because of the sin of all men, so that all may attain salvation. It is therefore, the duty of the Church's preaching to proclaim the cross of Christ as the sign of God's all-embracing love. . . . We cannot in truthfulness call upon that God who is the Father of all if we refuse to act in a brotherly way toward certain men, created though they be in God's image." There are, of course, passages in the declaration in which it is made clear that the Church, mindful of its own origin in the revelation of the Old Testament and aware of its authority, repeats what St. Paul says on the hope of his own people. The duty of the Church's preaching to proclaim the cross of Christ to all nations is strongly emphasized.

However, the reviewer (Claud Nelson) of the declaration in the semi-official edition of "The Documents of Vatican II" by Abbot and Gallagher says correctly, "The Vatican Declaration avoided suggestions of conversion confining itself to the hoped-for reunion of all believers at the end of history" (p. 671). This corresponds to a significant change in the liturgy. Pius XII had already omitted the word "perfidi" for the Jews in the prayer of Good Friday, so now Pope Paul has altered the prayer "For the Conversion of Jews" into a prayer "For the Jews." To change a word that might unnecessarily hurt the feeling of the Jews is justifiable. But to avoid terms like "conversion of Jews" and "mission to the Jews" indicates a deeper theological change. "Since the spiritual patrimony common to Christians and Jews is so great, this sacred Synod wishes to foster and recommend that mutual understanding and respect which is the fruit above all of biblical and theological studies, and of brotherly dialogues."

In other words, the relationship between Christians and Jews is regarded as essentially the same as the relationship with other non-Christian religions. Dr. Nelson in his "Response" explains this quite correctly when he states, "A shift from Christian denunciation of the Jews to a Christian strategy of their conversion, advocated and practised by many Christians, would not improve relations and might greatly exacerbate them. . . . In a very long run, those sections of the Declaration dealing with Muslims, Buddhists, Hindus, and primitive religions may prove to be even more important than the section on the Jewish religion." Thus writes an experienced ecumenist, the official representative of "Religious News Service" at the council for the "National Conference of Christians and Jews" in the U.S.A. (Abbott, p. 671).

Here the real issue becomes clear. Dialogue with other religions rests on serious and sympathetic mutual studies. To understand the deepest nature of the religions involved and the serious desire to find out what they have in common and what separates them. The greatest example for this is perhaps Thomas Aquinas? *Summa contra Gentiles*, where he distinguishes between the dialogue with the Muslims, which must be conducted on a philosophical level, and the dialogue with the Jews, with whom we have in common the Old Testament. "Against the Jews we are able to argue by means of the Old Testament, while against heretics we are able to argue by means of the New Testament. But the Mohammedans and the pagans accept neither the one nor the other. We must, therefore, have recourse to the natural reason, to which all men are forced to give their assent." Thomas has rightly seen that the one and only question that separates

Church and synagogue is the understanding of the Old Testament. It is important to keep that in mind even when the question of the relation between Christians and Jews in the Middle Ages comes up. The terrible persecution of the Jews, whatever their social and political implications may have been, go lastly back to the question of the right understanding of the books of the Old Covenant. It should never be forgotten that the terrible religious wars and persecutions in the Middle Ages were accompanied by the theological and philosophical dialogue of the scholars who treated each other as colleagues—how respectfully spoke Thomas of "Rabbi Moses" (Maimonides) and of Avicennia while the respective rulers and their mobs fought their unholy wars.

6.

Thus it must be acknowledged that the dialogue between the Church and the Jews is essentially different from the dialogue with any other religion. Nor can its result be something similar to the results between Christian denominations and the interreligious dialogue. Of course, both can learn from each other. There is a fruitful collaboration possible between Old Testament scholars in Church and synagogue, as it is going on, and not only in our ecumenical age already in former times. One may think of such great scholars as Origen and Jerome in the Ancient Church or their medieval successors like the Victorinis. Luther himself has consulted Jewish scholars in matters of the translation of Hebrew words. He had a really deep interest in Judaism in the first period when he was very hopeful for the conversion of the Jews. But any dialogue must come to the point where the crucial question has to be answered: Who was Jesus? This question cannot be bypassed, least of all in such attempts as are made today to combine parts of the liturgies of either side. There are attempts being made to receive into the Christian worship prayers and even customs of the synagogue. This has, of course, happened already in the Ancient Church, but if a Jewish religious meal like Passover is combined with the Christian Eucharist or if, what happens in Germany, there are real common services between Christians and Jews, the limit of the dialogue is transgressed. Every Christian service begins with the trinitarian formula, "In the name of the Father and the Son and the Holy Spirit." This is unbearable for a Jew, a grave violation of the First Commandment. We pray the Psalms in our worship services. But to each psalm is the Gloria added, the praise of the Triune God. We can take part in a service in the synagogue, just as the Christian worship service is open to the public. But Christian and Jews cannot pray together as long as they take seriously the words of their prayers. Our declaration says about possible relationships: It may prove both with regard to the Jewish religion and to other religions that the currency given by the Second Vatican Council to the phrase and the spirit embodied in the "People of God" carries a more powerful psychological and spiritual dynamic than the declaration, "Who can set the boundaries of the people of God?" This is correct, as even in the Old Testament strange persons appear as, for example, Melchizedek and Bileam [Balaam] or the pagans who pray at Solomon's temple (2 Chron. 6:32) to the God of Israel. In the New Testament, the Holy Spirit has to teach even Peter concerning the borders of the people of God. But all this does not abolish the fact that there is one point on which the border becomes visible. This is the cross of Christ. Who was crucified at Calvary? Was it a great teacher and even a prophet who had not deserved such hard treatment as every decent Jew would today readily admit? Or was that man "the Lord of glory" (1 Cor. 2:8), which means very God from very God (comp. John 12:41 with the reference to Is. 6). We do not draw the borderline. The Church of all ages has known what the medieval theologians have expressed *"Deus non alligatur sacramentis suis."* In his sovereign freedom, he can give his grace where and when it pleases him. But we are bound to the borders he has set for us in His Word.

Thus no man who encounters Christ and his Church can escape the necessity to answer the question "Whom say you that I am?" If he is what the New Testament teaches him to be, then what happened at Calvary is more than a human tragedy. Many innocent men were crucified at that time. But this was more than a miscarriage of justice, committed by the representatives of the two nations of the ancient world, which, each in its way, claimed to be the guardian of law and justice. Whose guilt was it? The declaration protests in strongest terms against the insinuation that the Jews committed "deicide," which was used for so many centuries as a popular justification of the persecution they had to suffer at the hands of Christian people.

It was a grave sin of omission on the part of the Church, especially in the Middle Ages, but even in our lifetime, that the proclamation of the Gospel in the practice of life failed to emphasize that the Jews and the Romans who were responsible for the crucifixion have acted on behalf of all mankind, on behalf of everyone and of us. The Western Church at least has never failed to emphasize this in its liturgy. On Good Friday, the Improperia, the complaints of God against his faithless people taken from the Old Testament (beginning with Micah 6:3f.) are interrupted by the Trishagion with its "Have mercy on us." So guilt and forgiveness are referred to the Church, not, as in the Eastern liturgies, to Israel. [*continued in next article*]

THE REFORMED THEOLOGICAL REVIEW
Vol. XXXV, No. 2, May–August 1976

Ten Years After the Council (II):
Some thoughts for ecumenical discussion

VII.

It was right and proper to reject the old misuse of "deicide." Unfortunately this is done with a dangerous argument: "True, authorities of the Jews and those who followed their lead pressed for the death of Christ (cf. John 19:6), still what happened in his Passion cannot be blamed upon all the Jews then living, without distinction, nor upon the Jews of today." The writer of this article remembers a correspondence he had with Cardinal Bea when the issue was under discussion. He asked him not to forget what the Bible teaches about the sin and guilt not only of individual men, but of whole communities and nations, from the preaching of the prophets to the threatening words Jesus spoke over Chorazin, Bethsaida, and Capernaum (Matt. 11:20ff.), to the tears he shed over the Holy City (Luke 19:41ff), to the last "O Jerusalem, Jerusalem" (Matt. 23). Almost every page of the Bible, from Genesis to Revelation, knows of what we may call with a modern term "collective guilt." Even the Jews today pray on the Day of Atonement and on other occasions for forgiveness not only of each individual's sin, but for pardon of the sins of the people as a whole: "On account of our sins we were exiled from our land, and removed from our own country, and we are unable to fulfil our obligations in thy chosen house. . . ." *(New Year Service, Authorized Daily Prayer Book*, p. 867). The Church has no right to exonerate the people of Israel of the gravest of all sins, the rejection of the Messiah, though we, of course, do not blame each and every Jew of the past or the present, remembering that our Lord himself has prayed for their forgiveness. We cannot accept the excuse of modern Judaism for what happened on Good Friday. But this is what in a dialogue the Jews would demand from us. I suggested to the great Christian with whom I had this discussion that the Church should, instead of minimizing or even denying the guilt of the old people of God refer to the *"Felix culpa"* of the Easter Vigil: *"O felix culpa, quae talem ac tantum meruit habere redemptorem."* He accepted this suggestion in one of his publications. The Church can never do without the concept of collective guilt. Otherwise we would deny the original sin. How can Adam's sin, as even the Council of Trent (Sessio V. 2f. Denz. 789f.) teaches, be my own (*unicuique poprium*) sin if sin and guilt belongs only to the individual?

The question of Church and synagogue can fruitfully be discussed only by a study of history and thorough investigations of the Old Testament, not forgetting those parts that must be equally offensive to modern Jews and Christians. Why do the wars of *Jahve* belong to the bloodiest and crudest of the cruel Orient? Wulfila, the translator of the first Bible in a Germanic dialect had to leave out the historical books of the Old Covenant because he was afraid of their effect on his bellicose people when they heard of the heaps of corpses of the fallen enemies. The sins of the patriarchs, who after all are also our spiritual patriarchs, have posed serious problems to the great thinkers of the Middle Ages, as, for example, the lie of *"patriarcha noster Abraham."* The God-pleasing whore among the ancestors of Christ demands also a theological explanation. The providence in which Hitler believed has prevented him and Goebbels from realizing that the legislation of Ezra that demanded the divorce of valid marriages between Jews and non-Jews could be used as a biblical anticipation of the infamous laws of Nuremberg. The last verses of Psalm 137 cannot be christianized by the addition of the *"Gloria Patri . . ."* And so on. What an unscrutable mystery of the judgments and the grace of God lies behind these parts of God's Word that no human reason can ever understand (Rom. 11:33ff.).

If we look into the New Testament and investigate the use made of the Old Testament by the apostles, we can understand that the Jews would never recognize this kind of interpretation of the Psalms and Prophets. Such are the theological questions that would have to be discussed in a true dialogue between Church and synagogue, a dialogue that incidentally went on already in the first centuries. In what sense is the Old Testament the Bible of the Church, and in what sense the Bible of the synagogue? Very serious questions will have to be answered, questions that do not turn up in the encounter of the Church with other "Non-Christian religions." This fact already indicates that the problem of church and synagogue cannot be discussed on the level and in the terms of dialogue between two religions. If the fathers of the council were not aware of this, their learned theological advisers (the numbers given vary between eight hundred and fourteen hundred) should have told them what to do. But it seems that the understanding of the Old Testament in the present Roman Church is not very great. One of the reasons seems to be that modern Roman theology, after it had to give up its old traditional exegesis, has followed too easily and uncritically modern Protestant exegetes. We do not say one word against the great and serious work done during the last generations on the field of New Testament research. But the question must be asked whether or not the almost exclusive study of a small book, the "fragment of fragments," as the New Testament has been called, has lead to a loss of the broad horizon of true historiography. Great historians like Harnack, Holl and Eduard Meyer have complained about this. It was also the complaint of Rudolf Otto at Marburg. In his lectures on dogmatics, he tried to make up for the shortcomings of his young colleague on the New Testament chair, Rudolf Bultmann. Drawing on his wide knowledge of the world of Islam, from Marakesh and Mogador to East Pakistan, and of the manifold religions of India, he had a different understanding of the historical value of the Gospels. Harold Kiesenfeld, Uppsala, calls our attention to the fact that "none of the outstanding New Testament scholars of our generation has succeeded in giving a presentation of the person of Jesus which could make the impression that it does justice to the central figure of the mightiest movement in the cultural and spiritual history of mankind" ("*Bemerkungen zur Frage des Selbstbewusstseins Jesu*" in Ristow and Matthias, "*Der historische*

Jesus und der kerygmatische Christus," Berlin 1961, p. 333). He asks what the origin is of New Testament Christianity and whether it does not in its unity go back to a mighty, creative personality. He finds the modern pictures of Jesus too superficial and prejudiced to be credible. This criticism would also apply to Bultmann's great philosophical countryman Karl Jaspers, whose picture of Jesus is weak compared to the masterly portraits of Socrates, Buddha, Confucius, and other epoch-making thinkers (now in "*Die massgebenden Menschen*" from the great work "*Die grossen Philosophen*" Bd.I).

VIII.

The Catholic theologians should have noticed that and tried to give us a better presentation. But they are obviously too weak for such problems, as also in other documents of the council becomes painfully evident. The celebrated "Dogmatic Constitution on Divine Revelation" is certainly one of the weakest texts of the council. It does not give a picture of the tremendous work done during the last generations at the two biblical institutes, the Dominican school of Jerusalem, under the leadership of the great scholar Pere Lagrange, and the Pontifical Institute in Rome, whose soul the great Augustine Bea was. The document begins with a brief restatement of the traditional theory of a *revelatio generalis*, an astonishingly superficial mention of the Old Testament, and a discussion of the New Testament revelation. It ends with a Solomonic decision of the great issue of Scripture and tradition. The council began with the discussion and rejection of a proposed "scheme" on the sources (*fontes*) of revelation. It seemed that the majority favored the acceptance of Scripture as the one source, from which everything is derived. It was a general impression that one of the most fundamental questions was to be tackled. Heated discussions inside and outside the council followed. The result (after a last correction by the pope himself) is the formula "that sacred tradition, sacred Scripture, and the teaching authority of the Church . . . are so linked and joined together that one cannot stand without the others, and that all together and each in its own way under the action of the one Holy Spirit contribute effectively to the salvation of souls." Thus, instead of one or two sources, there are three (one may think of the Mariological dogmas of 1854 and 1950), "a cord with three strands." So the *sola scriptura* of the Reformation is finally defeated—no pious admonition to read and study the Bible can abolish this fact. The "Response" (Abbot's American Edition p. 129ff.) has been written by one of the oldest liberal professors in America, who uses this opportunity to combat the new biblical theology of the protestant "neo-orthodox" in favour of the oldest enlightenment with its belief in a natural revelation in all religions and the "suffocating" censorship of the great Cardinal Bea, who warns against the wrong use of superficial biblical "research." Is this Rome's answer to the Reformation?

IX.

Space does not allow us to go on with other important issues. Only one problem may be briefly hinted at that is of utmost importance for the future of the Roman Church. It was generally understood that the existing dogma should not be questioned. Thus the decrees of Trent and of Vatican I remained untouched, at least theoretically. This implied the recognition of the "*Constitutio Prima de Ecclesia Christi*" of 1870 with its dogma of the primacy of jurisdiction of the bishop of Rome over the whole Church and his infallible teaching office, whose definitions on matters of faith and morals are irreformable. One must keep this in mind when studying the documents of Vatican II. On several occasions this dogma of 1870 is expressly reaffirmed. It is not the lust for power, not the will of a human being that made Pope Paul very firm on this point. No man is probably more suffering from the yoke of this dogma than the pope himself. But he cannot revoke it without violating his solemn oath of accession and perhaps destroying the Catholic Church. As a matter of fact, this dogma is regarded as false by many Catholic theologians. Neither the flood of writings from the indefatigable pen of Hans Kueng nor the fraternal war between him and his teacher Karl Rahner have been able and will be able to revoke "*Pastor Aeternus*". If this dogma should ever die, it would die of a natural death because it is no longer accepted by the vast majority of Catholic Christians. Officially in such a case, Rome would let it die by what the jurists call "desuetudo." A law lapses by simply not being applied any more. Perhaps some day a Jesuit like Karl Rahner may find a theological solution.

Otherwise one must be satisfied with the certainty that no future pope would ever proclaim some new Mariological dogma.

Why has the dogma of the papacy as defined by "*Pastor Aeternus*" collapsed? It has collapsed because the proofs from Scripture and tradition of the document have been proved to be wrong. This is admitted even by the Catholic theologians.

To solve the knotty problem, it was suggested to supplement the incomplete dogma of 1870 by the new dogma of the bishops who as successors to the Twelve share with the bishop of Rome his great privilege. This suggestion was carried out by the "Dogmatic Constitution on the Church". It was a very important step, the beginning of a great constitutional reform of the Catholic Church. It was the tragedy of this council that also this step did not really solve the problem. The office of the bishop has gained a new importance. No one can say what a bishop said after Vatican I: "We came as bishops and went as curates." But now the office of the bishop must be developed in a way that no bishop becomes pope in his diocese. The council has seen the necessity of a thorough reform of the life and the work of the priests and also of the laity. Only time can show what the future development of the life of the Catholic Church in all its strata will be. No Christian can deny the Roman Church his admiration for the courage with which this church ventured to start its new course on the storm-tossed sea of the outgoing second millennium of Church history. And what the Roman Church needs is more than our Christian sympathy and the prayers of all Christendom, whose destiny is closely bound up with the destiny of the largest of the Christian churches. It was more than Church politics if the great council became the beginning of a new era of the Ecumenical Movement, which, so far, was mainly the work of Protestant and more and more Orthodox churches.

X.

However, also these aspects of the council demand more than good will, Christian love, and brotherly help. Even the brotherly help includes fraternal admonition, which does not forget the doctrinal side of the life of Christ's Church. If one reads the "responses" in the American edition, one misses painfully the *admonitio fraterna* in the question of doctrine, except in the article by Prof. Schmemann, the Russian theologian. The Eastern Orthodox churches in America seem to be the only ones that really takes seriously the fact that the Church of Christ is by nature a teaching, a dogmatic Church. The churches that claim to be the heirs of the Reformation have with very few exceptions lost the understanding of the doctrines of the Reformation and the binding force of the ancient creeds that they still nominally uphold but no longer really confess. One wonders why no synagogue belongs to the National Council of Churches. Dr. Blake, who always liked to preach occasionally in a synagogue and has even on a solemn occasion expressed in Berlin his desire that the Ecumenical Movement might also embrace the Jews, has certainly no theological objection against this broadening of the"*Oikoumene*." One must never forget that the Reformation is for the Americans an event that took place in a different country, far away from the shores of America, and at a time when the New World was just being discovered. The first settlements in New England and in Pennsylvania brought to the New World not the old European churches—if one leaves out for a moment the Catholic Church in Latin America—but groups of dissenters from the European state churches. Thus, America became the great paradise of dissent and very soon the melting pot not only of nationalities but also of all religious groups of the Old World. The immigrants from the established churches of Europe— Anglican, Reformed-Presbyterian, and Lutheran, became more or less the dissenters in that type of American Christianity that had its origin in the small groups of the "Third Reformation," which could never take really root in the European establishments. The two great types of Protestants in America became the Baptists and Methodists. Even the influence of European Calvinism, important as it was, has not really shaped American Protestantism. The European immigrants retained faithfully also their confessional heritage as long as this was enshrined in the native language. But one has only to look at the history of American Lutheranism in the last generations to realize what the transition to the English Bible and the acceptance of English as the language of liturgy and preaching was bound to mean. The formation of the new American nation was bound to reflect itself in the process of Americanization and de-confessionalisation of all churches. Even the Roman Church had to fight "*Americanismus*" as one of the most important forms of Modernism already in the nineteenth century. The process of assimilation and unionism that found its first climax in the creation of the Federal Council of Churches in 1908, the precursor of the present National Council, coincided with the Ecumenical Movement in Europe, which from the very beginning had the closest connection with the development in America. The two world wars that made the U.S.A. the leading political power of the Western world and helped to finalize the American civilization with its tremendous influence on the whole world have accelerated this process.

It is in this context that one must understand the great breakdown of dogmatic thought we observe throughout the Christian world in all churches. The vast volume of the documents of the Second Vatican Council contains innumerable theological thoughts and concepts. But one concept is totally missing: the concept of heresy. But how can one teach the nature of the Church and discuss its various functions if one does not think of the fact that the existence of the Church is always threatened by errors and heresies? Pope John in his opening speech regarded the preservation of divine truth as an unquestioned task of the Church. But by refusing to repeat the anathemas of former times, he forgot that if "the sacred deposit of Christian doctrine," to quote John himself, must be "guarded and taught," this cannot be done without clearly and unmistakably rejecting that which contradicts this deposit. It is true that the Church has overdone it in the past. When the Council of Trent was solemnly closed on December 4, 1563, the last words were the acclamation: "*Anathema cunctis haereticis, Anathema, Anathema.*" This was overdone. At the end of Vatican II, an informal service of prayer with the "separated brethren" was held by the pope. This was a noble Christian gesture. But the question remains whether there is no longer a border between Church and heresy. The council has not been able to state this clearly, and this will create grave problems in the future. Many Christians in the entire world think that it no longer exists.

In spite of all good will and so much theological work, the concept of "separated brethren" as it has been established in "Lumen gentium" remains a compromise that can be understood in various ways. It should be a manifestation of the love that should exist between all followers of Christ, the love we should give to all men and quite especially also to the erring brother. The concept of "separated brethren," however, will prove in the long run to be quite insufficient, as it was already not successful in the attempts by Augustine and Optatus, who coined it to overcome the split between Catholics and Donatists. In the coming years, Rome will have to rethink its relationship with the Christians of other churches. Thus far it seems that our Roman brethren are satisfied with the basis of the World Council of Churches, which is so vague as to be acceptable even to communities that refuse to accept the Trinity as more than a liturgical formula and reject the divinity of Christ and other basic truths of the Christian faith as they themselves disclosed at New Delhi in 1961. In this respect Rome may learn from the Eastern churches, which untiringly have stated where for them the border lies between Church and non-Church. There seems to be no hope that the Lutheran and the Reformed churches will return to what for their fathers was the truth of the Gospel on which no compromise is possible. Thus a tremendous responsibility lies on the shoulders of our Roman brethren. The future destiny of Christendom may be decided in Rome—not in the sense that Rome has retained the common heritage of our holy faith, but in the sense that it may have the strength to renew its own understanding of the faith.

A vast amount of theological problems will have to be faced by us all. The problem of the papacy, which is at issue also between Rome and the Christian East, cannot be solved by adding to the infallible teaching office of the bishop of Rome a more or less equally important teaching office of the college of the bishops as the successors of the college of the apostles. There has never been such a college in the Church of the New Testament, just as there was no Petrine office for the whole of the Church. A new and deeper study of the New Testament will be required if we want to attain a sound ecclesiology. A great problem is the question of the *communicatio in sacris*; this is nothing new. This question has been seriously discussed in Roman theology in connection with the relationship with Greek Christians in the eastern Mediterranean islands. The learned canonist Bevenot has in the beginning of this century clearly formulated the question. Is the old canon *"Nulla communicatio in sacris cum schismaticis et haereticis"* divine or human law? Is it based on the revealed will of God, or is it a law the Church has made to protect its members from infection by heretical views? While the Church at all times has accepted the rule as divine law, there is at present a tendency to accept the other answer. This would open the way to that intercommunion with all Christians that is urgently demanded by all liberal churches and by a growing number of Catholics. Rome has thus far definitely resisted the great temptation that seems to become the main issues of the Ecumenical Movement. As in all cases of such nature, emergency situations and borderline-cases, such as mixed marriages, are used to settle the question according to the wishes of the people. It might be hoped that the Eastern Orthodox Church in this as in other questions will prove itself as the true guardian of orthodoxy.

XI.

What Christian love in doctrinal matters is and is not may be illustrated by the great example of the apostle of love in the New Testament. His first epistle is perhaps apart from 1 Corinthians 13 the greatest document of the great love Christ expects from all his disciples. But the same apostle has spoken the harshest words against heresies and the most terrible anathema against stubborn heretics. "Beloved, do not believe every spirit, but test the spirits to see whether they are of God, for many false prophets have gone out into the world. By this you know the Spirit of God: every Spirit which confesses that Jesus Christ has come in the flesh is of God, and every spirit which does not confess Jesus is not of God. This is the spirit of antichrist of whom ye heard that he was coming. . . ." What was happening in the province of Asia? There were groups of Christians to whom John denied fellowship and in whom he recognized antichrist. If we could have met them, they would have told us that they believed in Christ as the Savior of the world no less than John and his people. They loved Jesus and put all their hope in him. There was only a slight difference in the understanding of the Body of Christ. Some regard it as an earthly body, others as a heavenly body. Is this really so great a difference? We all know that his body is now glorified and heavenly. Could we not arrange a brotherly dialogue in which agreements and disagreements would be discussed with the result that the agreements are greater, especially since this question has become obsolete? But the apostle of love remained adamant. He insists on the real incarnation. For he knows that on this "small" difference hangs the entire Gospel, the Christian faith in the world and our eternal salvation. Today every serious theologian who knows the history of the Church would admit he was right. There would not be a Christian Church in the world today if this dogma had not been kept faithfully. Christianity would have lapsed into that chaos of pagan religions that promised eternal salvation without the incarnate Son of God. In his second epistle, John repeats the commandment of love and continues, "Many deceivers have gone out into the world, men who will not acknowledge the coming of Jesus Christ in the flesh, and such a one is a deceiver and the antichrist." "If anyone comes to you and does not bring this doctrine, do not receive him into the house or give him a greeting, for he who greets him shares his wicked work" (2 John 4:11). So serious is the danger of heresy. So the law forbidding *communicatio in sacris* with heretics is clearly a divine law. We find it also with St. Paul (e.g., Rom. 16, cf. 1. Cor. 16), who always connects it with the eucharistic liturgy. There it has its "*Sitz im Leben*" at all times. If our Catholic brethren want real, true unity of the Church and fellowship with us, they owe us the great service of love that includes the warning against soul-destroying errors and heresies. For the churches are, in our opinion, sisters who have to help each other. Why do we not hear a word of warning against the destruction of the Sacraments in so many of our Protestant churches? Why do they not tell us what sin we are committing by ordaining women for the priesthood and give the *potestas ordinis* and the *potestas juridictionis* that Christ has not given to his own mother to hundreds of girls? And so we could go on. Is it only weakness if Catholic dioceses join the so-called Councils of Churches in America and now even in Australia and if Catholic bishops pave the way for the *communicatio in sacris* in which the true Church must disappear? For so far one has not heard that one of the member churches of the Ecumenical Movement has returned from heresy to the true faith of the Church, from the neglect and the destruction of the Sacraments to the true Sacraments of Christ, which are more than nice human ceremonies.

In one word: what we expect from our Roman brethren is brotherly love in the sense of the New Testament, not that substitute for Christian love that modern ecumenism—what a terrible word; it should be abolished as soon as possible—offers us, pious sentiments that are not the gift of the Holy Spirit. The love of the New Testament does never forget the seriousness of the quest for truth. St. Paul connects truth and love in his great chapter on the unity of the Church, Ephesians 4, by his admonition "not to be tossed to and fro and carried about with every wind of doctrine" (v. 14), and to speak "the truth in love" (15). And in his great High Priestly Prayer for his Church, our Lord connects the two petitions, "That they may all be one" and "Sanctify them in the truth; thy word is truth." This connection is forgotten by certain professional ecumenists of our day in all churches who seem to be able to solve any problem. We all have to remember it and perhaps reconstruct our ecumenical organizations along the lines suggested in 1920 by the Ecumenical Patriarchate, which envisaged a brotherly league of churches living together in peace and sharing their mutual charisms until the Lord himself fulfils the promises he has given to his Church. We all have to make our contributions. One of the contributions our evangelical churches will certainly have to make before admonishing others is to remember for ourselves the word with which the Reformation began: "Our Lord and Master Jesus Christ, when he said, repent ye, wanted the entire life of the faithful to be repentance"—the entire life of all Christians and of all churches.

THE SPRINGFIELDER
Vol. XXV, No. 3 (1961)

Theses on the Seventh Article
of the Augsburg Confession

The Augsburg Confession (Art. VII, VIII, and Apology) teaches as an article of faith that there is and always will be one holy, catholic and apostolic Church. This Church is properly or strictly speaking (*proprie dicta, stricte dicta*) an "association of faith and the Holy Spirit in men's hearts" (*societas fidei et Spiritus Sancti in cordibus*, Apol. par. 5), the congregation of saints, in other words, of true believers who are justified by faith. Since the Lord alone "knoweth them that are his" (2 Tim. 2:19), and since their faith and holiness is seen by him alone, the Church in this sense is hidden to human eyes. But we are bound to believe it to be present wherever the means of grace are administered. This is meant by the first part of the Seventh Article: "*Item docent quod una sancta ecclesia perpetuo mansura sit. Est autem ecclesia congregatio sanctorum in qua evangelium pure docetur et recte administrantur sacramenta.*" (According to the German text, which is the authentic commentary to the shorter Latin: "It is also taught among us that one holy Christian Church will be and remain forever. This is the assembly of all believers among whom the Gospel is preached in purity and the Holy Sacraments are administered according to the Gospel.")

II.

As the means of grace must be and are administered here in this world, by living persons among living persons, the Church is also an "association of outward ties and rites" ("*societas externarum rerum ac rituum*"), like other societies. This is the Church in a broader sense ("*large dicta*," "*late dicta*"). It is not church in the proper sense because it comprises also persons who are not members of the Body of Christ, hypocrites and evil men, unbelievers who only for outward reasons belong to the external organization. But even the believers are weak and sinful men. This means that they are constantly in danger of losing their faith, of falling away under the onslaughts of the devil, who always tries to destroy the Church. Hence it is the constant task of the Church as the "association of outward ties and rites" to see to it that the pure Gospel and the Sacraments as instituted by Christ are preserved. The promise of Christ that he will be with his Church until the end of the world and that the gates of hell shall not prevail against it is, therefore, inseparably bound up with his command to preach the Gospel in its entirety (Matt. 28:29; Acts 20:20), to continue in his Word (John 8:31), and to administer the Sacraments. This includes the most sacred duty to reject error and heresy. Promise and commandment, the gift of the Gospel and the command to proclaim and preserve it belong inseparably together.

III.

The Church of Christ is essentially one, *Una sancta*. The doctrine of the Church is, therefore, always also a doctrine of the unity, the oneness of the Church. Also, the unity of the Church is at the same time a gift and a task, an indicative and an imperative. This becomes clear in the Scripture passage that underlies *Confessio Augustana*, VII, Ephesians 4: "There is one body and one Spirit . . . one Lord, one faith, one baptism, one God and Father. . . ." This is the indicative. It is bound up with the imperative "that ye walk worthily of the vocation with which ye are called . . . endeavoring to keep the unity of the Spirit in the bond of peace." In the same way, in the Seventh Article we find the indicative "*quod una sancta ecclesia perpetuo mansura sit*" linked up with the imperative contained in the sentence: "*et ad veram unitatem ecclesia satis est consentire de doctrina evangelii et de administratione sacramentorum, nec necesse est.*" For this sentence tells us what we have to do in the "*societas externarum rerum ac rituum*," the Church broadly speaking, in order that "*societas fidei et Spiritus Sancti in cordibus*," the Church strictly speaking, the *Una Sancta* may remain *with us*.

IV.

The Augsburg Confession was written for a practical purpose that is described in the Preface as a restoration of an outward unity that had been lost: "to have all of us embrace and adhere to a single, true religion and live together in unity and in one fellowship and church, even as we are all enlisted under one Christ (Pref. par. 4). Which the corresponding Schwabach Article XII had to deal only with the question of what the Church is, the Seventh Article of the *Confessio Augustana* had to take up that practical question: how can the unity of the Church as a "*societas externarum rerum ac rituum*" be restored? Over against the Roman claim that this would require not only the acceptance of the doctrine and the sacraments of the Roman Church, but also of constitution, liturgy, and other traditions, *Confessio Augustana* VII declares, "For the true unity of the Church it is enough to agree concerning the teaching of the gospel and the administration of the sacraments. It is not necessary that human traditions or rites or ceremonies, should be alike everywhere. It is as Paul says, 'one faith, one baptism, one God and Father of all . . .'. This implies clearly that the *consensus de doctrina evangelii et de administratione sacramentorum* is absolutely necessary for the true unity of the Church. The "*Satis est*" in contrast with "*Nec necesse est*" means "This is enough because only this is necessary."

V.

The "*consentire de doctrina . . .*" of the Latin text must be understood in the light of the German text that explains the meaning authoritatively: "For it is sufficient for the true unity of the Christian Church that the gospel be preached unanimously according to its pure (true) meaning and the sacraments be administered according to the word of God." Not any consensus will do, but the consensus in the pure Gospel and the right administration of the Sacraments. As in the

New Testament (cf. the petitions of Christ, John 17, "sanctify them in the truth" and "that they all may be one" and the apostolic injunctions concerning heretics), so in the Augsburg Confession the quest for unity is the quest for truth. *Ubi veritas, ibi unitas.* If two church bodies find that they agree concerning the Word and the Sacraments and establish a union on this basis, this would not necessarily serve the true unity of the Church.

In America, Unitarians and Universalists have reached agreement. But this union has nothing to do with the unity of the Church of Christ. Even if two Lutheran churches reach an agreement in matters of doctrine and establish a merger on this basis, this does not necessarily mean true Church union. For it could be that they agree to disagree in such doctrines as the doctrine of Holy Scripture as the Word of God (is it the Word? or is the Word contained in it?), or the real presence. In the Church the association of external ties and rites only serves the true unity of the Church when such agreement preserves the means of grace in their purity. For these means of grace create and preserve the Church as the association of faith and the Holy Spirit in men's hearts, the true Church that always is one, the *Una Sancta. Ubi veritas, ibi unitas.* For only through the means of grace the one Lord builds his Church, the *Una Sancta,* which is his Body.

VI.

What does it mean that we must agree in the pure doctrine of the Gospel and in the right administration of the Sacraments? Is it enough that the article of justification, the *articulus stantis et cadentis ecclesiae,* is correctly preached and taught, or must there be also agreement in other doctrines. The answer must be that the article of justification cannot be rightly taught where the great articles of the Apostles' and the Nicene Creed are not kept. The denial of the virgin birth leads to a false doctrine of the incarnation. A false doctrine of the incarnation leads to a false understanding of justification and of the Sacraments. Thus the article of the standing and the falling Church keeps together all articles of the Christian faith and illuminates them.

For Lutherans the consensus required should always be regarded as the doctrinal content of the Book of Concord. For also the doctrinal decisions of the Formula of Concord concerning original sin and the will of man, Law and Gospel, the Sacrament of the Altar, the person of Christ, and predestination and election are nothing but explanations and safeguards of the article of justification. It is the dogma of what has to be accepted, not necessarily the theological terminology. As to the Sacrament of the Altar, it must be maintained that the doctrine of the real presence belongs to the "administration" because Christ himself has given an explanation in the Words of Institution. Since the Christian Sacraments are bound up with the Word and could not exist without the Word, the consensus of the Gospel cannot be separated from the consensus concerning the Sacraments.

VII.

The question is constantly being asked, especially by all union churches, whether it is not enough that the Word is preached and the Sacraments are administered, whereas the common confession does not necessarily belong to the essence of the Church. Our answer must be that the confessional writings certainly do not belong to the essentials of the Church, but that the dogma they contain must be preached, proclaimed to the world, and confessed, not only by the individual Christian and pastor, but by the church body as a whole in church and school, in oral proclamation and in writing. It cannot be left to the individual pastor whether or not he wants to preach this or that doctrine. It is the duty of the Church body to see that all congregations hear the true Gospel and receive Christ's Sacraments. While the form of such church government belongs to the adiaphora and traditions, the function of oversight must be exercised—"*non vi, sed verbo,*" *Confessio Augustana* XXVIII—in order to preserve the Gospel and with it the unity of the Church. Only where the Church as the "association of outward ties and rites" obeys the divine imperative, "endeavoring to keep the Unity of the Spirit," remaining in the Word of Christ, and rejecting false doctrine will the divine promise be fulfilled that the *Una Sancta perpetuo mansura* is with us.

THE SPRINGFIELDER
Vol. XXVII, No. 2

"The Future Reunited Church" and "The Ancient Undivided Church"

I.

"I BELIEVE in the Holy Catholic Church, and sincerely regret that it does not at present exist," was a favorite saying of William Temple.[1] It makes sense in the mouth of an Anglican only. For the nineteenth article of the Articles of Religion has altered, to the great distress of many evangelicals in the Church of England, its pattern (Art. VII of the Augsburg Confession) in a very characteristic way

---

[1]See F. A. Iremonger, "*William Temple, Archbishop of Canterbury: His Life and Letters*," Oxford, 1948, p. 387. It would be worthwhile to investigate the ecclesiology of this representative leader of modern ecumenical Anglicanism. Sometimes he was inclined to find the *Una Sancta* solely in the future, e.g., in an address at Lausanne, 1927 (H. N. Bate, *Faith and Order*, 1927, p. 488f.) where he points out that the divisions are "as old as the Church." Here he thinks of the split between Jews and Christians in the New Testament. "Only the truly Catholic, the truly Universal, Church can have a living grasp of the whole Christian faith. From this point of view it would be true to say that there is not in the world today a Catholic Church with many schisms around it; from this point of view it would be true to say that there exist only schisms, and that this must always be true as soon as any schism has taken place at all."

by speaking not of the "Church" but of the "Visible Church": "*Ecclesia Christi visibilis est coetus fidelium, in quo verbum Dei purum praedicatur et sacramenta . . . recte administrantur.*" If the Church in which we believe, the *Una Sancta*, is visible, where, then, is it today? Roman Catholics will answer, "The *Una Sancta* is the Church," or the churches in communion with the Apostolic See. According to the Tractarians and later Anglo-Catholics, the *Una Sancta* existed in three branches, the Eastern Orthodox churches, Rome, and the Church of England. Thus they excluded all Protestant churches from the true Church of Christ.

To the Anglican, for whom the episcopal office with the apostolic succession belongs to the very nature of Christ's Church, but who refuses to deny the existence of the Church among the Protestants, nothing is left if he wants to be consistent but to declare that the *Una Sancta* does not at present exist. To believe in the *Una Sancta Catholica et Apostolica*, then, means to believe that it has existed in the past and that it will exist again in the future. From the dogma of the *Una Sancta* follows for the Anglican the dogma of the "ancient undivided church" and the dogma of the "future reunited church." From this belief again follows the ethical duty of Christians to work for the restoration of the lost unity of the Church in a "future reunited church." This dogmatic conception of the union of Christians as a reunion of Christendom corresponds to the ecclesiastical situation in England. Already in the seventeenth century, continental observers have been wondering about the multitude[2] of sects that split off from the Church of England. As England and English-speaking Christendom has proved the most fertile soil of religious divisions, reunion has always been one of the most urgent problems of Church life.

II.

It is distressing to see how modern Lutheranism has taken over these Anglican ideas, as they were disseminated by the Ecumenical Movement of our century, without examining them in the light

---

[2]"*ingens numerus,*" A. Calov, *Historia Syncretistica*, 2nd edition, 1685, p. 859. Many similar utterances are extant.

of the doctrine of the Lutheran Confessions on the Church and its unity, without asking if that understanding of the *Una Sancta* is scriptural, and without investigating the historical tenableness of the idea of the "Ancient Undivided Church." One may well ask what deep-rooted disease of modern Lutheranism is revealed by the fact that our churches have uncritically accepted those foreign ideas and have allowed them to penetrate our congregations and especially our youth organizations as something taken for granted.

All Lutherans who are interested in ecumenical questions are reading now in the Foreword to *A History of the Ecumenical Movement* by R. Rouse and S. Neill that it is their "responsibility to pray and work for the restoration of the visible unity of all Christian people" (p. xxiv). They learn about the stages of ecumenical work: "(1) cooperation between Christians belonging to different confessions and churches, (2) cooperation between the several confessions and churches, (3) union or reunion of separated churches, (4) the full and final restoration of the unity of all Christendom."

The author of this preface is the Director of the Ecumenical Institute at Bossey, Dr. Reinold von Thadden-Trieglaff. What would his famous ancestor, that conservative Pomeranian nobleman, Adolf von Thadden-Trieglaff, who left in 1848 the Prussian Union for the Lutheran Free Church have had to say about this gigantic plan of a union for all Christendom? What Luther would have said we know. It is written in the Smalcald Articles (III, 8) where we read, "Enthusiasm clings to Adam and his descendants from the beginning to the end of the world . . . and it is the source, strength and power of all heresy, including that of the papacy and Mohammedanism" (*The Book of Concord*, ed. Tappert, p. 313).

Enthusiasm, as Luther describes it in this context, is that type of Christian piety that does not stick to the Word alone, but listens to other voices besides the voice of the Good Shepherd. It is that religion that finds the Holy Spirit not only in the Word and in the Sacraments, but, as many Anglicans in our day would say,[3] also in

---

[3] For instance Archbishop Geoffrey Fischer in *Redeeming the Situation: Occasional Sermons, 1927* (London, 1948), p. 43: "The Church of England believes that the Holy Spirit of God, the only final authority, speaks to us in Holy Scripture, in the tradition of the Church and in the living thought and

the tradition of the Church and in the living experience of today. This enthusiasm is a danger for all churches, "Catholic" or "Protestant," "older" or "younger." It has always been in a particular way a danger in English Christianity, though we must not forget how this enthusiasm in the sixteenth century was kindled by influences from the continent—Bucer and the Anabaptists—and how readily it was accepted by the continental churches when the tide turned back. Pietism, Christian societies and conventicles in the eighteenth, sects from England and America since the nineteenth century, missionary societies of pietistic character, Christian youth movements, and finally ecumenical organizations and movements: in all these manifestations of the religious life of modern Protestantism that enthusiasm asserts itself. One feature of this enthusiasm is "chiliasm," the hope for the realization of the kingdom of God on this earth.

In touching words John Mott closed the First World Missionary Conference on June 23, 1910: "God grant that we all of us may in these next moments solemnly resolve henceforth so to plan and so to act, so to live and so to sacrifice, that our spirit of reality may become contagious among those to whom we go: and it may be that the words of the Archbishop shall prove to be a splendid prophecy and that before many of us taste death we shall see the Kingdom of God come with power" (*Report*, Vol. IX, p. 351). He referred to the address with which Archbishop Davidson had greeted the conference at its opening session and which closed with the quotation of Mark 9:1. The great American leader of World Missions and the Archbishop of Canterbury agreed that it might be that during the lifetime of some of the delegates "here on earth, in a way we know not now," as the Archbishop said, "the Kingdom of God come with power" (*loc. cit.*, p. 150).

III.

It is this chiliastic enthusiasm that has found an expression in the modern idea of a "future reunited church." To deny the idea that

---

experience of today. Thus there is a threefold cord, each single strand of which, unrelated to the others, leads astray." There are, of course, many Anglicans who would protest against the idea that the *sola scriptura* should lead astray.

there will be one united church in which all present churches including Rome will be absorbed is regarded as blasphemy by those under
the spell of this modern form of chiliasm, just as forty years ago when
in America the "Social Gospel" began to reach its climax, we Lutherans were accused of blasphemy and unbelief when we doubted that
it was the task of the Church to transform human society into the
kingdom of God.

But is it not the will of Christ that the churches should be
united? Is not the idea of a "future reunited church" based on the
promise of Christ that there will be one flock and one shepherd?
Has he not prayed "that they all may be one"? Hardly any sentence is
being used—and misused—more often in our days than the great *Ut
omnes unum* of the High Priestly Prayer. Is it really necessary to offer
the assurance that it is neither from disregard of our duty to work
for peace and unity among Christians nor, least of all, from lack of
respect for the words of our Lord that we disagree with the popular understanding of that petition, which is taken for granted today?
Can the repeated petition of Christ in the great prayer of John 17,
one of the most solemn, almost unearthly texts of the Bible, really be
understood in that way that this petition would have found its fulfillment in a "future reunited church" in which all who call themselves
Christians would be united?

Those who envisage such a church understand it to be an ecclesiastical organization in which not uniformity, but rather unity
in manifoldness would prevail. It would be a church in which the
peculiar gifts of each of the previously divided churches should be
preserved. Their various forms of faith, order, liturgy, and community life would be no longer regarded as contrasts, exclusive of one
another, but rather as supplementing each other and growing, on the
basis of the experiences of a common life, into an always-deepening
unity. The controversies between the churches would dissolve into
the peace of a great harmony like the sound of the various instruments of an orchestra.

For the present we do not want to discuss whether it is really
possible to regard the varieties as forms and fragments of one truth
underlying all of them or whether there are contradictory forms
of the Christian religion that defy reconciliation in a higher unity.
We cannot enter here into the question of whether the conviction

that it must be possible to reach, by patient and brotherly discussion, agreement on any question at issue is not the consequence of the fact that modern Protestantism has lost the concept of heresy, of Church-destroying error that accompanies the history of the Church from the beginning to the end, a consequence perhaps, in the last analysis of the tragic loss of the great *charisma* "to distinguish between spirits" (1 Cor. 12:10, cf. 1 John 4:1) without which the Church cannot exist.

However, we must ask this: Suppose that all Christians were united in such an ecumenical body, the "future reunited church." Would this really mean that the prayer of Jesus Christ was fulfilled, "that they all may be one; *as thou, Father, art in me, and I in thee, that they may be one in us*; that the world may believe that thou hast sent me, and hast loved them, as thou hast loved me. And the *glory which thou gavest me I have given them*; that they may be one, *even as we are one: I in them, and thou in me*, that they may be made perfect in one; and that the world may know that thou hast sent me, and hast loved them, as thou hast loved me" (John 17:21ff.)? Why does the world now not recognize Jesus as the Christ, the Son whom the Father has sent? Could one say the world does not believe in Christ because it sees a divided Christendom but that this would be different as soon as a united Christendom would give a united testimony?

Certainly the sins of Christendom, including the sin of unnecessary divisions and of a lack of love, are always a most serious obstacle to faith. But who would dare to say that if today a united Church, instead of the many denominations, preached the Gospel the Buddhists would give up their Buddha, and the Mohammedans would abandon their prophet and confess Christ? Does anyone believe that the communists of Russia and China and all other atheists the world over would accept Christ and that atheism and paganism would disappear?

Unbelief is not caused by the sins of the Christians. "More redeemed should his disciples look if I were to believe in their Redeemer," says Nietzsche-Zarathustra. What an untruthful statement this is. Even if a man like Nietzsche would have met the greatest saints of all ages, this would not have caused him to believe. He would certainly have found another excuse. Faith is always the work of the Holy Ghost. What kind of Pentecost would be necessary if suddenly the entire world should recognize Christ! If the High Priestly Prayer means by "world" here not only those whom the Father has given to his Son "from the world" (cf. v. 20, with 6, 8, 9, 12), but the whole of mankind, including those who thus far have rejected Christ, then the fulfillment of Christ's prayer must be understood in a strictly eschatological sense. The world cannot see the glory the Father has given to his Son. How, then, would it see the glory Christ has given to his Church?

As men in this aeon cannot see the oneness that exists between the Father and the Son, so no human eye can see the oneness "in Christ" that binds together those who believe in him. Even to the believing Christian this oneness is an object of faith and not of observation. It is more than the human love and fellowship we may experience. The New Testament calls it the "communion of the Holy Spirit" (2 Cor. 13:13), a *koinonia* that the members of the Church have with one another and that is at the same time "our *koinonia* with the Father and with his Son Jesus Christ" (1 John 1:3), a communion connected with the communion that exists between the persons of the blessed Trinity, as is clearly indicated in John 17:21. "*Ubi trinitas, ibi unitas*," as an old hymn says. Christ says (v. 24) when we shall see his glory: "Father, I will that they also, whom thou hast given me, be with me where I am; that they may behold my glory which thou hast given me. . . ." This glory will become manifest to the world on the Last Day. Then the *regnum Christi*, which, as the Lutheran Confessions (*Ap. ad C.A.* f) put it, is now *cruce tectum*, hidden under the cross, will be revealed (*revelatum*). Only at the end of time will the world know Christ. Then "every eye shall see him, and they also that pierced him" (Rev. 1:7), and the confession of the Church will become the confession of the whole cosmos when "at the name of Jesus every knee shall bow of those in heaven, and those on earth, and those under the earth, and every tongue confess: Jesus Christ is Lord, to the glory of God the Father" (Phil. 2:10f.).

Christ's disciples must never cease to fight against the lovelessness of their own sinful human nature. They must never cease to try their best to overcome error and heresy through which the devil tries to corrupt our faith and to destroy the Church. But to think that our most faithful and patient endeavors to overcome unnecessary divisions could make manifest the *Una Sancta* in this world of sin and error would be chiliastic enthusiasm and not true Christian faith based on the Word of God. For our Lord himself has made it unmistakably clear that this world—by the way, not the Church—is that field on which not only the seed of Christ's Gospel grows, but also the seed sown by the devil, until the harvest at the end of the world will separate the wheat and the tares (Matt. 13:31ff.). Then with the hidden glory of the Church also its true unity will become manifest, a oneness that comprises not only one generation but all true believers of all generations of the world. Then in the consummation of all history, the prayer of Christ that they all may be one will have found its final answer.

IV.

The untenableness of the Anglican idea of a "future reunited church" is indirectly confirmed by the fact that its counterpart, the concept of the "ancient undivided church" is equally untenable. It is also a dogmatic idea, a conclusion from the understanding of the *Una Sancta* as *ecclesia Christi visibilis*, which does not stand the historical test. What should and could be that "undivided church" of the past? With an astonishing tenacity, the idea has lived on in the Anglican churches that the "ancient undivided church" was the Church of the first five centuries. This church, therefore, should set the pattern for the restoration of the lost unity. This idea goes back to the Christian humanists whose program for a reform of the Church as well as for the restoration of the unity lost in the Reformation was the return *ad fontes*, to the Church of the New Testament and the early fathers as the sources of pure Christianity. It has been cultivated in the later sixteenth and seventeenth centuries by the Latitudinarians in England, the Arminians in Holland, and the Syncretists of the school of Helmstedt in Germany. It was one of the opponents of Georg Calixtus, a theologian at Strassburg, who has coined the term "*consensus quinquesecularis*," which was never approved by G. Calixtus and expressly rejected as "nonsense" by his son Ulrich.[4]

---

[4] He called it "*ineptum quinquesecularium vocabulum*." See for details and references Otto Ritschl, *Dogmengeschichte des Protestantismus*, Vol. IV, 1929, pp. 400ff.

The idea was that the basis of the reunion should be the historic dogma of the Ancient Church in which the Lutherans and the Reformed churches agreed with Rome and even the Eastern Orthodox, the great doctrines of the Trinity and the person of Christ. This practically amounted to the reception of the dogma up to the Chalcedonian Creed that had been reaffirmed in all confessions of the sixteenth century. Calixtus's theory was rejected as inadequate because it did not meet the issues between Rome and the Reformation. To his Lutheran opponents, he was a "semi-papist," while the Jesuits of Mainz called him a "semi-Christian doctor and Supreme Pontiff of the Utopian-Oecumenical Church assembled in whatever faith you like."[5]

The historical inadequacy becomes evident in Calixtus's reluctance to define the exact date of the division of the Church. If one regards the dogma of the person of Christ as belonging to the consensus, then the Nestorians and the Monophysites must be regarded as such who have separated from the true Church, the *Una, Sancta, Catholica et Apostolica Ecclesia* in the sense of Catholic and Anglican ecclesiology. Apart from the problem of the person of Nestorius, who was not a real "Nestorian," as Luther already suspected and modern Catholic scholarship has shown, what must we think of the Church of Eastern Syria, which represented the Christian Church to Central and East Asia for centuries? In every liturgy it commemorated the "318 fathers" of Nicea whose faith it wanted to preserve undefiled.

Certainly there is a grave theological error in its understanding of the person of Christ. He who reads the reat hymns of that church notices the deviations from the orthodox doctrine, but cannot help feeling that this is an older type of Christology that no one would have regarded as heretical around A.D. 400. We Lutherans at least, though compelled to reject its heresy, would believe that also in this church the Church of Christ was present. The same is true of the Monophysite churches of the Armenians, the Jacobites, and the Copts. The theological reasons why their fathers did not accept the Chalcedonian Creed—there were non-theological reasons, too—one can learn from

---

[5]*"Calixtum Semi-Christianum Doctorem optimum et Ecclesiae Utopico-Oecumenicae in fide quodlibetana congregatae Pontificem Maximum,"* quoted by A. Calov, *Historica Syncretistica*, 2nd edition, 1685, p. 870.

their present theologians.[6] Even Roman Catholic scholars would not deny the strong Christian element that has always remained in spite of the heresy extant in their doctrine. Thus A. Fortescue could write in *The Lesser Eastern Churches*, 1913 (pp. 449–50), "At least for one thing we must envy them, for the *glory of that martyr's crown* they have worn for over a thousand years. We can never forget that. During those dark centuries there was not a Copt nor a Jacobite, nor a Nestorian nor an Armenian who could not have brought relief, ease, and comfort, by denying Christ and turning Turk. I can think of nothing else like it in the world. These poor forgotten rayas *in their pathetic schism,* for thirteen hundred years of often ghastly persecution, kept their *loyalty to Christ.* And still for his name they bear patiently a servile state and the hatred of tyrants."[7]

We have stressed the words that indicate the problem of Church and sect as it is seen by a Roman theology. If in such schismatic or even heretical bodies there can be the crown of true martyrdom, if true loyalty to Christ can coexist with christological heresies, then we Lutherans must confess that also in them the true Church of Christ exists, just as we believe that the true Church exists also in the Eastern Orthodox churches and in Rome despite all errors and heresies. We believe that the *Una Sancta* is hidden in the outward organizations that claim the name "church" wherever the Gospel of Christ is still being proclaimed and his Sacraments are administered. This is, indeed, a dogmatic statement. But it seems to us that it is consistent with the facts of Church history. No one has so far been able to show at what time the "ancient undivided church" was divided.

V.

From the fifth century, we go back to the century of the first ecumenical synods. Where was the undivided church during the two generations between the Council of Nicea, 325, and the council of 381? The

---

[6]See the illuminating article by Vardapet Karekin Sarkissian, "The Ecumenical Problem in Eastern Christendom," *The Ecumenical Review* Vol. XIII (July 1960), pp. 436–54.

[7]*Ibid.,* pp 441 f.

latter was actually only a council of the East but was later recognized as "ecumenical" on account of its creed, which since 451 by and by replaced the old Nicene Creed of 325, so much that it has even inherited its name. For our "Nicene Creed" is actually that of the "150 Fathers" of Constantinople. One must try to imagine the situation of the Christian religion after Constantine's victory in order to understand the tragedy of a divided Christendom. Has there ever been a greater missionary opportunity than at the time when Constantine called the Church out of the catacombs to become his strongest ally in building up a politically unified and morally strong empire? But the Church, instead of rallying all its forces for the great mission work, absorbed its strength for two generations in an almost suicidal *bellum omnium contra omnes.*

When Constantine after his accession in the East heard of the controversy about "the interpretation of one Bible passage" (Prov. 8:22ff.) that had arisen in Alexandria, he implored both parties, Bishop Alexander and his presbyter Arius, to find a compromise as philosophers would do in a similar case. But the fight had become unavoidable. It became even worse when later emperors who had not the wisdom and patience of Constantine tried to solve the problems of the Church by mere political means. Athanasius knew why he went from exile to exile. With the *homoousios,* the dogma of the full divinity of the Savior, the Gospel itself, and the existence of the Church of Christ was at stake. But how few bishops, to say nothing of the simple laity, could understand the implications of the theological terms? How few congregations were able to find their way between the ever-increasing factions into which Christendom seemed to be disintegrating. They all, adherents and opponents of the "*homoousios,*" the *homoios,*" "*homousios kata panta,*" "*homoios kata tas graphas,*" "*homoios kat' ousian,*" "*homoiousios,*" "*anhomoios,*" claimed to be "Catholic Church."

Where was the border-line between Church and heresy? It happened that an orthodox congregation discovered that their bishop was a radical Arian who did not believe in the divinity of Christ, but had hidden his true convictions (Theodoret, *Hist. Eccl.* II, 30). Our orthodox Lutheran fathers, when dealing with the problem of heresy, have always emphasized that the condemnation of some errorists by the Council of Nicea did not mean that the entire churches from which they came were heretical, just as the Preface to the Book of Concord declares that the condemnation of certain Calvinistic errors, such as those concerning the Lord's Supper, does not imply a condemnation of entire churches within or without the empire. If the Arians claimed to be the Catholic Church, one must admit that even in their churches there were not only simple Christians who did not understand the Arian heresy and were satisfied with a childlike faith in Jesus Christ as Savior, but that also among their theologians there were men to whom we must concede an earnest Christian faith.

Erasmus discovered that an unfinished commentary on the Gospel of Matthew, which has been preserved among the works of Chrysostom, was written by an Arian of the fourth century. Bardenhewer, the famous Roman Catholic Church historian, observes that "the author has deserved that protection." He praises highly his knowledge of Holy Scripture and his literary achievements, and he adds, "Behind that book there is a man of character and strong convictions, of moral strictness, an attitude and a burning zeal for the true Church of Christ, the little flock of the adherents of the 'homoios' is in danger to be absorbed by the vast host of the heretics, i.e., the Catholics."[8] Thus the problem of various confessions and denominations was already present in the Ancient Church. With great sympathy one must look at that ambassador of the Visigoth king of Spain to the Frankish court at Boitierr. He was seen in church every Sunday at the Catholic Mass, but he never went to Holy Communion. For there was no church fellowship between the Catholic Church of Gaul and the Arian Church of the Spanish Visigoths until in 589 a synod of Toledo accepted the Catholic creed. This did of course not mean that all Christians in the Visigoth Church suddenly changed their religious convictions.

VI.

That the "ancient undivided church" is a theological fiction becomes fully evident if we turn from the "heresies" to the great "schisms" of ancient Christendom. Socrates (*Hist. eccl.* I, 10) and Sozomen (*Hist.*

---

[8]O. Bardenhewer, *Geschichte der altkirchlichen Literatur*, Vol. III, 1912, p. 597.

eccl. I, 22) report that at the request of Constantine also Acesius, the Novatian bishop of Byzantium—soon to become Constantinople— was summoned to the Council of Nicea. It was obviously the wish of the emperor to abolish the Novatian schism as he had tried for many years to heal the split between Catholics and Donatists in Africa. When at the end of the synod, the bishop was asked whether he accepted the decisions concerning the "*homoousios*" and the date of Easter, he replied in the affirmative because these decisions affirmed only the old faith and practice. To the question "Why, then, Acesius, do you keep aloof from communion with others, if you are of one mind with them?" he replied by stating the reasons for the Novatian schism. To them it was not permissible to re-admit to Holy Communion persons "who, after Baptism, had fallen into those sins which the Scriptures declare to be unto death." For such sins only God can forgive in the Last Judgment. "O Acesius, take a ladder and ascend alone to heaven," was the reply of the emperor.

The Novatians have always been, as the Meletians in Egypt whose schism was based on constitutional questions, staunch defenders of the orthodox faith. They differed from the "Catholics" in that they had preserved a principle concerning church discipline that once had been recognized by the entire Church. If we are inclined to criticize their rigorism as irreconcilable with the Gospel, we should not forget that also the more lenient Catholic Church knew only of a *paenitentia secunda*, a second penance after the great penance at Baptism. Did this disagreement over the question whether after Baptism in the case of such sins no penance or one penance only was permissible really constitute a sufficient reason for a schism that since the middle of the third century lasted for some hundreds of years?

Socrates relates (*Hist. eccl.* V, 14) of Honorius around 400 A.D., "The emperor's veneration for religion led him not only to honor the bishops of his own communion, but to treat with consideration those of the Novatians also, who embraced the '*homoousion*' creed: to gratify therefore Leontius, the bishop of the Novatians at Rome, who interceded in behalf of Symmachus, he graciously pardoned him for that crime." If the pagan consul who is accused before the Catholic emperor of high treason enlisted the support of the Novatian bishop of Rome, Leontius, the latter must have been a man of influence. For until the fifth century, Novatians are mentioned not only in Italy, but also in Gaul (Rouen). In the East they merged with the Montanists and must have formed a by no means insignificant church, comparable to the Donatists in Africa, who claim that not the congregations but at least the clergy must be free of mortal sinners. All attempts to heal this schism in Africa, initiated by Constantine as soon as he became ruler of the West, faded. Shortly after Constantine's death, the Donatists, who regarded themselves as the Catholic Church and denied the validity of the sacraments in the Church, which for Augustine was the *communio catholica*, could muster 270 bishops at a synod that met at Carthage for two weeks. In many places they have been the majority. In such a state of an incurable division, Christendom existed in the Latin provinces of Africa until it was wiped out by the Arabic conquerors.

So we could go on reviewing the state of Christendom in the various parts of the ancient world. Everywhere we would find a divided Christendom. This is true also for the first centuries. Celsus, who about A.D. 180 wrote the first great polemical work against the Christians from the standpoint of a pagan philosopher, has this to say: "In the beginning they were a little company and were of one mind. But since they have become a widely spread multitude, parties and factionsare arising, each claiming followers. They separate from each other and condemn each other. Thus, so to speak, there is one thing only they still have in common, the mere name they are ashamed of abandoning. Otherwise each group goes its own way." Origen in his reply does not deny the fact of these divisions. He explains them by comparing them with the various schools of philosophy and medicine: "Since many of the Greek scholars saw in Christianity something venerable, sects (*haireseis*) were bound to arise, not because they liked splits and controversies, but because many scholars (*philologoi*) were eager to understand Christianity. Consequently the books that by all were recognized as 'divine' (*theious logous*) were understood in different ways. Thus sects (*haireseis*) arose which were named after those men who, though admiring the origin of the doctrine, for various reasons arrived at varying results" (Origenes, *Contra Celsum*, III, 12; ed. Koetschau, pp. 210ff.).

Whatever one may think about Origen's rather apologetic explanation, the quotation shows that both Christians and pagans knew of the divisions of Christendom. Schisms like that between Callistos and Hippolytus, between Victor and the Church of Asia, the division caused by the Montanist movement and, worst of all, the great Gnostic sects and the counterchurch of the Marcionites made Christendom in the second century chaotic. What we would call orthodox Christendom, the Church that existed amidst the great Gnostic movements and later rallied around the "rule of faith," the canon of the New Testament and the episcopal office, was in the middle of that century probably a minority. A pagan who wanted to join the Church in Rome about A.D. 150 was in a situation very similar to that of a prospective convert in one of the big cities in India or Japan today. He had to make up his mind which of the denominations that claim to be the Church of Christ he should join.

One has to read only the last epistles of Paul or the epistles of John in order to know that already the apostles died in a divided Christendom. And this goes back even into the beginning of the apostolic mission at the time when Peter in Antioch did not know exactly in which church he could and should participate in Holy Communion and Paul called him a hypocrite because he withdrew from the communion with the Christians of Gentile origin when Judases from Jerusalem arrived.

VII.

"By schisms rent asunder, by heresies distressed": This has been the situation of Christendom at all times. There has never been a visible "ancient undivided church." We must never forget that the scarcity of our sources makes it impossible to write a full history of Christendom in the ancient world. One of the reasons for the lack of source material is the fact that the writings of heretics and schismatics have been delivered to the *damnation memoire*. We have almost nothing except quotations from their adversaries. The great works written against the Gnostic and Marion (mainly Irenaeus, Tertullian, Hippolytus) and the comprehensive works against all heresies by later writers like Epiphanius provide us with a lot of material. What we can know on the basis of their quotations is quite astonishing, as Harnack's masterly book on Marion shows as it tries to give also a picture of the Church of Marion, the history of which, unknown in details, accompanies the entire history of the Church. But such material does not allow the writing of a full history of Christendom even in the apostolic and postapostolic age.

How close Gnostic communities could be to what we call the early Catholic Church, how difficult it often was to draw a borderline between "Church" and "heresy" appears from the few fragments of direct Gnostic origin we possess. Was Clement of Alexandria much more than a Gnostic? We have mentioned that Arian commentary on Matthew that seemed to be so valuable that it has been attributed to Chrysostom. Still more regrettable is the lack of sources in the case of the great schismatic churches. Some writings by Novatian have been preserved, such as the famous book on the Trinity and even some letters in Cyprian's correspondence. But the later literature of the Church of the "*katharoi*" has completely disappeared, just as the literature of the Donatists. What we have are quotations and some fragments (Ticonius). We cannot simply apply the "*Damnant Donatists*" of Conf. Aug. 14 to all those Christians who once belonged to that large African Church in which an older form of African Christianity survived. Where was—in those centuries in Africa—the true Church of Christ? We cannot identify it with either group. We can only say, as we have pointed out when speaking of the divisions of the East, that the *Una Sancta* was hidden in these church bodies as it is hidden in, with, and under the earthly churches wherever Christ is still present in the proclamation of the Gospel and in his Sacraments.

It is interesting how in the Donatist controversies for the first time the question was debated whether and how far the Church of Christ can exist also in a schismatic church body. The Donatists were consistent when they simply denied that the "*communio catholica*" *Augustines* could claim the name "church" and "catholic." They appealed to Cyprian's "*Extra ecclesiam nulla salus*," with which the great African father had rejected the validity of any Baptism performed outside the "catholic" Church. Over against them, Augustine developed the doctrine of the Sacraments as valid, even if not effective, in a separated body. In his encyclical "*Ad Petri Cathedrum*," John XXIII addressed, in connection with the announcement of the Second Vatican Council, those who are separated from Rome as "separated brothers" ("*fratres sejuncti*"): 'We address you, then, as brothers, even though you are separated from us"—this means

from the *Cathedra Petri*, and consequently from the true Church—
"For as St. Augustine said, 'Whether they like it or not, they are our
brothers. They will only cease to be our brothers when they cease
to say, Our Father.'" The quotation is from Augustine's *Enarratio* in
Psalm 32 (Migne, PL 36, 299). The whole chapter 29 of that exposition of the psalm (our Ps. 33) is an admonition to exercise Christian
charity toward all men, not only the fellow church members, but also
toward those "outside" ("*foris*"), "whether they are still pagans, not
yet believing in Christ, or whether they are divided from us, confessing with us the head, but separated from the body ('*nobiscum caput
confitentes et a corpore separati*')." Augustine has taken over this
idea from Optatus of Mileve, who insisted on calling the Donatist
bishop Parmenianus his brother and justified that elaborately in his
De Schmismate Donatistarum (IV, 2; Migne PL 11, 1029f.). He, too,
uses the "Our Father," which is prayed on either side as an argument
and emphasizes that both pray the Fifth Petition. The Donatists,
of course, refused to reciprocate since to them the "*catholica communio*"[9] does not belong to the Church. But it is certainly significant that the rejection of Donatism by all churches, Catholic and
Protestant, means not only the rejection of that particular error concerning the validity of Sacraments administered by a sinful priest,
but also the condemnation of any concept of the Church that limits
the validity of the means of grace to one particular denomination.

VIII.

If our observations are correct, what must be the practical conclusion
for the ecumenical work of the churches today? This question has
become even more urgent since Rome at the Second Vatican Council
entered the Ecumenical Movement. The Roman Catholic Church,
too, knows the undivided church of the past. It claims to be the
Church from which all the other churches and sects are supposed to

---

[9]Augustine calls Optatus "*Milevitanus episcopus catholicae communionis*"
(*Contra ep. Parmeniani* I, 3, 5). It is not necessary to show here that "catholic"
is used since the second century often to denote the "orthodox" church in a
particular place or area. Thus it becomes the name of a Christian communion,
a "denomination."

have separated, not only the heretical churches of the East, but also the Eastern Orthodox Church, to say nothing of the great divisions of the sixteenth century. Rome is hoping and working for "reunion." The great vision of a "future reunited church" has taken hold of the Catholic Christians the world over.

The amazing efforts made today by the Roman Church to pave the way for such reunion of the "separated brethren" with the "mother church" must be taken quite seriously. It would be wrong to see in them only church politics. The ecumenical enthusiasm of many Catholic Christians, including bishops and theologians (e.g., Hans Küng, *That the World May Believe*) shows that the modern Ecumenical Movement is one of those great religious movements which, as pietism and rationalism did, penetrate the whole of Christendom irrespective of denominational borders. No one can say what the outcome of such movements will be. They cannot be controlled by a program made by men or by the constitutions of the ecumenical organizations. It may well be that one day the Roman idea of the undivided church of the past will be so modified that it becomes acceptable to the Christians of the East and to the Protestants. Then the way to reunion is open. But reunion built on figments is never the true unity of the Church; true unity is based on the truth of God's Word.

If we are asked what our alternative is to the enthusiastic efforts to unite Christendom on the basis of the ideas of the "ancient undivided church" and a "future reunited church," we can only say that we have to go back from such human dreams to the reality of Christ's Church. What this reality is we must learn from Holy Scripture and from nowhere else. With our fathers in the Reformation, we find the doctrine of the *Una Sancta* in the words of St. Paul, who, in Eph. 4:1ff., speaks of the unity of the Church as a divine gift. "There is one body and one Spirit . . . one hope . . . one Lord, one faith, one baptism, one God and Father of all." The one Lord builds his Church through the means of grace in which He is present. The Holy Spirit creates and preserves the unity of this Body, the Church, in the bond of peace. Faith and the oneness of faith are created in the souls of the believers, as in the Church as a whole, by God the Holy Spirit. To this indicative, "There is one body," the one, Holy Church, corresponds the divine imperative, the apostolic injunction "that ye walk worthy

of the vocation . . . with all lowliness and meekness, with longsuffer-
ing, forbearing one another in love, endeavoring to *keep* the unity of
the Spirit in the bond of peace."

But how can we keep this unity if we do not keep that by which
the Church is preserved, the pure doctrine of the Gospel and the Sacraments as instituted by Christ? The exhortation to walk in brotherly
love and in meekness cannot be separated from the duty to keep the
one faith. Love we owe to all men, also to the erring brother and to
the heretic. But true love requires that I warn my brother and distinguish clearly between Church and heresy. How can I save my brother
from the danger of heresy if I refuse to make this distinction? In the
New Testament, the quest for oneness and the quest for truth always
belong together. It was the apostle of love who uttered the most serious warnings against heresy (1 John 4:1ff.; 2 John). And it was Christ
himself in whose High Priestly Prayer the two petitions "that they
all may be one" and "sanctify them in thy truth; thy word is truth"
belong together.

It may be that the great contribution Roman Catholicism has to
make to the Ecumenical Movement is that it compels the Protestant
churches, many of which have lost the sense for dogmatic truth, and,
therefore, think of the Church of the future in terms of chiliastic
dreams, to realize again what the New Testament teaches about the
reality of the *Una Sancta*.

THE SPRINGFIELDER
Vol. XXVIII, No. 3 (1964)

The Confession of Faith
According to the New Testament

The author of these pages remembers from his student days those happy years shortly before World War I when Protestantism had succeeded in getting rid of the dogma of the Church. "Not the Son, but the Father belongs to the Gospel as Jesus has proclaimed it." This was Harnack's great discovery. The dogma of the Triune God and of the God-man Jesus Christ was regarded as a product of the Greek mind in the Church. These doctrines were necessary for the preservation of the Gospel in the Ancient World. The Greeks had lent their philosophy to the Church, just as the Romans had put their gift of administration and organization into the service of the Gospel. These were temporary necessities, still of great importance to the Middle Ages, which had taken over the heritage of the ancient culture. But it was a misunderstanding if the reformers kept the ancient dogma. The Gospel no longer needs these obsolete means of defense. On the contrary, they have become a hindrance to its true understanding. Christianity is essentially not a dogmatic religion.

This view corresponded with the popular conviction that the dogma was a straightjacket that hindered the free development of true religion, an invention of priests, and a product of human speculation on mysteries that essentially are incomprehensible to the human mind. The man in the street who dislikes anything that goes beyond the narrow horizon of his pure or poor reason felt justified by the great discovery that one can be a good Christian without accepting the Christology of the Church.

The great scholars of that age themselves felt sometimes that something was wrong with their theology. There were moments when they were aware of their tragedy. Harnack was sometimes quite upset by the use liberal pastors and laymen made of his thoughts. Friedrich von Hagel felt the tragedy in the life of his great friend Troeltsch. The crisis of liberal theology—or rather of that "historism" in theology that was one of the great topics if not the real theme of Troeltsch's thought—became manifest in the pathetic life of Albert Schweitzer. He spoke the last word in an era of Protestant theology in the famous conclusion of his "The Quest of the Historical Jesus." He states that the names once given to Jesus in the terms of late Judaism, such as Messiah, Son of Man, Son of God, have become historical symbols to us. By referring these titles to himself, he indicated that he thought of himself as a commander, a ruler. We do not find a name that would express to us what he really is. "As one unknown and nameless he comes to us, just as on the shore of the lake he approached those men who knew not who he was. His words are the same: 'Follow thou me!' and he puts us to the tasks which he has to carry out in our age. He commands. And to those who obey, be they wise or simple, he will reveal himself through all that they are privileged to experience in his fellowship, of peace and activity, of struggle and suffering, *till they come to know*, as an inexpressible secret, *who he is. . . .*" (A. Schweitzer, *My Life and Thought: An Autobiography*. Transl. by C. T. Campion. London, 1933, pp. 71f.). This is the key to the understanding of the great turn in Schweitzer's life. The great historical theology had spoken its last word on Jesus. This great man drew the conclusion. There is no human greatness without consistency.

I.

In silent obedience to the call of that mighty ruler, Schweitzer hoped to reach that understanding of the secret of Jesus that historical research could not give him. Has he reached his aim? We cannot know. This is a secret between him and his master that we must not try to investigate. "*Secretum meum mihi.*" One thing, however, we must state. Schweitzer's thinking in so many fields of learning has not led to a new theology, and theology always includes Christology. What we read in his philosophical books, and especially in his ethical writings where his thought comes sometimes nearer to Indian thought than to the New Testament ethics, shows that, whatever he may have come to know of the mystery of Jesus has remained inexpressible, as he had predicted.

Why is that so? It is strange that a New Testament scholar of Schweitzer's rank has never seen that according to the Gospels discipleship is never silent obedience only. Human curiosity has not asked who this Jesus is. It was our Lord himself who asked his disciples, "Whom do men say that I am?" "Whom say ye that I am?" (Mark 8:27ff) and who put the question to his adversaries, "What think ye of Christ? Whose son is he?" (Matt. 22:42). Men are not responsible for the Christology. Christ himself has created it by claiming to be what he is, by demanding from men a clear statement as to whether they accept his claim.

It is generally acknowledged today by New Testament scholarship that not only the Father, but also the Son belongs to the Gospel as Jesus has proclaimed it. The names "Messiah," "Son of Man," and "Son of God" were to him not only symbols denoting an inexpressible fact, but titles that exactly expressed his divinity. He claimed to be the fulfilment of what the Old Testament had prophesied concerning the Messiah, the Servant of God, and the Son of Man. One can accept or reject that claim just as did the witnesses of his earthly life. One can regard it as blasphemy as the High Priest did when Jesus made his "good confession (*kalen homologian*) before many witnesses" (1 Tim. 6:13, cf. Matt. 26:63f. and parr.). One can regard him as possessed of the devil (Mark 3:22 parr.) as the scribes did, or, with modern scribes, as a psychiatric case. One can accept in simple childlike faith his claim as his disciples did. Whatever attitude men may take, they have to answer the question of who he was. This belongs to the mystery of his person. Wherever a man is confronted with Jesus, he cannot avoid answering the question "Who is he?" Buddha or Muhammad do not ask this question. Jesus does. Even his bitterest enemies have to answer it.

II.

"Thou art the Christ" (Mark 9:29). This was the answer Simon Peter gave to the question of his Lord. It was the first confession made by Simon, the spokesman of the Twelve, on their behalf and on behalf of the future Church. A personal beatitude is spoken to the first confessor (Matt. 16:17): "Blessed art thou, Simon Bar Jona: for flesh and blood hath not revealed it unto thee, but my Father which is in heaven." This answer is not the result of human thinking. It is given by God.

Thus the confession of faith is the answer to the question Jesus puts to man, either directly, or as a question implicitly contained in the Gospel. All creeds and confessions of Christendom are meant to be essentially a repetition and continuation of the confession that Jesus is the Christ. This first confession needed clarification and enlargement as soon as it was no longer understood properly. There were Christians of Jewish background who would accept Jesus as Christ, as the Messiah, but who thought of him as a man who had become Son of God by adoption. Thus very early, probably in Antioch before Paul, Hellenistic Christianity confessed him as "*Kyrios*," using this Greek word to render the Aramaic "*mar*." Thus the Aramaic-speaking church's "*maranatha*", which is still preserved in 1 Corinthians 16:22 became "*erchou kyrie Iesou*," as we find in Revelation 22:20. "*Kyrios*" is "the name which is above every name" (Phil. 2:9), God's own name.

It is wrong to understand "*kyrios*" as meaning less than "*theos*." "*Kyrios*" is the translation of *Yahve* in the Greek Bible. It means, as also "*kyrios*" means in the pagan mystery religions, "God in his revelation." In this sense the words "*theos*" and "*kyrios*" must be understood also in 1 Corinthians 8:6, where Paul interprets the "*heis theos*" of the Jewish creed, the schemata of Deuteronomy 6:4 in the Christian sense. To call Christ "Lord" means to apply to him the holy name of God in the Old Testament, as he himself in the Fourth Gospel uses the "*Ego eimi*," "I am," hinting at Exodus 3:14. "*Kyrios Iesous Christos*," Jesus Christ is Lord, is the second stage of the Christian confession. He who calls him Lord says no less than what the later creed says of him: "God from God, light from light, very God from very God."

III.

The confession is the answer to the question of Jesus, who he is. Who gives that answer? It is noteworthy that Jesus has asked the Twelve, "Whom say ye that I am?" He expects an answer given by all of them. It seems that he is not so much interested in what Simon or John or Matthew or Judas may believe and confess. It is in the name of the Twelve that Simon answers, "Thou art the Christ" (see also John 6:68f). How can he answer on behalf of them all? Has he made an enquiry? We in his stead would have called a meeting, perhaps appointed a committee to investigate the matter and to report to the full assembly of the Twelve. That is the way modern confessions are made. And this is the reason why modern confessions as a rule are no confessions at all. To give only one example, when the constitution of the "Federal Council of the Churches of Christ in America" was drafted in 1908, it had been proposed to speak in the preamble of Christ as the Son of God. This was unacceptable to many. So the constitution called him "divine Lord and Savior." What do the words "divine," "Lord," and "Savior" mean if Christ is not the Son of God?

The confession Peter makes is not based on inquiries and negotiations. It is not a compromise between various personal views—maybe there had been several personal views among the Twelve. Simon does not even ask his fellow believers. He speaks for them all as he speaks for himself. The true confession is always the confession of the individual—"Blessed art thou, Simon"—and the confession of all true believers. It is the confession of the individual believer and of the Church as a whole. A true confession can begin with the "I believe" of the baptismal creed, which is always confessed by the individual, or it can begin with the "*pisteuomen*" of the creed as it was formulated by a synod and confessed at the Eucharist. There is no essential difference between the "I" and the "We."

We modern men have understood the creed mainly in the sense of the individual confession. Today we are in danger of thinking only in terms of a collective society, the Church. In the former case, we forgot the reality of the Church. In the latter case, we forgot the conversion is always something that happens to the individual. Individuals only can be baptized, not tribes or families. Even if a whole family is baptized, Baptism is administered to each individual, and the formula is "I baptize *thee*." This fact that in the Church of Christ the "I" and the "We" belong together is no longer understood by modern Christians, because they no longer understand the work of the Holy Spirit. As we no longer realize the meaning of "*Kyrios*," so we no longer understand the "*Pneuma Hagion*," the "*Parakletos*," as our careless religious language shows.

If we take it seriously that faith in Christ is always the gift of God, then we understand why the true faith and confession of the individual believer must be the same as the faith and confession of the Church. In his exposition of the Third Article in the Small Catechism, Luther puts it this way: "I believe that I cannot by my own reason or strength believe in Jesus Christ, my Lord, or come to him; but the Holy Ghost has called me through the Gospel, enlightened me by his gifts, and sanctified and preserved me in the true faith; in like manner as he calls, gathers, enlightens, and sanctifies the whole Christian Church on earth, and preserves it in union with Jesus Christ in the true faith."

Modern Christendom has tried to understand faith, the work of the Holy Ghost, psychologically, and the Church, the work of the Holy Ghost, sociologically. Hence many Christians no longer understand that reality the New Testament means when it speaks of the Holy Spirit and his work. How often do we speak of something as being the work of the Holy Spirit when it actually is the work of the human mind without realizing that the name of the Holy Ghost also comes under the commandment "thou shalt not take the name of the Lord thy God in vain. . . ."

IV.

If the confession of faith is essentially the work of the Holy Spirit in the individual soul as well as in the entire Church, then we understand the first great function of a true confession: it binds believers together. This first function of the confession is nowhere better expressed than in the liturgy of the Eastern Church where the creed follows the kiss of peace. The deacon admonishes, "Let us love one another that we may confess in one mind." The choir continues, "The Father, the Son, and the Holy Ghost, the one and indivisible Trinity." Then follows the creed, originally in the form of the "we": *Pisteuomen eis hena theon . . . .*" At all times the confession of faith has been the strongest expression of that "unity of the Spirit in the bond of peace" that belongs together with the "one faith, one baptism."

It is not necessary to dwell upon this point any longer. But one thing must be said over against modern misunderstandings of the Christian faith. If on the one hand the confession is the point around which the Church gathers, it has on the other hand a critical function. The confession "Jesus is the Christ" expressed the unity of faith in the first Church. He who confesses this as the conviction of his heart belongs to the Church of Christ. At the same time, this confession drew the borderline between Church and synagogue, as John 9:22 shows: "for the Jews had agreed already, that if any man did confess him as the Christ (*auton homologese Christon*) he should be put out of the synagogue."

In the same way, the name "*Kyrios*" drew the borderline between the Church and the Hellenistic synagogue ("*kyrios*" was *Yahve* for the Greek-speaking Jews), but also between the Church and the many cults of other *kyrioi* (1 Cor. 8:4ff.; 10:20f.), or between the worship of the Lord Jesus and the worship of *Kyrios Kaisar* (see *Martyrdom of Polycarp* 8ff.). The truth cannot be confessed without rejecting error. Thus already in the most ancient eucharistic liturgy we find the "*Pax*," the Holy Kiss, side by side with the anathema against schismatics and heretics (1 Cor. 16:20–22).

It is the constant task of the Church to confess the truth and to reject error. Already, therefore, the apostles had to warn against heresies, as the Pastoral Letters of Paul especially show these having been written at a time when Gnosticism began to threaten the Christian faith. And it is certainly not accidental that the apostle of love had to reject and condemn in strong words those who denied the incarnation (1 John 4:1ff., 2 John 9ff.). We have no report of the reaction of those Christians who differed from John in that they assumed the body of Christ had not consisted of dirty, earthly flesh. Most likely they claimed to love their Savior just as well, and perhaps even more than that irreconcilable keeper of (what he regarded as) orthodoxy, who not only denied them the name of brethren, but even the courteousy of a greeting, claiming that they had the spirit of antichrist. However, one has only to ask what would have become of the Church if the apostles had been less orthodox and more tolerant. Supposing they had called ecumenical conferences between the various groups who claimed to be the true Church of Christ and that Christendom of the second century had been spared the terrific splits between Basilidians, Valentinians, Catholics, Marcionites, and all the other groups, then there would be no Church today. The same is true of the Church of Nicea. Without the anathema against the deniers of the *Homoousios* in the Nicene Creed of 325, there would not be a Church today.

It is quite clear that not every anathema that has been uttered in the course of the history of the Church was justified, as it is true, on the other hand, that there have been false, heretical creeds and confessions that have created not true unity but false unity, not the unity created by the Holy Spirit, but man-made unity. This, however, has always been the way God's revelation was received by men. The people in Jerusalem at the time of Jeremiah were confronted with the problem as to who really spoke the Word of God: the many prophets who proclaimed as God's the comforting message that once had been proclaimed by Isaiah that Jerusalem would be saved, or that lonely man who called those prophets liars and their visions and auditions dreams. God's Word can be misunderstood. There is no infallible magisterium that could decide for me what is truth and what not. This gives the confession of the Church its seriousness. That is the reason why the Church should confess nothing not contained in God's Word.

V.

It is significant that the words used in the New Testament for "confess" have several meanings. While "*homologein*" and "*homologia*" mean confessing the faith, confession of faith (the use of "*homologia*" for the "confession" Jesus made at his trial [1 Tim. 6:13] is unique, but quite pertinent), "*exhomologeisthai*," is used for the confession of sins (Mark 1:5; Matt. 3:6; James 5:16) and for the praise of God (Matt. 11:25; cf. Luke 10:21; Acts 19:18; Rom. 14:11; 15:9).

The second meaning is present in Philippians 2:11 together with the meaning "confess Christ." In this passage the Church's confession of faith is at the same time the"confession" of the entire universe at the end of the world, the acclamation of triumph and praise. In the Latin of the Church the three meanings are contained in the words"*confiteri*," "*confessio*," which is quite in accordance with the New Testament usage. The "*Te Deum*" is at the same time confession of faith—it has often been enumerated among the creeds—and praise of God: "*Te Deum Laudamus, te Dominum confitemur*" (*exhomologeisthai*, see Phil. 2:11).

The "*Confessiones*" of Augustine are "Praises of God," but they contain the "confession of his faith" and the "confession of his sins." In the Greek Church, "*exhomologesis*" is used for the sacrament of penance and for the praise of God. This usage points to a very important theological fact. Confession of faith, confession of sin, and praise of God belong together. When Peter, overwhelmed by the great miracle, addresses Jesus for the first time as "*Kyrie*," this confession is at the same time a confession of his sinfulness: "Depart from me; for I am a sinful man, O Lord" (Luke 5:8). In deepest humility only can we acknowledge Jesus as Christ and Lord. On the other hand, the confession of faith is praise of God. It is prayer. The first confession is addressed to Jesus: "Thou art the Christ," or according to John 6:67ff., "Lord, to whom shall we go? Thou hast the words of eternal life, and we have believed and come to know that thou art the Holy One of God."

Whether the confession is a simple acclamation like the earliest confessions of the New Testament, or a baptismal or other creed, or a doctrinal statement like the *Symbolum Quicunque*, or an elaborate confession like those of the sixteenth century, they all want, each in its way, to give Christ praise and honor. This explains the fact that the creed has its place in the liturgy. The close connection between liturgy and dogma, the fact that each dogma appears first in the liturgy (e.g., the trinitarian formula is older than the trinitarian dogma, the "*erchou Kyrie Iesou*" older than the dogmatic definition of the Lordship of Christ, the *homoousia* of the Holy Spirit appears first in the liturgy, as the Nicaenum of 381 suggests; the *sola gratia* and *sola fide* of the Reformation appears in the medieval liturgy, etc.) has been emphasized by the Liturgical Movement, though sometimes at the expense of the dogma.

"Orthodoxy" has always been understood in the Eastern Church as "right doctrine" as well as "right worship." The word "*theologia*"—which means with the fathers of the fourth century the doctrine of the Triune God and especially of the divinity of Christ—is originally praise of God. According to old liturgies (e.g., James) the *Sanctus* is sung by the Seraphim and Cherubim "*asigetois theologiais*," in never-ceasing "theologies." John the Apostle is "John the Divine" (*ho theologis*) because he is the liturgist, his language being the language of the liturgy (see the hymns of Revelation).

A confession, a theology, and an "orthodox" theology which do not contain the praise of God are most certainly wrong. A confessional or confessing church interested in the doctrinal confession only and not in confession as penance and as praise of God would not be a truly confessing church. The really great theologians of the Church have always been at the same time great liturgists, as Ambrose, Basilius, Thomas Aquinas, and Luther. Schleiermacher and Ritschl were no theologians at all in the old sense. One cannot sing or pray their theology.

VI.

A last aspect of the New Testament confession may be mentioned. A true confession has always an eschatological aspect. The confessing church, as the individual confessor, stands always at the border of time and eternity. That Latin "*confessio*" is also used for the "grave of the martyr" over which the Church is built. Thus the "*confessio*" of Peter is the grave under the main altar of St. Peter in Rome. The cathedral of Fulda is built over the "*confessio*" of Boniface. The confession is made before governors and kings.

This confession before the earthly judge is made with the help of the Holy Spirit, as every true confession (Matt. 10:18f.; comp. 1 Cor. 12:3). To confess Christ is dangerous. It involves a risk of life. Still more dangerous is it to deny Christ. This can happen very easily, as is indicated by the fact that Peter, the first confessor, became the first to deny his Lord, a sin that later incurred excommunication. More dangerous is it because eternal death may follow. For we confess not only before a human judgment seat, but also before the judgment seat of God.

Confession and denial follow us into eternity. There the earthly confession will be followed by the heavenly confession, not only by the eternal praise of God in the *ecclesia triumphans*, but also by the confession of Christ: "Whosoever shall confess me before men, him will I confess also before my Father which is in heaven." As our confession is the answer to the question of our Lord, so his confession will be the answer to every faithful confession made here on earth.

THE SPRINGFIELDER
Vol XXXV, No. 3 (1971)

Walther and Loehe: On the Church

Professor Hermann Sasse discusses the relationship of the pastor to the congregation against the historical background of the controversy between C. F. W. Walther and Wilhelm Loehe. It may be safely said that each man was a giant of Confessional Lutheranism, Walther in America and Loehe in Germany. Both men were agreed that church organization belonged to the class of adiaphora, things that are directly commanded by God, but, as Professor Sasse contends, both men failed to apply their own principles. Walther insisting upon the primacy of the congregation and Loehe the primacy of the pastoral office. This is also a footnote to the history of the seminary as Loehe was its founder and later Walther one of its presidents. Dr. Sasse is the former professor of theology at the University of Erlangen and the Immanuel Lutheran Seminary. He is now professor emeritus of Luther Seminary of the Lutheran Church of Australia. From time to time he has been guest lecturer and professor at Concordia Theological Seminary. The seminary awarded him an honorary doctor of divinity degree for his contributions to Lutheranism. This article was translated and prepared by students John Sipppola and John Drickamer

One of the most disrupting occurrences in the history of the Lutheran Church of the nineteenth century was the parting of the great churchmen Wilhelm Loehe and Ferdinand Walther after the great Missouri Synod leader had had such a promising meeting with Loehe in Neuendettelsau in 1851. It is not important that neither of these men were able to establish a relationship with the Erlangen school. For despite the importance its theology may have had and despite the human and scientific greatness of its representatives, its theology possessed faults that rendered it impossible for it to be the source of lasting renewal for the Lutheran Church. This theology had not been able to keep itself free from the seductive poison of Schleiermacher's subjectivism. Every serious attempt to hold fast to the objective truths of Scripture was doomed to fail when the methodology that began with Schleiermacher became a hermeneutical principle. If my subjective self becomes the proper object of my theologizing, then no earthly power can prevent theology from becoming the science of human piety. Another fault of the Erlangen theology was its restriction to the narrow borders of official German Lutheranism. In comparison, Loehe and Walther viewed the problems of worldwide Lutheranism as opposed to the ecclesiastical bureaucracy, a bureaucracy protected and directed by the German *summi episcopi*! Who would have guessed that out of the troubled congregations then being organized on the border of civilization would one day come the great church in whose hands the fate of Lutheranism rests today, as far as it rests in the hands of men. Neither could anyone foresee what the break between Walther and Loehe, between Missouri and Iowa, would mean for the future. We see its significance today and must answer whether or not the unification that failed then is possible today, a century later.

II.

It was by no means only the question of the relationship between the Church and the pastoral office that separated Loehe and Walther and led to the cleavage between Missouri and Iowa, but this question had especially great significance. It separated not only these men and their churches but Lutheranism in general. The widespread divisions caused by this question may at first be surprising. The Lutheran Church has always regarded church policy as adiaphora or *ritus aut ceremoniae ab hominibus institutae*, because Christ is not the legislator of a human religious community and the

Gospel contains no law concerning church polity. The implications
of this position must be clearly understood. Every other church recognizes, in Calvin's familiar words, an *ordo, quo Dominus ecclesiam
gubernari voluit* (an order, by which the Lord wants his Church to
be governed). This holds true for all Catholic churches, Eastern and
Western rites, as well as for the Reformed churches. The differences
of opinion concern themselves only with the nature of this *ordo*,
whether it is to to be the universal monarchy of the papacy, the
episcopal-synodical government of the Anglicans and the Eastern
Orthodox, the direction of the church through a senate of presbyters all of whom must be equal, or the congregational autonomy of
the Congregationalists and Baptists, to mention only a few of the
types of church polity allegedly prescribed in the New Testament.
Luther's greatness and the boldness of his basic theological principle of the differentiation of Law and Gospel become clear when one
sees how he goes his own lonely way outside of these possibilities:
Christ never gave his Church a law *de constituenda ecclesia*. Every
type of church polity is possible as long as the pure administration
of the means of grace is not hindered. To be sure, the Lord has given
his Church something that does not belong to her *bene esse* but to
her *esse*. In order that we may obtain the faith that justifies, the Gospel must be preached and the Sacraments must be administered,
and for this purpose God has ordained the ministry, through which
this comes to pass. Wherever the means of grace are rightly administered, there is, according to the divine promise that the Word shall
not return void, the Church, the communion of saints, of justified
sinners. There are just as few prescriptions concerning the nature
of congregational as there are concerning the form the *ministerium
ecclesiasticum* assumes. The apostles came to the realization that it
would be helpful in fulfilling the duties of the spiritual office if they
were freed from the tasks of caring for the poor and of financial
administration. This was the origin of the auxiliary office of the
deacons. Nevertheless the Church was the Church even before the
creation of this office. The Church is always free to create specific
offices out of necessity, for example, the bishopric or the office of
superintendent. All these offices retain their right to exist, however,
only as long as they serve the one great office of the preaching of the
Gospel and the administration of the Sacraments.

If there is agreement in the entire Lutheran Church on this point, how do we explain the divergence of opinion concerning the pastoral office and the congregation and therefore concerning church polity that has time and again divided our church since Loehe and Walther first disagreed? It seems certain to me that the polity problems of other churches and confessions have influenced Lutheranism. In the process Lutherans have not remained completely loyal to the magnificent freedom of the Reformation. When others were concerned with "genuine, biblical church polity according to the command of Christ," it was dangerous for our church on her part to want to enter the fray. As loyal as they were to the Lutheran confession, neither Walther nor Loehe avoided this pitfall, to mention just their names. This situation is analogous to the time of orthodoxy, when Lutherans often allowed Calvinists or Catholics to ask the questions without recognizing that the questions were not valid in themselves. Here, as in other points, the old orthodoxy was much too dependent on her opponents. Although the theologians of the nineteenth century accepted orthodox dogmatics, they were right when they believed that Christendom would be led to a deeper understanding of the Church in the midst of the immense political and social catastrophes in their time and in the near future. The Early Church had already known everything confessed in the Nicene Creed, but it was the titanic struggle with ancient paganism that enabled the Church fully to recognize the importance of the true divinity and the true humanity of Jesus Christ and to articulate the doctrine of the *homoousia*. If we are to speak of progress in the confession of faith, it must be understood in the sense of the Church meeting new situations and in no other. The parting of the two great schools of Lutheranism in the last century is without doubt related to the failure of the Lutheran Church to come to final clarity concerning the implications for church life of the ecclesiastical articles of the Augsburg Confession. And so it happened that the great Lutherans of the previous century, and more specifically those who were concerned not only with the theoretical but also had to build churches, have left us a legacy, far from unexhausted. The task that therefore faces our generation cannot be to repeat the formulations and pick up the discussion where it stopped one hundred years ago. Rather, we must, on the basis of the experience of the Church in the past century and with perhaps greater insight into the teaching of Holy Scripture, once more think through what has, since that time, remained an unsolved problem.

IV.

It is worth noting how modern historical research into the beginnings of church polity has confirmed Luther's deep exegetical insight: The New Testament recognizes no fixed church order and was therefore unable to canonize any such order. The history of church polity is similar to the history of the liturgy. The beginning of each was marked by diversity rather than unity. Therefore it was possible to read the most varied forms of church polity into the New Testament and to find them there again with satisfaction. No one who considers the biblical statements will readily presume today to find a complete and always binding form of church polity in the New Testament. Even the Lutherans of the nineteenth century, who did not escape the temptation to inquire cautiously into the correct biblical form of the Church and her order, would today simply accept the fact that there were in the Church of the New Testament several possibilities for the ordering both of the spiritual office and of the Church as the communion of saints.

V.

The point of disagreement between Loehe and Walther was the relationship between the pastoral office and the congregation. Where does the primacy lie? Does the congregation proceed from the pastoral office or the pastoral office from the congregation? At first this question seems to be related to that question: which comes first? the chicken or the egg? In reality, however, this question conceals a problem of deepest theological significance. The entire concept of the Church depends on it. When Walther and Missouri declared themselves in favor of the primacy of the congregation, they could legitimately look to Luther and the old Lutheran Church for support. In his treatise *Letter to the Christian Nobility*, Luther illustrates the doctrine of the universal priesthood with the example of a group of Christians who find themselves in the desert without an ordained priest. They elect one of their number, and through this election he becomes a legitimate office-holder, with all rights and duties pertaining only to the bearer of the *minisierium ecclesiasticum*. One's answer to whether Christians in such solitude are able to ordain a legitimate office-bearer depends on whether or not one is thinking evangelically. There has never been an evangelical theologian who has differed basically with Luther on this point, not even among the most high church among the Lutherans of the previous century, and certainly not Loehe. To be sure, Loehe, in agreement with the Lutheran Confessions, considered the ordination of pastors through pastors the normal practice. Here our church has expressed conformity to the practice of the old Catholic Church. The Church of the Lutheran Reformation has never doubted that the conferral of office is possible without traditional ordination through an ordained minister; in this matter even those agree who cannot see the universal priesthood as acting only through the office of the ministry. For offering sacrifice certainly is to the essence of the priesthood, and spiritual sacrifices, in the New Testament sense, are offered by the entire Church. The proclamation of the Gospel and the administration of the Sacraments are a part of spiritual sacrifice but are not in and of themselves the essence of the priestly function.

VI.

The identity of the great freedom of the Reformation with that of the Gospel becomes clear for the first time in the realization that the *potestas clavium* is entrusted three times in the New Testament: Matthew 16 to Peter, John 20 to all the apostles, and Matthew 18 to the whole Church. These three instances cannot be separated from one another, nor can there be any differentiation between them with respect to significance. None of them can be considered to be the only proper one. When Jesus gives the Twelve the task of preaching the Gospel to every creature and making disciples of all nations by means of Baptism, when he commands them at the Last Supper, "This do in remembrance of me," who are the Twelve? They are the first holders of ecclesiastical office. From them proceeds the *ministerium docendi evangelii et porrigendi sacramenta*. But they are at the same time certainly the Church, the ecclesia, the representatives of the new eschatological people of God. Thus it is plainly impossible to separate the pastoral office and the congregation in the New Testament. What is said to the congregation is said to the pastoral office and vice versa. The pastoral office does not stand above the congregation but always in its midst. How does the congregation at Antioch (Acts 13) happen to send Paul and Barnabas out on mission work? They had already been sent by the Lord long before. What could the laying on of hands by the congregation give Paul in addition to what he already had through a commission directly given by the exalted Lord himself? Nevertheless, commissioning and laying on of hands are consciously repeated here. The pastoral office and the congregation belong inseparably together. Church history confirms this. There is a living congregation only where there is a living pastoral office, exercising the full authority of its commission. And there is a living pastoral office only where there is a living congregation. Among all Lutheran churches, there is probably none that respects the office of the ministry as much as the Missouri Synod, in which the individual congregations stand so much in the center of all church thought. The pastoral office and the congregation are like reciprocal conduits; the life of the one is the life of the other. The congregation stands or falls with the pastoral office and vice versa. This argument is sufficient to demonstrate that the nineteenth century alternative, pastoral office or congregation, was falsely posed. At that time no one had the resources to draw the consequences from this relationship, and Loehe and Walther each misunderstood the motives of the other's doctrine. Mundinger has shown in his penetrating study concerning the constitution of the Missouri

Synod that this constitution had nothing to do with the democratic inclinations of Americans. Walther and his followers were definitely all anti-democrats! And Hebart has shown that in Loehe's case, at least, no conservative political thoughts specified the form of the church. Instead, both sides overemphasized in support of their position particular biblical truths to the detriment of others. These truths really belong together in the New Testament. This overemphasis occurred because each elevated one aspect of the New Testament statements as if it were the only proper pronouncement, to which the other was to be subordinated.

VII.

This problem becomes clearer when one asks how the conferral of the spiritual office occurs. There is a *vocatio immediata* in which God quite alone and without human mediation makes the call. This is true in the case of the apostles, prophets, and teachers, if we do not here consider those with healing gifts and other special charismata. Only Christ can make a man an apostle. In the calling of a substitute for Judas, he does it through the lot. God has reserved for himself the calling of men to be prophets. Neither in the Old nor in the New Testament can a human cooperate in this work. Those offices that are created through the *vocatio immediate* belong to the entire Church. In addition there is a *vocatio mediate* for the offices of an individual congregation. The Lord Christ confers these offices also, but he does it through men. According to Philippians 1, there were already in the Pauline congregations bishops and deacons who were chosen by the congregation. There were evidently congregations with episcopal-diaconal polity and congregations with presbyterial polity. Paul did not consider it important to eliminate this diversity, which first begins to grow into unity in the Pastoral Epistles. Nothing is more absurd than to impose the standards of modern political constitutions onto the polity of the New Testament Church. The *ecclesia* is not a democracy in our sense of the word. It is not a pile of individuals each of whom possesses the same rights as the other. Nor can it be characterized as an aristocracy. It rather is a jointed body with gradations in structure and rights. Acceptance into the positions and offices of the congregation generally follows from the laying on of hands accompanied by prayer. And again, it can be an individual, for example, the Apostle Paul (2 Timothy 1:6), who performs the laying on of hands, or the presbytery (1 Timothy 4:14), or, as in the case of Timothy, both, or a whole congregation through its representatives (Acts 13:1). It is indeed God, it is the Lord Christ, it is the Holy Ghost, who finally acts through men, through an individual, through a group, or through the entire congregation, or who sometimes *extra ordinem* gives his gifts directly, and with them an office. Therefore it is impossible, as the

Lutheran fathers correctly understood, to make an essential differentiation between vocation and ordination. It is even more impossible to let this differentiation become a divisive conflict in the

Church. God issues the call into his service, and as a rule he does so through men. But it is not the manner that is decisive. It makes no difference whether it is done through an individual, through a group, or through the entire Church assembled for the service of God. It all happens in the name of the Church, the whole Church, which is the Body of Christ, and therefore it happens in the power of the Holy Spirit.

When one becomes aware of this, the differences between the theological theories of the nineteenth century become quite small. Then one begins to understand the magnificent freedom of the Lutheran Church, which knows no law *de constituendis ministris* because Jesus Christ has given no such law, neither directly nor indirectly. Then the *ministerium ecclesiasticum*, standing not above but rather in the congregation, becomes quite important, for then all of the stress is no longer placed on the question of how the office came into being but rather on the question of what its content is. Its apostolicity is then no longer dependent on its more or less questionable apostolic origin but rather on its apostolic content. The ministry has precisely and only that task to do that was laid upon the apostles, namely to proclaim the pure Gospel, to administer those Sacraments that were instituted by Christ, and nothing more. Only from this deep understanding can the spiritual office be renewed. Many things have become attached to the spiritual office through the modern over-organization of the Church, even down to the ecclesiastical-political tomfoolery with which modern bishops squander their own and other people's time. These amount to no more than ecclesiastical shows with no substance. Every sermon, even those preached in the small parishes, has more worth than the conferences in which great ecclesiastical resolutions about the federal constitution or the atom bomb or Goethe's two hundredth birthday are discussed. And as always, taking the pastoral office seriously can only lead to taking the Christian congregation seriously. Then there is no longer possible that misunderstanding under which our German state churches so deeply suffer—the misunderstanding that views each city precinct as if it were a congregation in the New Testament sense, which one need only to activate through a few modern methods of *seelsorge*. This would spell the end to the misunderstanding that views the clever, oh, all too clever, administrative activities of the central ecclesiastical authorities as the church government of the Lutheran Confessions. All these must and will fall to pieces just as the church government of the princely *summi episcopi* fell apart overnight. However, the office that preaches reconciliation and the congregation of believing sinners justified in faith will remain in forms with which we are are not yet familiar but which the Lord of the Church is preparing amidst the thousands of griefs of the

Church today. He is the Savior of his Body even where we see only ruin. Luther's great word concerning the activity of God in history still holds true: *"Occidendo vivificat."* "In killing he makes alive." This faith in the activity of God in history does not, to be sure, free us from, but rather holds us to, the responsibility of renouncing everything that would destroy the genuine pastoral office established by Christ and the genuine congregation established by Christ, everything that makes what Christ has established a playground for the human lust for power, whether clerical or congregational. The pastor is not lord over the congregation (2 Corinthians 1:24). The congregation is not lord over the pastor (Galatians 1). Both have rather over them the one Lord in whom they are one.

These are only a few thoughts about the Church and the pastoral office that may help you read with new attention what God's Word says to us on this matter.

THE LUTHERAN THEOLOGICAL JOURNAL
Vol. 1, No. 1, August 1967

What Is the Sacrament of the Altar?

The following, with some small alterations, is
reprinted with permission of the author and the editor
(Dr. H. P. Hamann) of LUTHERAN THEOLOGICAL
JOURNAL, August 1967, Adelaide, Australia.

I.

The Lutheran Church of Australia accepts unanimously and whole-heartedly the doctrine of the Lutheran Confessions on the Lord's Supper. It confesses unambiguously, in the sense in which Luther understood the words, concerning the Sacrament of the Altar: "It is the true body and blood of our Lord Jesus Christ under the bread and wine, given to us Christians to eat and to drink, instituted by Christ himself." It is not conservatism and theological traditionalism that causes us to take this stand. We are fully aware of the problems, exegetical and historical, dogmatical and ecclesiastical, implied in such a confession in our time. We have learned to regard this consensus not only as a great inheritance of our history, but as a gift of divine grace. We are a small church, a minority within a small nation at the fringe of the vast world of the non-Christian nations of Asia. We have grown together out of many traditions. Our early fathers came from Prussia to find a country where they were able to live without the interference by the state, according to the dictates of their conscience, and to build up the Lutheran Church. They were later joined by immigrants who for different reasons were seeking a new home but who had a Lutheran background in Germany or Scandinavia. When our church had become English speaking, Christians who came from other denominations joined us. Our first pastors came from Prussia. They were joined by men who had been trained at great mission centers such as Hermannsburg, Basel, and Neuendettelsau. Others came from America, partly after years of missionary service in India. The great conservative synods of the American Middle West—such as Missouri, Iowa, and Ohio—also exercised a strong influence,. This variety of backgrounds and theological traditions explains why deep theological differences have often divided us. These differences, however, have not destroyed our loyalty to the Lutheran doctrine of the Sacrament. Luther's simple and (as we believe) biblical doctrine on the Sacrament of the Altar in the words of the Small Catechism—as our children learned them and as they even belonged to the act of confession with which many of our synods were opened—has proved to be one of the great unifying factors in our history, as also men who came from other ecclesiastical traditions, among them Reformed pastors, have accepted it. The common understanding of the Cacrament and its meaning for the Church has also been a strong bond of spiritual unity with our brethren in the faith abroad. In our long striving for true unity, we have learned to understand what the Seventh Article of the Augsburg Confession teaches about what is sufficient and necessary for the true unity of the Church, namely that "the gospel be preached with great unanimity in its purity and that the sacraments be administered in accordance with the divine word."[1] If anywhere in the world this great doctrine has been tried out, then it was in Australia. It has proved to be the only means of establishing true unity among Christians and of preserving the Gospel and the Sacraments of Christ.

---

[1] This is the correct translation of the German text that was not fully understood by the translator in the *Book of Concord* (ed. Tappert), p. 32, who did not understand the word *"eintrichtiglich,"* which is rendered in the Latin text by *magno consensu.*

II.

Now we are having the perturbing experience that we are more and more isolated from the rest of the Lutheran world not on account of what we are doing or not doing, but by the fact that the Sacrament of the Altar, as it has been celebrated in our churches, is vanishing in many parts of the Lutheran world and with it the unity of the Church, which it has helped to preserve. The Lutheran Sacrament is being replaced on one hand by semi-Catholic masses or by ecumenical mystery rites, which neither Rome nor the Christian East would recognize, and on the other by Reformed communion rites. While the Roman Mass is today of an almost puritanical simplicity, the liturgical tinsel of ages past finds a place in Lutheran churches. But the clouds of incense that prevent us from seeing exactly what is going on at the altar cannot hide the fact that the nature of the Sacrament has changed. If we ask these people what the Sacrament of the Altar is, we no longer get the simple answer of Luther's Catechism, but a long discourse on the representation of the sacrifice of Christ and on our participation in this sacrifice as the true nature of this Sacrament. If we ask whether the bread is the body and the wine is the blood, we receive various answers. Some would say yes, others would say "yes, but," which is the fashionable substitute for no, introduced by Karl Barth. In any case they would find the answer of the Catechism too simple, insufficient, and in need of a reinterpretation in the light of modern thought. For we are told even today by an over-enlightened Dutch Catholic Professor of Dogmatics, "Every human statement, including that of a dogma is time-conditioned. It is limited by the possibilities of language and style, by the subleties that can or cannot be adequately expressed. . . ."[2] That we have to use human language in theology is a truism. That human language

---

[2] Quoted by Arnold Lunn in a letter concerning the Dutch Catechism with its ambiguous statement on the virgin birth. Lunn replies, "The dogma of the virgin birth is either true or false. If true, it is as true today as when the gospels were written. It is a truth which is in no sense 'time-conditioned' or 'limited by the possibilities of style and language,' still less by 'subleties that can or cannot be adequately expressed'" (*Herder Correspondence*, May 1967, p. 161).

should be unable to express objective truth would mean the end not only of theology, but of all science.

III.

Like every great change in the history of the Church, so also this one began slowly and almost imperceptibly. But now the results are conspicuous in the entire Lutheran world. When the Church of Sweden in 1922 accepted intercommunion with the Church of England as had been proposed by the Lambeth Conference of 1920, Söderblom had to defend this against what he called "a narrow Lutheran institutionalism." But the confessional protest ceased during the following years. When some time ago Sweden established in the most solemn way intercommunion with the Church of Scotland, even Bishop Giertz, the leader of the *Kyrkliq Samlinq* had no objection. None of the Lutheran churches of Scandinavia seem to have been able and willing to maintain the basic requirements of the Augsburg Confession for altar and church fellowship. Consensus concerning the Gospel and the Sacraments is no longer required as a condition of church fellowship. The American Lutherans of Scandinavian background obviously had no objection to raise against the flagrant violation of the Augsburg Confession in their home churches. So the first pillar of the Lutheran Church of the world collapsed. The other churches of Europe followed. The customary intercommunion between the Reformed (*Hervormde*) and the Lutheran Church in the Netherlands was justified in 1953 by an agreement that leaves the difference between the sacramental doctrines unresolved. The Lutherans "ask" the Reformed whether they can maintain what is taught in question 47 of the Heidelberg Catechism about Christ's human nature being in heaven and not on earth. The Reformed "ask" the Lutherans whether "an omnipresence (ubiquity) of the human nature of Christ does not actually mean an abolition of the incarnation." Obviously the Lutherans were not quite clear about their own doctrine; otherwise they would have answered that the "ubiquity" is not a dogma of the Lutheran Church and that their doctrine that the body of Christ has more ways of being in one place than the local presence does not deny the reality of the incarnation. But the level of this discussion obviously did not permit an intelligent investigation of the problems.

The aim was not to solve the problem, but to have a document that could be used to justify what had been practiced through ignorance for so long a time.

Much more serious was the attempt made in Germany in the so-called Arnoldshain Theses." When in 1948, the new "Evangelical Church in Germany" was established, which comprises all territorial churches of Germany—Lutheran, Reformed and United—the decisive hour of the churches of the Reformation in the world had struck. These are the Lutheran and the Reformed Presbyterian churches, for Anglicanism ceased to be a church of the Reformation when it *de facto* abolished the Articles of Religion, and the majority of the Protestant churches of America are only indirectly related to the Reformation or are the descendants of the Radical Reformation in Europe, which could not develop in the Old World. It was German-speaking Europe where Lutheranism and Calvinism first met in the tragic encounter that has proved so fateful for the history of the Church. It is understandable that time and again attempts have been made to overcome the great schism of the Reformation. But the theological means of the sixteenth and seventeenth centuries were insufflcient for a settlement of the great controversy. And the eighteenth and nineteenth centuries could find nothing but political solutions, based on the ignorance of the churchmen and the indifference of the masses in these territorial churches. Nothing is more significant of the tragic situation than the fact that the unions that began in 1817 in Nassau, 1817–36 in Prussia, 1818 in the Palatinate, 1821 in Baden and Waldeck, and simultaneously or soon after in other territories had an entirely territorial character. Each of the newly circumscribed states of Germany wanted to have its own church, its confessional character being merely based on the local conditions and not on a real theological consensus. Hence in the middle of the nineteenth century, Germany had about seven different union churches with different theological bases, the largest being the Union Church of Prussia, which theoretically did not abolish the authority of the old confessions in the individual congregations, but *de facto* soon became the great unifying factor in Germany, especially since the majority of the universities and their theological faculties was in the hands of the Prussian State. The Lutheran churches joined forces in 1868 by forming the "General Evangelical Lutheran Conference" in close connection with Sweden and the General Council in the

U.S.A. In 1933, Hitler forced all territorial churches into the "German Evangelical Church," which in 1948 transformed itself into the present EKiD after the last attempts of Lutherans in Germany to maintain their identity in a federation between a Lutheran, a Reformed, and a United Church had been defeated. The new body with an ambiguous constitution, which could and can be interpreted as a federation or as a unified church, decided that a colloquy on the Lord's Supper should be held with the aim of bringing about a common statement on the Sacrament that would justify full intercommunion between all parts of the EKiD. Thus the Arnoldshain Theses were written mainly by theologians of the Union Faculties of Heidelberg and Bonn. Among them were outstanding representatives of Lutheranism within the Union, namely, Peter Brunner and Edmund Schlink, the latter, however, being more and more influenced by the Ecumenical Movement. Theologians from Lutheran churches like W. Ehlert declined the invitation because they knew nothing else but a formula of compromise could be the result. The author of this article refused to take part because he could not recognize the right of the EKiD to arrange an official colloquy on the Sacrament. E. Sommerlath accepted the invitation but could not accept the result. However, for the majority of the German churches, their leaders, and their theologians, the theses are sufficient basis for establishing full intercommunion between all parts of the EKiD, which then would become the great union church of Germany. While these lines are being written, the bishop and synod of Bavaria, the last of the Lutheran territorial churches in Germany that thus far had officially refused to declare intercommunion with non-Lutherans, decided that henceforth all members of any church within the EKiD will be invited to Holy Communion in Bavaria. (They declared that doctrine and order of the Sacrament should remain Lutheran. But how can you retain the Lutheran doctrine of the Sacrament of the Altar if you declare that people who do not believe they receive the true body and blood of Christ, and regard this as nonsense, are invited to join in the Sacrament?) With this decision the borderline between Lutheran and Reformed churches within the EKiD has been abolished and "The Evangelical Church in Germany" has become the great union church in which the old churches of the Reformation have become one church in the theological sense of the word "Church" according to Conf. Aug. VII.

V.

What do the theses of Arnoldshain teach? The main thesis meant to settle the old controversy is Thesis 4, which reads,

> The words which our Lord Jesus Christ speaks when he offers the bread and the cup tell us what he himself gives to all who come to this supper: He, the crucified and risen Lord, permits himself to be taken in his body and blood given and shed for all, through his word of promise, with the bread and wine, and grants us participation, by virtue of the Holy Spirit in the victory of his lordship, so that we, believing in his promise, may receive forgiveness of sins, life and salvation.[3]

This thesis must be read together with the rejection of certain erroneous views in Thesis 5: Therefore what happens in the Lord's Supper is not adequately described,

(a) when it is taught that, by means of the Words of Institution, bread and wine are changed into a supernatural substance, thus ceasing to be bread and wine;

(b) when it is taught that a repetition of the act of salvation takes place in the Lord's Supper;

(c) when it is taught that in the Lord's Supper either a natural or a supernatural "matter" is distributed;

(d) when it is taught that there are two parallel but separate processes, one an eating on the part of the body and the other an eating on the part of the soul; and

(e) when it is taught that the eating on the part of the body as such saves us, or that participation in the body and blood of Christ is a purely mental process.

These theses contain a clear rejection of the Roman and the Zwinglian doctrines. But what about the doctrine of the Lutheran

---

[3]We quote from the official English translation contained in "*Lehrgesprach uber das Heilige Abendmahl. Stimmen and Studien zu den Arnoldshainer Thesen der Kommission fur das Abendmahlsgespraich der EKiD*," herausgegeben von Gottfried Niemeier (München, 1961), pp. 332ff.

and of the Reformed churches? The Reformed have given up the idea of two parallel but separate processes of eating—a bodily and a spiritual one. They admit that what is given in the Lord's Supper is given with the bread and wine. The Lutherans have given up the doctrine that the consecrated bread is the body of Christ and the consecrated wine is the blood of Christ. The words "through his word of promise" cannot hide the fact that the Lutheran doctrine of consecration has been abandoned. For even if by "word of promise" the Words of the Institution are meant, for Luther and the Lutheran Church the Words of Institution are more than that. They are "the word and institution of our almighty God and Savior, Jesus Christ, which always remain efficacious in Christendom" (FC, Sol. Decl. VII, 89), "in virtue" of which (Luther in his last offer at Marburg—see below) the body and blood of Christ are present in the Sacrament. The strict denial of the gift of the Sacrament being either a natural or supernatural "matter" shows how remote the new theory is from all previous doctrines of the Sacrament: Catholic, Lutheran, and Reformed. Even Calvin is nearer to Rome and Luther than to this new theory. If the body of Christ is not the body that was born of the Virgin Mary, hung on the cross, raised from the dead and sits at the right hand of the Father, what then is meant by "body" and "blood"? In what sense are these words being used? Would it not be much more honest to replace them with other words? What is meant by the statement that Christ "permits himself to be taken in his body and blood . . . with the bread and wine" (German: ". . . lässt sich in seinem für uns alle in den Tod gegebenen Leib und seinem für alle vergossenen Blut durch sein verheissendes Wort mit Brot und Wein von uns nehmen. . . .")? What we receive is "He," the person, "in his body and blood." This is obviously a compromise between the view that the gift in the Lord's Supper is the body and blood of Christ and the view that the gift is he himself, his person. The Arnoldshain Theses belong together with many modern statements on the Lord's Supper that try to substitute the presence of the person for the presence of body and blood. Arnoldshain agrees substantially with the statement in the report of an American Faith and Order Conference of 1957 on "The Table of the Lord":

> (2) Jesus Christ on the night in which he was betrayed chose bread and wine as the elements of the first Eucharist at

the Last Supper. Rejecting any one-sided preoccupation with the elements in isolation, we agree that in the entire Eucharist action the whole Christ is personally present as both subject and object, i.e., as the One who is at the same time the Giver and the Gift.

(3) In view of our belief in Christ's active presence in the whole Eucharistic action, we agree that this action is our participation in his risen life and the fulfillment of his promise to his Church.

(4) Christ's presence at his table follows from his promise and command. It is only in repentance and faith that the believer . . . receives the fruits of redemption, including the forgiveness of sins, justification, sanctification, newness of life and communion with his brethren . . . The Holy Communion is a means of placing us in the presence of Christ in a total way. In his presence we are judged as well as forgiven (1 Cor. 11:17–34).[4]

If the American churches and sects that met at Oberlin make such a statement, this might be understandable because most of them have never taught the real presence of the body and blood of Christ, though it is neither understandable nor pardonable that the Anglicans and the Lutherans (American Lutheran Church, Augustana Lutheran Church, United Lutheran Church) failed to follow the example of the Quakers who did not take part in the negotiations of this Section, but confessed later in a statement added to the report, their "belief in the non-necessity of the outward elements of bread and wine to mediate the living presence of Christ to the believer in the act of communion with him."[5]

But how is it to be explained that the German theologians with their thorough historical training do not understand the connection between the presence of body and blood of Christ and the presence

---

[4]*The Nature of the Unity we Seek.* Official Report of the North American Conference on Faith and Order, Sept. 1957, Oberlin, Ohio (ed. by P. S. Minear, 1958), pp. 199–205; the quotation from p. 202.

[5]*Ibid.*, p. 205.

of the whole divine-human person? Do they not know the Roman doctrine of the concomitance? Do they not know any longer the eucharistic hymns and prayers—the greatest of which are common to Catholics and Lutherans—in which the presence of body and blood is always understood as including the presence of the person? Does not at least Mozart's (since most of them are Barthians, Mozart must belong to their saints) *Ave verum* ring in their ears:

Ave verum corpus natum ex Maria Virgine
Vere passum, immolatum in cruce pro homine. . . .
O Jesu dulcis, O Jesu pie,
Fili Patris et Mariae.

Or do we no longer remember the German version of Aquinas's *Lauda Sion Salvatorem*, which is to be found in every German hymnbook: *Schmücke dich, o liebe Seele*? The consequence of the Arnoldshain Theses, with their clear rejection of the old Reformed as well as of the Lutheran doctrine, would be that we should have to give up our Catechism. Wilhelm Niesel (*Lehrgesprach*, ed. Niemeier, p. 293) discusses whether the acceptance of the theses with their rejection of the doctrine of question 47 of the Heidelberg Catechism does not necessitate an alteration of this catechism. The same has to be said concerning Luther's Catechism. Its clear confession of the real presence of the true body and blood of Christ, its affirmation of the old "Substantialism" in favor of a mere "Personalism," the reaffirmation of the Lutheran *Est* in the words "It is the true body and blood of Christ" cannot be reconciled with Arnoldshain. Honesty would demand that we give up Luther's Catechism, but theologians have long ago learned to confess with the mouth what they do not believe with their heart. For what is the deepest reason for this new attempt to find a new doctrine of the Sacrament? It is not respect for the Word of God. For everybody knows that the literal understanding of "this is my body" is the simplest way of doing justice to the text. It is not possible to deny that according to 1 Corinthians 10:15f. the eating and drinking of bread and wine constitutes the participation of the body and blood of the Lord. It cannot be denied that 1 Corinthians 11:27ff. has the same realistic meaning. One could argue, "This is Paul's view, but what did Jesus mean?" Can we really assume that Paul, who is so careful in rendering the genuine *paradosis* (11:23, cf. 15:1ff.), should have smuggled in a different, "Hellenistic" interpretation of the words of Jesus? Would none of his adversaries have noticed this, even if we could assume that Paul was capable of what amounts to a forgery? But Jesus as a Jew could not have meant that, we are told. Why not? In this most solemn moment, he did not speak as a Jew only, but as the God-man. And if he really meant something different, what did he mean? Up to this very day, no one has been able to give another explanation acceptable to all New Testament scholars, to speak only of them. Even the men of Arnoldshain have not found a common explanation. For their theses are differently understood even by their authors. As to the respect for the Word of God, have we not in Holy Scripture a Word of God that is not only the word of Jesus or the word of Paul or the word of another apostle, but the Word that may find its expression in different terminologies (1 Cor. 3:5ff; 4:1ff.) while essentially one in the whole New Testament? But the scholars of Arnold-shain have obviously lost this Word. Let us be quite frank: behind this chaos of opinions, there is not historical "scholarship" but unbelief. In the discussion of the theses, it happened that some naive readers understood the words of Thesis 1, "The Lord's Supper which we cele-brate is based on its having been instituted and commanded by Jesus Christ," as referring to the institution at the Last Supper. They had to learn that the authors of the thesis were by no means agreed on this. Some find the roots of the Sacrament in previous meals; others regard it as instituted by the Risen Lord in the earliest Church. What kind of historical scholarship is this? In all churches of Christendom, in every mass, in every celebration of Holy Communion since the apostolic age, the words occur *qui pridie quam pateretur*, "in the night in which he was betrayed." Must Christendom now stop saying this because some German "scholars" think this sacrament is an invention of the first Church? But the churches will probably not be convinced that for almost two thousand years in the most solemn worship of the Church they have told a story that is not true. For this statement is the unanimous statement of the New Testament. This is not historical scholarship but a frivolous playing with the Word of God.

No one who knows German church life and German theol-ogy would have expected anything better. We know the tragedy of German Protestantism. There are faithful pastors. There are also professors who still take their churchly obligations seriously. There are some bishops whose eyes have not yet been blinded by the brilliant stars in their faculties and by the fireworks of the Ecumenical Movement. And there are, above all, *die Stillen im Lande* who pray for the Church and who sometimes cease to be silent and make a loud public confession. But how Luther's Catechism can again become the confession of the Christian people in Europe nobody can see.

VII.

Deeply saddened, though not surprised by the development of the Lutheran churches of the Old World, we turn to America to experience our deepest disappointment. If we ask the great Lutheran churches of America, "What is the Sacrament of the Altar"? we hear confused voices that are tantamount to the answer, "We do not know exactly what it is except that it is not quite what Luther believed and what our fathers have confessed it to be. We can no longer express the mystery of this Sacrament in the simple words of the Catechism: 'It is the true body and blood of our Lord Jesus Christ. . . .' We have seen light, for we have revisited Marburg." *Marburg Revisited* is the title of a book that appeared in 1966 at Minneapolis (Augsburg Publishing House), jointly edited by James I. McCord, President of Princeton Theological Seminary, and Paul C. Empie, Executive Director of the National Lutheran Council. It contains the official report (lectures and summary statements with some additional statements) on "conversations between members of the Lutheran and the Reformed traditions" (tradition is the new term for what formerly was called confession) under the auspices of the "North American Area of the World Alliance of Reformed Churches Holding the Presbyterian Order" and the U.S.A. National Committee of the Lutheran World Federation from 1962 to 1966. Churches outside these two ecumenical organizations, such as the orthodox Presbyterian, the Christian Reformed Church and The Lutheran Church—Missouri Synod, had been invited and took part. "It was clear from the start that the individuals named to participate would speak for themselves, their conclusions neither necessarily representing nor binding the respective churches which appointed them" (Preface). "During these four meetings we have examined carefully the major issues." At some points it was "discovered that our respective views of each other have been inherited caricatures, initially caused by misunderstanding or polemical zeal." In other instances the differences are in fact complementary. Some difficulties remain, but "we have recognized in each other's teachings a common understanding of the gospel and have concluded that the issues which divided the two major branches of the Reformation can no longer be regarded as constituting obstacles to mutual understanding and fellowship." This is then confirmed in the final Report to the Sponsoring Confessional Organizations (p. 190): "We see no insuperable obstacles to pulpit and altar fellowship and, therefore, we recommend to our parent bodies that they encourage their constituent churches to enter into discussions looking forward to intercommunion and the fuller recognition of one another's ministries." May it be understood from the outset that, whatever has to be said about this document, we regard the split between the two great churches of the Reformation as one of the major catastrophes of Christendom, in its consequences comparable only to the split between Rome and the East and between the Orthodox and the Monophysitic churches in the Orient. For this split has been and is still the great obstacle that has prevented the message of the Reformation to penetrate the whole of Christendom. This split was especially fateful for America. One may well ask whether the absence of *one* great Church of the Reformation has not made America the land of innumerable groups and sects in which the Gospel of Jesus Christ and the Sacraments of the New Testament were bound to be lost. And we must examine ourselves and ask whether this split has not made the Lutheran as well as the Reformed churches in Europe and in America the playground of an unbiblical, sectarian enthusiasm. What would Luther and Calvin say about the claim that the discussion in America has been a "confrontation under the guidance of the Holy Spirit" and that God is praised "for the evident working of his Spirit in our midst"? Is it an unbiblical enthusiasm that speaks here and not the Reformation. For to the reformers, the Holy Spirit was always an object of faith and not of observation. There may be, and there is indeed, in the world an unrepentant, stubborn confessionalism. But we would not find it in a church that faithfully, and not only nominally, holds the confession of the Reformation, be it the Reformation of Wittenberg or that of Geneva, because these confessions know of the authority of the Word of God that judges us all and reveals to us all the merciful Savior. The word "Lutheran" does not appear in the Book of Concord except in a passage of the Apology where Melanchthon makes the complaint that the adversaries call the dear Holy Gospel "Lutheran." The Church we believe and confess is never our denomination, but the one Church of Christ, which is not identical with any individual denomination. Our reformers died as ex-communicated members of the Catholic Church. They were not conscious of being members of a new church, although they had to organize their emergency churches. No one would deny the grave sins that have been committed in the polemics between the confessions. But it may well be asked whether they were greater than the sins that are today committed on behalf of ecumenicity: the destruction of the doctrinal substance of the Christian faith by our compromises and the misleading of Christian souls by allowing any kind of false teaching. What is worse, to fight against heresies or to declare that there are no heresies but only different "traditions"? One advantage the old Geneva had over the Geneva of today: the fathers of the Reformed Church knew the seriousness of the question "What is truth?" The Lutheran fathers were prepared to die for the doctrine they had confessed in the Augsburg Confession. Who would die for the Theses of Arnoldshain?

VII.

What we have to say by way of criticizing the new document is not directed against a serious discussion of the issues that divide our churches, nor against the attempt to find an agreement. The author of this article does not despair of the possibility of reaching unity between the separated churches of the Reformation. What we are criticizing is solely the method. In four sessions the committee was able to solve, or nearly solve, the problems of four centuries. In four sessions they covered all the issues that stood between our churches: Gospel, Confession and Scripture; Eucharist and Christology, and all the problems connected with this topic, including Justification and Sanctification; Liturgy and Ethics; Law and Gospel; Creation and Redemption; and the problem of the Two Kingdoms. As *donum superadditum*, we get in the last part a paper on "Confessional Integrity and Ecumenical

Dialogue" by Professor W. A. Quanbeck, who also wrote the opening chapter on "Gospel, Confession, and Scripture." We take from this paper one example to illustrate our criticism of the method of these discussions. We read in p. 186,

> 'We can see clearly that the Nicene Creed uses the theological method and vocabulary of the fourth century to assert the truth about Jesus Christ and to reject misunderstandings of his person and mission which threatened the clarity and power of the gospel. Those who drew up the creed were compelled to use non-biblical language to assert the truth of the biblical message. The language of the creed is not biblical language, but that of fourth century philosophy.'

This statement is crude dilettantism. The Creed of Nicea was a liturgical formula consisting of biblical words (e.g., 1 Cor. 8:6; Col. 1; Heb. 1; 1 Cor. 15). The fathers of Nicea added the famous *homoousios*, which is not a philosophical term. It was used to express the biblical idea that Jesus Christ is Lord and God. Bishop Alexander was no philosopher. His sole interest was to save the Church. For if Christ is not God, the entire Christian liturgy that treats him as such becomes a sin against the First Commandment. The *anathematismata* added to the creed in its first form said nothing else. And they do not contain philosophy. Professor Quanbeck is obviously a victim of some obsolete books on the history of dogma. If the Nicene Creed uses concepts like *ousia*, "substance," it uses words used already in the New Testament. Was the author of Hebrews a philosopher? Athanasius did not go from exile to exile because of a love for the word *homoousios*; in fact, he did not like it and used it sparingly, and never in his early writings. But it summarized briefly the biblical doctrine of the relationship between Father and Son. Quanbeck reveals the deepest reason for his criticism of the allegedly unbiblical language of the Nicene Creed in this sentence: "The problems of theology have a certain consistency from age to age, and yet the shift from substantialist, static thinking to developmental, dynamic categories means that every problem appears in a new light and from a different perspective" (p. 187). This is the philosophy of Prof. Quanbeck. His developmental, dynamic categories replace what he regards as the substantialist, static thinking of the past.

A new philosophy produces a new theology. Every problem appears in a new light and from a different perspective. This, then, applies also to the problem of the Lord's Supper. The old understanding is accused of resting on a substantialist, ontological philosophy. Now we apply the philosophy of our time, Personalism and Existentialism, to the doctrine of the Sacrament, in Arnoldshain, in Oberlin, and now in Princeton and Minneapolis. The gift of the Sacrament is not a "substance," but the "person." A new philosophy has freed us from the *skandalon*, which the words of our Lord, "This is my body," must be to our human reason.

Space does not permit us to discuss the entire content of the book. We must be satisfied with this question: How does this theology understand the one and only question of Marburg 1529? The title *Marburg Revisited* is misleading in so far as the discussion covers the whole range of the issues between the Lutheran and the Reformed churches. Instead of traveling to Marburg and listening attentively to what was said there, these theologians have rather made a quick jet flight over the whole area between Wittenberg and Geneva, high up in the air. They have not seen very much of the issue of Marburg. Clouds seem to have sometimes obscured their sight. There are, of course, some good passages, especially in the Reformed contributions. But the articles could not exhaust so many subjects. The question we have to ask is the question of Marburg: What did Jesus mean when he said, "This is my body," and when he made the corresponding statement on his blood? The answer is distressingly weak. Christ is present in the Word and in the Sacrament. "The sacrament is a form of visible, enacted word, through which Christ and his saving benefits are effectively offered to men" (p. 104). "The assurance of his presence is given in the self-witness of Christ in the instituting rite: This is my body, this is my blood." The realization of his presence in the Sacrament is effected by the Holy Spirit through the Word. "The significance of christology in the Lord's Supper is that it provides assurance that it is the total Christ, the divine-human person who is present in the sacrament, but it does not explain how he is present." This is the answer. The Lutherans who have accepted this document are no longer able to confess with a clear conscience concerning the Sacrament of the Altar, "It is the true body and blood of Christ. . . ." Individual persons may believe that. But it is not essential for the Sacrament. It cannot, therefore, be the dogma of the Church. All that the Church can teach is the presence of the person of Christ. "Christology" may give us the assurance that the Christ present is the total Christ. But "Christology" is for Professor Quanbeck and his followers theological speculation. So we are left with the "consolations of philosophy" and have no longer the firm foundation of the Word of the Lord himself. Luther never based his doctrine on philosophical-theological speculations, nor has the Lutheran Church after him. The one and only basis of the Lutheran doctrine of the real presence of the body and blood of Christ has always been the words in which Christ himself once and for all gave the definition of this Sacrament: "This is my body; this is my blood."

Marburg Revisited, with its papers and recommendations, is now before the Lutheran churches of America. No church has so far committed itself to it, but only to its study. It will be put into the hands of all students of theology in the Lutheran and Reformed churches. It will be discussed on all levels of the churches. It will have far-reaching effects. As these discussions will coincide with the discussions now happening on a worldwide scale between Lutherans and Reformed—discussions in which the Lutheran churches in Europe have already surrendered the Lutheran doctrine of the Confessions—our brethren in America are facing a tremendous responsibility. It seems that the Lutheran World Federation and the Reformed World Alliance are—as far as their ecclesiastical and theological leadership is concerned—determined to carry out the great union in the spirit of modern ecumenism. So the hour of confession has come for the Lutherans in America. The hour of confession and not of mere discussion. No one wants to discourage a serious and thorough-going dialogue between the Lutheran and Reformed churches. On the contrary, we regard that as necessary. But this document cannot be the basis for such a dialogue. It can serve as an instrument to stir up churches and theologians, to help them to realize the great task that lies before them. But it cannot do more. It takes up too many problems, each of which needs a much more elaborate treatment than it could receive here. What we need for a real dialogue is, first of all, a clear statement on the issues to be discussed and a frank realization of the existing agreements and disagreements. What we need, further, is thorough research. It is not enough that two men each write a paper and that these papers are then discussed and a few theses set up. The problems of sacramental theology must be more thoroughly studied in biblical, historical, and dogmatic research. The philosophical aspect, too, must be investigated much more thoroughly. What is the use of basing our discussions and their result on modern Existentialism, if, as every philosopher knows, Existentialist philosophy is already on the way out? There are signs indicating that the future will belong to a new metaphysics, and this would include a new ontology. Christian theology can make use of many different philosophical systems, using what truth is contained in each of them. But it should never be married to one system, which happens to be in fashion at the time. Hence it is our considered opinion that, though *Marburg Revisited* should be read for a start, there should not be a formal discussion of its findings. They have, by the way, no authority whatever. The participants were present as private theologians and not as representatives of their churches. No one knows who is responsible for the results. There is a list of participants and consultants. But we do not know who was present when a certain "summary statement" was accepted nor whether it was accepted unanimously. In the list of the participants, we find names of men from very conservative churches with deep dogmatic convictions. Did these men accept the results? If so, in what sense? I cannot imagine that any New Testament scholar is satisfied with the way in which the exegetical problem, which was after all the problem of Marburg, was brushed aside. Whoever may be responsible, documents of this nature have no validity in the Church unless they are signed. This is a rule of the Church of all ages. The creed and the canons of Nicea had to be signed by all members of the council. Everyone knows what the signatures under the Confessions of the Reformation have meant. Only in modern ecumenical conferences are resolutions adopted for which nobody is responsible.

VIII.

In our opinion, what the Lutheran churches in America that were involved in these negotiations ought to do is to bring the semiofficial discussions out of the twilight of non-committal ecumenical conversation between private theologians into the daylight of responsible discussions and negotiations from church to church. We are not interested in what this or that professor, president, or pastor thinks but in the doctrine of their churches. Only then can we find out whether there is still a consensus on a basic doctrine such as the dogma *De coena Domini* among the Lutherans and the Reformed respectively. What we want to know is whether the Lutheran churches in America as churches still confess of the Sacrament of the Altar what our Catechism teaches, or whether the disintegration of the Lutheran doctrine in these churches has reached the degree that we find in European Lutheranism. We are very much concerned. For a document published some years ago by the former United Lutheran Church was indicative of such disintegration. What we hear of the younger churches of Lutheran background is alarming. It seems that the Lutherans in India in their negotiations with the United Church of India, a definitely Reformed body now being left even by thousands of Anglicans, have let the Lutheran *est* be negotiated away. We ask our brethren in America to understand our deep concern. We refuse to believe that any of the Lutheran churches in America would endorse the results of *Marburg Revisited*, even if private persons accept them. Why are we so concerned? It is our deep conviction that in defending the literal meaning of "This is my body," Martin Luther did not defend a theological view of his own or of a theological school, but a basic dogma of the Christian Church. With this *est* stands and falls the incarnation. And with the reality of the incarnation stands and falls the Church of Jesus Christ. This is why we are concerned about the development in India. We do not want to make the people of India Lutherans. But we know that the highly spiritualizing Indian soul needs the real Christ, not Christ as one of the *Avataras*, a divine being that for a while descends to the earth later to return to the spiritual and divine world, but Christ Incarnate, the Son of God who accepted real human flesh and who never put aside what he once accepted, Christ who remains our brother in heaven. This is why we are afraid to take away from India the real Sacrament with its full assurance of the real presence of the Incarnate One. We are confirmed in our concern when we read that a Lutheran professor in India has proposed to abolish Christian Baptism as a condition of membership in the Church. A very similar concern causes us to insist on the *est* when we think of our Reformed brethren. We do not want to make them Lutherans but to help them to regain what in the tragic history of the Reformation they have lost. The present doctrine of the United Presbyterian Church in the U.S.A. is contained in the "Confession of 1967."[6]

It is certainly nearer to Zwingli than to Calvin and reveals, like all modern substitutes for the old confessions, the loss of the old dogmatic substance. We should ask ourselves whether the rise of unhealthy, unevangelical high church movements, the "catholic" revivals in the once Reformed Church of England, but also in many other Protestant churches, including such as claim to be Reformed or Lutheran, is not the reaction to the loss of a Catholic truth. The Lutheran Church has often been blamed for having retained in its doctrine of the real presence a "popish remnant." We should say what we have retained or tried to preserve is a truth the Catholic churches in East and West have retained. For with them we are convinced that the real presence in the sense that the bread in the Supper is the body of Christ is the doctrine of the New Testament. Whether this is true or not was the issue under discussion at Marburg, the only issue. When Luther's sacramental realism met with Zwingli's spiritualizing, humanistic idealism, it was the realism of the Bible that met with a spiritualizing and rationalizing Christianity, which had been a latent danger to the old Christian faith for centuries. This "flight into reason" (*fugere ad rationem*) had come to the fore in the eleventh century with Berengar. This spiritualizing Christianity found its home later in the lowlands from where Cornelis Hoen passed on to Zwingli his doctrine of the merely significative character of the

---

[6]Art. 4, "The Lord's Supper": The Lord's Supper is a celebration of the reconciliation of men with God and with one another, in which they joyfully eat and drink together at the table of their Savior. Jesus Christ gave his church this remembrance of his dying for sinful men so that by participating in it they have communion with him and with all who shall be gathered to him. Partaking in him as they eat the bread and drink the wine in accordance with Christ's appointment, they receive from the risen and living Lord the benefits of his death and resurrection. They rejoice in the foretaste of the kingdom he will bring to consummation at his promised coming, and go out from the Lord's Table with courage and hope for the service to which he has called them. *The Proposed Book of Confessions of the United Presbyterian Church In the U.S.A.* (Philadelphia, 1966), p. 186.

Sacrament. It is strange to see how in the same country today Roman Catholic theologians try to replace the theory of "transubstantiation" with their theory of "transignification." If our Reformed brethren tried to take into account for a moment the possibility that what happened at Marburg was the encounter of a realistic and an idealistic understanding of God's revelation in Christ, they would have a better understanding of Luther's stand at Marburg, even if they could not approve of it. It was perhaps the greatest moment in the tragic days of the colloquy, when the Lutherans, after the discussions had broken down, made their last offer. Since this offer corresponds exactly to what Luther had repeatedly declared to be his condition for a union in the question of the Sacrament, it may be assumed that also here he was the author of the formula. The proposal was that either side should declare, "We confess that by virtue of the words 'this is my body', 'this is my blood' the body and the blood are truly—*substantive et essentialiter non autem quantitative vel qualitative vel localiter*—present and distributed in the Lord's Supper." Neither at Marburg nor later on any other occasion did Luther demand that his theory on the "ubiquity"—this term was coined by his adversaries—which he had developed to refute those who denied any possibility of the presence of Christ's body other than the local one, had to be accepted as dogma of the Church. Even the Formula of Concord did not dogmatize it, but only the sentence "that God has and knows more ways to be present at a certain place, not only . . . the one which the philosophers call local or spatial" (*Sol. Decl.* VII, 97). What he demanded as necessary was the affirmation that the true body of Christ, that means the body that was born of the virgin, hung on the cross, and was raised from the grave, was present by virtue of the Words of Institution. This presence was to be understood not as a presence in "quantity" or "quality" and not in the sense of a local presence, as medieval theologians had already limited the "in" and "under."[7] In other words, what Luther always demanded was that the words of Christ should be accepted in simple faith, while the "How" remained God's mystery. Oecolampadius was prepared to accept the proposal, Zwingli could not agree because anything that

---

[7]See for details H. Sasse: *This Is My Body* (1959), pp. 266ff.

was called "substance" was unbearable for him—as for the Zwinglians at all times.

It is this last offer of Luther at Marburg that the Lutheran Church has to repeat today in the negotiations and discussions with the Reformed churches. This does not mean that we only repeat an old formula. We have first to regain the doctrine contained in it for ourselves. We shall never succeed in persuading anyone to accept it because it was Luther's doctrine or by showing its profound philosophical presuppositions and consequences. The contention will be, as it was at Marburg, a contention about the meaning of the Sacrament in the New Testament. One does not have to be a Lutheran to believe in the real presence. Many a thorough exegete has found in the New Testament the doctrine that bread and wine in the Lord's Supper are the body and blood of Christ. Even modern scholars who reject the doctrine for themselves admit that somewhere in the New Testament this view is present—some find it with Paul, others with John. But since they know only writings and strata of writings in the Bible and no longer the New Testament as a whole, they do not draw the necessary conclusions from their observation. The day may not be far off when the crisis becomes manifest in which modern theology finds itself because it has lost the authority of the Bible as such. Much more promising than the discussions of our dogmaticians might be a thorough investigation of what the New Testament has to say about the Sacrament. The day when we shall have again a great theology of the New Testament may be nearer than many are inclined to think. And perhaps the time is not far away when Christendom can confess as an ecumenical article of faith concerning the Sacrament of the Altar: "It is the true body and blood of our Lord Jesus Christ, under the bread and wine, given to us Christians to eat and to drink, instituted by Christ himself." In fact, this is already the faith of the majority of all Christians on earth.

CONCORDIA THEOLOGICAL MONTHLY
Vol. 20, No. 8 (1949)

Concerning the Status of the Lutheran Churches in the World

Dear Brethren in the Ministry:

The following lines and letters that, God willing, are to follow this one, are addressed to Lutheran pastors in totally different churches and nations, in Germany and in the remaining Europe, in North and South America, in Africa and Australia. They are addressed to fellow ministers who together with the undersigned know themselves bound by their ordination vow to the Holy Scriptures as the *norma normans* of all the doctrines of the Church and to the Confessions of the Evangelical Lutheran Church as the true interpretation of the Scriptures. They are addressed to brethren whose hearts bleed whenever they see the condition in which the Lutheran Church of our day and of our world finds itself. We know full well: Not only we as theologians see and labor under these distressing conditions. Numberless members of our congregations share our experience and sense the reason for the Church's distress. But we, as the incumbents of the *ministerium ecclesiasticum* defined by Article V of the Augustana, have this duty toward the Christian congregation: to gain a clear understanding of the status of the Lutheran Church in the world, of the cause and ultimate reason for her distress, and to do our utmost, as far as mortals can do anything in this matter, to overcome this distress.

I.

At first glance we may gain the impression that the status of the Lutheran Church is a more splendid one than ever before in her history. We can point to the "Lutheran World Federation," which represents an organized merger of the churches of the *Invariata* as has never before been realized in the history of our church, not even in the most favorable times of the old "Lutheran World Council." This world federation and its constituent churches have evolved into efficient organizations, which are without comparison in the history of our church. We have but to remind ourselves of the large relief organizations of American fellow believers, who came to the aid of the needy churches of Europe, or of the colossal work being conducted from Geneva by Dr. S. C. Michelfelder and Dr. Stewart Herman. One can also point to clear signs of a considerable outward progress in the Lutheran churches of other lands, as, for instance, the union movement of the Lutheran churches of America. This movement at least had this result: that the relationship of the Lutherans, who had stood in sharp opposition to each other, has become an entirely different and better one. This is perhaps the deepest impression of the fully altered church conditions of Lutheranism in the United States gained by the undersigned when he for the first time after twenty-two years was permitted to visit the Lutheran churches of the New World at the exceedingly friendly invitation of The Lutheran Church—Missouri Synod. Even in Germany, Lutheranism occasionally shows signs of life, although it has been robbed of its influence on the world and although its most recent history is one large chain of ecclesiastical political defeats. That a number of professors as members of a non-Lutheran faculty like that at Heidelberg, which legally can never become Lutheran, personally subscribe to the *Augustana Invariata* and teach accordingly—even more so than is done on old faculties nominally still Lutheran—who would not find in this a cause for rejoicing. And also in the Ecumenical Movement of our day, in the recently established Council of Churches, the Lutheran churches are well represented and are the recipients of many a compliment. At first glance everything seems to be in the best of order, the Lutheran Church even in the ascendency. What do we mean when we, in view of these circumstances, speak of a dire distress of our church? That there should be a distress, even an urgent distress of the Lutheran

Church, is that not perhaps only the view of a few malcontents and pessimists whom no one has to take seriously?

II.

The distress of the Lutheran Church becomes apparent in that she is denied the right to exist as a church and that she has put up with it more or less. It is the Reformed Church or, to be more exact, the Reformed churches of various shades of confession who are willing to tolerate Lutheranism as an imperfect semi-Catholic form of evangelical Christianity, even as they also put up with Anglicanism. This is only done under the condition that the Lutheran Church considers herself as one section and one form of the one Evangelical Church and therefore remains with the Reformed Church in the *communio in sacris*. For according to the opinion of the Swiss reformers, as it especially becomes apparent in the far-reaching church politics of Calvin, the Evangelical Church is the church of the *sola scriptura*, different types of interpretation of the Scriptures having led to different formations of this one Evangelical Church, which do not exclude but supplement each other. In this sense all great Reformed theologians have understood the coexistence of Lutheran and Reformed churches. Schleiermacher and Karl Barth, both living in lands of the German tongue—despite the differences otherwise existing between them—have said it with almost the same words, namely that the difference in doctrine between Lutherans and Reformed is one of the theological school but not one of the church. Both have brought their theological convictions to bear on church politics: Schleiermacher as one of the founding fathers and as the actual church father of the Prussian Union; Barth as the founder and sponsor of the "Confessional Union," which in 1934 was formed at Barmen in opposition to the confessional Lutherans, in that a mixed synod composed of Lutherans, Reformed, and United theologians framed a doctrinal declaration and thereby claimed the right to judge between pure and false doctrine in the Evangelical Church. If even in Germany the significance of this step was not understood—which in 1948 logically led to the founding of the Evangelical Church in Germany, including Lutheran, Reformed, and United churches, as the legal and actual successor of the German Evangelical Church of

1933—how was one to understand this step in foreign countries, where one was not able to see anything else in regard to Barmen than the courageous protest against the encroachments of the state on the legal sphere of the Church and where one knew nothing or little of the conflict confessional Lutheranism carried on in favor of a confessional solution of the church problem? We repeat, no one knew anything or little of the conflict because of the wholly one-sided information transmitted by the international press, which again was under the control of the sponsors of this new union. In the Nordic lands, with a few laudable exceptions, Calvinistic church-politics were not known, because Calvinism never had been in the land. In America, Lutheran and Reformed churches exist side by side as separate churches and, apart from a few territories like Pennsylvania, the question of a union between Lutherans and Reformed has nowhere really ever arisen. Added to this the Lutherans in the other parts of the world—whose forefathers at one time emigrated because of the secularization and the unionism of their home churches and founded Lutheran confessional churches in their new homelands—lost, by failing to retain their German language, a knowledge of the above-mentioned events of German church history. Therefore we are face to face with the fact that world Lutheranism, occupied with the task of setting up an imposing outward structure, does not at all become aware of having lost the ground under its feet, in that the Christian world contested its right to exist as an independent church. In Germany of the nineteenth century, the claim of an independent church existence was made in such a manner that the Lutherans demanded a church government in accord with the Lutheran Confessions, claiming that "the church government as an important part of the Church must also, as far as orthodox doctrine and administration of the sacraments are concerned, be in harmony with the church which it is to govern. Therefore it is not permissible to unite, by means of a common church government, churches which are not in agreement with one another as to doctrine and the administration of the sacraments." With these sentences Theodor Kliefoth at the General Evangelical Lutheran Conference, the first ecumenical organization of Lutheranism in 1868, opposed the theological statement of the Prussian unionists that the Lutheran Confessions do not demand a confessional church government, since the unity of the church consists in the *consentire de doctrina evangelii et de administratione sacramentorum* and not in a fixed constitution. That this *consentire* can also be obtained under a mixed church government was the opinion of the sponsors of the union at that time and is their opinion today. But if the conflict in the German Church since 1933 had one definite result: the knowledge that a church cannot adhere to its confession for any length of time as long as only the pastors and the congregations are bound to the confession, but not also the church government. Therefore the newly formed EKD actually does regard its church government as bound not only to the Holy Scriptures, but also to the confessions of the Ancient Church and to "the decisions of the first confessional church passed at Barmen." In other words, practically speaking, the church government is bound to the doctrinal decisions of the "Theological Declaration" of Barmen, which have been taken over by many land churches into the ordination formulas and vows of the church elders. Now as regards the Confessions of the Lutheran Reformation, they are still being recognized in the Lutheran territories of the EKD. But since the Reformed and United Confessions in the respective constituent churches within the EKD are regarded as having equal rights, the Lutheran Confessions are actually being robbed of that binding dogmatical force whereby the unity of the church is safeguarded. With it Lutheranism ceases to be a church. From the Reformed viewpoint, it is understood to be a movement of the Evangelical Church, a theological school. Indeed, it regards itself as just that since the factual recognition of Barmen, and only in this sense some Lutheran land churches have united as the "United Evangelical Lutheran Church of Germany" to represent the union of Lutheranism in the EKD. Concerning this EKD, its founders, also the Lutheran bishops of Germany, say only with somewhat different words, exactly what Frederick William III declared in regard to the Prussian Union as introduced by him: "It does not purpose and signify a relinquishing of the hitherto existing confession. Also the authority which the two evangelical creeds had till now has not thereby been annulled. By joining it one merely expresses that spirit of moderation and charitableness which no longer regards the differences between the two creeds in point of doctrine as a reason to deny each other outward church fellowship." Consequently, unionism in Germany actually has gained a victory

THE JOURNAL ARTICLES OF HERMANN SASSE

over confessionalism. Likewise the Reformed conception of the Evangelical Church and of the church confessions has gained a victory over the Lutheran. The conception of the Confession of the Church, as we find it unequivocally expressed in Luther's Large Confession of 1528, in his Smalcald Articles, and in the Formula of Concord, and as it is also presupposed in the Augustana, is now quite impossible. What Karl Barth calls the "pious and free relativism" of the Reformed Confession has now taken the place of that definiteness with which the Lutheran Confession regards its doctrinal content as the doctrinal content of the Holy Scriptures, from which one "cannot depart or give way in anything" and with which Luther and the confessors of the Formula of Concord wanted "to appear with intrepid hearts before the judgment seat of Jesus Christ, and give an account of it." The *quia* of the confessional oath has given way to the non-obligatory *quatenus*. From this attempt at making the Confessions something relative, it is only a short step to its invalidation, a step that has been taken already in large parts of Reformed Christendom. But this development means practically nothing less than that in the Lutheranism of the German churches the heretofore valid and legally accepted Formula of Concord has been invalidated. For no theologian will earnestly maintain that the spirit of moderation and charitableness, which once gained command in Prussia and now in all of Germany, can be brought into accord with the condemnations the Formula of Concord has voiced against Calvinism and Crypto-Calvinism, although with the express reservation that it does not intend to deprive erring Reformed churches of the character of a church of Christ.

Now the shocking part of this development is that it has not only taken place in Germany. It was not a mere chance occurrence that neither from Nordic Lutheranism nor from the Lutheran churches of America including The Lutheran Church—Missouri Synod has a loud warning been voiced in regard to this wrong undertaking. Also no definite repudiation of the "Evangelical Church of Germany" and of the "United Evangelical Lutheran Church of Germany," which is very closely joined up with the former, has been voiced. One can explain this in part because of the extraordinary difficulty to understand the development in Germany and to correctly evaluate its significance. But this difficulty is not the only explanation.

The deepest reason is rather to be sought in the fact that a similar development, although in a different manner, has taken place also in these churches. In the Nordic churches it is a result of the Reformed influences in the Ecumenical Movement. Here one understands Lutheranism as one of the great historical growths of Protestantism, which can be blended with other forms into a higher unity without losing its own peculiar rights and manner of existence. Especially in the Church of Sweden, it has been forgotten that there is also an Ecumenical Movement, which, of course, seeks a new relationship of the creeds, but which also knows that the great creeds do not only supplement but also exclude one another. The strong dogmatical character of the Confessions and with it the import of the condemnations, which exclude church union, have been forgotten. Apparently both in Scandinavia and in Germany, this is the result of an influence of liberalism within the Church. This liberalism, which, it is true, is publicly being declared dead, has in reality permeated all theology and thereby has conquered the church in a seemingly harmless and yet extremely dangerous manner. And something quite similar has taken place in America. There, strange enough, liberalism calls itself neo-orthodoxy, and as such it has gained access to Lutheran faculties that formerly were inaccessible to all liberal influences. Step by step one can trace the weakening of the dogmatical heritage in the inability of the old orthodoxy to win the youth and to render an explanation of the present-day problems. This change has become evident in the fate of the Galesburg Rule of 1875, which conforms to the above-cited principle of the German Lutherans of 1868: "Lutheran pulpits are for Lutheran ministers only; Lutheran altars are for Lutheran communicants only." While already the matter of fact way with which the abolition of this principle was accepted in America, no conclusions being drawn from it in regard to church unity predicted a weakening of the approved rule on which in the United States the valid existence of a real Lutheran Church as church depends. The American conditions themselves make it apparent that it was not anymore understood and taken seriously. But not only on special occasions do American Lutherans, as the Scandinavians are wont to do, practice communion-fellowship with those of another persuasion, but one can, for instance, read in the church bulletin of one of the largest Lutheran churches of Philadelphia: "Members of other churches who believe in Jesus Christ, the Son of God, and in the forgiveness of sin through him are welcome to join with us in this sacred Sacrament." Instances could readily be adduced to show that in regard to pulpit-fellowship matters are still worse, which should cause every Lutheran theologian to blush for shame. But all this happens in churches that play a leading part in the Lutheran World Federation. Not in order to carry on polemics, but to understand the ailment of Lutheranism, to which virtually all Lutheran churches in the world are prone, we state the objective and historic-dogmatical facts of the case, namely that the Lutheran churches of our time—with exceptions which we do not want to mention here—that at least the leading churches of the world are not any longer churches in the light of the Formula of Concord. And if we hear the rejoinder that the Formula of Concord is not being accepted by all churches, that the Lutheran Church is the Church of the Augustana, then we must join our fathers in answering that one can be a Lutheran without the Formula of Concord, but one cannot be a Lutheran in opposition to it. We must answer that the Augustana is no longer understood as Luther and the confessors of 1530 understood it if one no longer understands the *improbant secus docentes* of its Article X as a demarcation line of the Church, but only as a boundary line of the theological school. This, then, is the dire need of our church, that in that very moment in which she begins to step before the world as one of the great confessions of Christendom to testify to the world and to the Ecumenical Movement the truth of the Lutheran Reformation, she is about to lose, or to a great extent already has lost, that very truth.

III.

How are we to explain this distress? Where are its roots? They cannot be sought in one country only. If German Lutheranism disintegrated through National-Socialism, if the Nordic state and land churches not influenced by National Socialism and if the American free churches have also fallen prey to the disintegration of Lutheranism, then the cause must be sought in Lutheranism itself. It cannot possibly be found in the church politics of Calvinism. For then we would have to ask at once why the Lutheran churches no longer had that power of resistance they had in the sixteenth and seventeenth century. We, of course, have to admit that the events in Lutheranism about which we are concerned also have their parallels in other creeds, and therefore some of the reasons are at least to be sought in a development that is running through all of modern Christendom. The clearest example of this is the noteworthy fact that the present pope had to proceed with all means of Roman Church discipline against certain excesses of the liturgical and the so-called Una Sancta movement in which the dividing line separating from Protestantism also became doubtful for Catholics, even for truly pious Catholics so that they crossed it in conscious opposition to the canonical law. Did it not happen in the eastern parts of Germany—it had already happened in the Siberian prison camps of World War I—that Catholic communion was administered to Protestants? Without a doubt, a weakening of the fixed confessional boundary lines has come about in all of modern Christendom. The Ecumenical Movement has contributed its share, especially since its leadership has been transferred from the Anglicans, who were still interested in regulations and dogma, to the truly Reformed churches. And what would the fathers of the Faith and Order Movement say to the fact that the great event of the World Council of Lausanne in 1927, the renewed acceptance of the Nicene-Constantinopolitan Confession as the basis for the ecumenical work, was so rapidly bypassed in favor of what had now become the order of the day? But beyond this, there must be in Lutheranism itself a reason for the weakening of its dogmatical substance. In Germany it can be explained in part by the extinction of two theological generations. Whole families in which Lutheran theology and Lutheran faith were a living tradition, died out in the two World Wars. In America the decline of the German language played an important role. Not one of Luther's great writings on the Lord's Supper has been put into English. But this does not explain everything. Why were these writings not translated? Why do Anglo-Catholics and Roman Catholics believe in the real presence? Why do leading Scandinavian bishops—concerning those who are less renowned one knows nothing, at least they have not voiced their opinion—reject Luther's teachings on the Lord's Supper in their own church? One cannot explain all this by saying that the untenableness of Luther's exegesis has become apparent. For no serious-minded exegete, even in the Reformed Church, will understand the *est* of the Words of Institution as *significat*. That was reserved for the Lutheran "dogmaticians" of today who know nothing of exegesis. The question also has to be raised whether the Benedictine esoteric theology—which was recently appraised by a German "Lutheran" theologian in the official organ of the German Lutheran bishops as the real meaning of the Lutheran doctrine of the Lord's Supper—has, after all, the least foothold in the Holy Scriptures. No, this whole decaying of Lutheran doctrine must have another reason for which there is no rational explanation. It is the dying away of a faith that hides itself, as many another decline in the spiritual life of Christendom, behind a theological trend that seems to be on the up-grade. And as is the case with every decline in Christian life, so also this one goes hand in hand with a shocking weakness of character. To put it very frankly, the present-day theologians no longer believe what they say and no longer say what they believe. What great characters were the liberals of the past century who in public worship refused to confess the Apostolic Creed because they did not any more believe some of its pronouncements! Today no theologian stumbles over such thin threads. We have no Sydow, Schrempf, or Knote incident anymore; not because our times have a greater desire for dogma, but because theologians are no longer serious-minded in regard to their own confession and to confession as such. This is true despite all confessional movements of our times. No confessional church would dare to exclude one from its midst who denies the Trinity or the Incarnation of Jesus Christ. And that heresy has not yet been discovered that would compromise a pastor in one of our Lutheran land churches. At the most it could only be the very untimely and inopportune loyalty to the Formula of Concord. Here, of course, all tolerance ceases and for no other reason than that it would involve insubordination toward a practically unconfessional church government. Proudly our churches acknowledge the fact that errorists are no longer being disciplined. They do not suspect that they are leaving it to Rome to defend the fundamental truths of the Apostolic and the Nicene Creeds without which there is no Church. And they do not realize that thereby they are placing themselves into an impossible contrast to the Scriptures, which, as is well-known, very earnestly war against heresy and urge such warfare upon the Church of all times.

What would have become of the Church if she had not taken up arms against the heresies of the second, fourth, and sixteenth centuries but had hoped, as present-day bishops are doing, that of itself the truth would carry the day. Thus it is a serious weakness that has befallen our church, and which is undoubtedly to be associated with the fate of Christendom as such. God has not blessed Christianity with a new revival as he had done in the decades following the Napoleonic era. It may be that it will come yet, but till now we are not aware of it. The spiritual life of the Catholic Church of the world, excepting in a few countries like Germany, which, however, are not being heard, shows signs of an apparent decline. The present pope when elected in 1939 was one of the intellectuals of Europe. Today, because of his political undertakings and his superstitious belief in the Madonna of Fatima as the liberator from Bolshevism, he has lowered himself to the level of a Pius IX. What human respect did one have in the twenties for the preachers of the Social Gospel in the Reformed churches of America! They at least had the courage of an independent conviction. Today they have the conviction the daily press may momentarily have, which, so to speak, is no conviction at all. Where in the independent America is there a Reformed churchman who has the power and the courage with which Karl Barth as a lone "voice in Switzerland" spoke to his people and its church? There were men in the Reformed world who once spoke so courageously against the destruction of the dignity of man and the disregard of human rights in National Socialism. Where are the men today who now do not criticize Communism only, but also oppose in no uncertain terms the trampling underfoot of people in Spain and by Latin American Neo-Fascism? There were such voices, but they are silenced. No, the appearance of Christendom today is everything else but uplifting, even in the most elevating moments of a convention like that of Amsterdam. The distress of the Lutheran Church is *mutatis mutandis* the distress of all churches.

4.

We must keep all of this in mind when putting the question, what is to be done? What are we to do, dear brethren, who have been entrusted with the ministerial office of the Lutheran Church in times so decisive for the Church and the world? Nothing would be more wrong than if we would wait for that which others will do. The World Conference will take its course in accordance with the law by which it was guided at the outset. We cannot expect it to know what the church of the Formula of Concord is and to act accordingly. This does not imply that we do not support and aid it everywhere where we are able to do so. From it we can expect an inner renewal of Lutheranism as little as from any other ecclesiastical organization, not even from the organization of our own church. Also from our bishops, synods, church presidents, and faculties we can expect nothing, nothing at all. We are not to wait for an extraordinary miracle, for a new out-pouring of the Holy Spirit. That would be altogether un-Lutheran. If God should once more grant us a revival and thereby a renewal of our church, that rests with God's omnipotence alone. That which we are able to do is threefold. First of all we can make ourselves see the status of our church and of Christendom. We must understand, of course, that the question is not how the legendary eighty million Lutherans of the world, who really are not in existence but have been invented by exceedingly superficial and thoughtless statistics, can be merged into a powerful organism. We must know, however, how those can be congregated from the midst of that poor, stricken, and feeble Lutheranism for whom the

Lutheran Confessions are no mere pretense, but, as they were for Luther and the signatories of the Confessions, a matter of life and death, of eternal life and eternal death, because it is a matter pertaining to the everlasting truth of the Holy Scriptures, which concerns all peoples and all churches of Christendom. Indeed, not such a one thinks and acts in an ecumenical fashion who looks upon the Confessions as something relative, who reduces them to a low level and practically does away with them, but who, like Luther, searches for the one truth of the one Gospel for the one Church. Let us again become confessional Lutherans for the sake of the unity of the Church.

The second thing we must do to attain this end and the thing that we can do without difficulty is to once more study the Confessions, that we again and again compare them with the Holy Scripture, and that we constantly learn to gauge their interpretation of the Scriptures and their Scripture proofs more profoundly. As the Roman Catholic has the daily duty to read his breviary, a tedious and difficult task, thus our duty must be, next to the thorough study of the Scriptures, the unflagging study of the Confessions. In this manner let us begin prayerfully to read Luther's Large Catechism, even as Luther, although an old doctor, still was not ashamed to pray the Catechism daily. The deepest cause for the failure of the German church conflict is none other but that everyone always spoke about the Confessions, appealed to them, but knew them too little. We not only need this insight for ourselves, our teaching, and our preaching, but very much so for our congregations. At the last large convention of the United Lutheran Church in America, an engineer made the statement—by the way in agreement with the president of the church, Dr. Fry— that the church is in need of theologians, that it calls for theologians. The Christian congregation of the present day in all lands and of all creeds is tired of the undogmatical, devotional character of the ethical sermon, which changes its theme every year. It demands in a manner we pastors frequently do not at all understand a substantial dogmatical sermon, a doctrinal sermon in the best sense of the word. If our contemporaries do not find it in the Lutheran Church, then the hunger for doctrine drives them into other denominations. Therefore lay hold of the Confessions, dear brethren in the ministry, by yourselves and together with others.

The third thing, however, that we must learn anew is Luther's invincible faith in the power of the means of grace. Whatever the Church still has and still does should not be minimized. But she does not live from mercy or from political and social activity. She does not subsist on large numbers. When will the terrible superstition of the Christendom of our day cease that believes Jesus Christ is powerful only where two or three millions are gathered together in his name. When will we again comprehend that the

Church lives by the means of grace of the pure preaching of the Gospel, the divinely instituted administration of the Sacraments, and nothing else. And for no other reason but because Jesus Christ the Lord is present in his means of grace and builds his Church on earth, being as powerful as ever before in the history of the Church— even if his power and glory, to speak with our Confessions, are *cruce tectum*, hidden under the cross. Oh, what a secret unbelief and what little faith we find in the church that calls herself the church of the *sola fide*! May God in his grace eradicate this unbelief and strengthen this little faith in our soul and renew us through the great faith of the New Testament and the Reformation. That and that alone is the manner of overcoming the urgent need of the Evangelical Lutheran Church in the greatest and weightiest crisis of her history.

To all of you, whether I am acquainted with you or whether you are strangers to me, wherever you may be sojourners, in whichever Lutheran Church you may be serving, I in the fellowship of the Lutheran faith extend my most heartfelt greetings for the Advent Season and for the beginning of the New Church Year.

Your devoted and faithful,
Hermann Sasse Translated by P. Peters.
(*Quartalschrift*, April, 1949, pp. 81–95.)

[*Note. Dr. P. Peters rendered a service to the Lutherans of America by translating the remarks of Dr. Sasse, and the* Quartalschrift *is to be thanked for publishing this English version and for inviting other journals to copy it. Dr. Sasse takes for granted that EKD (Evangelical Church in Germany) is a church, while many other German theologians look upon it as a mere federation. We trust that this point will gradually be fully clarified. A.*]

CONCORDIA THEOLOGICAL MONTHLY
Vol. 30, No. 1 (1959)

A Lutheran Contribution to the Present Discussions on the Lord's Supper

I.

The Lord's Supper has again become one of the main issues among the churches of Christendom as well as within individual denominations. This is the result of two movements which, though deeply rooted in the nineteenth century, have shaped the life of all Christendom since the beginning of this century: the liturgical and the Ecumenical Movement. Since the deepest motive underlying both is what has been called "the awakening of the Church in the souls," future Church historians may regard them as branches of one great movement, which, like all great movements in the Western Church (Reformation, Pietism, Rationalism, etc.), sweep through the whole of Christendom regardless of national or denominational borderlines.

The modern liturgical movement in the Roman Church began with Pius X. It is certainly not accidental that the "pope of the Eucharist" was also the stanch fighter against Modernism. He started the fight in 1903, a few weeks after his great reform of the liturgy had begun. The longing of the best minds of the Roman Church for a closer contact with, and a greater influence on, modern man (which at that time could not be satisfied in the fields of biblical studies and dogmatics) found an outlet in the field of the liturgy. Whilst theological scholarship turned from the danger zone of doctrinal Modernism to the less dangerous fields of liturgiology and there achieved surprising results, the devotional life of the entire Roman Church since the end of World War I underwent a profound change, the characteristic feature of which is an astonishing renewal of the Eucharistic life at the expense of lower forms of devotion.

The parallels in the Protestant churches are evident. They can by no means be explained by Roman influence, though the impact of the Roman movement has become strong in the course of time. For even outside the churches there are most interesting parallels indicative of a deep change in the inner life of modern mankind. This change may be called the turn from subject to object. At the same time when in Roman Catholic churches the high altar began to be replaced by the *mensa* of the ancient Church, the priest saying Mass facing the people, it could happen that in a "Scoto-Catholic" church the Reformed table was replaced by a high altar. In either case the ecclesiastical authorities had great difficulties in turning the minister around. It may be a consolation to other churches that Rome even today, thirty years after the constitution *Divini cultus* and despite the rules laid down in *Mediator Dei* (1947), has to combat "certain misguided enthusiasts" who "interfere with the liturgy in an unauthorized way," as Archbishop Simonds of Melbourne has put it in May 1958. Pius XII, continuing the work of his predecessor, has strongly emphasized that the rule of Celestine I, "*Legem credendi lex statuat supplicandi*" (Denzinger 139 and 2200) must also be inverted: The rule of faith constitutes the rule of prayer. It is most significant that the present pope in *Humani generis* (1952) had to defend even the real presence against certain trends in modern Catholicism that would make "the consecrated species . . . merely efficacious signs of the spiritual presence of Christ."

Similar difficulties that have arisen in many Lutheran churches are due to the neglect of the truth that the rule of faith must remain the rule of prayer. It is a deplorable fact that some Lutheran theologians, while accepting Roman, Eastern, and meaningless Anglican elements, have left it to Roman Catholic scholars to discover Luther's greatness as a liturgist and the importance of the old Lutheran liturgy. A liturgical movement not based upon the confession of the church is bound to go astray. A renewal of the Sacrament of the Altar in the Lutheran Church must go hand in hand with a new understanding of the doctrine of the Sacrament.

If, thus, the liturgical movement was bound to provoke new discussions of the doctrine of the Lord's Supper, the Ecumenical Movement has had the same effect. It is true that this movement, as long as it was dominated by Anglican theology, was interested in the practical issues of intercommunion rather than in doctrinal discussions on the Sacrament. The Eucharist, so we are told, has been instituted to be celebrated, not to be speculated on. Nowhere did the *lex orandi lex credendi* play a greater part than in the Anglican churches after they had practically abandoned the Thirty-nine Articles with their definitely Reformed doctrine on the Lord's Supper. The modern union churches that follow more or less the Anglican pattern (South India, Ceylon, the proposals for North India-Pakistan and for Australia) determine the liturgical requirements and the *minister sacramenti* but leave the understanding of the presence of Christ and of the gift of the Sacrament to the individual minister and communicant.

However, as soon as Lutherans or serious Presbyterians and Reformed are invited to join such a union, doctrinal discussions become inevitable. This is also the experience of the European churches. When in 1933 the Federation of the Evangelical Churches in Germany (*Deutscher Evangelischer Kirchenbund*) of 1922 was transformed into the German Evangelical Church (*Deutsche Evangelische Kirche*), a discussion of the problem of the Lord's Supper was not envisaged, though the question of intercommunion had become urgent. Even when in the following year, the Confessional Synod of Barmen, under the leadership of Karl Barth, gave its interpretation of the new body in the Barmen Declaration, no mention was made of the Sacrament, since "the controversy was not about the Lord's Supper" (Barth).

But soon the question came up and divided the Confessing Church. When a confessional synod of the Prussian Union in 1937 declared full intercommunion among the various denominations, a new discussion of the Sacrament of the Altar began, with the result that when after the war the German Evangelical Church was to be replaced by the Evangelical Church in Germany (EKiD), an "obligatory discussion of the Lord's Supper" (*verbindliches Abendmahlsgespracb*) was demanded to settle the question that had divided Protestantism since 1529. Several official meetings of theologians were held, but no result has been reached. However, the literary discussion is going on in Germany as well as throughout the world.

II.

It is one of the great tragedies of Lutheranism that this challenge comes to it at a moment when it may be least able to meet it. What a revelation is contained in the words spoken by Dr. H. W. Gensichen of Heidelberg, formerly of Madras, at Minneapolis ("The Unity of the Church in Christ," *Messages of the Third Assembly* [Minneapolis: The Lutheran World Federation, 1957], p. 48):

> On the one hand, we Lutherans claim that our doctrine of the Lord's Supper approaches most closely the intentions of the Lord, and we have in the course of history drawn very sharp lines of distinction over against those who disagree with our doctrine. But, on the other hand, we ourselves are today perhaps further than ever removed from complete agreement on the traditional Lutheran doctrine of the Lord's Supper. Today there is at least one Lutheran Church which has reached agreement on the Lord's Supper with its Calvinistic neighbor church, not to mention various types of "emergency" intercommunion practiced in diaspora regions or in young churches. There are Lutheran churches which "really see no obstacle to intercommunion with the Anglican Church." Some present-day Lutheran exegetes assert that the Lutheran doctrine of the Lord's Supper, as stated in the Confessions, does not do full justice to the biblical witness. And then there are many other Lutherans who view all this as deplorable apostasy from the faith of the fathers.

The proper way to redeem this situation would seem to be a thorough re-examination of the doctrine that every Lutheran has learned from the Catechism and every pastor has solemnly pledged to teach upon his ordination. How can Lutheranism speak to other churches without having first reached agreement within its own ranks? It is most disappointing that the corresponding thesis of Minneapolis (II, 6, p. 106) does not envisage an attempt to heal this wound of our own church. Rather it pushes on the problem to an ecumenical level:

In an *ecumenical study of the Scriptures* we find the most helpful means towards a fuller realization of the unity in Christ and towards a fuller realization of our faith as found in and behind our confessional statements. *On this basis also the question of intercommunion and the nature of the Sacraments can be brought out of the present deadlock.* For our Lutheran churches it is a congenial and timely task to participate in and initiate such *ecumenical studies—on the highest theological, as well as on the parish level.* [Emphasis added]

In order to avoid any misunderstanding, the present author wants to emphasize that he has no objection against an "ecumenical study of the Scriptures"—to his knowledge all true biblical scholarship since the Reformation has been a constant exchange of thought between the theologians of various churches, including Rome. He himself confesses that he has learned much from other churches, precisely with regard to the Sacraments, and that he has never published anything on that subject, including this article, without having talked it over with Reformed and Roman Catholic colleagues. He does object to the superficial methods of modern conferences in which the profoundest questions are briefly debated and hurriedly decided, and to the superstitious belief that if Christians of different persuasions are gathered around the Bible, the Holy Spirit will certainly guide them into truth. He can do that, but *ubi et quando visum est Deo*, and he will most certainly not do it if on the "parish level" Lutherans, Presbyterians, Anglicans, Baptists, and Quakers meet in order to bring "out of the deadlock" insoluble problems, especially if they do not realize that they have quite different ideas of the authority of Holy Scripture and that they do not understand one another's language when using terms like "Gospel," "Church," "Sacrament," and "real presence." Such methods will not lead to another Pentecost but to a Babylonian confusion of tongues.

III.

Under these circumstances, what can the Lutheran contribution to the worldwide Eucharistic discussions of our time be? If the present generation of Lutherans cannot speak because the *magnus consensus* of the Confessions has been lost, we could perhaps learn something from the fathers and ask, What do the controversies of the sixteenth century teach us? Why were the discussions of that time bound to fail? We should never forget that they failed to reach the much-desired unity, although the participants were nearer to one another than we are to them.

When in 1929 at Marburg, the fourth centenary of the great colloquy was celebrated, it was the delegate from Zurich, Emil Brunner, who called the attention of that big meeting composed of representatives of many Protestant churches of Europe and America to the necessity of first reaching the amount of agreement that existed among the reformers before we could hope to solve the problems they had not been able to solve.

How can we hope to reach agreement on the Lord's Supper as long as we are not agreed on the authority of the Word of God? May I be allowed to make clear what this means by relating a personal experience? When the great discussion on the Lord's Supper was going on after the last war in Germany, I met an outstanding New Testament scholar whose personal piety, learning, and character are held in high esteem by all who know him. As we both had written on the Eucharist in the New Testament and were continuing our studies, our conversation soon turned to that problem. I asked him whether he still maintained that the Last Supper must be understood as a parabolical action of our Lord and the Words of Institution consequently must be taken in a figurative sense. He replied in the affirmative. To the question of whether 1 Corinthians 10:16f. and 11:27 taught clearly that the bread is the body, because partaking of the blessed bread is partaking of the body, and unworthy eating and drinking involves a sinning against the body and blood of the Lord, he answered that he had not yet reached a full explanation of the latter passage but was convinced that Paul, on the whole, had a parabolical and figurative understanding. The question whether somewhere in the New Testament the literal and realistic understanding was present was answered again in the affirmative. This was to be found John 6:51b–58, where Jesus speaks no longer of his person but suddenly of his flesh as the bread of life. This passage, with its realistic understanding of the Eucharist, however, ought to be regarded as an insertion into the original text of the Fourth Gospel, he added, a view held by many scholars, such as Bultmann. He knew, of course, that this is a mere hypothesis without any basis in textual evidence.

The theological objection that for the Lutheran Church the text, as contained in the best manuscripts, is the normative Word of God was pushed aside, and the question of what then the normative authority was met with the answer "the words of the historic Jesus." This had been the answer given by Harnack at the beginning of the century.

This episode reveals more than anything else the tragedy of much modern Lutheran theology. No revival of biblical studies, no rediscovery of the Reformation, no Luther renaissance, has been able to restore the *sola scriptura*. We should not have mentioned that episode were it not characteristic of the discussions that have been going on since 1937. Many scholars, even very critical scholars, find somewhere in the New Testament that realistic concept of the Sacrament that is, as St. Ignatius shows, present in the liturgy of Antioch at the beginning of the second century. Some found it with St. Paul (Heitmüller, Weinel, Lietzmann, Kasemann), others with St. John (Bultmann, Jeremias, and many others). Lohmeyer in his commentary on Mark realizes that in 14:22 "is" cannot mean "signifies."

Just as in the sixteenth century the adversaries of the Lutheran doctrine were agreed on the rejection of the literal understanding of the Words of Institution but disagreed as to what they actually meant, so today the exegetes are not able to find agreement as to what the alleged parable contained in those words actually means. In the sixteenth century, Luther and Zwingli, Oecolampadius and Bucer, Melanchthon and Calvin, Andreae and Beza, the Anglican and, in this case, even the Roman theologians, were convinced that there is one doctrine of the Lord's Supper in the New Testament, that St. Paul's commentary on the words of Jesus cannot contradict our Lord himself. This common conviction was the basis of all debates. Modern Protestantism has lost that basis. There is a doctrine of Jesus, a doctrine of Paul, and of John, but where is the doctrine of the New Testament? Along with the authority of the Scriptures, with the *sola scriptura*, the Bible itself is destroyed.

Nobody denies the achievements of exegetical and historical scholarship. We know better than anyone in the sixteenth century was able to know the linguistic and historic background of the New Testament passages, the Jewish and Old Testament presuppositions, the eschatology of the New Testament and the liturgy of the earliest Church. But all these great achievements, instead of helping us to reach a fuller understanding of the Sacrament, lead us away from the main issue, because we are so remote from an understanding of the authority of Holy Scripture that the question must arise whether this authority has not been better preserved by Rome than by modern Lutheranism.[1] There is no possibility of bringing "out of the present deadlock" the question of the Sacrament unless we have first rediscovered what for our fathers was "the only judge, rule, and standard according to which, as the only test stone, all dogmas must be discerned and judged."

IV.

The second thing we have to learn from our fathers is the clear statement of the *status controversiae*. The issue is not whether the Lord's Supper is a remembrance of Christ's atoning death. All churches of Christendom are agreed on that. One has only to think of the *anamnesis* in the various liturgies or the doctrine of Trent on the Mass as the *memoria* of the sacrifice of Calvary. Gratefully we accept what modern linguistic scholarship has discovered concerning the biblical meaning of ἀνάμνησῃ as something more than a mere remembrance of a historic event or person. But we all agree that to remember Christ means more than to remember Socrates. That is the reason why all churches teach a presence or even a real presence of Christ in the Lord's Supper.

---

[1] Another example is the discussion of the problem of ordination of women. One of the oldest Lutheran churches has put the question, after its bishops failed to reach unanimity on that issue, to the LWF, the WCC, and even to secular organizations. Even if it were technically possible for the ecumenical organizations to give a reply—the LWF comprises churches that have no objection against such ordinations, and others that have, to say nothing of the WCC—the fathers would have consulted Holy Scripture. For them the question would have been definitely settled by the apostolic injunction (1 Cor. 14:34ff.), especially since Paul, who in such cases clearly distinguishes between his counsels and the commandments of the Lord (1 Cor. 7:10ff.), in this case expressly states that "the things that I write unto you are the commandments of the Lord." This is the answer Rome would give.

Nor is the issue the understanding of this Sacrament as "Communion." How much Luther made use of the beautiful old imagery of the bread made from many grains, the wine made from many grapes, his sermons on the Sacrament show. This side of the Sacrament could have been stressed more in the Confessions, but it is there, as the quotation from St. Cyril of Alexandria on John 15 in the Apology (X:3) shows. In the Middle Ages also, this aspect of the Sacrament is not dealt with in the doctrinal works (e.g., Aquinas's *Summa theologica*) but in the devotional literature. Even the eschatological aspect of the Sacrament is present in the old doctrine and in the liturgy. The "Come, Lord Jesus" has always belonged to this Sacrament, in which our Lord anticipates his coming in glory on the "Day of the Lord" (cf. Rev. 1:10 and Amos 5:18) by coming in the Lord's Supper to his Church: "*Benedictus, qui venit in nomine Domini.*" Thus the future glory becomes in a way a present reality, the Lord's Supper becoming "heaven on earth" (*Le ciel sur la terre*, as S. Bulgakow has described it in harmony with Scriver's prayer, *Dass dein Abendmahl mein Himmel auf Erden werde*).

Also as to the fruits of the Sacrament, there is hardly any difference, except that the Lutheran Church, with the Eastern Church, emphasizes the importance of this Sacrament for our eternal life (see the understanding of the *caro vivifica* of John 6, Formula of Concord, SD VIII 59, 76; Large Catechism, Sacrament of the Altar, 68; cf. Catalog of Testimonies III).

There is much more agreement on the Sacrament of the Altar between the churches than generally is assumed, and such agreement may be stated for encouragement. Such statements, however, should never be made for the purpose of minimizing or concealing the real point at issue. The *status controversiae* is today, as it was in the sixteenth century, the question of whether the consecrated bread is the body and the consecrated wine is the blood of Christ. This all-important issue should not be obscured by employing terms like "real presence" or "eating the body in a spiritual manner" before their meaning is clarified. For these terms are used by various churches in various meanings. The *status controversiae* must be as clear as it was at Marburg when Luther at the beginning of the colloquy took chalk and wrote on the table the words *Hoc est corpus meum* and covered them with the tablecloth to produce them at the decisive moment of the debate.

436 THE JOURNAL ARTICLES OF HERMANN SASSE

V.

It is not customary today when speaking of the Eucharistic controversies of the sixteenth century in view of a continuation of those discussions to look first at Marburg. There Luther and Zwingli met. The present Reformed churches are not Zwinglian but Calvinist. They even reject Zwingli. However, it must be asked whether Calvin's negative verdict on Zwingli was wholly justified. Has the reformer of Geneva, who was not able to read Zwingli's German, done full justice to the reformer of Zurich? Since the second volume of W. Kohler's standard work *Zwingli and Luther* has appeared in 1953 (ed. by E. Kohlmeyer and H. Bornkamm), and since Zwingli research on the basis of the new edition of Zwingli's works in the *Corpus reformatorum* in Switzerland has produced remarkable results, the encounter between Luther and Zwingli can no longer be regarded as a mere prelude to what used to be regarded as the real controversy between Calvin and his Lutheran opponents. On the contrary, these later controversies appear as tragic attempts to unmake a decision definitely made in 1529.

It has been stated that Luther went to Marburg with the result in his pocket. This is an impermissible simplification. Luther, it is true, had first refused the colloquy. His reason was that every possible argument had been brought forward already in the preceding literary controversy. In addition to that, he disliked the political aspect of the enterprise. In either respect he was right.

Philip of Hesse was a great politician. He was not so much interested in the truth. What he wanted was an alliance between all those estates that had signed in April 1529 the "Protestation" of Speyer and the "Protestant" cantons of Switzerland. "The Marburg Colloquy was largely a political action, born of the situation after the Diet of Speyer, which made an alliance of all Protestants imperative," as W. Koehler (*Huldrych Zwingli*, 1943, p. 199) puts it.

For Zwingli, too, it had this aspect. To save the Gospel, he had made his alliance in Switzerland over against the Papalist cantons and Ferdinand and had in June even started his war, which to his great disappointment at Kappel was terminated by a negotiated peace. He could not see how the cause of the Reformation in Europe could be saved except by an alliance of all anti-Habsburg powers, including the King of France, who persecuted the Protestants, and even the Sultan. At Marburg on the last days of September, before the Lutherans arrived, he had come to a full political agreement with Landgrave Philip. For the sake of such a political alliance he was prepared to tolerate Luther's doctrine of the Sacrament of the Altar, though he strongly disagreed with him. The colloquy should lead, if not to an agreement, to a *syncretismus* (the technical term for what we would call "union"), a formula of compromise or a statement that a disagreement on such a matter was not church-divisive. To Luther this was not acceptable, not only because to him a dogma of the Church was at stake on which compromise was not permissible, but also because the idea that the Gospel could be defended by political means was contrary to the Word of God. In this connection he always quoted Isaiah 7 with its serious warnings against political confederations in the alleged interest of the Church: "If ye will not believe, surely ye shall not be established."

What, then, was the theological issue at Marburg? To understand that, one must try to get rid of the old prejudices that still play a great role, not only in historical works whose authors have no understanding of theology but also in the accepted textbooks on Church history. It was not Luther who started the controversy. For a long time he ignored the attacks from Zurich. However, the controversy had become unavoidable because it was a real *contentio de fide*. "Today it is generally acknowledged that it is not permissible to speak of obstinacy, of stubborn insistence on the letter of the Bible on the part of Luther. What to him was at stake was the root of our communion with God, which cannot be separated from the Lord's Supper and its gift. It must, on the other hand, be admitted that we owe also to Zwingli the recognition that his conviction was formed under an inner compulsion, and we should cease to reproach him with superficial rationalism" (W. Koehler, *Zwingli und Luther*, II, 133).

In point of fact, in these two men two different concepts of Christianity met. While Luther's faith in Christ was bound up with a strong sacramental realism, Zwingli was the representative of a spiritual concept of Christianity that was no longer able to understand the Sacrament. As a reaction against certain doctrinal and devotional exaggerations of the Middle Ages, this spiritualistic movement accompanies as an undercurrent the main stream of medieval theology and piety. It becomes visible first in the "dialectic," rationalistic doctrine of Berengar in the eleventh century. In the era of late scholasticism, it reappears in Wycliffe. It becomes manifest in some kinds of German mysticism, in aspects of the *devotio moderna* of the Lowlands, in the more radical forms of the Hussite movement, in the piety of the Bohemian and Moravian Brethren, in much Christian humanism, and in the various Spiritualist and Anabaptist movements at the time of the Reformation. There is always a radical wing (e.g., in the "Pickards" or "Beghards" in the Lowlands and in Bohemia who rejected all Sacraments) and a moderate one that retains the Sacraments with a different understanding. Thus Zwingli persecuted the Anabaptists, although he was not able to defend infant Baptism.

It is this great movement whose representative Zwingli was at Marburg. Luther, on the other hand, became the defender of the Catholic dogma. It is a strange spectacle to see these two men and their companions at the great debate. One must never forget that this was not a discussion between churches, as later colloquies were. There was at that time, before the Augsburg Confession was written, neither a Lutheran nor a Reformed Church. The colloquists at Marburg considered themselves Catholic Christians, though excommunicated. But no one at that time doubted that the unity was only temporarily lost and would be restored by an ecumenical council that was generally demanded. The Marburg Colloquy was an event within the Catholic Church of the West.

Thus the doctrine Zwingli defended was not "Reformed" in the later sense. It was, strictly speaking, not even Zwinglian. For Zwingli had taken it over from the Dutch humanist Hoen. Nor was the doctrine of Luther "Lutheran." It was simply the dogma of the entire Church since the days of the apostles that Luther defended against Zwingli, just as Nicholas II and Gregory VII had defended it against Berengar. This sounds strange, but it is true. Luther has always praised Pope Nicholas for his most Christian action against the French Modernist. Here lies the deeper reason for Melanchthon's request that a few "decent papists" should participate, while there was agreement on both sides that no Anabaptist could be admitted. Against this historic background, it is to be understood that Luther chalked on the table of Marburg the words containing the *status controversiae* as well as the dogma on which there could not be a compromise: *Hoc est corpus meum.*

VI.

"This is my body." That the consecrated bread in the Lord's Supper is the body and the consecrated wine is the blood of Christ, this is the doctrine of Luther in which he agrees with the entire orthodox Church throughout the ages. All thoughts and theories he developed in connection with this fundamental dogma are only explanations of this doctrine, which he had to put forward as answers to questions asked by his opponents.

In the centuries before the Reformation, there had always been people who doubted the real presence. There have always been theologians who wanted to know too much and, while trying to explain what defies all explanation, have suffered shipwreck in the faith. Even some of the Church fathers, especially those who were influenced by Neoplatonism, have given false or insufficient answers that later were used by the deniers of the real presence. But the dogma of the Church was not affected by that. It was and is binding on all Christians because it is the doctrine of the apostles and the explanation of the Sacrament given by our Lord himself at the institution. Either he meant what he said, or he has left to his Church a puzzle that thus far nobody has been able to solve.

This dogma was contained and expressed in all liturgies, Eastern and Western. It had to be defined by the Church only when it was attacked. This was the case in the East when the Seventh Ecumenical Council of 787 had to refute the decision of a synod of 754 that the consecrated bread and wine are symbols, images of the body and blood of Christ. In the Western Church, the dogma had to be defined against Berengar and his followers almost three hundred years later. For the controversies of the Carolingian Age were theological discussions only. As the dogma was contained in the liturgy, it was taught in the catechetical instruction, either immediately before or as, for example, in the case of the *Mystagogical Catecheses* of St. Cyril of Jerusalem, after Baptism and first Communion.

Since the Eucharist was celebrated behind closed doors, the dogma was not taught publicly. Only when the rumors about cannibalism had become too dangerous, St. Justin Martyr felt constrained to tell the public in his Apology what was going on in that service and to state, in a somewhat involved sentence, what "we have been taught," namely, that the bread and wine are the body and blood of

Christ. He referred to the Words of Institution as recorded by the apostles in the Gospels.[2] His statement of the doctrine is confirmed

---

[2]Apol. I,65 f. – There can be no doubt *Quevsteia dei`pna and Oi*dipovdeiai mivxeiò* (Athenagoras, 3,1) refer to the Eucharist, the latter approach being a misinterpretation of the "holy kiss" (Rom. 16:16; 1 Cor. 16:20; 2 Cor. 13:12; 1 Thess. 5:26; 1 Peter 5:14), that preceded the Communion. The strict rule that men and women have their places on different sides so that "brothers" and "sisters" could not exchange the liturgical kiss was not sufficient to suppress the rumor of incest. It is always connected with the reproach that a child is killed in the service and its flesh and blood are eaten and drunken, a misinterpretation of John 6:53. All apologists from Aristides to Origen had to reject these reproaches. They go back to the first century and are probably willful slander on the part of the Jews, whose burning hatred against the Christians who had apostasized from the synagogue caused the persecutions. This hatred was especially strong in Asia (Acts 21:27). This explains how John speaks of the Jews in his Gospel and passages like Rev. 2:9; 3:9. Those terrific experiences in Asia still resound in the Eastern Church. When antisemitism spread in the West in the thirteenth century, the old slander of ritual murder and eating of children was turned back upon the Jews. We mention all this here because (1) it confirms indirectly the sacramental realism of the earliest Church (it is worth noticing that throughout the sixteenth century the old word *Thyestes* was used in the polemics against the Lutheran realism. Cf. WA 54, 156: *Uns biessen sie Fleischfresser, Blutsaufer, Anthropophagos, Capernaiten, Thyestas, etc.*) and because (2) it is important for the understanding of John 6. This chapter was originally understood as dealing with the mystery of the Eucharist. The way John relates a discourse of our Lord on the "bread from heaven," which in the first part is he himself, in the later part is flesh, and the way this discourse is brought into connection with the miracles of the feeding of the 5,000 (multiplication of the bread, the *reliquiae sacramenti*, w. 12f.) and Jesus walking on the water (His body not necessarily obeying the laws of a natural body), furthermore the use of eucharist (w. 11,23), the dispute with the Jews, and the offense that even "many of his disciples" took at the "hard saying," have always been suggestive of the Eucharist, until Origen, Eusebius, and Augustine introduced a different interpretation. How the early Christians understood such texts is shown by the earliest representation of the *fractio panis* in the Capella Graeca (second century) of the catacomb of St. Priscilla in Rome. John could not include a narrative of the institution of the Lord's Supper in his Gospel, which was written not only for Christian readers who had gone through a course of catechetical instruction (Luke 1:4) but obviously for a wider public. Instead he inserted the discourse that seems to indicate that Jesus had prepared his disciples for their first Holy Communion.

by Irenaeus (*Adv. Haer.*, IV, 18, 5). Much confusion has later been caused by the fact that Augustine was never able to reach clarity in regard to the Sacrament of the Altar. His attempt to build up a theory of the sacraments in terms of Neoplatonism and to apply it to the Lord's Supper was most unfortunate.

The Reformed theologians could, indeed, refer to Augustine as their authority, as Berengar and Wycliffe had done. They could do so also with regard to another fateful heritage the great father left to the Western Church: the idea that the body of Christ, since it is in heaven, cannot at the same time be here on earth. It is noteworthy that this argument is the basis not only of the Reformed doctrine but also of the doctrine of transubstantiation. Since Christ's body, as a true body, must be in heaven, it can be on the altar, and on so many altars simultaneously, not by a change of its place (*per motum localem*) but only by the conversion of the substance of the bread into the substance of the body (*perconversionemsubstantiae pants in ipsum*), as Thomas (*Summa theol.*, III, qu. 75, art. 2) points out. Although Augustine was never able to solve the problem of the relation between the body in heaven and the body in the Sacrament theologically, he kept his belief in the real presence as it was expressed in the liturgy. The formula of distribution in Africa was the same as in the Eastern churches: *Corpus Christi*, whereupon the communicant answered Amen. The cup was given with the words *Sanguis Christi*, which also was answered by Amen. This Amen was always understood as a confession: Yes, I believe that. Can one imagine a man like Augustine for so many years distributing the Sacrament without firmly believing what he said and made his people confess? There is a lack of clarity, a gap between his faith and his theological thinking, as is often found in the history of the Church.

But it is impossible to claim Augustine with his neoplatonic mysticism for a rationalizing or merely spiritualistic understanding of the Lord's Supper. He emphasized, it is true, the spiritual manducation, for example, in the famous *Crede et manducasti*. It must not be overlooked that this word is to be found in his exposition of John 6:27.

But in addition to this *manducatio spiritualis*, he knows and emphasizes, especially in his later years, the sacramental eating to such a degree that he teaches—and this distinguishes him from the

Reformed churches—a *manducatio oralis*, the *manducatio impiorum*, and even the necessity of this Sacrament for salvation. The Jews who at Pentecost were converted were now eating the body they had killed. Even Judas had received the body of Christ. The Sacrament is necessary even for infants. Hence the early practice of giving the Holy Eucharist to the children after Baptism, as the Eastern Church still does. But even if Augustine's doctrine had not this other side, even if he were a mere symbolist like Origen, this would not alter the dogma of the Church. This was the same in the liturgies Eastern and Western and had been proclaimed by the Second Council of Nicea for the East and in *Ego Berengarius* of 1079 (Denzinger, 355) for the Medieval Latin Church.

Luther, like others, had his misgivings concerning the later dogma of 1215. By introducing the idea of "transubstantiation," this dogma tried to give a theological and even a philosophical answer to the question of *how* the elements after consecration could be the body and blood of Christ. The simple declaration of 1079 was never rejected; even Wycliffe accepted it, though he did not quite understand it. This doctrine is expressed in the medieval German hymn "*Gott sei gelobet und gebenedeiet*," which Luther accepted and enlarged. It is the conviction that after consecration the bread is truly the body of our Lord that hung on the cross and is now on the right hand of the Father, the wine the true blood of Christ that was shed at Calvary. No mention was made any longer of the statement of 1059 that the body is crushed by the teeth, this being against the view (which meanwhile had been generally accepted) that this would be an overstatement, because the presence is not a local one in the sense that Christ's body can be divided when the host is divided. The entire body is present "in, with, and under" each particle of the host.

VII.

It was this doctrine of the entire Church of almost fifteen hundred years that Luther at Marburg defended against Zwingli and Oecolampadius. Over against their objection that Jesus could not have meant the Eucharistic Words literally because God does not propose to us incomprehensible things (*Deus non proponit nobis incomprehensibilia*) he could simply answer that all great truths of God's revelation are incomprehensible, as the incarnation, the virgin birth, the bodily resurrection, and so on.

Zwingli, of course, never doubted such doctrines. He even maintained the ecclesiastical tradition of Mary's perpetual virginity. He was not a rationalist but rather what later has been called a supranaturalist. He was a Biblicist. But his understanding of Scripture was, to a greater extent than he was able to realize, determined by his humanism and that amount of rationalism that is inherent in all humanists and that was bound to produce the rationalistic philosophy and theology of the later seventeenth and eighteenth centuries. "God is Light and leads into light" was his answer to Luther's "One must close one's eyes when God speaks," as Abraham hid himself in the darkness of faith when God commanded him to sacrifice his son, thus obviously making impossible the fulfillment of his own promise. Over against the old Augustinian argument (which plays such a great role with Zwingli and Calvin) that the body of Christ cannot be on earth, since it is in heaven, "it being against the truth of Christ's natural body to be at one time in more places than one" (*1662, Book of Common Prayer*), Luther pointed out that he would not listen to mathematical arguments, for "God is beyond all mathematics" (we would today use the word *physics*). He was, however, prepared to enter this field, if that was desired, not to prove with "mathematical" arguments what no human reason can prove but rather to show that mathematics cannot disprove the real presence.

Perhaps the deepest motive of Zwingli's view is to be found in the objection based on John 6:63 ("The flesh profiteth nothing"): "Spirit eats spirit, it does not eat flesh." It is, in other words, the problem of what should be the use of such eating even if it were possible. It was easy for Luther to show that John 6:63 could not mean that Christ's flesh profiteth nothing. Otherwise the entire doctrine of the incarnation would break down. The passage could only be a warning against the "Capernaitic" misunderstanding of the sacramental eating, as if Christ's body were eaten like ordinary food. But here the real issue became quite clear. When Oecolampadius asked Luther not to stick to the humanity of Christ, but rather to lift up his mind to his divinity in heaven—who is not reminded of Calvin's use of the *sursum corda*?—the reply was that he could not separate the divine and the human nature in Christ in such a way. How could space separate that which had become one in the hypostatic union? Besides, he knew of no other God but him who has become flesh, and he wanted to have no other God.

Here the two ways of understanding Christianity met: on Luther's part the realistic understanding of the incarnation and of the Sacrament as the continuation of the incarnation, on Zwingli's part the idealistic separation of body and soul, the visible and the invisible, the finite and the infinite, and, consequently, of the human and divine natures of Christ. Zwingli, of course, did not want to be, and was not, a Nestorian. He could still, in contrast with Calvin, speak of Mary as the mother of God, which has always been the test of orthodox Christology. And yet such language given by theological tradition was actually, as he called it, *alloiosis*, a mode of speech in which when speaking of one nature of Christ we use words that properly can be applied only to the other nature.

When reading Luther's criticism of this *alloiosis*, one has the impression as if Luther anticipated the future development that was bound to lead to the modern Protestantism that can no longer understand that the person of Christ is the eternal Son, who has accepted our human nature without ceasing to be true and real God. Such Protestantism can, of course, no longer understand and preserve the Sacrament in Luther's sense. This modern Protestantism must see in Luther's doctrine a regrettable relapse into Romanism, though it should not be forgotten that the Roman doctrine of transubstantiation is more spiritual than we are inclined to believe. This is at least the opinion of Eastern Orthodox theologians, who maintain that after all Aquinas is perhaps not very far from Calvin, owing to their common Augustinian heritage. In some respects Luther is nearer to the Eastern Church, which has never formulated a dogma concerning the *how* of the real presence.

But Luther could never accept the understanding of the Eucharist as a propitiatory sacrifice, which was to him the great corruption of the Sacrament, far worse than transubstantiation. The medieval doctrine of transubstantiation he rejected as "a sophistic subtlety" meant to explain philosophically that which defies any explanation. Besides, "it is in perfect agreement with Holy Scripture that there is, and remains, bread, as Paul himself calls it, 1 Corinthians 10:16: 'The bread which we break.' And 1 Corinthians 11:28: 'Let him eat of the bread'" (Smalcald Articles, Part Three, VI, 5). Luther has no doctrine on the how of the real presence. Neither "consubstantiation" nor "impanation" is the doctrine of the Lutheran Church. These are medieval theories. If Luther in *De captivitate Babylonica* refers to Peter d'Ailly, he does so in order to show that even this distinguished cardinal had his doubts concerning transubstantiation and would prefer consubstantiation if that were possible. Nor does Luther teach an *inclusio* or any kind of "local" presence. Luther has never demanded from anyone the acceptance of his theory of omnipresence, which he had developed only to show that the philosophical, mathematical arguments of his opponents could be refuted. Even the medieval terms "in," "with," "under" are by no means characteristic of the Lutheran doctrine. Just as Luther in his *Last Confession* (1544–45), referring to Aquinas and the Medieval Church, rejected the idea of a "local" presence or *inclusio*, so Nicholas Selneccer, one of the authors of the Formula of Concord, in harmony with Luther's Last Confession, points out, "Though our churches use the old words 'In the bread, with the bread, under the bread the body of Christ is received,' they do not thereby teach an *inclusio* or *consubstantiatio*. . . . They rather intend to say not more than this, that Christ is veracious and that when giving us the bread in his supper, he gives us simultaneously his body to eat, as he himself says. Whether one says 'in the bread,' 'with the bread,' 'under the bread,' we do not care if only we keep the Lord's body in the supper. That we would not allow anyone to take from us. . . ." (*Vom Heiligen Abendmahl des Herrn. . . . Wiederholete kurze und letzte Bekenntnis und Testament D. Nicolai Selnecceri* [Frankfurt-am-Main: 1591], fol. E3)

It was this simple understanding of the Sacrament of the Altar that was contained in the last offer Luther made after the Marburg Colloquy had failed. The Marburg Colloquy was bound to fail because Zwingli could not accept the real presence, and Luther could not accept a compromise that left the question open. But would Zwingli not perhaps be prepared to accept the real presence if formulated in such a way that no Capernaitic misunderstanding was possible? The formula suggested by Luther and his colleagues was this: "We confess that by virtue of the words 'This is my body, this is my blood' the body and blood of Christ are truly—*hoc est: substantive et essentialiter, non autem quantitative vel qualitative vel localiter*—present and distributed in the Lord's Supper." *Substantive et essentialiter* means the true body and blood in the sense of the old hymn *"Gott sei gelobet und gebenedeiet"*: *"Herr, durch deinen heiligen Leichnam / Der von deiner Mutter Maria kam / Und das heilige Blut . . ."* (see *Ego Berengarius*, Denzinger 355). Body and blood are present not quantitatively or qualitatively. This means that Christ's body in the Sacrament has not the extension, weight, and other properties of a natural, earthly body. Luther and the Lutheran fathers (e.g., Johann Gerhard, *Loci* XXI, cap. 26; ed. Preuss V, 252) could refer to Aquinas's Adoro devote with the words *"Visas, tactus, gustus / In te fallitur / Sed audito solo in te creditur / Credo quidquid dixit / Dei filius / Verbo veritatis nihil verius."* The body of Christ is present in the *usus*—which is not identical with *sumptio*.[3] It is there where the bread is. But this *ibi eucharisticum* is not a local *ibi*.

---

[3]Neither Luther nor the Lutheran Confessions have identified *usus* with *sumptio*. When explaining the rule *"Nihil habet rationem sacramenti extra usum a Christo institutum"* or *"extra actionem divinitus institutam,"* the Formula of Concord (SD VII 85ff.) gives the definition: "The use or action here does not mean chiefly faith, neither the oral participation only, but the entire external, visible action of the Lord's Supper instituted by Christ, the consecration or Words of Institution, the distribution and reception (Latin text: *consecratio seu verba institutionis, distributio et sumptio*), or oral partaking. . . ." This is important for the problems of the "moment of consecration" 'and the "duration" of the real presence. They cannot be defined. All attempts to give an exact definition are bound to fail because nothing has been revealed to us concerning these questions. This must be said also of the view of later orthodox theologians who limited the real presence to the moment of the *sumptio*. This is not the view of the Lutheran Confessions. The Formula of Concord, in harmony with Luther and the entire Western Church, teaches that the words of consecration are the Words of Institution. The view of some schoolmen that the consecration at the institution was effected by the eucharist Christ spoke before the Words of Institution should not be accepted by Lutherans. Therefore the introduction of an *epiclesis* of the Holy Spirit upon the elements should be avoided in a Lutheran liturgy. The alternative form of consecration in the new *Service Book of the Lutheran Church in America* is a strange mixture of Western (*benedictione coelesti et gratia repleamur*) and Eastern elements (*e&pivklhsiòof* the Logos and of the Holy Spirit).

VIII.

The connection between the elements on the one hand and the body and blood on the other is rather the true *unio sacramentalis*. And this presence is effected through the words of Christ, which, once spoken at the institution, are effective at all times when spoken by the minister of the Sacrament *ex persona Christi*.[4]

All this is contained in the Lutheran formula, which was the last possible offer Luther could make. It was not accepted by Zwingli. Kohler has shown why he could not accept this offer. Even in this form the doctrine of the real presence was unacceptable to him. He could not return to Zurich with a formula that contradicted everything he had taught in the previous years, especially since the words "by virtue of the words of Christ" could be understood only in the sense of a consecration. The Words of Institution were addressed in the liturgy of Zurich, as in all Reformed liturgies, to the people as a proclamation of the Gospel. "Consecration" in the Reformed liturgies and confessions means "setting apart for a sacred use by prayer." The "consecration," even where the word is retained, does not effect the real presence. One must keep this in mind in order to do justice to Zwingli. He could not accept this offer.

IX.

It is in this last offer made by Luther and in its rejection by Zwingli that the real result of the Marburg Colloquy is to be found, and not in the Marburg Articles, which used to be regarded as the real outcome, a promise for a future understanding, which, though not reached in the sixteenth century, should be possible today. The fifteen (not fourteen, as in older printings) articles Luther drafted at the request of the Landgrave (on the basis of the articles that the Lutheran theologians

---

[4]Here lies the reason why the denial of the real presence on the part of the officiating minister is, according to Luther, a destruction of the institution of Christ. He speaks not *ex persona Christi* who does not mean what Christ meant by his words. If these words could be used without this meaning, they would be a sort of magic formula. Nor do the words effect the presence but Christ, who speaks them through his minister.

formulated in summer 1529 and that the Lutheran estates formally adopted after the Marburg Colloquy at Schwabach) show how far Luther could go in the interest of the true union that he was still hoping for despite the failure of the colloquy.

At the same time, they are a testimony to the political cleverness of Philip of Hesse. Only a great politician was able to interpret an obvious failure as a seeming success. He wanted a result, a statement of agreement, even if only of a partial agreement. The colloquy was originally planned for a week. The negotiations began on Friday, October 1; the formal discussions were held on Saturday and Sunday. The colloquy broke down on Sunday afternoon. In the evening the Lutheran proposal was made and discussed.

The reason for the hurry in which everything had to be done was the appearance of an epidemic, the sudor Anglicus, at Marburg. The Landgrave wanted his guests to depart safely as soon as possible, as he himself wanted to leave Marburg. He was the first to depart on Tuesday morning.

Thus the articles were formulated and discussed on Monday. It is not surprising that they proved to be insufficient, since no full and proper consideration could be given to them in so short a time. Otherwise it would have become apparent at Marburg already what became obvious when Zwingli published them with his *notae* (WA 30, III, 160ff.), that important passages were understood differently by either side. Article XI, to take an example, deals with "confession or seeking of counsel and consolation from one's pastor or neighbor" and speaks of the comfort "of the absolution or consolation of the gospel, which is the true absolution." Luther understood this in the way of real confession and real absolution, while Zwingli thought of the fraternal seeking of counsel and consolation and not of an absolution in the sense of the proclamation of divine forgiveness through a human mouth.

The masterpiece of diplomacy was Article 15, probably formulated by Philip himself. This deals with the Lord's Supper and states that there is agreement in five points, which indeed were recognized by either side. Two of them could even be accepted by the pope ("that the Sacrament of the Altar is the sacrament of the true body and blood of Christ"—it all depends on what one understands by the word "sacrament," whether a mere sign of grace or a means of grace—and that the spiritual manducation is necessary for every Christian).

Among all these real or alleged agreements there disappears almost the one point of disagreement, namely, that "*at present* we are not agreed whether the true body and blood of Christ are bodily present in the bread and wine," but both parties should "earnestly implore Almighty God to confirm us by his Spirit in the sound doctrine." Agreement in 14 out of 15 articles, agreement in five out of six points of the Fifteenth Article, Zwingli almost a 99 percent Lutheran—what a marvelous achievement! Already at Marburg it had become quite clear what the controversies and negotiations of the subsequent four hundred years have time and again confirmed and what Luther had seen from the beginning: There is no middle road between *est* and *significat*, between *is* and *is not*, between yes and no.

It is the tragedy of Protestantism that this was not realized. All attempts to find such a middle road were and still are bound to fail. One must have high respects for Calvin's endeavor to solve the problem of how a real reception of the true body and blood of Christ, which are in heaven, can be reconciled with the view that what we orally receive is only bread and wine. From Bucer he had learned to teach a reception of the body and blood by faith. But the New Testament as well as the Church of all ages teach that we receive Christ's body and blood orally and that they are received by all communicants. Even Augustine had taught the *manducatio oralis* and the *manducatio impiorum*.

Calvin attempted to solve the problem of bridging the distance between heaven and earth, between Christ's body in heaven and the believer on earth, by his interpretation of the *sursum corda* and by the idea of the Holy Spirit as the *transporteur* who brings Christ's body to us. But this attempt has no biblical foundation. He was unable to reconcile the *est* and the *significat*. The same is true of all later attempts, also of many formulas suggested today.

What can we do in this really tragic situation? What can and must the Lutheran contribution toward the present Eucharistic discussions be? It cannot be a continuation of the fruitless attempts to reach a compromise or to take up and improve the Fifteenth Article of Marburg. What we can and ought to do is rather to renew the offer Luther made on the evening of October 3, 1529. Zwingli could not accept it. But the time has come to again ask the question of whether this is not the only possible solution and whether it is not acceptable to many Protestant churches also outside the orbit of Lutheranism: "We confess that by virtue of the words 'This is My body,' 'This is My blood,' the body and blood of Christ are truly—*hoc est: substantive et essentialiter, non autem quantitative vel qualitative vel localiter*—present and distributed in the Lord's Supper." This is not a specifically Lutheran doctrine, not the doctrine of one of the many Christian denominations. It has been the doctrine of the entire Christian Church for fifteen hundred years and is still the doctrine of the vast majority of Christendom today. It is, as we are convinced, the doctrine of the apostles and of our Lord himself. It is in its simplest form stated in the answer to the question "What is the Sacrament of the Altar?" and in the Lutheran formula of distribution. In this sense we enter the discussion of the Lord's Supper, writing with Luther on the table the *status controversiae: Hoc est corpus meum.*

CONCORDIA THEOLOGICAL MONTHLY
Vol. 31, No. 2 (1960)

The Ecumenical Movement
and the Lutheran Church

Editorial Note: This article was presented as an essay to the 1959 convention of The Lutheran Church—Missouri Synod at San Francisco by request of President J. W. Behnken.

Church history knows of great movements that sweep through the whole of Christendom, irrespective of national and denominational lines, and bring about profound changes in the inner life and the outward appearance of all churches. Such movements were Pietism and Rationalism in the seventeenth and eighteenth centuries, and the great European Awakening in the nineteenth century. Such a movement is the Ecumenical Movement, which in our time is penetrating all churches of Christendom, including Rome and the Eastern churches. The effects may prove to be as far-reaching as those of the great movement of the sixteenth century, which we call the Reformation in its widest sense.

At that time the breakdown of the Medieval Church, long overdue and foreshadowed by minor upheavals, resulted in a complete change in the religious life and the ecclesiastical scene of the world. Within two generations a large part of Europe was lost to the papacy. Out of the Catholic Church of the West new churches have issued, Lutheran and Reformed churches, the Church of England, besides

451

a number of smaller groups and sects. What remained of the Papal Church underwent such a profound change in the Roman Catholic reformation at the Council of Trent that in many respects it may be regarded as a new church, the modern Roman Church, which found its completion at the Vatican Council of 1869–70, the largest of the confessional churches of Christendom. To make up for the losses suffered in Europe, this church took up mission work in Asia and the Americas and thus inaugurated an era in which the entire earth, the οἰκουμένη, to use the Greek word for the inhabited earth, was to become the scene of Church history.

This great era of four hundred years seems now to be drawing to its end. In the second half of the twentieth century, we are witnessing not only the most revolutionary changes in the social, political, and economic life of mankind but also one of the greatest religious revolutions in human history. This revolution has often been described by our missionaries. We call to mind only a few bare facts. The ratio between Christians and non-Christians in the world is rapidly changing in favor of the non-Christians, no mission work being able to cope with the growth of mankind. The decline of Christianity in the old Christian countries makes these countries mission fields. The great religions of Asia are reviving in connection with the growth of nationalism and anticolonialism. And who would have expected when the Communist *Manifesto* appeared in 1948 that this booklet would become the creed of one third of mankind only a century later?

I.

The Ecumenical Movement must be seen against this background. For in this movement Christendom is trying to solve the problems presented by those facts. It is essentially a spiritual movement and cannot be understood only from its organizational aspects. A new relationship between the Christians throughout the world is developing, a new relationship also between the churches. Would it have been possible fifty years ago for German Roman Catholic bishops to speak of the Protestants as "our separated brethren"? Would it have been possible to sing hymns by Luther in Roman Catholic churches? A remarkable fellowship has grown out of theological conferences between Roman Catholics and Lutherans in Germany and between Reformed and Roman Catholics in France, to say nothing of the fellowship experienced by members of various churches in prisons, in concentration camps, and in the emergencies of the war.

Apart from this change of the spiritual climate, a complete transformation of the external setup of Christendom is taking place. Think what it means for America that the venerable church of the pilgrim fathers, which has meant so much for the formation of the American nation, is now disappearing, as it has already disappeared in Canada and will disappear in Australia and New Zealand, being absorbed by a large united church. At the same time, some millions of Eastern Christians have transplanted their old churches to the New World. The same process is going on in South America, in Australia, and on the mission fields of Asia and Africa, where out of the missions of the Protestant denominations new churches, and perhaps new types of Christianity, are growing. If we take into account, furthermore, the tremendous growth seen in the world, we understand that no human mind is able to imagine what Christendom will look like when in about forty years it enters the third millennium. If of this movement is true what is true of every great religious movement in the world, we see the beginnings, but we do not know where it will end, then where will the movement represented by the WCC and the LWF end? Nobody knows. Conferences may make constitutions and programs, define aims and purposes. Executive secretaries may travel through the world and proclaim these aims. Conferences may appoint committees, and the committees may appoint subcommittees, to investigate the nature and purpose of what actually is going on. Of Randall Davidson, the great archbishop of Canterbury (1903–28), they said in England that were he in office when the last trumpet sounds, "he would be sure to nominate a representative committee to consider and report whether it was the last trump or the last but one."[1] The real history is beyond the reach of man. As all history, so also the history of the Ecumenical Movement is a battle between God and Satan. Good and evil, blessing and curse, grace and

---

[1] F. A. Iremonger, William Temple, Archbishop of Canterbury: His Life and Letters, 1948, p. 356f.

judgment, are hidden in what is going on in the Ecumenical Movement of our age.

Time does not permit us to relate here the history of the Ecumenical Movement. Only a few lines can be drawn. This movement is deeply rooted in the European awakening of the 1800s, when after the icy winter of Rationalism the Christian faith was revived. It was around 1830 that suddenly the Church was rediscovered as one of the great articles of faith and as a reality by Roman theologians in Germany (Mohler) and France (Lacordaire, Lamennais) and by great thinkers in Russia (Chomjakow), in the Church of England (Keble, Newman, Pusey) as well as in the Lutheran (Scheibel, Vilmar, Löhe, Rudelbach, Walther) and Reformed (Vinet, Kohlbrügge) churches of Europe. The Lutheran Church—Missouri Synod owes its existence to that European awakening, just as our Lutheran churches in Australia and the free churches in Germany do. For it was the quest for *the true Church* that caused our fathers to leave their country, their people, their earthly possessions, after they had come to the conviction that the territorial churches of the Old World, which comprised all the people irrespective of their actual faith, could no longer be what they claimed to be: churches confessing before God and the world the truth of the Gospel as it was testified to in the *Book of Concord*. Some people call that separatism. You know from the history of your church how seriously your fathers searched their own conscience, asking themselves in the sight of God whether they were right or whether they were guilty of the sin of schism. Thank God for these consciences! Thank God for that holy separatism! The blessing of their faithful confession is still a very great reality in your church. And it is generally admitted that the faithful witness of the true confessors of that time has saved what has remained of the Lutheran Church in the old country.

Another example is the "Disruption" in the Church of Scotland in 1843, when "no less than 474 ministers—two-fifths of the entire number in the Church—left manses, stipends, and all the earthly goods the state had given and, under Dr. Chalmers, went forth to continue the Church of Scotland Free.[2] They did so because their con-

---

[2]P.C. Simpson, *The Life of Principal Rainy*, Popular Edition (1904), p. 67.

science did not allow them to sacrifice the confession of their church to an arbitrary law made by Parliament in London. Their confessional loyalty saved the Reformed faith in Scotland for the coming generations. Even a separation can be a great service to true ecumenicity if it is a separation from that which is bound to destroy the true Church. The Ecumenical Movement is not primarily a union movement, though it might lead to unions, true or false unions. As old Bishop Palmer of Bombay said at the First World Conference on Faith and Order at Lausanne, 1927, when he opened the discussion on the controversial subject "The Church's Ministry," "This is a conference about truth, not about reunion. We engage in it because we desire the visible unity of Christ's Church on earth. . . . As we differ greatly about cardinal matters, some of us must be wrong, and all may to some extent be wrong. We come here expecting to learn, and that must mean hoping to be corrected if we are wrong.—We seek God's truth about the whole of Christendom."[3] This is true ecumenicity, the concern for the *una sancta*, "which is the Church of the living God, the pillar and ground of the truth" (1 Tim. 3:15). In this sense I venture to say that the Synodical Convention of The Lutheran Church—Missouri Synod at San Francisco, 1959, is one of the very few really ecumenical events of this year.

The quest for the Church always involves the quest for the unity of the Church, for it belongs to the very nature of the Church that it is the *una sancta*, the one, holy, catholic, and apostolic Church. Thus also in Europe the rediscovery of the Church in the nineteenth century made the unity of the Church one of the great topics of theology and one of the great practical problems of church life. In a special way, however, this question was bound to come up in America. Europeans have always been surprised by, and have even mocked at, the variety of religious communities in the New World. What most of them failed to realize is that this is not altogether the fault of the Americans. On the contrary, they have inherited almost all of these divisions from European Christendom. The tragic situation of a divided Christendom in countries like America

---

[3]*Faith and Order, Proceedings of the World Conference, Lausanne, August 3–21, 1927*, ed. H. N. Bate (1927), p. 233.

and Australia is caused by the fact that the groups and communities, which in Europe were and are separated by geographical and national boundaries, here live in the same city, in the same street, in the same house. This state of division is—and this should never be forgotten—the price that had to be paid for that great contribution America has made not only to Western civilization but also to the life of the churches, of all churches: freedom of conscience, freedom of religion. Europe has never been quite able to get rid of the terrific heritage of the Roman Empire, which claimed the rule also over the souls of men. Neither the Lutheran nor the Reformed churches of Europe have been able to attain that freedom from secular powers that the confessions of the Reformation claimed for the Church of Christ. In what a terrific slavery these churches live is apparent when in Norway the minister of the State for Church Affairs could decide that it is not a violation of the confessional obligation of a bishop to deny the biblical and confessional doctrine of hell and eternal damnation. In Sweden, likewise, the Riksdag makes a law permitting the ordination of women, and the church follows and alters its constitution and its liturgy accordingly. Who possesses the "freedom to reform the church" of which Bishop Giertz spoke so convincingly at Minneapolis? The state, and that means, the ruling political party. The Church has this right only as far as the state permits it. Or one may think of the terrific slavery of the Church of England, which is not able to bring about a real reform of the *Book of Common Prayer* because Parliament would not allow it. Only if one has lived in the slavery of the *cuius regio eius religio,* can one understand what religious freedom, freedom of conscience, is. And one who has lived in the world of religious freedom can understand why in America the quest for the Church became the quest for unity and why America has given birth to the modern Ecumenical Movement. In speaking of the Ecumenical Movement we must here confine ourselves to two great ecumenical programs that originated in America and that have produced the movement as it presents itself today.

II.

The first of these programs has its origin in American Reformed Protestantism. When Zinzendorf came to Pennsylvania, that great paradise of dissent and cradle of religious freedom, he conceived the strange idea of asking the governor to see to it—what a European he was! —that the children of God in all denominations should attend the meetings of the *Brüdergemeinde*, not to become its members but to express the essential oneness of God's children in the various denominations. For the *Brüdergemeinde* was not to be a new denomination but a place where Lutherans, Reformed, Roman Catholics, and other Christians should meet as children of their heavenly Father, as souls redeemed through the blood of the Lamb. To Zinzendorf the various churches were *trovpoi paideivaò*, ways of education, schools, as it were, in which God educated his children. According to Lutheran doctrine, it is indeed true that children of God, true believers, exist in all churches wherever the means of grace still exist. It is, however, un-Lutheran to assume that we are able to see and to make visible what only God can see. This is sheer enthusiasm, and this enthusiasm is the contribution of Pietism to the modern Ecumenical Movement. You find this enthusiasm in the Evangelical Alliance, which from 1846 on spread from Britain to Europe and America. You find this idea still as one of the strongest elements of modern ecumenicity, for instance, when in 1950 the member churches of the Federal Council merged their organization with the new National Council of Churches of Christ in the USA with the intention to "manifest more fully oneness in Jesus Christ as their divine Lord and Savior." I have never been able to understand how the president of the United Lutheran Church could solemnly inaugurate that council that has this formula as its basis. How can we manifest oneness in Jesus Christ between Lutherans, Presbyterians, Anglicans, Methodists, Baptists, Congregationalists, Disciples, Quakers, and all sorts of sects, among them such as deny the *sola scriptura*, the *sola fide*—Anglo-Catholics—and reject the Sacrament of Christ, as the Salvation Army does? How can we manifest "oneness in Christ" with those who deny the deity of Christ as taught in the New Testament and the creeds of the Church? Here lies one of the deepest of the problems that divide the Lutheran churches today, one that must be solved before we can talk of Lutheran unity.

I must resist the temptation to speak on such an interesting attempt to establish Christian unity as was made by the Disciples of Christ, who wanted to go back behind all man-made creeds and constitutions to what they regarded as the Church of the New Testament. Serious and important as this attempt has been, it was bound to have the same result as Zinzendorf's endeavors. You cannot diminish the number of Christian denominations by founding a new one. This is a simple arithmetical truth. But I want to mention briefly at least one man whose significance for the rise of American ecumenism has been generally recognized nowadays. This is the tragic figure of Samuel Simon Schmucker, for forty years president of the first Lutheran seminary in this country at Gettysburg. The Lutheran churches had to reject his so-called *Definite Platform*, which appeared anonymously in 1855, the program of the so-called American Lutheranism, the Lutheran version of that "Americanismus" the Roman Church rejected in 1899. It was a sort of *Confessio Augustana Variata Americana* in which the distinctive doctrines of the Lutheran Reformation, such as baptismal regeneration, the real presence of the true body and blood of Christ in the Lord's Supper, and private confession and absolution, had been given up. The Schmucker of the *Definite Platform* is a pathetic figure, one that should not be forgotten, for his life and work has clarified the situation of the Lutheran Church in your country. Just as the question has been asked, "Can a Roman Catholic be a good American citizen?" so the question is, "Can the Lutheran Church be truly American without giving up what distinguishes it from the Reformed denominations in the midst of which it lives?" At a time when Schmucker's ghost seems to haunt the Lutheran churches of America, it is worthwhile to study him again. Such study would reveal him as one of the fathers of the Ecumenical Movement in the U.S.A.[4] From his *Fraternal Appeal to the American Churches* (1838) to his book on *The True Unity of Christ's Church* (1870) and his last addresses, he developed the idea that all Protestant churches are essentially one. He tried to express their common doctrine in a United Confession, in which he combines articles from the various Protestant confessions. The churches should remain what they are but were called upon to do away with their sectarian names, with the man worship of Luther,

---

[4]See D. H. Yoder in *A History of the Ecumenical Movement*, ed. R. Rouse and S. C. Neill, p. 241ff.

Calvin, and Wesley. They were to grant one another pulpit and altar fellowship. Schmucker is one of the fathers of the idea of federal union, the precursor of men like E. Stanley Jones.

Schmucker's plan of a "Protestant Apostolic Church of America" on a federal basis could not be carried out in the nineteenth century, confessionalism in all churches being too strong. Thus another version of federal union won the day: Let us not discuss doctrine, but rather work together in practical fields. "Doctrine divides, service unites," as one of the slogans at the beginning of this century puts it. This idea was first realized in the Federal Council of the Churches of Christ in America of 1908, one of the most important ecumenical organizations of our time. If we cannot have a common confession of faith, we can at least together follow our Lord in practical work. However, it became obvious—what later became apparent also in the World Conference on Life and Work at Stockholm, 1925—that even common work among churches presupposes some kind of doctrinal agreement. Thus membership in the Federal Council was limited to churches for which Christ is the "divine Lord and Savior," whatever that may mean. For this formula was chosen after some churches declared that they could not accept the term "Son of God." But what does "divine" mean if it does not mean the deity of Christ as the Son of God? What does "Lord" mean if not the Christ of the New Testament who bears the name *kurios*, Lord, the holy name of God in the Greek Bible? What does "Savior" mean if not Christ as the Lamb of God that taketh away the sins of the world? The entire tragedy of the modern Ecumenical Movement becomes clear at this point. And a very serious question arises. Neither the Protestant Episcopal Church nor the United Lutheran Church was able at that time to become a member of the Federal Council, though they found some way of cooperation. What changes have made it possible for these churches now to be members of the National Council of the Churches of Christ? No basic changes have taken place in the ecumenical organization. They have taken place in these churches.

Before we go on, an appraisal of these attempts to achieve Christian unity may be in place. If we criticize them from the point of view of the Lutheran Confessions, we must realize that the majority of American Protestants are quite unable to understand our criticism. The Congregationalists, Baptists, Disciples, Quakers, and many other churches do not possess a confession and cannot possess one. Even for the Reformed and Presbyterians, a confession has not only a different content but even a different function in the church. I remember one night during one of the confessional synods in Germany when a theological committee had to formulate certain suggestions. It was in the small hours when I said to Karl Barth: "Herr Barth, you cannot expect us to abandon the Augsburg Confession just at the moment when our bishop is a prisoner of the police because he adheres to that confession." His reply was "Why not?" He was unable to understand that a Lutheran Church cannot confess before the world the truth of God's Word if it does not take quite seriously the Augsburg Confession, to which it has pledged itself because (*quia*, not only *quatenus*) it is the pure exposition of the Word of God. Also the Anglicans cannot understand our attitude toward our Confessions. For most of them, the *Thirty-Nine Articles*, which they have signed, have merely a historical meaning. They fail to understand, like other churches, that the confession binds together not only the living generation but all generations of the Church, because it expresses the eternal truth of the Gospel, which is the same for all ages.

This explains the fruitlessness of so many ecumenical discussions. When the Lutheran churches in India had reached an agreement on the Lord's Supper with the Church of South India, the then secretary of the Commission on Faith and Order visited me in Adelaide and produced the document. He was overjoyed. I showed him that certain terms had different meanings on either side. I called his attention to the fact that even if it were a real agreement, it could have no binding force for the Church of South India, because the liturgy and the constitution of this church allows for several doctrines on the Sacrament. Then we both felt what the French call "*la tristesse ecumenique,*" the ecumenical sadness, the distress that comes over us when we look into the depth of the gulf that still separates Christians. We do not speak the same language. We do not mean the same things when we use the same words: Gospel, Sacrament, consecration, real presence, and so on. This is the real tragedy of our divisions, which we must bravely face if we are to overcome them.

Much remains to be said on this first program of federal unity, for instance, on the deep influence exercised on it by the ideas of the

Enlightenment of the eighteenth century, which have played such a great role in the making of the United States of America and her institutions. We could refer to the close connection between the idea of freedom of religion and the rights of men or to the assumption of the men who have shaped the young American nation: that there is behind all historic religions one religion in which all men agree. Without this belief in an almost religious belief inone can understand neither the ecumenical organizations of America nor the tenacity with which American Protestants believe that eventually the Roman Church will commit suicide and join the united church of the future.

III.

The second ecumenical program on which we now have to speak briefly is the plan for organic unity. Behind it there is the Anglican concept of the one, holy, catholic, and apostolic church as was developed in the seventeenth century and renewed with great power in the Tractarian Movement since 1833. The article on the Church in the *Thirty-Nine Articles of the Church of England*, shaped like the corresponding articles in all confessions of the sixteenth century, including the *Catechismus Romanus*, after the pattern of the seventh article of the Augsburg Confession, begins with the words "*Ecclesia Christi visibilis est coetus fidelium. . . .*" "The visible Church of Christ is a congregation of faithful men, in the which the pure Word of God is preached, and the Sacraments be duly administered. . . ." According to the Lutheran Confession, the one, holy, catholic Church, the congregation of saints, that means of true believers, is a reality in this world, not a utopia, a "Platonic state." But this Church, the "society of faith and the Holy Spirit in the hearts," is hidden in the outward church, the "society of external things, and rites." "*Abscondita est ecclesia, latent sancti,*" as Luther puts it. "Hidden is the Church, hidden are the saints." We cannot see the faith and holiness of any man. We cannot feel the Holy Spirit. We can only believe in him. Therefore also the Church in its "strict" sense remains an article of faith and never becomes in this world an object of observation. As the sacramental body of Christ is hidden in, with, and under the earthly elements, so also his mystical or spiritual body, the Church, is hidden in, with, and under the visible earthly church bodies.

Over against this Lutheran view, which is closely linked with the article on justification, the Anglican Church insists on the visibility of the *una sancta*. Hence men must be able to say where it is. The Anglican divines of former centuries would say that the one, holy, catholic, and apostolic Church exists on earth. It consists of three branches, the Eastern Orthodox, the Roman, and the Anglican Church. Today they would be more broad-minded and not exclude other churches so definitely. Thus William Temple, the late archbishop of Canterbury, used to say, and he said it quite seriously, "I believe in the Holy Catholic Church, and sincerely regret that it does not at present exist."[5] At present there is no *one* church; there are many churches. The Church, the Body of Christ, is divided. But the creed's article "I believe in one, holy, catholic Church" implies the conviction that once there has been one church and that eventually it will again exist. There must have been an "ancient undivided church," whatever that may mean. Some have thought of the Church of the first four or five centuries. But was there one church at that time? Every student of Church history knows that ancient Christendom, too, was a divided Christendom. When Celsus about A.D. 180 wrote his book against Christianity, he did not fail to mention this dividedness. Origen, in his great answer to Celsus, did not deny it, but he tried to explain it. When a pagan about A. D. 150 wanted to become a Christian, he was in exactly the same position as a pagan is today in Calcutta and Bombay. He had to make up his mind as to which was the true Church of Christ among the several bodies—at that time three or four, and soon even more—each of which claimed to be the true Church. The people whom John, the apostle of love, called false prophets and antichrists must have been quite upset by his lack of ecumenicity. For they, too, professed to love their Lord Jesus Christ. They certainly wanted to be Christians. The only difference seemed to be that they did not assume that the Lord's body had been a natural body of human flesh. Is that really church-divisive, as John thought? Or look into Paul's Epistle to the Galatians. When Peter came to Antioch, he was not quite sure with whom he could and could not eat and drink, and that meant, since

---

[5]Iremonger, *William Temple*, p. 387.

the Lord's Supper was still connected with a meal, where he could participate in Holy Communion. He did so in the Greek Church. But when people arrived from Jerusalem, he switched over to the church in communion with James, and Paul called him a hypocrite. No, the "ancient undivided church" is an unproved axiom. The same is true of the "reunited church of the future." "It is an article of faith that the followers of Christ should form one united body on earth," so begins the book of a learned English historian on the schism between East and West.[6] Really? The name "followers of Christ" has always been claimed and is being claimed today by the most dangerous heretics. When our Lord prayed, "that they all may be one," He did not think of all who would call themselves Christians but of all true believers. He prayed for the apostles whom he was sending into the world: "Sanctify them through thy truth, thy word is truth," and he prayed "for them also which shall believe on me through their word, that they all may be one, as thou, Father, art in me, and I in thee, that they also may be (one)[7] in us." The oneness Christ has in mind is the oneness of those who believe in him through the apostolic word of truth. At no time have these words been understood as referring to the whole of outward Christendom. They have always referred to the true Church of Christ, which has kept the Word (John 17:6, cf. 8:51; 14:21; 15:20; Matt. 28:20; 2 Tim. 4:7; Rev. 3:10).

Naturally, there have always been different opinions as to where the true Church of Christ is. Novatians, Catholics, Donatists, adherents of the Nicene Creed, the various groups of Arians, Nestorians, Monophysites, adherents of the Chalcedonense, to mention only a few of the ancient "denominations," were disagreed on that, just as the modern denominations of Lutherans, Anglicans, Presbyterians, Methodists, Baptists, Roman Catholics, and Eastern Orthodox are today. The idea that the petition of our Lord "That they all may be one" would have been fulfilled if all denominations were absorbed in one big body that would comprise all who called themselves

---

[6] L. Runciman, *The Eastern Schism* (1955), p. 1.

[7] The second "one" (e{n) seems not to have been a part of the original text of John 17:1.

Christians is foreign to the Church fathers as well as to the reformers and to the Church of all ages up to the modern Ecumenical Movement. It overlooks the fact that there are, and always will be, heresies that the Church has to anathematize and heretics and schismatics for whose return to the Word and to itself the Church has to pray and to work in the spirit of charity. But this Church will always remain the "little flock," despised by the world, even the ecclesiastical world. That Christ in his High Priestly Prayer cannot have thought of a oneness and glory that will be visible before the Last Day appears from the fact that this oneness comprises the believers of all generations of the Church and that it is at the same time the oneness with the Son and the Father (cf. John 17:21ff. with 1 John 1:3) that is naturally invisible. On the Last Day only, with the advent of Christ in glory, the hidden glory and oneness of his Church will be revealed (cf. John 17:21–26 with Phil. 2:10f., Col. 3:3f.). The idea of a glorious "future reunited church" in this world is a chiliastic dream.

It was out of the Anglican doctrine of the *ecclesia Christi visibilis*, with its assumption of an "ancient undivided church" and a "future reunited church," that in America the concrete program for reunion arose. At the request of the then Church of England in Canada, the Anglican bishops of the world met for the first time in 1867 at Lambeth Palace, the residence of the Archbishop of Canterbury in London, for a free conference. The Lambeth conferences, held, as a rule, every ten years, not only have been the instrument in creating the Anglican Communion as one of the great confessional bodies of the world but also have been of utmost importance to the Ecumenical Movement. A proposal for reunion, drafted in 1886 by the Protestant Episcopal Church in the U.S.A. on the basis of a document of 1870, was adopted by the Lambeth Conference in 1888. It has been improved and reaffirmed by all subsequent conferences, with greatest emphasis in 1908, the year of the creation of the Federal Council. Thus the idea of federal union, the product of American Protestantism, was supplemented by the Anglican concept of organic union.

What does this program, the "Lambeth Quadrilateral," contain? It proposes that agreement in four points is necessary, but is also sufficient to establish full fellowship between the churches and so to unite them. There must be a common acceptance of (1) the Holy Scriptures, (2) the Apostles' and the Nicene Creed, (3) the Sacraments of Baptism and the Holy Communion, (4) a generally acknowledged ministry that includes the historic episcopate. This program is the basis of all unions inaugurated by the Anglican Church. It underlies the constitution of the Church of South India, the "Scheme for Church Union in Ceylon," the corresponding plan for North India and Pakistan, and similar proposals for Australia, New Zealand, and New Guinea.

Let us briefly look at these points. The first is the acceptance of Holy Scripture. Since every church accepts the Scriptures, the question arises, in what sense must they be accepted? The first draft of the Quadrilateral spoke of "The Holy Scriptures of the Old and the New Testament as the revealed word of God." This was already in 1888 changed into the Scriptures "as 'containing all things necessary to salvation,' and as being the rule and ultimate standard of faith." The definitive form of 1920 reads, "The Holy Scriptures, as the record of God's revelation of himself to man, and as being the rule and ultimate standard of faith." The development of the formula reveals a significant lack of clarity. It does justice neither to the Catholic churches nor to the churches of the Reformation. Why has the original "the revealed word of God" been changed into "the record of God's revelation of himself"? The Scriptures are no longer regarded as the Word of God, given by the inspiration of the Holy Spirit, but only as a record of God's revelation. This is equally unacceptable to the Eastern, the Roman, the Lutheran, and the Reformed churches. It is not necessary here to show how for all churches of the Reformation the Bible was the Word of God, given by the inspiration of the Holy Spirit. If the Lutheran Confessions do not contain an explicit article on the inspiration and inerrancy of Scripture but mention it only incidentally (e.g., Apology IV 108; FCSD VI 14; XI, 12; LC V 75), the only reason for that is that this common Christian doctrine was *extra controversiam* in the sixteenth century. Nor does the Council of Trent mention it expressly, though it is presupposed in the decree on the Holy Scriptures. It was over against the modern denial of the classical doctrine on the Scriptures that Rome in the *Constitutio de fide catholica* of the Vatican Council spoke an anathema against the denial of the inspiration of the Bible. The positive doctrine is contained in the statement that "the Church regards the books as sacred and canonical, not as books written only by human diligence, and later approved by the authority of the Church; nor for that reason only that they contain the revelation without error (*quod revelationem sine errore contineant*), but rather because they, written by the inspiration of the Holy Spirit, have God as their author, and as such are given to the Church (*quod Spiritu Sancto inspkante conscript* Deumhabentauctorem, atque ut tales ipsi Ecclesiae traditi sunt*)" (Denzinger 1788, cf. the canon Denz. 1809). Hence even Rome would have to reject the Quadrilateral's view of the Scripture "as the record of God's revelation," because it is insufficient and unable to establish the authority of the Scriptures. Lutherans and Reformed, on the other hand, would ask whether a mere record can be "the ultimate rule and standard of faith." Only God's Word can be that. Thus the first point of the Quadrilateral is unacceptable to both Catholics and orthodox Protestants. As it denies the teaching of all Christendom of the Scripture as the Word of God, so it is unable to maintain the *sola scriptura* of the Reformation. This is confirmed by a statement made by the present Archbishop of Canterbury, under whose presidency the Lambeth Conference of 1958 reaffirmed the Quadrilateral. In reply to the question of what the beliefs of the Church of England are, he said among other things, "The Church of England believes that the Holy Spirit of God, the only final authority, speaks to us in Scripture, in the tradition of the Church, and in the living thought and experience of today. Thus there is a threefold cord, each single strand of which, unrelated to the others, leads astray."[8] The *sola scriptura* leads astray. What would the fathers of the English Reformation, men like Tyndale, Barnes, Latimer, Ridley, and Hooper, who became martyrs of the *sola scriptura*, say to this doctrine, which adds to the Scriptures "tradition and contemporary reason"? What is here actually "the rule and ultimate standard of faith"?

The second point of the Quadrilateral calls for agreement on the Apostles' and the Nicene Creed, the latter being regarded as "the sufficient statement of the Christian faith." This is the old idea of the Latitudinarians and syncretists of the seventeenth century: Let us be satisfied with the doctrines of the ancient creeds that were sufficient until the sixteenth century. Let us regard the confessions

---

[8]G. F. Fischer, *Redeeming the Situation. Occasional Sermons* (1947), p. 43f.

of the Reformation, the Augsburg Confession, the Anglican articles, the various Reformed confessions as valuable documents, but not as containing binding doctrine beyond the reaffirmation of the ancient creeds. This idea is proposed in all union plans for South East Asia, Australia, and New Zealand. Every Church entering these unions is free to retain its historic confessions and catechisms, provided their distinctive doctrines are not regarded as binding dogma. It is essentially the same idea that we find in the official definition of the Prussian Union, which does not abolish the authority of the existing confessions but demands only that the differences be not regarded as justifying the refusal of intercommunion. This idea underlies also the Declaration of Barmen, which on the one hand expresses loyalty to the existing confessions but on the other hand abolishes their exclusive character.

When Leibniz in the last negotiations with the Roman theologians proposed that the Lutherans should give up the Augsburg Confession and Rome should abandon the decrees of Trent, it became apparent that it is impossible to wipe out the sixteenth century from the history of the Church. As Rome can never revoke the decrees of Trent and the Vatican Council, the great doctrines of the Reformation would at least be preserved in the condemnations proclaimed by these councils. If the Protestant churches could forget the *sola fide* and *sola scriptura*, the anathema by Rome would stand, and there would remain the question of whether the *sola fide* is a heresy or the *articulus stantis et cadentis ecclesiae*. This question cannot remain unanswered. And so it is with all doctrines of our Confessions. The real presence cannot be declared an open question. Why is that so? It is so because the doctrines of the Reformation were not new doctrines but eternal truths, contained in Holy Scripture and, at least implicitly, also in the ancient creeds. This is confirmed by the fact that no church that has discarded the confessions of the sixteenth century has been able to preserve the creeds in their integrity. This is not only true of so many Reformed churches that have abolished, along with the confessions of their Reformation, the creeds of the Ancient Church. It is also true of the Church of England, which practically has discarded the *Thirty-Nine Articles* as binding dogma while emphatically claiming loyalty to the Nicene Creed and its central dogma of the incarnation. It would be interesting to find out what people understand by the incarnation who deny the virgin birth and the bodily resurrection of Christ, or who regard the Church, and that includes the Church of England, as a continuation of the incarnation. How doubtful even the authority of the Nicene Creed can be in the Anglican Church may be illustrated by a personal experience. I asked an eminent theologian of an Australian diocese of mainly Anglo-Catholic character, "What actually is the doctrinal standard of this diocese? Is it the *Thirty-Nine Articles*?" The answer was a definite no. "Is it the Nicene Creed?" The answer again was no. "We do not know whether we should accept it in the Western or the Eastern form, with or without the *filioque*. The former would block the way to a union with the Orthodox churches, the latter the way to a union with Rome." "What, then, is your standard?" I went on. "The doctrinal content of the *Book of Common Prayer*," I was told. But the English *Book of Common Prayer* contains not only the Nicene Creed in the Western form but also the *Symbolum quicunque*. In such a church, dogma has become a liturgical formula. With the teaching of the Reformation also the understanding of the teaching of the universal Church has disappeared. This would be the destiny of all churches that regard the second point of the Quadrilateral as sufficient.

The third point is the Two sacraments of Baptism and Holy Communion. They are, indeed, essential for the Church and its unity. But what is Baptism? In all the proposals and plans for a "reunited church," the necessity of Baptism, performed with water and the trinitarian formula, is recognized. The most advanced of these plans is the *Plan of Church Union in North India and Pakistan*, which has been recommended by the Lambeth Conference of 1958. Its significance lies in the fact that here for the first time are included Baptists and Disciples, who as a matter of principle reject infant Baptism. This new church is to have room for them as well as for Anglicans, Methodists, Brethren, and the various groups existing in the United Church of South India (among them former Presbyterians and Lutherans). Its statement on Baptism is a masterpiece of compromise. "Both infant Baptism and believer's Baptism shall be accepted as alternative practices." This is acceptable to the Anglicans because in either case the rite of initiation is completed through the confirmation by the bishop. It is acceptable to the Baptists because the admission to full membership in the Church presupposes a personal confession of faith. Provision is even made for the case of a person who has been baptized as an infant and later regards this Baptism as invalid, or for the case of a minister who refuses to baptize infants. This is possible because Baptism is not regarded as the washing of regeneration, not as necessary for salvation. "Baptism is a sign of cleansing from sin, of entrance into the covenant of grace, of fellowship with Christ in his death and Resurrection and of rising to newness of life" (*Plan*, etc., pp. 5f.). Baptism is no longer a real means of grace, but only a sign. It is no longer "the washing of regeneration and renewing of the Holy Ghost." How could this be acceptable to Lutherans and to Roman Catholics? Similarly, in all these attempts to carry out the third point of the Lambeth Quadrilateral, the Lord's Supper loses its character as a Sacrament. It must be celebrated with the proper elements and the Words of Institution. But what the Sacrament is, this is an open question, to be answered privately by the individual minister and Christian. This destroys the character of the Sacrament. For it belongs to the very nature of the Sacraments and rites of the Church that they are not mystery rites but actions in which the minister as well as the recipient know what is happening: "I baptize thee in the name. . . ." "Take, eat, this is my body, which is given for you. . . . If a pagan in India asks the question, "What is the Sacrament of the Altar?" neither the Church of South India nor the Church of North India could give him an authoritative answer.

The most important of the four points of the Quadrilateral for the Anglicans is the last one. Its formulation has varied, but the idea has always been this: that the Church must have a generally recognized ministry with the historic episcopate as its center. This would imply a reordination of the ministers not ordained in the apostolic succession by a bishop who enjoys that privilege. Attempts have been made to make this acceptable by denying that this would be a reordination or by introducing a rite of mutual laying on of hands. Thus far all such attempts have failed—even in South India not all ministers are episcopally ordained—and they are bound to fail because no one is able to say what, for example, a Presbyterian minister would receive when he undergoes such a rite and what the apostolic succession claimed by an Anglican bishop actually is. This became clear when the negotiations between the churches of England and Scotland that had gone on for many years broke down this year (1958). No church of the Reformation can accept this point of the Lambeth Quadrilateral. Nor can any Catholic Church, Eastern or Western. For even if these churches could recognize the validity of the Anglican orders, which is at present not the case, or if these orders could be validated in a technical sense, these churches would not be satisfied with the mere possession of the so-called apostolic succession. Important and indispensable as the *apostolicitas successionis* may be to them, it has never played such a role in Rome or in the Eastern churches as it plays in Anglicanism, especially since the first of the "Tracts for the Times" of 1833 based the claims of the Church of England and the rights and duties of its clergy on it. At the latest negotiations between a delegation of the Church of England and the Patriarchate of Moscow, it was made clear to the Anglicans that the Orthodox Church is primarily interested in the doctrine. What do you teach? This was the question addressed to them, as it also is the main question put to the Anglican Church by Rome. Organic union presupposes unity in doctrine, as also we Lutherans would point out. It is the tragedy of the union negotiations based on the Lambeth Quadrilateral that they necessarily end in compromise on the doctrine of the Church, and that means in the loss of even the most elementary truths of the creeds.

IV.

In a very rough outline we have spoken of the program of organic union Anglicanism has contributed to the Ecumenical Movement as a supplement to the plans of federal union. It is worth remembering that both plans have grown in America. The Anglican Church of England in Canada and the Protestant Episcopal Church in the United States have developed the Quadrilateral. It took a long time until the Church of England overcame its reluctance to accept what some people called an American utopia. Thus America is the real home of the modern Ecumenical Movement with its two branches, federal and organic union, "Life and Work" and "Faith and Order," Stockholm and Lausanne, which have grown together into the World Council of Churches in 1948, forty years after the establishment of the Federal Council and of the Fifth Lambeth Conference.

This movement, which has shaped the history of the Church in the twentieth century, has become the greatest challenge to the Lutheran Church.

One year after the First Lambeth Conference, in which the Anglican churches began to rally, the first ecumenical Lutheran organization was founded, *Die Allgemeine Evangelisch-Lutherische Konferenz* of 1868. This alliance of the Lutheran churches of Germany at once took up relations with the Church of Sweden and with the General Council in America. Out of this work grew, again under American leadership, the Lutheran World Convention, founded at Eisenach in 1923. Time does not permit to tell the story how men like Morehead, Reu, Long, and Knubel, together with the leading Lutherans in Germany and the Scandinavian countries, built up the first loose alliance of Lutheran churches and how these Lutherans faithfully testified to the Lutheran doctrine before the other denominations at Lausanne, 1927. Nor can we discuss here the question of why the Lutheran World Convention, in spite of serious attempts, was not able to meet the challenge of the Ecumenical Movement by developing a Lutheran program of interchurch relationship over against the dogmatically impossible programs of American Reformed Protestantism and Anglicanism. Perhaps it was too late. When in 1947 the World Convention was transformed into the Lutheran World Federation, the Lutheran churches had already been influenced by the foreign ideas of American and Anglican ecumenism to such a degree that the new organization was unable to produce a clear testimony to the Lutheran and biblical doctrine of the Church.

But this testimony must be given inside and outside the Lutheran World Federation. For as there are Lutherans within this federation who want to preserve the confessional and biblical heritage of the Church of the Augsburg Confession, so there are others who for reasons of conscience cannot belong to that federation so long as it does not take a clear stand against the errors and heresies of the modern Ecumenical Movement. This testimony, if it is to be truly Lutheran, can be nothing else but a testimony to the biblical doctrine of the Church. It belongs to the very nature of the Lutheran faith that it is not interested in the Lutheran Church as such. We do not believe in a Lutheran Church but in the *una sancta catholica*. Of this our Confessions speak when in the Augsburg Confession and in the Apology they explain the "comforting and highly necessary article of the catholic or universal Church." One must compare these passages with the corresponding articles of the other confessions of the sixteenth century in order to understand what belief in the Church, a profound faith in the divine mystery of the Church, has meant to the Church of the Lutheran Reformation. In this world of sin and death there exists God's holy people, the congregation of saints, Christ's kingdom in which he reigns through the inconspicuous means of grace, forgiving sins and redeeming from eternal death. This kingdom is *cruce tectum* until at the end of the world with the glory of Christ also the glory of his Church will be revealed. This doctrine of the *ecclesia abscondita* is not a Lutheran invention. Like the doctrine of the justification of the sinner, like the Lutheran doctrine of the Sacraments, and like the entire *theologia cruets* of our reformers, it is a rediscovery of the eschatology of the New Testament: "Beloved, now are we the sons of God, and it doth not yet appear what we shall be" (1 John 3:2). The Church lives always "in these last days" (Heb. 1:2), in the "last hour" (1 John 2:18), on the border between time and eternity, in the twilight between this world and the world to come. That is the reason why its nature cannot be expressed in the terms of human sociology. In, with, and under the earthly organization we call "church" or "churches"—the *ecclesia late dicta*—there lives the true Church of Christ, the *ecclesia stricte dicta*. This Church is among us. It consists of actual living men, women, and children, even infants. We do not know who they are. God only knows them. They are saints in his judgment, real saints though they know themselves only as sinners. They are the salt of the earth, the light of the world, the church within the Church. We cannot speak too realistically of these children of God, "which were born, not of blood, nor of the will of the flesh, nor of the will of man, but of God" (John 1:13), "born again," which means at the same time "born from above," "born of water and the Spirit" (3:2ff.). These people, real people here on earth, outwardly just like other people, are the holy people of God, not a nation after the flesh, like Israel of old, but the Israel after the Spirit. They are God's people, not in a figurative sense or in the sense of what human sociology calls a people. They are the Body of Christ, which again is no figurative speech. A human society can be figuratively called a body, a corporation, with its constituents as members. In this sense the outward organization of Christendom, the Church as the "society of external things and rites," can be understood as a social organism and may be called a body with members. The modern way of speaking of the whole of Christendom, the sum total of ecclesiastical organizations, as the Body of Christ of which the individual churches are members, cannot be justified from the New Testament. There the "members" of the Church as the Body of Christ are always the individual believers, "for by one Spirit are we all baptized into one body . . . and have been all made to drink into one Spirit" (1 Cor. 12:13). Nowhere does the New Testament teach or presuppose that the individual "churches" are members of the Church as the Body of Christ. It is highly significant that the New Testament does not distinguish terminologically between the Church as a local church and as the Church universal. This is due not to an undeveloped terminology but rather to the fact that the Church cannot be understood as a quantity in terms of human sociology. The Church, the *una sancta catholica,* is there where two or three are gathered in Christ's name, and it is present in the entire world, wherever the people of God exist. The Church as the spiritual or mystical Body of Christ exists wherever members of this Body are, but it exists also in the smallest local church, just as the sacramental body of Christ is in its entirety in, with, and under each consecrated host and in each particle of the host. And just as the sacramental body of Christ remains unbroken, undivided, so the spiritual Body remains one. Paul's pleading with the Corinthians to avoid schisms rests on the conviction that Christ is not and cannot be divided (1 Cor. 1:13) because the Body is essentially one. What a schism can destroy is the unity of the outward ecclesiastical organization. That it cannot destroy the unity of the Church of Christ was the common conviction of all Christendom until at least the seventeenth century. The schismatic separates himself from the unity of the Church, but he cannot destroy this unity. This is the teaching of the Primitive Church, which emphasized, when speaking of schism, that the Church is and remains one. When Cyprian occasionally speaks of heretics that are splitting the "Body of the Church" (ep. 44, 3, cf. 46, 1), he significantly avoids the term "Body of Christ" (see also 1 Clement 46). A body of men, a social organism, can be divided, but not the Church as the Body of Christ.

This, then, would be the pre-eminent task of the Lutheran Church in view of the present Ecumenical Movement, to testify to the biblical doctrine of the Church. This requires the humble confession on the part of Lutheran theology that also our thinking on the Church and its unity has been deeply influenced by modern secular sociology, which can just as little understand the mystery of Christ's Church as psychology can understand the work of the Holy Spirit. It requires a fresh study of the Word of God and the humble readiness to submit to this Word alone. The study of the Word of God can and will, where and when it pleases God, renew our faith in the great reality of the one, holy, catholic, and apostolic Church. And such faith will find means and ways to work for the outward unity of God's people. It is wrong to conclude from the reluctance of Lutherans to cooperate in certain ecumenical organizations of our time that our church is not interested in the outward unity of the children of God and does not feel its ecumenical obligation. On the contrary, no church has a broader ecumenical outlook than the Church of the Augsburg Confession. Lutherans do not refuse to cooperate with other churches in such matters as do not involve the recognition of heresy. Such recognition would be the end of the Church. In an age when large parts of Christendom have lost the biblical distinction between truth and error, Church and heresy, and have lost or are in danger of losing, with this distinction, the pure Gospel and the Sacraments of Christ, the means of grace by which the Church lives, it is the highest ecumenical duty to call all Christians back to the truth of the Gospel—all Christians, including ourselves. In deep humility only, always aware of our own shortcomings, of the weakness of our faith, our lack of love, our failure to confess where we ought to have confessed, in deep repentance of our manifold sins and with continuous prayer that God may keep us steadfast in his Word can we and must we ask our fellow Christians to submit with us to the Word that, as it maintains and saves the Church, judges us all.

Where will the great Ecumenical Movement lead to? What will Christendom look like at the threshold of the twenty-first century? No human eye can see what the results of this movement will be. Church history is unpredictable. It was almost fifty years ago that the first of the great ecumenical gatherings of our century was held, the World Missionary Conference of Edinburgh in 1910.

Everyone had the feeling that this was a turning point in the history of the Church. It was indeed a turning point. But what it meant no one was able to see. The conviction seemed to prevail that a new era of world missions had begun, the final battle for the Christianization of mankind. The time seemed to be at hand when the nations and races of the world would accept with the Western civilization also its finest flower and the secret of its greatness, the Christian religion. The vision of a Christian world appeared on the horizon. In a touching address on June 23, John Mott closed the conference: "The end of the conference is the beginning of conquest. The end of the planning is the beginning of doing." Then he called upon every one of his hearers to resolve before God to plan and to act as best he could. And referring to an address Archbishop Davidson had delivered at the opening of the conference, he concluded, "And it may be that the words of the Archbishop shall prove to be a splendid prophecy, and that before many of us taste death we shall see the Kingdom of God come with power."

As one of the last survivors of the conference of Edinburgh, the great American leader of world missions died some years ago. The prophecy had not come true. The kingdom had not come with power. Four years after the conference, the Great War broke out. Again three years later began the greatest persecution that the history of the Church has known. More martyrs have died in this century than in all previous centuries of the Church. It was the way of the cross the Church had to go. But this is the way of the true Church at all times, the Church of the crucified and risen Lord. *Cruce tectum*, hidden under the cross, is his kingdom in this world, until with his advent in glory, the hidden glory and unity of his Body, the Church will be revealed.

THE REFORMED THEOLOGICAL REVIEW
Vol. XXXVII, No. 1, January–April 1968

Dr. Hermann Sasse "In Statu Confessionis"

Lutherisches Verlagstiaus, Berlin and
Hamburg, 1866, pp. 380; DM 32

In Statu Confessionis is the title of a large volume in German containing twenty-seven essays of Dr. Hermann Sasse, Professor in Luther Seminary, North Adelaide, S.A. The volume was edited by his friend and former student Friedrich Wilhelm Hopf and published on the occasion of the author's seventieth birthday. The editor of our journal has asked me to write a review article on this volume and in this way to express the appreciation of our journal, which has so greatly benefitted from the many contributions the author has given to it since 1953.

CURRICULUM VITAE.

Some time ago Dr. Sasse wrote me in a personal letter, "I belong to that generation of theologians who were trained in the liberal theology of pre-war Berlin, though I had excellent teachers and was never a radical liberal. I studied with Holl and Harnack. My main interest was the New Testament and the Early Church. I took my Lic. degree (which is now, as you know, the Dr. Theol.) with Deiss-mann. More and more I studied Luther while in the ministry. This and my

experience in the ecumenical work (I was one of the German delegates at Lausanne 1927 and was active, until I was forbidden to leave
Germany, in the Continuation and Executive Committee) made me
a confessional Lutheran. I believed strongly that the future of Christianity depended in Germany and in the world on those churches,
which still dare to confess their dogma. I had learned in America,
where I spent a year at Hartford (1925/26), what undogmatic Christianity is and where it ends."

In 1933, Dr. Sasse was called to a theological chair in the University of Erlangen. From the beginning he played an important
part in the socalled "Kirchenkampf," yes, he was one of the founders of the "*Bekennende Kirche*" (Confessing Church). Its first doctrinal statement, the socalled Bethel Confession, was to a large degree
based upon his preparatory work. When the movement was "taken
over" by Karl Barth, who used it to promote his ideal of a confessional union of Lutheran, Reformed, and United churches, Dr. Sasse
went into the opposition. He openly voiced his criticism of the Barmen Declaration, not because he disagreed with its contents (on the
contrary, he fully approved its theses and its rejections of errors),
but he believed that this United Church had not right to draw up
confessions (cf. pp. 280ff.). The United Church was nothing else
than a compromise. The greater part of the members of the Barmen
Synod belonged to churches whose doctrine had been rejected in the
Lutheran Confessions.

After the war Dr. Sasse, together with many other conservative Lutherans, tried to remedy the situation. At the request of some
Lutheran bishops, he wrote a new constitution for German Protestantism, which envisaged the following situation: a United Lutheran
Church, a Reformed Church, and a United Church, each under its
own church government. These three churches were to replace
the old territorial churches and form a "Council of Evangelical
Churches" of Germany. But under the influence of Karl Barth, the
majority of German Protestants opted for one United Evangelical
Church. Thus in 1948 the Evangelical Church in Germany was formed.
Dr. Sasse then left the Church of Bavaria and joined a Lutheran Free
Church. Since there was no teaching position available for him in the
Free Church he decided to emigrate. At that time there was no opening
for him in the U.S.A. (where in 1939 he had received an appointment,

but the outbreak of the war prevented him from going), and in 1949 he accepted the invitation to join the Faculty of Immanuel College, Adelaide, the seminary of the United Evangelical Lutheran Church of Australia. Last year this church merged with the Evangelical Lutheran Church to form the Lutheran Church of Australia. The seminaries of the two churches have also merged into the new Luther Seminary, on the staff of which Dr. Sasse still serves in a full time capacity.

Dr. Sasse himself has been one of the leading figures behind the union of the two Lutheran churches of Australia. But his influence has also been felt outside his own denomination. Through his "Letters to Lutheran Pastors," which have appeared since 1948 and several of which have been published in this volume, he has given leadership to Lutheran churches in Germany, Scandinavia, and the United States. Through many other publications, both in German and in English, he has continuously propagated and defended the doctrines of the (Lutheran) Reformation. The bibliography, added to this volume, numbers 333 books, articles, and major reviews! Unfortunately this volume contains only a selection of his articles. Several important sections have been left out, such as articles dealing with the doctrine of Scripture. We know, however, that Dr. Sasse is preparing a volume "De Sacra Scriptura" to which we are looking forward with great expectation. It is our sincere prayer that the Lord may grant to Dr. Sasse many more years of work and study and that the promise of Psalm 92:4 may be fulfilled in his life: "They still bring forth fruit in old age"!

A CONFESSIONAL THEOLOGY.

The volume opens with an article on "Church and Confession." This choice is a very happy one, not only because nearly all essays in this volume, one way or another, deal with these concepts, but also because they are representative of Dr. Sasse's whole theology. As we shall see presently, he has always concerned himself with the problems of the Church, both theologically and practically. The doctrine of the Church is one of the main foci of his theology.

But this is no less true of the confession. Contrary to the main theological trend of our day, Dr. Sasse is an ardent defender of the authority of the confession in the Church. To him the confession is not a fetter or shackle that hampers him in his work as a theologian and therefore has to be cast off, but it is rather the reliable and authoritative guide that helps the theologian find his way into the mystery of God's revelation in Scripture. On purpose we connect confession and Scripture in this way. Although Dr. Sasse is a confessional theologian, he is definitely no confessionalist. He knows too well that the confession is not the *norma normans*, but only the *norma normata*. But this *norma normata* has been derived from Scripture itself and it only desires to express the truth of Scripture. For this reason he can write in the essay on the decision of Chalcedon, "The experience of the Christian Church shows us that everywhere, where the authority of the ancient confessions was given up, the biblical doctrine of the incarnation of the eternal Son was also abandoned. It is impossible to maintain the authority of Holy Scripture, when one rejects the authority of the confession, and this is so because the authority of the confession is nothing else than the authority of the contents of Scripture to which the confession testifies" (35/6). All this does not mean that the confession, in this case the Lutheran confession, is infallible or that the fathers of the sixteenth century have spoken the last word (cf. 24, 279). But as long as it has not been proved that the confession is contrary to the Word of God, every theologian should be bound by it and every member of the Church should accept it as the expression of his own faith.

THE DOCTRINE OF THE CHURCH.

There is a close connection between the foregoing and Dr. Sasse's doctrine of the Church. His starting point is the definition of article 7 of the Augsburg Confession, "the first dogmatical formulation in the history of Christianity concerning the nature and the unity of the Church" (51). Article 7 reads, "Our churches also teach that one holy Church is to continue forever. The Church is the assembly of the saints in which the gospel is purely taught and the sacraments are administered rightly. For the true unity of the Church it is enough to agree concerning the teaching of the gospel and the administration of the sacraments. It is not necessary that human traditions or rites and ceremonies, instituted by men, should be alike everywhere. It is, as Paul says, 'One faith, one baptism, one God and Father of all,' etc. (Eph. 4:5, 6)."

Dr. Sasse first points out that this article does not distinguish between an invisible and a visible Church. The one Church, as we are taught by the New Testament, is both "a real, concrete fellowship of people, which one can see" and "the congregation of the saints, the people of God, the body of Christ, which one must believe" (55). In other words, the Church is always at the same time an object of faith and a reality in the world. The same is true of the unity of the Church. "As the Church itself, so also the unity of the Church is an object of faith. As no one can see the body of Christ, so no one can see its unity" (58). "The one Church is hidden under the external denominations with their differences in language and nationality, in Church, polity and cult and other human traditions" (59). Yet at the same time it is also a reality. For this unity binds together people throughout the world who believe in the one Christ, the only Holy Spirit, the one Gospel, the one Baptism, and the one Sacrament of the Altar. In spite of all the differences in ceremonies and traditions, this unity is present as a reality in the world.

This unity, however, is only present where there is a real oneness in the teaching of the Gospel and the administration of the Sacraments. When article 7 says that "it is enough" (*satis est*) to agree concerning this, we should realize that this *satis est* implies a *necesse est*. For this reason there are also limits to the unity. "There is unity in the Church only when heresy is rejected. Thus the Lord himself in his high priestly prayer connected the petition for the unity of the believers with the other petition: 'Sanctify them in thy truth; thy word is truth.' Truth was served and therefore the unity of the Church was served, when John separated from the deniers of the incarnation; the Ancient Church from Marcion and the Gnostics; Augustine from Pelagius; Luther from the pope, Zwingli and the Anabaptists. In the ecclesia militans here on earth we cannot serve the truth without rejecting that which contradicts the truth" (62; cf. 300f).

This view of the Church and its unity explains Dr. Sasse's attitude in practical ecclesiastical matters. This was the reason why he could not possibly join the United Church in Germany, in which the confessional differences between Lutheranism and Calvinism had been relegated to mere controversies between different theological schools. This is the reason why gradually he has turned away from the modern Ecumenical Movement, in which he wholeheartedly participated in the early stages. The great thing of the World Conference of Lausanne (1927) was "the seriousness with which the Orthodox, Lutheran and Anglo-Catholic delegates raised the question of the truth over against the superficial ecumenism of the Americans who were only interested in the quick appearance of a syncretistic union church" (8). But in later years, the question of the truth has been pushed into the background; unity itself has become the great goal.

OPPOSITION TO NATIONAL SOCIALISM.

This concern for and obedience to the truth of God's Word was also the reason why from the very beginning Dr. Sasse opposed the claims of the national-socialists. Very illuminating is the essay on "The Church and the Political Powers of Our Time," written in 1932. Openly and fiercely he rejected the Fuehrer idea, which was so common in Germany at that time and became embodied in Hitler. "The sun of freedom has set in Europe" (255). When some theologians called Hitler "the Fuehrer sent by God," Sasse simply asks, "How do you know this?" He speaks of the "false racial theories" (257). When article 24 of the National Social party program speaks of religious freedom, in as far as the churches do not speak or act against "the morality of the German race," Dr. Sasse declares that a discussion between church and party must begin with the clear statement from the side of the church that its doctrine is a permanent offense against this "morality of the German race"; that the baby of the noblest German parents with the most beautiful racial virtues is just as much subject to eternal condemnation as the descendant of the most decadent race; that the doctrine of the justification *sola gratia, sola fide*, is the end of all German morality just as it is the end of all human morality; that the Jews have crucified Jesus because he destroyed such human morality and that they have done this also on behalf of the German nation and the Nordic race (262/3). At the end of this very same article he quoted some words that were prophetic indeed: "Over the shoulders of these blind people we see the burning eye of the murderer and arsonist of the future" (264).

In another article, written after the Second World War and surveying the situation of Lutheranism throughout the world, he again refers to National Socialism and with great sadness admits that Lutheran theology in particular opened the door through which National Socialism and the movement of the so-called German Christians could get a hold in the evangelical church of Germany. This did not happen because National Socialism developed from Lutheranism or because there was an affinity between the two, but the reason was that the Lutheran theology of the period between the two wars was a truncated theology that showed serious weaknesses on decisive points. There were weaknesses especially in the view of the Old Testament (e.g., W. Elert) and in the anthropology (P. Althaus, who declared that Paul's view of man was much more optimistic than that of the reformers, 294f.). The former was the open door through which the modern Marcionitism of the antisemites, the national-socialists, and the German Christians could enter the Lutheran churches. The latter fostered the pride of the German race and closed the eyes of the people to the depravity of the human heart. And so, utterly blinded, many Christians in Germany supported Hitler and his National Socialism. "For such a blindness there is no human explanations any more. It is more than a mistake, more than a sickness. It is guilt—the guilt of us all" (299).

LUTHERAN AND REFORMED.

As a Reformed theologian, I was naturally interested in what Dr. Sasse has to say about the Reformed churches and Reformed theology. As is to be expected from one who believes that the Lutheran Confessions represent the truth of Scripture, he openly and strongly condemns those aspects of Reformed theology that he believes to be contrary to the Word of God. At times he even goes further. In an article on the Union of 1933, he seems to deny that there is a common understanding of the Gospel in the Lutheran and Reformed confessions (270). From the reference to Luther at Marburg, however, it is clear that the author thinks in particular of the differences in the doctrine of the Sacraments. He believes that at this point Luther walked "a lonely road" between Rome on the one hand, and the enthusiasts on the other. For Luther, Zwingli and his adherents (and no doubt also the Calvinists, if he had known them) belonged to these enthusiasts (97). He further wonders whether in the doctrine of Baptism

Barth is not more Reformed than the Reformed churches and whether he has not seen the consequences of the Zwinglian and Calvinist doctrine better than any Reformed theologian before him (91).

The great heresy of the Reformed churches is found in the doctrine of the Lord's Supper. Dr. Sasse believes that both Zwingli and Calvin, each in his own way, were already representatives of the modern humanistic and rationalistic culture. Zwingli in particular had a rational-philosophical element in his hermeneutics, which led him (and also Calvin and Reformed theology in general) to the following three great objections to the Lutheran doctrine of the Lord's Supper: it is absurd, impossible, and unnecessary (107). For Dr. Sasse this is much more than a difference between two theological schools within the same church. He believes that it is impossible to have altar fellowship between those for whom the consecrated bread is the body of the Lord and those for whom it is only a sign of the body of the Lord (87). He even writes, "It is impossible for a Lutheran Christian, even in periculo mortis, to participate in a Reformed communion" (118). He does not deny that the Lord's Supper celebrated in the Reformed Church is a real Lord's Supper, but this does not alter the fact that the view held by this church is a serious, Church-destroying heresy. Dr. Sasse realizes that at this point there is a difference in evaluation between the Reformed and the Lutheran churches. For the former the Lutheran refusal of church and altar fellowship is only a matter of schism; for the latter the Reformed doctrine is a heresy, which automatically excludes church and altar fellowship.

It cannot be denied that there is such a difference in evaluation between Reformed and Lutheran theology. Although I can understand Dr. Sasse's judgment of the Reformed position and, in a way, respect his frank condemnation, yet I cannot share his evaluation of this controversy. On some points, I believe, he sees differences that do not exist. For example, his description of the Reformed conception of the confession in the first essay does no justice to the original Reformed position. It is definitely not true that from the beginning the Reformed held the *quatenus*-position over against the *quia*-position of the Lutherans (cf. 23). No more is it correct to say that where the Lutheran Confessions confirmed the ancient creeds, the Reformed confessions stated the biblical canon (21). Many Reformed confessions did both. The French Confession of 1559, for instance, enumerates the books of the canon in article 3, but likewise states in article 5: "We confess the three creeds, to wit: the Apostles', the Nicene, and the Anthanasian, became (*quia*) they are in accordance with the word of God." I have the impression that on this point Dr. Sasse has confused the Barthian view with the original Reformed view of the confession. Likewise it is not true to say that Reformed theology teaches an invisible and a visible Church (53). Reformed theology has never done this, but it always stressed that the one Church has two sides, an invisible and a visible, which actually corresponds with Dr. Sasse's own distinction between the Church as the object of faith and as a reality in the world. To mention one more point, no Reformed theologian would hold the view that the Sacraments are no real means of grace but only mere signs (77, 95).

On the other hand, there is still the deep gap between the Lutheran and the Reformed view of the nature of the Sacraments. On this point Wittenberg and Geneva are still apart. But is it a soul-destroying and Church-destroying heresy? Does the author himself still hold this view? Nearly all the articles from which I quoted are more than fifteen years old. The editor of the volume says in his preface that in many respects the author's thoughts have developed beyond what is said in these essays. Is this also true of his view of the controversy between Lutheran and Reformed theology?

On the basis of personal discussions with the author, I would venture to say yes. This is confirmed by an article of Dr. Sasse in the *Lutheran Theological Journal* (August 1967), in which he discusses recent attempts to bridge the gap between the Lutheran and the Reformed doctrine of the Lord's Supper. He writes, among others, that he "does not despair of the possibility of reaching unity between the separated churches of the Reformation" (p. 11). He still upholds the original Lutheran doctrine, the doctrine of the "*est*," but adds in a truly ecumenical spirit, "We do not want to make our Reformed brethren Lutherans, but to help them to regain what in the tragic history of the Reformation they have lost" (p. 14). On such a basis there is indeed place for a dialogue.

FROM POLEMICS TO DIALOGUE.

Reading through this rich volume I could not help noticing a certain development in Dr. Sasse's theological method. While all the earlier articles are strongly polemical, the later ones tend increasingly more to the approach of the dialogue. This becomes very clear in the essays that deal with the doctrines of the R. C. Church. The 1961 article on the new dogma of the assumption of Mary is very sharp in tone and contents. It begins with this question: Who is speaking here? Is it really the Vicar of Christ or is it the antichrist? *Tertium non datur* (205). Dr. Sasse believes that both in the cult of Mary and in the sacrifice of the Mass the old, hidden heathenism has wedded itself to the Christian faith. At this point the antichrist has set himself in the temple of God. But then he immediately adds that evangelical Christians should not forget that this still happens in the temple of God; it happens in the one, holy Church of God, which is still present in Rome, because the Gospel and the Sacraments are still in this church (211).

In more recent years, however, the approach to Rome has changed. Although the differences are still clearly recognized and the heresies are unequivocally stated, the polemical tone is making way for that of the dialogue. This new approach becomes particularly evident in the 1965 article, "After the Council." Dr. Sasse believes that a tremendous change is taking place in the Church of Rome. "Rome is on the road to a reformation" (234). He fully realizes that this reformation has not yet taken place. Better than anyone else, he knows about the *irreformabilis* of Vatican 1. He himself writes, "No dogma of the Church has been revoked, no dogma can be revoked." But then he adds, "But new dogmas will no longer be produced, at least not for a long time" (239). His new evaluation of Rome, however, is not based on merely negative considerations. The main thing is the new discovery of the Bible in Rome (236). As a Lutheran theologian, Dr. Sasse knows the power of the Word. Was it not the power of this Word that changed Luther and led to the Reformation of the sixteenth century? There is still the same power in this Word. And so there is hope for the future, also with regard to the Church of Rome. It is therefore no wonder that in this article all of a sudden the word "dialogue" appears in Dr. Sasse's writings. "The great council is closed. The dialogue begins" (247).

Dr. Sasse himself is a redoubtable partner in such a dialogue. With his tremendous knowledge of the history and the dogma of the Church, both of the Ancient Church and of the Lutheran Reformation, and above all with his profound understanding of God's Word, he is a partner who can make a great contribution to every dialogue. Although he is in his seventies, he is still remarkably open for new insights and new approaches. But in all discussions there remains one norm: *secundum Sacram Scripturam.*

> "The dialogue has begun and it will be the theme of the coming decades. It will be a dialogue between separated brethren. In the tension between separation and brotherhood lies the secret of true ecumenical labour. In this tension we have to do our work, each the keeper of his separated brother. It cannot be a matter of indifference for us Lutherans what will happen to the Roman Catholic Church. It cannot be a matter of indifference for our separated Catholic brethren what will happen to the Lutheran Church. And the same is true with regard to the Reformed churches of the West and the Orthodox churches of the East. In this spirit we engage in the dialogue. But the answer to the questions asked in this dialogue comes from the Lord" (248).

BOOK REVIEWS

THEOLOGIE DER LUTHERISCHEN BEKENNTNISSCHRIFTEN [XIII:3]

By Edmund Schlink, Third Edition (Chr. Kaiser Verlag, Muenchen) 1948, pp. 435, D.M. 12.

It is to be regretted that this book has not yet been translated into English and published by one of the great Lutheran publishing houses in America. For it is more than a textbook for Lutheran students. It is the best introduction into Lutheran theology that at present exists, and as such of great value for every theological student who wants to understand the Lutheran Church, which thus far more than other churches has preserved the doctrinal heritage of the Reformation. Schlink began his spiritual pilgrimage as scientist and philosopher until, under the influence of Karl Barth, at that time at Muenster, he became a student of theology. As a decided and active member of the "Confessional Church" he was forced to give up his lectureship at the University of Giessen and found a sanctuary at the "*Theologische Schule*," a private faculty connected with the Bodelschwingh Institutions of the Inner Mission at Bethel in Westphalia, until this school, a center of the Confessional Church, was closed in 1939. He became a pastor at Bielefeld, and Fr. von Bodelschwingh, the leader of Bethel, made it possible for him to write this book, which appeared in 1940, just before theological books were no longer allowed to be printed. Since 1946, Schlink has been Professor of Systematic Theology at Heidelberg and is well-known in ecumenical circles. He belongs to those disciples of Barth who found the way not only to Luther but to the doctrine of the Lutheran Church.

Schlink's book is not a sort of commentary to the Augsburg Confession or even to the whole Book of Concord, comparable to Barth's Gifford lectures on the "*Confessio Scotica*." It is rather the first part of his lectures on dogmatics. It was an event in the history of German systematic theology, a result of the new studies of the Confessions in the "Confessional Church," that a dogmatician ventured to go this unusual way of starting with the doctrine of the Church instead of making his own philosophy the starting-point for presenting "dogmatics." This way corresponded to what the philosophers after the First World War in Europe called the "turn from the subject to the object." Whether Schlink's way is wholly successful can be seen only when, as we hope, his work on dogmatics will be published in its entirety.

The introduction makes it clear that and why the Lutheran Confessions—the same would have to be said of the corresponding confessions of other churches—cannot be understood as historical documents only. They claim to give, in essential points, the correct, and therefore binding, interpretation of Scripture. This claim may be rejected, but it cannot be passed by. The relationship between Scripture and confession is discussed in the first chapter, which makes it quite clear that Scripture is by all means the only source, rule, and standard of doctrine for the Lutheran Church. If written today, the book would perhaps still more emphasize how the Confessions refute the idea of tradition as a possible source of doctrine. This idea at present seems to find access even into some parts of the Lutheran Church, as though the Bible were only written tradition and the authority of the Scriptures were based on the judgment of the Church, which established the canon, this being even according to the Vatican Council (Densinger 1787) a grave heresy. From what this chapter says about the nature of an ecclesiastical confession in the Lutheran sense, it becomes quite clear that the confession of faith, deeply related to the confession of sin and the praise of God (cf. the biblical usage and the meanings of the Latin "*confiteri*"), wants to be nothing else but the sum total of the Gospel. Chapter II on "The Revelation of God, the Creator" presents the doctrine of the Confessions on the much-debated problem of natural theology. It is most interesting to compare the doctrine on the lost image of God with the writings of Barth and Brunner. Schlink criticises Brunner's understanding of the traditional doctrine of original sin and the fall, as if this classical doctrine of the Reformation denied the actual character of all sin and minimized our responsibility. Over against Barth it is made clear what the confession means that "a dim spark of the knowledge that there is a God" has remained even in man after the fall. The same chapter makes it clear that belief in God the Creator is always belief in Christ and in the Holy Ghost. The core of the Lutheran understanding of the Gospel is given in two chapters on "Law and Gospel," the distinction—not separation—of which was for Luther the mark by which a real theologian could be recognized. It is remarkable how the sixteenth-century theologians have avoided the danger of trying to understand psychologically the relationship between justification, regeneration, and sanctification. Luther's paradoxical understanding of the essential identity of forgiveness and regeneration has been preserved. Chapter V deals with Baptism and the Lord's Supper, avoiding a doctrine on the Sacraments as such, which never has officially existed in the Lutheran Church. It is impossible to go into details here, though this chapter might be of special interest to a Reformed reader. The Chapter VI on the Church starts with the contrast between the *regnum diaboli* and the Church as the *regnum Christi*. It presents the doctrine on the Church, which as a great reality is hidden in, with, and under the earthly ecclesiastical organisations. Chapters VII and VIII deal with "Secular and Ecclesiastical Authority" and "The Last Day." Chapter VII should help to overcome the popular prejudices as if Erastianism and adoration of the state had anything to do with the Lutheran doctrine.

How independent Schlink is from the Confessions themselves is shown in the appendix where he points out a number of questions modern exegesis would put to the theologians of the sixteenth century and that have to be answered today. The work as a whole is by no means an uncritical glorification of the Confessions of the Lutheran Church. There are, of course, questions that must be put to the author from the Lutheran side, such as what the Confessions teach on intercommunion, and whether he has fully understood the Formula of Concord. For the non-Lutheran scholar who is able to read German, it is not only the best introduction into Lutheran theology, but also an encouragement to study again the confessions of his own church.

CHRIST AND THE CAESARS.
HISTORICAL SKETCHES [XIV:3]
By Ethelbert Stauffer (S.C.M. Press), 1955, pp. 293; 18/-.

I take pleasure to introduce to the readers of this review a book by my former colleague E. Stauffer, Professor of New Testament at Erlangen and at the same time lecturer in numismatics. Written in a brilliant style, which has been preserved in the masterly translation by K. and R. G. Smith, the book contains sixteen "sketches," the form of which reminds the reader of the best essays of French literature. They are parerga of the work done by the author in his two fields of research. These essays, independent from one another, are knit together by the common theme "Christ and the Caesars," which has become so important to the witnesses and victims of modem Caesarism. They are full of detailed historical information without the burden of a learned apparatus and should make interesting reading to anyone who wants to get a deeper understanding of the first five hundred years of Christianity. To the student of the New Testament, the essays VIII ("The Story of the Tribute Money": a thought-provoking explanation of Mark 12:13–17) and XI ("Domitian and John": an illuminating sketch of the political background of Revelation) may be of special importance. The great essay XIV on "The Last Struggle" is perhaps one of the best presentations of the eventful third century that we possess. Here, as in all essays that cover the time from Augustus to the Christian emperors, the author shows an amazing ability of drawing vivid pictures of past history. Thus the book is a valuable supplement to textbooks of Church history and deserves to be recommended to the students in our country who are so remote from the scenes of early Church history. However, this thought-provoking book should also find many readers among Christian laymen, especially historians and politicians.

It would not be fair to criticize details of these sketches, which necessarily are fragmentary in many respects. A few questions, however, must be asked. As to numismatics: Why did the author in discussing Constantine not take into account the masterly attempt by the late Hans Lietzmann to describe the development of Constantine's church politics from the development of Constantine's coins ("*Der Glaube Konstantins*," a paper read in 1937 at the Berlin Academy of Sciences). The main objection against the book is the author's attitude toward Caesarism as such. His predilection for Caesar himself prevents him from realizing that, after all, the assassination of Caesar, a crime though it was, delayed for at least two centuries the introduction of Asiatic despotism into the Roman Empire, notwithstanding such figures like Domitian, who was so severely criticised by Trajanus. The astonishing amount of practical freedom Christianity enjoyed during the first centuries in spite of the persecutions is due to the remnant of human freedom Augustus had secured for the new empire. The author even has sympathy for Cleopatra and applies to her verses Rilke in a poem on Michelangelo wrote on the great man in history. Paul and John would have used a much simpler term to describe that corrupt oriental woman. Constantine is glorified in the manner of Eusebius under the title Imperium Gratiae. The relatives whom he had assassinated would probably have had their own ideas of the "reign of grace." "The guilt of Constantine was perhaps greater than that of any other ruler" (p. 271). But perhaps the "Uebermensch" must not be measured by Christian standards. "The first Christian emperor was no saint, but a great stateman who was aware of the inherent tragedy of politics with its involvement in sin and violence." Does not this imply that a criminal is not a criminal if and as long as he happens to be a successful statesman? Is this ethics still alive in spite of all that has happened during the last decade? "This very awareness made the grace of God in the cross of Christ the *conditio nine qua non* of his political life, which played an increasing part, subjectively as well as objectively, in his own career." This means to read religious convictions of a modern statesman like Bismarck into the soul of an ancient man for whom the "cross" was not more than the swastica for Hitler, a symbol of victory and the expression of the belief to be elected by providence for a great political work. The author's sympathy with the more cultured, or even Christian, Caesars has its counterpart in his understanding of Christ as Imperator. This idea, though based on Revelation, is only one side of the Early Church's understanding of Christ. K. Holl is criticized (p. 205) for holding the view that the victory of Christianity over the ancient religions is to be ascribed to the fact that the Gospel is the message of a merciful God.

Its victory should rather be ascribed to the Gospel as being the message of incarnation. Does the author not realise that according to the early fathers God became man *propter immensam suam dilectionem*? He is wrong when he states that the Gospel of mercy was first understood by Augustine and Luther. Among the excellent illustrations with which the publishers have embellished the book there is a most impressive one, "The Face of the Third Century," taken from a pagan sarcophagus and expressing the terrible fear of a generation that saw the first downfall of the Roman Empire. There is another "Face of the Third Century" to be found on contemporary Christian sarcophagi, faces of men and women that express a supernatural peace. And it should not be forgotten that the first representations of Christ in Christian art do not show the Pantokrator of the Byzantine era, but rather Christ at the Eucharist and the Good Shepherd who carries home his lost sheep.

These criticisms are not meant to question the value of this book. Their intention is only to show that the problems it raises are perhaps greater than those which it solves. It calls our attention to the deepest question of our age, that of a new merciless Caesarism.

THE EUCHARISTIC WORDS OF JESUS [XV:1]

By Joachim Jeremias, translated by A. Ehrhardt,
with an Introduction by John Lowe
(Oxford, B. Blackwell), 1955, pp. 195; 18/-.

The Eucharist is still today, and certainly to the Last Day, one of the foremost problems of Christian theology. Thus we owe a debt of gratitude to the publisher and to the able translator for having made available in English the second edition of a book that since its first appearance in 1935 has played a great role in the discussions on the Sacrament of the Altar in continental theology. The Dean of Christ Church, Oxford, calls it in the introduction rightly "a weighty and indispensable contribution in any discussion of the background, nature, and interpretation of the Last Supper." It is the mature fruit of prolonged studies by a scholar in the field of New Testament research who has distinguished himself in elucidating the Jewish background of the Gospel. His archaeological studies on "Golgotha" and his investigation of the modern Samaritans show him as a historian who always asks for facts. This factual character, as far as it goes, is the strength of the present book.

Chapter I, "Was the Last Supper a Passover Meal?" answers the question in the affirmative. The material, put forward in support of the synoptic tradition, is so exhausting and the refutation of the objections so convincing that in future it will be very difficult to defend the historicity of the tradition of John (and perhaps Paul, 1 Cor. 5:7); however, its origin may be explained, according to which Jesus died in the very hour of the 14th of Nisan when the Passover lambs were killed in the Temple. The attempts made to harmonize these traditions are shown to be untenable, and the

"*Passsover-Kiddush*," a sanctification of the feast twenty-four hours before its beginning, which has played such a great role in modern discussions, is rejected as "a product of fancy, for which there is no evidence" (p. 24). The astronomical investigations as to when in those years the 15th of Nisan was a Friday are discussed. Though they are not conclusive, they yield as an interesting by-product the result that Jesus probably died on April 7 of the year 30, whether this was the 14th or 15th of Nisan. Chapter II discusses "The Account of the Last Supper within the Framework of the Passion Story." Chapter III tries to establish "The Earliest Text of the Words of Institution." The silence of the Fourth Gospel is explained as *disciplina arcani*. New light is shed from Jewish sources, including the Dead Sea Scrolls, on the problem of this discipline in the time of Jesus and the apostles. In a new and thorough examination of Luke, Dr. Jeremias, revising his former views, maintains the authenticity of the Longer Text. A thorough discussion of the problem of the oldest form of the Words of Institution shows the substantial agreement of the two forms represented by Paul-Luke and Mark-Matthew. "The earliest text of the words of institution ("interpretation" would have been here the correct translation) which can be established is: *labete; touto estin to soma mou 2. touto estin to haima mou tes' diathekes to ekchynoomenon hyper pollon*. This means—and this result has surprised me very much—that the earliest text of the words of interpretation which can be established by comparison of the texts is identical with the text of Mark" (p. 114f.). The Aramaic text of the decisive words, as spoken by Jesus, was probably: "*den bisri*" (not "*guphi*" as the author, following G. Dalman, in the first edition suggested) and "*den idmi*" (p. 141). The last chapter, "The Meaning of the Eucharistic Words of Jesus," though containing very valuable material, shows the weak spot of Professor Jeremias's otherwise great scholarship. To establish by means of careful examination of the sources the historical facts concerning the Last Supper, including the words actually spoken by Jesus on that occasion, is one thing. To interpret the facts and the words is another thing. Such interpretation requires not only historical but also theological understanding. Now Dr. Jeremias is, of course, a theologian who takes the Messiahship and the atoning death of Jesus quite seriously. But to say nothing of the interpretation of the Last Supper as a mere parabolic action to be repeated, indeed, by the Church, is it possible to understand the words "in remembrance of me" as meaning "that God remember me"? "He desired that his disciples should continue to meet together daily as the table fellowship of the Messiah during the short interval between his departure and the *parousia*, and thereby to remember his Messiah by bringing the consummation to pass" (p. 165). Apart from the christological implications of this sentence, is it believable that all Christendom throughout the ages should have misunderstood those words? Another question: Can sound historical research declare that John 6:51c–58 does not originally belong to the discourse on the bread of life, but comes from a pre-Johannine eucharistic homily (p. 73)? How can that be proved? One must compare such exegesis of John 6 with the profound theological insights of the late Sir Edwyn Hoskyns in order to understand in what direction the present book needs supplementation.

Further studies concerning the question of the day of the Last Supper should deal with the rich patristic literature on the Christian "*pascha*" and the many attempts of the fathers and the schoolmen (Aquinas Summa theol. III, qu. 46,9; 74,4 and Summa contra Gentiles IV cap. 69) to harmonize the Synoptists and John. The use of leavened bread by the Eastern Church (p. 6) seems to have nothing to do with the Johannine tradition. The entire Ancient Church used ordinary bread; the "*asyma*" were introduced in the West only in the early Middle Ages. By the Ancient Church they were regarded, as the wording of the canons forbidding the partaking of the Jewish *azyma* suggests (Apost. 70. Laodicea 38, Quinisextum 11), as something Jewish.

LUTHER'S WORKS. VOL. 12, SELECTED PSALMS I [XV:2]

Edited by Jaroslav Pelikan (Concordia Publishing House, Saint Louis), 1955, pp. 418.

In his excellent Luther studies, *The Righteousness of God*, Dr. Gordon Rupp has told the interesting story of the surprisingly large number of translations of works of Luther published in England in the course of centuries. Some American translations might be added to that list. However, none of these earlier attempts to introduce Luther to the English-speaking world can compete with what promises to be the future standard edition of Luther's works in English. Concordia Publishing House, St. Louis, and Muehlenberg Press, Philadelphia, have joined forces to bring out, within about fifteen years, fifty-five volumes. Concordia, following the great tradition of The Lutheran Church—Missouri Synod, which published in the nineteenth century Luther's works in German on the basis of the Walch Edition with a vast amount of other sources of the history of the Reformation that otherwise are inaccessible (the original Walch Edition is to be found in the Public Library of Melbourne), will bring out thirty volumes of exegetical works under the competent editorship of Professor J. Pelikan, now at Chicago. Muehlenberg Press is to publish twenty-four volumes of other works, thus continuing the endeavors that have begun with the Philadelphia edition of *Selected Works of Luther* in English by Holman. The editor of these volumes will be Dr. H. T. Lehmann, also well equipped for this scholarly work. Both editors will be supported by a large staff of translators. The whole edition can be purchased at an extremely low price by way of a subscription that can be cancelled at any time. Taking in account the usual deduction for ministers, the price of the individual volume will not be much more than £A2.

The edition is based on the Weimar Edition (W.A.), that unique and unrepeatable critical edition of all of Luther's writings that was started in 1883 and is now being completed. The W.A. with its constant improvements and additions will always remain the basis of Luther research. For the average theologian in the English-speaking world, however, even Lutherans, it is even if accessible hardly readable as far as the German text with its old orthography is concerned. Luther's German is, by the way, not as the General Introduction calls it, "Middle High German," but rather what is technically called "Early New High German," the first stage of modern German as was created by Luther himself in his translation of the Bible. How difficult Luther's language sometimes is may be illustrated by the curious fact that still A. Smyth in his learned book *Cranmer and the Reformation under Edward VI* (1926) speaks of "Suvermarianism" and "Suvermarians" as a sect in Germany. This is a misunderstanding of Luther's "*Schwaermeri*," a latinized form of "*Schwaermer*," which means the "enthusiasts" (this is a better translation than "fanatics," which occasionally is used still in this volume, following old Latin translations), the "Free Spirits," as R. Bainton calls them. The linguistic difficulties are sometimes so great that even German scholars have to consult, just as in the case of Zwingli's writings, special dictionaries. It would be a great help if each of the translators had on his desk at least A. Goetze's *Fruehneuhochdeutsches Glossar*. Since almost all of Luther's Latin works have been translated into German, such translations may be consulted with great care. "*Doctrina pietatis*" (p. 197) is rendered with "doctrine of eternal salvation," probably because the older translations give the translation "*Lehre de Gottseligkeit*." But this latter word corresponds to "godliness" in the English Bible. This should not be understood as a pedantic criticism, but rather as a hint at the amazing difficulties the editors and translators will have to overcome. On the whole, the translation is admirable, especially those done by Prof. Pelican himself. Luther in a good idiomatic English without losing anything of what is characteristic of the German reformer: this is, indeed, a great achievement.

While W.A. presents the writings of Luther in historical sequence, this edition returns to the practice of all older editions that arrange Luther's works according to subject matters. The readers of this review will look forward with special interest to volumes 35–38 with the writings on "Word and Sacrament" and 39–41 on "Church and Ministry." The exegetical works are arranged in the sequence of the biblical books, thus furnishing the reader with a sort of commentary (for certain parts of the New Testament the sermons on the Gospels and Epistles must be added) on the Bible. This has the disadvantage that Luther's last lectures (on Genesis), which have been edited and somewhat melanchthonized by younger men, precede the early lectures on Romans and Hebrews that show Luther's progress from medieval theology to the rediscovery of the Gospel. However, just this way of presenting the material may help to overcome the modern exaggeration of the difference between the "young" and the "old" Luther. Despite the development he underwent as every great man, the reformer has remained essentially the same. His *theologia crucis* so often regarded as characteristic of the young or even of the pre-Reformation Luther has still found perfect expression in his lectures in Genesis.

When at the end of his life the first edition of his works was begun, he did not like the idea—a German professor who was absolutely free from vanity—stating that only two of his books were worth preserving: the Catechism and *De servo arbitrio*.

The present volume (12 in the series) contains expositions of Psalms 2, 8, 19, 23, 26, 45, and 51 (from 1525-38) taken from several volumes of W.A., but contained in vol. V of the St Louis Edition (Walch). Some are sermons, some lectures. The latter were based on the Latin text the students had while Luther gave his Latin explanation on the basis of the Hebrew text and correcting the Vulgate constantly. Time and again he admonished his students to learn Hebrew, which for him was always more important than Greek, just as the "Scripture" proper was for him, as for Jesus and the apostles, the Old Testament, read, of course, in the light of the Gospel. This distinguishes him from Zwingli and other reformers of humanist background. In his exegesis first a line from the Vulgate text was read. It is always used as subtitle. In cases when these subtitles, as taken from the Vulgate, differ from Luther's own understanding of the Hebrew text (p. 198), they should be given in quotation marks. More notes might be useful, and those taken from the W.A, should be examined.

Other suggestions for an improvement will be made directly to the editors. On the whole it must be said that the present volume gives to the English reader an impression of the amazing work done by one of the greatest exegetes of Christendom. Even where we cannot accept the details of Luther's interpretation, Luther can teach us what all churches of Christendom, and especially all preachers, have to learn after so much damage has been done by a mere historical approach to Scripture: a real theological understanding of the Bible as the Word of God and the book of the Church. Space does not allow us to give some examples of the rich contents of this volume. We can only suggest that the exposition of Psalm 2 or the powerful interpretation of the "Miserere" may be read as specimens.

The publishers as well as the editors deserve not only our gratitude, but also encouragement of the great task that lies still before them. Not only the Lutheran churches will profit from their work, but, as we hope, the whole of English-speaking Christendom. For a man like Luther belongs to the entire Church of Christ.

THEOLOGISCHE ERKENNTNISLEHRE. VERSUCH DOGMATISCHER PROLEGOMENA [XVI:1]

By Hendrikvan Oyen (Zwingli-Verlag, Zurich), 1955, pp. 244; Fr. 14.50.

This "Theological Epistemology" with the modest subtitle "An Attempt at Dogmatic Prolegomena" is another hopeful sign of the great awakening of dogmatic studies that began with Karl Barth's *Commentary on Romans* in 1919 and that since has influenced the whole of Protestantism, and has become a challenge even to Roman theology. It is certainly no easy task to teach theology at Basel side by side with Barth. Prof. van Oyen, however, holds, as this outstanding book shows, his own as an independent disciple of his great master and colleague. He brings a fresh impetus to dogmatic studies from Dutch theology, which is comparatively unknown to other churches except for its traditional interest in comparative religion and missions. Half the book comprises chapter I, "Orientation," which deals with "The Task of Theology," "Theology and Religions," "Theology as a Science," "Dogma and Dogmatics," "Dogmatics and Apologetics," and "The Task of Dogmatic Prolegomena." The "prolegomena" proper, as contained in chapter II ("Unfolding") want to show the character of the Christian faith as a phenomenon *sui generis* wrought by the Holy Spirit and implying a certain knowledge (*Erkenntnis*). "Just as Christ is man, the Word a book, so faith is experience" (p. 116). Section A of this chapter (117–71) deals in several paragraphs with "The Revelation in Christ," B with man as "mandatary" of God (the "old" and the "new" man) (172–209), C with the Holy Spirit and his work (210–29), while the brief chapter III "Epilegomena" gives a concluding paragraph on "Faith and Knowledge" (*Glaube and Erkennen*) (230–36). Every reader will be impressed by the spirit of impartiality and humility with which the author approaches one of the most difficult tasks of a theologian, namely, to justify dogmatics as the core of theology. He sees the danger of theology becoming a sort of esoteric gnosis within the Church (p. 16) and realises with K. Jaspers that pride and fanaticism, so often connected with dogmatic thinking inside and outside the Church, may impair the concept of truth (71). Yet he demonstrates convincingly the necessity of dogmatics as the presupposition of all true preaching, the function of dogma being the establishment of agreement between the kerygma of the Church and the revelation of God as given in Holy Scripture (70). This books shows again that the renaissance of dogmatics in modern theology has its roots not in any speculative interests of some incurable theoretical thinkers on the European continent, but rather in the most serious practical problem confronting the Church in the one great vital question of the preacher, which is not "How shall I cry" in order to be heard by men?, but rather "What shall I cry" (Is. 40:6) as God's messenger? As soon as this question is seriously asked, the objective, dogmatic character of the biblical *kerygma*, even of the preaching of Jesus himself, becomes evident (67).

The main problem to be answered by the prolegomena of dogmatics is this question: What is God's revelation, and where is it to be found? As a Reformed theologian, van Oyen can find it in Scripture only. In interpreting the biblical revelation he seeks to avoid the dangers of a relapse into the *analogia entis* of a *theologia naturalis* on the one hand, and of the dissolution of the dogmatic substance in a mere existentialist interpretation of Scripture on the other. The criticism of Bultmann's "de-mythologization" and his attempt to understand the N.T. kerygma as a mere interpretation of man's existence belongs to the best ever written on that problem. Over against the *analogia entis* (this term has been coined, as far as we know, by E. Przywara, S.J., to denote the Catholic understanding of revelation on the basis of the scholastic, especially Thomistic, doctrine of the analogia between God and man, which makes it possible for man to know of God), the author rejects the ontology of Aquinas as canonized by modern Catholicism. The "I AM" of Exodus 3:14, which resounds in the self-predications of Jesus does not mean "I am," "I exist" in the sense of Greek ontology. It rather means "I am there" in the sense of the personal presence of him who speaks to man, comes to man. The pages 117 and following, where the biblical counterpart to Platonic-Aristotelian ontology is shown by an analysis of concepts like "truth" (*emet*), belong to the most illuminating parts of the book. The author solves the problem by interpreting the relation between God and man as an *analogia verbi* or *communicationis* that safeguards the ontological content of revelation without forgetting that the *esse* of God is totally different from the *esse* of the creatures. Space allows only a few further remarks. With Barth, van Oyen shares the conviction that God's revelation is essentially revelation in Christ; for also the revelation that occurred to Israel is related to Christ. As to the great problem of the *theologia naturalis*, he sides with his master in rejecting it absolutely. However, he corrects him by repudiating certain overstatements, as Barth's interpretation of Romans 1:18ff. There is a revelation of God in the works of creation, as also the O.T. teaches. The interpretation of Romans 1 would have been more convincing, especially as far as the rejection of Althaus and Brunner is concerned, had the author consulted Luther's interpretation of Romans and his treatment of the First Commandment in the Large Catechism. The whole problem of an "original revelation" remains in a certain twilight as long as there is no clear understanding of the fall, of the *status integritatis*, and the *status corruptionis*. The solution of this problem again depends on our understanding of Holy Scripture. We may hope that the author will be able to answer these questions in his future dogmatics. The section on the Holy Spirit, which also corrects somehow Barth's one-sidedness, entitles us to such hope. There are some minor desires that might be fulfilled in future volumes. References to the schoolmen should be given in a more complete way. The terminology should be watched carefully. Thus the *assumptio* of Mary must not be called *ascensio*. We should also avoid the term "parthenogenesis," which has a definite meaning in biology, for the virgin birth on which, by the way, the author writes in a really theological way that would please T. Berdjajew, who took so strong exception to what Brunner had to say about it. When criticizing Anselm's doctrine on satisfaction, we should never overlook what he has to say about God's mercy and about Christ taking our place (see p. 148): *Deus pater dicit: accipe unigenitum meum et da pro te; et ipse filius dicit: tolle me et redime te* (*Cur Deus Homo* 1. I, cap. 20). It is the sincere wish of a representative of "Lutheran Confessionalism" (see p. 90) that we soon may be able to read a work by Hendrik van Oyen in English.

KINGDOM AND THE CHURCH: STUDY IN THE THEOLOGY OF THE REFORMATION [XVI:2]

By T. F. Torrance (Oliver and Boyd, Edinburgh and London), 1956, pp. 168; 16/-.

This thought-provoking book presents in a comparatively small space a wealth of historical information, illuminated by the systematizing power of a great dogmatician. It deals with the teaching of Luther, Butzer (this correct spelling of the name is applied), and Calvin on "Kingdom and Church," showing the indissoluble connection between ecclesiology and eschatology, which characterizes the theology of the reformers in contrast with Rome. The chapter on Luther, whose doctrine is characterized as "eschatology of faith," gives a fair and comprehensive presentation of just those points of his theology that were not so well understood on the British Isles until scholars like G. Rupp inaugurated the British version of the "Luther Renaissance." The attention of the reader is especially called to what Professor Torrance has to say about the eschatological dialectic of *justus et peccator*—the very key to Luther's theology—and about the much-debated doctrine on the "two kingdoms." More emphasis should have been placed on Luther's understanding of history and on the meaning of his doctrine on antichrist. The brief chapter on Butzer and his "eschatology of love" cannot be more than an introduction into the problems of Butzer's concept of the *Regnum Christi*. The observations of the author are illustrated and corroborated by the discovery of the far-reaching influence the reformer of Strassburg has exercised not only on Puritanism in England, but via England again on European Pietism. The investigation of Butzer's *ecclesiola* and its program at Strassburg by W. Bellardi (*Quellen und Texte zur Reformationsgeschichte*, vol. XVIII, 1934), and the last work by the late Professor of Reformed Theology at Halle, August Lang (*Puritanismus und Pietismus*, 1941) have shed a new light on this man who came into his own when Pietism and Methodism defeated the theology of Luther and Calvin. The chapter on Calvin and his "eschatology of hope" is full of most valuable information on this reformer whose theology was broader and more complex than the classical Calvinistic orthodoxy would make us believe. It has, however, to be asked whether the sudden change that has obviously taken place with regard to the interpretation of Calvin's doctrine on predestination is not due rather to a change of mind on the part of modern Reformed Christendom than to a discovery of the real theology of Calvin by modern historians. Karl Barth's biting remarks on what he calls

"Neocalvinism" (see the interesting report on the discussion of predestination since 1936 in *Kirchliche Dogmatik*, vol. 11/2, p. 207ff.) suggest to him who thus far took Calvin's statements at their face value that Calvin would take the side of the "Neocalvinists." Are we not all, Lutherans as well as Reformed, in the great danger of selecting from our reformers that which appeals to us and calling this their true theology? This is most certainly true of historians and dogmaticians in present-day Lutheranism, especially with regard to the doctrine on the Sacrament of the Altar. But probably it is true of all theologians, theology being a *scientia practica* that cannot be separated from our lives and from the life of the Church. This, then, explains also the ethos and pathos of this book, which aims at a closer understanding of the Lutheran and Reformed churches and at the achievement of that unity that was unattainable in the sixteenth century. This deepest interest of Professor Torrance's book becomes evident not only in the entire setup—for there can be no separation between faith, love, and hope—but in a special way in his dealing with the problem of the Sacraments. We cannot enter into a discussion of this problem here. Suffice it to say that his interpretation of Luther's doctrine on the real presence is historically untenable, though many Lutherans today would accept it. Luther and the Lutheran Church have always rejected consubstantiation— the contrary opinion is due to a misunderstanding of a passage in

"*De Captivitate Babylonica*." Even the medieval terms "in," "with," and "under" are not characteristic of the Lutheran doctrine. Strictly speaking, there is no specific Lutheran doctrine on the real presence. Luther demanded nothing but the acceptance of the literal meaning of the "*est*." Calvin could never accept that, as on the other hand the Lutherans could never accept as biblical Calvin's doctrine of the Holy Spirit as the "*transporteur*" who brings the body and blood of Christ to our souls or accept Calvin's interpretation of the *Sursum corda*. In this respect the learned author, despite all attempts to do justice to both reformers, has not been able to give more than a formulation of a problem that, as it has occupied the greatest minds of the sixteenth century, seems to become again a central issue of modern theology. Professor Torrance may be assured that his voice will be attentively heard by all who take part in these discussions.

THE CHRISTIAN ETHOS [XVI:3]

By Werner Elert. Translated by Carl J. Schindler
(Muhlenberg Press, Philadelphia), 1957, pp. 451; $6.

These "Outlines of Lutheran Ethics," as the subtitle of the German original (*"Das Christliche Ethos. Grundlinien der lutherischen Ethik,"* p. 595; 1949) reads, may later be regarded as one of the theological classics of our time. One wonders why this subtitle has been deleted in the English translation and replaced, on the dust cover only, by the meaningless "The Foundations of the Christian Way of Life." The cause seems to be a certain disdain of modern Lutheranism for the old "confessionalism," as appears from the foreword in which Bishop Lilje in his non-committal way appraises the book as at least "ecumenical in outlook" and defends it against the suspicion of being "a product of denominational exclusiveness"—whatever that may be. What would the author, who died in 1954 after he had been for more than thirty years professor of historical and systematic theology at Erlangen, think about this sort of "Imprimatur"? Where will Protestant theology end if we can no longer listen to the genuine voice of another confession? True ecumenicity demands that we carefully study the best books the theology of other churches can offer us. Even where they provoke our opposition, they help us at least to clarify our own thoughts. Thus every serious theologian will be grateful to the enterprising Muhlenberg Press and to the translator for having made available in English this new approach to the problems of theological ethics.

While Elert's Dogmatics ("Der Christliche Glaube," 1940) had to be written in too short a time and was, therefore, as the author himself realized, not free from structural and other weaknesses, this work may be regarded as the maturest fruit of the life's work of a

THE JOURNAL ARTICLES OF HERMANN SASSE

great scholar who was equally at home in the fields of theology, history, and sociology, an independent thinker who nevertheless takes a firm stand in a church bound to a strictly scriptural confession. Written in a beautiful, pointed, concise style whose brilliancy still shines through the translation, this book is not what usually is understood as a textbook on ethics. "Ethics" is defined as "the science of ethos," ethos being "the established behaviour of man as far as it is subject to being judged qualitatively." "The Christian ethos conceives of itself as the quality of man according to the divine judgment." Thus theological ethics is wholly different from philosophical ethics, which does not know of a divine judgment. Since "dogma" and "behavior" are incommensurable, dogmatics and ethics cannot be regarded as parts of one "systematic theology," nor can ethics, as with K. Barth, become a part of dogmatics. Thus ethics becomes a theological discipline in its own right, though its content is closely bound up with dogmatics.

The arrangement of the subject matter results from the fact that God's judgment is of a twofold nature. "It appears as condemnatory or guilt judgment in the law, as forgiveness in the gospel." The distinction between Law (every Word of God that tells us what God commands us to do and what his punishment will be if we fail to do it) and Gospel (every Word of God that tells us what Christ has done for us) is for Luther and the Lutheran Church the mark of true theology. This distinction, which does not mean separation, provides the disposition of the book: "Ethos under Law" and "Ethos under Grace" are the main parts. They are followed by a third part, "Objective Ethos," which deals with the ethos of the Church as a corporate community and the relationship between the Church and the forces of history. This does not mean that a sort of social ethics follows the ethics of the individual. For already part I contains what used to be understood by social ethics. We give first a brief outline of the rich contents. "Ethos under Law" gives in chapters 1 ("The Creature") and 4 ("Sin and Guilt") a reinterpretation of the anthropology of the Bible and the Reformation. Chapter 2 deals with the "Law of God," chapter 3 with "The Natural Orders" (family; marriage; "the people"; State and Law; economic interdependence; truth, oath and honor). "Ethos under Grace" describes in four chapters ("Encounter with Christ," "The New Creature," "The New Obedience," "The Invisible

Struggle") the ethos of the believing sinner who, justified by faith and endowed with the gifts of the Holy Spirit, lives still in this world of sin and death. The spiritual background that lies behind every great theology becomes visible especially in the paragraph on prayer, which, born out of the *De profundis* of a Christian life, may serve as a first introduction into the spirit that pervades this book. "Objective Ethos" is a notable contribution to a new ecclesiology. The paragraphs on the "We" of the apologists, martyrs, and confessions, and on "The Liturgical We" are highly illuminating.

One of the great achievements of this ethics is the clarification of the concept of "collective guilt" at the end of the first part and in "The Liturgical We." The paragraph on "Natural Law" is too short, but it shows why this idea has been preserved in the Lutheran Confessions. A thorough discussion of the book is highly desirable, but it should avoid current prejudices. There is no real difference between Lutheranism and Calvinism of the sixteenth century regarding the attitude towards secular authority, even the terms of the confessions are almost identical, and Calvin's great chapter Inst. IV, 20 could have been written almost entirely at least by Melanchthon. There is on either side the same horror of a revolution. Barth has misinterpreted the Confessio Scotica (art. 14 and 24) in this respect. That there might be an active resistance against a power that has ceased to be authority in the sense of Romans 13 (the classical text also for all Reformed confessions) is admitted also by Elert as by many earlier Lutheran theologians. Both Luther and Calvin had to fight the theological errors of the revolutionary enthusiasts, and only later the ideas of the Anabaptists and Quakers became a power in Reformed Christendom. As to the alleged servile attitude of the Lutheran Church toward the state, one has only to ask whether Luther's strong criticism of the princes would have been possible in England, even at the time of Elizabeth. The problem of the two realms, should be reconsidered in the light of Niebuhr's recent criticism of Barth. The real issue between the churches and within the churches is the problem of the "orders" and the problem of the law. We should distinguish between the "orders," which go back into the *status integritatis* (Gen. 1:28) and orders of history like "people" (Amos 3:2; 9:7) and state. It is significant that the divine ordinance ("*Dei ordinatio*," "diatage" Rom. 13:2) is, according to the N.T., not what we call "state," but rather the "*exousia*," "*potestas*," the secular authority within the state. The "state" of the Christians is in heaven and not on earth ("*polite-uma*" Phil. 3:20; "*polis*" Heb. 13:14). Here lies one of the great weaknesses of Elert's ethics. His doctrine on the Law will meet with strong criticism on the part of Reformed theologians, but also of Lutherans. The clear distinction between Law and Gospel is essential for Lutheran theology and should be regarded by Reformed theology as a challenge, especially in view of the legalism of Puritanism. The real issue is the question of the uses of the Law. Luther and Calvin agree on the "*usus politicus*" and the "*usus elenchticus*," as Inst. II, 7 shows. The "third use," the use of the Law for the regenerate as a rule of life, is strongly emphasised by Calvin. Luther does not speak directly of a third use as the Formula of Concord does. The passages from Luther adduced by the Formula are not genuine but are added to the texts of Luther by adherents of Melanchthon, as Elert has definitely proved. This, however, does not mean that the substance of the doctrine is not present with Luther. His explanation of the Decalogue should be sufficient to prove that Luther also knew of what was later called "the third use," though he never could separate the *usus elenchticus* from the *usus tertius*: The Law always accuses. Whether or not we should use the word "law" for the admonitions addressed to the believers is a matter of terminology. The N.T. knows of the "Law of Christ," the "Law of the Spirit," and the apostles made ample use of the commandments to instruct their young churches. The whole question is connected with the problem of the authority of the Decalogue, which can be deduced only from the use Christ has made of it, as Elert clearly sees. A new investigation of this problem is needed. Reformed theology should ask itself whether Puritanism has not destroyed the freedom with which Calvin still declared the Fourth (our third) Commandment to be fulfilled in Christ (Inst. II, 8, 32), and whether one has not to go further than Calvin by assuming that the entire ceremonial content of the Decalogue has been abrogated in the N.T. For Calvin as well as Barth (Dogmatics III, 4 p. 51ff.) and Elert are mistaken when they assume that for the Primitive Church the Lord's Day was a substitute for the Sabbath. Jewish Christians celebrated both the Sabbath and the Lord's Day. Only the later Church regarded Sunday as the Christian Sabbath. On the other hand, Lutherans of Elert's persuasion must ask themselves why the Church since the days of the apostles has made so much use of the Decalogue. The great commandment of love is not sufficient, unless it is illustrated by the individual commandments. Why am I allowed to kill a wounded horse on the battlefield, while I must refuse the coup de grace to a soldier who in a situation where no medical help is available suffers unspeakable pains until he dies? Because there is a commandment of God. This aspect of the divine Law has not been sufficiently realized by Elert.

The translation is on the whole admirable. Some important passages have been omitted. The paragraph on "Natural Law" suffers from such omissions and even from mistakes (e.g., "social use" for "*proprius usus*," p. 72, and the confusion of "*para physin*" and "*kata physin*," p. 75). A short list of "*corrigenda*," printed on a separate sheet, would be a great help to the readers of this otherwise highly commendable English edition.

LUTHER ON VOCATION [XVI:3]

Gustav Wingren. Translated by Carl C. Rasmussen
(Muhlenberg Press, Philadelphia), 1957;
XII and 256 pages; $3.50.

This excellent translation of one of the outstanding works of present-day Swedish theology is perhaps the best introduction into the theology of the Reformer. It is more than the modest title suggests. By examining one basic thought of Luther's in the context of his whole theology, the author, professor of systematic theology at Lund, has elucidated the sometimes embarrassing wealth of Luther's thoughts. He has avoided the dangers of systematizing and modernizing Luther on the one hand, and of writing a mere historical monograph on the other. Luther uses "vocation" ("*Beruf*") in three meanings. Vocation can mean the calling of man by God to faith. It can mean the calling of a man into the ministry of the Church. It can mean the "calling" in the sense of work, occupation, "vocation," as Luther found it, in harmony with the translators of the King James version, in 1 Corinthians 7:20. (An English counterpart of K. Holl's examination of the history of the world "*Beruf*" in *Gesammelte Aufsoetze zur Kirchengeschichte*, vol. Ill, pp. 189–219 would be most illuminating.) Only in this sense the word is meant here. While every man, Christian or non-Christian, has his "station" ("*Stand*") as father, wife, son, farmer, judge, and so on, the Christian's "station" implies his vocation, the work he has to do. As vocation in the Middle Ages primarily denotes the "call to the cloister," it is not surprising that Luther developed his idea of the "vocation" of each individual Christian after he had rejected the validity of monastic vows (1521). The meaning of this concept is discussed in three chapters. "Earth and Heaven" discusses the problem from the point of view of the two realms or kingdoms in which the Christian lives "with the

Spirit in the paradise of grace and peace and with the flesh in the world of toil and cross" (Luther). This chapter should destroy many current prejudices, especially if read in comparison with Calvin's doctrine on the two realms ("*duplex regimen*," "*duo regimina*," "*regnum spirituale*" and "*regnum politicum*"; Inst. III, cap. 19, 15). While these two kingdoms "stand side by side and are not hostile to one another per se," there is at the same time to be distinguished two other kingdoms, the kingdom of Christ and the kingdom of the devil. These are antagonistic. The situation of the Christian who lives on the battlefield where the fight goes on is described in chapter II, "God and the Devil." The last chapter, "Man," summarizes the results and presents at the same time new aspects of the situation of man between heaven and earth, God and the devil. It is impossible to give a full account of the rich contents of each of these chapters. Suffice it to say that almost all aspects of Luther's theology are discussed (Law and Gospel, the "orders")—in a very sober way—including the problems of secular government and forgiveness as the core of the Gospel. Special attention may be called to the paragraphs on "Faith and Love," "Cross and Desperation" (chap. I), "Regeneration" (chap. II), and "Prayer" (chap. III). Everywhere the spiritual background of Luther's theological thinking becomes visible. It is obvious that the Reformation can be understood only if we understand what realities "God," "Christ," "The Word," and "The Devil" for Luther must have been. Some questions remain open. Wingren, like Elert, shows that Luther did not speak of a "third use of the Law." How, then, is his explanation of the Decalogue to be understood? While the meaning of Baptism is made clear, the question remains as to what absolution and the Sacrament of the Altar mean for the Christian. In a book that sees the weakness of the modern emphasis on the young Luther, this question should not be passed over, especially in view of what the Sacrament meant for Luther himself in his situation between heaven and earth, God and the devil. The book in its English form should find many grateful readers. In a new edition, Luther's "*Schwaermer*" should be rendered by "enthusiasts" (instead of "fanatics"). As it always gives the title of the writings of Luther from which the quotations are taken, this book can lead to a real study of Luther. It should be read together with such writings like the explanation of the Magnificat or Luther's sermons on Matthew 5–7, which now are available in the new English edition.

LUTHER'S WORKS, VOL. 22. [XVII:2]

Sermons on the Gospel of St. John, Chapters 1–4. Ed. by Jaroslav Pelikan (Concordia Publishing House, St. Louis), 1957; XI and 558 pp.; $4.50.

This interpretation of John 1:1–4:10 is a reconstruction by J. Auri-faber, the eager and able collector of Luther's letters and table talks and author of two volumes meant to supplement the earliest editions (Wittenberg and Jena) of Luther's Works (Eisleben 1564/65) of sermons preached by the Reformer in 1537–40. Since it is based on reliable notes taken by serious students independently, this reconstruction is generally accepted as a faithful rendering of what Luther said. "The hands may sometimes be the hands of Aurifaber; but the voice is the voice of Luther," as Prof. Pelikan remarks. The sermons were preached on Saturdays. Thus Luther was here free to use the method of homilies, explaining sentence after sentence that the division of the chapters into verses was at that time not yet made. It might perhaps have been better to put the numbers of our verses, as given in the subtitles, in brackets. The interpretation is incomplete because Luther left out the pericopes contained in these chapters (1:19–28, Last Sunday in Advent; 2:1–11, 2nd post Epiph.; 3:16–21, Monday in Whitsun-Week). For these texts the reader must turn to Luther's Gospel Sermons proper. The volume gives an excellent picture of Luther, who as preacher had the great ability of every great theologian to put the profoundest truths of the Gospel into such a language as could be understood by the simplest layman. Special attention should be given to the explanation of the prologue with its christological problems and to what Luther has to say on the Lamb of God (p. 159ff).

The translation by M. H. Bertram is on the whole excellent, especially when it comes to the rendering of difficult idiomatic and picturesque phrases. In some cases, however, and this applies to all modern translations of theological texts of the sixteenth century, either experts in the field of "Early New High German" in that period of the formation of a new German language should be consulted or the historical dictionaries. At least the "*Fruehneuhochdeutsches Glossar*" by A. Goetze (H. Lietzmann, *Kleine Texte*, No. 101) should be on the desk of every translator of Luther, Zwingli, or the Anabaptists. Then it could not happen that the word "*berichten*," which means "to give the Sacrament" is not understood and a conjecture is made to make the text understandable (p. 418, note 120). Even the old St. Louis Edition provides in such cases the correct information in the short glossaries contained in several volumes. A great problem is the use of the American Revised Standard Version for the biblical text. This version has its merits, but it seems that its authors did not understand much of the *theology* of the New Testament. Besides it is liturgically impossible. One should have chosen the Revised King James Version to render the Bible quotations in Luther's sermons. One of the great shortcomings in the R.S.V. is the loss of the distinction between "thou" and "you." Thus the transition from "*su*" to "*humeis*" in the discourses of Jesus, which is so significant, can no longer be expressed. As we may expect that this edition of Luther's Works will survive the present R.S.V., it is to be regretted that the translators did not follow at least the example of Ronald Knox's translation in keeping this important differentiation. A comparison of John 3 and 4 in R.S.V. and the version of Knox shows what here is at stake.

In the interest of the future volumes, a word must be said about the footnotes. Some of them are meant for scholars, as, for example, references to passages in the *W.A.*, in Aquinas's *Summa th.* or in the fathers. Others are necessary in the interest of the average reader. Thus the false conception of the Gentiles who worshiped the God of the Jews (p. 251) would need an explanatory note in view of what Luther in other passages says correctly about the proselytes (p. 97). Without such clarification the modern reader gets a wrong picture. If historical information is given to explain Luther's necessarily wrong or incomplete views of Church history (he had to reply on the

Historia Tripartita), it should be reliable. Unfortunately this is not always the case. The note on p. 67 on the ancient heretics, obviously based on obsolete textbooks, is untenable. It seems to confirm the erroneous assumption that Novatus was the author of Novatianism. Note 83, p. 110, confirms Luther's error that Apollinaris taught that the Logos assumed a human body only but not a human soul (as Arius thought). The difference between *"psyche"* and *"nous"* should have been made clear by referring to the anthropology of St. Paul. Page 327 seems to suggest to the uninformed reader that Augustine held traducianist views over against Pelagius's creationism. In actual fact Augustine had never been able to decide whether traducianism or creationism is right, as he himself confessed. As to the doctrine of concomitance (p. 266, note 44), it should not have been forgotten that it was already defined by the Council of Constance, even if the word *"concomitantia"* is not used. It is this council that Luther attacks, as he had done so forcefully already in 1535. However, not the doctrine of concomitance is for him the real issue, but rather the arbitrary law that withholds the cup from the laity. It took a long time for Luther to see that the *communio sub una* was contrary to Christ's institution (it should not be forgotten that the daily Communion of the early Christians was a Communion under the species of bread only, as also the Communion that, still in the Middle Ages, the infant received after Baptism when it was given a drop of consecrated wine), and still in the Smalcald Articles of 1537 he leaves open a remote possibility that we receive under one species as much as under both. Also in his writing against the Council of Constance the question of concomitance is only a sideline.

We have mentioned these shortcomings not to disparage the great work that lies behind this volume and the great service its editor and its translator have rendered to English-speaking Christendom. We want only to encourage the men who are in charge of this monumental work to think of means and ways how the edition can be brought to that level of scholarship that must be expected, even if this should mean a slower process of production.

SPIRITUAL AND ANABAPTIST WRITERS
[XVII:2]

Documents Illustrative of the Radical Reformation,
ed. by George H. Williams, and Evangelical
Catholicism as represented by Juan de Valdes, ed.
by Angel M. Mergal. The library of Christian Classics,
Vol. xxv (S.C.M. Press, London), 1957, pp. 421.

America, the sanctuary of all dissenters of the Old World, has more and more become the center of intensive studies in the "Left Wing" R. Bainton or "Radical Reformation," as Prof. Williams calls the movements of the "Anabaptists," "Spirituals" and "Evangelical Rationalists" of the sixteenth century. This is primarily due to the endeavors of churches like the Mennonites and the Schwenckfelders to preserve the heritage of their fathers, the greatest achievement in this respect being the monumental *"Corpus Schwenckfeldianorum."* A surprisingly large number of primary sources in English translation are listed in the important bibliography (pp. 285–93). These studies have grown beyond denominational boundaries into a comprehensive investigation of that "Fourth" Reformation (beside the Lutheran, Calvinist, and Anglican reformations) that has helped to shape American religion and culture. Prof. Williams of Harvard is one of the outstanding scholars in this important field of theological and historical research. In the present volume he presents, with informative introductions into the whole work and the individual documents, well-chosen selections from Swiss, German, and Dutch Anabaptists (Blaurock, Grebel, Hubmaier, Denck, Stadler, M. Hofman, Obbe and Dietrich Philips, Menno Simons) and Spiritualists (Müntzer, Franck, Schwenckfeld). The spirit of the early

Anabaptists is shown by the most touching human document of this movement, the "Trial and Martyrdom of Michael Sattler," the author of the Seven Theses of Schlatt (i.e., Schlaten in Baden, not Schleitheim!), 1527. If anywhere the restriction put on the editor by lack of space is to be regretted, then it is here where Sattler's letter with the theses should have been inserted. Of great importance for the historian are Obbe Philips's recollections of the fateful years 1533–36 (pp. 182ff.). The main purpose in selecting the material was to give an insight into the theological thought of these men. It is impossible to give an account of the various theological topics concerned. They cover all issues of the Reformation and are easily accessible through the topical and analytical index. It is interesting to meet as theologians some men who otherwise are only known from their lives and their fate. One has the impression that the theological tradition plays a greater role in their thinking than might be expected from revolutionary minds. The connection with the Middle Ages, so conspicuous in Holland and Moravia, needs further investigation, and by no means only with regard to the medieval sects. The allegorical use of Levitcus 11:3, which Williams finds "widely employed in Anabaptist exegesis" (p. 134, n. 14), goes back via the schoolmen and the fathers to the pre-Christian synagogue. Also the influence of Augustine is conspicuous. Most of the German texts have been translated by the editor, on the whole a marvelous work in view of the difficulties of the Early High German. In some cases he has read too much into the text, for example p. 150, where *der einige Geist* is translated "the unitary Spirit" instead of "the only Spirit" and the question is asked whether this might be "in contrast with the septiform Spirit of sacramental theology."

Professor Williams's excellent presentation of Northern representatives of the "Radical Reformation" is supplemented by some selections from Juan de Valdes from Spain (about 1500–41). Prof. Mergal of Puerto Rico has looked after this second part (pp. 297–394), which contains three selections with introductions and bibliography. It gives an insight into a type of evangelical piety in which evangelical biblicism, humanist clarity, and Spanish mysticism form a wonderful harmony. It is regrettable that space did not allow the insertion of some passages on Valdes's view of the Sacraments. The passage on Law and Gospel (p. 366) sounds remarkably Lutheran.

The volume as a whole is an outstanding contribution to the "Library" and will serve as a means to provoke self-examination on all sides. Why did the sixteenth century produce five reformations instead of one—for also the Roman Church was after Trent no longer what it had been in 1517? Why had Luther, Zwingli, and Calvin to reject the Anabaptists? Why was the "Radical Reformation" bound to disintegrate from the beginning? Was it a "reformation?"

"FUNDAMENTALISM" AND THE WORD OF GOD [XVII:2]

Some Evangelical Principles. By J. I. Packer (Inter-Varsity Fellowship, London), 1958, pp. 191; 4/6.

Is this the first of the new Tracts for the Times we have been waiting for? If so, another "Second Spring" may be in the air, this time a renewal of evangelical piety and theology. For this book, small in size, but rich in content, persuasive in argument and, above all, pervaded by the freshness of a young spiritual movement, is a clarion call to the defeated and scattered sons of the Reformation to rally again around the Bible as the infallible Word of God. Its background is the new discussion of "Fundamentalism" in Britain caused by "Billy Graham's evangelistic crusades, the growth of evangelical groups in schools and universities, and the increase of evangelical candidates for the ministry" (p. 9). Dr. Packer clarifies the issue by discussing various misinterpretations of the movement even by such outstanding scholars as Archbishop Ramsey and especially Father Herbert to whose "Fundamentalism and the Church" this book is an answer. The new Evangelicalism does not want to be equated with American Fundamentalism, which arose fifty years ago. This "Fundamentalism" in which great theologians like Warfield and Machen played a prominent role is regarded as "a recent chapter, now closing, if not already closed," of that Evangelicalism, which appeared in sixteenth century Protestantism, in Puritanism and Methodism, and will continue in new forms. "We honor Fundamentalism for its witness at a time when militant Liberalism threatened to sweep the historic faith away. But we honor it best not by perpetuating its weaknesses but by frankly acknowledging them and taking pains to avoid them" (38). The theological argument is given in the chapters "Authority," "Scripture," "Faith," and "Reason." The main problem underlying the fundamentalist-modernist controversy, theproblem of authority, can neither be solved by the "traditionalist view," which practically subordinates the Bible to the Church, nor by the "subjectivist position," which destroys the objective truth, but solely by the "evangelical view," whose basic principle is that "the teaching of the written Scriptures is the Word which God spoke and speaks to his Church and is finally authoritative for faith and life." "What Scripture says, God says." "The Bible is inspired in the sense of being word-for-word God given." It is sufficient and perspicuous. "The Holy Spirit, who caused it to be written, has been given to the church to cause believers to recognize it for the divine word that it is, and to enable them to interpret it rightly and to understand its meaning" (47). Such sentences sound strange to modem Protestants. However, before dismissing them one should carefully read what Dr. Packer says (pp. 54–64) on the teaching of Christ and his apostles. What Scripture is must be learned from what Scripture teaches about itself. The strongest point made against Dr. Hebert is that he "writes a complete book on 'Fundamentalism' without discussing at all the avowed biblicism of our Lord and his apostles, nor the biblical concepts of Scripture and of its authority" (144). The urgent plea made by the author in another context (144) when he quotes Cromwell writing to the Church of Scotland, "I beseech you in the bowels of Christ, think it possible you may be mistaken," should be heeded by all modern Protestants and especially by the representatives of "neo-orthodoxy" or British "Biblical Theology." The chapter "Liberalism" puts really heart-searching questions to us all. The plea could have been made even stronger if the author had realized the development in the Roman Church since the Vatican Council, whose statement on the authority of the Scriptures may prove in the future to be of far greater importance than the dogma on the infallible magisterium of the pope, which after all was nothing new and is only the Roman version of the infallibility of the Church. Since 1870, Rome, notwithstanding its errors, has been the guardian of the doctrine of the Church Universal, expressed in the New Testament, confirmed by the Nicene Creed ("Who spake by the prophets"), and held by all orthodox Christians, that the Scriptures have to be accepted as sacred not because they have been approved by the authority of the Church, "and not only because they contain the revelation without error, but rather because they, having been written under the inspiration of the Holy Spirit, have God as their author and as such have been given to the Church" (Denzinger 1787). The amazing work that has been dedicated by Roman Catholic theology to the doctrines of the inspiration and inerrancy of the Bible since Cardinal Newman's last essays were bypassed and the Modernist Movement had to be rejected now begins to bear fruit (see the documents collected in *Rome and the Study of the Scriptures*, a Grail Publication, St. Meinrad, Indiana). It is the greatest challenge to the churches of the Reformation in this "Post-Protestant Age" of which American Protestants begin to speak. In this situation the present book and the movement it represents are most timely.

It must be left to our readers to see for themselves how the author successfully overcomes the limitations of the old fundamentalism concerning nature: The Bible does not teach science. The book is not satisfactory when it comes to the problem of the inerrancy concerning history. In this respect the author does not quite do justice to a biblical scholar of the stature of Dr. Hebert, though he rightly rejects the alleged pseudonymity of the Pastorals. Dogmaticians and historians have to learn from each other and have to resist the temptation either to overcome history by dogma (as the Vatican dogma on the papacy was justified), or to overcome the dogma by history (as the Modernists did). Here lie the great tasks of the future that have not yet been realized by the new movement. Dr. Packer does not see, to take one example, the problem of the canon. East and West have different canons. Even the apostles had two Bibles, for the Septuagint is not only a translation of our Hebrew text and yet is treated in the New Testament as the authoritative Word of God even where it deviates from the Hebrew Bible (Acts 7). The question of whether the "antilegomena" like 2 Peter, which by the Reformation (at first even by Calvin) were regarded as deuterocanonical, are Holy Scripture cannot be answered by assuming that the Holy Spirit would not have allowed the Church to be misled in receiving them (p. 185). This would bring us perilously close to Rome. Here, as in other points, a lack of a detailed knowledge of the reformers becomes manifest. What after all does "evangelical" mean if we share with Rome the doctrine of the inspiration and inerrancy of Holy Scripture, and if the *sola scriptura* could be taught even by good Catholics in the Middle Ages? Thus the new movement will have to go a long and stony road until it reaches the goal for which it is striving in a courageous and really promising way.

CORRESPONDENCE

DR. SASSE'S REVIEW OF DR. PACKER'S BOOK [XVII:2]

Sir, since in Dr. Sasse's review in your last number of Packer's book, *"Fundamentalism" and the Word of God,* I come in for my share of blame, and since the issue raised queries the validity of all our Bible study, it seems to be my duty to enter a protest, even though it be against our beloved and revered Dr. Sasse. I am astonished that he should be so carried away by Dr. Packer's most attractive style as to bestow so glowing an encomium on his book and on the utterances of the papal magisterium about the Bible since 1870 and that he should reserve till the end two criticisms, of which the first, that the book "is not satisfactory when it comes to the problem of the inerrancy concerning history" involves a major criticism of its whole argument. With the second criticism there is not space to deal here.

He endorses Packer's judgement that in my own book I do not discuss "the avowed biblicism of our Lord and his apostles, nor the biblical concepts of Scripture and its authority" (p. 142). With regard to the first of these points, it is necessary to enter a strong protest when Packer equates our Lord's view of Scripture with "the Jewish doctrine of Scripture, the only one the Bible knows" (p. 142). Others are saying this, too, and Packer, in other writings of his. But in fact our Lord roundly condemns the "Jewish" (rabbinic) doctrine of Scripture when he says, as in Mark 7:6–14; 12:24–27 and 35–37, the Pharisees and the Sadducees both misinterpret the Bible. As for St. Paul, I would refer Dr. Sasse and Dr. Packer to Earle Ellis's investigation into Paul's use of the Old Testament, of the fact that St. Paul is again and again at no pains to quote his O.T. texts accurately. He says that in Paul's eyes the Jews stood on the Scripture and not under it; "though they extolled it, they erred because they did not know it . . . and its true meaning remained hidden from them" (cf. Rom. 2:27, 29; 7:6; 2 Cor. 3:6–7, on the "letter" and "the Spirit"). "In Judaism the synthesis of 'word and 'spirit' had been lost, and the Scriptures had become mere 'letters;' the law had become an end in itself rather than a means to evoke faith in God's grace; through their false interpretations the word of God had become ineffectual. The issue of 'the law versus Christ' here passes into Paul's understanding of Scripture itself. Graphe is the Spirit-carried letter, the Spirit-interpreted letter. Therefore, Paul does not hesitate to give his O.T. citations as interpretative renderings, and he is convinced that he conveys the true (i.e., the Spirit's) meaning best in this way. Thus Paul rejects the law, yet he uses the law; the apparent antinomy is resolved by distinguishing between the Jewish and the spiritual authority of it," (cf. [1] Cor. 2; 2 Cor. 3:14). What the Spirit meant is known through the messianic fulfilment, as, for example, in Romans 15:4.

Then I am told that in my book I do not deal with "the biblical concepts of Scripture and its authority." But what are these "biblical concepts"? I find all through Dr. Packer's book the assumption that revelation is "Propositional Revelation" (p. 91), and "the word of God consists of revealed truths"; and so "the evangelical faith is a systematic and integrated whole" (p. 17). Is it, then, that what is revealed is not God himself, and the way by which we may come to him, but truths about him? Is it that the formula of the creeds, "I believe in . . ." is incorrect, and that it ought to have been "I believe that . . ."?

I am convinced that the issue between us is that of the meaning of "Truth," and that he and his friends are at present wholly tied to a notion of propositional truth that is an uncriticised and unexamined legacy from Scholasticism and Aristotle. On this question see A. C. Outler, *The Christian Tradition and the Unity We Seek*, esp. ch. III and pages 86ff., to which it seems to me that there is no reply. The Bible for its part is innocent of Aristotelian logic, and it contains no "system" of theology; it speaks of divine things by means of paradoxes such as "God was in Christ reconciling the world to himself," because it is only by such logically "impossible" language that the mysteries of God can be set forth. On this, see Prof. I. T. Ramsey, Religious Language (S.C.M. Press).

It is strange that a major controversy such as this between Christians should appear to center in a problem of logic and epistemology; for, honestly, I feel that I have no other major difference with Dr. Packer except this, that he is tied to an ideology, to a very questionable philosophical opinion.

There is very much more to say, but this must suffice. And what does Dr. Sasse say?

A. G. HEBERT, S.S.M.

REPLY TO FATHER HEBERT [XVIII:3]

Sir, Father Hebert does me the unusual honor of putting before our readers his complaints concerning my review of Packer's *"Funda-mentalism" and the Word of God.* I must confess that at first I was a little distressed to hear from a highly esteemed man who knows me as belonging to a church that has solemnly pledged itself to the doctrine of the verbal inspiration and inerrancy of Holy Scripture that in my review I had been "so carried away by Dr. Packer's most attractive style as to bestow so glowing an encomium on his book and on the utterances of the papal *magisterium* about the Bible since 1870." Dr. Packer will be surprised to read about the dangerous effect of his style even on critical readers. But I think our Venerable Father Hebert has rendered to us all a great service by compelling us to state clearly the REAL *status controversiae.*

The strength of Dr. Packer's argument lies in the fact that he defends an old dogma of the Church, indeed a doctrine older than the Church, and that he proves it from Scripture. It is the doctrine confessed by all "Catholic" churches, East and West, and equally by the churches of the Reformation, that Holy Scripture in its entirety and in all its parts is the Word of God, given by the inspiration of the Holy Ghost and, therefore, infallible. The importance of Packer's book lies in the seriousness with which he tries to restore this dogma at a time when many churches—Anglican, Reformed, and Lutheran in the same degree—seem to have given it up as untenable in view of modern science and historical scholarship. What would the fathers of the Church of England, the martyrs of the sixteenth century who died for the *sola scriptura,* as well as the great Anglo-Catholics of the nineteenth century say about the Resolution on the Bible by the Lambeth Conference of 1958? Though the latter would accept the statement that the Church is both guardian and interpreter of the Holy Scripture, they would ask whether this guardianship can be in keeping with the failure to confess the Catholic dogma of the Bible as the Word of God. The Evangelicals, on the other hand, would ask what it means that "the Church may teach nothing 'as necessary for eternal salvation but what may be concluded and proved by the Scripture.'" The fathers who formulated Article VI (speaking of "read in" instead of "concluded") believed in the possibility of scriptural proof because to them Scripture was the inerrant, sufficient, and perspicuous Word of God. If this understanding of Scripture is abandoned, then another authority must be added, be it the Church (Lambeth, 1958) or tradition, as it is done in the following statement by Archbishop Fisher: "The Church of England believes that the Holy Spirit of God, the only final authority, speaks to us in Holy Scripture, in the tradition of the Church and in the living thought and experience of today. Thus there is a threefold cord, each, single strand of which, unrelated to the others, leads astray" (*Redeeming the Situation*, 1948, p. 43). Here the *sola scriptura* of the Reformation is lost. Packer's book is the most forceful and the most convincing attempt to restore this fundamental principle of the Reformation, also the English Reformation. "The supreme Judge . . . in whose sentence we are to rest, can be no other but the Holy Spirit speaking in the Scripture." Commenting on this quotation from the Westminster Confession (1, 10), Packer says, "Tradition may not be so lightly dismissed. But neither may it be made a separate authority apart from Scripture. Like every commentary on the Bible, it must itself be tested and, where necessary, corrected by the Bible which it seeks to expound" (p. 48). "The Church collectively, and the Christian individually, can and do err, and the inerrant Scripture must ever be allowed to speak and correct them" (*ibidem*).

This is the real issue. Has Father Hebert seen it? His own doctrine on the relationship between Church and Scripture (Fundamentalism and the Church, p. 34) suffers from the same lack of clarity as that of the utterances of the papal *magisterium* he quotes in support of his view. On the one hand, the superiority of the Scriptures is recognized: they are given to the Church. On the other hand, "the Church did exist before the Bible, and the books were written within the Church and later formed into a canon . . . by the Church; but the

Church is subject to the Lord, and depends on him for her salvation. So, living by the tradition of faith, that is of faith in him, and indwelt by the Spirit, she has known and knows now what are the books that testify of him." Does she know that with absolute certainty, as Rome thinks? If not, must we then not clearly reaffirm the *sola scriptura* of the Reformation? And is it really true that the Church existed before the Bible? This is most certainly not true of the Church of the New Testament. The entire preaching of our Lord from the beginning (Luke 4:17ff) to the end (Matt. 24:15, 30) is exposition of the Scriptures. And as the Risen Lord explains the Law, the Prophets, the Scriptures (Luke 24:25ff.; 44ff), so the preaching of the apostles since Pentecost (Act. 2:16ff) is exposition of the Scriptures of the Old Testament. It is not necessary to remind a scholar like Father Hebert who always has emphasised the connection between the Old and the New Testament of the fact that the entire life, work, and suffering of our Lord was meant by himself to be the fulfilment of Scripture. However, if that is so, we must draw our conclusions for the doctrine *de Sacra Scriptura*. If the Scriptures were to him the Word of God, they must be that to us. There can be no faith in Christ without acceptance of everything that to him was the Word of God. I fail to see how it can be denied that he and his apostles shared the belief of the Old Testament people of God in the inspiration of the Scriptures. His terminology (e.g., "How then doth David in spirit call him Lord," Matt. 22:43, comp, "the Holy Ghost by the mouth of David spake," Acts 1:16) corresponds exactly to that of the Rabbis (see for details the material collected by Billerbeck vol. IV, pp. 415–51). This view of the Bible is the common basis of the controversies of Jesus with his adversaries and of the controversy between Paul and the Judaists and between church and synagogue. The issue is always the right understanding of the Scripture whose divine origin and authority is recognized by either side.

As to the understanding of the nature of inerrancy, this is, indeed, the great problem for all churches today. We agree with Father Hebert about the impossibility of a rationalistic equation of the biblical idea of truth with what we understand in ordinary life or even in philosophy by truth. He himself has shown that there is no faith in the biblical sense without the acceptance of historical facts, without the assent of the intellect. He as well as Dr. Packer and the reviewer are agreed that there is not such a thing in the Bible as truth that would not include also "propositional truth." Also Father Hebert knows that I cannot believe in God without believing "that he is" (Heb. 11:6) and that X cannot believe in Christ without accepting the facts of his life (John 20:31; 21:28). We are furthermore agreed that we must not allow the belief in the truth of the Bible to deteriorate into a supranaturalistic philosophy, a sort of gnosis as we find it in certain sects that claim to teach the truth of the Bible, and that, on the other hand, we cannot accept a "theology" in which the factual content of the Christian faith has evaporated in a philosophy of values (Ritschl's school) or in existentialism (Bultmann). We disagree in the question of inerrancy. What constitutes an error that would destroy the divine character of the Scriptures? What do we mean by error? Is it an error if the Old Testament gives, in the way of ancient historians, figures that are not meant to be statistical figures in our sense? Did the Holy Ghost commit or permit errors when he allowed Stephen and Paul to so use the Greek Bible with its deviations from the Hebrew text? All these problems must be investigated. However, they can be fruitfully discussed only if we are one in the acceptance of the Bible as the Word of God, given by inspiration, not because this is the dogma of the Church from the beginning, but because Jesus Christ, who is content and Lord of the Scriptures, tells us so. If we fail to listen in obedient faith to this voice, then our churches are most certainly going to lose the Scriptures and to leave them to Rome. This should be, and certainly is, our common concern.

LUTHER'S WORKS, VOL. 14. [XVIII:2]
SELECTED PSALMS III

Edited by Jaroslav Pelikan (Concordia Publishing House, St. Louis), 1958; XII and 368 pp.; $5.00.

If the greatness of a theology can be measured by its ability to understand the Psalms, then our modern theology is at a very low ebb and needs a new study of the great exegetes of the Church who were able to penetrate into the depth of this timeless hymn and prayer book of the people of God of all ages, of the Old and the New Covenant, from which our Lord prayed himself even in his agony on the cross. Outstanding among these exegetes is Luther. His exposition of the Psalms becomes theology in the old sense of Anselm and Augustine who wrote their deepest thoughts in the form of prayers, and of the Ancient Church, which understood by "theology" the praise of God.

The present volume contains Psalms 117 and 118—Luther's favorite psalm—and 147 (Vulgate, our Ps. 147:12–20). Then follows the explanation of the so-called "Seven Penitential Psalms" (6, 32, 38, 51, 102, 130, 143), which Luther as a monk had prayed in the Laudes of the Fridays of Lent. All these expositions have been translated from German, as also "The Four Psalms of Comfort" (37, 62, 94, 109). They combine profound theological insights with the practical aspects of true pastoral care. The collection is concluded with the exposition of Psalms 1 and 2 from the second Lectures on the Psalter in Latin. They show the Reformer as lecturer. It would be impossible to enter here into a discussion of the rich content of this volume that in a certain way is a climax of the growing series of this edition. All aspects of Luther's theology are to be found in this volume, which may well serve as an introduction into the biblical theology of the

Reformer. The reader may begin with Psalms 18 and 2 and from there proceed to the Penitential Psalms. A careful study of this volume will show how the Church could and can pray the Psalms, including the vindictive prayers against the enemies of God as prayers of faith (p. 244ff.). The translators (G. Beto, A. Guebert, J. Pelikan, E. Sittler) have again done an admirable work, though, of course, their individualities are perceptible. The introductions are excellent, the footnotes illuminating and to the point, with the exception of p. 204, n. 29, where such an important doctrine as that of justification seems to have been misunderstood in the sense of Osiander. It is not the doctrine of Luther that in the act of justification Christ's righteousness becomes our righteousness through "the personal presence of the indwelling Christ." This mystical misunderstanding of our unity with Christ has been read into Luther. Its danger has been clearly seen, not only by the Lutheran Church (*Form. Conc.* III), but also by Calvin in his elaborate rejection of Osiander *Inst.* III, ch. II. The outward appearance of the volumes is very good, the constant reference to the Weimar Edition is a great improvement. German words like the name Weiss must never be printed "Weisz" according to the rules of German printing.

THE NATURE AND AUTHORITY OF THE BIBLE [XVIII:3]

By Raymond Abba (James Clarke & Co., London), 1958, pp. XVI and 333; 21/-.

The former students of Camden College, Sydney, where the author was principal in 1948–55, as well as his many friends in Australia will welcome Professor Abba's book. It will win him more friends among the educated laymen who are longing for better information on the vital religious questions. It is to them that the author wants to pass on "the chief fruits of twentieth century biblical scholarship" (p. XI). In eight chapters (What is the Bible?; The Interpretation of the Bible; Revelation through History; Myth, Legend and History; Miracles; The Old Testament and the New; Differing Levels of Truth; The Word of God) the great problems the Bible presents to modern man are discussed in a very lucid way. A lot of information is given, especially on problems of Old and New Testament introduction. Almost everywhere the author proves himself as well informed, especially in biblical theology proper. Not so good are the historical remarks on the reformers where the author had to rely on secondary literature that does not do justice to Luther and Calvin. Naturally, the dogmatic problems, as for example the problem of the authority of the Bible, cannot be solved in such a comprehensive volume. But the author shows, by wrestling seriously with them, what the problems are and encourages the reader to think for himself. An appendix summarizes some results from the investigations of the Dead Sea Scrolls. Excellent indexes follow. Ample and well-chosen quotations show the wide reading of the author. As in almost all English books on such a topic, the great contribution of modern Roman theology is completely overlooked. We should ask ourselves whether this can go on and whether the thorough discussion of all our problems in the works on Theologia Fundamentalis is not more important than the theologically poor products of our "Fundamentalism." The author is a representative of modem English biblical theology, which combines biblical scholarship with a real theological understanding of the divine revelation. His judgments (e.g., on Fundamentalism, p. 63f.) are well-balanced and fair. Wherever our Australian laymen are still under the spell of the old liberalism, this book should be recommended to them for study and for group discussions.

FROM ROUSSEAU TO RITSCHL [XIX:2]

Being the translation of eleven chapters from *Die protestantische im 19 Jahrundert*. By Karl Barth. Translated by Brian Cozens. Library of Philosophy and Theology (S.C.M. Press, London), 1959, pp. 435; 42/-.

When Professor in Munster and Bonn, Karl Barth lectured on the history of modern Protestant theology, following the custom of German faculties, which offer such a course as an important supplement to the lectures on dogmatics and history of dogma. These lectures, first published in 1947, dealt in nine chapters with the theology of the eighteenth century, followed by nineteen chapters on the nineteenth century from Schleiermacher to Ritschl. The present English book contains seven chapters from the introductory part and only four (Schleiermacher, Feuerbach, Strauss, Ritschl) from the main part. This selection is reasonable because some stars of the galaxy of the nineteenth century are of third or fourth magnitude and have not shone in the English-speaking world, which, incidentally, raises the question whether we shall ever possess a history of modern theology that would cover not only Germany and Switzerland, but also the French- and English-speaking world, the Netherlands, and Scandinavia. In making their selection, the editors have shifted the emphasis from the nineteenth to the eighteenth century, and thus put into the foreground the great problem of the relationship between philosophy and theology. Thus they have given to the English public one of the finest works ever written in this field.

A later biographer of Barth may try to explain the predilection of this archenemy of the misunderstanding of the Christian faith by modern Protestant theology for the eigheenth century that has produced this misunderstanding. Barth's remarkable interest in, and knowledge of, the age of Enlightenment is known to every reader of his *Die Kirchliche Dogmatik* (e.g., vol. III, I where p. 465 even his beloved Mozart, "the incomparable," appears as the climax of the music of all times till now). The opening chapter of this book, one of three important chapters of the German edition, on "Man in the Eighteenth Century" describes this man as the man of "absolutism" in the broadest sense. The chapter on Rousseau belongs to the best essays on the life and thought of this great Frenchman who also belongs to Switzerland. Lessing, Kant, Herder, Novalis, and Hegel (a chapter on Goethe was planned for the original book, but never finished) are the great representatives of German thought on the border of philosophy and theology. They are followed by the comprehensive genius Schleiermacher, the radical atheist Feuerbach, the unfortunate D. F. Strauss and Ritschl whose "rounded, transparent and compact . . . train of thought" attracted followers but has not given birth to an epoch as the theology of Schleiermacher did. The chapters are of unequal length according to the importance of the subject and the interest of the author. They are all informative, most of them even very stimulating as it may be expected if the greatest theological thinker of our time reveals something of his encounter with great minds of the past. There is a strong autobiographical element in these essays as every reader of Barth's books will feel.

The most important chapters for the systematic theologian are naturally those on Kant, Hegel, and Schleiermacher. It is impossible to discuss them here. Barth shows how Kant, standing on the border at philosophy and theology, does not claim that his interpretation of religion as phenomenon of reason leaves no possibility of any revelation, "since it might be after all, that the teachings of revelation stem from men supernaturally inspired" (quoted from "*Disputation of the Faculties*" on p. 193). Kant who never went to church recognized the existence of the Church that has its foundation in the Bible. Hence he envisaged "the possibility of a theology which would be different from the philosophical theology he himself was propounding. He explicitly calls this other theology, which limits philosophical theology, 'biblical theology,' and it is his wish that the affairs of this biblical theology should not be 'allowed to mingle' with those

of philosophy" (p. 192). In the case of Schleiermacher, Barth emphasises rightly Schleiermacher's profound interest in the Church and
rejects E. Brunner's criticism for Schleiermacher's understanding of
religion as mysticism. While he describes with great sympathy the
attempt of Schleiermacher to reconcile Christianity with modern
culture ("Shall the knot of history be thus loosed: Christianity with
barbarism and learning with unbelief?" quoted p. 321), he shows
why the great thinker was not able to retain the objective Word of
God, the reality of Christ and the biblical understanding of sin and
grace. The tragedy of idealistic philosophy in its attempts to interpret
the Christian faith is made clear in the chapter on Hegel. It would
have become still clearer if the development of the school of Hegel
had been taken into account, which ended in the final breakdown of
metaphysics in European philosophy and in the claims of modern
Communism that Marx and Lenin are the legitimate heirs of Hegel's
philosophy and that Marxist Communism is the necessary product
of Western, Christian civilization.

This outstanding book will find many grateful readers. The
translation is good; even misprints in the German text have been
corrected. Schleiermacher's "Glaubenslehre," the popular name for
his main work *Der Christliche Glaube*, should not be rendered with
"Doctrine of Faith," but with the English title (see p. 424) "The Christian Faith," to avoid misunderstandings.

THE FAITH OF THE CHURCH [XIX:2]

Report of a Joint Commission on Church Union set up by The Congregational Union of Australia and New Zealand, The Methodist Church of Australasia, The Presbyterian Church of Australia (Melbourne, 1959), pp. 44; 2/6.

This report, soon to be followed by a "Second Report on THE STRUC-TURE OF THE CHURCH," is one of the most important documents of Australian church history. What distinguishes it favorably from similar union documents in other parts of the world is its spiritual character: "We make this poor offering to the Lord of the Church and ask him to take, correct and use it, praying that what we have spoken in error may perish from men's memory, and, if it be his will, what we have here done be taken in its imperfection and used for the building up of the Body which is the Church" (p. 7). The whole document is pervaded by a spirit of genuine piety, humble self-criticism, and the serious desire to listen to the Word of God. It deserves the attention of all Australian churches, who, indeed, "would do well to ask themselves" the four questions (p. 26): (1) "Is our message unequivocally conditioned by what God said to man in Jesus Christ?" (2) "In listening to that word have we sought the aid and guidance of our confessing forebears?" (3) "Are those of us who value the traditions of the past and cherish them, equally prepared to confess the faith afresh in the present? Are we only confessionalists, or are we also confessing Christians?" (4) "Are we facing the world, or just facing each other?" As these questions are the climax of Part I, "The Faith We Have Received," so "Our Confession" (pp. 37–40) is the climax of Part II, "The Faith We Affirm in Common." Since our readers know the report and since space does not permit discussion of the numerous historical problems touched upon in a document that is the result of the work of two years by more than twenty theologians, we confine ourselves to those four questions and ask how they have been answered in the new confession.

Ad I. This question can be answered properly only if the scriptural principle of the Reformation is upheld. While the report states clearly (e.g., p. 14) that the Church is always under the Scripture, the relationship between Scripture and the Word of God is not clarified. "To recognize in Scripture the Word of God" (14) seems to mean that the true Word of God is found in Scripture because it is "the unique earthly instrument through which the Church hears the living Word" (34) that is "mediated through the Scriptures" (33). This view, held also by Anglican and Lutheran theologians, abolishes the truly ecumenical doctrine that the Bible is the Word of God.

Ad 2 and 3. Of the creeds and confessions it is said, "The Church cannot afford to ignore these. Nor can she be content simply to repeat them. . . . God is calling his Church to declare the ancient faith anew" (27). No Church wants "simply to repeat" the Nicene or the Apostles' Creed when they are Sunday by Sunday repeated in the divine service. The Church confesses them, and that implies the praise of God, as the report points out (p. 13). If we do that, why should we not accept the full dogmatic content of these creeds? Are they not thoroughly biblical? God does not call us to "declare the ancient faith anew" by leaving out in our new formulas biblical doctrines like the virgin birth of our Lord or his bodily resurrection. If one compares the "confession" (p. 37ff.) with the creeds, it is obvious that the scriptural content of the creeds is not rendered, probably because the authors did not want to make declarations that by some or many of their people could not be honestly accepted. Does this mean to declare the faith anew? They should have made it clear why these doctrines are contained in the creeds, which contain nothing but what is essential. Without the virgin birth, as K. Barth (*Dogmatics I*, 1, par 15, 3) shows, the incarnation becomes ambiguous or even doubtful. What do we celebrate at Christmas if "conceived by the Holy Ghost, born of the Virgin Mary" becomes a myth? What is Easter if the holy sepulchre is like the grave of a martyr in which his body decays while, according to the belief of the Ancient Church, he has already been raised to heaven in the "first resurrection" (Rev. 20:4)? This is the reason why we, instead of formulating the creeds anew, are better off simply confirming them unequivocally, as our fathers did in the Reformation. The same we should do with the content of the confessions of our fathers, as far as the fundamental doctrines of the Reformation are concerned, such as the *sola gratia*. In the absence of a clear statement that man is saved by grace alone without any doing of himself lies the greatest weakness of the new confession. Arminianism seems to be taken for granted, and the comforting biblical doctrines of predestination (Election) seem to have disappeared. The strangest misunderstanding of the Reformation is the reference to the doctrine of justification (p. 41). "We would demonstrate our justification by faith through seeking further to demonstrate the Church's unity." How can we demonstrate God's judgment through which he makes Christ's righteousness our own? What would Luther and Calvin (Inst, m, cap. II) say about this *theologia gloriae*? Here speaks "a church which is seeking to recover a message of justification by faith" (41). But can a church make a new confession without having understood the heart of the Gospel? Can we claim to continue the work of our fathers without having understood their confession?

Ad. 4. We ought, indeed, to remember that the Church has to confess facing the world. Grateful for this admonition we must ask, to take one instance, whether we fulfil our missionary task over against the peoples of Asia if we repeat the old prejudice as if Christianity were a Western religion whose doctrine must be translated from "West European terms" into a language understandable to Asians and Africans. Whatever may be Western in our churches, our dogma is thoroughly Asiatic, as all adversaries of the Christian faith in Europe from Nero and Tacitus to Nietzsche and Hitler have known. The fathers of the Nicene Creed were Asians. Even of the Greek philosophy they are supposed to have used, nothing is Greek except the language. As to the Latin Church, it arose in Africa while the Church of Rome for some generations still consisted mainly of Greek-speaking Asian immigrants. The father of Western theology, Augustine, who has determined the theology of the Middle Ages and of the Reformation, was an African who felt about the Romans very much the same as his present countrymen about the French. Would it not be better to bring to the peoples of Asia and Africa the great Christian theology of their forbears instead of the diluted eighteenth-century Pietism and Rationalism that speaks in many a confession of these younger churches?

We do not want to minimize what is great in the present report. It is outstanding in many respects, also in its honesty. Its shortcomings are the shortcomings of all our modern churches of Reformed, Anglican, and Lutheran origin. We are strong in putting questions and weak in answering them. We have lost the understanding of the dogma of the Church. Consequently we have lost the distinction between Church and heresy. Discussing the biblical idea of the confession, Luther says to the first representative of modern enlightened Christianity, Erasmus: "Take away the firm statements, and you have destroyed Christianity" (*Tolle assertiones, et Christianismum tulisti*). This is the great danger in which we all are. The report should be understood as a challenge to us all. A confession is demanded from all our churches. But a new confession will come to us, as gift of the Holy Spirit, only if we have thoroughly understood the old one and are able to judge it by the ultimate rule and standard of all doctrine, the Scriptures as the Word of God.

THE NOTION OF TRADITION
IN JOHN DRIEDO [XIX:3]

Dissertatio ad Lauream in Facilitate Theologica Universitatis Gregorianae. By John L. Murphy (The Seraphic Press, 1501 So. Layton Blvd., Milwaukee 15, Wis.), 1959, pp. XIV and 321; $3.

The Roman dogma of tradition as a second source of revelation, unknown to the Middle Ages, has been defined in the decree *De Sacris Scripturis* of the Fourth Session of Trent in 1546 against the *sola scriptura* of the Reformation. The decree speaks of "traditions" as truths once delivered to the apostles either by Christ or by the Holy Spirit and handed down to the future generations of the Church. It leaves open the question of what tradition as the act of handing down is, and it does not define the actual relationship between the content of Scripture and the content of tradition. Hence the meaning of the decree is under discussion, especially in view of the ecumenical situation that has made tradition an issue also in the Anglican, Reformed, and Lutheran churches.

The present book is a very important contribution not only to the clarification of the doctrine of Trent, but also, just in its concentration on one important point, to the understanding of the complicated history of doctrine in the sixteenth century. Since it is not allowed to read into the texts of the sixteenth century the idea of a "living tradition" that was developed in the nineteenth century by Mohler and Newman under the influence of the Romantic understanding of the living organism of the Church, the doctrine of Trent must be elucidated first of all from the theological milieu out of which it grew. This the author has tried to do in his well-written and highly

interesting book on John Driedo (1480–1535), one of the outstanding theologians of Louvain along with Adrian of Utrecht (Hadrian
VI.), D. Latomus whom Luther praised as his finest adversary, and
Pighius with whom Calvin took issue. A comprehensive chapter,
"Life, Times and Works of Driedo," is followed by a penetrating analysis of his views on tradition as expressed mainly in "*De ecclesias-
ticis scripturis et dogmatibus*" (1533). Driedo uses the singular and
the plural of *traditio* interchangeably, "meaning either that complex
of truths and practices handed down by the apostles, or perhaps in
some instances, the act of handing down" (72). We have added the
emphasis to indicate that on the whole Driedo has the same use as
Trent. The chapter "Scripture and the Church" shows how Driedo
coordinates both: "Scripture is nothing other than the testimony of
the Church itself, testifying and speaking, written under the Holy
Spirit" (78). To avoid misunderstandings, Driedo emphasises the
inspiration of the whole Bible. The question of whether Scripture
or the Church is the higher authority can be answered in either way.
The Church cannot teach contrary to Scripture, but what Scripture
is and how it must be interpreted we know from the Church. Both
authorities proceed from the same Holy Spirit (97). The relationship
between Scripture and tradition is determined by this sentence: All
truths necessary for salvation are somehow contained in the Scriptures (136), either expressly or tacitly (132ff.), even if only under the
general admonition of hearing the Church. Driedo is, however, far
from the medieval view that a dogma must be taken from Scripture,
though under the authority of the Church. "The authority of the universal Church is to complete the Scriptures, to bring to full light that
which the inspired books mention only in germinal form," as the
author interprets Driedo (129). Besides liturgical and disciplinary
traditions, there are such important doctrines as the perpetual virginity of Mary, the sacrificial nature of the Mass, and purgatory
that cannot be proven from Scripture, but are only insinuated in it
(129). "We may not conclude, therefore, that Driedo held to a totally
extrascriptural source of revealed truth, even though—taken apart
from his general teaching—isolated statements may seem to indicate this" (137). A definite answer to the great problem "Holy Writ
or Holy Church" has never been found, neither by Driedo, nor in
the discussions at Trent, nor at the Vatican Council. It is one of the

fundamental questions debated by modern Roman theologians who (e.g., Geiselmann) try to show the unity of the two sources of revelation by denying that the doctrines of the Church can be ascribed to either Scripture or tradition alone.

This highly informative and thought-provoking book should be studied by every theologian interested in the doctrine *de Sacra Scriptura*. It contains important material on the Council of Trent in some appendices ("'Traditions' and the Council of Trent," "'Faith and Morals' at Trent.") Driedo has rightly been called "the inspirer of the Fourth Session." His writings must have been widely studied in the decade between his death and the council. The prevailing opinion that Pighius is the author of the juxtaposition of Scripture and tradition must be revised in favour of his teacher Driedo. Whoever might have inspired him, it is now evident that the doctrine of Trent on Scripture and tradition is the product of that conservative Catholic humanism that was inspired by the new editions of the Church fathers and had its great center in Louvain.

ZWINGLI'S LEHRE VON DER GOETTLICHEN UND MENSCHLICHEN GERECHTIGKEIT [XIX:3]

By Heinrich Schmid, Zurich (Zwingli Verlag), 1959, pp. 269; Sw. fr. 19.

This thorough investigation of the ideas of divine and human righteousness in the theology of Zwingli deals with a central problem in the thought of the Swiss reformer who in his life as churchman and politician personified his theocratic concept of a Christian society. Three factors have determined this concept: the medieval heritage of the idea of the *"corpus Christianum,"* a society that is simultaneously Church and state; the humanistic biblicism that characterizes Zwinglias reformer; the encounter with the Anabaptists who confronted him with a different understanding of the Bible. What he has in common with the Anabaptists is the attempt to derive the entire human law from the divine revelation and the conviction that the Sermon on the Mount is binding on all Christians. What distinguishes him from them is the recognition that it cannot become public law, as is already shown by the fact that the Anabaptists had to abstain from participation in civil government and had to build up their own religious society separated from the people. With Aquinas and Luther, Zwingli must distinguish between two parts of the divine Law and between two types of righteousness. There is a law that concerns the outward man. Its fulfilment is possible. But the "human righteousness" we acquire by obeying this law does not justify us before God. There is another law, or rather part of the divine Law that commands love of God and of one's neighbour. No man can fulfil it. The righteousness it requires, the "divine righteousness," is a gift of God in Christ, who alone is righteous, a gift of the divine grace received through faith. (To justify means to Zwingli always to make righteous.) Both laws constitute the one Law of God binding on all men. This doctrine must not be confused with the doctrines of Aquinas and Luther. Zwingli teaches with Luther against Aquinas that there are not two states of perfection. Against Luther he teaches that there are not two sources of the divine Law, not two realms or "governments," not a Church distinct from the state. Both Church and state are the same community.

The first part of the book deals in five chapters with all aspects of "The Divine Righteousness." It discusses Zwingli's understanding of revelation, the Law of God, justification and the relationship between grace and human activity, faith and works. The second deals in eight chapters with all problems of "The Human Righteousness," culminating in a discussion of the religious task of the state, the political task of the Church, and the dialectic between Church and state. These chapters are of great actual significance and may be read first as an introduction into the theoretical chapters. It is the duty of the people, to take one example, to depose a secular government that opposes God's Commandments. Since such a deposition should not be made in a disorderly way, practical problems arise that Zwingli was not able to solve. It is noteworthy that just in this context the Law is always equated to the Gospel. Luther's distinction between Law and Gospel has always been foreign to Zwingli.

It is not possible to enter here into a discussion of the rich content of this important contribution to modern Zwingli research. The book gives an impression of Zwingli as a thinker in his own right, but also of his limitations. The epilogue shows why Zwingli's solution of the problems with which he had to wrestle is not applicable to our time. The philosophical presuppositions of his thought—the Thomistic background is everywhere noticeable, especially in his understanding of predestination—are no longer tenable, and the social and political developments have destroyed not only the ideal of a Christian society in which Church and state coincide, but also the possibility of a secular authority bound to one religious confession. The book confirms the fact that Zwingli who otherwise seemed to be the most progressive among the reformers was actually more bound to the medieval world than Luther and Calvin. The tragedy of his theology has become the tragedy of his life. The deepest reason of this tragedy must be found in his understanding of the Word of God and not in the circumstances of his time.

THE CHRISTOLOGY OF
THE NEW TESTAMENT [XX:1]

By Oscar Cullmann. Translated from the German
"Die Christologie des Neuen Testaments" (1957) by
Shirley C. Guthrie and Charles A. G. Hall (S.C.M.
Press, London), 1959, pp. XV and 342; 42/-.

This comprehensive study of the central theme of biblical theology starts with two important observations: "Early Christian theology is almost exclusively Christology" (p. 2f.), even the work of creation being related to Christ, and "The New Testament hardly ever speaks of the person of Christ without at the same time speaking of his work" (p. 3).

The method followed in elucidating the Christology of the N.T. is the investigation of the christological titles. They are divided into four groups, as they refer to the earthly work of Jesus (Part I: Jesus the Prophet, the Suffering Servant, the High Priest), on the other hand the author is compelled to include in his chapters designations like "king" or "judge" which are related to the main titles.

Of special interest to the general reader as well as to the preacher are the chapters on the "Lord," the "Son of God," and on "The Designation of Jesus as 'God.'" The discussion of the title of "*Kyrios*" is a masterpiece of biblical theology. It refutes definitely all attempts to derive the concept of Jesus as the Lord from Hellenism (Bousset). The title goes back to the "*maran*" of the Aramaic-speaking church and has its root in the earliest liturgy. Cullmann makes quite clear that "*kyrios*" is not less than "*theos*" (just as in John 1:1 "*theos*" is not less than "*ho theos*"—p. 265f.—against Origen's famous misinterpretation). The most important result of Cullmann's work is the proof that the New Testament teaches the full divinity of Christ.

What Cullmann says (p. 294f.) of the virgin birth will not satisfy him who realizes the Jewish background of the nativity stories and sees the difference between these narratives and "oriental and Hellenistic themes" that have been adduced as parallels and sources. Nor does it justice to the remarkable fact that there never seems to have been a Christological confession of the Church without the "*natus de Maria virgine*," while none of the classical creeds mentions the "Logos." The doctrine of the incarnation was for the Church always bound up with the doctrine of the virgin birth. This fact should make us more reluctant to make use of the *argumentum e silentio*.

The full value of this mature fruit of many years of thorough research will be appreciated by the reader who studies Cullmann's exegesis of the classical passages like Philippians 2:5ff. or the prologue to St. John. This book should be on the desk of everyone who has to preach the Gospel. It leads back from the Christological myths of modern Christianity to the real Christ, the Christ of the New Testament. The latest of these myths is the demythologized Jesus of Bultmann. It is refreshing to see how Cullmann deals in a most chivalrous manner as a real historian with that great unfortunate thinker who has become a symbol of a certain Protestantism that has lost with what it regards as myth the real Jesus of history. At the same time, the book should be helpful to all those who today speak again of the incarnation of the Word, of Christ as Lord and Savior, without realizing the profound meaning of the biblical terms.

In the preface the author asks his critics not to dispose of his interpretations with apodictic assertions and verdicts without exegetical grounds. For he has written as an exegete, knowing "no other 'method' than the proven philological-historical one." The few remarks we can make here are not meant as a criticism of Cullmann's great book, but only as questions that occur to him who reads the book from the point of view of the history of dogma. What is the actual relationship between the Christology of the New Testament and the classical Christology of the Church as it was developed in the centuries up to Chalcedon? Cullmann says of the latter, "that although the Church attempted a solution of the problem by reference to the New Testament, its statement of the problem was nevertheless oriented all too exclusively in a direction which no longer completely corresponds to the manner in which the New Testament itself states it"

(p. 3). The difference lies in the fact that the later Christological controversies "refer almost exclusively to the person or nature of Christ," while the New Testament speaks of the person of Christ always in connection with his work. New Testament Christology is "*Heilsgeschichte*" (in the twofold sense of "history of salvation" and "saving history"), as the concluding chapter, "Perspectives of New Testament Christology," points out. No one will deny that the fathers of the fourth and fifth centuries did not simply repeat the Christology of the N.T. But it was nothing but this Christology that they defended with the means at their disposal. For a man like Basil, "theology" is, as his terminology shows, essentially Christology that has now grown into the doctrine of the Trinity since the biblical view of the Holy Spirit, the person of the Paraclete, has been taken into account. And this doctrine is deeply rooted in the liturgy ("who together with the Father and the Son is worshiped and glorified"), just as the Christology of the New Testament is rooted in the earliest liturgy ("*maranatha*"). Apart from the word "*homo-ousios*"—which even a man like Athanasius has used very rarely—there is not one word in the creed that is not biblical. Peter, Paul, and John would certainly not have found fault with our Nicene Creed. Even the work of Christ they would have found in the phrases, "who for us men and for our salvation came down from heaven . . . who for us, too, was crucified under Pontius Pilate." If the full meaning of this "for us" has not been understood in the Ancient Church, it must not be forgotten that the man who was to have brought it up at the Council of Ephesus in 431 had died a year before while his town, Hippo Regius, was besieged by the barbarians. And as to "*Heilsgeschichte*," one has only to look into the great Eucharistic Prayers of the Ancient Church (e.g., Apost. Const. V33I, 12 where almost the O.T. is epitomized) in order to know that this was a living reality to the Church, the liturgy being, as it were, re-enacted *Heilsgeschichte*. Only if we realise that the Christology of the Church is essentially the Christology of the New Testament shall we be able to avoid one great danger. If it is true that Christology is *Heilsgeschichte* and *Heilsgeschichte* Christology, what, then, is the source of our Christology? The first Christians, so we read in the concluding sentences of Cullmann's book, found their conviction in a threefold way: "Through the acceptance of the witness given in the life of Jesus with the events of Good Friday and Easter; through the powerful experience, both personal and in common worship, of the presence of the *Kyrios* . . . through the reflection, carried out in faith in the present Lord and the crucified Son of Man, concerning the relation of this Jesus Christ to all the rest of God's revelation. These are the sources of early Christian Christological conviction. For the modem man there are no others." If we could ask Peter, John, and Paul how they got their convictions concerning Christ, they would certainly confirm that statement, but they would add another source: He opened to us the Scriptures (Luke 24:32). Certainly he did this: the Jesus of history who is the Lord whose mighty presence has become a reality to us. When "he opened their understanding that they might understand the Scriptures, and said unto them, thus it is written . . . ," their Christology was finished. How could Paul and John otherwise know that all things were created through him, had they not found it in the Scriptures (e.g., Prov. 8)? And how can the modern man who is separated from the Jesus of history by almost two thousand years achieve a Christology except by the Scripture, which is not only a record of a divine revelation in the past, but at the same time the living and powerful Word of God? The theological rule must be this: The only source of Christology is the Holy Scriptures of the Old and New Testament, "opened" by Christ.

REVELATION AND THE BIBLE [XX:1]

Contemporary Evangelical Thought.
Edited by Carl F. H. Henry (The Tyndale Press, London), 1959, pp. 413; 17/6.

The writer of this review belongs to the generation of continental theologians who as students went directly from Harnack's lecture-room to the battlefields of the First World War to discover that on the theology they had learned one could perhaps live, but not die. This highly idealistic and optimistic "theology for good boys" failed to see the realities of this world of sin and death and came under the judgment of Anselm's word, *Nondum considerasti quanti ponderis sit peccatum.* It took not less than the great breakdown of humanity in our age to teach us that the object of theology is not man and his religion, but God and his Word. To this generation Karl Barth became teacher and leader. Future Church historians will evaluate the work of this great man and the influence he has exercised even far beyond the Protestant churches. They will also recognize and explain the limitations of the "theology of crisis" in Europe and the school of "Neo-Orthodogy" that grew out of it in the English-speaking world. The development of men like Brunner and Niebuhr, the failure of the "Confessional Church" in Germany, the astonishing rise of Bultmann and Tillich after the Second War point to the fact that Barth's theology, great and influential as it is, has not been able to fully achieve that "turn from subject to object" that was its original aim.

Today it is obvious that one of the reasons for the failure of Barthian and neo-orthodox theology was its inability to understand why for the reformers as for the Christian Church of all ages Holy Scripture is the Word of God without any qualifications. In this situation a new movement was bound to come that would try to restore a truth that had been neglected by European theology in such a way that even Barth had to pay his tribute to that liberalism against which he had revolted. This new movement, noticeable in the English-speaking world for years, presents itself in a most impressive way in the present symposium. Dr. Henry, the well-known editor of *Christianity Today* has proved again his ability to bring together for common work theologians of various backgrounds on the basis of a common recognition of the unconditional authority of Holy Writ. His preface describes the background and origin of this book in which twenty-four contributors from various countries (England, Scotland, America, Holland, France, South Africa) and of different denominational background (Anglican, Presbyterian, Reformed, Lutheran, Baptist) make their contributions to the problems of "Revelation and the Bible." The first six chapters deal with the problem of revelation (Berkouwer, Clark, Jewett, Martin, Stonehouse, Packer). Professor Berkouwer, the theological leader of the Reformed Free Church in Holland who has made a deep impression even on K. Barth (see the touching passage on the new Fundamentalism in the Preface to Vol. IV, 2 of Barth's Dogmatics) deals with "General and Special Revelation" in a way that does justice to the fact of the general revelation as taught in Holy Scripture, while rejecting the *theologia naturalis* of Rome and Protestant Modernism. The subsequent contributions show how the special revelation is rational (Clark), historical and personal (Jewett), objective (Martin) and scriptural (Stonehouse), while J. I. Packer gives a review of contemporary views of revelation. Besides the return to the reformers, there is noticeable a promising attempt to solve the philosophical problem after existentialism has failed. The limited space allows not for a full solution of the problems. The authors know that their work cannot be more than a beginning. The major part of the book is dedicated to the problem of the revelation in Scripture. Stibbs ("The Witness of Scripture to Its Inspiration"), Marcel ("Our Lord's Use of Scripture"), and Nicole ("New Testament Use of the Old Testament") give the scriptural basis of a doctrine of Holy Writ. Young deals with the canon of the O.T., Young with the Apocrypha, and Ridderbos with the canon of the N.T. Here one feels the limitations of the space available. The problem of the Septuagint as well as the problem of the understanding of the canon by the reformers require a more elaborate treatment than can be given on a few pages. The same is true of "The Church Doctrine of Inspiration," by Bromiley (pp. 205–17). Finlayson's valuable review of "Contemporary Ideas of Inspiration" is followed by contributions by Harrison, Ramm, Mueller, Kevan, Wiseman, Bruce, Ridderbos, Tenney, which mainly deal with concrete problems of interpretation. Of special interest are the discussions of archaeological confirmation of the Old and New Testament (Wiseman, Bruce) and on reversals of Old and New Testament criticism (Ridderbos, Tenney). "Authority and the Bible" by Geldenhuys and "The Unity of the Bible" by Gaebelein provide a fitting conclusion.

This book is a testimony to the great seriousness with which the doctrine of revelation and the Bible is being investigated throughout Christendom. More attention could have been paid to what Roman Catholic scholarship is doing on the same questions. What strikes the reader is the spirit of humility that pervades the book. Criticism becomes nowhere unnecessary polemics. This symposium is a great promise. The extraordinary cheap price will make it available to the widest circles, especially also among non-theologians.

LUTHER'S WORKS, VOLS 2, 9, AND LUTHER THE EXPOSITOR [XX:2]

Edited by Jaroslav Pelikan and Daniel E. Poellet (Concordia Publishing House, St. Louis). Vol. 2: *Lectures on Genesis*, Chapters 6–14, 1960, pp. X, 433; $6.00. Vol. 9: *Lectures on Deuteronomy*, 1960, pp. X, 344; $6.00. Companion Volume: *Luther the Expositor. Introduction to the Reformer's Exegetical Writings*, by Jaroslav Pelikan, 1959, pp. XH, 286; $4.00.

The new standard edition of Luther's Works is making good progress. More and more of the volumes published by Muehlenberg are appearing on the shelves of the Australian libraries. As they are accessible to the reviewer only there, he can only recommend them briefly in our review on the basis of his own experiences and those of his students. They are indispensable for the study of the Reformation, especially the three volumes on the "Career of the Reformer" with many important documents. Concordia has brought out two more volumes of Old Testament lectures, Deuteronomy and the continuation of Luther's great lectures on Genesis, chapters 6–14. Luther is at his best as exegete in explaining the Old Testament. No one would expect from him information that could not be given in an age that had not yet learnt to think in terms of historical research. But many years will elapse before a modem exegete arrives at such profound theological insights as Luther shows in interpreting what the Old Testament tells about Noah, Abraham, and Moses, or about the Gospel in a book that at first sight seems to be only a book of the Law. Again the editors and the translators (R. Caemmerer and G. V. Schick, St. Louis) have rendered us a great service, though some corrections may be needed in future reprints. Space does not allow us to quote from texts that may become now classics for English-speaking Christians, for example from the great passages on Abraham that begin in Genesis 12.

A question of principle is raised by the "companion volume" in which Professor Pelikan wants "to provide the reader and student of Luther's Works with some of the tools he needs for an appreciation of Luther's exegesis. These tools should enable him to identify Luther's procedures in these commentaries on the Scriptures." This is indeed a task, but not a task that can legitimately be performed within the framework of an edition of Luther, even in a "Companion Volume." By being published in a series of Luther's works, in the same wonderful binding as all the other volumes, even with the signature "Martinus Luther," it claims an authority it never can have. The first principle of editorship, emphasised by Luther himself—he did not like the idea of his works being printed because he regarded only his Catechism and *De servo arbitrio* as deserving survival, but had to give in in order to avoid the dangers of unauthorised spurious editions—is the presentation of the text without comment, excepting illuminations of difficult words and sentences and historical or other factual notes including historical introductions. What would the *"Kirchenvaterkommission"* say if the editor of the new edition of the works of Athanasius would offer them a companion volume discussing the theology of the father with references to his favourite colleagues? Text and commentary must be distinguished, or a work comprising text and commentary must be written. Professor Pelikan will see that for himself if in a few years' time he notices that this volume has become obsolete in view of the advanced research. The edition itself will remain, with improvements in the case of reprints—as also the Weimar Edition is going through a process of revision—but this volume would at least have to be rewritten. One wonders who actually are the responsible bodies behind this edition. But perhaps our American friends have still to learn this aspect of an edition that is not only one man's work. Every great edition of this kind needs a patronizing and responsible body.

The book has grown out of lectures held on various occasions during five years. Part I deals in six chapters with "The Principles" of Luther's exegesis. Chapter 1 gives some very good observations on the problem "Exegesis and the History of Theology" up to Augustine. None of the great exegetes of the Middle Ages is dealt with, not even in the later parts, such as in the discussion of Luther's exegesis of the eucharistic texts. No one can understand the exegesis of the reformers and of the Old Protestant churches without the great exegetical tradition of the Middle Ages. Also the short chapter 4, "Scripture and Tradition," suffers from an insufficient treatment of the problem in the Middle Ages. Pelikan sees the difference between East and West in the emphasis of tradition. But he fails to see why the Latin theology develops a theory on tradition only after the Reformation and under the influence of the first printed editions of the fathers who up to that time were known mostly in fragments and quotations. A clarification of the various concepts of tradition (N.T. *paradosis*, *paradosis* in the Ancient Church, in the East since 787, with the reformers and the completely different concept of tradition and traditions as a source of doctrine since Trent, the modern attempts on the part of Roman theology to interpret Trent in the direction of the pre-eminent authority of Scripture, and the Anglican views) must precede any fruitful discussion of the burning issue of today. Chapter 3, "The Bible and the Word of God," will be a disappointment for many who seek an answer to that problem. Pelikan tries to find the right balance between the Word of God as deed, as oral Word and as written Word, but he does not do justice to the written Word. Inspiration and infallibility of the Scriptures, the unquestioned basis of Luther's view of the Bible, which he shares with the Catholic Church of all ages, are, as far as I can see, not even mentioned. This may partly explain Pelikan's untenable juxtaposition of Scripture and tradition that he wants to find in Luther. It may also explain his failure to understand why for Luther the authority of the Scriptures is the authority of Christ. One has the impression as if too many subjects have been touched upon in these chapters to allow for a sufficient treatment. The second part, "The Practice of Luther's Exegesis: A Case Study," tries to show how Luther applied his principles to one great problem, the exegesis of important passages connected with the Lord's Supper from Matthew 26; John 6;

1 Corinthians 10 and 11; and Hebrews 9. Here lies the strength of the book, and nobody will read these chapters without getting an impression of Luther's profound searching of the Word of God, which perhaps meant more to him than to any of his contemporaries, as even a Roman Catholic scholar like J. Lortz says when he speaks of the unique relationship between Luther and the Bible. This would have come out still more clearly if Pelikan had not read into Luther's words foreign ideas. "Luther's exegesis was based on the presupposition that a human being became an authentic person only when he was brought into participation in the life of God, and that this happened in and by the Church" (p. 203). So we read in an explanation of "Participation in the Body of Christ" (1 Cor. 10.16). Luther would never have understood that. Besides it is wrong. Instead of asking what modern existentialist theologians may think of "*koinonia tou somatos Christou*," one should better consult what Chysostom has to say in his homily on 1 Corinthians 10, on "*koinonia*" and "*metalepsis*." Another case in point is Pelikan's attempt to read into Luther the idea that the "remembrance of the death of Christ is a pleading with God." Referring to the interpretation of "remembrance" by Gregory Dix, he finds in Luther's exposition of Psalm 111 the idea "that God remembered the death of Christ and that the Church was to remind God of it" (p. 209). Luther says expressly in the passage referred to (WA 31, 1; 417–18; Luther's Works 13,377) of this remembrance: "This takes place through the preaching and the word of God." It is a public remembrance, a public proclamation that takes place to the end of the world: "And thus in the sacrament there is not merely food but also the word of God." The remembrance is preaching. There is not the slightest hint at a pleading with God. The same is true of the passages from the commentary on Isaiah and the lectures on Genesis Pelikan quotes. It is difficult to understand how a scholar like Professor Pelikan could misunderstand the texts so obviously. We can only hope that this theologian from whom we expect great things will not be absorbed by the requirements of too many duties.

THE LIVING WORD.
A THEOLOGICAL STUDY OF
PREACHING AND THE CHURCH [XX:3]

By Gustaf Wingren. Translated from the Swedish
PREDIKAN by Victor O. Pogue (S.OM., London),
1960, pp. 223; 25/-.

The English version of Wingren's "*Predikan*" (1949); German translation "Die Predigt" (1954 and 1959) appears under a new and well-chosen title that indicates the scope of the book better than the original title, which cannot be well translated. The division into sixteen chapters, each comprising three or four paragraphs, instead of the original seven chapters with numerous subtitles, makes it easier to read. The translation is complete except for the omission in footnotes of titles and references, which are not available to the English reader. Scholars will have to look for them in the German edition. The book is prefaced by Alan Richardson.

English-speaking theology is so accustomed to connecting the revival of a "theology of the word" with the names Barth and Brunner that it will be a surprise to many to discover how theologians of a definite Lutheran tradition have approached the same problems from a different angle. For nothing less than a theology of the Word is the aim of Wingren, and this book is an attempt to pave the way for it by clarifying theologically what it means that the Church has the task to preach the Word. He tries to overcome the dualism of object and subject, of the Word and the hearing man, by the thesis that the Word and man belong always together. In the Bible God's Word and God's people are inseparable. The Word is addressed to man, and man becomes what he is and what he is meant to be through the creative and living Word. From this starting point, Wingren goes on to a discussion of almost all topics of the Christian doctrine in their relation to the preaching task of the Church. Creation and redemption, death and resurrection of Christ, Law and Gospel, Baptism and the Lord's Supper, the Ministry of Reconciliation, and the communion of Saints are some of the main topics of this far-flung discussion of the Church's preaching.

The book shows the strength and the weakness of the "Lundensian School" of modem Swedish theology. Its strength is what this school has learned from Luther: the centrality of Christ, the condescendence of God who enters the human flesh, who is present in the Word. If real presence is a characteristic feature of Lutheranism—Wingren speaks of "*communication idiomatum*" instead—then this book is a witness to Luther's understanding of the divine revelation. On this point Wingren sees the great difference over against Barth and classical Reformed theology. Characteristic of the Lundensians is the emphasis on Christus Victor as the Savior and a lack of understanding of Christ's atoning death as satisfaction.

The weakness of this theological school and also the weakness of this book is a lack of understanding of the Holy Spirit. This would perhaps be the main objection by Reformed theologians, but not only by them. It becomes obvious in the misunderstanding of the inspiration of the Bible. Wingren rejects it, admitting only the view "that God directed the events that resulted in the writing of the books of the Bible and the work that in time resulted in their being collected into one" (p. 47). This cannot be reconciled with Luther's understanding of the Bible as "the Holy Spirit's book." What modern Lutheranism reads into Luther's utterances about the human side of the Scriptures is absolutely un-Lutheran. He had no theory about the "how" of the inspiration, but he has never doubted the dogma of the entire Church that the Holy Spirit is the divine author of the Scriptures.

The lack of an understanding of the Holy Spirit becomes obvious also in Wingren's understanding of the Church. He knows what the ministry of the Church is. What he says about that (pp. 96ff.), including his criticism of the apostolic succession (pp. 101ff.), belongs to the best parts of the book. But the idea that the Church must be "open," "without questions of membership being raised or . . . being answered" amounts to a glorification of the system of national churches and local parishes that today should have become suspect also to the Christians of Sweden. "The priest exists that the word and sacraments may move outwards. Out there in many parishes, in homes, in places of work the conflict between God and Satan is being decided. . . . Even the bishop himself exists, first of all, for the congregations. . . . Afterwards the consequences of all hidden decisions will follow. They follow in the church assembly or in parliament" (p. 189). But parliament decides, or rather the political powers behind parliament have decided, whether God's Word permits or forbids the ordination of women to the office of a pastor. And the church assembly follows suit. And suddenly the congregations are told that they must accept women as pastors. The decision has been made, definitely and irrevocably. This is the "open" church. Is it really Christ's Church? If Wingren should bring out in Sweden a new edition of his book, will this answer our question?

THE REUNION OF THE CHURCH. A DEFENSE OF THE SOUTH INDIA SCHEME [XXI:1]

By J. E. Lesslie Newbigin (S.C.M., London), 1960, pp. XXXVI and 192; 21/-.

The new edition of Bishop Newbigin's *Apologia pro ecclesia sua* will be welcomed by all who are engaged in the ecumenical and ecclesiological discussions of our day. It reveals the theological background of the much-debated union of South India and should be regarded as the most important supplement to the history of that union by B. Sundkler, (Church of South India, *The Movement toward Union, 1900–1947*, London, 1954). This second edition is a reprint of the book that was written when the union was being completed in 1947 and in view of the decision to be expected from Lambeth 1948, augmented by an introductionthat takes in account the development since 1947 (W.C.C., Lambeth, 1958, Church of South India). It was wise not to alter the old text, which in freshness, its keen argumentation, and its character as a personal confession is itself an important document of the origin of the C.S.I.

Since the book is known to our readers, we limit ourselves to the question, "How has the program of reunion it contains stood the test of the years since 1947?" It must be said that the theology, and especially the ecclesiology, underlying the scheme and presented in Newbigin's book has proved a sufficient basis for what may be called "home reunion on a mission field." What in England has thus far been impossible, has been achieved on the mission fields of South India, where the split between the Church of England and her dissenting daughters and again the differences between the various types of British Protestantism had created a situation in which the Christian mission as such was at stake. Deep sympathy with the Christians in India who suffered for divisions they had not caused but inherited from their missionaries and the serious desire that a child of so many prayers should not be lost have restrained many from criticizing the scheme and have caused the Church of England and the Lambeth Conference of 1948 to go to, and even beyond, the limits of what they could concede. Bishop Newbigin expresses his deep disappointment with the action of Lambeth 1958, "advising negotiators in West Africa to abandon the South India pattern and follow that of Ceylon" (p. XXVI). This action seems indeed to suggest "that the method of supplemental ordination is to be the basis for all future unions in which Anglicans are involved." It is hardly to be expected that the urgent plea to reconsider what amounts, however the rite may be called, to a second ordination will be heeded. Newbigin's argument is to us theologically correct, but it will be unacceptable to Anglicans with definite "Catholic" convictions.

Here the limitation of the unique and unrepeatable experiment of South India becomes manifest. The new church—one of the finest of the younger churches, as everyone knows who has met its representatives, studied its literature and taken part in its liturgy—belongs, seen from the point of view of the Church historian, to the "family of Reformed churches" in a broad sense: Reformed Evangelical without the distinctive doctrines of the classical Reformed confessions, spiritually shaped by the modem missionary and ecumenical movements and with strong Anglican elements in its liturgy and its constitution. While the life of this church justifies the union of the churches that have entered it, it must, on the other hand, be stated that this union is not and cannot be what the book tries to prove: "a valid attempt, within the conditions of a particular part of the world, to restore the visible unity of the Church" (p. 187). Newbigin's ecclesiology is an attempt to do justice to what to him seems to be the truth of Catholicism and the truth of the Reformation concerning the nature of the Church. Over against the Protestant understanding of the Church and its unity as something "spiritual" and therefore "invisible," he points out that in the New Testament "spiritual" and "bodily" belong together. Against the Catholic understanding of the Church as the extension of the Incarnation, the Church, which is at the same time "divine" and "human" like Christ, he emphasises the sinfulness of the Church, which is, like the individual Christian, holy and sinful simultaneously. No one can read the book without being impressed by the energy with which the author, an ecclesiologist in his own right, tries to build up a doctrine of the Church as the visible people of God and Body of Christ as determined by the doctrine of justification by faith. This emphasis on the *sola fide* is Newbigin's contributionto modern ecumenical theology, as it is the contribution of the C.S.I to the practical work of church union. And yet one has the impression that this doctrine of the Church cannot be the last word of the author himself and should not be taken as the basis of the work to be done by the International Missionary Council in its new connection with the W.C.C. In some passages lack of clarity seems to point to deeper mistakes. In rejecting the idea that the Church is the extension of the incarnation, the author states that "the Incarnation was an event, the crucial event, within this whole history. It had a beginning and an end. It was something done 'once' (1 Peter 3:18; Heb. 9:26–28), in the sense of 'once for all'" (p. 60). The incarnation had, of course, a beginning, but what should its end be? That Christ with his human nature was raised from the dead, ascended into heaven, and sitteth on the right hand of the Father: this distinguishes the true incarnation of the Son of God clearly from all imagined incarnations, as, for example, from the avataras of Hinduism. This example shows, by the way, how necessary it is for the younger churches that they preserve the clear theology of the creeds and how dangerous the "reasonable liberty of interpretation" is that the CHX allows and that is defended in this book (p. 124ff.). We have certainly to understand the confessional obligation in an evangelical way. But we should not forget that without the "*conceptus de Spiritu Sancto, natus ex Maria virgine*" and without the empty grave out of which Christ was bodily raised, the Christian faith loses its meaning. Another case in point is the strange treatment of the classical doctrines of justification. "In what sense can God accept men as righteous? Is it because they are already righteous, or being made righteous, as Catholic theologians teach? Or is it because God 'imputes' to them, in his mercy, a righteousness which they do not in fact possess, as some Protestant theologians teach?" (p. 86). This is what the reformers (e.g., Calvin, Inst, m, II) and all confessions of the Reformation from Conf. Aug. IV to Westminster Conf. XI teach on the basis of the New Testament.

This raises the question of whether it is possible to preserve the historic faith of the Church while dispensing with the historic creeds and confessions in such a way as it is done by Bishop Newbigin and the C.S.I. Even where the Church confesses today, it cannot ignore that which the fathers have confessed, for example, concerning the Sacraments. Maybe the present generation will not accept their faith. In that case we must confess our faith in a new confession. But this can be properly done only if we are clear about what the Church before us has taught and why we must retain or reject it. Otherwise the continuity of the Church is destroyed and the consensus that binds together the generations of the Church is replaced by the short-living consensus of those who at a given moment constitute the Church in a given area. The result is not a "reunited" church, but a variety of union churches with different bases replacing the old denominations with their confessions. Bishop Newbigin has already to defend the scheme of South India against those who recommend the schemes of Ceylon or of North India as the better ones, though he does so in a spirit of open-minded brotherliness and ecumenicity. But is present-day Christendom not in danger of repeating on a worldwide scale the mistake German Protestantism made in the nineteenth century, when in various territories the Lutheran and the Reformed Church were united with the result that within a few decades there arose, side by side with the old confessional churches, seven United churches that up to this day nobody has been able to unite in one faith? Who will unite the united churches of India, Ceylon, Africa, Canada, U.S.A., and soon perhaps Australia and New Zealand? Should this tragic situation not cause us all to examine the axioms that underlie our ecumenical endeavors? Is it God's will that all who call themselves Christians should recognize each other and their views, or are there heresies that have no room in the Church? Is the outward ecclesiastical organization the Body of Christ? Is organic union the only way in which Christian unity can express itself? There is perhaps no other book that makes these questions more urgent than Bishop Newbigin's confession.

PETRUS: JUENGER, APOSTLE, MAERTYRER [XXI:2]

Das historische und das theologische Petrusproblem. Zweite ungearbeitete und ergelnzte Auflage. By Oscar Cullman (Zwingli Verlag, Ztirich-Stuttgart), 1960, p. 287; 24 Swiss Fr. [English translation by Floyd V. Filson: *Peter: Disciple, Apostle, Martyr.* (S.C.M., London), 1962, p. 252. 25/*]

What Professor McCaughey [attached below] has written in this review (Vol. xiii, No. 1, pp. 21f.) on the English version (1953) of Cullmann's important book on Peter (1952) is valid also for this revised edition and need not be repeated here. The old text is almost entirely preserved. The revisions are limited to a brief discussion of new literature and new archaeological material (e.g., the proof that the cult of Peter and Paul in the catacomb of San Sebastiano goes actually back to the year 258) and to clarifications (e.g., the enlarged discussion of the relationship between Matt. 16:17ff.; Luke 22:31f; and John 21:15ff. in the chapter on the narrative framework of Matt. 16). Since Cullman in the preface makes the complaint that the reviewers, preoccupied with the theological problem of Matthew 16, have failed to deal sufficiently with the historical chapters, we concentrate on the problems presented by this book to the Church historian, though space does not allow to do justice to the amazing amount of information and investigation embodied in these chapters.

On the basis of a thorough examination of the entire literary (New Testament, apostolic fathers, patristic literature, apocryphal acts of apostles, etc.), liturgical (*"Depositio martyrum,"* *"Catalogus Liberianus,"* etc., with reference to the feasts of January 18, February 22, and June 29) and archaeological (catacombs, excavations at St. Peter) sources, Cullmann arrives at the following results. Already in the earthly days of Jesus, Simon Peter held a unique position in the circle of the disciples as the spokesman and representative of the Twelve. This pre-eminence of Peter cannot be explained as a predating of the position he held in the Primitive Church. Jesus himself had given him the name *"Kepha."* Peter was the first to see the Risen Lord. He was the leader of the Primitive Church in Jerusalem until after the martyrdom of James the brother of John, and at his own imprisonment, the leadership passed over to James the brother of the Lord, while Peter became the leader of the mission to the Jewish diaspora, as Paul was recognised as the apostle of the Gentiles. Much more broad-minded than James, he was nearer to Paul not only in his attitude toward the converts from the Gentiles, but also in his theology. He was a theologian in his own right: the first witness of the resurrection was also the first interpreter of the death of Christ as that of the Servant of God (*"pais theou"*). At the Apostles' Council he, like Paul, appears to be subordinate to James. In his later years he came to Rome and died there as a martyr, after a very short work, under Nero. His grave cannot be identified. "The excavations speak in favor of the report that the execution of Peter took place in the Vatican district" (English Translation p. 152).

This last statement is Cullmann's answer to the great problem that has occupied Church historians since Lietzmann in "Peter and Paul in Rome" (1915) on the basis of thorough historical and liturgiological studies came to the conclusion that the graves of Peter and Paul in St. Peter in the Vatican and St. Paul outside the walls off the road to Ostia are genuine. On June 29, 258, during the persecution of Valerian, he maintained, the remnants of the two Roman martyr-apostles were transferred into the catacomb at St. Sebastian, from where Constantine brought them back to the original burial places on which he built the famous basilicas. Lietzmann's ingenious reconstruction of that chapter of Church history could be corroborated only by excavations under the churches. What the excavations at St. Peter, which began in 1939, have revealed needs still a definite interpretation. Pius XII's enthusiastic announcement that the grave of Peter had been found and with it proof the Christ wanted the government of his Church transferred from Jerusalem to Rome was an overstatement in every respect. Even Catholic scholars have expressed doubts as to whether the discoveries permit to speak of Peter's grave. Cullmann gives a report of the discussions, which have been going on at a very high scientific level and without any prejudice on the part of the archaeologists. His own well-balanced judgment is perhaps too negative. What seems to have been found is the "*tropaion*" of Peter, which together with the corresponding "*tropaion*" of Paul at the Via Ostiensis was mentioned by a Roman writer around A.D. 200 as an argument against the Church of Asia, which proved its apostolicity from the graves of great Christian leaders in Asia. Eusebius understood the word "*tropaion*" as referring to the graves of the apostles, but it could refer to the places of execution. A definite verdict could be reached only by excavations at St. Paul. Cullmann's careful evaluation of the facts shows that the witness of mute monuments has natural limitations. Our literary sources prove sufficiently the reliability of the tradition of the martyrdom of Peter and Paul in Rome.

The most important problem of the book is the nature of the "primacy" of Peter. On the whole we can agree with Cullmann's interpretation, especially with the statement that the New Testament does not know of the perpetuation of this primacy in an individual bishop of any local church. Some historical questions, however, seem to need further investigation. In what sense is Simon "primus," the first, "who is called Peter" (Matt. 10:2)? If he exercises a jurisdiction, as every apostle does (Acts 5:1ff. comp. 1 Cor. 5:1ff.) as shepherd of his flock who has to give account to the chief Shepherd (1 Peter 5:4), this jurisdiction does never extend over another apostle. It seems to be significant that in the circle of the Twelve time and again the question is raised, "which of them should be accounted the greatest" (Luke 22:24) and that each time Jesus rejects such hierarchic claims among those whom he appoints judges or rulers in his kingdom (v. 30). It is worthwhile to consider the structure of the whole body of Jesus' disciples. There is a wider circle of the Seventy around the circle of the Twelve, the apostles in the proper sense and again a narrower circle of three within the Twelve, comprising the "first," *Kepha*, and the sons of Zebedee, John and James, who also receive a surname from Jesus. These three accompany the Master at special great events, as the Transfiguration and Gethsemane.

Are they the first stage of what later was the college of the "*styloi*" in Jerusalem, James the brother of the Lord, Peter, and John? At least John accompanies Peter in Acts on very important occasions, as the journey to Samaria. This leads to the important question of the relationship of Peter and John in the Fourth Gospel. If it foreshadows the relationship between the churches of Rome and Asia, how was the primacy of Peter understood in the Church of the East? Perhaps one may say that the riddle of the primacy of Peter will not be solved before the greatest of the riddles of the New Testament has found an answer: the origin of St. John's Gospel. To us who are accustomed to find in the Synoptics the Gospel proper to which the Fourth Gospel gives a commentary, it seems strange that John's has always been regarded in the Church as the main Gospel. This will never be understood unless we learn to take seriously its claim to be inspired by the Paraclete, the Spirit of Truth, whose witness supplements and interprets the witness of the apostles (John 15:26f.; 16:12ff). Another riddle is the position of James the brother of the Lord as head of the Church to which Cullmann has called our attention. When the apostles left the earthly Jerusalem to call the Jewish diaspora and the Gentiles to the heavenly Jerusalem, "which is the mother of us all," the church that thus far had been "mother and head of all churches" lost its original importance. We shall probably never know what caused, with the accession of James as its first bishop, that strange development that led to what has been called the beginnings of a Christian "caliphate," relatives of Jesus becoming the leaders. Eusebius is not right when he thinks of the house in which they were educated. It is an oriental idea that the spirit is bound up with the blood, the office with the family. Still in the later church of Eastern Syria, it was the rule that the Katholikos (Patriarch) was succeeded by a nephew.

A last question may be raised. The historian must ask whether the modem approach to the texts of the Gospels in the "*Formgeschichte*" does really justice to their contents. There is, of course, a truth in this method. But its danger is the atomization of the Gospel and an arbitrary construction of an alleged history. Cullmann accepts as historical the confession of Peter and the answer of Jesus in Matthew 16. But he distinguishes between the event of Caesarea Philippi, which is historical only as far as it corresponds to Mark, and a later event. The confession that Jesus is not only the Messiah, but also the Son of God, and the answer in Matthew 16:17ff. belongs to another occasion that Cullmann finds, on account of an inner relationship between Matthew 16:17ff.; Luke 22:31ff.; and John 6:66ff; 21:15ff. in the Last Supper. This duplication of the confession of Peter is a mere hypothesis that robs it of its meaning. For what is the confession that Jesus is the Messiah if it does not imply that he is the Son of God? That Matthew 16:17ff and Luke 22:32 are two parallel sayings belonging closely together and yet each having its own meaning, has lately been shown by I. Salaverri in a structural analysis that owes much to Cullmann's book (*Sacrae Theologiae Summa*, Madrid, 1958, Vol. I, pp. 573 and 703) and is instructive even to him who does not find in Luke 22 the doctrine of infallibility. The deeper reason for Cullman's construction seems to be the difficulty of explaining why Mark has left out what Matthew has preserved. Should it be an intentional omission, one of those omissions we find with regret in so many passages of the New Testament, the greatest of which is the omission of the first appearance of the Risen Lord to Peter? There is no lost end of the Gospel of Mark. That greatest event in the life of Peter and in the history of the First Church is mentioned as a fact. It is reflected, or anticipated, in narratives like Matthew 14:22 and the parallels, Luke 5:1ff. and John 21:1ff. But this climax in the life of Peter is not told. Why not? Maybe he who gave us the New Testament did not want us to believe in saints, to search for their tombs, and to venerate them, but to believe in the Holy One, as Peter calls him (John 6:69), who the third day rose from the dead according to the Scriptures.

One last question: Should not we all give up the way of speech that seems to become a habit among us when reading even in a book like this of the "Incarnate One" in the sense of "Christ in his earthly days" in contrast to the "Risen One." We must distinguish between "after the flesh" and "incarnate." Also the Risen and Exalted Lord does not cease to be the Incarnate. In this all churches agree: *Quod semel assumpsit, numquam deposuit.*

PETER: DISCIPLE, APOSTLE, MARTYR.
By Oscar Cullmann (S.C.M.), 1953, pp. 252; 18/-.

This latest work of Cullmann to appear in an English edition consists of a lengthy historical study of 150 pages, followed by 80 pages on the exegetical and theological questions involved in the discussion. Part I—the historical section—contains three chapters in which the author, using the techniques of historical enquiry, asks what can be surely known or properly inferred about Peter as a disciple of Jesus, as apostle in the Primitive Church and as martyr. The sources of our knowledge of Peter as disciple and apostle are the documents of the New Testament. Our information about his residence in Rome and his martyrdom depends on traditions preserved in later literary sources, though his martyrdom is at least hinted at in certain N.T. passages. Cullmann examines all these documents again and places beside them the evidence of liturgical sources and of recent excavations in Rome—this last not the least interesting and informative section of the book.

Throughout, Cullmann's conclusions are very much more positive than Protestant scholars have sometimes allowed themselves to be about the significant role played by Peter among the disciples and apostles and about his stay in Rome and his martyrdom there. His representative position in the circle of the disciples, articulating their hopes and fears; his leadership of the Primitive Church in Jerusalem, derived as it was from the double commission at the hands of the Incarnate and the Risen Lord; his subsequent handing-over of the leadership to James in order that he (Peter) might lead the Jewish Christian mission; the assertion that Peter stood much closer to Paul theologically than did other members of the Jerusalem Church mission: all this and much more, as described by Cullmann, will cause many readers to revise their understanding of authority within and of the developing mission of the Early Church. The last ghosts of Tuebingen seem to have been laid.

Having cleared the ground by minute and careful historical enquiry, Cullman begins his theological section (Part II of the book) with a careful exegesis of Matthew 16:17–19. Here he can agree neither with the more radical modern critics who deny the genuineness of the saying, nor with the reformers and their modern counterparts who see in Jesus' saying little more than the declaration that it is on faith such as Peter's that Christ's Church it to be built. The saying is genuine but (suggests Cullmann, making a positive use of form-critical methods) misplaced: his own suggestion is that it belongs to the dialogue found in a Passion context at Luke 22:31ff.; it was found by Matthew as an isolated fragment in his independent source and incorporated by a characteristic Matthaean method into the story of the confession of Peter at Caesarea Philippi. But be that as it may, the saying refers to Peter as a person, to his personal pre-eminence among the apostles. This pre-eminence was confirmed by the fact that he was the first to whom the risen Lord appeared. He was to assume the leadership of the post-Ascension Church. On the foundation (in terms of chronology as well as faith) of the apostles and of this apostle in particular is built the faith and life of the whole Church from then until now.

Readers of Cullmann's "Christ and Time" will not be surprised to find in his final doctrinal chapter a distinction between the one-for-all element in Peter's apostolic commission (what belongs to the mid-point of time) and what belongs to the Church of subsequent generations, and of the relation between the two. This chapter defines in a fresh way the theological grounds for controversy between the reformed theologian and the upholders of Roman Catholic claims. Indeed one of the two most interesting things about this book as a whole is the tone of friendly controversy in which it is written. One can believe that the hope expressed by the author in his foreword, that his frank statements will be welcomed by his Roman Catholic friends and fellow-theologians, has been fulfilled. We must be grateful that the best writing on this as on so many other theological subjects is in our day no longer polemical. The other fascinating matter raised by this book is the relation between a historical and a theological question. There is no simple way of defining this relation, but in this book Cullmann has once more (in company with many other leading biblical theologians of our day) shown that many of our problems arise from confusions and unexamined assumptions about the nature of the two activities and the relation between them. Whether Cullmann's own implied redefinition is entirely satisfactory is a question requiring further consideration.

The book is lucidly written and, even when the method of presentation leads to some repetition, is always readable. The copious footnotes and many sections of the text give us cross-references to other recent work, continental European, British, and (to a lesser extent) American—though some Anglicans may demur at the use of the definite article in the sentence: "The Anglican standpoint (on apostolic succession) is represented by K. E. Kirk, *The Apostolic Ministry*, 1945, especially the essay by G. Dix, 'The Ministry in the Early Church.'"

J. D. McCAUGHEY.

KARL BARTH'S DOCTRINE OF HOLY SCRIPTURE [XXI:3]

By Klaas Runia (William B. Eerdmans Publishing Company, Grand Rapids, Michigan), 1962, pp. 225; $4.00.

It is the historic significance of Karl Barth that he with prophetic power has called back Christendom to the *sola scriptura* of the Reformation. His tragedy is that of many a great man who has shown to others a goal he himself has not been able to reach. Barth has never reached a full understanding of Holy Writ as the Word of God as the reformers understand it. This is what the reader of this penetrating study of Barth's doctrine of Holy Scripture feels. The author is theologically and, what in this case is of special importance, linguistically fully equipped for his task. He knows the entire oeuvre of Barth and approaches the thoughts of the greatest theologian of our age respectfully and sympathetically even there where he cannot agree with them. In the concluding chapter, "Basic Motifs," he discusses briefly the astonishing development of Barth's theology since the first volume of his *Kirchliche Dogmatik* (1932). "All changes that are found in Barth's thinking are related to the increasing concentration of all his theology upon christology" (p. 209). The question of whether the stronger emphasis on the objective work of Christ (which leads to consequences reminding of the old Swiss anti-Calvinist theologian Huber and is bordering on Universalism, as E. Brunner thinks) contradicts and eliminates the former emphasis of the freedom of God's grace is answered in the negative. And this is most certainly true of Barth's doctrine of Scripture, which is elaborately and with great precision discussed under the headings, "Scripture as a Witness to Divine

591

Revelation," "The Humanity and Fallibility of the Bible," "'Proofs' of the Fallibility of the Bible," "The Bible as the Word of God, "Inspiration or Theopneustia," "The Authority of the Bible." The author listens very attentively to, and accepts to a large degree, Barth's criticism of orthodoxy, which made the same mistake, though in a different manner, as liberalism made, in trying to control the divine revelation, forgetting that God's revelation is God himself (p. 3 comp. 164). All the more convincing is Dr. Runia's irrefutable proof that Barth's understanding of God's revelation as always being an event is untenable because it contradicts the Bible. "The witness of the prophets and the apostles, that is in concrete, the Bible, does not only constitute the area or sphere where the divine revelation may take place, but this witness itself is included in the revelation, belongs to it, is revelation" (p. 47). Overwhelming evidence from all strata of the New Testament is adduced to show that for Jesus and the apostles and the earliest Church, the Bible is the Word of God. Barth's view that it is called the Word of God because it can become the Word of God "where and when it pleases God," from time to time, just as the water of the pool of Siloah became powerful from time to time, is not the view of Scripture itself. (May it be added here that the famous "*ubi et quando visum est Deo*" Barth takes from the Augsburg Confession, Art. V has there a totally different meaning: "Through the word and the sacraments, as through instruments, the Holy Spirit is given, and the Holy Spirit produces faith, where and when it pleases God, in those who hear the gospel." Where the Word of God is, there is the Holy Spirit. The "*ubi et quando*" limits not the Spirit, but the effect of the Spirit. Barth understands it as meaning that the Holy Spirit is given where and when it pleases God.) Great and new over against the theology of the preceding generations was Barth's rejection of what the author calls the "horizontal" (static) dualism that distinguished between divine and human words in the Bible. "Barth maintains that all biblical passages are fundamentally the same" (p. 123). He replaces it by a "vertical" (dynamic) dualism, the fundamental separation between man's word and God's Word: "The first can become the medium for the latter, but as such and in itself it is not God's word. Runia points out the consequence of such dualism: the lack of understanding for the continuity of the faith of the Christian. ("Does the hearing of God's word not become an endless dotted line with Barth?" p. 127.) He could have added the consequences for the church that loses its continuity and becomes an endless dotted line of "events." Barth has been asked by some of his best friends whether his actualistic understanding of the Word of God, his dualistic separation of the divine and the human word must not eventually lead into that enthusiastic understanding of the Church against which Luther and Calvin had to fight. What is the church, where is the church whose *Church Dogmatics* K. Barth wrote? Is it accidental that Barth does not know the continuity of the confession that is important not only to Lutherans, as he seems to think, but also to all conservative Reformed churches?

The consequences of Barth's basic understanding of revelation as an act of God's freedom for the problems of the infallibility, the inspiration, and the authority of the Bible are thoroughly discussed. Barth's assumption that the Bible as human word must be fallible is rejected. Runia points out that Barth has failed to give any concrete example of the alleged fallibility of the Bible even as to its religious and theological contents. "It is noteworthy that in the eleven volumes of *Church Dogmatics*, so far published, we hardly find any instance of actual criticism" (p. 105). But even where Barth finds a false view of the world or historical errors he does not see the difference between false doctrines and necessary human limitations that do not abolish the truth of what the writer intended to relate. Deeper than what Barth says about the fallibility of the Bible is his doctrine of inspiration where he tries to reconstruct the classical doctrine by adding to the "theopneustia" of the authors "a second moment in the event of inspiration, namely when the books are read and heard" (p. 138). The necessity of the operation of the Holy Spirit for our understanding of the Scriptures must be recognized, as it has been recognized by the reformers. But this 'Illumination" should be distinguished from the "inspiration" that makes the Scriptures the Word of God. Tiff's well-written book is one of the most important works on Barth's theology. At the same time, it is the contribution by an independent theological scholar toward a solution of the great problem of the doctrine of Holy Scripture, which today occupies all Christendom. A new generation of the Reformed Church that confesses the doctrine of the Church faithfully and without narrowness begins to speak in this book. May it succeed in answering the questions Barth was unable to answer. Some problems may be mentioned briefly that need reconsideration if the work is to go on successfully. What is the canon of Holy Scripture, and what does the distinction made by the reformers between protocanonical and deuterocanonical books in the New Testament mean? How do we justify, if we can do it, our use of the word "revelation," which is clearly distinct from the usage of the New Testament, where *apokalyptein* and *phaneroon* are not used for what we call "revelation of God"? The Church can certainly introduce theological terms not found in the language of the Scriptures, but only if the doctrine of the Bible is fully preserved. In any case we should not take it for granted that the medieval term *revelatio* does really illuminate the biblical "Word of God."

THE DOCTRINE OF FAITH IN
THE REIGN OF HENRY VIII [XXII:1]
By David Broughton Knox (James Clarke, London), 1961, pp. XI and 294; 18/6.

This highly informative book gives a history of the doctrine of the justification by faith in the early period of the English Reformation. The first chapters are dedicated to the theology of Tyndale and his contemporaries (W. Roye, S. Fish, J. Frith, G. Joye, R. Barnes, Coverdale). They give an impressive picture of the consensus concerning the fundamental doctrine of the Reformation as well as of the individual character of each of these men. Chapter III deals with "English Precursors" of the doctrine (evangelical elements in medieval orthodoxy, especially in pastoral and devotional literature), the Lollards representing the religious movement that stemmed from Wycliffe and "still had a vigourous though undistinguished life in England at the eve of the Reformation" (p. 89); the mystic Julian of Norwich, Colet who "was not afraid of the phrase 'faith only,'" understood faith in a fiduciary sense and taught total depravity and total predestination; Erasmus and Bilney who had learned the doctrine of grace "not from Luther but from the Scriptures and no doubt also from the religious ideas of the Lollards" (p. 107). Chapter IV deals with the opposition (Henry Vm, Fisher, Whitford, Rastell, Barlow, More). Chapters V and VI deal with the "Acceptance of the Doctrine in the Church of England," culminating in the Ten Articles and with its "Consolidation," especially in the religious literature of 1534–40. Chapter VII describes the "Renewed Controversy" after the burning of Barnes, Garrett, and Jerome. It is followed by a brief chapter on "The New Reign." The modest title does not betray the full content of the book. Since the doctrine of justification is not an isolated chapter but the heart of the Reformation, other doctrines are repeatedly touched upon, such as the Sacraments. So it becomes in some chapters a history of English evangelical theology in the tragic era of Henry VIII. This theology could not find the perfection it would have reached under more favorable political conditions. Broken reeds and unfinished lives are the mark of this period. The limitations of the book are the limitations of present-day Reformation research. The author has proved his thesis that the Edwardian reform was due to the work of the early English reformers and that the foreign refugees have played a secondary role. The actual relationship between the continental influences and original English thought remains to be investigated. A comparison between Luther's and Tyndale's prefaces shows that the English reformer kept his independence in important points. The author gives some examples. The influence of Oecolampadius and Bucer in the earliest period is still to be investigated. This book should be carefully studied by the theologians and historians on the continent as an important contribution to the history of the Reformation as an event in the whole of Western Christendom.

REFORMATION STUDIES
SIXTEEN ESSAYS IN HONOR OF
ROLAND H. BAINTON [XXII:1]

Edited by Franklin H. Littell with a Biographical
Appreciation by Georgia Harkness. (John Knox
Press, Richmond, Va.) 1962, pp. 285; $5.50.

Seventeen of the former doctoral students of Professor Roland H.
Bainton have joined forces to produce this remarkable Festschrift in
honor of their beloved teacher. A biographical appreciation by Georgia Harkness draws a vivid picture of the charming personality, the
great scholar, and the conscientious and inspiring teacher Bainton,
whose name will forever be connected with Yale Divinity School
where he taught Church history for forty years. Bainton was born in
1894 as son of a Congregational minister in England, who migrated
in 1898 to Canada and later to the United States. Himself a Congregational minister, Bainton became, as a convinced pacifist, an affiliated
member of the Society of Friends. With this background in the two
most American of all American churches, he became one of the most
outstanding scholars in the field of Reformation research of our age,
recognized as such on both sides of the Atlantic. That a man of his
religious convictions to which Luther was stronger opposed than to
Rome could write one of the best biographies of Luther shows his
greatness as historian. His main interest, however, was focussed in the
"Left-wing Reformation," which, more or less suppressed in Europe,
has become a world power in American Protestantism.

It is not possible to evaluate or even to enumerate the contributions to this rich book. They deal with problems of the theology of

Luther (Bendtz, Robert Fisher, Hovland, J. von Rohr, Toth) and Calvin (Kuizenga, Leith), with "Other Men and Movements" (Brush on Lefevre d'Etaples); Krumm on "Continental Protestantism and Elizabethan Anglicanism," which sheds new light on the church history of England, as also Norwood's interesting article on "The Strangers' 'Model Churches' in Sixteenth Century England" does; Manschreck on "Reason and Conversion in the Thought of Melanchthon," while Littell's "New Light on Butzer's Significance" is of great importance because it gives a translation of Butzer's "Disputation with the Anabaptists at Marburg, 1538." The last part of the essays deals with the "Left Wing of the Reformation" (Schwab, Wray, Zuck) with a most illuminating and timely article by Walso Beach on the problem of religious freedom and toleration in America, "Sectarianism and Skepticism." This book, in the diversity of topics and in the scholarship with which they are treated, reflects the greatness of Roland Bainton as founder of a historical school. A bibliography of his writings on the Reformation period is added. This work should have a place in any theology library.

THE WORD OF GOD ACCORDING TO ST. AUGUSTINE [XXII:2]

By A. D. R. Polman (Hodder and Stoughton, London), 1961, pp. 242; 52/- Aust.

This book fills a real gap in the vast literature on the great Church father whose theology plays still a fundamental role in all Western churches: Catholic, Lutheran, and Reformed. In view of the many investigations of Augustine's doctrine of the Sacraments, it was necessary to write a thorough examination of his doctrine of the Word of God. The author, professor at the John Calvin Academy at Kampen, Holland, was well equipped for this task. His book appeared in Dutch at Kampen, 1955. For this English edition, which is a very good translation by A. J. Pomerans, he has rewritten one of the chapters.

Chapter I, "The Word of God—Christ," describes the development of Augustine's doctrine of Christ as the Logos from a first stage in which under Neo-Platonic influence Christ is understood as precept and example to a stage where the deeper understanding of the Scriptures leads to a doctrine of Christ, the Logos, as Savior. Chapter II, "The Word of God as Holy Scripture," discusses the fact, nature, extent and effect of inspiration, and the divine authority, perspicuity, sufficiency, and necessity of Scripture. Chapter III, "The Word of God as the Word of Christ," shows how Augustine developed his Christocentric view of the Scriptures against the Manichaeans, Jews, and Pelagians, and discusses such problems as "Christ in the Old Testament" and the relationship between the two Testaments. Chapter IV, "The Word of God as Proclamation," gives Augustine's theology of preaching, a highly informative presentation that shows the actuality of Augustine's theology. In Chapter V, "The Word of God and the Church," we have a clear and convincing discussion of the true relationship between the two great authorities in Augustine's thought. Two smaller chapters—VI, "The Word of God and Spiritual Life of the Individual," and VII, "The Word of God without Holy Scripture" (when Holy Scripture has fulfilled its task)—conclude the book, which combines deep scholarship with a very clear and interesting presentation. We cannot discuss the rich content, especially of chapters III and IV, but must limit ourselves to two remarks. Chapter II gives a good presentation of Augustine's doctrine on Holy Scripture, but it does not go into the question of the sources of this doctrine. Otherwise the limitations of Augustine's view of inspiration would have become clear. The problem of why Augustine regarded the Septuagint as inspired has been touched upon but should be examined further. His view of prophecy does not do justice to the Bible. His failure to understand the inspiration of Holy Scripture from the doctrine of the Holy Spirit, the Paraclete, has been fateful for the later Church, which has canonized his view in a tradition that has even determined the classical doctrine of the churches of the Reformation. Polman's material should lead to a closer examination of the background of Augustine's doctrine of the Scriptures. Chapter V should be helpful in rejecting the claims by Roman theologians who read the modem dogma into Augustine, but it should also be of great importance in present-day discussions in our circles on the nature of the Church and the relationship between the Word of God and the Church. "Questions as to whether the Church is superior, equal or inferior to the Scriptures were never even raised by St. Augustine. Both work in harmony. The words of God are entrusted to the Church, so that from her hands we may safely receive the divine books and submit to their authority" (p. 207). Most Protestant churches are at present leaving the study of the fathers to the Roman Church—with detrimental effects. This book, which requires no Latin from the reader, could help us to realize what the fathers can and must mean to us, even in the practical ministry. It is a gift worthy of the great tradition of the theological school of Calvin.

MUT ZUR KATHOLIZITAET [XXII:2]

Geistliche und theologische Erwagungen zur Einigung der Christen. By Thomas Sartory, O.S.B. (Salzburg, Otto Muller Yerlag), 1962, pp. 475; 89 sh. Austrian.

Professor Thomas Sartory, O.S.B., Salzburg, is one of the outstanding theologians of Austria, one of the leaders of the young ecumenical movement in the Catholic Church of the German-speaking countries. He is editor of a series, "Oekumenisches Gesprach," in which the present book has appeared. It contains "spiritual and theological considerations with regard to Christian unity," arranged in three main parts: "Access to the Father," "Apprehended of Christ" (Phil. 3:12), and "The Spirit Who Unites." One of the chapters, "The Manifold Grace of Christ" contains a personal confession by a Greek theologian (A. Theodorou, Athens), "Why I am Orthodox" and a letter by an old-Catholic priest, "The Task of the Old-Catholic Church." The Benedictine tradition of the author finds a wonderful expression in the chapter "Monasticism in the Midst of the World" with an appreciation of the brethren of Taiz—whose rule is quoted—and comments on the Rule of St. Benedict. The book, obviously based on essays and talks of some years, is pervaded by a genuine biblical theology, deeply influenced by the work of Protestant scholarship. The chapter "The Mother Who Separates Us" deals with the problems of Mariology, calling the Protestant theologians who deny the virgin birth back to the authority of Scripture and to the Mariology of Luther, which, however, he does not fully understand. The chapter "Unity in the Truth" discusses *inter alia* the biblical concept of truth in comparison with the philosophical concept. The problem of the formulation of the dogma is discussed with reference to Karl Bahner's investigation of the formula of Chalcedon.

This must suffice to indicate the rich content of the work. What interests us here is the spirit in which the book is written. The new Catholic theology finds a different expression in the various countries. German-speaking Catholicism is at present very close to the modern French theology, while Catholicism in the English-speaking world (Leeming, Weigel), though fully sharing the ideals, seems more occupied with practical solutions than with the theological reform that must precede any practical steps. What is most impressive in Sartory's book is the awareness of the difficulties. His interpretation of John 17 is much deeper than Küng's understanding of "That the World May Believe," which obviously makes an impression on Americans but is theologically untenable. What will happen if "*la tristesse ecumenique*," which we have experienced in the Protestant churches, follows the present optimism? For there is no possibility of a doctrinal agreement between those who confess the *Professio Fidei Tridentina* and the confessors of the doctrines of the Reformation. What is possible is a new Christian relationship between both sides and a deeper mutual understanding. It is the theology of men like Sartory that then will survive, a theology prepared to learn from "separated brethren" is not satisfied with quick results. "Here is the patience and the faith of the Saints." This must be the watchword of all true ecumenical work. And we all have to learn that the goal of all Church history is in heaven and not on earth.

THE HARVEST OF MEDIEVAL THEOLOGY
[XXII:3]

Gabriel Biel and Late Medieval Nominalism, by Heiko Augustinus Obermann. The Robert Troup Paine Prize-Treatise for the year 1962 (Harvard University Press, Cambridge, Mass., distributed in Great Britain by Oxford University Press, London), 1963, pp. XV, 459; $9.25.

It is certainly not accidental that the period of transition from the Middle Ages to the Reformation is attracting so many Dutch scholars as the Netherlands late medieval piety reached its climax. The Netherlands are the homeland of that Christian humanism that has helped to shape the Reformed churches of Western Europe as well as the Catholic Reformation of Trent. In the spirit of this tradition, the recent book has been written. Meticulous historical research, the broad horizon of great historiography and penetrating elucidation of difficult philosophical and theological problems, make it one of the outstanding works in the field of the history of Christian thought. It gives not only an analysis and historical investigation of the thought of "the last scholastic," who died in 1495, but finds in him a vantage point from which to look at the great problem of the relationship between late medieval theology and the Reformation. The title itself contains a program. "The Harvest of Medieval Theology" suggests that the late medieval Nominalism must not be seen as a theology of decay, but as a legitimate product of medieval thought, the last fruit of the Middle Ages, closely connected with the achievements of this colorful period in other fields. Biel, born at Speyer, preacher at the cathedral of Mainz, later professor at Tubingen, was a member of the Brethren of the Common Life, a representative of the *Devotio Modema*, as theologian not an innovator, but a man of astonishing knowledge of the older medieval theology, a faithful, though never radical, adherent of the Via Moderna of Occamism. He has influenced Luther indirectly through Usingen in Erfurt and directly through his writings, especially the exposition of the Canon Missae that Luther studied in preparation for his ordination. From Melanchthon we know that Luther even in later years could quote Biel (and Peter d'Ailli) extensively from memory. However, this influence is not investigated in the present book, which (it is scheduled to appear still in 1963 at Zürich-Zollikon in German) is only one of three volumes that will come out under the general title "Scholastik und Reformation." The scope of the present volume is to analyze the thought of Gabriel Biel as one of the key figures of the fifteenth century against the background of the Middle Ages and thus to shed light on a period of the history of Christian thought that has been neglected as hardly any other period.

The reason for this neglect is not only the deplorable fact that the sources are for the average scholar inaccessible, either very old and rare prints or still unprinted. Only by and by do new editions appear, as, such as a new edition of Biel's *Expositio Canonis Missae* in four volumes, edited by Obermann and Courtenay. The deeper reason was the lack of interest in a period that for the churches of the Reformation was the darkest age of theology and which even Roman Catholic theology regarded as defection from the great normative schools of the thirteenth century. The consequence of this neglect was the inability of Protestant and Catholic scholars to reach a balanced judgment on the relationship between the Middle Ages and the Reformation. The dialogue that is going on between the Christian churches in our time has greatly encouraged the historical investigation of the late Middle Ages, and it is to be expected that the work of the historians will greatly benefit the churches in their attempts to reach a better mutual understanding. Hence the work by Obermann must be regarded as a most timely one.

It is impossible to give a report of the rich content of this book that deals with all questions of medieval theology and always in such a way that Biel's doctrine is seen in the great context of the whole of medieval thought, including the early schoolmen like Anselm and the great representatives of high scholasticism. Since the presentation of Biel is always substantiated in the footnotes by quotations from the original writings, the reader gets firsthand information about Biel that is otherwise not available. Chapter 1 gives a biography with a discussion of the literary problems. A touching "Letter to the Church at Mainz under Interdict" (1462), in which Biel warns against the reception of the Sacraments from schismatic priests, reveals not only the Catholic piety of Gabriel, but also his view of the Church and the papacy. Chapter II, "Prolegomena," discusses the basic concepts of nominalistic theology, such as God's *potentia absoluta* and *ordinata*, the natural knowledge of God, the meaning of *"ex puris naturalisms"* —an especially illuminating discussion of "the state of pure nature" and "nature and grace." The following chapters deal with "Faith and Understanding," "Natural Law as Divine Order" (with a discussion of "Law and Gospel"), "Man Fallen and Redeemed" (the doctrine of sin, the disposition for justification), "The Process of Justification," "The Riddle of Predestination," "Christ and the Eucharist" (including a discussion of the "two offerings," the cross and the altar, which shows that Biel has understood the sacrifice of the Eucharist as *"repraesentatio"* of the sacrifice of the cross), "Mariology," "Nominalistic Mysticism," and "Holy Writ and Holy Church."

Could we enter into a discussion with Obermann, we should have to ask whether he does full justice to the fact that for the Catholic churches, Eastern and Western, Chalcedon is not the end of the Christological development because to them the interpretation of the Chalcedonense by the Fifth Ecumenical Council is normative. Also the Lutheran Reformation did not regard Chalcedon as the last word but understood that great council in the light of Constantinople II, of Cyril and John of Damask. It is perhaps significant that the problem of Mary as the Mother of God is hardly touched, not even in the chapter on Mariology. We mention this only because it will be an important issue when Obermann in the next volumes comes to grips with the Christological problems of the Reformation. Of highest significance is the chapter on "Holy Writ and Holy Church." Obermann thinks rightly that Geiselmann's interpretation of the decree of Trent in the sense of the "one source theory" is historically untenable. He does not accept Tavard's assumption that there has been "a classical

principle of coinherence of Scripture and Church" which disintegrated in the fourteenth century. What Obermann has to say about
this much-debated problem is of great importance. It seems that the
rise of the problem in the theology of late Middle Ages is connected
with the great crisis of the authority of the papacy in the century
of Occam, Wiclif, and the Great Schism, which Obermann "rightly
regards as the great turning point of the Middle Ages." But the great
thinkers of the High Middle Ages, such as Aquinas, were not yet
aware of the problem of "Scripture and Tradition," which the Church
had to settle in the sixteenth century.

A concluding chapter deals with "The Catholicity of Nominalism." It rejects the thesis that the theology of Occam and his followers
is essentially un-Catholic as modern Catholicism believes. Deni-
fie and Lortz, antipodes in the understanding of the Reformation,
were agreed in the thesis that the theology Luther rejected was not
true Catholicism at all. If however Nominalism was an essentially
Catholic theology in spite of its neo-Pelagianism—one has only to
think of the theology of the Eastern Church, which Rome has never
rejected—then the question arises of whether Luther's fight against
Rome was only a misunderstanding, as modern Catholics want us to
believe. This question will find an answer in the coming volumes of
Obermann's *magnum opus*.

FAITH AND ORDER FINDINGS [XXIII:1]

The Final Report of the Theological Commissions to the Fourth World Conference on Faith and Order, Montreal 1963, edited by Paul S. Minear (S.C.M. Press, London), 1963; pp. 219, 21/-.

This volume contains the Faith and Order Papers Nos. 37, 38, 39, and 40, as they were published by the Commission on Faith and Order at Geneva, 1963. Each paper is given with its own table of contents and its separate pagination. They are the Report of the Study Commission on "Institutionalism" (pp. 31) and the Reports of the Theological Commissions on "Christ and the Church" (pp. 62), "Worship" (pp. 62), and "Tradition and Traditions" (pp. 64). A short review cannot do justice to the rich content of these documents in which the research work and the discussions by many scholars have been condensed. Written as the basis for the Conference at Montreal, they ought not now after Montreal be discussed without the report on that World Conference that has not yet appeared. One may well ask whether it would not have been wiser to delay this publication in book form until the discussions and decisions of the World Conference could be incorporated. The most satisfactory of these reports is that on "Worship," which consists of the reports of the European Section whose personnel (chairman, Professor Prenter, Denmark) was especially well chosen, the East Asian Section, which presented in spite of great external difficulties it had to overcome a very good statement on the liturgical problems of the younger churches of Asia, and the American Section, which was especially interested in how to make the liturgy intelligible to modern man. The work of the European Section in its practical and its theological aspects can be regarded as a masterpiece of what can be done by a ecumenical committee. This paper as a whole seems to indicate that the liturgy may be the most fruitful field for a real ecumenical encounter. The parallels in the treatment of the subject by the Second Vatican Council are obvious, especially as far as the problems of the mission field abroad and at home are concerned. The study of the liturgy leads necessarily to the great doctrinal problems. The reports dealing with them are weaker. While the report on "Christ and the Church," at least as far as the European part is concerned, shows a real progress in theological thought over against current ecumenical terminology ("the church is not the extension of the Incarnation or the prolongation of Christ in the world," Paper 38, p. 48), it is obvious that what has to be said in this paper on the Sacraments is differently understood by the various churches represented. The emphasis on the Sacraments becomes a problem if the meaning of the Sacrament is not clarified or if it is even misunderstood. What a strange error underlies the statement on Baptism by the American Commission: "The meaning of the sacred rite is properly understood only when it is seen not primarily as either a gift or an action of the individual recipient, but as an act of God in the whole process of building up of the body of Christ" (p. 20), which is confirmed by the Europeans: "Baptism is the sacrament of the church's incorporation, once and for all, in Christ and marks out in the world the covenanted mercies of God . . ." (pp. 40f.). Have we forgotten that the Church confesses the "one baptism" of Ephesians 4:5 in the Nicene Creed, on the basis of the whole New Testament as "one baptism for the forgiveness of sins?" The weakest of the theological papers is that on "Tradition and Traditions." The issue between Rome and the East on the one hand and the Reformation on the other is whether the *sola scriptura*, —in the sense that canonical books of the Old and New Testament are the only source, rule, and norm of all doctrine of the church—is correct, and that means in harmony with what Jesus and the apostles have believed and taught and what the Church has confessed in the Nicene Creed. The answer, hidden behind complicated discussions of what "tradition" may mean, can be reduced to the simple word no. What the consensus in this "no" may mean in the future of the Ecumenical Movement history will tell. The first paper, "Institutionalism," a report given by a special commission, contains some valuable thoughts on the sociology of ecclesiastical institutions and their problems (e.g., on unions p.1ff.), but it shows to the theologian that sociology can never grasp let alone clarify the nature of the Church. The distinction between Church and sect in the thought of Weber and Troeltsch has appealed to modern American Protestantism, which does no longer understand the biblical distinction between Church and heresy. But would the Study Commission really think that Eastern and Western Catholics or conservative Lutherans and Reformed Presbyterians can ever give up that basic distinction?

NEW TESTAMENT APOCRYPHA [XXIII:1]

By E. Hennecke, new edition by
W. Schneemelcher, English translation edited
by R. McL. Wilson. Volume One: *Gospels
and Related Writings* (Lutterworth Press,
London), 1963, pp. 531; 75/6 (Aust.).

When the writer of this review took up his studies more than fifty years ago at Berlin, one of the first books he bought was the first edition (1904) of the New Testament Apocrypha, edited and translated in cooperation with other scholars by the learned Hannoverian pastor E. Hennecke, who died in 1951. This work was regarded as one of the indispensable tools of the student of theology. We can only wish that this masterly work, brought up to date and enlarged by newly discovered writings by the German editor and his staff of experts, in its English edition by Dr. Wilson may in future play a similar role in the English-speaking world. A general introduction to the whole work, which will also contain the non-canonical, apostolic, and pseudoapostolic literature and the apostolic fathers and the oldest church orders is followed by the introduction to the present volume on the Gospels. Both are of great importance for the history of the canon and the origins of the Gospel literature. The texts are always preceded by scholarly introductions. This volume contains not only the well-known apocryphal gospels and the isolated sayings of the Lord and the logia contained in papyri, but also the most complete collections of the numerous fragments of the vast gnostic gospel literature. An appendix contains the much-discussed Gospel of Thomas in a fresh translation from the Coptic text and a precis of the Gospel of Truth, both by the editor. Of special historical interest are the chapters on the relatives of Jesus and the traditions on "The Work and Sufferings of Jesus" (Jesus' earthly appearance and character, the alleged testimony of Josephus, the Abgar Legend, the Gospel of Nicodemus, the Acts of Pilate and other Pilate literature, the Gospel of Bartholomew a.o.). Among the German co-editors are W. Bauer, O. Cullmann, and J. Jeremias. The entire Patristic material is carefully collected in the introductions. Hence the work is of importance also for the Church historian. We all owe a great debt of gratitude to the editor, who in his work combines competence as New Testament scholar and as linguist in modern and ancient languages, such as Coptic, with that great measure of unselfishness such editorship requires. In the translations he was ably assisted by Drs. George Ogg and Richard E. Taylor. The work is an outstanding example of international cooperation. It must be regarded as a standard work for many decades to come. With great expectations we are looking forward to the appearance of the Second Volume.

REVOLUTIONARY THEOLOGY
IN THE MAKING [XXIII:3]

Barth-Thurneysen Correspondence, 1914–1925. Translated James D. Smart (John Knox Press, Richmond, Virginia), 1964, pp. 249: $5.

A great debt of gratitude is due to Professor Smart of Union Seminary, New York, for having made accessible to English-speaking Christendom these highly important documents. It was a good idea to publish in one volume Thumeysen's contribution to "Antwort," the symposium dedicated to Barth on his seventieth birthday in 1956, and Barth's contribution to the Festschrift for Thumeysen in 1958. Under the title "The Beginnings," Thumeysen published letters from Karl Barth from the years 1914–1922 with a concise and illuminating introduction on the beginnings of Barth's theology. In return Barth published under the title "The Living Past" fragments of a correspondence from the years 1921–1925 between him and Thumeysen, including some circular letters he wrote to his friends, with a short introduction. These publications form the two parts of the present book, pp. 7–61 and 65–249. The reader should always keep in mind that he has not before him everything that the future biographer of Karl Barth will have before him. But just this selection made by Thumeysen and Barth themselves for these festive occasions gives a living picture of the rise of the new theology in those fateful years of Europe. It was a turning point in the life of our generation when the light of these Dioscures began to outshine not only the will-o-the-wisps of that time, but also the great stars of the generation of "the lions" Hamack and Troeltsch. The first part of the book reveals the secret of their success. Two young pastors, neighbors in the canton Aargau, Barth at Safenwil (1911–21) and Thumeysen at Leutwil (1913–20), men who had received the highest training the best universities of Switzerland and Germany could give in the years preceding the Great War, both theologians with a wide horizon, aware of the cultural and social problems of their time and more or less engaged in public affairs, found themselves confronted with the task to preach to their people Sunday by Sunday. What shall I preach? This became their great question. We ministers in Australia, where the content of the sermon is so often—in spite of all "Biblical Theology"—"plain Christianity," or religious sentiments, or the awe of God diluted to ethical platitudes, will benefit from the experience of these men. "The Second Letter to the Corinthians sweeps over me like a torrent. Only the smallest part can flow on in the form of sermons," writes Barth (p. 51). And Thumeysen describes the work of his friend as preacher in words which also apply to himself: "In preparation for his work of preaching he sat down before the Bible each day of the week and in his own new way ploughed like a farmer who goes out into his fields in the early morning and makes furrow after furrow. He had to recognize that this work cannot be done without making thorough use of the Bible commentaries, above all those of the reformers" (p. 12). Out of this sermon work grew his *Commentary on Romans* and his entire thelogy. Still his *Dogmatics* shows that (see M. W. J. Geursen in the previous issue of this review, p. 56f.).

The second part shows Barth at Gottingen as professor of Reformed Theology. It covers the years until 1925 when he was called to Munster. His position in Gottingen was originally a very humble one, his professorship being an appendix to the Lutheran faculty, mainly maintained by the "Reformierter Bund" in the interest of the small Reformed Church in the North West of Hannover. Of the Reformed Church in those parts of Germany with its strong Calvinistic tradition, we receive a very vivid description (pp. 112f.). Soon the hard-working young professor who had to work until the small hours and sometimes even unto 5 a.m. for the lecture he was to give at 7 a.m. became the center of a theological movement that spread through all churches of Germany. His letters give a necessarily incomplete but vivid and colorful picture of the discussions that were going on between two generations, neither of which could understand the other. Also the background becomes alive, the Germany of the inflation and the occupation of the Ruhr by the French; state, church and universities without that generation that had fallen in the war and therefore coming under the leadership of the same forces that had led the German people into the first World War. The person of Karl Barth with his pipe never going out—he seems to have not yet discovered Mozart at that time—steps out of the pages of this book, a lovable man also in his shortcomings, his politics as a Swiss who is not directly engaged in the wars and revolutions of his time, his anti-Lutheranism and anti-confessionalism.

A "revolutionary theology" is what the editor calls the new theology that arose with Barth and Thurneysen during those years. One may dispute the applicability of the word "revolutionary" because it has too many shades of meaning. If one applies it, it must be understood in all these senses. Its greatest weakness is, as also the Reformed theologian will admit in view of Barth's poor doctrine of Baptism, the lack of understanding of the Sacraments. But perhaps the rediscovery of the Word was enough for one generation. Theology has not come to the end of its history. Keeping this in mind, we shall apply to this theology the words Charles Péguy addressed to the critics of Bergson: "A great philosophy is not a philosophy against which nothing can be said. It is a philosophy which says something, which brings unrest into the world and even shatters it." This can be said of the theology the making of which comes to light in this book. We hope to see it soon in a cheap edition and with an index of names.

THE PROBLEM OF CATHOLICISM [XXIV:1]

By Vittoria Subilia. Translated from the Italian
(*II Proglema dell Cattolicesimo*, Turin, 1962) by
Reginald Kissack (S.C.M. The Library of History
and Doctrine, London), 1964, pp. 190; 30/-.

Half a mile from the Vatican stands the Theological College of the Waldensian Church of Italy, the oldest evangelical church of Christendom. This is certainly an ideal place for mutual observation and for theological conversation between Roman Catholicism and Reformed Protestantism. Professor Subilia, the dean of the faculty, has not failed to make full use of the unique facilities offered by this neighborhood when he published, on the eve of the Second Vatican Council, this book that now two years later has appeared in a good English translation by R. Kissack, Methodist minister in Rome. The author has meanwhile been an observer at the council. When reading the proofs of the English translation after the first session of the council, he said "that nothing yet had happened to make him want to change a word." One wonders whether he would say that now after the third session.

The book is "an attempt to understand the religious and theological bases of the Catholic-Protestant disaccord, and to trace out (at least faintly) their consequences for civilization." The introductory chapter, "Roman Catholicism and Ecumenism," tries to explain the rise of the new ecumenical mood in the Roman Church mainly from a careful interpretation of utterances by John XXIII. However, it is too short (pp. 13–31) to give a satisfactory answer. Modern Roman Catholic ecumenism has its origin not in Rome. Coming from Germany, France, Belgium, and the Netherlands, it has conquered Rome and has found in Pope John its protector and champion. One of the limitations of this learned and highly informative book lies in its local Roman outlook. This becomes already clear at the starting point, the distinction between two attitudes towards the ecumenical problem: "The first goes by the name of *Integrism*, the second is known as the process of *integration*. . . . By *integrism* is meant a pure and simple submission to the claims of Roman authority. . . . By *integration* is meant a process of taking the gospel truths professed by non-Catholics and inserting them into the framework of Catholic doctrine and the Catholic hierarchical system." Apart from the question of how an English pen can write such an impossible word as "integrism," where outside Rome are these terms "known?" Since Benedict XV in his first encyclical has disavowed the "integralists," who played such a fateful role under Pius X, words like "integrists" or "integralists" are no longer in use in the Catholic world. And the ideas of a return to Rome and an integration of the heritage of non-Catholics in the Roman Church have never been mutually exclusive. Today they have become one in the program of Paul VI as well as in the actions of the council.

The core of the book is the chapters that describe the theological problems of the program of integration ("The Evolution of Dogma," "Roman Catholic Biblicism," "The Doctrine of Justification," "Mariology," "The Reassessment of Episcopacy," "The Discovery of the Laity," and "*Ecclesia Reformanda*") and the "Reforming Tendencies in Roman Catholicism" ("Subjective Faults—The Reformation of Life"; "Institutional Faults—The Cleansing of the Temple"; "Historical Faults—The "Westernizing" of Christianity"; "The Reform of Forms—The Significance of the Use of a Dead Language"; "The Intellectual Framework—The Necessity of Setting the Christian Message Free from the Framework of Ancient Thought, and of Expressing It in Contemporary Language"; "The Dogmatic Reformation—Its Basic Impossibility"). Some of the paragraphs suffer from the limitation of the space available, but they are all full of good observation and well-supported by quotations from sources not available to the average reader. Special attention must be called to the paragraph "The Intellectual Framework" (pp. 85–95), which discusses the problem of how Roman theology tries to get rid of the fetters of Aristotelian philosophy, mainly on the basis of French-speaking theology.

Karl Rahner—he is not included in the index of names, though his "*Kirche der Suender*" is mentioned (p. 67)—has meanwhile made important contributions the author could not take into account. These chapters give an impression of the tremendous work being done by Roman theology during the last decades. They show at the same time how fast Roman Catholicism is moving in the direction toward a goal that neither the pope nor the council knows. If somebody had told Archbishop Roncalli or Archbishop Montini at the time of Pius XI and Pius XII what they would be doing as Pope John and Pope Paul, they would certainly have declared that they never would do such things.

For the author of greatest importance is the last chapter of his book in which he tries to explain the nature of Roman Catholicism and the theological disagreement between Roman Catholicism and Protestantism. He sees clearly the great error of Rome, the identification of the Church with Christ, and traces its origin in the early Catholic Church. Whether his own ecclesiology, which is determined by definite Reformed convictions and by a modern theology, that thinks "God cannot be objectified either in church or in a book" is tenable in the light of the Reformation is questionable. Protesting against ecclesiologies based either on the doctrine of Christ or on the doctrine of the Holy Spirit, Professor Subilia wants to build the doctrine of the Church on the doctrine of God, the Father: "The God of the Church is and remains God, the Father, *Yahve*" (p. 178). To this we reply that the Church is always the Church of the Triune God. *Yahve* is not "the Father," but God as he reveals his name, *Kyrios*, Lord. It has a deep meaning if the New Testament refers the name *Yahve*, *Kyrios* to Christ. "I am the good shepherd"; this is the New Testament counterpart to "*Yahve* is my shepherd." Even the "*Kebod Yahve*," the glory of the Lord of hosts that the prophet saw, is referred to Jesus in John 12:39ff: "These things said Esaias when he saw his (i.e., Christ's) glory and spoke of him." This book, in its rich content and with its limitations, is a lasting contribution of modern Waldensian theology to the great dialogue of the Christian churches. Would it not be the historic mission of the oldest church of the *sola scriptura* to lead us all back to the written Word of God as the authority in the Church?

THE REFORMERS AND
THEIR STEPCHILDREN [XXIV:3]

By Leonard Verduin (Eerdmans Publishing Company, Grand Rapids), 1964, pp. 292; $5.75.

This book contains lectures, amplified and furnished with illuminating notes, which the author, a minister of the Christian Reformed Church, and translator and editor of Menno Simon's writings, gave in 1963. Sponsored by the Calvin Foundation, they deal with "the rift that developed between the reformers of the sixteenth century and the men of the Second Front" (Postscript, p. 276ff. where the scope of the book is clarified). This is not only a historical problem of great significance, but also a very practical issue for the remnants of the churches of the Reformation (Lutheran, Anglican, and Presbyterian-Reformed), which in America are surrounded and constantly influenced by that American Protestantism that has its roots in the religious revolution of the seventeenth century in England and is to a large degree dominated by the religious thought of the "second front." The author himself with his Calvinist background and his enthusiastic love for those whom Luther, Calvin, and even Zwingli have regarded as the worst enemies of the Reformation— "a child's play" called Zwingli in 1525 the fight against the pope in comparison with the struggle with the Anabaptists—reflects in his person and in his book this situation of evangelical Christianity in the United States. It is praiseworthy if after all the slanderous treatment of the "stepchildren" in centuries past he acts according to Luther's explanation of the Eighth (the Ninth in the Reformed Church) Commandment, "but apologize for our neighbour, speak well of him, and put the most charitable construction on all his actions." He is right when he says, "One can speak very well of them indeed before he becomes guilty of a bias as pronounced as that of those who have long spoken evil of them" (p. 276). But he goes further than that: "A second reason for the sympathetic treatment given these Radicals of the Reformation is that history has to a large extent demonstrated that they were in a large way right. Little by little, step by step, item by item, Protestantism has, at least in the New World, come to endorse the very emphases for which these men pioneered." He mentions the free church, the church by voluntary association, the separation of state and Church in the First Amendment, the recognition of a pluralistic society as the achievements we owe to them. There is certainly much truth in that. But this does not answer who was right and who was wrong in the great controversy between the reformers and their "stepchildren." All those achievements lie entirely in the field of sociology. What about the theological issues?

With this question we look into the eight lectures that form the body of the book.

Each bears as title one of the nicknames used in the polemics in the German-speaking countries. They do not denote particular groups, but rather tendencies that appeared in various places of the "second front." The reproaches contained in each of these bad words are discussed and refuted. In doing this the author draws heavily on his knowledge of the sources, printed and imprinted, the latter being taken mainly from Holland. The titles are 1. Donatisten! 2. Stabler! (staff-bearers; a wooden staff was carried by medieval heretics instead of a weapon); 3. Catharer! 4. Sacramentschwarmer! ("*Schwarmer*" was Luther's favourite name for these "enthusiasts" who were not satisfied with the external word of Holy Scripture, but appealed to an alleged *verbum internum* as the highest authority. He could even latinize the name to Svaermeri, which occurs in England as "Suvermeri" and Suvermerians" without being understood there); 5. Winckier! (holding secret meetings) 6. Wieder-taufer! (Anabaptists) 7. Kommunisten! 8. Rottengeister! (factious spirits). These chapters with their explanatory notes contain a wealth of information. Old slanders that the Jews first levelled against the Christians and later the Christians against the Jews and against each other are revived in these polemics. Special attention may be called to the chapter "Communists," where the problem of poverty and property is discussed, but the question is not answered why later all Social-ists and Communists in Europe have regarded Thomas Münzer as their great forerunner, the first great revolutionary of Germany. The reader gets a deep impression of the determination with which not only Luther, but also the entire Reformed Church, including men like Zwingli and Bucer, who in many respects were not so far from them, fought the fight against those whom they never could recognize even as their stepchildren—one must not forget that the heresies these radicals represent had been disturbing Christendom already in the Middle Ages. What is most saddening is the inability of the author to understand the motives of the reformers. No one would today defend Calvin's action against Servet and Melanchthon's approval of it. But to understand it, one must know that the denial of the trinitar-ian faith was to them, and is in fact, the end of the Church of Christ. It can perhaps no longer be understood in wide circles of modern American Protestantism where the dogma of the Church has long since vanished and Servet's doctrine is being taught and preached because theology has been replaced by psychology and sociology. Thus the only explanation our author has for the attitude of the reformers is that they wanted to maintain at all costs the Constantin-ian establishment. This is why they maintained infant Baptism and the Lord's Supper as Sacrament, why they refused to reject military service and the oath to the magistrates. In all these points Verduin accepts the attitude of the "step-children" uncritically without tak-ing into account the differences and contradictions existing between them. They are unimportant to him as long as agreement exists in the opposition to "Constantinianism" and "Sacralism."

Theology has been replaced by sociology, and antiquated at that. Verduin refers occasionally to Karl Holl (not mentioned in the index). But he has not taken cognizance of Holl's critical examination of the theories with which thinkers in the fields of church law (Sohm, Riecker) and sociology of religion (Weber, Troeltsch) in the nine-teenth and the early twentieth centuries have tried to illuminate the social forms of life in the history of Christianity. He takes for granted the distinction between "Church" and "Christendom," which were used synonymously by Luther, between the Corpus Christi, which is a biblical and theological concept, and the *Corpus Christianum*, which is a modern term that, as far as we know, was never used in the Middle Ages. That the idea of a Christian, in other words, Christianized society is not identical with the Church was unknown to former centuries. Least of all have the Sacraments anything to do with a "Christian" society as distinct from the Church. No theologian of whatever persuasion should dare to contrast "salvation by believing response to the word" and "salvation by sacramental manipulation" (pp. 136, 156, 158). To create "the monolithic society," "the first thing that had to be done was to appropriate the pagan word *sacramentum* (recall that it occurs nowhere in the Scriptures) and to let it replace the word *agape* of the authentic tradition. This was a clever stroke; every Roman citizen knew what a *sacramentum* was and what it was supposed to do and achieve; he needed only to hear the word to know the theology, that of 'tasting the sacrificial victim,' a transaction signifying the participant's solidarity with the society of which he was a part" (138). It is not a "sacralist hangover" if we refuse to discuss this amazing discovery. "The Christian Supper had been changed into a sacralism-serving thing. Very similarly was the already existing institution of infant Baptism laid hold of . . . in order that it too might serve the cause of 'Christian Sacralism.' Men took the existing institution and made of it a 'christening,' that is, a ritual whereby every child in the empire was taken and 'made a Christian of' . . ." (190). It is certainly not astonishing that Verduin does neither understand the practice and doctrine on infant Baptism in his own Reformed Church nor the discussion of the biblical question by Luther in WA 26, which he quotes (p. 203f). (There is no direct biblical command to baptize infants, nor is there any prohibition. The question for us is whether we have the right to abolish the custom).

It might be wise to separate entirely the question of infant Baptism from the question of the "Christian" Empire that began under Constantine. Infant Baptism and adult Baptism have always existed side by side. From very early times, infants were baptized in the same ceremony with adults. The Church baptizes infants as if they were adults, and adults as if they were infants. The only difference was and is that the infants express their desire to be baptized and confess their faith through the mouth of their parents and sponsors. To understand why this is regarded as possible, one should rather look into the Old Testament, as the old Reformed Church did, than into the *Codex Iuris* of Justinian. There have been times and parts of the

Ancient Church in which the one or the other was preferred. Just in the times after Constantine many pious families deferred Baptism to a maturer age. There have been Christians who did not like infant Baptism at all. But as far as I know, nobody has ever denied the validity of a Baptism received in infancy. It could never be repeated. The Donatists whom Verduin regards as the forerunners of his stepchildren did not recognize any Baptism or other sacrament received in the synagogue of the *traditores* as they called the "*catholica communio.*" Behind this stands a long tradition of the African Church, which, following Cyprian for a long time, did not recognize Baptism performed by heretics or schismatics. It is against such people that the laws are directed that forbid re-Baptism.

But the refusal to recognize the Baptism of the Catholic Church on the part of the Donatists has nothing to do with a rejection of the Constantinian (or Theodosian) establishment. When Constantine supported the Church of Africa financially, the Donatists had no objection against such support. Their complaint was only that the money had been given to the wrong church. They were the first to appeal to the emperor. When Constantine later in the *Civitas Constantina* (Cirta) built a church for the Catholics, the Donatists occupied it so successfully—they were in the majority—that the Emperor had to build a second church for the Catholics. There was no objection on the part of the Donatists against this *Donatio Constantini*, as pious Catholics all over the world began to complain of the damage the Church had suffered from the rich gifts of the state. But these people did not found an anti-Constantinian Church, but rather went into the deserts as hermits or into the monasteries. The "Christianisation" of the Empire, which was really carried out only under Justinian, was the unavoidable destiny of Christianity in the ancient world that—Verduin mentions the Babylonian Empire and quotes Plato—regarded religion as a function of the state, as today the state claims education that in the ancient world was left to private enterprise. That the Middle Ages did not follow the principle expressed by Theoderic the Great in the words "*Religionem imperare non possumus,*" but rather the law of the Christian Roman Empire was the consequence of Charlemagne's renewal of the empire in the West. Nobody denies the importance of the "stepchildren" for the separation of Church and state and the freedom of religion—also we in Australia know that, living under a constitution whose section 116 is an almost literal quotation of the First Amendment and of the clause on religious tests in Art. VI of the Constitution of the U.S.A. But we cannot accept their views on Church and sacraments as normative. And we Lutherans cannot forget that one of the principles of Luther was *"Gott will keinen erzwungenen Dienst,"* "God does not want worship which is enforced." The book as a whole, in spite of much valuable detailed information for which we are indebted to the author, confirms the view expressed by outstanding Church historians of our day that the time has not yet come for a comprehensive presentation of the "Radical Reformation" in its context with the history of the Late Middle Ages.

THE SECOND VATICAN COUNCIL
AND THE NEW CATHOLICISM [XXV:1]

By G. Berkouwer, translated by Lewis B. Smedes, (Eerdmans, Grand Rapids), 1965, pp. 264, $5.95.

Holland is becoming more and more a center of profound theological studies by Protestant and Catholic scholars. So we take gladly cognizance of what a recognized master of Dutch Evangelical Reformed theology has to say about the New Theology of Roman Catholicism in which some of his countrymen have begun to play an outstanding role. The book was written in Dutch and appeared in English during the council before the final results had become known. This has disadvantages that are outweighed by the fact that the freshness of the theological discussion has been preserved. As an observer at the council, the author could gather first-hand impressions and information that make the first chapters ("The Unexpected Council" and "The Changed Climate") very interesting reading. With the chapter "Unchangeability and Changeability of Dogma" begins the discussion of the problem presented by the "New Theology" in what sense there can be and is a true progress of Roman theology. Chapter 4 on "Scripture and Tradition" sketches the debate on the meaning of Sessio IV of Trent, which began with Geiselmann's thesis. One wonders how the representatives of the "One Source Theory" will interpret the compromise reached by the council as a victory. In "Exegesis and Doctrinal Authority," one of the deepest problems of all Christian churches today is dealt with. The chapter on "The Pope and the Bishops" contains excellent observations on the Early Church and "primitive Catholicism." "The Mystery of the Church" shows how the new theology tries to overcome the "triumphalism" of the traditional ecclesiology. "Catholics are reminding each other that the Church is on a pilgrimage and of how different it really is from the glorious kingdom of God. They are reminding each other that the confession reads: I believe the Church and not I believe in the Church" (p. 185). The author could have reminded them that the original text of the Nicene Creed has "in the . . . Church." One should not make too much of this terminological difference. This problem and also the great problem of the *extra ecclesiam nulla salus* is carefully discussed. But the author is certainly, as we all are, disappointed with the solution of the problem in the "Constitution on the Church," which opens the gate of heaven to all decent pagans, as also Küng does in his little book *That the World May Believe*. In spite of all attempts to claim the *sola gratia*, there remains, as Karl Barth has rightly seen in his criticism of Küng, that deep belief of Catholicism in the cooperation between God and man in the process of salvation. This should have been brought out more clearly perhaps in the otherwise excellent chapter on Mary. It is astonishing what a wealth of theological insights and information—especially in the discussion with Catholic authors of many countries—Professor Berkouwer has been able to put into these chapters. They will remain a monument to the *theologie nouvelle*, even if the limitations of this theology will become more and more manifest. And it will be one of the indispensable tools of those who are engaged in the great dialogue with Rome in the years following the council.

OBEDIENT REBELS [XXV:2]

Catholic Substance and Protestant Principle In Luther's Reformation. By Jaroslav Pelikan (S.O.M., London), 1964, pp. 212; sh. 25.

"This volume unites two of the deepest concerns of my thought and scholarship, the Reformation of the sixteenth century and the Ecumenical Movement of the twentieth, and studies each in the light of the other." So begins the preface. It ends with the confession, "I dedicate this book to one who was neither my professor nor my colleague, but who is none the less my teacher, the theologian who taught me to speak of 'Catholic substance and Protestant principle,' Paul Tillich." Hence the book has an autobiographical character without which it cannot be understood properly. An introductory chapter, "The Paradox of Luther's Reformation" ("Martin Luther was the first Protestant, and yet he was more Catholic than many of his Roman Catholic opponents," which shows that the whole terminology of Catholic substance and Protestant principle is not applicable to the Reformation), is followed by Part One, "Critical Reverence toward Tradition" (pp. 27–104), which discusses problems as "The Meaning of Tradition," "The Authority of the Councils," "The Preservation of Catholic Liturgical Substance," and "The Protestant Principle in Worship." While these chapters repeat in revised form much of what the author had written twenty years earlier in an excellent doctoral dissertation with Wilhelm Pauck at Chicago, Part Two contains four later essays on Luther's endeavors to reach union with the Bohemian Brethren and on the Consensus of Sendomir in 1570 ("Unity despite Separation," pp. 105–69). Part III ("Catholic Substance and Protestant Principle Today" pp. 159–206) adds some articles on the present ecumenical issues between Catholicism and Protestantism.

Professor Pelikan, the highly gifted son of one of the finest Lutheran churches in America, the Church of the Slovaks, has become one of the outstanding scholars in the field of the history of the Reformation in his country. But his great historical knowledge, his astonishing literary productivity, his broad reading, and his linguistic abilities have never found the supplementation by a great theology a first-rate dogmatician as teacher or as friend would have provided. Hence there's a strange lack of clarity about "Which was the real Luther?" (p. 12, p. 146). The real Luther was always the Luther who speaks in his catechisms. Hence the inability to understand the motives of Luther's Last Confession (141), which had been necessitated by the church politics of Bucer. The difference between the Bohemians on the one hand and Zwingli and Bucer on the other is made quite clear by Luther himself. It might help the author to a better understanding of Luther's doctrine of the Sacrament and its consequences if he made more use in this respect of his great knowledge of the Eastern Church. And how does the problem "Catholic substance and Protestant principle" look if seen from the East? For the Eastern Church, Roman Catholicism and Protestantism belong together as the two great heresies of the Western Augustinian Church, which started with what the East regards as the breach of ecumenicity in 1054. Whatever we may think of this view that we, of course, cannot make our own, it shows that the problem of Catholicism is much more complicated than we Westerners used to think. Hence we cannot accept Tillich's scheme. We shall always honor the late Paul Tillich as one of the great philosophers of religion in our time. Religion was the topic of his thought. But he was not a theologian in the strict sense of the word. For a theologian is an interpreter of the Word of God. And this did not exist for him as it existed for Augustine and Thomas, for Luther and Calvin. Neither Luther nor Calvin was a Protestant in Tillich's sense. This applies also to the churches that still today seriously confess the faith of the Reformation as the faith of the one, holy, catholic, and apostolic Church. We may hope that Professor Pelikan will outgrow the limitations of his teacher Tillich.

ASIA AND THE ECUMENICAL MOVEMENT
1895–1961 [XXV:3]
By Hans-Ruedi Weber (S.C.M. Press, London), 1966, pp. 319; 50/-.

This is one of the best books ever written on the Ecumenical Movement as understood in the circles of the World Council of Churches
and on the history of Christianity in modern Asia, seen both from
the historical and the theological point of view. An introductory
chapter (pp. 15–51), "Changing Asia," gives a concise sketch of the
scene of "Asiatic Asia," which comprises mainly East Asia, excluding
the Near East and Russian Asia, from John Mott's arrival in China
1895 to the revolutionary Asia of our days. This is followed by a
thoughtful discussion of the nature of the Ecumenical Movement.
Part One (53–111), "Ecumenical Youth Movements Set the Pattern,"
destroys the myth that the Edinburgh World Missionary Conference
of 1910 is the beginning of the Ecumenical Movement by giving an
accurate and well-documented history of the ecumenical thoughts
and endeavors of the Christian Youth Movement, mainly the World
Student Christian Movements and the Y.M.C.A./Y.W.C.A. in West
and East. Part Two, "Missions and the Asian Church" (113–63),
starting from a short glimpse into the early Asian churches, deals
with "the Ecumenical Significance of the Missionaries," their glo-
ries and their failures, with the era of missionary cooperation since
1910 and with the era of the Indigenous Church, with special
emphasis on the World Missionary Conference at Jerusalem 1928.
Part Three, "Witness and Service in Unity" (165–248), groups its
rich material around the Asian participation in the International
Missionary Council (especially the Conference of Tambaram), the

participation in the Movement for Life and Work (Kagawa), in Faith and Order, and deals in the last chapter elaborately with the relationship between Asia and the World Council of Churches.

The highly informative Part Four describes the Asian contribution to the Ecumenical Movement, dealing with Japanese, Chinese, and Indian pioneers with a glimpse at the incoming new generation, with the East Asia Christian Conference, and ends with what the author in great modesty calls an annotated bibliography, "Some Asian Convictions and Questions." This brief outline cannot give a full picture of the rich content of the well-written and substantial book that in masterly concentration and on the basis of a rich first-hand material discusses all problems connected with the subject.

One of the great merits of the book is the emphasis placed on the Christian Youth Movements for the rise of the Ecumenical Movement in West and East. The World Council has often been called the Student Christian Movement in long trousers. But we change with the length of our trousers. Bishops and professors are no longer students. It is an experience that nothing ages more quickly than youth movements. Their changes may mean a loss of spiritual substance. The late Karl Heim, the grand old man of the S.C.M. in Germany, had to say some very serious things about that at the end of his life. What has the Y.M.C.A. in America today to do with the Y.M.C.A. of 1895? What has the World Student Christian Movement of today with the S.C.M. and the student volunteers of young John Mott and Robert Wilders? Wilders has told me himself of the time when the whole archive of such a movement found sufficient space under his college bed. He explained to me also the original meaning of the slogan "Evangelization of the world in this generation." It had indeed, contrary to what Weber thinks (p. 59, footnote 3), a chiliastic meaning, being based on Matthew 24:14. Still in his closing words at Edinburgh 1910, John Mott, quoting Archbishop Davidson who in his greetings at the beginning of the conference had referred to Mark 9:1, ventured to prophesy that "before many of us taste death they shall see the kingdom of God come with power." The story of the S.C.M. as well as of the whole Ecumenical Movement is to a large degree the story of the secularization of the Christian hope and its degeneration in the Social Gospel and later in an enthusiastic ecclesiology. What this has meant in China, Japan, and India is not told and could not be told in this book. The development of Christian missions in Asia and the world during the last decades was certainly not only progress, but it has implied a decay of the Christian message. This message was bound to decay with the decline of the doctrinal substance of the sending churches, their missions, and their ecumenical organizations. This book gives an insight into the unions and plans of South India, Lanka, and North India, none of which has been able to preserve the purity of the Gospel. Here lies perhaps the reason why the Asian churches have so far not been able, with the remarkable exceptions of Japan, to make real theological contributions to Christian theology. For the new interpretation of the Gospel of St. John by Indians, to which my teacher Banninga at Hartford has always been looking forward, has never appeared. What men like Appasamy have achieved goes not beyond a new syncretism, which is threatening everywhere where the dogmatic substance of the Christian faith is not preserved. Asia and especially India has shown in the long, tragic history of Christian missions a tremendous ability to assimilate elements of Christianity. What has survived of the religion of the old Chinese and Mongolian churches are certain elements of Northern Buddhism, in especially the transformation of Gautama Buddha into a sort of savior. The great ecumenical problem of Asia is whether the churches in Asia will be Asian without ceasing to be truly Church of Christ also in the preservation of the Christian dogma. We make these remarks in true gratitude for the thought-provoking book.

LUTHER'S WORKS, VOL. 4 [XXVII:2]

Lectures on Genesis, Chapters 21–25. Volume 5: Lectures on Genesis, Chapters 26–30. Edited by Jaroslav Pelikan and Walter A. Hansen. (Concordia, St. Louis), 1964 and 1968, XI plus 433 and XII plus 412 pp.; each volume $6.00.

Modern Luther research began with the study of the young Luther, whose early lectures had been rediscovered and for the first time published in this century. Meanwhile a shift of emphasis has taken place. A new investigation of the theology of the reformer in his mature years has shown that the contrast between the "young" and the "old" Luther is after all not so great. The essential thoughts of his early years are to be found also in his later writings, as the lectures on Genesis that occupied Luther from 1535 to 1545. The editor gives, as in the previous volumes, a short, but exhaustive introduction in the historic background and in the textual problems. The able translator was until his death Dr. George V. Shick of St. Louis. His work was at once expertly continued by Dr. Paul D. Pahl, Luther Theological Seminary, North Adelaide. As Luther in his lectures sometimes goes over from Latin to German, the translator had to be at home equally in both languages. To the painstaking work of the two translators we owe a great debt of gratitude. To illustrate the importance of these lectures, which are much more than a commentary on Genesis, we quote from Shick's translation of an excursus ad Genesis 26:9 on God's revelation in the Gospel: "Thus God reveals his will to us through Jesus Christ and the gospel. But we loathe it and, in accordance with Adam's example, take delight in the forbidden tree above all the others. This fault has been implanted in us by nature. When paradise and heaven have been closed and the angel has been placed on guard there, we try in vain to enter. For Christ has truthfully said, 'No one has ever seen God' (John 1:18). Nevertheless, God, in his boundless goodness, has revealed himself to us in order to satisfy our desire. He has shown us a visible image. 'Behold, you my Son; he who hears him and is baptized is written in the book of life. This I reveal through my Son, whom you can touch with your hands and look at with your eyes.' I have wanted to teach and transmit this in such a painstaking and accurate way because after my death many will publish my books and will prove from them errors of every kind and their own delusions. Among other things I have written that everything is absolute and unavoidable; but at the same time I have added that one must look at the revealed God, as we sing in the hymn: *Er heisst Jesu Christ, der HERR Zebaoth, und ist kein ander Gott*, 'Jesus Christ is the Lord of hosts, and there is no other God'— and also in very many other places. But they will pass over all these places and take only those that deal with the hidden God.

Accordingly, you who are listening to me now should remember that I have taught that one should not inquire into the predestination of the hidden God but should be satisfied with what is revealed through the calling and through the ministry of the word. For then you can be sure of your faith and your salvation and say, 'I believe in the Son of God, who said (John 3:36), 'He who believes in the Son has eternal life.' Hence no condemnation or wrath rests on him, but he enjoys the good pleasure of God the Father. But I have publicly stated these same things elsewhere in my books, and now I am teaching them vive voce. Therefore I am excused." Joh. von Walter (*Christentum und Frommigkeit, Gesammelte Vortrage und Aufsatze*, 1941, p. 261) asks whether Luther had in mind Calvin's *Institutio*. In any case this passage shows how Luther to the end of his life retained the view of predestination he had confessed in "The Bondage of the Will" of 1525.

A HISTORY OF CHRISTIAN THOUGHT
[XXVIII:1]

By Paul Tillich. Edited by Carl E. Braaten
(London, S.C.M.), 1968, pp. Vni and 300; 45/-.

During the spring semester of 1953, Tillich delivered at Union Theological Seminary, New York, a series of lectures on the history of
Christian thought (corresponding to the "history of dogma" in the
faculties in Germany). They were taken down in shorthand, revised,
and circulated. They appeared again in print in 1956. The present
book is a revision of that second edition, edited by a faithful friend
and student of Tillich, Professor Carl B. Braaten, Chicago. Tillich
himself could not finalize this work.

It is not only the origin of this book that reminds of Harnack's
famous lectures of the winter semester of 1900–1901 on *"Das Wesen
des Christentums"* ("What is Christianity?"), re-edited by Bultmann
in 1951, which owe their publication to a stenographic transcription
by one of the students. As Harnack, the Church historian, ventured
to enter the field of the systematician to answer with the means of
historical scholarship a basic question of dogmatics, so in this case
a great systematic thinker tried a hand in historiography, a trade
he had not learned. But such trespasses are sometimes necessary if
theology should not end in a sterile departmentalization. Also Karl
Barth had to write a "History of Protestant Theology," though his
book is not what the title promises, but rather a collection of highly
important and interesting essays on the great theologians of the
eighteenth and nineteenth centuries, corresponding to the systematician Tillich's "Perspectives on Nineteenth and Twentieth Century

Protestant Theology" in which Tillich could rely on his own comprehensive studies in modern theology.

Although the present volume will be read with interest by those who want to understand Tillich, it cannot be regarded as a substitute for a textbook on the history of Christian dogma. Most of the chapters are too short to give a real picture of the development of the dogma of the Church. Tillich is at his best where he speaks as a teacher of philosophy, for example, making clear in concise chapters certain problems of mediaeval philosophy, such as the nature of medieval "realism," which is exactly the opposite of what our modern language understands by realism and is what we would call idealism. Illuminating is also the presentation of the conflict of the Platonic-Augustinian tradition (e.g., Bonaventura) and Aristotelian Thomism. Weaker is the understanding of medieval theology that finds an expression sometimes in a confused terminology. So we read on p. 157 that above all the sacraments is the Sacrament of the Mass. This is the sacrifice of Christ repeated every day in every church in Christendom, in terms of transubstantiation of bread and wine into body and blood. This sacrifice is the foundation of the presence of the divine and of the sacramental and hierarchical power of the Church. Officially it was a part of the Lord's Supper, but objectively it was and is the foundation of all sacraments, for here the priest has the power to produce God, *facere deum*; making God out of bread and wine is the fundamental power of the Church in the Middle Ages." "The Mass, which is a part of the Lord's Supper" occurs again p. 231 in the discussion of Luther's theology. On p. 190, it is stated that "the word 'person' was never applied to God in the Middle Ages. The reason for this is that the three members of the trinity were called personae ('faces' or 'countenances'): the Father is persona, the Son is persona, and the Spirit is persona. Persona here means a special characteristic of the divine ground, expressing itself in an independent hypostasis." This is Tillich's interpretation. It is not the doctrine of the Middle Ages "that God has three personae, three expressions of his being." What Tillich was unable to understand is that the doctrine of the Trinity has its roots not in philosophical speculation, but in the liturgy. Father, Son, and Holy Spirit are mentioned first in liturgical formulas, in prayers, in the liturgy that invokes the Father as God, the Son as God (e.g., the binitarian "Great Gloria"), and after Nicea also the Holy Spirit as God and Lord ("Who with the Father and the Son is worshiped and glorified"). Arius was excommunicated because his theology made the whole Christian liturgy one great lie. That was the origin of the Arian controversy. Hence the first part of the book that deals with the Ancient Church is the weakest. "The 'Son of God' is an adequate term because of the special relationship and intimate communion between Jesus and God. At the same time, it is inadequate because 'Son of God' is a very familiar pagan concept. Because of this, the words 'only begotten' were added and he was called 'eternal'" (p. 15). This is sheer dilettantism, just as the translation of "*homoios*" (in "*homoi-ousios*") as "similar."

Homoios in this context means always "equal" (p. 75). Of the Nicene Creed we hear, "The statements were made in philosophical, non-biblical terms" (p. 72). The creed was a liturgical creed, consisting almost entirely of literal quotations from the Bible, including the "visible and invisible" of the first sentence (Col. 1:16 comp. 2 Cor. 4:18). It has no "reference to the Platonic ideas." Into this liturgical creed the "*homoousion to patri*" was inserted and the condemnations were added to safeguard the full divinity of Christ. One may find philosophical speculation with the theologians, but to speak of philosophical language in the creed is not allowed. This old prejudice of Harnack's great work, which still now, eighty years after its appearance, enjoys a sort of canonical dignity in America is untenable. That Tillich stuck to what he as a young man had learnt from Harnack may be understandable, but that the editor and the whole set of young theologians in the U.S.A. accept today uncritically what a great German scholar wrote almost three generations ago is unpardonable. It could not possibly happen in any other branch of American scholarship. We could go on and deal with the treatment of Chalcedon, which remains entirely within the clichees of the past. It seems that neither Tillich nor the editor have ever read the full dogmatic statement of that great council that consists of three parts, the creed of the 318 fathers of 325 (Nicea), the creed of the 180 fathers of Constantinople, which was now elevated to the rank of the old Nicenum, so that both enjoyed the same authority, and the Chalcedonian Formula. The problems of this formula can be understood only by him who has read the sources and knows that the entire controversy between the schools of Antioch and Alexandria was a controversy on the exegetical understanding of the Gospels. Should not the time have come in America when the theologians must read the sources?

Space does not permit us to deal with Tillich's treatment of the Reformation. We who have followed his theological development since his early days in Berlin have often wondered why Tillich (in contrast to his contemporaries, Barth, Brunner, Holl, and his school, Elert, Althaus, Aulen, Nygren) has never shared the great theological and spiritual experience of those years after World War I of rediscovering the message of the Reformation. He has, of course, read all the books that appeared during those exciting years. But his understanding of Luther and the Reformation remained within the limits of what he had learned from Harnack and Troeltsch. He was never touched in the depth of his soul by the rediscovery of the reformers, of the Bible as the objective Word of God, of the confession of the Church and its dogmatic content. He has never learned what evangelical faith is. He remained with what in the first decade of the twentieth century was regarded as Christianity, an immediate mystical experience of "the Divine." Thus it was a logical step that he changed over from theology to philosophy until the enforced migration to America brought him into a religious world where he could become a theological leader. For American Protestantism, and this seems to be true today even of American Catholicism, is far more remote from Wittenberg, Geneva, Canterbury, and Rome than European Christendom is from Nicea and Chalcedon. Not Luther and Calvin, but the "Third Reformation" of the sixteenth century, the sects of the great religious revolution of seventeenth-century England, and the religion of the Enlightenment of the eighteenth century have shaped the American Protestantism that speaks in this book. Tillich has himself repeatedly remarked that this Protestantism is closer to Thomas Muentzer than to Luther and Calvin. So he found a spiritual and theological home in the New World in which now the snipers of Los Angeles and Chicago try to execute Thomas Muentzer's last will and testament.

REFORMATION TODAY [XXVIII:3]

By Klaas Runia (London, Banner of Truth Trust), 1968, paperback, pp. 147; £5.

A lethal disease is spreading through Christendom: the disintegration of the doctrinal substance of the Christian faith. While this process is hailed by theologians as the great renewal of the Church and as the beginning of a new era in which Christianity become again relevant to modern man, that man who allegedly has come of age, the laity in all churches Catholic and Protestant is becoming restless. Making use of the rights now generally accorded to them, they begin to question the blessings of a renewal that ends in empty churches (more than eighty Roman Catholic churches are reported to have been closed in August in Amsterdam in the heavily renewed Catholic Church of Holland), empty pulpits (only a small percentage of the students of famous Protestant seminaries in America intend to enter the parish ministry), and empty sermons and "sermonettes," soon to be replaced by free discussions, as it has been done already with little or no success in some places in Lutheran Germany. If this is the renewal of the Church, then indeed the hour of the laymen has struck with Roman Catholics and Protestants, with the Presbyterians from America to Australia and New Zealand.

For all those who are concerned about the future of the Church, ministers of the Word and church elders, laymen young and old, this exciting small book has been written by one of the best dogmaticians of the younger generation of the Reformed Church who combines deep evangelical piety with a thorough theological training and has the rare gift of modern theologians to write about the most difficult theological problems in a simple language every Christian who knows his Bible and his catechism can understand. It may serve as an eye-opener also to those who are still satisfied with their church but a little bit uneasy as far as the future is concerned. In short but well-substantiated chapters, the author describes the rise of "Heretical Theology" up to Bultmann, Tillich, Robinson, and Van Buren, and "The Failure of the Church" to cope with the problem. Over against the slogan "No Creed, but Christ," he shows convincingly that a mere revival will not help the Church unless it is at same the time a revival of sound evangelical doctrine. This thesis sounds through the whole book and is elaborated in a thorough discussion of the problems of "The Unity of the Church" (3), "The World Council of Churches" (4), and "Union Discussions between Denominations" (5). The last chapters show the validity of this thesis and the possibilities of its practical application in the life of the individual church. Special attention is called to "The Question of Separation," a careful discussion of the problem by a man who comes from the largest free church of the European continent.

The author represents a Reformed Church in which the deepest reverence for the written Word of God goes hand in hand with a strong emphasis on its confession, mainly the Heidelberg Catechism, which is taught every Sunday. His confessional loyalty allows him to be very broad-minded in all questions that have divided the Reformed churches. He sides with the Reformed Church of the century rather than with the later orthodoxy even in such questions as the episcopal office. His great aim is a truly evangelical Reformed Church. "Within the framework of our essential unity there are some fundamental differences among us. Let me mention some of them. There is the contrast between Calvinism and Arminianism. There are our differences concerning Baptism. Some believe that the infant children of believers should be baptized, while others contend that Baptism is for professing believers only" (p. 130). But these differences as also the problems of the millenium, are not sufficient reason to stay apart. They should be discussed with the open Bible before us. He thinks ultimate agreement is possible with the help of the Holy Spirit.

The reviewer is not quite sure whether this optimism will be shared everywhere. The question of whether Baptism is an act of God, which it is in the last analysis for Calvin and the Heidelberg Catechism, or an act of man as for the Baptists and the late Karl

Barth (Dogmatics IV 4) would seem to many deeper than Professor Runia is inclined to believe. This book deserves thorough discussion in all churches of the Reformed tradition. Unfortunately the binding is very poor. If the reviewer reads it once more, as he intends to do, it will fall apart into loose leafs. The publishers should treat such books with more respect for the author and with more consideration for the reader.

LUTHER AND ERASMUS [XXIX:3]

By E. Gordon Rupp and Philip S. Watson in collaboration with A. N. Marlow and B. Drewery. The Library of Christian Classics, Vol. XVI (London, S.C.M. Press), 1969, pp. vx and 348; £5.

This outstanding volume of the well-known "Library of Christian Classics" contains the full text of Erasmus "*De libero arbitrio diatribe*" and Luther's "*De servo arbitrio*" in a new translation with explanatory notes and an introduction. Professor Rupp, of Cambridge University, is responsible for the translation and edition of the Erasmus Diatribe and for the corresponding chapter of the Introduction, "The Erasmian Enigma" (pp. 1–12). Professor Watson, now of Garret Theol. Seminary, Evanston, IL, is the translator of Luther's famous reply. He wrote the second chapter of the introduction, "The Lutheran Riposte"(pp. 12–28). The two great Luther scholars were supported by two younger men who teach at Manchester University, A. N. Marlow, senior lecturer in Latin, and B. Drewery, lecturer in Ecclesiastical History. Both contributed the third part of the Introduction (pp. 28–32), "The Language of the Debate." A. N. Marlow wrote as a small donum superadditum an "Appendix: On the Adagia of Erasmus" (pp. 335–9).

No better team could be found for this English edition of the greatest debates in the history of Christian thought. For a really great event was this discussion of freewill between the prince of the humanists and the leading man of the Reformation. Certainly it was not a flawless *disputatio in forma*. Both men were under the stress of those turbulent years 1524 (On Free Will) and 1525 (On the Bondage of the Will). One may find fault with the passion of Luther and the lack of passion with which Erasmus spoke of the great mysteries of the depth of human sin and the overwhelming marvel of God's forgiveness. Luther did not think very highly of his own literary achievements. Only two of his books did he want to be preserved: "*De servo arbitrio*" and the catechism for the children. Erasmus would never have regarded his diatribe as the climax of his literary work. Neither Luther nor Erasmus were able to understand the other's thought perfectly, as we would expect a Church historian to penetrate the thoughts of the great men of the past irrespective of his own preferences. Karl Barth has said of the debate between Luther and Zwingli: "They are not the worst theologians who simply are not able to rethink the thoughts of other men." He should have known. "Their debate slammed the door on any reconciliation between two great men," we read right in the beginning (p. 1f.). But we should realize that some slamming of doors must be done in the Church if the truth of the Word of God and the existence of Christ's Church is at stake. Why have all those literary discussions and colloquies of the sixteenth and seventeenth centuries since Marburg ended in what, humanly speaking, was failure? Perhaps God has a different judgment on what failure and success is. The present reviewer looks back at fifty years of ecumenical discussions. He has never seen a document that could have solved one of the great doctrinal problems that are troubling Christendom. No real consensus has been reached on the Sacraments, the ministry, the doctrine of justification, the nature of the Church, or the last things. All the new formulas proved to be either short-living compromises or the agreement to disagree in doctrine altogether. How often have we been reminded of Luther's word "*Non in doctrina, sed in disputatione veritas amittitur*," "Not in teaching, but in disputation the truth is lost." There have been cases when real union and full agreement have been reached after thorough, patient theological work of many years. One case in point is the synod of Alexandria in 362, when the staunch defender of Nicean orthodoxy, Athanasius, came to terms with the Cappadocians. Agreement on the *homoousion-humoiousion* question was reached and the full divinity of the Holy Spirit was recognized. Such cases have occurred time and again. They may happen also today. They will certainly not happen if we believe that any question can be solved by means of the dialogue. It is with deepest concern only that one can observe the development of the Roman Church since the Vatican Council II that opened doors that had been rightly slammed, with the result that the borderline between Christianity and paganism begins to fade away.

"At best, Erasmus prodded Luther into some splendid epigrams and into uttering hermeneutical principles of worth." These epigrams contain Luther's doctrine of the revelation of God, who comes to us hidden under the cross: Luther's *theologia crucis*, the key to his understanding of God's revelation. The "hermeneutical principles" contain his doctrine of Holy Scripture. He has clearly seen that Erasmus's rejection of the total depravity of man, his view that our salvation rests on our cooperation with the divine grace, and his rejections of predestination are closely bound up with the view that the Bible is a dark book that cannot be understood properly without the help of the teaching office of the Church. The *sola gratia*, the *sola fide*, and the *sola scriptura* belong inseparably together. This leads Luther to his doctrines of the clarity of Holy Scripture. It is not the clarity Erasmus was looking for, the absence of any dark passages. What Erasmus was looking for in the Bible was the clarity of a scientific textbook or the clarity of a great work of poetry. The clarity Luther found was the clear presentation of the great dogmas of the Church, the Trinity, the person and the work of Christ. Christ as the true content of the Bible, of the entire Bible, Christ who shines through all Scriptures and illumines them (in the sense of 2 Cor. 3:12ff. 1): this is more than a hermeneutical principle. It is the rediscovery of the Scripture as the Word of God.

May this book find many readers who try to penetrate into the thoughts of two great men: the reformer who rediscovered the *sola gratia*, the *sola fide* in its inseparable unity with the *sola scriptura*, and the prince of the humanists, one of the greatest men of letters Europe has seen, who approaches the Bible with all the means with which rising modern scholarship had provided him, but could not find the Gospel of God's grace in its fullness. It has a deep significance that the debate was never finalized in their days. It goes on today and is perhaps the great theme of the history of the Church today. *Tolle, lege.*

Made in the USA
San Bernardino, CA
10 September 2016